International Mergers and Acquisitions:
a reader

International Mergers
and Acquisitions:
a reader

Edited by
Peter J. Buckley
and
Pervez N. Ghauri

THOMSON

Australia • Canada • Mexico • Singapore • Spain • United Kingdom • United States

THOMSON

International Mergers and Acquisitions: a reader

Copyright © 2002 Peter J. Buckley and Pervez N. Ghauri for the collection. Refer to end of chapters for individual copyrights.

The Thomson logo is a registered trademark used herein under licence.

For more information, contact Thomson, High Holborn House, 50/51 Bedford Row, London, WC1R 4LR or visit us on the World Wide Web at:
http://www.thomsonlearning.co.uk

British Library Cataloguing-in-Publication Data
A catalogue record for this book is available from the British Library

ISBN 1–86152–800–0

Typeset by Photoprint, Torquay, Devon
Printed in Singapore by Seng Lee

Contents

Preface

The Financial Times of 19th September 2001 announced the UNCTAD World Investment Report for 2001 with the headline "Global foreign investment flows set to fall by 40%". This was before the impact of the events of September 11 in New York and Washington DC could have been felt. A primary reason for the projected fall in foreign direct investment is given as the drop in merger and acquisition (M&A) activity. "The drop, the first since 1991, was almost entirely accounted for by the fading of last year's merger boom in the industrialised world" (p. 12). It is fair to assume that the current merger wave is over.

There will be another merger wave in the near future and this book of readings provides guidance, food for thought and evidence for managers engaged in M&A choices. It shows that the overall record for M&A outcomes is mixed, with many studies finding that the bulk of gains accrues to the acquired firm. Bettering the record of incumbent managers is difficult, beating the market (for the acquiring firm has to pay the market price for the assets and then still achieve a positive return) is inordinately difficult. This book counsels caution as well as opportunity in M&A activities.

The book will be useful for practising managers, for business students particularly at MBA level and for focussed short courses (including Executive MBA modules) on international M&As. It has relevance for students of international business, finance, strategic management, HRM, marketing and industrial economics. The study of M&A activity is, as these readings show, necessarily interdisciplinary and it is offered in the hope that its use, particularly on focussed short courses, will enable a deeper understanding of the importance of M&A activity and its outcome, in an increasingly volatile world economy.

Peter J. Buckley
Leeds

Pervez N. Ghauri
Manchester

September 2001

Introduction 1

Peter J. Buckley and Pervez N. Ghauri

OVERVIEW

Mergers and acquisitions have become the most dramatic demonstration of vision and strategy in the corporate world. With one single move you can change the course of your company, the careers of your managers and create value for your share-holders (Puranam et al., 2000). Time and again, we have seen how share values increase or decrease due to the mergers announced and completed. Daimler-Chrysler, a $38 billion merger, is a good example, where the share values dropped by almost 40 percent from the time of the announcement of merger, May 1998 to December 2000 (Bert and Tait, 2000). More than 50 percent of the mergers so far have led to a decrease in share value and another 25 percent have shown no significant increase.

Throughout the last decade mergers and acquisitions (M&A) have dominated the world economic scene. In 1998, mergers were worth US$ 2.4 trillion worldwide, a 50 percent increase on 1997, which was itself a record year. This list also included the mega merger announced between Exxon and Mobil. In 1999, this figure exceeded $3.3 trillion and in 2000, $3.5 trillion. In Europe, a major M&A activity area, the value of M&A rose to $1.2 trillion. The pace of M&A has slowed down in the last two years, mainly because no mega mergers, over $50 billion, were announced in these years.

Types of merger and acquisition (M&A)

In a merger, the assets of two previously separate firms are combined to establish a new legal entity. In a takeover or acquisition, the control of assets is transferred from one company to another. A complete takeover involves all the assets of the acquired company being absorbed by the acquirer and the takeover "victim" disappears.

Acquisitions differ according to the scale of the acquired assets in relation to the acquiring firm. Where the firm can leverage its assets to buy a firm which is as big or bigger than itself, the problems posed are quite different from "bolt-on" deals where the new assets can be integrated with an existing part of the buying firm.

In fact, the number of mergers in "mergers and acquisitions" is almost vanishingly small. Less than 3 percent of cross border mergers and acquisitions by number are mergers (UNCTAD, 2000: 99). In reality, even when mergers are supposedly between equal partners, most are acquisitions where one company controls the other. The number of "real" mergers is so low that for practical purposes, "M&As" basically mean "acquisitions" (UNCTAD, 2000: 99). Indeed full or outright acquisi-tions (100 percent control) accounted for more than half of all cross border M&As in

1999, although the proportion was lower in developing countries, largely because of legislation.

Mergers and acquisitions (M&As) are conventionally classified as:

- horizontal M&As, between competing firms in the same industry;
- vertical M&As, between firms in buyer–seller, client–supplier and value chain linkages; and
- conglomerate M&As, where the companies are unrelated businesses.

Takeovers

Firms which carry out a takeover of another firm make two very strong statements. The first is that the acquiring firm can extract more value from the same assets than can the current owners. This is a strong statement of comparative management ability; "We can manage the assets more effectively than you can!". The second statement is even stronger. It is that the acquiring firm can pay the market price for the asset and can even then extract further value. This is the core reason why many mergers fail – if the market price fully reflects the future profit stream of the acquired assets, then there is no scope for profit from the merger. An acquiring firm is saying "our valuation of the assets is superior to the current valuation". Where assets do not have a market price, as is the case with private firms, or divisions of multi-unit companies, then "guesstimates" have to be made of the market price, which provides scope for some firms to be more skilled than others in this estimation.

The role of uncertainty in the valuation of future income streams looms large in takeovers. Superior competitive performance may well be unique to the firm, viewed as a team, which is not obtainable by others except by the purchase of the whole firm (Alchian and Demsetz, 1972). The firm may have a reputation or goodwill that is difficult to separate from the firm itself (and which should be carried at higher value on its books). Possibly members of the employee team derive their productivity from the knowledge they possess about each other in the particular environment of that unique firm. This gave rise to concern about "knowledge management" within firms and may be difficult to transfer piecemeal to other firms by M&A, or by any other means. The complexity of the modern firm defies easy analysis so the inputs responsible for (long term) success may be difficult to identify and may be overvalued or undervalued for some time. The success of firms will be reflected in higher returns and stock prices, not higher input process. This is compounded by the fact that inputs are acquired at historic cost, but the use made of these inputs yields only uncertain outcomes. The acquisition cost of these inputs may fail to reflect their value to the firm at some future date. By the time their value is recognized, they are beyond acquisition by other firms at the same historic cost and meanwhile the shareholders of this lucky firm have enjoyed higher profits. When such input acquisition decisions are made, they can give rise to high accounting returns for several years (or a once for all capital gain if accountants could value *a priori* decisions that turn out to be correct *ex post*). [This paragraph is a paraphrase of Demsetz 1973, p. 1.]

By the same token, once assets are embodied into a firm, their value becomes difficult to separate from the other assets which comprise the firm. Takeovers often involve the search for undervalued assets packaged into an existing firm. In a takeover, the potential acquirer is seeking some otherwise unavailable asset (or one which is only available elsewhere at a higher price). Key examples of such assets are brand names, distribution networks, R&D facilities, management team skills, a loyal customer base, or specific knowledge. Often, the only way to acquire such assets is to purchase the whole firm. On the positive side for the acquiring firm, all the other assets of the acquired firm which are not required can be sold off. This gives rise to the phrase "asset stripping". On the negative side, once acquired, these assets may not provide the value which the purchaser envisaged. This may be due to a simple misvaluation of the assets or it may result from the inability of the acquirer to release the synergy between the new assets and the firm's existing ones.

Thus the problems of *ex ante* valuation and *ex post* integration (releasing synergy) are related. The problems of integrating a previously separate unit into the acquiring firm are many, varied and ongoing. The previous owners may have had different goals, procedures, technologies (including IT systems), management styles, corporate cultures, operating languages and routines. If the takeover was hostile, residual bitterness may be involved. The strategy of acquiring management skills by takeover often fails because the newly acquired management team often walks away in disgust, or is fired because of incompatibilities which emerge in the post merger situation.

Acquisition strategies

There are several motives for these M&A activities. The most important, as seen from the experience of the last decade, has been economies of scale and scope. Companies aim to achieve economies of scale by combining resources of the two merging companies or create economies of scope by acquiring a company allowing product/market diversification. Daimler's merger (acquisition) with Chrysler and AOL's merger with Time Warner are good examples. Other motives include access to each other's technology or market reach, achieving a dominant position in the industry, consolidation of the industry, and manipulating rules of competition and antitrust. Value creation for either company, or at least for the acquiring company, in fact is the underlying reason. This value creation has to come through either cost cutting or through added value due to increased scope. Finally, too often fashion has led managers to pursue a strategy of M&A, as mergers or acquisitions have become an end in themselves or a means of empire-building.

Friendly M&As can be distinguished from those that are hostile. In a friendly M&A, the Board of the target firm agrees to the transaction (this may be after a period of opposition to it). Hostile M&As are undertaken against the wishes of the target firm's owners. The price premium tends to be higher for hostile rather than friendly M&As even where only one bidder is involved. The overwhelming proportion of both international and domestic M&As are friendly. In 1999, there were only 30 hostile takeovers out of 17 000 M&As between domestic firms. Hostile cross-border-completed M&As accounted for less than 5 percent of total value and less than 0.2 percent of the total number of M&As during the 1990s (UNCTAD, 2000: 105, figures from Thomson Financial Securities Data Company). There are of course some high profile battles which attract attention to hostile M&As.

The six cases from *The Economist* presented here as Chapter 2 illustrate the varied motives and backgrounds of firms engaged in M&As. They include the iconic Daimler-Chrysler case and AOL's merger with Time Warner. Most of the mergers were defensive in nature, often occurring in response to a threat. As the covering article points out, this often means that the problems are not solved, but are imported into the emergent firm. Losses of key personnel post-merger often compromise its potential success and this is part of the human relations problems which can be inimical to a successful venture. The importance of a clear vision pre-merger and a clear strategy, rapidly implemented, post-merger are lessons from these cases.

Assessing the impact of M&As

A simple static trade-off model compares the allocative efficiency losses from merger-related increases in market power with merger-related gains in cost efficiency (arising from scale effects, learning effects, and the reallocation of output from firms of differing efficiency in the post-merger world) (Williamson, 1968; Farrell and Shapiro, 1990). This model applies most easily to horizontal M&As, but in principle it is also applicable to vertical and conglomerate M&As. Unfortunately, its static nature leads to a preoccupation with static concentration measures and monopoly power. The relationship of the M&As to profitability is not clear in a welfare sense because the outcome is a result of both monopoly power and efficiency gains.

Mergers in the long run: merger waves

M&As are clustered in time, giving rise to the notion of "merger waves". Exhibit 1 shows successive waves of merger activity in US industry and features five such waves – the latest running from 1997–2000 and continuing into 2001.

EXHIBIT 1 Merger waves in US industry

	Merger wave approximate dates	Current $ amount billion	Constant (2000) $ amount billion	Number of deals*
1.	1898–1902	6.9	136	3012
2.	1926–1939	7.3	69.3	4828
3.	1966–1969	46	236	NA
4.	1983–1986	618	NA	9617
5.	1997–2000	4500	4500	31 152

Source: Derived from *Mergers & Acquisitions*, Vol. 35, No. 8, September 2000.
Note: * Involving US companies

THE ORGANIZATION OF THIS VOLUME

Principles of selection

Our selection followed four key principles:

(1) The pieces selected should have genuine academic worth, be based on careful empirical work and be relevant to managerial problems in M&A activities.
(2) The selected works should not be available in other books of readings. (This principle is only violated where the works are out of print and unavailable).

(3) The selected pieces should not peddle "M&A nostrums" but should be challenging, critical and original.

(4) The volume should be complementary to monographs on M&As such as Haspeslagh and Jemison (1991), Child, Faulkner and Pitkethly (2001) and Hitt, Harrison and Ireland (2001). We also have a bias towards recency where there is a choice of pieces to illustrate key issues. This does not preclude enduring classic works.

The readings

The readings in this volume are planned so as to show the different stages in the M&A process. Section 1 examines the general issue of growth by M&A, the market for corporate control, the advantages and disadvantages of M&As, both systematic and for the firms involved. In addition, it examines international M&As from the point of comparison with alternative means of entering foreign markets – greenfield ventures and acquisitions. Section 2 on "motives and targets" examines hostile and friendly takeovers, the role of uncertainty in M&A strategies and the role of M&As in acquiring intangible, knowledge-based assets which are notoriously difficult to value. Section 3 approaches strategic planning, tactics and valuation from a number of different viewpoints including an examination of service industries, the role of control mechanisms and the defensive strategies (and their consequences) employed by potential acquisition victims. Section 4 examines merger processes, paying particular attention to the impact of cultural differences. The managerial and social consequences of M&As are the subject of Section 5, including a paper on post-acquisition managerial learning in Central Eastern Europe. Finally, the summary and conclusion are enhanced by a recent round table of executives giving their views on how to make mergers succeed.

    The intention of the volume is sequential, moving through M&A from general issues of strategy to implementation of the acquisition and finally to post-merger integration and consequences. Naturally, this sequence is not made up of utterly discrete stages and many of our readings spill out into other questions.

SECTION 1: GROWTH BY M&A

The market for corporate control

The key argument here is "that control of corporations is a valuable asset; that this asset exists independently of any interest in either economies of scale or monopoly profits; that an active market for corporate control exists; and that a great many mergers are probably the result of the successful workings of this special market" (Manne 1965: 112 in original, Chapter 3 below). Thus, management teams compete for the right to control this asset and operating efficiency is ensured by a natural selection mechanism in which the threat and act of a takeover by raiders ensures the survival of the fittest management teams. The key mechanism here is that low past performance due to inefficiency or the abuse of managerial discretion leads to weak share prices; potential raiders see the opportunity to alter policies and make capital gains as share prices respond to their improved management of the victim's assets.

    Several conditions are required if this stock market selection process is to work (Hughes, 1993).

(1) Share prices should reflect the relative expected profitability of firms.
(2) Raiders should be able to distinguish managerial shirking from poor performance arising from external circumstances.
(3) Raiders should be motivated by the desire to remove non-shareholder maximizing policies.
(4) Raiders should be able to obtain a sufficient payoff to make their activities worthwhile.

If (1) does not hold, scope for changes in corporate control occurs because of differences of opinion about the accuracy of stock market valuations between seller and raiders, rather than (potential) changes in managerial objectives or corporate efficiency. Failures in the market for corporate control also arise because of transaction costs and because acquiring companies cannot capture all the benefits of the raid. In practice, there are huge transaction costs for acquisition (legal, advisory, and information costs). Defensive tactics on the victims' part aim to increase these costs. They include: "shark repellents," constitutional or voting arrangements to protect incumbents; "golden parachutes" to raise the costs of firing incumbent managers; counterbidding; seeking a "white knight" to contest an unwanted bid or raiding a third party. (See Kosnik and Turk, 1994) on the antecedents and consequences resistance to takeovers).

EXHIBIT 2
Poison pills and other defence mechanisms

Companies adopt various measures to avoid takeovers. Poison pills are used by companies that fear hostile takovers to ensure that a bid, if successful, will trigger events that will significantly reduce the value of the firm. For instance, *flip-in* poison pills allow all existing holders of target company shares to buy additional shares at a bargain price. *Flip-over* poison pills allow holders of common stock to buy (or holders of preferred stock to convert into) the acquirer's shares at a bargain price. This defence measure has been installed in many companies, in particular United States companies. Although it is not certain how much poison pills alone have contributed to the low number of hostile takeovers, they have forced raiders to negotiate with the board of target firms to agree to a fair market price for the acquired firms' shares.

Another type of defence mechanism is when a target company warns an acquirer that in the event of a successful takeover, the entire management team will resign at once, leaving the company without experienced leadership.

Other measures include selling off "crown jewels" (dilute the intention of the acquirer by selling the assets of the target firm to a third party); and calling in "white knights" (find a preferable firm and ask it to acquire the target firm).

Source: UNCTAD World Investment Report, 2000, p. 104.

It has been suggested (Grossman and Hart, 1980) that the incentive structures in bids may lead to too few M&As from the point of view of disciplining inefficient managers. There can be an incentive for individual shareholders to "free ride" on post-merger gains rather than to sell out. In this case, the private return to the raider

is less than overall return which is split between the raider and the free riders. The observation of huge "merger waves" suggests that free riding may not be a major problem. Alternatively, partial bids (eg. 51 percent acquisitions) may be undesirable given that they incur transaction costs and may merely redistribute wealth between the raiders and the "oppressed" minority shareholders. Smaller companies with substantial owner control may be overvalued by the owners such that the costs of disciplinary M&A action may be prohibitive.

There are many pitfalls in the assessment of the impact of M&As on efficiency and economic performance. In terms of the stock market selection process, the choice of the control group is critical. Classification includes acquirers, acquired, and neither acquiring nor acquired. Some firms may be in both the first two categories. Characteristics of firms may affect the relevant comparisons – the size of firms, industry, and time may affect the choice of the most appropriate control groups. Outcome, too, can be measured in various ways – profitability, growth, and changes in profitability are possible measures as well as market value. The impact on technical change may also in certain contexts be relevant, and again, it is important to choose the appropriate counterfactual.

Empire building

M&As actually may be the result of empire building behaviours by managers. Growth maximizing implies that some management teams have a lower discount rate than the market as a whole. Such teams are then faced with a wealth of "under-valued" takeover opportunities.

In the international arena, the explanation of takeovers can have a two-fold aspect. If we use the simple formula for capitalizing a future income stream:

$$C = \frac{I}{r}$$

where C is the value of a capital asset, I is the stream of income it produces and r is the rate of return on investment, then a foreign firm can successfully buy out a domestic one if *either* I is higher *or* r is lower (or both). International business theory suggests that I will be higher where the foreign firm can raise the income stream by infusing the victim with better management, technology, organizational skills or superior marketing (Kindleberger, 1969). Alternatively, the capital market may apply a lower discount rate to the asset when it comes under foreign ownership (perhaps in the belief that higher returns will result). Thus Aliber (1970, 1971) suggests that a foreign asset owned by a US firm will be evaluated by the capital market as if it were a dollar asset. Differences in capitalization ratios set by the market on the basis of ownership may, on this reading, provide a rationale for foreign takeovers *even if* no increase in earnings occurs.

Success and the time horizon

Researchers using "event study methodology" have found that acquiring firms generally lose value as a result of merger activity (see Table 2 in Reading 5, p. 98). This research examines the short-term reaction of the prices of stock to merger announcements. The studies found that the price of the victim's stock rises while the price of the acquirer's stock stays about the same. The targets' share price rises

because the market expects the bid to be successful and that it will involve a premium above its current market price. The market also reacts conservatively to the impact of the bid on the market price of the acquirer. The results of longer-term studies are mixed. Some evidence is cited that if strategic, operational, and cultural fit are present, then cross border mergers may outperform domestic M&As.

The piece by Jensen (Chapter 4) is a ringing affirmation of the positive role of takeovers as a logical outcome of competitive struggles in the free market. "The takeover market provides a unique, powerful, and impersonal mechanism to accomplish the major restructuring and redeployment of assets continually required by changes in technology and consumer preferences".

Chapter 5, formulated by Hopkins, is unusual in that it combines a structured review of the literature with extensive executive comments, using the former as a skeleton for the latter to good effect. Particular attention should be drawn to the section on merger and acquisition related problems which highlights inspection (and its associated information problems), negotiation, and integration as key issues in the M&A process.

Alternatives to M&As

Two Chapters (6 and 7) examine the alternatives to international M&As: joint ventures and greenfield start-ups. Kogut examines joint ventures as an option to acquire. Kogut's paper seeks to explain joint ventures as "real options" to expand in response to future technological and market developments. In this sense, the exercise of the option is the move to acquisition. Joint ventures thus reduce the risk of entry into a new (national) market or technology. Investment in acquisition then becomes a second stage choice when the firm acquires new information from its initial venture. Such a strategy is useful in times of great volatility (Buckley and Casson, 1998) but entrant firms should be aware of the risk of being locked into a joint venture where it is captured by the local partner.

EXHIBIT 3
To what extent are greenfield FDI and cross-border M&As alternatives?

A comparison of the impact of FDI through cross-border M&As with that of greenfield FDI assumes that the two modes of foreign entry constitute alternatives from the perspectives of both host countries and TNCs. In principle and even in practice this may be the case, but they are rarely perfect substitutes for each other. From a host country's perspective, substitutability depends on its characteristics, including its level of economic development, FDI policy, the institutional framework and specific circumstances.

Level of economic development. While both modes may be options in developed countries with a large pool of strong private enterprises and well-functioning markets for corporate control, this is not always the case in developing countries and economies in transition. For example, M&As are typically not a realistic alternative to greenfield investment in the least

developed countries, in which investment opportunities may exist but there are few firms to acquire. In other development countries with a more advanced industrial sector and more developed capital markets, the acquisition of a local firm can represent a realistic alternative to greenfield FDI. Mergers between local firms in many developing countries and developed country firms are typically not feasible because of large differences in size, technology or management experience. In general, the higher the level of development of a host country, the larger the supply of firms that may be targeted for cross-border M&As.

FDI policy. Another obvious prerequisite for cross-border M&As is that they have to be permitted by the national regulatory framework. The liberalization of FDI regimes has gone far, and most countries now actively promote the inflow of FDI. In many cases, liberalization applies to both greenfield FDI and cross-border M&As. However, in a number of developing countries, foreign takeovers are *de facto* (if not *de jure*) restricted. Even in some developed countries, authorization is needed for the acquisition of companies in certain industries. Policy liberalization as regards foreign acquisitions has been shown to have a strong impact on the pattern of inward FDI in countries with a strong industrial base. In Argentina, for example, cross-border M&As accounted for almost 60 percent of total FDI inflows between 1992 and 1999. While privatization was initially responsible for the bulk of M&As, foreign acquisitions of private firms have gradually increased in importance, accounting for more than one-third of total inflows between 1996 and 1998 (Chudnovsky and López, 2000).

Institutional framework. The balance between cross-border M&As and greenfield FDI is also related to the institutional environment. For example, even among developed economies, the use of M&As is affected by differences in corporate governance and ownership structure. These help to explain the diverging patterns of M&As in the United States and the United Kingdom, on the one hand, and Germany and Japan on the other. In developing countries, underdeveloped asset markets and poor accounting standards may make it more difficult to assess accurately the value of corporate assets.

Exceptional circumstances. Examples include financial crises (as in Asia in 1997–1999) and large privatization programmes (as in Latin America or Central and Eastern Europe). Both produce, though for different reasons, a large one-off supply of firms in financial or competitive trouble. In both sets of circumstances, policy-makers have welcomed the cross-border acquisitions of local enterprises. Greenfield FDI could not in these circumstances play the role of cross-border M&As in rescuing ailing companies and restructuring state-owned firms.

To sum up, even though there are a number of situations in which the two modes of FDI entry are not realistic alternatives, they remain alternatives often enough to justify the comparison of their impacts on development. From a host-country perspective, this also means that host countries can influence both forms of entry through various policy measures. Such measures, however,

should be based not only on a realistic assessment of a host country's locational advantages, but also on an awareness of factors guiding firms' choices.

Firm-level factors can vary from industry to industry, depending on market structure and industry characteristics. High market concentration and high barriers to entry limit the probability of greenfield investment. This is the principal reason why, in such service industries as telecommunications, power generation and financial services, cross-border M&As are a predominant mode of entry. Similarly, in industries characterized by slow growth or excess capacity, firms are not likely to add new productive capacity if they can acquire existing assets. It should be noted that the market power of existing firms can be affected by the introduction of new technology (like cellular phones in telecommunications) or removal of barriers to entry and increasing the scope for greenfield investment.

The emergence of a knowledge-based economy and the liberalization of markets favour cross-border M&As. The former underlines the significance of skills and other knowledge-based assets for competitiveness and, consequently, leads to the increasing importance of asset-seeking FDI: of the two modes of FDI entry (leaving aside other modes and especially strategic alliances), only M&As can be used to access assets embodied in firms. The latter has increased competitive pressures, forcing firms to access assets or restructure *rapidly* and consolidate their operations in strategic response to competitors' moves, actual or expected. As *speed* has become a critical parameter, the greenfield option is often ruled out as an entry mode at an early stage of corporate decision-making.

Source: UNCTAD World Investment Report, 2000, pp. 161–2 (abridged).

Brouthers and Brouthers (1999) examine the impact of institutional cultural and transaction cost factors on the "buy or build" (acquire or establish new facilities) choice. As joint venture and wholly owned subsidiaries are ownership choices, this decision can be combined with the entry mode choice of acquiring existing assets versus establishing new facilities or a "greenfield" site. Greenfield entry is more likely to take place in high tech industries where the entrant firm has strong intangible competitive advantages.

The option perspective is widely recognized as a means of understanding the dynamics of joint ventures as the partners have the option to acquire, divest, and expand their stake. However, as Chi (2000) points out, the nature of the option, its value to the "buyer" and the "seller" varies markedly with its structure (including the structure of uncertainty and the terms of the option contract). "Even the most commonly recognized option in a JV – the option to acquire the partner's stake – tends to have some unique structural attributes" (Chi, 2000: 665). A typical JV contract, as Kogut points out, does not give either partner the right to acquire or divest the venture at an *ex ante* specified price. Thus, the partners have to negotiate a price *ex post* making the options exercise price indeterminate *ex ante*. Partners have good reasons for believing that new information will arrive during the operation of the JV which can result in one of them moving to full acquisition.

Hennart and Reddy (1997) examine the choice between "two alternative methods of pooling similar and complementary assets: the merger/acquisition and the greenfield equity joint ventures" (p. 1). This conflates the ownership choice (wholly owned versus joint venture) with the entry choice (takeovers versus greenfield entry). In fact, there are technically four potential choices of entry mode viz: (1) Greenfield/ Wholly Owned, (2) Greenfield/Joint Venture, (3) Takeover/Wholly Owned and a partial takeover, (4) Takeover/Joint Venture. Hennart and Reddy compare (3) with (2) leaving out wholly owned greenfield entry and partial acquisitions presumably because it is not a method of "pooling similar and complementary assets"! Hennart and Reddy contrast "two competing theories of why joint ventures exist" (p. 1): asymmetric information in the pre-merger situation versus "indigestibility" which refers to the (post-merger) problems of acquiring indivisible resources. In a commentary, Reuer and Koza (2000) point out that these views are complementary and overlapping.

Kogut and Singh (1988) examine the effect of national culture on choice of entry mode after accounting for firm and industry level variables. Their classification of entry is "greenfield" (equals wholly owned greenfield ventures), "joint venture" (greenfield shared ownership), and "takeovers" (purchase of stock in an already existing company in an amount sufficient to confer control). They claim that all acquisitions in the sample conferred a controlling equity share so the partial takeover (takeover/joint venture) category conveniently disappeared. After allowing for the impact of firm and industry variables, cultural distance is significant in influencing the entry mode choice into the US. The measure of cultural distance is a conflation of Hofstede's (Hofstede, 1980) four cultural dimensions (power distance, uncertainty avoidance, masculinity/femininity, and individualism) and is open to great objections even if the separate relevance of the four dimensions to the decision is accepted.

We have chosen the piece by Barkema and Vermeulen (Chapter 7) because it covers the foreign market entry choice (greenfield ventures versus takeovers) in an imaginative fashion. The authors show that the multicultural diversity leads to foreign start-ups rather than acquisitions but that product diversity has an inverted U-shape relationship with start-ups and acquisitions. The interaction between the explanatory variables is explored and an additional hypothesis is that unrelated expansions are more likely to be acquisitions whilst horizontal, related and vertical expansions are more likely to be greenfield start-ups. Their piece also contains an excellent bibliography and literature review so that the interested reader can trace the development of the role of acquisitions in international entry strategy.

SECTION 2: MOTIVES AND TARGETS

In Chapter 8, Baumann sets out a theory of (international) mergers. He examines "monopoly power, economies of scale, synergistic effects" and "non-profit maximising behaviour, differences in attitudes towards risk" and economic disturbance theory as alternative explanations for mergers, and applies property rights theory to foreign direct investment. The theoretical base, following an early version of internalization theory (McManus, 1972, following Coase, 1937; see also Buckley and Casson, 1976) is tested on US FDI in Canada. Both the improvement in the profit stream and the lower discount rate for assets denominated in stronger currencies are included as explanatory variables as are improvements due to superior management post take-over. Although Baumann's model is unable to distinguish between M&As and greenfield FDI, he is able to show the close relationship between the determinants of M&As and of FDI. This article, of course, pre-dates all but Manne's classic analysis (Chapter 3) and shows the importance of the valuation gap between buyer and seller (paralleling the gap between the foreign direct investor and the owners of host country resources either in packaged (M&A) or unpackaged (greenfield) form).

Following the distinction above between hostile and friendly takeovers, Morck et al. (1988) align these categories with disciplinary and synergistic motives. "Disciplinary takeovers" are aimed at correcting non-value-maximizing practices of the managers of target firms. Here, the actual integration of the acquirer and the target firm is not really essential. A takeover is the best way to change control and therefore strategy. "Synergistic takeovers" are motivated by the possibility of benefits of combining the businesses of the two firms. Morck et al. forcefully suggest that hostile and friendly takeovers should not be lumped together in an analysis of M&As but that they should be separated and inferences about one type should not be drawn on takeovers undertaken for the other motive. The empirical work analyses firms in the Fortune 500 in 1980 and examines takeovers 1981–85. They found that firms which were the target for hostile takover bids compared to the universe of firm, were smaller, older, more slow-growing and having lower Tobin's q, more debt and less investment of their income. They were less likely to be run by the founding family and had lower officer ownership than the average firm. Compared to the universe of Fortune 500 firms, friendly targets were smaller and younger but had comparable Tobin's q values and growth rates. The friendly targets were more likely to be run by a member of the founding family and had higher officer ownership than the average firm. The decision to retire of a CEO with a large stake in the firm or with a relationship to the founder often precipitated a friendly takeover – high officer ownership was the most important attribute predicting friendly acquisitions.

Coff (Chapter 9) takes on a theme that runs through many of the Readings – the idea that knowledge is frequently the target of corporate acquisitions. Knowledge is a key focus because often it cannot be acquired in efficient factor markets because it is bundled with other assets and because of asymmetric information. This leads to the risk of overbidding. The response of buyers was threefold: lower bid premia, contingent buy-outs, and lengthy negotiations designed to elicit tacit information. Where the firms drew on unrelated forms of expertise, these strategies were not used, leading to the conclusion that either lower post-merger integration was envisaged or that unrelated buyers were simply unaware of extra information needs.

Laamanen (Chapter 10) addresses the nature of acquisitions of small firms as growth options. Acquisitions were used as options to enter a new technology or business area. The option nature was related to technology-based variables such as low levels of maturity of the acquired competencies, possibility to patent these competencies, and the R&D intensity of the acquiring company. Key variables in achieving success were the relatedness of the acquirer and acquired, industry trends, and the marketing competence of the acquirer. In examining the foreign acquisition of US technology assets, Inkpen et al. (Reading 11) emphasize the organization and governance issues that are central to the acquisition process. Demoralization of staff and employees can be critical in technology-based industries where the main assets are knowledge related, residing in people.

Seth et al. (2000) examine the motives for the foreign acquisitions of US firms in terms of three hypotheses – synergy, managerialism, or hubris. The synergy hypothesis proposes that M&As take place when the value of the combined firm is greater than the sum of the values of the individual firms (see above for the difficulties of establishing this in practice!). The managerialism hypothesis suggests that managers embark on an acquisition to maximize their own utilities at the expense of the firm's shareholders. The hubris hypothesis suggests that bidding firm managers make mistakes in evaluating the target firm, but undertake the acquisition presuming that their valuations are correct. There is something of a conflation of these motives with outcomes in the empirical testing where positive and negative gains are attributed to acquirers and targets and total gains and losses are distributed among motives on a somewhat arbitrary basis.

SECTION 3: STRATEGIC PLANNING, TACTICS AND EVALUATION

Chapter 12 (Keenan) touches one of the most difficult issues in M&As, valuation problems. The paper examines a situation in which real economic adjustments evolve from the mergers and focuses on the valuation problems related to synergistic benefits arising from M&A. The paper analyses an acquisition of a service firm and contrasts it with an entry into an industry by starting a new firm, and is a valuable piece on valuation problems. It claims that capital budgeting theory is not very well developed to handle such "multi-period" problems where risk levels are shifting and where project-tied financing consideration exists. Moreover, the theory is rather generalized at the firm level, considering equations for demand, supply, and budget constraints in the economy. The valuation of M&As becomes particularly complex as the real economic markets for labour and capital are not strongly efficient. While reviewing existing studies, the authors explain that most of the research on M&As since the 1960s focused on two questions: (1) Are there any real benefits to conglomerate type mergers? and (2) What are the portfolio implications of a merger between two firms? It claims that according to these studies, statistically there are few valuation benefits and that many M&As are in fact detrimental to profit maximizing goals; while the stockholders of the acquired firm may reap some benefits, the stockholders of the acquiring firm do not.

The paper presents some examples of situations where the cost of labour is not in equilibrium, discussing the expected value, the market value, and what stages the process goes through. It highlights the complexities of valuation in a hypothetical case where a firm (A) wants to take over a firm (B) and becomes a new firm (C). It claims that a merger between two firms with different constant growth rates yields a firm that does not have a constant growth rate. The question thus arises, as to whether there are real benefits from mergers. It also builds up a scenario with acquisition of labour-intensive firms and demonstrates how the value of the acquired firm may, in fact, decrease. This suggests that there may be serious problems in the expected-value determination, negotiated-price determination, and accounting standards applied to the acquisition of a service firm where the value of the labour product is greater than the wage rate paid. Although the paper does not provide a solution as to how to solve these problems, it does a good job of highlighting the complexities. Moreover, considering the difficulties with goodwill evaluation and accounting, it stresses the need for a new accounting system applicable to these problems as well as new negotiation strategies and tactics.

Singh and Montgomery (Chapter 13) compare related with unrelated acquisitions (in product/market or technological terms). They find that acquired firms in related acquisitions have higher returns than acquired firms in unrelated acquisitions. For acquiring firms, abnormal returns directly attributable to the acquisition transaction are not significant. However, announcement effects are less easily detectable for the acquirers rather than targets because the acquisition affects only part of the acquiring firm but the whole of the target firm. In addition, as the acquisition is an event in a series of an implicit diversification programme, its effect as a unique market signal is mitigated. Expected gains for acquiring firms are thus often competed away in the bidding process, while stockholders of the target firm obtain high proportions of the gains.

Calori et al. (Chapter 14) examine the influence of national culture on the integration mechanisms used by French and US entrants into Britain and British and US acquirers in France. They find that firms are influenced by their national administrative heritage when they acquire foreign firms. In the UK comparison, the French acquiring firms relied more on formal control of strategy and of operations than US firms (as perceived from respective acquired firms). The American acquiring firms relied more on informal communication and cooperation (teamwork) with the French. In examining the acquisition of French firms, it was found that the US acquiring firms relied more on formal control by procedures than the British, and American managers became more personally involved, suggesting a "hands off" attitude from the managers of British acquiring firms. In terms of impact on post-merger performance, the article is suggestive. It points out that the health of the acquired firm prior to the merger is negatively correlated to improvements in attitudinal performance and both informal communication and cooperation (teamwork) and informal personal efforts from the managers of the buying firms are positively correlated with improvements in attitudinal performance. This confirms the view that socialization is a key factor in reducing post-merger conflicts and demotivation (Haspeslagh and Jemison, 1991). Two other variables are significant in economic performance of the acquired firms – time elapsed since acquisition and the level of shared resources and transfers. Thus the implementation of synergies between the merging firms contributes to economic performance but there seems to be a delay before the economic performance shows through. Two measures of control mechanisms also are correlated with economic performance. Informal personal effects of the buying firm's managers positively affect performance and the level of control of operations exercized by the buying firm is negatively correlated with performance. The authors suggest that, as far as international acquisitions are concerned, operational decisions should not be centralized.

In examining cross-border mergers, Gonzalez et al. (Chapter 15) suggest there might be systematic undervaluation of assets at national level, which result in acquisitions being the most cost-effective way of penetrating certain national markets. This arises because of the existence of market imperfections that cause friction in the product and service markets leading to asset undervaluation.

SECTION 4: MERGER PROCESS

The first chapter in this section by Buono et al. (Chapter 16) deals with culture as a phenomenon in a merger context. As we can see from this volume and other writings on M&A, culture is one of the dominating factors that influences performance. Buono et al. have studied a merger between two banks from the perspective of organizational culture. Data on organizational culture is collected and analysed through pre- and post-merger interviews. The interesting point is that the study shows that culture is an important issue even when the firms come from the same

country and same industry. The study thus enhances our understanding of culture and its consequences on the merger process. It also clarifies and helps us understand how a new culture emerges in a newly formed organization. It looks at objective and subjective organizational culture and suggests that although both aspects of culture are important, subjective culture provides more distinctive interpretations of similarities and differences among people in different groups, as it is particularly unique to an organization. Another issue discussed is the organizational climate: whether people's expectations in that organization are met or not. This study has outlined the real issues that emerge during and after the merger process. These are the issues that influence behaviour, satisfaction, expectations of organizational members and thereby success or failure of a merger.

As illustrated throughout this volume, the importance of knowledge transfer for the success of acquisitions is regarded as critical to achieving synergy and creating value. Bresman et al. (1999) focus on the factors facilitating the post-acquisition transfer of knowledge over time. They find that the transfer of technological know-how is facilitated by communication, visits and meetings and increases as time elapses. The transfer of patents is associated with the articulability of the knowledge, the size of the acquired unit and the recency of the acquisition. High-quality reciprocal knowledge transfer takes time to develop but it gradually replaces the one-way transfer of knowledge from acquirer to acquired. This parallels the increasing transfer of tacit knowledge which is more time-consuming to transfer than knowledge which is more articulated. The human relations processes across the merged unit develop in similar fashion (see Buono and Bowditch, 1989).

Chatterjee et al. (1992) dealt with the compatibility of the merging firms and its relationship to shareholder gains and relatedness. They surveyed the perceptions of top management teams in 168 M&As. Based on the response from 73 firms, their findings show an intense relationship between the acquired managers' perceptions of cultural difference and shareholder value. Their results support the hypothesis that changes in shareholder value of acquiring firms are directly related to the degree to which the buyer's top management team tolerates multiculturalism. Their findings also show that a lower cultural tolerance will influence shareholder value negatively. This study provides a systematic evidence linking equity and human capital in M&As.

Morosini et al. (Chapter 17) examine cross-border acquisition activity in Italy. They measure post-acquisition performance using the percentage rate of growth of sales over the two-year period following the acquisition. This is clearly a less satisfying measure of performance than stock market pricing or profitability. On this measure they found that national cultural distance enhances cross-border acquisition performance. They explain this result by the argument that cross-border acquisition in more culturally distant countries might provide a mechanism for multinational companies to access diverse routines and repertoires which have the potential to enhance the combined firm's performance over time. Post-acquisition strategies are also adduced to enhance this result. The quantitative findings are supplemented with interviews with acquiring companies from a number of source countries.

SECTION 5: MANAGERIAL AND SOCIAL CONSEQUENCE OF MERGERS

The first chapter in this section (18) deals with an important, but often ignored, aspect of M&A activity; its social and political consequences. The Reading by

Siegfield and Sweeney is a comprehensive account of these consequences. As there are competing views, the authors point out that we have to depend on the judicial system which is unfortunately not well equipped to weigh competing claims. They discuss the most important characteristics of M&A, namely, market concentration, firm size, product diversification and geographic dispersion, and discuss the consequences of each. Based on empirical evidence, they then assess other social consequences such as effect on workers, distribution of income, and on community welfare and explain reasons why M&A might increase and/or decrease social goals. Finally, they stress the need for more systematic research in this area that will assist policymakers in handling these problems.

The Reading by Deepak Datta (Chapter 19) connects organizational fit to acquisition performance. Based on 173 US acquisitions it evaluates post-merger performance of the firms involved in an acquisition. His findings demonstrate that differences in top management styles have a negative impact on post-merger performance as well as integration. Secondly, it examines difference in reward and evaluation systems and suggests that these differences do not have the same kind of negative impact on performance as differences in management styles. A possible reason is said to be that differences in reward and evaluation systems are more easily and quickly reconciled following an acquisition than are differences in management styles. Although the study only takes two aspects of organizational fit and there are some flaws in data collection, it brings forward important issues in post-acquisition integration of firms.

The study by Villinger (Chapter 20) is an important one as it deals with post-acquisition learning in Central and Eastern Europe. It examines post-acquisition learning by Western firms in Hungary, the Czech Republic, Slovakia and Poland. That means that it covers the most important market area for M&A activity in the region. He points out that in these countries cross-border management skills seem to be more important than general business skills for post-acquisition management efforts. The knowledge of acquired partner's language and sensitivity about cultural issues are crucial. It claims that learning is the central aspect rather than integration, at least in the earlier phases of post-acquisition as it is more important to transform the East European acquiree than to integrate it with its Western parent. It then proposes three levels of learning based on Senge (1968) and Child et al. (1992) as "single-loop learning"; "double-loop learning"; and "deuterolearning". These different levels pose different problems for learners and learning entity, but in Eastern Europe context and for a successful transition, this framework is considered to be the most "elegant". Based on an empirical study of 35 cases, the study concludes that a dominance of general business competence over cross-border skills is more prevalent, which creates post-acquisition problems. A lack of communication and understanding is generally blamed for insufficient learning. Language and cultural awareness are thus considered the most important issues for post-acquisition integration in Eastern Europe.

PRIVATIZATION

Privatization represents a special case of acquisition activity where the acquiring firm takes over part or the whole of the equity of state-owned firms. Where foreign firms are the buyers this represents an international M&A. In contrast to other forms of

international M&A, the foreign buyer is welcomed by the host government rather than, as is often the case, treated as a predator.

The rapid growth of privatization following the collapse of communism in Central and Eastern Europe has now subsided and although privatization in developed economies outweighs that in developing countries, several Latin American (notably Brazil) and Asian developing countries are pressing ahead with privatization programmes (UNCTAD, 2001). Foreign acquisitions of privatized firms as a percentage of the total value of cross-border M&As reached about one-tenth in the mid 1990s but fell to 6 percent in 1999. In developed countries, the bulk of privatization sales are to domestic buyers while in developing countries foreign participation has been higher than domestic (UNCTAD, 2001: 131). In Central and Eastern Europe, privatization has been an integral part of the transition to a market economy, accounting for a substantial share of cross-border M&As, but the majority of privatized assets have been acquired by or distributed to domestic shareholders. In the period 1987–1999, 11 countries sold more than $5 billion each of privatized firms with Brazil, Argentina and Australia the largest sellers (see UNCTAD, 2001, Annex Table A. IV.21 p. 262).

The industries involved include capital intensive infrastructural activities such as telecommunications and utilities and industries requiring substantial restructuring such as automobiles, energy related industries including petroleum and mining. Most of the cross-border mega deals in developing countries are privatizations. While the value of cross-border M&As through privatization has continued to increase in recent years, the number of deals reached a plateau by the early 1990s (UNCTAD, 2001, Figure IV. 22, p. 132).

DIFFERENCES IN INTERNATIONAL REGULATION OF M&As

Franks and Mayer (1993) examine the relationship between capital markets and corporate control. They compare the relationship in France, Germany, and the UK and include buy-outs and buy-ins by managers. Regulation (company laws, competition policy, stock exchange rules and labour laws) explain much of the difference in control and ownership changes across countries, even within an economic area such as the European Union (EU). The EU's Competition Commissioner heads a competition authority which is currently "seen by business as overburdened and unpredictable in its decision making" (Hargreaves, *Financial Times* 18.9.2000: 16). The EU's merger regulation has a theoretically clear remit to prevent mergers which inhibit competition and allow others to proceed. In practice, European mergers still need clearance from several national competition authorities. The unit that reviews mergers, the Merger Task Force, is under resourced. The absence of a single European regulatory organization, let alone a global one, vastly increases the transaction costs of M&As. In practice, European authorities veto very few mergers (of 1500 deals during the 1990s only 13 were vetoed and 12 more withdrawn after it became clear that the Commission would intervene over excessive market power). The increase in number and complexity of deals is putting pressure on regulatory authorities – particularly those like the EU which wants to examine ever smaller-sized M&As. In Europe in particular, labour organizations play a role in M&As. Given the high rate of failure because of the human factor, this is perhaps to be welcomed. The International Labour Office (ILO) is currently calling for increased

dialogue between management and workers in the M&A process in an attempt to minimize the negative effects.

The number of significant regulatory authorities in the world has mushroomed. Reports of the deal between Coca-Cola and Cadbury-Schweppes suggest that their lawyers sought anti-trust approval in more than 40 jurisdictions around the world. In the failed effort to merge, Alcan Aluminium of Canada, Pechiney of France and Algroup of Switzerland, lawyers from 35 firms filed for regulatory approval in 16 jurisdictions and 8 languages. Pernod Ricard's £2.1 billion purchase of 38.6 percent of Seagram's drinks portfolio (with Diageo) has required filing for regulatory approval in 70 countries (Kemeny, *Sunday Times* 21.1.01: 3/6). Simplification of competition laws and creating a consensus among regulators to make antitrust laws coherent and predictable is the current extent of feasibility. There is little current prospect of a new international bureaucracy to oversee mergers. The United States has recently opposed a European proposal to give the World Trade Organisation (WTO) a central role in policing mergers. Harmonization is made urgent by the increased number of merger cases which amounted to 26 000 filings between 1994 and 2000 with the US Department of Justice and the Federal Trade Commission (FTC).

GAINS FROM M&A?

Seth et al. (2000) estimate total gains in cross-border acquisition to be 7.6 percent of the pre-acquisition value of the combined firm. This is similar to the estimate of total gains for domestic acquisitions (Bradley, Resai and Kim, 1988) but larger than that reported by Eun et al. (1996). Seth et al. find that positive total gains occur in 74 percent of the acquisitions in their sample, similar to the proportions reported by Berkovitch and Narayanan (1993) at 76 percent and Bradley, Desai and Kim (1988) (75 percent). However, Seth et al. find that targets realize the majority of the gains, whilst acquirers appear to neither gain nor lose on average. Successful acquirers in single bidder acquisitions retain around 40 percent of the total gains on average, whilst acquirers in multiple bidder transactions make small losses.

Only about one-third of recent M&As were found to have positive effects on the shareholder value for the buying firm (Schenk, 2000). Performance results, reported by earlier research, are quite mixed (Cowling et al., 1980; Magenheim and Mueller, 1988; Sirowar, 1997). Dickerson et al. (1997) show that company growth through acquisition yielded a lower rate of return than growth through internal investment. A survey of 22 accounting data studies from nine countries showed that the average acquiring firm does not earn a significantly higher profit than the industry average (Bild, 1998). Earlier results from Mandelker (1974) found that the market for acquisitions can be regarded as perfectly competitive, supporting the hypothesis that information regarding mergers is efficiently incorporated into the stock price. Stockholders of acquiring firms seem to earn normal returns from mergers as compared to other ventures of similar risks. Stockholders of acquired firms earned abnormal returns of approximately 14 percent on average in the seven months preceding the merger. The fact that the market anticipates mergers (at least three months on average according to Franks et al. (1977)) before announcement further complicates the analysis. Aiello and Watkins (2000) suggest that leveraged buy outs (LBOs) are more successful than M&As in general. "Between 1984 and 1994, some 80 percent of LBO firms reported that their fund investors had received a return that

matched or exceeded their cost of capital, even though in many cases the prices paid for the companies those funds acquired were pushed up by competing bidders" (p. 101). This, they suggest, is due to the fact that senior managers at financial investors (like the most successful corporate acquirers) approach potential acquisitions with sensitivity and a well-established process. They contrast this approach with that of "most corporate managers" who try to beat down prices and often delegate actual deal management to outside experts (investment bankers and lawyers). Ashkenas and Francis (2000) suggest that specialist integration managers with real leadership qualities and considerable discretion should be appointed to manage post-deal integration processes.

As for achieving efficiency gains (the most cited justification for M&As), the scope for rationalization and improving company performance by achieving an international specialization of the value chain can be particularly high in M&As (UNCTAD, 2000). Moreover, size can have a large influence for R&D and the expansion of distribution networks as well as adoption of new information and innovations.

In sum, empirical literature from the field of finance generally finds that the significant gains from mergers go to the acquired firms. However, the literature from the strategic management and international business fields suggest that mergers are not a uniform phenomenon (Lubatkin, 1983). They can lead to a range of possible outcomes depending on the strategic fit between the firms and the quality of pre- and post-merger management, as this volume shows. Halpern (1973) showed that since most mergers occur in rising markets, this effect needs to be removed in estimating gains and premia. Size of company too is a factor. If we accept that acquisitions are often a search for a unique asset embedded in a company, then returns from that asset will vary as the size of the unique element varies as a proportion of the total company. Because quality of management, too, is a factor, uncertainty about when that management will be replaced will be reflected in the current stock price (the present value of an uncertain event). When the merger is announced, there is a positive total adjusted gain which reflects the markets' re-evaluation of the company under its new management. Bargaining strategies will also affect the distribution of gains.

REFERENCES

Aiello, Robert J. and Michael D. Watkins (2000) "The Fine Art of Friendly Acquisition" *Harvard Business Review* 78(6), Nov–Dec, 101–107.

Alchian, A. A. and Harold Demsetz (1972) "Production, Information and Economic Organization" *American Economic Review*, 62, 777–95.

Aliber, Robert Z. (1970) "A Theory of Direct Foreign Investment" in Charles P. Kindleberger (ed.) *The International Corporation*, Cambridge, Mass: MIT Press.

Aliber, Robert Z. (1971) "The Multinational Enterprise in a Multiple Currency World" in John H. Dunning (ed.) *The Multinational Enterprise*, London: George Allen & Unwin.

Ashkenas, Ronald N. and Susanne C. Francis (2000) "Integration Managers: Special Leaders for Special Times" *Harvard Business Review*, 78(6), Nov–Dec, 108–116.

Berkovitch, Elazor and M. P. Narayanan (1993) "Motives for Takeovers: An Empirical Investigation" *Journal of Finance and Quantitative Analysis,* 28(3), 347–362.

Bert, Tim and Nikki Trait (2000) "Kerkorian versus Schrempp May Add to Chrysler's Woes", *Financial Times*, November 28, 24.

Bild, Magnus (1998) *Valuation of Takeovers*, Ph.D dissertation, Stockholm School of Economics, Stockholm: Elander Gotalo.

Bradley, M., A. Desai and E. H. Kim (1988) "Synergistic Gains from Corporate Acquisitions and Their Division between the Stockholders of Target and Acquiring Firms" *Journal of Financial Economics* 21(1), 3–40.

Bresman, Henrik, Julian Birkinshaw and Robert Nobel (1999) "Knowledge Transfer in International Acquisitions" *Journal of International Business Studies*, 30(3), 439–462.

Brouthers, Keith. D. and Lance Eliot Brouthers (2000) "Acquisition or Greenfield Start-up? Institutional, Cultural and Transaction Cost Influences" *Strategic Management Journal* 21, 89–97.

Buckley, Peter J. and Mark Casson (1976) *The Future of the Multinational Enterprise*, London: Macmillan.

Buckley, Peter J. and Mark Casson (1998) "Models of the Multinational Enterprise" *Journal of International Business Studies*, 29(1), 21–44.

Buono, A. F. and J. L. Bowditch (1989) *The Human Side of Mergers and Acquisitions: Managing Collisions Between People and Organizations*, San Francisco: Jossey Bass.

Chatterjee, Sayan, Michael H. Lubatkin, David M. Scheweiger and Yaakov Weber (1992) "Cultural Differences and Shareholder Value in Related Mergers, Linking Equity and Human Capital", *Strategic Management Journal* 13, 319–344.

Chi, Tailan (2000) "Option to Acquire or Divest a Joint Venture" *Strategic Management Journal* 21, 665–687.

Child, John, David Faulkner and Robert Pitkethly (2001) *The Management of International Acquisitions*, Cambridge: Cambridge University Press.

Child, John, Markocy, Livia and Tony Cheung (1992) "Management Adaptation in Chinese and Hungarian Strategic Alliances with Culturally Different Foreign Partners", Working Paper, *The Judge Institute Management Studies at St. John College*, University of Cambridge: UK.

Chudnovisky, Daniel A. L. and Fernando Porta (1995) "New Foreign Direct Investment in Argentina: Privatization, the Domestic Market, and Regional Integration" in Manuel R. Agosin (ed.) *Foreign Direct Investment in Latin America*, pp. 39–104. Washington DC: Inter-American Development Bank.

Coase, Ronald H. (1937) "The Nature of the Firm" *Economica* (ns) 4, 386–405.

Cowling, Keith, Paul Stoneman, John Cubbin, John Cable, Graham Hall, Simon Domberger and Patricia Dutton (1980) *Mergers and Economic Performance*. Cambridge: Cambridge University Press.

Demsetz, Harold (1973) "Industry Structure, Market Rivalry, and Public Policy" *The Journal of Law and Economics* 16: 1–3.

Dickerson, Andrew P., Heather D. Gibson and Euolid Tsakalotos (1997) "The Impact of Acquisitions on Company Performance: Evidence from a Large Panel of UK Firms" *Oxford Economic Papers* 49, 344–61.

The Economist (2000) "The Great Merger Wave Breaks", Jan. 27, 59–60. .

Eun, Cheol S., Richard Kolodny and Carl Scheraga (1996) "Cross-border Acquisitions and Shareholder Wealth: Tests of the Synergy and Internalization Hypotheses" *Journal of Banking and Finance*, 20, 1559–1582.

Farrell J. and C. Shapiro (1990) "Horizontal Mergers: An Equilibrium Analysis" *American Economic Review*, March, 107–26.

Franks, F. R., J. E. Broyles and M. J. Hecht (1977) "An Industry Study of the Profitability of Mergers in the United Kingdom" *The Journal of Finance*, XXXII(5) December, 1513–1525.

Franks, Julian and Colin Mayer (1993) "European Capital Markets and Corporate Control" in Matthew Bishop and John Kay (eds) *European Mergers and Merger Policy*, Oxford: Oxford University Press.

Grossman S. J. and O. D. Hart (1980) "Takeover Bids, the Free-rider Problem, and the Theory of the Corporation" *Bell Journal of Economics* 11(1), 42–64.

Halpern, Paul J. (1973) "Empirical Estimates of the Amount and Distribution of Gains to Companies in Mergers" *Journal of Business* 46(4), Oct., 554–575.

Haspeslagh, Philippe and David Jemison (1991) *Managing Acquisitions: Creating Value through Corporate Renewal*, New York: The Free Press.

Hennart, Jean Francois and Sabine Reddy (1997) "The Choice Between Mergers/Acquisitions and Joint Ventures: The Case of Japanese Investors in the United States" *Strategic Management Journal* 18, 1–12.

Hitt, Michael A., Jeffrey S. Harrison and R. Duane Ireland (2001) *Mergers and Acquisitions: a Guide for Creating Value for Stakeholders*, Oxford: Oxford University Press.

Hofstede, Geert (1980) *Culture's Consequences: International Differences in Work Related Values*, Beverly Hills: Sage Publications.

Hughes, Alan (1993) "Mergers and Economic Performance in the UK: A Survey of the Empirical Evidence 1950–90" in M. Bishop and J. Kay (eds) *European Mergers and Merger Policy*. Oxford: Oxford University Press.

Kindleberger, Charles P. (1969) *American Business Abroad*, New Haven: Yale University Press.

Kogut, Bruce and Harbir Singh (1988) "The Effect of National Culture on the Choice of Entry Mode" *Journal of International Business Studies* Fall, 411–432.

Kosnik, Rita D. and Thomas A. Turk (1994) "The Antecedents and Consequence of Resistance to Takeovers" in Georg von Krogh, Alessandro Sinatra and Harbir Singh (eds) *The Management of Corporate Acquisitions: International Perspectives*, London: Macmillan, pp. 170–190.

Lubatkin, Michael (1983) "Mergers and the Performance of the Acquiring Firm" *Academy of Management Review* 8(2), 218–225.

Mandelker, Gershon (1974) "Risk and Return: The Case of Merging Firms" *Journal of Financial Economics* 1, 303–35.

Magenheim, Ellen and Dennis C. Muller (1988) "Are Acquiring Firm Shareholders Better Off After an Acquisition?" in John Coffee, Louis Lowenstein and Susan Rose-Ackerman (eds) *Knights, Raiders and Targets*. Oxford: Oxford University Press.

McManus, J. C. (1972) "The Theory of the International Firm" in Gilles Pacquet (ed.) *The Multinational Firm and the Nation State*, Toronto: Collier–Mcmillan.

Morck, Randall, Andrei Shleifer and Robert W. Vishny (1988) "Characteristics of Targets of Hostile and Friendly Takeovers" in Alan J Auerbach (ed.) *Corporate Takeovers: Causes and Consequences*, pp. 101–118. Chicago: University of Chicago Press.

Puranam, Phanish, Harbir Singh and Maurizio Zollo (2000) "Bringing Some Discipline to M&A Mania", *Financial Times: Mastering Management*, October 30, 2–4.

Reuer, Jeffrey J. and Mitchell P. Koza (2000) "On Lemons and Indigestibility: Resource Assembly through Joint Ventures" *Strategic Management Journal*, 21, 195–7.

Schenk, Hans (2000) "Are International Acquisitions a Matter of Strategy Rather than Wealth Creation?" *International Review of Applied Economics*, 00–00.

Senge, Peter (1968) "The Leader's New Work: Building Learning Organizations", *Sloan Management Review*, 7–23.

Seth, Anju, Kea P. Song and Richardson Pettit (2000) "Synergy, Managerialism or Hubris? An Empirical Examination of Motives for Foreign Acquisitions of US Firms" *Journal of International Business Studies*, 31(3), 387–405.

Sirowar, Mark I. (1997) *The Synergy Trap: How Companies Lose the Acquisition Game*. New York: Free Press.

UNCTAD (2000) *World Investment Report 2000*, New York and Geneva: UNCTAD.

von Krogh, Georg, Alessandro Sinatra and Harbir Singh (1974) *The Management of Corporate Acquisitions: International Perspectives*. London: Macmillan.

Williamson, Oliver E. (1968) "Economics as Anti-Trust Defence: The Welfare Trade-Offs", *American Economic Review* 58 (March), 18–36.

2 *The Economist* cases: how mergers go wrong

It is important to learn the lessons from the failures and successes of past mergers

They are, like second marriages, a triumph of hope over experience. A stream of studies has shown that corporate mergers have even higher failure rates than the liaisons of Hollywood stars. One report by KPMG, a consultancy, concluded that over half of them had destroyed shareholder value, and a further third had made no difference. Yet over the past two years, companies around the globe have jumped into bed with each other on an unprecedented scale. In 1999, the worldwide value of mergers and acquisitions rose by over a third to more than $3.4 trillion. In Europe, the hottest merger zone of all, the figure more than doubled, to $1.2 trillion.

Can today's would-be corporate partners avoid repeating yesterday's bad experiences? To help answer that question, *The Economist* recently published a series of case studies of mergers, most of which happened at least two years ago so that lessons can safely be drawn. None is in the *Titanic* league of merger disasters on the scale, say, of AT&T'S 1991 purchase of NCR, the second-largest acquisition in the computer industry, which was reversed after years of immense losses. But none has gone entirely smoothly either; and all offer useful insights.

Most of the mergers looked at were defensive, meaning that they were initiated in part because the companies involved were under threat. Sometimes, the threat was a change in the size or nature of a particular market: McDonnell Douglas merged with Boeing, for example, because its biggest customer, the Pentagon, was cutting spending by half. Occasionally the threat lay in that buzzword of today, globalisation, and its concomitant demand for greater scale: Chrysler merged with Daimler-Benz because, even as number three in the world's largest car market, it was too small to prosper alone. Or the threat may have come from another predator: Bayerische Vereinsbank sought a merger with a Bavarian rival, Hypobank, because its management was scared of being gobbled up by Deutsche Bank.

When a company merges to escape a threat, it often imports its problems into the marriage. Its new mate, in the starry moments of courtship, may find it easier to see the opportunities than the challenges. Hypobank is an egregious example: it took more than two years for Vereinsbank to discover the full horror of its partner's balance sheet.

As important as the need for clear vision and due diligence before a merger is a clear strategy after it. As every employee knows full well, mergers tend to mean job losses. No sooner is the announcement out than the most marketable and valuable members of staff send out their resumés. Unless they learn quickly that the deal will give them opportunities rather than pay-offs, they will be gone, often taking a big chunk of shareholder value with them.

The mergers that worked relatively well were those where managers both had a sensible strategy and set about implementing it straight away. The acquisition of

Turner Broadcasting by Time Warner comes in this category: Gerald Levin, Time Warner's boss, had developed in the late 1980s a vision of the modern media conglomerate, offering one piece of content to many different audiences. At DaimlerChrysler, too, merger integration was pursued with Teutonic thoroughness – although not skilfully enough to avoid the loss of several key people. And after Citibank merged with Travelers to form Citigroup, the world's biggest financial-services firm, it quickly reaped big profits from cost-cutting – though rather less from its original aim of cross-selling different financial services to customers.

As in every walk of business, luck and the economic background play a big part. Merging in an upswing is easier to do, as rising share prices allow bidders to finance deals with their own paper, and it is also easier to reap rewards when economies are growing. But companies, like people, can make their own luck: Boeing's Phantom Works, an in-house think-tank that has speeded the integration process, developed new products and refocused the company on its diverse customers, was a serendipitous creation in the turmoil that followed its deal with McDonnell Douglas.

Above all, personal chemistry matters every bit as much in mergers as it does in marriage. It matters most at the top. No company can have two bosses for long. So one boss must accept a less important role with good grace. After many months of damaging dithering, Citibank's John Reed eventually made way for Sandy Weill of Travelers. It helps if a boss has a financial interest in making the merger work, as the success of the union of Time Warner and Turner shows: few people would have bet at the outset that the mercurial Ted Turner would have been able to work with the stolid Mr Levin. Without leadership from its top manager, a company that is being bought can all too often feel like a defeated army in an occupied land, and will wage guerrilla warfare against a deal.

The fact that mergers so often fail is not, of itself, a reason for companies to avoid them altogether. But it does mean that merging is never going to be a simple solution to a company's problems. And it also suggests that it would be a good idea, before they book their weddings, if managers boned up on the experiences of those who have gone before. The six merger briefs which follow were published in July and August 2000.

MERGER BRIEFS

1   THE DIGITAL DILEMMA

Our new series of six briefs looks at big mergers of the recent past: what was the strategy behind them, and did it work? We start with Compaq's ill-fated takeover of Digital Equipment, the biggest merger in the history of the computer industry. As companies so often do, Compaq tried to buy a new future. So was the deal bad strategy, or just bad timing?

It was just two and a half years ago, but it seems another age. In January 1998 the king of the business world was Compaq Computer. The Texan giant, the world's largest PC maker, had just overtaken IBM. It had been growing by 30% a year, twice the industry average, and its skyrocketing share price had made more millionaires in Houston than oil ever did.

Forbes magazine had just crowned Compaq its "company of the year", saluting its "exceptional" chief executive, Eckhard Pfeiffer. And then, as if to prove that this was

just the beginning, Compaq announced that it would buy Digital Equipment, a company with nearly twice as many employees, for an industry record of $9 billion, at a stroke reshaping the computer world. Mr Pfeiffer predicted that the Microsoft-Intel "Wintel" duopoly would soon give way to "Wintelpaq".

Today Compaq is a shaken company with an uncertain future. It has lost more money since the merger than in all its previous history: more than $2 billion in all. It is no longer America's leading PC maker, having been passed by both Dell and Hewlett-Packard in the retail market. Its shares are at about half their peak. And Mr Pfeiffer is gone, ignominiously fired by the board last year and eventually replaced by a little-known Compaq executive, Michael Capellas, after months of looking for a high-flying outsider.

From afar, the cause and effect seem clear: Compaq bought Digital and choked on it, losing its way. But look closer and another possibility emerges: Compaq was already living on borrowed time, which expired before the Digital deal could be made to work.

Over the past two years, the PC has fallen out of favour, as has the increasingly commoditised business of making it. Having the leading PC brand, as Compaq did, became less attractive once most PC makers were losing money.

Credit Mr Pfeiffer for one thing: he was among the first to spot that the PC industry was reaching the end of its golden age. Buying Digital was his bid to migrate to a more profitable market: services and sophisticated high-end hardware that would not be cannibalised by Intel's next mainstream chip or by the relentless pricing pressure of a swarm of hyperefficient competitors. Like any big merger, it was hugely risky – but so was doing nothing.

This reading leads to a more charitable view of events. "What happened to Compaq's PC business was going to happen anyway – everyone else in the industry is now feeling the same pressure," says Howard Elias, who heads Compaq's storage business (and came from Digital). "If anything, the merger came too late." On this

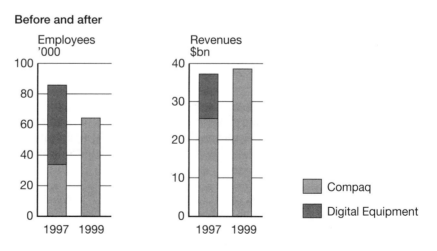

Source: Company reports

Figure 1

interpretation, the deal was not a mistake; but it came as Compaq hit an internal crisis, distracting it when it needed to focus on making the acquisition work.

Delled

In truth, the Compaq of early 1998 was already stumbling. The system it had perfected – manufacturing PCs to meticulous three- and six-month forecasts and then selling them via a hard-won network of retailers, systems integrators and distributors – had passed its prime. The rise of the sub-$1,000 PC spelled the end of the 30% gross margins that had supported Compaq's distribution chain, and an increasingly global market had made forecasting harder. When Compaq started missing profit targets, its share price fell sharply.

The new way to do things was devised by Dell, whose direct-to-consumer model allowed it to manufacture a PC only when it had an order in hand. This meant the near-elimination of unsold stock, the bane of the industry (PCs lose about 1% of their value every week they stay on the shelf). Dell's technology was no better than Compaq's, but consumers loved being able to design their own PC and get it within a week. Wall Street was dazzled, too: soon, Dell had about the same market capitalisation as Compaq on just half the revenues. The differences between the firms grew more striking: while Dell was winning admiration for its web strategy, Compaq was signing deals with Tandy to sell computers through Radio Shack in shopping malls.

It was a classic instance of "channel conflict". Compaq could not switch to Dell's direct model because this would mean undercutting the 11,000 retailers and other channel partners that had been so much a part of Compaq's success to date. But neither could it continue as before. Compaq tried to fine-tune its manufacturing system by, for example, building to dealers' forecasts rather than its own. When there was an unexpected dip in PC demand in late 1997, Dell was flexible enough to cut production, but Compaq, with months of inventory, was hit hard.

Short of abandoning the desktop PC market, the only alternative seemed to be to expand beyond the low-margin PC-making business, into services and equipment for corporate customers. The real giants of the computer industry, firms such as IBM and Hewlett-Packard, already offered such breadth. They make equipment from PCs to supercomputers; and they have a huge service, support and sales operation. Most of IBM's recent growth has come from its services side.

Compaq itself already had the core of such a diversified operation. Its Intel-based hardware extended from laptops to mid-range servers. To serve more demanding users it had in 1997 bought Tandem, a maker of "fault-tolerant" servers that run such critical operations as Nasdaq's trading system and airline-booking networks. In the long term, Compaq was betting that Intel-based systems would continue to move upstream as Microsoft's NT operating system began to approach the capabilities of Unix, the leading system for high-end servers. But the big missing piece was a global services organisation that could support both the complex systems and the demanding corporate clients it brought them.

From 1995 onwards, Compaq was looking for ways to get such a service and support operation, which would inevitably mean an army of people far larger than the existing Compaq workforce. Building one from scratch seemed too slow, especially for a firm growing so fast. The natural place to look was Digital, a $13 billion behemoth that was number three in the industry. But Digital rejected Compaq's offer

for its services division twice, in 1995 and 1996, on the ground that it was worth more than Compaq would pay.

Fortunately for Compaq, Digital was rapidly self-destructing. The Massachusetts-based firm had been the Compaq of its day, an upstart that grew huge by betting on an industry shift (in this case from mainframes to minicomputers, in the 1970s and early 1980s). Now, it was entering a difficult middle age. It was fat: despite shedding over 75,000 employees in 1993–97, it still had 55,000. Its own PC operation was a chronic money-loser. Since 1991 it had suffered cumulative net losses of nearly $6 billion.

As the rest of its business declined, Digital had bet its future on a high-performance, 64-bit processor called Alpha that had yet to take off. To pay for Alpha's research and manufacturing facilities, it had sold off many of its best technologies. Headhunters were circling hungrily round its most highly skilled people.

Life after the PC

In Digital, Compaq saw a future beyond the PC. Its services organisation was still one of the industry's best. Its salespeople were known for their loyalty to their customers and knowledge of their needs. Digital's customers were fiercely loyal in return.

Digital's products were largely complementary to Compaq's. Its high-performance notebooks were thin and light, especially compared with Compaq's clunky offerings. Its Alpha chip and servers were technically impressive. And Digital's search engine, Alta Vista, created to show off the power of Alpha servers, was one of the top destinations on the web even though Digital had done virtually nothing with it (astonishingly, it had not even bought the altavista.com address).

Even better, with every stumble and financial blow, Digital became less resistant to takeover talks. In 1995, when its market capitalisation was around $6 billion, its board had felt its shares were undervalued. After three more years of losses, they were less sure. Compaq offered a 20% premium and, after four days of talks in early 1998, the companies had a deal.

And then: nothing. Mr Pfeiffer wanted to wait until the merger was final, in June, before making any announcements. This was bizarre – plenty of other companies in the industry, especially such serial acquirers as Computer Associates, send in rapid action teams within days to brief employees on the broad outlines of the merger plans. In spite of hiring three consultancies and setting up more than 200 internal committees to advise on its merger integration, Compaq froze.

After years of internal decline, Digital's people were tired of uncertainty. The one sure outcome of the merger would be massive lay-offs (more than 15,000 to date). Just before the completion of the merger, Digital had promoted a number of managers to vice-president, a title that carried a preferential severance package. Most of those newly minted vice-presidents resigned from Compaq in June 1999, a year after the merger and just days before their severance packages were due to expire.

Even after the deal went through, Compaq moved slowly. By now it was distracted by emerging problems in its core PC business. As Dell's direct model flourished, Compaq half-heartedly tried to respond. It launched its own direct-sales programme, under which customers could order and configure PCs from its website and get them delivered to their home within a week or two. But Compaq's existing logistics

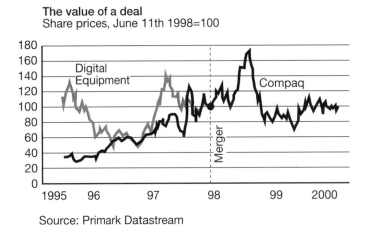

The value of a deal
Share prices, June 11th 1998=100

Source: Primark Datastream

Figure 2

software was not flexible enough to handle batch-of-one orders. Orders often took a week longer to fill than with Dell.

Worse, Compaq had not resolved its channel-conflict problem. Rather than offend its sales partners, it created a new line of direct-only PCs. Consumers could buy one product range in stores and another online, but if they saw a product they liked in a store, they could not usually order a customised version online; nor could they take an online product to a local Compaq dealer for service. It was the worst of both worlds: a fragmented channel strategy, poorly executed.

Trouble at the top

At the same time, Compaq's high-end strategy was also in trouble. The main problem was that, in the minds of the big corporate customers that the company was now wooing, Compaq still stood largely for PC hardware and servers. Compaq now had more than 30,000 service consultants and more than 14,000 salespeople in the field, but most had come from Digital and were finding it tough to win new customers. Worse, although Digital's name still carried a cachet, Compaq had erased it by rebranding all products and services as "Compaq".

Within the company, the divisions between the two survived. Most "Digital Heritage" people were still in New England and most "Compaq Classic" folk in Texas. Aside from the geographic distance, there was a cultural one. Digital people tended to have joined early in their careers and planned to stay for life; Compaq people had the PC industry's more dynamic instincts.

Compaq knew about the cultural differences but did little to break them down. "The follow-up didn't happen aggressively enough, in part because of the geographies involved," says Jeff Lynn, who now runs Compaq's services unit, after being wooed from IBM. "There were such strong cultures and pride in brand, and it didn't help that at the same time [after Mr Pfeiffer's departure]. Compaq was changing its entire senior management team." Mark Coggin, a former Digital manager who now works for Meta, a consultancy in Connecticut, says that "Compaq completely

underestimated the complexity of taking on a company that was at least half again as large."

Despite two years of lost opportunities, the two companies now at last seem to be coming together. A new management team led by Mr Capellas is winning praise for an open, informal style (in marked contrast to the German-born Mr Pfeiffer, who was driven but stiff). A new advertising agency and public-relations firm plan to sell Compaq as an Internet e-business company, taking a page out of IBM's (expensively produced) book.

Internally, too, the scars are healing. Mr Lynn, who arrived three months ago, says he banned the words "Digital" and "Classic", "unless they're used in opposition to analogue or in reference to a sort of Coke." Everybody has a Compaq namecard. The product lines have largely been integrated; the research teams work together. This is way better than the second-largest acquisition in the computer industry – AT&T's purchase of NCR in 1991 – which proved a disaster of epic proportions (it was reversed after several years and billions of dollars of losses).

Financially, the deal seems sure to be a winner. After sitting on Alta Vista for a year, Compaq last year sold 83% of it to CMGI for an 18% stake in the Internet holding company, a share that is now worth over $2.5 billion, more than a quarter of Digital's purchase price. It also sold most of Digital's factories and some technology, recouping another third of the price. Digital had $3 billion in cash and the same again in tax-loss "carry-forwards" that Compaq can use to offset tax over the coming years. Alpha and the rest of the Digital technology, people and patents have, in effect, cost nothing.

Whether the acquisition will achieve its main aim of taking Compaq from PC maker to the top of the broader computer industry, with IBM and Hewlett-Packard, remains to be seen. Alpha and Tandem's Himalaya servers are technically un-matched, but the market for such specialised high-end machines is small. And, in its lower-end Intel-based server market, Compaq is facing stiffer competition, not least from Dell.

As long as the Internet world is mostly based on Unix, Compaq will continue to struggle. But if Microsoft's NT operating system continues to improve, eventually unseating Unix as the market leader, no company is better placed than Compaq to benefit. With Microsoft's future in doubt, this is a risky bet. But so was the Digital deal. It is a sign of the times in the PC industry that even giants have to take such risks to survive.

Seen this way, Compaq's failures were more of poor implementation than of strategy. The same moves a few years earlier might have ensured a successful future. The company's two years of hell were mainly the result of what Mr Coggin calls a "misalignment of the planets" – the PC industry sagged just as Compaq embarked on what would have been one of the toughest mergers in the technology industry even at the best of times. Mr Pfeiffer paid the price. He also took a bet on a different future, in which even Dell will one day be punished for eschewing services and sticking to hardware. That vision might yet come to pass. Only then will the costs of "Pfeiffer's folly" be forgotten.

2   THE DAIMLERCHRYSLER EMULSION

Our second merger brief asks whether cross-border deals are different from other mergers, or just harder to carry out. DaimlerChrysler may offer an answer

When, two years ago, Daimler-Benz, Germany's most profitable car company, and owner of the world-beating Mercedes marque, revealed that it was merging with Chrysler, the smallest but most efficient of America's Big Three car producers, the two companies embarked on a cross-border deal based on what seemed to be impeccable industrial logic.

Cross-border mergers are notoriously tricky. For DaimlerChrysler to succeed requires cohesion not just between two headquarters, in Stuttgart and Auburn Hills, Michigan, but also between a host of offices and factories with different national and corporate cultures. To overcome such differences, the merged company took an unusual approach.

In its pre-merger planning Daimler put little weight on the fact that the deal would be a cross-border one. Apparently, it assumed that this would create no special problems. According to Eckhard Cordes, one of three Daimler managers to take part in the pre-merger discussions with Chrysler (the others were Jürgen Schrempp, the group's chairman, and Jürgen Hubbert, a board member responsible for Daimler's Mercedes-Benz car division), questions raised by the deal's cross-border nature were not specifically asked until after its broad terms had been agreed.

Mr Cordes says that three big issues preoccupied the Daimler team. First, against a background of consolidation in the car industry, they were trying to put together two companies with strong and distinctive heritages, so how best could they do this? Second, given that there was no precedent for such a merger, was the deal at all feasible? And third, were Daimler and Chrysler bold enough to manage the difficult task of post-merger integration successfully?

None of these issues, says Mr Cordes, had an explicit cross-border element: they would have applied equally had the deal been between two German companies. The solution to post-merger integration, for instance, was to be ruthless over efficiency and planning, no matter where the deal. At the same time, however, the questions were formulated in the knowledge that profound difficulties over differing locations and cultures would have to be tackled if the merger were to succeed.

These difficulties were aggravated by a justifiable feeling among those on the American side that this was no merger of equals, but rather a deal in which Daimler was calling the principal shots. Chrysler's middle managers and engineers saw it as a sell-out to foreigners, and feared an invasion of rigid Teutonic working practices into their own rather freewheeling company. The potential clash of cultures was thus corporate as well as national: could a bunch of process-led German engineers work effectively with Chrysler's hunch-inspired, risk-taking bosses?

Two cultures, one company

By some measures, the fact that DaimlerChrysler has got as far as it has since 1998 has been nothing short of miraculous. Despite plenty of bumpy moments, the combination has held together. "We are absolutely happy with the development of the merger," says Mr Hubbert. "We have a clear understanding: one company, one vision, one chairman, two cultures."

DaimlerChrysler has surmounted barriers as simple but important as the time difference between Germany and America. Managers from both firms criss-cross the Atlantic in a stream of meetings and workshops, seeking ways to drive down expenses and share future development costs. To reduce the wear-and-tear of constant travel, a specially converted aircraft helps them to catch up on sleep. In an

ironic twist, DaimlerChrysler has leased space in New York's Chrysler Building so that travel can be further reduced.

Moreover, the new firm has continued to expand. On March 27th, for example, it announced a deal with loss-making Mitsubishi Motors of Japan, which should strengthen DaimlerChrysler's plans for small cars. And on June 26th it spent $428m on a 10% stake in Hyundai of South Korea.

But by other measures, the merger has fallen far short of its designers' vision. Until last autumn the companies were talking about maintaining two head offices, and the word "merger" was still in use. In fact, it is now acknowledged by people such as Mr Hubbert that Daimler, seeking to solve strategic problems of its own, had engineered a friendly takeover of America's third car maker.

Two years on, problems abound. Some are financial. DaimlerChrysler has abandoned detailed discussion of the cost-saving targets it set for the new company, even though investors remain intensely interested. But the group has admitted that renewed and deep cost-cutting efforts have had to be undertaken to shore up the group's operating results.

On July 26th DaimlerChrysler duly announced second-quarter profits of $1.7 billion, slightly ahead of expectations. But it also said that it was struggling to meet earlier projections of operating performance for the full financial year. And, tellingly, Mr Schrempp said the group urgently needed to improve its efforts to communicate its story to investors. This remark came after an abysmal period for the group's share price, which has now fallen by more than 40% from a high of 95.5 Euros ($106) in 1999 (see chart on p. 32). The stock-market, at least, seems sceptical about the prospects for the merger.

Other problems are operational. Rumblings of discontent within the firm can still be heard. Competition in the car market is intensifying, especially in Chrysler's home market and in the high-margin minivan sector that it has long dominated. As competitors such as Honda of Japan have produced their own vans, Chrysler's efforts to hang on to market share have consisted largely of giving ever bigger discounts to

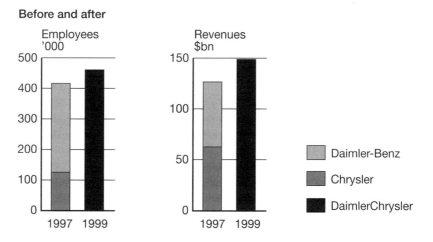

Source: Company reports

Figure 3

dealers. But sales have stalled, and Chrysler recently began a new $2 billion cost-cutting programme to shore up its performance. A few vehicles, notably the retro-styled PT Cruiser, have been successes, but the firm's main roll-out of new models is still several months away.

Even the deal with Mitsubishi is an admission that the transatlantic marriage was not enough: it united two complementary sets of products in America and Europe, but failed to remedy the weakness of both companies in the faster-growing Asian and Latin American markets. Eighteen months ago, Mr Schrempp wanted to invest in Nissan as an answer to Daimler's Asian shortcomings. But he was overruled by his management board, which decided that Daimler could not digest two big acquisitions at once. To the surprise of Renault, the rival bidder, Daimler walked away from a deal that would have made its reach global in a way that its takeover of Chrysler has not.

Yet, despite these problems, it is too early to conclude that the merger has failed. Its true test will come in the next two or three years, when the first products developed entirely since the merger should start to roll off the production lines. If DaimlerChrysler can show that it has translated operational efficiency into successful new cars and higher levels of profit, it will have proved that the deal's underlying logic was sound. Even at this early stage, however, the merger offers some powerful lessons in the problems of combining firms in different countries.

Two sets of problems

The business background to the deal shows why both companies were willing to take on such problems. By the mid-1990s Chrysler had survived near bankruptcy and a failed hostile buy-out launched by Kirk Kerkorian, a corporate raider who was its biggest single shareholder. Chrysler was lean and had trendy designs, but where was it going? Its advisers, Credit Suisse First Boston, prepared a paper outlining six strategic options. According to a recent book by two *Detroit News* journalists, they all consisted of some form of alliance with the Germans.

Desultory talks had taken place between the two companies in 1995. But Bob Eaton, Chrysler's chairman, believed that sooner or later he would have to throw in his lot with another car company. So when, in 1997, Mr Schrempp sought to reopen talks with Chrysler, he got a friendly reception. Not that everything was friendly thereafter. In particular, Mr Eaton took plenty of personal flak after he announced that he intended to stand down as co-chief executive within three years.

Yet, judging by DaimlerChrysler's performance since the merger, Mr Eaton may deserve more credit for strategic insight than he has had. In return for accepting junior status in the merger, he obtained a big premium for Chrysler shareholders. Had it remained independent, Chrysler would be in a horrid position today.

Even so, the merger could have been better handled. By focusing on general issues rather than cross-border ones, the two companies underestimated a factor that would define, and could even scupper, the entire deal. Throughout the negotiations, even after integration began, cross-border problems surfaced, demanding attention. But top managers on both sides seemed to prefer sidling up to potential hurdles rather than meeting them head on.

Consider, for instance, the task of melding two distinct ways of doing business. Old Daimler was bureacratic and formal. A standard meeting of senior managers would generate thick wads of papers and lengthy minutes. After months of influence

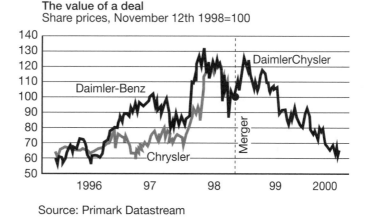

The value of a deal
Share prices, November 12th 1998=100

Source: Primark Datastream

Figure 4

by the American's more spontaneous behaviour, most presentations are now oral, and a one-page memo then summarises proceedings.

Some barriers have been harder to overcome. At the time of the merger, senior Chrysler managers became rich, as share options suddenly became hugely valuable. That triggered concern in Germany that Daimler bosses might become greedy. But it also served to highlight deep-rooted differentials in pay. Typically, the Americans were taking home two, three or even four times as much as their German equivalents. At the same time, the Americans were aghast at what they viewed as German profligacy over expenses. Some Daimler executives routinely travelled first class to get to meetings, or stayed at top-flight hotels over weekends. For these cultures to meet in the middle will take time and the acceptance by both sides of new approaches.

One thing that has made the merger easier is that neither company conformed entirely to the American or Teutonic stereotypes, particularly at the level of top management. By the time the two got talking, Chrysler was no longer the funky Detroit company that in the 1980s had come back from the dead through then chief executive Lee Iacocca's sheer flair. Its chairman, Mr Eaton, was a cautious, reserved former GM manager with all the buttoned-down instincts of a GM engineer. Daimler-Benz, for its part, was under the spell of Mr Schrempp, who had spent the formative periods of his adult life in South Africa and who still goes there to relax. He is a gutsy, earthy, wilful leader whose style is to listen before making up his mind and then dominate.

Viewed from outside Detroit, the merger seems to have caused relatively few arguments. DaimlerChrysler has had some high-profile departures, most of which occurred at the time of the merger when senior jobs were allocated. The exception was the controversial exit of Thomas Stallkamp, former president of Chrysler and a fervent believer in the importance of thoroughly integrating the two companies. He left last September, to be replaced by Jim Holden. Mr Stallkamp had been undermined by the Germans for weeks before Mr Schrempp gave Mr Eaton the order to fire him.

There has, however, also been a slew of departures further down the ranks. At one stage last year, talented Chrysler designers were defecting in droves. The flow has slowed to more of a trickle these days. Mr Hubbert says the Germans have learnt an important lesson: that they should not take workers' loyalty for granted. But it is also possible that the departures have distracted top managers' attention from the underlying problems in Chrysler's business.

The German dominance in the deal has also led to uncomfortable moments, such as when Mr Hubbert asserted last year that DaimlerChrysler would have a single headquarters in Stuttgart. But generally the Germans have been diplomatic, sensible even. From the outset, Daimler tried to apply lessons learned from other troubled deals. Hence, for instance, the insistence on clarifying in advance which managers would occupy which slots.

Hence, too, a determination to centralise and control decisions that might otherwise chip away at cohesion. To handle the hundreds of integration projects, DaimlerChrysler has formed a powerful automotive council of five senior managers to which all projects must report every four to six weeks. Mr Cordes, who sits on the council, says it has been critically important in helping the group to stay on course.

Cross-border conundrum

In the end, the lesson of DaimlerChrysler's merger may be that cross-border deals are, in essence, the same as all other mergers, only with extra layers of difficulty. Mr Schrempp and his team have concentrated on the deal's operational parts, downplaying cultural problems and management jockeying as inevitable but manageable.

The trickiest problems seem to have been largely about the details of doing things effectively. In May 1998, the merging companies forecast $1.4 billion of cost-savings during 1999, a figure they duly delivered. Having set internal goals for further cost synergies by 2000 and 2005, DaimlerChrysler then decided not to make these public. One reason was that, to management's growing discomfort, investors and journalists alike were interested in little else. A second, more acceptable, reason was that defining a true synergy becomes ever harder the more time has passed since a merger.

But another reason was more subtle. As DaimlerChrysler has tried to produce workable and cost-efficient ways of doing business as a single entity, it has run into a level of difficulty that was not anticipated when the deal was struck. Consider the apparently simple idea of component sharing. If Daimler and Chrysler have two similar vehicles, in theory they can save money by using the same component – an axle or fuel pump, say – in both. But what if one vehicle is scheduled for launch this year, the other not until next year? Should the product launches be co-ordinated to maximise efficiency? And how are development costs to be allocated?

It is on these nitty-gritty details that the deal's fate ultimately rests. If DaimlerChrysler gets it right, the merger might yet come to be seen as a masterstroke. If it fails, doubtless some blame will be laid on cross-border differences such as language and culture. And that, perhaps, is the true lesson of such mergers: the cross-border angle comes to the fore only when other things are already going wrong.

3   A BAVARIAN BOTCH-UP

Our third merger brief is a reminder that, when couples mate in a hurry for the wrong reasons, things can go wrong – as two Bavarian banks proved when they formed HypoVereinsbank

Last May, Germany's second-biggest bank, HypoVereinsbank (HVB), announced a surge in profits in the first quarter. The bank "goes from strength to strength," declared its boss, Albrecht Schmidt, proudly. Last week Mr Schmidt was looking even prouder, as HVB snapped up Bank Austria, that country's biggest bank.

Yet any pride at HVB is heavily tinged with relief. The bank is only now clawing its way back from a dark period of losses and infighting inextricably linked to the merger that created it: the marriage of Bayerische Vereinsbank and Bayerische Hypotheken- und Wechselbank (Hypobank), announced in July 1997.

HVB's rebound is a sign that the merger may yet prove worthwhile. But it has already become a textbook case of how not to bring together two banks. It serves as a lesson in what can go wrong when corporate couples leap too hastily into each other's arms. It is also a reminder that old rivals can turn out to know much less about each other than they thought.

Mr Schmidt, who formerly ran Vereinsbank, insists that the deal was right, for all its low points – including a bad-loan scandal that blew apart the merged bank's board. But even he admits that "there were times when we wondered if it was all worth it."

Early applause

The deal got off to an auspicious start. It was applauded as the long-awaited first move to consolidate Germany's fragmented and inefficient banking market. Now that two banks had taken a bold step to cut overlapping costs, others were bound to follow suit. There was talk of a ripple effect through Europe, as restructuring in its largest financial market sent banks elsewhere scrambling to the altar.

The merger was touted by some as a match made in heaven. Here were two cross-town rivals (based on different sides of Munich's Englischer Garten) that had long known and respected each other, but had only just realised they were in love. There was plenty of scope to cut costs, as the banks had branches on the same high streets and a similar mix of businesses, centred on property financing, retail banking and fund management. Apart, the two had been modest regional banks. Together, they hoped to become a European "super-regional". With a combined 12% of the German market, they were an unmatched force in residential mortgage-lending.

Yet this was not a love match. Although it had a strategic logic, both Mr Schmidt and Eberhard Martini, the boss of Hypobank, would have preferred to stay independent, other things being equal. But other things were not equal.

Vereinsbank went a-wooing mainly because it was the object of an unwanted suitor: Deutsche Bank, Germany's largest bank. In 1996 Vereinsbank executives were alarmed to find that Frankfurt-based Deutsche – seen in Munich's banking circles as almost foreign – had bought 5% of its shares. They became even more agitated when it hinted it wanted to build a strategic stake.

Desperate to avoid Deutsche's clutches, Mr Schmidt talked to Commerzbank, a similar-sized bank. But Commerzbank got cold feet. Hypobank, far from being the dream partner, was just next on his list. When Mr Martini agreed, says one adviser,

a deal was hammered out over a weekend. "It was clear that it had to be done quickly, even if corners were cut," he says.

There was some surprise that Hypobank was so eager to oblige. It seemed to be doing well on its own: profits were healthy and its cost base was the leanest of any German bank. Known for taking big risks, some of its new ventures were doing nicely, such as Direkt Anlage Bank, a telephone-banking unit. But Hypobank was becoming worried that Allianz, a giant Munich-based insurer with a 10% stake, might push it into a merger with (ie, takeover by) the much bigger Dresdner Bank, which was also in the Allianz stable. A deal with Vereinsbank would help Hypo to weaken its ties to Dresdner, and would be a more equitable merger.

Add to this a dose of political intervention. With the big Frankfurt banks closing in, Munich's politicians were keen to create a Bavarian champion, whatever the cost. The state's prime minister, Edmund Stoiber, had long wanted to turn Munich into a financial centre to rival Frankfurt, home to Germany's main stock exchange as well as its largest banks. When Mr Schmidt played the regional card, says one HVB insider, asking Mr Stoiber to "smooth the way or we become a satellite of Frankfurt", the prime minister was happy to oblige with a one-off tax waiver on the exchange of shares in the merger transaction. Without this incentive, which has since been outlawed, the merger might not have happened.

In the rush to create a Bavarian superbank, many loose ends were left hanging. At the signing ceremony, it was not clear who would get which top jobs or how some divisions would be integrated. One investment banker who worked on the deal says: "A lot was left vague, on the assumption that, since they were all local buddies, it

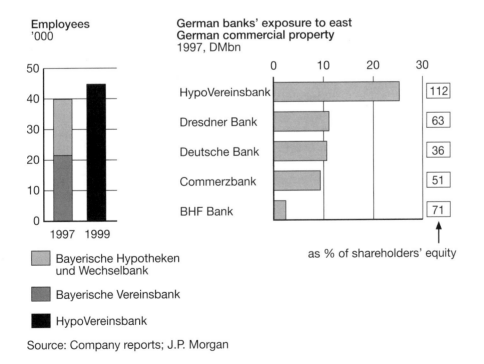

Source: Company reports; J.P. Morgan

Figure 5

could be worked out later." This sign-now, talk-later approach to mergers is common in Germany: a merger between Deutsche Bank and Dresdner Bank collapsed earlier this year because they had not decided the fate of Dresdner's investment bank. More recently, a mooted deal between Dresdner and Commerzbank also fell apart.

The most worrying loose end for HVB concerned the nature of the transaction. It was billed as a merger of equals, and Messrs Schmidt and Martini called it a "merger of the best", explaining that the new bank would fuse the best people and ideas from each side. But there was soon unease that Vereinsbank's goal was a no-premium takeover of its slightly smaller rival. It took nine of the 14 seats on the managing board and most of the senior positions in several key departments. Mr Martini agreed to let Mr Schmidt run the bank, and moved to the supervisory board. Morale among old Hypo hands sank.

Why had Mr Martini given in so easily? The answer lies partly with personality. Although he and Mr Schmidt seemed to have much in common, and had even studied together, they were very different managers. Unlike the workaholic, details-obsessed Mr Schmidt, who fought his corner on every point, Mr Martini was a *bon viveur* with little time for the fine print. He was happy to give way on individual appointments; it was overall strategy that interested him more.

Tick, tick, tick

There was another reason for Mr Martini's flexibility: his bank's balance sheet contained a time-bomb. The detonator, as so often in commercial banking, was property lending. All the big German banks rushed into eastern Germany in the unification boom and lent heavily to developers. Under the flamboyant Mr Martini, Hypobank was particularly bullish, throwing money at projects with no tenants and guaranteeing rents for up to 25 years. The euphoria evaporated when the property market turned down in 1993, leaving Hypobank with an exposure to east German commercial property that exceeded shareholders' equity (see chart on p. 35).

Vereinsbank knew that Hypobank had property problems. But the full extent of those problems did not become clear until over a year after the merger's announcement. In October 1998, following a string of audits, Mr Schmidt announced that HVB would need extra loan-loss provisions of DM3.5 billion ($2.1 billion) to cover holes in Hypobank's property book. Unable to hide his anger, he told a press conference that he had a "bellyfull of rage". He hinted that losses may have been intentionally concealed. Munich's state prosecutors launched a probe.

This led to a bust-up with Mr Martini, who, despite moving to the supervisory board, was still seen as guardian of Hypobank's interests in the merger. Taking the comments as personal criticism, he denounced Mr Schmidt as "consumed by vanity" and unfit to run a bank. Spin-doctors now insist that this was all just a communications breakdown. Mr Schmidt, they say, was about to make it clear that he did not blame Mr Martini, when the latter heard (from a part-time secretary) that the canteen gossip suggested otherwise, and flew into a rage.

Although the two men made up within a week, their war of words did enormous damage to the new bank's reputation and share price – arguably as much as the bad loans themselves. Already worried about the state of HVB's loan book, investors now became spooked by the prospect of a long-drawn-out, backroom power struggle

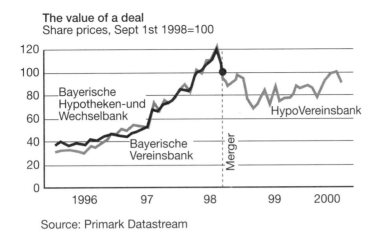

The value of a deal
Share prices, Sept 1st 1998=100

Source: Primark Datastream

Figure 6

between Vereinsbank and Hypobank people. Many assumed that such a public spat, in a country where bankers tend to close ranks in times of turmoil, could only mean one thing: that the problems were much worse than they appeared.

Indeed, Mr Schmidt's outburst, intended to show leadership and draw a line under the bad-loan fiasco, had the opposite effect. Investors wanted a definitive figure put on the losses, not just some guesstimate. Countless accountancy firms and property experts were brought in to decipher Hypobank's red-stained ledgers.

It was not until October 1999, nearly two-and-a-half years after the merger's announcement, that the matter was laid to rest, with a thick report by BDO, a Munich-based auditor that had been given unprecedented access to Hypobank staff. The report vindicated Mr Schmidt's conservative assessment. Mr Martini and the four remaining managing-board members from Hypobank resigned.

Why did it take so long for Vereinsbank to discover the problems at its partner? One reason is that valuing a loan portfolio can be more art than science. This is especially true of property loans, which are horribly cyclical. A loan assessed during a recession on the basis of low current rents and occupancy looks far less healthy than one based on likely future income. Germany's finance professors are still arguing about HVB.

German law is also to blame. Unlike Britain or America, data-protection laws make it hard for a company to conduct proper due diligence on a competitor until after a deal is struck – sometimes several months later. And Germany's antiquated accounting rules do not fully recognise "mergers of equals", an increasingly popular accounting concept. "You have to rely on the good faith of your counterparty," says a member of HVB's supervisory board. "That's hair-raising stuff when billions are on the table."

Vereinsbank was certainly over-reliant on the good faith of Hypobank. According to another board member, it decided to halt its review of Hypobank's books in the early stages of the merger after Hypobank said it planned to clean up its portfolio with a DM2 billion provision. Had Vereinsbank's auditors, KPMG, continued their probe, they might have discovered much earlier that that provision was woefully inadequate. The decision to stop was "tragic", says the board member.

Repair job

Mr Schmidt now has to repair HVB's image with investors and customers. According to John Leonard of Schroder Salomon Smith Barney, the bank's shares have continued to lag behind those of rivals because of heavy loan provisioning and all the bad publicity. The recent jump in profits is no great triumph, as HVB's return on equity last year was a paltry 4.4%. Investors remain anxious: property lending, after all, is the bank's bread and butter. Stains that disfigure an organisation's birth often prove particularly stubborn (just ask the European Bank for Reconstruction and Development about marble). HVB claims to have lost "very few" of its 4m customers during the merger process, but it offers no figures.

There is internal damage to repair too. The merger debacle has hampered efforts to forge a new culture. After initial distrust, fuelled by anger over a Vereinsbank takeover, the two sides were starting to work more closely together when Messrs Schmidt and Martini lashed out at each other, turning the merger back into a case of "us and them". Their timing could not have been worse.

Mr Schmidt has subsequently tried to rebuild bridges – for instance, by putting ex-Hypobankers in charge of the revamped property division and giving them half of the top jobs in accounting and controlling. But there is a long way to go. It is not hard to find old Hypobank folk who insist, in private, that Mr Schmidt – or Little Napoleon, as he is known among the troops – exaggerated their bank's losses to make it look as weak as possible. That, they say, made it easier for him to purge the board of Hypobankers, a move he had planned from the start.

Mr Schmidt dismisses this theory as "nonsense" and insists that morale at the bank is "no longer an issue". He says staff are fired up at the prospect of creating Europe's best "bank of the regions", offering retail financial products in and beyond Germany. And he likes to think that the culture clashes that caused the merger's worst problems can be turned to HVB's advantage: with Vereinsbank's rigorous risk controls, Hypobank's tradition of free-wheeling and product innovation could bring profits, not just losses.

From a technical standpoint, the merger has even had some bright spots. Some 500 overlapping branches have been closed, confounding sceptics who predicted that cost-saving closures would be politically tricky. The bulk of the systems integration has been done in less than three years, far ahead of schedule. Even the bank's detractors admit that its computer systems are now second to none, and that it has as good a picture of its credit risks as any other European bank.

Still, HVB's merger will be studied chiefly for its failure to grasp the softer factors. Among its many lessons: leaving the terms of a deal vague stores up trouble; takeovers disguised as mergers of equals do little for staff morale and can lead to intolerable management strain; and appearances count. Far from being passing annoyances, public slanging matches can do lasting damage to both image and the bottom line.

The most important lesson of all seems to be: know your partner. When asked what was most likely to ruin financial mergers, Carl Fürstenberg, a noted pre-war German banker, once answered: "Overestimation of the one bank for the other." As they will tell you in Munich, that still holds true.

4   BUILDING A NEW BOEING

Our fourth merger brief explores what happens in an industry where government is the marriage broker. Was Boeing wise to team up with McDonnell Douglas when that company's biggest customer had cut its spending in half?

The defence industry is not a business driven purely by commercial logic. Many of its companies have only one big customer. If the American Defence Department wants a change, change is what it gets. The merger in 1997 of Boeing and McDonnell Douglas was, like much of the industry's consolidation in the 1990s, a product of the peace dividend. But, while the other mergers brought together two or more defence companies, this one was different: it united a defence firm with a largely civilian company. Unexpectedly, it may be a success.

In 1993, the Pentagon summoned America's main defence contractors to a meeting that has gone down in legend as "The Last Supper". With the end of the cold war, the military procurement budget was being cut in half; the administration made it clear that it would prefer to deal with a smaller number of suppliers. So 32 defence companies consolidated into nine.

For McDonnell Douglas, the prospect was alarming. The company had grown out of the merger, in 1967, of California's Douglas Aircraft company, which made civil jets, with the McDonnell company, a leading maker of military aircraft. The marriage was a disaster: the new company never defused the antagonism of the old Douglas employees at Long Beach, California, who felt they were ignored by the dominant military types back in St Louis.

As for Boeing, Phil Condit, its president, was worried about the consequences of remaining concentrated mainly in the highly cyclical market for civil aerospace. "That would have meant Boeing being a bit player in military aircraft and space, while its fortunes ebbed and flowed with the commercial aircraft cycle," he says. In search of stability, he contemplated a bold move: to buy-in space and military aircraft expertise by acquiring, first, most of Rockwell International, a medium-sized American defence business; and then, in a much bigger deal, McDonnell Douglas. The result would be to create the world's second largest defence company and the largest aerospace group.

The American Defence Department gave the plan an unexpected fillip. In 1996 it held a competition to develop the Joint Strike Fighter (JSF), which will eventually be the biggest defence procurement deal ever, worth up to $300 billion for the winner. McDonnell Douglas failed to reach the final round. Instead, the two finalists chosen to develop competing prototypes were Lockheed Martin – and Boeing. The Defence Department was intrigued by Boeing's ability to apply civil aerospace manufacturing techniques to keep down the fighter's price.

For McDonnell Douglas, exclusion from the competition's last round marked its final fall from grace. Harry Stonecipher, McDonnell's boss, had tried in 1995 to fashion a deal with Mr Condit, who had been a friend for 20 years, but they could not agree on a price. They had another conversation a year later, and agreed to try once more, but only after Boeing had completed the purchase of Rockwell, announced in August 1996.

Meanwhile, Mr Stonecipher needed a fallback position, in case the Boeing deal failed. He pondered making a pre-emptive bid for the defence activities of Hughes Electronics and Texas Instruments, before they were snapped up by Raytheon. The chairman and board of McDonnell Douglas more or less gave Mr Stonecipher carte blanche to negotiate a deal that would salvage the company.

At that point Mr Condit telephoned to suggest a meeting at the Four Seasons hotel in Seattle where they worked out the outline of a deal, even agreeing on the share price Boeing would pay. For its part, Boeing calculated that its options were to do a deal then or to stand by and see McDonnell secure its future by buying TI and Hughes Defense. That would have put the company out of Boeing's reach. Had Boeing chosen that route, it would have remained largely a civil aerospace company, with less chance of winning the deal for the JSF against Lockheed.

A friend in court

All big mergers face regulatory hoops, but defence companies face more than most. Announced in mid-December 1996, the Boeing-McDonnell Douglas deal took until August 1997 to clear regulatory hurdles in America and Europe. Even the structure of the merged firm, something that is usually a matter for companies and their consultants, had to pass muster with the Defence Department. The two companies brought in a former Pentagon official, Paul Kaminski, to advise them on how to satisfy his old department.

Mr Kaminski's solution was to split Boeing into two divisions: Information Space and Defence Systems, and Boeing Commercial Airplane Group (BCAG). This was rather rough-and-ready, with little focus on products, let alone customers, outside the civil business. It took a crisis – aggravated by the merger – to create the structure that the new company needed. Together, the merger, and the crisis that followed it, also led Boeing to do something altogether more fundamental and more ambitious than most merging companies do.

Billions of problems

It was not defence, the business Boeing had bought into, which caused problems; it was the market for commercial aircraft, whose cycles had worried Mr Condit before the deal. Harried by competition from Airbus, in 1997 Boeing fought to protect its dominant market position by slashing prices for its civil jets. Demand expanded out of control. The factories in Seattle could not keep up with the blistering pace; nor could suppliers. So aircraft sold too cheaply had to be expensively completed outside the normal production sequence because of a shortage of parts.

The upshot was expensive delays, and then huge write-offs, of some $4 billion. And in vain: Airbus still grabbed about half the market, up from its one-third share in the mid-1990s. By September 1998, Boeing was on the ropes.

Arguably, the task of making the merger work distracted top management from the basic task of making and selling jet aeroplanes at a profit. Mr Stonecipher, now Boeing's president, predictably denies that. He claims it was just a coincidence that the civil-jet crisis came along at the same time. The whole board had agreed to expand production of 737s to counter Airbus's incursions into the American market with its A320 aircraft. "The same would have happened without the merger," he insists.

However, the merger's legacy of uncertainty and wrenching change may have triggered Boeing's second post-merger crisis. Earlier this year, just as the company seemed to be recovering from the first crisis, Boeing's white-collar engineers embarked on a bitter strike, which will dent Boeing's profits. The company's recovering share price fell back, but has since recovered.

Phantom in the works

The crisis on the civil-aircraft side of the business had another, more benign effect. It became obvious that Ron Woodard, the super-salesman who ran the civil business, was incapable of getting things under control. Wall Street was baying for blood; Mr Woodard was fired. In the management reshuffle to replace him, Mr Condit and Mr Stonecipher decided to give the company a clearer focus.

The obvious choice to repair the dented airliner business was Alan Mulally, who initially made his name with the successful launch of the Boeing 777, the star new aircraft in Boeing's fleet. Immediately after the merger, Mr Mulally had been put in charge of the sprawling defence division. Now, a new boss had to be appointed to that job. Instead of sticking with the crude separation of defence and civil aircraft, undertaken to pacify the Pentagon, Boeing decided to create a third division to tackle the space and communications markets. That meant everything from launching satellites to providing high-powered data links to and from aircraft, using satellites.

Boeing thus became a company that had a variety of customers: government in the case of defence, government and private business in space, and increasingly privatised airlines in the case of commercial jets. The business became reshaped around these different sets of customers, each of which had different requirements.

The new focus this created allowed Mr Condit to develop another strain of post-merger thinking: Boeing needed to harness its technical expertise and knowledge of defence and airline customers to move into aerospace services. Lots of much smaller businesses around the world make a living repairing or servicing Boeing products, in the process earning better profit margins than Boeing: why should Boeing not do the same, if its customers in the American air force or the world's big airlines would accept it? They did, and Boeing's military businesses now earn around a fifth of their revenues from services such as running bases for the air force.

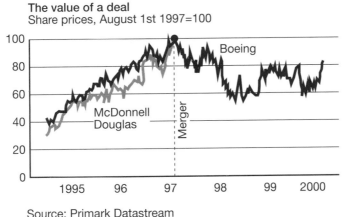

The value of a deal
Share prices, August 1st 1997=100

Source: Primark Datastream

Figure 7

Another opportunity to create a new business emerged in the civil-aircraft side, where Boeing now offers broadband communications for aircraft, using satellites. This business, called "Connexion by Boeing", is also set to take advantage of Boeing's planned purchase of the space and communications businesses of Hughes Electronics, the world's leading supplier of commercial satellites.

Next in Boeing's sights is air-traffic control. Satellite navigation offers dramatic possibilities for improving air-traffic management, dispensing with much ground control and allowing aircraft to choose their own paths through the sky. Governments, balking at the huge investments involved, are keen to privatise air-traffic control. Boeing will probably join BAE Systems to bid when Britain privatises its system.

The gains of serendipity

Boeing would never have begun supplying services to its traditional customers without the more precise focus it developed after its merger. Nor would it have planned a totally new communications service or an air-traffic management contract, had it not developed, in the process of post-merger integration, a tool for sucking knowledge out of different parts of the huge company and squirting it into a business plan. The device for doing that is called Phantom Works.

Like the famous Lockheed Martin "Skunk Works", where secret defence systems are developed as "black programmes" for the Pentagon, Phantom Works was the research and development heart of McDonnell Douglas. Messrs Condit and Stonecipher decided not only to make this the R&D organisation for the company as a whole, but to use it as a way of integrating the company.

Astonishingly, Phantom Works was never part of the post-merger plan. Mr Condit admits he stumbled on the idea of using it more widely as an engine to integrate the company, rather than as just an R&D centre, only about a year ago. Now, as well as helping to split Boeing's operating units in three divisions to develop new products, Phantom Works acts as a general technology generator to improve manufacturing processes around the group.

With about 4,500 staff scattered across a handful of locations around America, it has become a key to the integration of Rockwell, McDonnell Douglas and Boeing. It works both on short-term programmes to improve rockets or fighters such as the JSF prototype, and on projects to apply to civil aircraft technical lessons learned in military applications. This is also where futuristic projects such as the Blended Wing Body, which may replace conventional airliners, are being developed. Scientists and engineers from the different parts of Boeing are to come into this unit on three- or four-year assignments before returning to operating businesses.

The balanced scorecard

Against this background, it may seem odd to suggest that things are going well at Boeing. Plainly, despite the company's recovering margins and profits, the financial markets are still not entirely sure that a profitable aerospace manufacturer and service company is firmly established. The share price slid after the merger, but is now reviving (see chart on p. 41).

At the least, Boeing is confronting post-merger integration head-on. Mr Condit argues that the moulding of three sets of employees into one team is only 40%

successful. "It takes time. After all, they were bitter rivals. Each lot thought, since our product was better (human nature), when the other guy won it was only by playing dirty." The engineers' strike, he thinks, was caused by fears that Boeing, with its new emphasis on services, would neglect product development, compromising the engineers' careers. But he reckons that Boeing's performance is twice as good as that achieved by other merged companies.

As for the company's senior management, Mr Stonecipher points out that the top dozen or so executives in the enlarged Boeing group emerged from, but do not specifically represent, the three companies that came together three years ago to form the Boeing defence and aerospace company. "It's not about making everybody from McDonnell Douglas, Boeing or Rockwell happy," he says, "it's about making one new Boeing company with the best people in the best place."

The best hope for shareholders, employees and managers is that the integrated new Boeing is greater than the sum of the parts. For the moment, the financial evidence does not point in that direction. But that may change. After a slow start, Boeing is moving on to a new phase of using the pooled technical and business talents now at its command to develop completely new activities. But only when these start delivering better returns and faster growth than Boeing's traditional business, will investors be impressed.

In February 1999, when Boeing's share price was last almost as low as it was recently, Mr Condit warned his top managers that the company was theoretically a takeover target, as its market capitalisation fell below net asset value. The only company ever thought likely to take on Boeing was General Electric. Although GE never normally comments on such rumours, this time it denied it had any intention of making a move. It has nevertheless grown much closer to Boeing, developing a super-powerful jet engine at its own expense to power a new long-range version of Boeing's 777, and, in effect, helping to finance the new model. The Boeing-GE rapprochement is still one to watch.

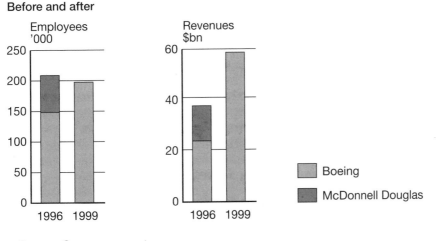

Before and after

Source: Company reports

Figure 8

The other big mergers that resulted from "The Last Supper" meeting produced Raytheon and Lockheed Martin. Both have suffered from confusion, falling profits and diving share prices. They have failed to integrate their enlarged operations enough to take full advantages of economies of scale and of scope.

Lockheed in particular ran into problems last year, apparently because it had scarcely tried to integrate its merged companies. Boeing, by contrast, has seized every opportunity for integration while focusing business units on precise markets. Perhaps that was largely serendipity, but it shows why opportunism can be a perfectly valid reason for a merger. It will work, though, only if management has the wit and will then to seize the unexpected opportunities brought by a merger – even one created by government intervention.

5   ONE HOUSE, MANY WINDOWS

The modern media company is based on the notion of offering one piece of content to different audiences. But, as our fifth merger brief, on the union of Time Warner and Turner Broadcasting System shows, combining media folk is like herding cats. Will the latest deal, with AOL, be different?

The men who drive America's media business tend to be larger-than-life figures: characters such as News Corp's Rupert Murdoch or Sumner Redstone, head of Viacom, whose legendary grit was most famously demonstrated when he survived a hotel fire by clinging to a window ledge with his fingertips. But the figure whose vision has done most to shape the media mergers of the past decade is a man who did not survive: Steve Ross, the boss of Warner Communications, America's most powerful movie studio and music company, who died suddenly in 1992.

Of the many industries being reshaped by changing communications, few have altered as fast as media. Disney bought ABC, CBS and Viacom merged, Seagram took over Polygram, Bertelsmann bought Random House. The basic strategy behind the mergers, though, has been the one Mr Ross spotted more than a decade ago: different media platforms should be brought together within one company, so that the same piece of content could be used in different ways, and the different products could promote each other.

Mr Ross's own attempt to create his vision never quite succeeded. In 1989, he merged Warner with Time Inc, the country's largest magazine publisher. Somehow the reality didn't match up to the dream. The two companies did not have enough in common. Their cable assets fitted together reasonably well, but the publishing and the movie businesses had little to do with each other. The cultures of Burbank, California, the movie business's home, and New York, home of the publishing business, did not get on. Culture clash is a danger in most mergers, but it is a particular hazard in the media business, with its disproportionate supply of large egos.

When Mr Ross died, the company was in disarray. Nobody could remember why the merger had been pushed through in the first place – nobody, that is, except Gerald Levin, who had been Mr Ross's head of strategy at the time, who wrote the paper that first suggested the merger, and who took over Mr Ross's job after his death. It was Mr Levin who eventually achieved the merger that turned the Ross vision into reality: the biggest media merger of its time, the marriage of Time Warner and Turner Broadcasting System (TBS).

That deal has been the more remarkable because of the scepticism that greeted it at the time. For it involved one of the largest egos in the entire well-stocked media business: that of Ted Turner, creator of TBS. It thus demonstrated not only that the content-sharing principle could work; but that even someone as self-important as Mr Turner could be persuaded to accept a deal, if the logic and structure were sufficiently attractive.

An improbable visionary

When Mr Levin stepped into Mr Ross's shoes, neither the investors nor the press thought much of him. Arguably the worst public speaker in the entertainment business, he was a grey, corporate sort of figure, who lacked the Ross charm. Newspapers were peppered with quotes such as that from the head of a rival entertainment company, who said, "When you think of visionaries in the entertainment business, Jerry Levin is not a name that usually makes the list."

What's more, Mr Levin's judgment seemed seriously awry. He was investing heavily in upgrading the company's cable infrastructure at a time when the analysts universally agreed that "content is king." Time Warner's debt grew and its stock price suffered.

Yet Mr Levin's unpopularity strengthened his resolve, rather than weakening it. He concluded not that his strategy was wrong, but that it had not gone far enough. The model was incomplete. His eye strayed to Mr Turner's empire, the world's biggest producer of cable-television programming.

Moreover, while Time Warner had become the acknowledged giant of the media world, it was overtaken in the summer of 1995 by the creation of an even larger and more promising realisation of the Ross vision: the takeover by Walt Disney of Capital Cities/ABC: Hollywood's most famous film studio with America's most successful television network.

Mr Turner also needed a merger that summer – even more than Mr Levin did. He had built up the biggest cable network company in the country from scratch, starting with CNN in 1980, but was dependent for distribution on the two big cable-systems companies – Tele-Communications, Inc (TCI) and Time Warner.

He was also in financial difficulties. In 1986, he had bought MGM, a large Hollywood studio, principally for its library, and had got heavily into debt. He sold on most of MGM, keeping the library, and was bailed out by a consortium of cable-systems companies, who wanted him to survive because they needed his programming. Time Warner and TCI took sizeable stakes and three seats each on the board.

It was not a comfortable situation. "There are natural constraints," says Terry McGuirk, chairman of TBS and Mr Turner's long-time friend and lieutenant, "that go with having the customer being the governor on your board. Turner was fulfilling the role that the cable industry wanted, but not the role that Ted wanted." Among the constraints was Time Warner's obstruction of Mr Turner's ambitions to buy a television network. Over the years he tried and failed to buy both CBS and NBC. In the bid-fevered summer of 1995, Westinghouse Electric had snapped up CBS, scotching Mr Turner's vain efforts to mount a counterbid.

His debts large, his television ambitions thwarted, Mr Turner concluded that he would have to merge with one or other of the big cable companies. His first instinct was to go with John Malone of TCI, a friend, but Mr Levin was eager, pressed his suit and won.

Jilted, jolted

When news of the merger slipped out in the summer of 1995, investors were underwhelmed. Time Warner's stock slipped further. Several interested parties were hostile to the proposed merger.

Mr Malone, on Mr Turner's board, was furious: his biggest competitor in the cable-systems business would own the biggest programmer. US West, a telecoms company which owned a quarter of Time Warner Entertainment, the subsidiary which in turn owned many of the company's cable systems, filed a suit against the merger, on which it had not been consulted. Mr Malone was squared through a deal that gave him a large chunk of stock in the merged company. As for US West, it lost its suit, and its holdings were eventually disentangled from Time Warner's.

Few people in 1995 thought that Mr Levin and Mr Turner would be able to work together for long. Mr Turner had been less than warm about the Time Warner chief executive, in the days when his network-television ambitions were still smouldering. How would he fit into Time Warner's corporate bureaucracy? "Nobody had ever seen a character like Ted do something like this, so there was no script," says Mr McGuirk. "He willed himself to do it because he wanted to make the union work."

TBS itself buckled down to the new way of working. "At Turner," says Mr McGuirk, "there was a lot of seat-of-the-pants initiative. We just felt something needed to be done, and we'd do it." Within Time Warner, Turner executives found themselves having to justify themselves more in front of their new colleagues. Managers had to subject their decisions to more rigorous analysis. It was, says Mr McGuirk, good for them.

In gluing the merger together, it helped that Mr Turner had become not just vice-president of the merged group, but its largest individual shareholder. It helped, too, that TBS was expert in the art that was the essence of the Ross vision: repackaging the same content into many forms, and creating a whole family of cable news channels aimed at different audiences.

Connective tissue

It also helped that there were real synergies of the sort that Mr Levin had foreseen. Richard Parsons, Time Warner's president, describes Turner as the third side of the triangle. Its cable networks buy material from Warner's movie business; they use Time's publishing assets, such as *Time* and *Sports Illustrated*, as brands to strengthen their television offerings. "What you have to realise", said Steve Heyer, one of the TBS team, shortly after the merger went through, "is that Turner's fit with Time and its fit with Warner are more powerful than their fit with each other."

A Warner brand such as Batman, for instance, could be exploited by the movie studio, the publishing and cable television. Such multiple use of brands has two virtues: it brings in new revenue streams, and it strengthens brand recognition. Batman is better known because he has been on television, in print, in the movies, on pencil-cases and T-shirts; and Batman has also made more money for the company because he has been used in those different ways. So the Turner cable systems were

Before and after

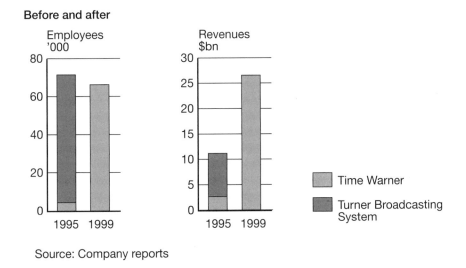

Source: Company reports

Figure 9

able to add value to Warner and Time content, and Warner and Time distribution platforms could enhance Turner content.

For Turner, having access to cable systems made all the difference. "We can get into any area of the business more cheaply than anybody else," says Mr McGuirk. "But the basic cable industry is a crowded one. For most people, it's difficult to get carriage." Once Turner was part of Time Warner, carriage was no longer a problem.

Being in both content and distribution, Time Warner was able to change the relationship between the two, to its advantage. The movie business, for instance, has a rigid series of "windows" through which films are shown on different media. First they go to American cinemas for around three months; then to foreign cinemas; then

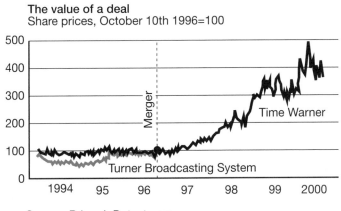

Source: Primark Datastream

Figure 10

to pay-per-view; then to home video; then to the broadcast networks; then to cable. Until recently, by the time they reached the cable stations, they were six to eight years old.

The windows were regarded as immutable, but Mr Turner was determined to move cable up the food chain. Before the merger with Time Warner, however much he bid, he was turned down. Cable was regarded as the end of the line. Now, however, movies regularly appear on cable television channels before they are broadcast. That has helped to build viewers for cable, which has both increased subscription revenue and boosted cable advertising.

Nevertheless, there are risks in vertical integration. The principal one is that the content does not get the best distribution, or the distribution network does not get the best content. Mr Parsons recognises the danger, but says, "We sell enough of our product outside to know what market values are. We don't necessarily put everything out for bid, but we like to have a benchmark."

Still, in this model, a poor-quality piece of content that comes out of one bit of the machine can damage other outlets. Time Warner discovered that when CNN put out its fallacious "Tailwind" story claiming that America used nerve gas in Vietnam. *Time* carried the story too, and so had to share CNN's embarrassment when the cable network retracted the story, even though its journalists had not been involved in the research.

Despite the evident dangers, investors' attitudes to Time Warner improved markedly after the merger (see Figure 10). Time Warner came to be regarded as Mr Ross hoped it would be, as the model of the modern media company. It now has every bit of distribution that is regarded as essential: publishing, movie and television production, music, a small television-broadcast network, cable systems and cable networks.

For the next trick

And now, assuming its merger with AOL goes through, it will have a huge online business. Some see AOL as another way of distributing Time Warner content; others are sceptical. Either way, cross-promotion should benefit both, as AOL advertises the old media outlets on the Internet, and Time Warner's old media outlets push the Internet service.

So Time Warner's earlier mergers set the pattern for the current one. And those experiences also, according to Mr Parsons, taught the company about the practicalities of implementing mergers.

During the Time and Warner merger, he says, "we erred on the side of sorting out who's going to do what upfront." The Turner merger taught them to be more relaxed about allocating roles. "That's one of the reasons we did so little of that with AOL. We wanted to wait until people got together and sorted things out themselves."

This lesson will help with the integration of Time Warner and AOL; but it does not guarantee that it will proceed smoothly. If the informal culture of Turner was hard to reconcile with that of a big media corporation, the speed-of-light agility that an Internet company needs will be even harder to meld with Time Warner. "The speed at which AOL is used to change is unknown at Time Warner," says an insider.

Nor will the Mouth of the South necessarily buckle down to this merger as willingly as he did to the previous one. When the deal with AOL was first announced, Mr Turner said with characteristic panache that it was the most exciting thing that had happened to him since the first time he had sex. Since then, the temperature has cooled.

In May, a restructuring was announced that deprived Mr Turner of an operational role. He has been noisily unhappy about that (for instance at a banquet at the cable industry's get-together in New Orleans). At the party for the 20th anniversary of CNN recently, he was obviously, and uncharacteristically, avoiding journalists who were trying to talk to him about the merger. When one of them cornered him, he grabbed Steve Case, AOL's chief executive, around the shoulders, pulled him close, and said fiercely, "See? I'm happy!"

Whether Mr Turner buckles down or not depends on whether AOL and Time Warner can do as much for each other as Time Warner and Turner did. The logic of the merger is as strong, but the cultural differences are even greater; and, with the implementation of the merger under way, the two companies will work out whether or not the sum is greater than the parts. It is a delicate time to have an angry Ted on the loose.

6   FIRST AMONG EQUALS

Our sixth and final merger brief shows why true mergers of equals are rare. The union of Citicorp and Travelers, initially equal partners, became a takeover as one of its co-chief executives took sole command

It was the most extraordinary merger ever, or so it seemed back in April 1998. The marriage of two financial-services giants, Citicorp and Travelers, was the biggest to date, with a combined market capitalisation of $84 billion on the day it was announced. The vision behind it was just as large: the newly created Citigroup would be an entirely new sort of global business, a financial-services supermarket selling every financial product under the sun to individual, corporate and government customers in every corner of the earth.

As if that were not enough, the marriage was structured as a genuine "merger of equals" – a phrase often used, but usually only to soothe the ego of the boss of a company that is being taken over. In this case, every effort was made to ensure that both sides really were equal partners, starting at the top, with the bosses of the two merging firms becoming co-chairman and co-chief executive.

But the omens were bad. Announcing the merger, Sandy Weill (of Travelers) quipped that he was used to "sharing power and responsibility as I've been married to my wife for 43 years". This metaphor may have jarred on John Reed, who had divorced in 1991 and married a stewardess on the Citi corporate jet.

Barely 15 months after the deal was done, the two co-heads agreed, under pressure from shareholders, to separate their roles. Divorce followed in April this year, when Mr Reed retired, at the request of the board, leaving Mr Weill as lone chief executive.

For the moment, Citigroup is an undeniable success: in the first quarter of 2000, it was the world's most profitable company. But the power struggle at the top delayed integration and discouraged "cross-selling" the financial products of one part of the merged firm to customers of another, one of the key goals of the merger strategy. It has also prevented the emergence of a strong Internet strategy.

Mr Weill admits only that "we have taken longer to get places than we might have." In fact, the costs may have been greater than that implies, not least in missed opportunities. Citigroup's management is now dominated by people from Travelers. The loss of the Citibank talent may yet cause problems, especially outside America. The stellar performance hoped for by the stockmarket may not happen.

Citi and Travelers came to the altar with different experiences of mergers. In the 1990s Citi, which traces its origins back to 1812, went from near bankruptcy to being the leading global consumer bank. But big mergers were not central to this success. Indeed, the mergers it undertook went badly – notably the acquisition of Quotron, a securities data firm.

By contrast, a knack for acquisitions enabled Mr Weill to build up Shearson Loeb Rhodes, a brokerage, which he merged with American Express in 1981. He quit in 1985, after falling out with James Robinson, the boss of Amex, thereby learning a valuable lesson: do not be the junior partner in a merger. In 1986, he bought Commercial Credit, a small consumer-lending firm, which through mergers became Travelers, an insurance and brokerage conglomerate. And even as the merger with Citi was announced, the recently acquired Salomon Brothers investment bank was still being integrated with Travelers' Smith Barney. In June 1998, Mr Weill added a stake in and a joint venture with Nikko Securities, a Japanese stockbroker.

Mr Weill's merger technique was based on having a clear strategy – including cutting fat out of undermanaged businesses – and implementing it fast. He tried to minimise cancerous uncertainty by selecting the management team to run the merged businesses as soon as possible, usually on merit and loyalty to him.

Yet integrating Citigroup was never going to be straightforward. Citibank was not flabby or undermanaged – or at least, did not see itself that way. It was possible that the merger would be called off by regulators, a danger that fostered hesitancy over integration. In the event, the Citigroup merger helped secure the scrapping of America's Glass-Steagall act, which had separated commercial banks, insurers and investment banks. But above all loomed the problem of this being a genuine merger of equals.

Two heads better than one?

The to-be-merged company quickly adopted a "Noah's Ark" approach to top management – everything in twos. As well as Messrs Weill and Reed, half the new board's members came from Citibank and half from Travelers. The global consumer business was headed by Bob Lipp (Travelers), and William Campbell (Citi). The global corporate and investment banks had three heads – Victor Menezes (Citi), Deryck Maughan (Salomon Smith Barney) and Jamie Dimon (Travelers), long regarded as Mr Weill's heir apparent.

As a result, every decision became a lengthy philosophical discussion. This partly reflected the personalities of the two co-chief executives. Mr Reed is the sort who loves to discuss management with academics. A loner in leadership, he tended to invite people into his inner management circle only to expel them soon after. Mr Weill is guided more by gut instinct than by briefing papers, and relies on a small group of loyal managers.

Indecision at the top soon led to trouble in the global corporate and investment bank: Travelers' Salomon Smith Barney investment bank, plus Citi's corporate relationship bank. Integration had been half-hearted: SSB's well-paid investment bankers regarded their new colleagues as stuffy corporate folk. Staff in the Citi operation were proud of the 1,500 leading global firms that were their main customers, and looked down on traders at Salomon, with their lower-grade corporate-bond clients. They wanted their services to continue under the Citi brand, not to be switched to SSB. They were aghast at the huge losses run up by Salomon during the financial-market crisis in 1998. Meanwhile, Salomon itself resented Mr Weill's decision to close its American bond-arbitrage operation only a few months after buying the firm.

Things came to a head in late October 1998 at a weekend of golf and spouses in West Virginia, where senior executives complained about how the merger was proceeding. Scuffles broke out. The two leaders reacted with unusual decisiveness. A week later, a new management team was appointed. Mr Dimon left the company, his ambition having reportedly annoyed Mr Weill. Mr Menezes was joined as co-head of global corporate and investment banking by Michael Carpenter, a Weill loyalist. The pair at once set about fully integrating the two businesses, selecting a new top management team, and identifying a dozen big issues that needed urgent action.

In July, after Citi's biggest shareholder, Prince Alwaleed bin Talal of Saudi Arabia, fretted in public about the relationship between the firm's co-heads, Mr Weill took charge of day-to-day operations. Mr Reed was left with strategy. In October 1999, Robert Rubin, a former Treasury secretary and co-head of Goldman Sachs, was appointed to the "office of the chairman", apparently to broker peace between the two bosses.

By now, the tensions at the top were public. Mr Reed had told the Academy of Management that, although the "wisdom of the merger is even more compelling" than when it began, it "is not 100% clear to me that it will necessarily be successful". He drew telling comparisons with step-parenting. "Sandy and I both have the problem that our 'children' look up to us as they never did before, and reject the other parent with equal vigour, saying 'Sandy wouldn't want to do this, so what do I care about what John wants?'"

The reality was that Sandy's children were increasingly winning the top jobs, and John's were quitting in droves. Citigroup was rapidly becoming Mr Weill's creature. One top-notch Travelers person did leave, however: Heidi Miller, Citi's chief finance officer, quit for Priceline, an e-commerce firm. Mr Weill blamed her departure on irritation with Mr Reed. But that was the last straw: the board asked Mr Reed, 61, to retire. The 67-year-old Mr Weill became sole boss, supported by Mr Rubin. All Mr Reed salvaged was a promise (which few now believe) that Mr Weill would go within two years, and that the search would begin for a successor.

Mr Weill soon completed his domination of Citi. In July, the last of the post-merger top-job splits ended. Mr Carpenter became sole head of the global corporate and investment bank; Mr Menezes, the last remaining Citibanker at the top, was packed off to head corporate and consumer banking in emerging markets. Mr Lipp, another Weill loyalist and head of consumer banking, joined the office of the chairman, with a brief to co-ordinate cross-selling.

As for cross-selling, the vision that ostensibly motivated the merger, this has worked better in some parts of the merged company than in others. The greatest success has been achieved where it was least expected – in corporate and investment banking. Wall Street analysts initially hated the decision to axe Mr Dimon and to promote Mr Carpenter. In the event, it proved inspired. Aided by the link with Nikko Securities and a merger with Schroders, a British investment bank, in January 2000, the now Schroders Salomon Smith Barney has moved from being a middle-ranking

Before and after

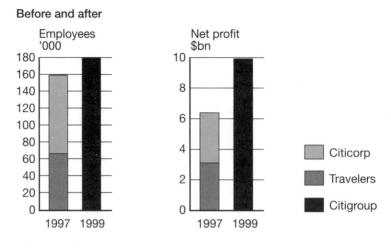

Source: Company reports

Figure 11

firm to the brink of – or even into – the so-called "bulge bracket" of top global investment banks.

Blurred vision?

Mr Carpenter says his business was involved in some 300 transactions during 1999 that both Citi and Salomon folk agree could not have been done without each other, and that the firm is now in the top four in every product category, in every geographical region of the world. This may be stretching it – SSSB is still not a first-tier adviser on mergers and acquisitions, for example, though it is gaining on rivals

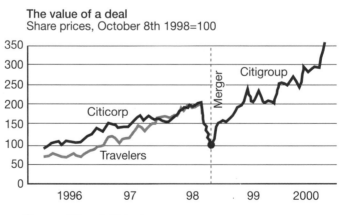

Source: Primark Datastream

Figure 12

such as Goldman Sachs and Morgan Stanley by using its huge balance sheet to offer corporate clients credit lines during mergers.

The potential for cross-selling was supposedly greatest in consumer finance. Citi's strong global brand provided a superb platform for selling Travelers and Salomon Smith Barney products through its branch network, which spans over 100 countries, and to Citi's 42m credit-card account-holders (more than any other credit-card provider). But cross-selling is something that many financial institutions, across the globe, have attempted, with little success.

Citi claims a few modest achievements. Some wealthy Salomon Smith Barney customers have been given 100% mortgages by Citibank, secured against their brokerage accounts. Salomon Smith Barney mutual funds have been sold to Citibank branch customers. Within months of the merger announcement, Travelers annuities were selling in the Citibank branch network, and now generate revenues of $750m a year.

Travelers has now "pre-under-written" all of Citi's credit-card customers, and whenever somebody with an attractive risk profile calls to discuss his credit card – there are 80m such calls a year – he is invited to buy a Travelers home or car insurance policy. Travelers says that sales by this channel have minimal incremental cost, making them particularly profitable. It now sells almost 5,000 policies a month, and expects $200m in premiums by 2002 (6% of current revenues).

Travelers has started to expand abroad, primarily in emerging markets rather than in the already highly competitive continental European market. Once only a domestic American insurer, Travelers now expects to win the lion's share of the $400m a year in commissions currently earned by the global Citibank branch network from selling competitors' products.

According to Mr Weill, integration in the corporate and investment-banking business happened faster than in retail because it had to. "If we'd gone slower, we would have lost a lot of people." There have been huge technology challenges, such as incompatible computer systems. Citi remains confident that retail cross-selling will bear more fruit, but progress has been slow. It has been hard to integrate systems, and business units have warred over which brands to cross-sell and which to ditch.

Adding to the frustration has been the group's muddled Internet strategy. Mr Reed, who took sole charge of it in July 1999, believed that Citi's Internet potential would best be fulfilled by developing from scratch an entirely self-contained, state-of-the-art online retail financial-services provider. More than $500m was spent developing "e-Citi" – a classic example of the big-bang innovation strategy pursued by Mr Reed decades earlier when he installed thousands of ATMS in Citi branches, and transformed the way people used their bank.

E-Citi attracted few customers, and was resented by Citi's established businesses. Since Mr Reed's retirement, it has been downgraded to a sort of incubator, and 1,400 of its employees have been despatched to other Citigroup brand businesses. Now, ownership of Internet strategy is left with the top executives in individual businesses. This caution may be a mistake. Asked in June whether Mr Weill could take Citi into the Internet age, Mr Reed said, "This isn't Sandy's deal. He is not going to personally design the Internet company that is going to do this." Mr Reed's boldness might eventually have brought rewards – as did his huge spending on ATMS, which initially meant huge losses.

Despite the infighting, strategic mishaps and delays in integration, Citigroup has prospered, with both profits and the share price soaring. Mr Weill has, as usual, cut costs and made undermanaged assets sweat. New managers from Travelers have instilled a more aggressive sales culture in Citibank branches.

But the Travelers people who now lead Citibank lack experience in overseas markets, where the group expects its main growth. Citibank's institutional memory, which gave some protection from bad lending decisions, has gone. So has Mr Reed's vision. Mr Weill is skilled at fixing and then expanding undermanaged companies. But he has yet to show that he can fix and expand an already successful global giant.

Section 1
Growth by M&A

Mergers and the market for corporate control[1]

3

Henry G. Manne

In recent years many of the traditional economic justifications of our antitrust laws have been seriously questioned. A new sophistication has developed, and economic activities frequently held illegal by the courts are now thought by many to be consistent with our antitrust goals. The rules against tie-ins, vertical mergers, predatory competition, among others, have to a greater or lesser degree had their theoretical foundations considerably weakened. Recently even cartels, the most venerable victim of American antitrust laws, have found their near champion.[2]

One practice, however, remains generally condemned in both the economic literature and the most recent Supreme Court rulings. Mergers among competitors would seem to have no important saving grace. The position has gained considerable legal currency that any merger between competing firms is at least suspect and perhaps *per se* illegal. The latter result seems especially likely when one of the combining firms already occupies a substantial position in the relevant market. Antitrust problems in the merger field seem more and more to be confined to discussions of relevant product and geographic markets and perhaps to the issue of quantitative substantiality.[3]

Presumably there is still a so-called failing-company defense to an illegal merger charge. The announced justification for this doctrine was that, if indeed the merged company was failing, then it was not actually a competitor in the industry.[4] But there are strong suggestions that even that defense may be unavailable when a large corporation is making the acquisition, or when there is any chance of absorption by a non-competing firm, or when the acquired company has not "failed" enough.[5]

There is general agreement among economists that the courts' approach to horizontal mergers is correct.[6] Professor Donald Dewey, who appears slightly regretful about the severe treatment of mergers by our courts and administrative agencies, concedes that no important economies can be attained through a merger which cannot be gained either by internal growth or, at worst, by a cartel, if that were legal. But Dewey is certainly not as severe in his personal indictment of horizontal mergers as most other economists. He has argued that most mergers "have virtually nothing to do with either the creation of market power or the realization of scale economies. They are merely a civilized alternative to bankruptcy or the voluntary liquidation that transfers assets from falling to rising firms."[7]

Consistent with his alternative-to-bankruptcy explanation of mergers, Dewey points out that, "[i]f the capital market were perfect and a merger conferred no monopoly power, a rising firm would be indifferent between the two forms of expansion."[8] Thus a rapidly expanding industry with a relatively short life cycle of its firms would be characterized by substantial external growth of successful firms. Mergers then would "most commonly indicate not the decline of competition but its undoubted vigor."[9]

Dewey's argument is, however, only a partial redemption of mergers, since a great many have occurred in industries in which the life cycle of firms is not as short as in the southern textile industry, which he mentions as his example. Further, Dewey's defense of mergers seems to be limited to those cases in which bankruptcy or liquidation is imminent. But, if a merger can be justified at this stage of the firm's life, presumably it is also desirable before bankruptcy becomes imminent in order to avoid that eventuality. If, as Dewey suggests, mergers actually are superior to bankruptcy as a method of "shifting assets from falling to rising firms," and if mergers were completely legal, we should anticipate relatively few actual bankruptcy proceedings in any industry which was not itself contracting. The function so wastefully performed by bankruptcies and liquidations would be economically performed by mergers at a much earlier stage of the firm's life.

THE CORPORATE-CONTROL MARKET

The conventional approach to a merger problem takes corporations merely as decision-making units or firms within the classical market framework. This approach dictates a ban on many horizontal mergers almost by definition. The basic proposition advanced in this paper is that the control of corporations may constitute a valuable asset; that this asset exists independent of any interest in either economies of scale or monopoly profits; that an active market for corporate control exists; and that a great many mergers are probably the result of the successful workings of this special market.

Basically this paper will constitute an introduction to a study of the market for corporation control. The emphasis will be placed on the antitrust implications of this market, but the analysis to follow has important implications for a variety of economic questions. Perhaps the most important implications are those for the alleged separation of ownership and control in large corporations. So long as we are unable to discern any control relationship between small shareholders and corporate management, the thrust of Berle and Means's famous phrase remains strong. But, as will be explained below, the market for corporate control gives to these shareholders both power and protection commensurate with their interest in corporate affairs.

A fundamental premise underlying the market for corporate control is the existence of a high positive correlation between corporate managerial efficiency and the market price of shares of that company.[10] As an existing company is poorly managed – in the sense of not making as great a return for the shareholders as could be accomplished under other feasible managements – the market price of the shares declines relative to the shares of other companies in the same industry or relative to the market as a whole. This phenomenon has a dual importance for the market for corporate control.

In the first place, a lower share price facilitates any effort to take over high-paying managerial positions. The compensation from these positions may take the usual forms of salary, bonuses, pensions, expense accounts, and stock options. Perhaps more important, it may take the form of information useful in trading in the company's shares; or, if that is illegal, information may be exchanged and the trading done in other companies' shares. But it is extremely doubtful that the full compensation recoverable by executives for managing their corporations explains more than a small fraction of outsider[11] attempts to take over control. Take-overs of corporations are too expensive generally to make the "purchase" of management compensation an attractive proposition.[12]

It is far more likely that a second kind of reward provides the primary motivation for most take-over attempts. The market price of shares does more than measure the price at which the normal compensation of executives can be "sold" to new individuals. Share price, or that part reflecting managerial efficiency, also measures the potential capital gain inherent in the corporate stock. The lower the stock price, relative to what it could be with more efficient management, the more attractive the take-over becomes to those who believe that they can manage the company more efficiently. And the potential return from the successful take-over and revitalization of a poorly run company can be enormous.[13]

Additional leverage in this operation can be obtained by borrowing the funds with which the shares are purchased, although American commercial banks are generally forbidden to lend money for this purpose. A comparable advantage can be had from using other shares rather than cash as the exchange medium. Given the fact of special tax treatment for capital gains, we can see how this mechanism for taking over control of badly run corporations is one of the most important "get-rich-quick" opportunities in our economy today.

But the greatest benefits of the take-over scheme probably inure to those least conscious of it. Apart from the stock market, we have no objective standard of managerial efficiency. Courts, as indicated by the so-called business-judgment rule, are loath to second-guess business decisions or remove directors from office. Only the take-over scheme provides some assurance of competitive efficiency among corporate managers and thereby affords strong protection to the interests of vast numbers of small, non-controlling shareholders. Compared to this mechanism, the efforts of the SEC and the courts to protect shareholders through the development of a fiduciary duty concept and the shareholder's derivative suit seem small indeed. It is true that sales by dissatisfied shareholders are necessary to trigger the mechanism and that these shareholders may suffer considerable losses. On the other hand, even greater capital losses are prevented by the existence of a competitive market for corporate control.[14]

There are several mechanisms for taking over the control of corporations. The three basic techniques are the proxy fight, direct purchase of shares, and the merger. The costs, practical difficulties, and legal consequences of these approaches vary widely. The selection of one or another or some combination of these techniques frequently represents a difficult strategy decision. An attempt will be made in this paper to analyze some of the considerations involved in a selection of one device over another.

PROXY FIGHTS

The most dramatic and publicized of the take-over devices is the proxy fight; it is also the most expensive, the most uncertain, and the least used of the various techniques. Indeed it is somewhat difficult to describe the necessary conditions under which a proxy fight rather than some other take-over form will be indicated. At first blush, the proxy fight appears to be inexpensive since one does not have to own a large number of shares (or for that matter any shares) in order to wage a fight. But this fact is most relevant when the take-over is for the purpose of gaining the incumbents' compensation. If the outsider wants capital gains, he will be interested in owning more, not fewer, shares. This suggests that proxy fights will be relatively more often used when the issue is not one of management policies but of distribution of insiders' compensation.[15]

Even as a device for settling internal power struggles, actual proxy fights constitute only a small percentage of threatened fights.[16] The parties will generally prefer to negotiate a settlement in accordance with their respective strengths than incur the costs of soliciting proxies. The more reliable the information about relative strengths available, the more will settlement be likely to occur. This suggests that proxy fights will be relatively more common when there is widespread distribution of the company's shares than when there are relatively large holdings.

In a number of cases the outsider would probably like to own more shares and take over control without waging or threatening a proxy fight. But if he is unable to accumulate sufficient capital to purchase control directly, he may settle for half a loaf. In effect he indicates his willingness to share the capital-gain potential with all other shareholders in exchange for enough of their votes to put him into control.

When a proxy fight is announced, the shares tend to rise in price, reflecting a rise in both the market value of the vote and the discounted value of potential gain in the underlying share interest if the outsider wins.[17] Other outsiders will find it in their interest to retain their shares or purchase shares, to vote for the outsider seeking control, and to share in the capital appreciation. It may be cheaper to elicit the support of these voters through expenditures on persuasion than through outright purchase of the shares. But to the outsider seeking control, every voter represents another person with whom he must share the potential gain resulting from his more efficient management. These voters are analogous to, or substitutes for, the capital or credit with which the outsider would otherwise purchase control directly.

Proxy-fight expenses have always included direct expenses of mailings, advertising, telephone calls, and visits to large shareholders. But since the Securities Exchange Act of 1934, the cost of waging a proxy fight has probably increased substantially. Prior to the act, the proxy system operated largely through broker intermediaries acting as full agents for the beneficial owners of the shares. To the brokers was delegated not merely the ministerial job of voting but the more important responsibility of deciding how to vote. That practice has been largely replaced because of the SEC philosophy that the proxy system should duplicate actual meetings of shareholders as closely as possible. Thus, today, "giving a proxy" is really tantamount to voting. And, since the shareholder himself is voting, it is also felt that he should be fully and truthfully informed about all aspects of the corporation's affairs. This has tremendously increased the cost of soliciting proxies. But while the incumbents finance the bulk of their proxy solicitation expenses from corporate funds, the outsider will have this advantage only if he wins.[18]

DIRECT PURCHASE OF SHARES

The second mechanism for taking over control of a corporation is the direct purchase of the requisite number of shares of the corporations. There are several techniques that may be used in the direct purchase of shares. The most obvious is outright purchase on the open market of the requisite percentage of shares.[19] The outsider might also try to buy the shares from large individual owners, thus preserving secrecy and allowing negotiation on price. Finally, he may make a bid for tenders, that is, a request that shareholders make an offer to sell their shares to him at a certain price, usually above the market. This last form of direct purchase is most apposite when the shares are widely held and there is a chance of a fast increase in market price if the news spreads that there is a heavy buyer in the market for the company's shares. A tender bid is usually stated to be effective only if a minimum percentage of shares is offered at the announced price. Also, the bid will ordinarily be for less than 100 per cent of the shares in order to avoid the problem of many individual shareholders trying to be the sole hold-out. In practice, private negotiation for large blocks of shares may be combined with either open-market purchases or a tender bid.

There are few serious legal problems with any of the direct purchase techniques. In fact, about the only one which has arisen with any regularity in recent years results from Professor Adolf A. Berle's contention that control is a corporate asset.[20] The implication of this notion is that any premium received by an individual for a sale of control belongs in equity to all of the shareholders. As a general proposition, the courts have refused to follow this thesis; and there are numerous judicial statements to the effect that one may claim a premium for control.[21]

A number of legal writers, following Berle, continue to press for a rule of equality in share purchase price when an outsider buys control in a corporation.[22] The economic results of such a rule could be most unfortunate. Many holders of control blocks of shares would refuse to sell at a share price which did not pay them a premium at least sufficient to compensate them for the loss of net values presently being received from their position in the corporation. If all non-controlling share-holders must accordingly be paid a premium over the market price of their shares, then in a substantial number of cases the purchaser will not conclude the bargain. This further suggests that, if control is securely held in one block, the "market price" of traded shares is the price for an underlying share interest without an aliquot portion of control. That is, if one person owns 51 per cent of the shares of a company, nothing will be paid for the vote attached to the other shares,[23] no matter how actively the shares may be traded on the market. The less securely control is held in one block, the more likely are non-controlling shareholders to participate in the "premium," and the less will an outsider be willing to pay one shareholder for control. Both proxy fights and competitive tender bids are more likely to occur under these conditions, since each of them gives shareholders the power to sell their votes at a premium.

MERGERS

The third major mechanism for taking over control of the corporation is the merger. Here, by definition, the acquiring concern will be a corporation and not an individual, and the medium of exchange used to buy control will typically be shares of the acquiring company rather than cash. Another major difference between the merger and other take-over forms is that, almost without exception, a merger requires the explicit approval of those already in control of the corporation.[24] And most statutes require more than a simple majority vote by shareholders to effectuate a merger. If the merger occurs after an acquisition of shares in a tender bid, then the tender bid and not the merger is the actual mechanism for changing control.

The requirement of management's approval for a merger generates some peculiar results. Generally speaking, managers' incentives and interests coincide with those of their shareholders in every particular except one: they have no incentive, as managers, to buy management services for the company at the lowest possible price.[25] Even if the market for corporate control is working perfectly, so long as the cost to the corporation of the incumbent managers' inefficiency is below the cost to an outsider of taking over control, the insiders will remain secure in the positions with protected high salaries.[26]

In the case of tender bids, as we have seen, a premium for control may be paid; and in the proxy fight situation, in one sense at least, the premium is paid in the form of expenditures necessary to persuade shareholders to vote a certain way. But the merger has considerable cost advantages over the other two forms of take-over, not the least being the ability to use shares rather than cash as the purchasing medium.

The shareholders should ordinarily be willing to accept any offer of a tax-free exchange of new marketable shares worth more than their old shares. But the managers are in a position to claim almost the full market value of control, since they have it in their power to block the merger by voting against it.[27] When we find incumbents recommending a control change, it is generally safe to assume that some side payment is occurring.

Side payments are often not simple transactions at law because of the rule that directors and officers may not sell their positions shorn of the share interest necessary to ensure a transfer of control.[28] The most obvious kind of side payment to managers is a position within the new structure either paying a salary or making them privy to valuable market information.[29] This arrangement, easily established with mergers, can look like normal business expediency, since the argument can always be made that the old management provides continuity and a link with the past experience of the corporation.

There is still another very important reason why mergers may be more desirable than proxy fights or take-over bids as a way of operating in the corporate-control market. This is a market in which reliable information about valuable opportunities will be extremely difficult to discover. For reasons already mentioned, the corporate insiders will generally have no incentive to advertise this kind of information. Blatant cases will, of course, be evident from casual observation of industrial affairs and the stock market.[30]

The great problem in the corporate-control market is finding reliable information about new opportunities. There have generally been a few individual operators in this market, and perhaps they have found the more obvious cases of bad management. But to guarantee effective competition in the market for corporate control, it seems clear that corporations must be allowed to function therein. Managers of a competing firm, unlike free-wheeling individual participants in the market for corporate control, almost automatically know a great deal of the kind of information crucial to a take-over decision. Careful analysis of cost conditions in their own firm and the market price of shares of other corporations in the same industry will provide information that can be relied upon with some degree of confidence.

Since, in a world of uncertainty, profitable transactions will be entered into more often by those whose information is relatively more reliable,[31] it should not surprise us that mergers within the same industry have been a principal form of changing corporate control. Reliable information is often available to suppliers and customers as well. Thus many vertical mergers may be of the control takeover variety rather than of the "foreclosure of competitors" or scale-economies type. Undoubtedly many more mergers, both horizontal and vertical, would have occurred but for our antitrust laws. The managers of corporations have considerable incentive to exploit such opportunities for their corporation, just as they are motivated to find any good new investment opportunity. And there are both legal and practical barriers to the individuals' utilizing such opportunities for themselves.

CONCLUSIONS

Mergers seem in many instances to be the most efficient of the three devices for corporate take-overs. Consequently, they are of considerable importance for the protection of individual non-controlling shareholders and are desirable from a general welfare-economics point of view. Certainly they are more desirable than the increased number of bankruptcies that would undoubtedly ensue if this avenue of taking over control were totally closed.

This is not to suggest that the anti-trust norm of competition in the product market need be entirely sacrificed to the norm of competition in the market for corporate control. Rather it points up some of the serious problems with current antitrust doctrine. The market for corporate control implies a number of important advantages which must be compared to those existing in present antitrust enforcement. Among the advantages of the former, as we have seen, are a lessening of wasteful bankruptcy proceedings, more efficient management of corporations, the protection afforded non-controlling corporate investors, increased mobility of capital, and generally a more efficient allocation of resources.

The greatest difficulty in assessing the proper role for the market for corporate control comes in the area of horizontal mergers, where, as previously indicated, this market may operate most effectively.[32] It may be that, so long as entry into an industry is kept open, there is no reason at all for rules against mergers, at least short of a monopolization charge under Section 2 of the Sherman Act. It is extremely unlikely, however, that Congress or the courts would ever adopt such a rule.

Far more likely is an *ad hoc* recognition of the importance of the market for corporate control in individual cases.[33] Courts or agencies might begin to look at such factors as the average life cycle of firms in the industry, the amount of total new investment in the industry, the condition of the acquired firms in terms of both financial and managerial strength, the number of bankruptcies in the industry, and the amount of proxy-fight and tender-bid activity. These factors would then have to be weighed on the scales with the more traditional approach in terms of number of firms in the industry, concentration ratios, size of the acquiring firm, and its acquisitions history. But no longer does the tendency to hold most mergers illegal *per se* seem justified.

One real problem will be in devising statistical methods for distinguishing mergers motivated by a quest for monopoly profit from those merely trying to establish more efficient management in poorly run companies. But if the theoretical aspects of these transactions are well enough understood, this should not be insuperable. There may be different effects on the prices of shares depending on the motive behind the merger. In the normal merger for acquisition of control, something will be paid by the acquiring company for the control opportunity. Since this factor does not figure largely in the market price of even badly run companies until the possibility of a take-over is known, the exchange ratio in the merger will appear to be too favorable to the acquired company, judged by the relative premerger announcement prices. The price of the shares of the acquiring company in such a merger should then tend to decrease and those of the acquired company to increase upon the announcement of the merger. If, on the other hand, the merger is motivated by a quest for market power, or by economies of scale available to both corporations, then the price of stock of each company should increase on the announcement of the merger terms. The first of these two results conforms to what seems most frequently to occur when mergers are announced, though no data are presently available on this subject.[34] The study of the economics of the market for corporate control is still in its infancy.

NOTES

1 Helpful criticisms and suggestions on this article by Professors Armen A. Alchian, Joseph Aschheim, Donald Dewey, and Joseph P. McKenna are gratefully acknowledged.

   A companion article to this one by the same author, entitled "Some Theoretical Aspects of Share Voting," appears in *Columbia Law Review*, LXIV (1964), 1427–45. That article analyzes the strategies available to shareholders when different techniques for taking over control of a corporation are used.

2 Donald Dewey, "The Economic Theory of Anti-Trust: Science or Religion?" *Virginia Law Review*, L (1964), 413–34. This article also contains references to the other iconoclastic literature (pp. 426–27).

3 Among the recent articles and cases bearing out this conclusion are the following: Donald Dewey, *op. cit.*; Richard E. Day, "Conglomerate Mergers and the 'Curse of Bigness,'" *North Carolina Law Review*, XLII (1964), 511–66; James A. Rahl, "Current Anti-Trust Developments in the Merger Field," *Anti-Trust Bulletin*, VIII (1963), 493–515; United States v. El Paso Natural Gas Company, 376 US 651 (1964); and United States v. First National Bank and Trust Company of Lexington, 376 US 665 (1964).

4 International Shoe Company v. Federal Trade Commission, 280 US 291, 294 (1929); but see Derek C. Bok, "Section 7 of the Clayton Act and the Merging of Law and Economics," *Harvard Law Review*, LXXIV (1960), 226–355, esp. p. 340, where concern for the interests in the failing company is argued to be the most likely reason for the doctrine.

5 Derek C. Bok, *op. cit.*, pp. 339–47; and see cases cited in anonymous comment, "An Updating of the 'Failing Company' Doctrine in the Amended Section 7 Setting," *Michigan Law Review*, LXI (1963), 566–83.

   There is also a "solely for investment" defense to Clayton Act charges. This appears as an explicit proviso in the third paragraph of Section 7, 15 USCA sec. 18 (1962). But the famous du Pont–G. M. case, United States v. E. I. Du Pont de Nemours and Company, 353 US 586 (1957), seems to have very substantially weakened the force of this proviso. Also see Swift and Co. v. FTC, 8 Fed. 2d 595, 599, reversed on other grounds, 272 US 554 (1925), where it is stated: "It would be difficult to conceive of any case where one corporation purchased all the stock of its competitor solely for investment. Such a case would be a rare one."

   There was once thought to be an illegal purpose requirement for convictions under the Sherman Act. See Eugene V. Rostow, "Monopoly under the Sherman Act: Power or Purpose?" *Illinois Law Review*, XLIII (1949), 745–92. But recent Supreme Court decisions in the merger field have left little vitality to that notion. Cf. United States v. First National Bank and Trust Company of Lexington, 376 US 665, 669 (1964).

6 See George J. Stigler, "Mergers and Preventive Anti-Trust Policy," *Pennsylvania Law Review*, CIV (1955), 176–84 (Stigler too recognizes the possibility that some mergers may increase competition, but he finds it "most uncommon" [p. 181]); M. A. Adelman, "The Anti-Merger Act, 1950–60," *American Economic Review*, LI (May, 1961), 236–54 ("The horizontal elements of mergers . . . have been treated severely and – if maintaining competition is the object – rationally" [p. 238]).

7 "Mergers and Cartels: Some Reservations about Policy," *Market Economic Review*, LI (May, 1961), 257. Dewey analyzed four relatively unimportant cases of scale economies that can be realized only through a consolidation, but he concluded, in substantial agreement with Stigler and Adelman, "that

the present experiment discouraging growth by mergers should be continued" with a ban in any industry not generally considered a good example of workable competition (p. 261).

Jesse W. Markham has remarked that some mergers are the "means by which some entrepreneurs make their exit from the industry, selling their undepreciated assets to other entrepreneurs. . . . Since 1930 most mergers appear to have been of the ordinary business variety in that they had neither monopoly nor promotional gains as their objective" ("Survey of the Evidence and Findings on Mergers," in *Business Concentration and Price Policy* [New York: National Bureau of Economic Research, 1955], p. 181). He concluded that "while some mergers impair a competitive enterprise system, others may be an integral part of it" (p. 182).

8 "Mergers and Cartels . . .," *op. cit.*, p. 257.

9 *Ibid.*

10 The claim of a positive correlation between managerial efficiency and the market price of shares would seem at first blush to raise an empirical question. In fact, however, the concept of corporate managerial efficiency, with its overtones of an entrepreneurial function, is one for which there are no objective standards. But there are compelling reasons, apart from empirical data, for believing that this correlation exists. Insiders, those who have the most reliable information about corporate affairs, are strongly motived financially to perform a kind of arbitrage function for their company's stock. That is, given their sense of what constitutes efficient management, they will cause share prices to rise or decline in accordance with that standard.

The contention is often made that stock-market prices are not accurate gauges, since far more trades take place without reliable information than with it. But there is reason to believe that intelligence rather than ignorance ultimately determines the course of individual share prices. Stock-market decisions tend to be of the one-out-of-two-alternatives variety, such as buy or not buy, hold or sell, or put or call. To the extent that decisions on these questions are made by shareholders or potential shareholders operating without reliable information, over a period of time the decisions will tend to be randomly distributed and the effect will therefore be neutral. Decisions made by those with a higher degree of certainty will to that extent not meet a canceling effect since they will not be made on a random basis. Over some period of time it would seem that the average market price of a company's shares must be the "correct" one.

11 "Outsider" here refers to anyone not presently controlling the affairs of the corporation, even though it may include one or more individuals on the corporation's board of directors.

12 To the extent that executive compensation increases with higher share prices, the take-over is most attractive at the time when it is also most expensive. Indeed, the danger of a take-over may account for managers' voluntarily decreasing their compensation when the company's share price is down.

13 The clearest modern illustration is probably furnished by Louis Wolfson's successful venture into Montgomery Ward. For details of this and other large stock price gains associated with corporation "raids" see David Karr, *Fight for Control* (New York: Ballantine Books, 1956).

14 Unfortunately the suppression of this market would be the consequence of proposals made by several writers in the field. For a review and a criticism of this literature see Henry G. Manne, "The 'Higher Criticism' of the Modern Corporation," *Columbia Law Review*, LXII (1962), 399–432. For another defense of this market see Harry G. Johnson, *The Canadian Quandary* (Toronto: McGraw-Hill Book Co., 1963), pp. xvii-xviii.

15 The courts draw a similar distinction for purposes of determining when contestants in a proxy fight may recover their expenses from the corporate treasury. Generally they may recover if the contest is found to be one of policy rather than a "purely personal power contest" (Rosenfeld v. Fairchild Engine & Airplane Corp., 309 NY 168, 129 NE 2d 291 [1955]). It does not seem to be too difficult, however, to establish the existence of a "policy" controversy to the court's satisfaction.

16 In the SEC's fiscal year 1962 seventeen companies were involved in proxy contests, while a total of 253 persons, both management and non-management, filed statements as participants. The respective figures for 1961 were thirty-two proxy contests and 463 participant filings. Many non-management filings are multiple; that is, several people are involved in the same fight. But no breakdown beyond the total number of participants is available. Therefore, it is impossible to prove the point made in the text from published data. See *27th and 28th Annual Reports* (Washington: Securities and Exchange Commission, 1961 and 1962).

17 See Henry G. Manne, *op. cit.*, pp. 410–13. It is possible, of course, for the vote price to be rising while the market value of the underlying investment interest is declining, though this would seem to be uncommon.

18 The SEC rules on proxy solicitations have aided the insiders in unexpected and curious ways. Outsiders in a proxy fight are not privy to the particulars of corporate information as are the insiders, so they must frequently "guess" why the company is not doing as well as it should. These "guesses" will take the form of broad accusations and innuendoes directed at the incumbents. Outsiders would like the opportunity to include in their proxy solicitation such general statements as "the incumbents are wasting corporate assets"; "the incumbents are paying themselves fraudulently high salaries"; or "the officers of the company have been negligent in failing to acquire new opportunities for the corporation." The SEC generally refuses to allow such statements to be mailed to shareholders unless the insurgents can prove the truthfulness of the allegations. Frequently there is no way the insurgents can find that proof, short of discovery proceedings in a suit, though they might in all good faith suspect the facts alleged. Therefore, the practice has developed of filing shareholder derivative suits when a proxy fight is decided upon. Then the solicitation materials may legally say, "A shareholder's derivative suit is presently pending in the Federal District Court for the Southern District of New York charging the officers and directors with waste of corporate assets"; or "a suit to force the officers to pay back part of their salaries has been filed by a shareholder in Delaware"; etc.

Not only has the Securities Exchange Act increased the cost of waging a proxy fight because of the additional materials that must be cleared through the SEC, but it has also increased uncertainty because of the panoply of SEC regulations. For instance, the Chicago and North Western Railroad's successful fight against the Union Pacific's first bid for control of the Rock Island Railroad was recently voided on the grounds, among others, that unsolicited advice by a broker to his customer advising acceptance of the C. & NW's offer constituted an illegal solicitation of proxies (Union Pacific Railroad Company v. Chicago and North Western Railway Company, 226 F. Supp. 400 [ND, Ill., 1964]).

19 This percentage may range from less than 51 per cent if the purchaser is only interested in establishing a foundation for a proxy fight; to 51 per cent when only simple control is desired; to $66\frac{2}{3}$ or 75 per cent, when state law requires that percentage for approval of a merger or reorganization; to 80 per cent, the figure required for consolidation of income statements under the Internal Revenue Code as well as for tax-free reorganizations; to 90 per cent, the figure required for simplified mergers of subsidiaries into parent companies in Delaware (95 per cent in New York); or 100 per cent if no minority interests are wanted.

20 Adolf A. Berle and Gardiner C. Means, *The Modern Corporation and Private Property* (New York: Macmillan Co., 1933), p. 244; Adolf A. Berle, " 'Control' in Corporate Law," *Columbia Law Review*, LVIII (1958), 1212–25, esp. 1221.

21 The difficult cases have been those in which control carried with it peculiar advantages not normally assumed to be part of the standard compensation of corporate managers. The problem is illustrated by the now classic case of Perlman v. Feldmann, 219 F. 2d 172 (2d Cir., 1955), in which only a controlling block of shares was purchased, but at a price reflecting the value of the right to allocate the company's steel production to the purchaser at a time when quasi-official price controls existed. The court found the control seller liable to the other shareholders for a part of the premium received over the normal market price of the shares. The most convincing factor, not emphasized by the court, was that the company had probably been receiving a full free-market price for its steel, with the difference over the controlled price taken in the form of interest-free loans and guaranteed future orders. Indications were that the new controllers would sell to themselves at the "quasi-legal" price and discontinue these other valuable practices. Thus the premium paid for the control block of shares was given partly in exchange for a right more appropriately thought of as belonging equally to each share than to the control group. That is, if a "gray-market" profit was to be made, it should go to all the shareholders. The court was explicit, however, that the seller could retain that part of the premium received for control not covering the power to allocate steel.

22 Richard W. Jennings, "Trading in Corporate Control," *California Law Review*, XLIV (1956), 1–39; and Noyes Leech, "Transactions in Corporate Control," *University of Pennsylvania Law Review*, CIV (1956), 725–839. For a sharply opposing view-point see Wilbur G. Katz, "The Sale of Corporate Control," *Chicago Bar Record*, XXXVIII (1957), 376–80; also Alfred Hill, "The Sale of Controlling Shares," *Harvard Law Review*, LXX (1957), 986–1039.

23 This holds true only to the extent that 51 per cent is the relevant majority. If a higher percentage is necessary for some purpose, minority votes will have some value so long as the requisite percentage is not already controlled.

24 There is a slight possibility that outsiders might be able to force a merger vote by shareholders under the Securities Exchange Act's "Stockholder's Proposal" Rule, although the SEC seems to take the position that such a proposal may only be advisory, not mandatory, on the board, if passed. See Louis Loss, *Securities Regulation* (Boston: Little, Brown & Co., 1961), p. 908.

25 To the extent that the same individuals are also shareholders, their motivation will reflect a conflict. If their ownership interest is great enough, they may sacrifice the emoluments of management in order to improve their position as shareholders. The decision will simply reflect the greater of the two conflicting interests.

26 This may furnish some proof for the notion that executive compensation is a function of size. If the cost of taking over control is a function of the number of shareholders, as it certainly is in the case of proxy fights, it is likely that managers may be able to claim larger compensation to the extent of the higher cost to outsiders of buying control.

27 The greater the shareholdings of management, the more likely they are to approve a merger offer with little or no side payment.

28 Essex Universal Corp. v. Yates 305 F.2d (2d Cir., 1962).

29 See, e.g., Smith v. The Good Music Station, 129 A.2d 242 (Del. Ch. 1957), and Borak v. J. I. Case Co., 317 Fed. 2d 838, at 844 (7th Cir., 1963), aff'd 377 US 426 (1964). There are no reported cases of differential numbers of shares being offered controlling and non-controlling shareholders in a merger. Such an arrangement may be illegal under state statutes, and it is not likely to receive the high-majority-share vote required for most mergers.

30 The most obvious example is that of a corporation whose total assets in liquidation would be worth more than the aggregate market value of all of its shares. This situation can continue to exist only because no individual shareholder believes there is any way of claiming the premium, since the managers will take no step toward liquidation and there is no indication that the corporation will not continue to be badly run. Perhaps the classic case of this sort was the take-over by Louis Wolfson of the Capital Transit Corporation. For this and other examples see Karr, *op. cit.*, p. 150.

31 Cf. H. B. Malmgren, "Information, Expectations, and the Theory of the Firm," *Quarterly Journal of Economics*, LXXIX (1961), 399–421; and George J. Stigler, "The Economics of Information," *Journal of Political Economy*, LXIX (1961), 213–25.

32 The case for a free market in corporate control as between supplier and customer firms seems quite strong, since the arguments in favor of present anti-merger policy are perhaps weakest there. See Robert Bork, "Vertical Integration and the Sherman Act: The Legal History of an Economic Misconception," *University of Chicago Law Review*, XXII (1954), 157–201.

33 This might be done either through the resurrection of the "business-purpose" doctrine or, in Clayton Act cases, by beefing up the "solely-for-investment" proviso. See n. 5 above.

34 A study of the effect of mergers on stock prices has been completed by the staff of the Subcommittee on Anti-Trust and Monopoly of the Senate Judiciary Committee. That study was unavailable at the time of writing this article.

   Another possible approach to proof in this area is to determine if actual changes in the management personnel ultimately follow the merger. In mergers for market power, there is little reason to believe that this will occur very quickly; whereas, if the position is in the nature of a side payment, as it would be if the merger was motivated more by the control potential, we might anticipate somewhat earlier efforts to "ease out" the old managers of the acquired company.

Manne, H. G. (1965) "Mergers and the market for corporate control". *Journal of Political Economy*, 73(2), April: 110–120. Reproduced with permission.

4 Takeovers: folklore and science

Michael C. Jensen

From 1981 to 1983, the number of large US corporate acquisitions grew at a rate roughly double that of the 1970s and even exceeded the one realized during the famous merger wave of the 1960s. The drama of 2100 annual takeovers valued at more than $1 million – much of it played out in heated, public battles – has generated an enormous amount of criticism, not only from politicians and the media but also from high-level corporate executives.

Commenting in the *Wall Street Journal* on the Bendix and Martin Marietta takeover battle, for example, Lee Iacocca, chairman of Chrysler, argued:

> It's not a merger. It's a three-ring circus. If they're really concerned about America, they'd stop it right now. It's no good for the economy. It wrecks it. If I were in the banking system I'd say no more [money] for conglomerates for one year.

A former director at Bendix added:

> I think ... it's the kind of thing corporate America ought not to do, because the poor stockholder is the one whose interest is being ignored in favor of the egos of directors and executives. And who the hell is running the show – the business of making brakes and aerospace equipment – while all of this is going on?

In a 1984 *New York Times* piece on the "surge of corporate mergers," Felix Rohatyn noted:

> All this frenzy may be good for investment bankers now, but it's not good for the country or investment bankers in the long run. We seem to be living in a 1920s, jazz age atmosphere.

Just as the public outcry over excesses on Wall Street in the early 1930s led to the Glass-Steagall Act regulating banking, so the latest criticisms of mergers have brought enormous political pressure to bear on Congress to restrict takeovers. The July 1983 report of the SEC Advisory Committee on Tender Offers contained 50 recommendations for new regulations. Democratic Representative Peter Rodino has cosponsored a bill that would require advance notice of proposed acquisitions resulting in assets of $5 billion and 25 000 employees and a judgment by the Antitrust Division of the Justice Department or the FTC whether such acquisitions "serve the public interest."

The popular view underlying these proposals is wrong, however, because it ignores the fundamental economic function that takeover activities serve. In the corporate takeover market, management teams compete for the right to control – that is, to manage – corporate resources. Viewed in this way, the market for control is an important part of the managerial labor market, which is very different from, and has higher stakes than, the normal labor market. After all, potential chief executive officers do not simply leave their applications with personnel officers. Their on-the-job performance is subject not only to the normal internal control mechanisms of their organizations but also to the scrutiny of the external market for control.

Imagine that you are the president of a large billion-dollar corporation. Suddenly, another management team threatens your job and prestige by trying to buy your company's stock. The whole world watches your performance. Putting yourself in this situation leads to a better understanding of the reasons behind the rhetoric, maneuverings, and even lobbying in the political and regulatory sectors by managers for protection from unfriendly offers.

The Bendix attempt to take control of Martin Marietta in 1982 gained considerable attention because of Marietta's unusual countertakeover offer for Bendix, called the "Pac-Man defense," whose principle is: "My company will eat yours before yours eats mine." Some describe this kind of contest as disgraceful. I find it fascinating because it makes clear that the crucial issue is not whether the two companies will merge but which managers will be in control.

At the end of the contest, Bendix held 67% of Martin Marietta while Martin Marietta held 50% of Bendix. United Technologies then entered as Martin Marietta's friend and offered to buy Bendix. But it was Allied, coming in late, that finally won the battle with its purchase of all of Bendix's stock, 39% of Martin Marietta's, and a promise not to buy more. When the dust had cleared, shareholders of Bendix and Martin had both won; their respective shares gained roughly 38% in value (after adjusting for marketwide stock price change). Allied's shareholders, on the other hand, lost approximately 8.6%.

Given the success and history of the modern corporation, it is surprising how little the media, the legal and political communities, and even business executives understand the reasons behind the complexities and subtleties of takeover battles. Prior to the last decade, the academic community made little progress in redressing this lack of understanding. But research efforts in business schools across the country have recently begun to overcome it.

In this article I summarize the most important scientific evidence refuting the myths that swirl around the controversy. The research shows that:

- Takeovers of companies by outsiders do not harm shareholders of the target company; in fact, they gain substantial wealth.
- Corporate takeovers do not waste resources; they use assets productively.
- Takeovers do not siphon commercial credit from its uses in funding new plant and equipment.
- Takeovers do not create gains for shareholders through creation of monopoly power.
- Prohibition of plant closings, layoffs, and dismissals following takeovers would reduce market efficiency and lower aggregate living standards.
- Although managers are self-interested, the environment in which they operate gives them relatively little leeway to feather their nests at shareholders' expense. Corporate control-related actions of managers do not generally harm shareholders,

but actions that eliminate actual or potential takeover bids are most suspect as exceptions to this rule.

- Golden parachutes for top-level executives are, in principle, in the interest of shareholders. Although the practice can be abused, the evidence indicates that shareholders gain when golden parachutes are adopted.
- In general, the activities of takeover specialists benefit shareholders.

Before exploring the evidence, I consider why shareholders are the most important constituency of the modern corporation and why their interests must be held paramount when discussing the current wave of acquisitions and mergers.

THE NATURE OF THE CORPORATION

Stockholders are commonly portrayed as one group in a set of equal constituencies, or "stakeholders," of the company. In fact, stockholders are not equal with these other groups because they are the ultimate holders of the rights to organization control and therefore must be the focal point for any discussion concerning it.

The public corporation is the nexus for a complex set of voluntary contracts among customers, workers, managers, and the suppliers of materials, capital, and risk bearing. The rights of the interacting parties are determined by law, the corporation's charter, and the implicit and explicit contracts with each individual.

Corporations, like all organizations, vest control rights in the constituency bearing the residual risk. (Residual risk is the risk associated with the difference between the random cash inflows and outflows of the organization.) In partnerships and privately held companies, for example, these residual claims and the organizational control rights are restricted to major decision agents (directors and managers); in mutuals and consumer cooperatives, to customers; and in supplier cooperatives, to suppliers.

Corporations are unique organizations because they make no restrictions on who can own their residual claims and this makes it possible for customers, managers, labor, and suppliers to avoid bearing any of the corporate residual risk. Because stockholders guarantee the contracts of all constituents, they bear the corporation's residual risk. The absence of restrictions on who can own corporate residual claims allows specialization in risk bearing by those investors who are most adept at the function. As a result, the corporation realizes great efficiencies in risk bearing that reduce costs substantially and allow it to meet market demand more efficiently than other organizations.

Although the identities of the bearers of residual risk may differ, all business organizations vest organizational control rights in them. For control to rest in any other group would be equivalent to allowing that group to "play poker" with someone else's money and would create inefficiencies that lead to the possibility of failure. Stockholders as the bearers of residual risk hold the right to control of the corporation, although they delegate much of this control to a board of directors who normally hire, fire, and set the compensation of at least the CEO.

Proof of the efficiency of the corporate organizational form shows dramatically in market performance. In principle, any marketer can supply goods and services. In reality, all organizational forms compete for consumers, managers, labor, and supplies of capital and other goods. Those that supply the goods demanded by customers at the lowest price win out. The dominance of the corporate form of organization in large-scale nonfinancial activities indicates that it is winning much of this competition.

ACQUISITION FOLKLORE

Takeovers can be carried out through mergers, tender offers, and proxy fights, or sometimes through elements of all three. A tender offer made directly to the stockholders to buy some or all of their shares for a specified price during a specified time period does not require the approval of the target company's management or board of directors. A merger, however, is negotiated with the company's management and, when approved by its board of directors, is submitted to the shareholders for approval. In a proxy contest the votes of the stockholders are solicited, generally for the election of a new slate of directors.

Takeovers frequently begin with what is called a "friendly" merger offer from the bidder to the target management and board. If management turns down the offer, the bidder can, and often does, take the offer directly to the shareholders in the form of a tender offer. At this point, target company managers usually oppose the offer by issuing press releases condemning it as outside the shareholders' best interest, by initiating court action, by requesting antitrust action against the bidder, by starting a countertakeover move for the bidder, and by other actions designed to make the target company a less desirable acquisition.

Target company management often casts about for a "white knight" – a friendly merger partner who will protect the "maiden" from the advances of the feared raider and, more important, who will pay a higher price. When the company doesn't find a white knight, and an unfriendly bidder takes it over, its leaders will likely look for new jobs. The takeover process penalizes incompetent or self-serving managers whose actions have lowered the market price of their corporation's stock. Although the process operates with a lag, the forces are strong and persistent. Of course – as a result of economies of scale or other efficiencies – some efficient managers lose their jobs after a takeover through no fault of their own.

This kind of romantic language has been used to offer comic relief, but it contributes to the atmosphere of folklore that surrounds a process fundamental to the corporate world. The resulting myths and misunderstandings distort the public's perception and render a meaningful dialogue impossible.

> **Folklore**: Takeovers harm the shareholders of target companies.
>
> **Fact**: The pejorative term raider used to label the bidding company in an unfriendly takeover suggests that the bidder will buy control of a company, pillage it, and leave the stockholders with only a crumbling shell.

More than a dozen studies have painstakingly gathered evidence on the stock price effect of successful takeovers (see Exhibit 1 for a summary of the results). According to these studies, companies involved in takeovers experience abnormal increases in their stock prices for approximately one month surrounding the initial announcement of the takeover. (Abnormal stock price changes are stock price changes customarily adjusted by regression analysis to eliminate the effects of marketwide forces on all corporations.) The exhibit shows that target company shareholders gain 30% from tender offers and 20% from mergers.

Because tender offers are often extended for less than 100% of the outstanding shares and because not all takeover announcements result in acquisitions, stock

Exhibit 1 Abnormal stock price increases from successful takeovers*

	Target companies	Bidding companies
Tender offers	30%	4%
Mergers	20%	0%
Proxy contests	8%	NA[†]

Notes:
* Adjusted to eliminate the effects of marketwide price changes.
[†] Not applicable.

prices do not increase at the announcement of the offer by the full amount of the premium offered. Consequently, average target stockholder returns in takeovers are actually higher than the estimates in Exhibit 1 because the abnormal stock price changes it summarizes generally exclude the purchase premiums shareholders receive when they surrender their shares.

The shareholders of bidding companies, on the other hand, earn only about 4% from tender offers and nothing from mergers. If the much feared raiding has taken place, it seems to be of a peculiar, Robin Hood variety.

When an insurgent group, led by a dissatisfied manager or a large stockholder, attempts to gain controlling seats on the board of directors of a company (thereby taking over the company through an internal proxy fight), shareholders also gain. As Exhibit 1 shows, the stock prices of these companies gain 8% on average.

Because target companies are usually a lot smaller than the bidders, you cannot calculate total returns to both parties from the data in Exhibit 1. An analysis of more than 180 tender-offer acquisitions, however, indicates statistically significant gains to target and acquiring company shareholders equal to an average 8.4% of the total market value of the equity of both companies.

In sum, contrary to the argument that merger activity wastes resources without benefiting stockholders, stockholders earn substantial gains in successful takeovers. In the Texaco takeover of Getty, for example, Getty Oil shareholders realized abnormal stock price gains of $4.7 billion, or 78.6% of the total equity value, and Texaco shareholders, abnormal returns of $1.3 billion or 14.5%. Gains for both totaled $6 billion, 40% of the sum of their equity values. Gulf stockholders earned abnormal returns of $6.2 billion (79.9%) from the Socal takeover, and Socal stockholders earned $2.8 billion (22.6%). The total gains of $9 billion in this merger represent a 44.6% increase in the total equity values of both companies.

In light of these shareholder benefits, the cries to eliminate or restrain unfriendly takeovers seem peculiar (and in some cases self-serving). In a January 5, 1983 *Wall Street Journal* article, Peter Drucker called for such controls: "The question is no longer whether unfriendly takeovers will be curbed but only when and how." He went on to say:

> The recent shoot-out between Bendix and Martin Marietta has deeply disturbed even the staunchest laissez-faire advocates in the business community. And fear of the raider and his unfriendly takeover bid is increasingly distorting business judgment and decisions. In company after company the first question is no longer: Is this decision best for the business? But, will it encourage or discourage the raider?

Such arguments may comfort concerned managers and board members who want protection from the discipline of competition in the market for managers. But they are based on false premises. The best way to discourage the competing manager (that's what raider means) is to run a company to maximize its value. "Will this decision help us obtain maximum market value?" is the only logically sensible interpretation of "What is best for the business?".

Folklore: Takeover expenditures are wasted.

Fact: Purchase prices in corporate takeovers represent the transfer of wealth from the stockholders of bidding companies to those of target organizations, not the consumption of wealth. In a takeover, the resources represented in the cash received by the target shareholders can still be used to build new plant and equipment or for R&D.

The only resources consumed are those used to arrange the transaction, such as the time and fees of managers, lawyers, economists, and financial consultants. These expenses are often large in dollar terms; the financial fees of the US Steel/Marathon Oil merger were more than $27 million, and those received by four investment banking firms in the Getty takeover hit a record by exceeding $47 million. But they are a tiny fraction of the dollar value of the acquisition; total financial and legal fees usually amount to only about 0.7%. More significantly, they help shareholders achieve their much larger gains of 4% to 30%.

In fact, the stock price change is the best measure of the takeover's future impact on the organization. The vast scientific evidence on the theory of efficient markets indicates that, in the absence of inside information, a security's market price represents the best available estimate of its true value. The evidence shows that market prices incorporate all current public information about future cash flows and the value of individual assets in an unbiased way. Stock prices change, of course, in response to new information about individual assets. Because market prices are efficient, however, the new information is equally likely to cause them to decrease or increase, after allowing for normal returns. Positive stock price changes, then, indicate a rise in the total profitability of the merged companies. Furthermore, because evidence indicates it does not come from the acquisition of market power, this increased profitability must come from the company's improved productivity.

Folklore: The huge bank credit lines used to carry out large takeovers siphon credit from the financial system and crowd out "legitimate" borrowing for productive investments.

Fact: First, the increases in shareholder wealth I've discussed indicate that takeover activities are productive investments; credit lines are not wasted. Second, companies that make acquisitions with stock or other securities, or with cash on hand or capital acquired from the sale of assets, do not use bank credit.

More important, even when companies accomplish takeovers with bank loans, they do not waste credit because most, if not all, of it is still available for real investment such as new plant and equipment. Let me illustrate the point by using a simple example.

When an acquiring company borrows from a bank for an acquisition, it receives the funds in the form of a credit to its bank account. When target company stockholders deposit receipts from the takeover in their accounts, the bank's total deposits remain unchanged because the acquirer's deposits are reduced by the same amount.

Now, however, the portfolios of the target company shareholders are unbalanced. In response, they can make new investments either directly or by purchasing newly issued shares, and if they do so the credit goes directly into productive real investments. If they take the opposite course of action and reduce their bank debt, the bank will have the same amount of loans and deposits as before the acquisition; total outstanding credit is unchanged and there is no waste.

Alternatively, target company shareholders can purchase securities from other investors, but the sellers then are in the same position as the target company shareholders after the acquisition.

If the recipients of the funds from the takeover don't make new investments or pay down debt, they must increase either their cash holdings or their consumption. If their wealth hasn't changed, they have no reason to change either their cash balances or their consumption, and, therefore, the proceeds will go to make new investments and/or reduce debt. If investor wealth increases, investors will increase their consumption and their cash balances. The value of the consumption and cash balance increases will only be a small fraction of the wealth increase (the capital gains, not the proceeds) from the takeover; the remainder will go for new investments and/or debt reduction. The increase in cash balances and consumption will be the same as that coming from increases in wealth generated by any other cause. Thus, takeovers waste no more credit than any other productive investment.

> **Folklore**: By merging competitors, takeovers create a monopoly that will raise product prices, produce less, and thereby harm consumers.

> **Fact**: The evidence from four studies of the issue indicates that takeover gains come not from the merger's creation of monopoly market power but from its productive economies and synergy.

If the gains did come from the creation of companies with monopolistic powers, industry competitors would benefit, in turn, from the higher prices and would enjoy significant increases in profits and stock prices. Furthermore, the stock prices of rivals would fall if the FTC or the Antitrust Division of the Justice Department cancelled or challenged the merger. The evidence indicates, however, that competitors gain when two other companies in the same industry merge. But these gains are not related to the creation of monopolistic power or industry concentration. Moreover, the stock prices of competitors do not fall on announcement of antitrust prosecution or cancellation of the acquisition. This evidence supports the hypothesis that takeover gains stem from real economies in production and distribution realized through the takeover and that it signals the availability of similar gains for rival companies.

In fact, the evidence raises serious doubts about the wisdom of FTC or Justice Department policies concerning mergers. The cancellation of an acquisition erases virtually all the stock price increases occurring on its announcement – with no apparent offsetting benefits to anyone.

> **Folklore**: Consolidating facilities after a takeover leads to plant closings, layoffs, and employee dismissals – all at great social cost.

Fact: No evidence with which I am familiar indicates that takeovers produce more plant closings, layoffs, and dismissals than would otherwise have occurred.

This charge raises a serious question, however, about the proper criteria for evaluation of the social desirability of takeovers. The standard efficiency yardstick measures increases in the aggregate real standard of living. By these criteria the wealth gains from takeovers (and their associated effects) are good as long as they do not come from the creation of monopolistic market power. Therefore, even if takeovers lead to plant closings, layoffs, and dismissals, their prohibition or limitation would generate real social costs and reduce aggregate human welfare because of the loss of potential operating economies.

Some observers may not agree that the standard efficiency criterion is the best measure of social desirability. But the adoption of any other criterion threatens to paralyze innovation. For example, innovations that increase standards of living in the long run initially produce changes that reduce the welfare of some individuals, at least in the short run. The development of efficient truck and air transport harmed the railroads and their workers; the rise of television hurt the radio industry. New and more efficient production, distribution, or organizational technology often imposes similar short-term costs.

The adoption of new technologies following takeovers enhances the overall real standard of living but reduces the wealth of those individuals with large investments in older technologies. Not surprisingly, such individuals and companies, their unions, communities, and political representatives will lobby to limit or prohibit takeovers that might result in new technologies. When successful, such politics reduce the nation's standard of living and its standing in international competition.

Folklore: Managers act in their own interests and are in reality unanswerable to shareholders.

Fact: Because executive compensation is related to company size, critics charge that a top officer's desire for wealth and an empire drives merger activity while the stockholders pay the bill. But as Exhibit 1 shows, there is no systematic evidence that bidding company managers are harming shareholders to build empires. Instead, the evidence is consistent with the synergy theory of takeovers. This theory argues that the stock price increases for target companies come from the increase in value obtained by consolidating or altering control of the assets of the companies involved, perhaps because of cost savings from economies of scale or from a highly complementary combination of employees and assets in production and distribution.

The evidence shows that target companies get a large share of the gains; indeed, the gains in mergers go to the target companies while virtually none accrue to bidding companies on the average. Bidding wars such as the DuPont-Seagram-Mobil competition for control of Conoco push up the gain for target companies.

The zero returns to bidders in mergers noted in Exhibit 1 are puzzling. For several reasons, however, this particular estimate has more uncertainty built into it and is probably biased downward. My own assessment is that the returns to bidding companies in mergers are closer to the 4% shown for bidders in tender offers. An examination of the total dollar gains to both bidding and target company shareholders shows that both get about the same amount of dollars but not of percentage gains. The disparity results because bidding companies are generally larger than target companies and the same dollar gains translate into different percentage gains. Because the stock prices of larger companies vary more widely relative to gains in an acquisition than do the stock prices of target companies, their returns cannot be estimated as precisely.

Furthermore, bidders often engage in a prolonged acquisition program. The benefits for target companies from a particular merger occur around the time of the takeover announcement and therefore can be more easily estimated than the bidders' benefits, which may be spread out over several acquisitions.

Often the stock price of a company that seeks several acquisitions reflects the projected benefits of future deals at an early date. When a particular acquisition is announced, the bidder's stock price will change only to the extent that there is a difference between the actual and the previously expected profitability of the merger and on average this will be zero in an efficient market. And because mergers involve negotiations that do not occur in tender offers, more information about the intentions of bidders will leak than will information about the identity of the target; the effect on the bidder's price will therefore be spread out over time.

The record of several large takeovers shows mixed evidence on the returns to acquiring shareholders. In the $13.2 billion takeover of Gulf, Socal shareholders earned $2.77 billion (22.6%) after adjustment for the effects of marketwide price changes (from January 23, 1984 to May 3, 1984). Similarly, in the $10.1 billion takeover of Getty Oil, Texaco shareholders earned $1.3 billion (14.5%, from December 13, 1983 to February 7, 1984). In contrast, Allied shareholders lost $100 million (−8.6%) in the acquisition of Bendix; DuPont lost $800 million (−10.0%) in the takeover of Conoco, while Conoco shareholders realized a gain of 71%, or about $3.2 billion.

On the other hand, Occidental Petroleum shareholders did not lose in Occidental's takeover of Cities Service, whose shareholders gained about $350 million (12.5%). Mesa Petroleum initiated the Cities Service war with a bid of $45 per share. Cities Service countered with a bid for Mesa Petroleum. Gulf Oil then announced completion of negotiations to merge with Cities Service for $63 per share; Cities Service stock immediately gained over 43%, or $1.25 billion. In contrast, the Gulf stock price fell over 14%, or slightly over $900 million. The $350 million difference between the gain to Cities Service shareholders and the loss to Gulf shareholders measures the market's estimate of the net increase in value from the merger.

Citing antitrust difficulties with the FTC, Gulf cancelled its acquisition of Cities Service seven weeks later. Cities Service countered with a breach of contract suit against Gulf for $3 billion. All the earlier gains in the price of Cities Service stock were eliminated, but only one-third of the Gulf loss was recovered – perhaps because the market forecast that legal action might hold Gulf liable for part of the premium offered to Cities Service shareholders or that Gulf would make more overpriced takeover attempts. Within four weeks of the Gulf cancellation, Cities Service merged with Occidental for a $350 million premium – an amount identical to the estimated value of the net merger gains from the aborted combination of Cities Service and Gulf.

A good way for a company to become a takeover target is to make a series of acquisitions that reduce value but allow the value to be recovered through divestiture. A bidder that realizes it can make money by selling off the pieces at a profit will likely seize the initiative. Victor Posner's attack on Marley Company in 1981 is an extreme example. Marley, which manufactured water-cooling towers and heat exchangers, took control of Wylain, a manufacturer of air conditioning, heating, and pumping systems, for an 87% premium over Wylain's previous market value. Marley's stock price fell 21%. Posner bought 11.2% of Marley during the first six months of 1980. Unable to find a white knight, Marley sold its assets, dissolved, and distributed the proceeds in June 1981. Posner received $21.9 million for his investment of $12.5 million in Marley.

MANAGER–SHAREHOLDER CONFLICTS

The interests of managers and shareholders conflict on many, but certainly not all, issues. The divergence intensifies if the company becomes the target of an unfriendly takeover. Exhibit 1 indicates that target shareholders benefit when the bidders offer substantial premiums over current market value. During a takeover top managers of target companies can lose both their jobs and the value of their talents, knowledge, and income that are particular to the organization. Threatened with these losses, such officers may try to reduce the probability of a successful unfriendly takeover and benefit themselves at the expense of shareholders.

MANAGEMENT STRUGGLES

The attempt by Carter Hawley Hale to acquire Marshall Field is an interesting example of a management struggle to retain control. Marshall Field, a high-quality department and specialty store chain, enjoyed less growth than other retailers but consistently rejected merger bids. In early 1978, Carter Hawley Hale, another retailer, offered $42 per share for Marshall Field stock, which was selling for less than $20. Resisting, Marshall Field filed a lawsuit that argued the acquisition would violate securities and antitrust laws. It informed shareholders that the asking price was inadequate and made several defensive acquisitions that aggravated potential antitrust problems and made it less attractive to Carter Hawley. Marshall Field's board authorized top officials to take "such action as they deemed necessary" to defeat the offer. After Carter Hawley withdrew the offer, Marshall Field's stock fell back to $20 per share.

In April 1984, another retailer, The Limited, tried to take over Carter Hawley Hale, whose stock then experienced abnormal gains of 49% in the ensuing conflict. Carter Hawley filed suit against The Limited, claiming securities law violations and antitrust problems, and gave up 33% of its voting rights through the sale of $300 million of convertible preferred stock to General Cinema Corporation. Carter Hawley then gave General Cinema a six-month option to buy the Waldenbook chain, one of its most profitable subsidiaries, and repurchased 51% of its own shares. As a result The Limited withdrew its offer in May and Carter Hawley stockholders lost $363 million – the entire 49% abnormal stock price gain.

Both of these cases show what happens to stock prices when acquisition bids fail. Exhibit 2 summarizes the general evidence obtained from ten studies on stock price behavior during unsuccessful takeover attempts. The average abnormal stock price changes surrounding unsuccessful takeover bids are uniformly small and negative, ranging from −1% to −5%. The exception is the 8% positive return to shareholders of companies subjected to unsuccessful proxy contests. It is interesting that a proxy

Exhibit 2 Abnormal stock price changes from unsuccessful bids*

	Target companies	*Bidding companies*
Tender offers	−3%	−1%
Mergers	−3%	−5%
Proxy contests	8%	NA[†]

Notes:
* Adjusted to eliminate the effects of marketwide price changes.
[†] Not applicable.

contest causes an abnormal stock price gain even when the challengers fail, perhaps because the contest threat motivates incumbent managers to change their strategies.

The uncertainty of the estimates, however, means that only the −5% return for unsuccessful bidders is statistically significantly different from zero. The other negative returns can arise by chance if the true returns from such unsuccessful offers are actually zero. In conclusion, the Marshall Field experience that target company shareholders essentially lose all the offered premiums when an acquisition bid fails, fits the general evidence.

Exhibit 2, however, simplifies the story. Sometimes stockholders benefit greatly from opposition to takeover bids.

Uncoordinated, independent decisions by individual shareholders regarding the acceptance or rejection of a tender offer can cause most of the takeover gains to go to bidding company stockholders. If target managers act as the agents for all target shareholders in negotiating with the bidder for a higher price, however, this "free rider" problem can be alleviated.

Empirical evidence also indicates that some managerial opposition benefits target shareholders. For example, on the failure of a tender offer, target stock prices do not on average immediately lose the 30% average increase in price they earned when the offer was made. In fact, they generally stay up, apparently in anticipation of future bids. And target companies that receive at least one more bid in the two years following the failure of a tender offer on average realize another 20% increase in price. Those targets that do not receive another bid, however, lose the entire initial price increase. Apparently, a little opposition in a merger battle is good, but too much can be disastrous if it prohibits takeover of the company.

THE CORPORATE CHARTER

Corporate charters specify governance rules and establish conditions for mergers, such as the percentage of stockholders who must approve a takeover. Since constraints on permissible charter rules differ from state to state, changing the state of incorporation will affect the contractual arrangement among shareholders and the probability that a company will be a takeover target. It is alleged that some states desiring to increase their corporate charter revenues make their statutes appealing to corporate management. Allegedly, in doing so they provide management with great freedom from stockholder control and therefore provide little shareholder protection. Delaware, for example, has few constraints in its rules on corporate charters and hence provides much contractual freedom for shareholders. William L. Cary, former chairman of the Securities and Exchange Commission, has criticized Delaware and argued that the state is leading a "movement towards the least common denominator" and "winning a race for the bottom.".

But a study of 140 companies switching their state of incorporation reveals no evidence of stock price declines at the time of the change, even though most switched to Delaware. In fact, small abnormal price increases are usually associated with the switch. This evidence is inconsistent with the notion that such charter changes lead to managerial exploitation of shareholders.

Without switching their state of incorporation, companies can amend corporate charters to toughen the conditions for the approval by shareholders of mergers. Such antitakeover amendments may require a "super majority" for approval or for the staggered election of board members and can thus lower the probability that the company will be taken over and thereby reduce shareholder wealth. On the other hand, the amendments can also benefit shareholders by increasing the plurality required for takeover approval and thus enable management to better represent their common interests in the merger negotiations.

Two studies of adoption of antitakeover amendments in samples of 100 and 388 companies reveal no negative impact on shareholder wealth. One exception may arise if the super-majority provisions grant effective power to block mergers to a managerstockholder. The market value of R. P. Scherer, for example, fell 33.8% when shareholders adopted an 80% super-majority merger approval provision. Because the wife of Scherer's CEO owned 21.1% of the stock, she then had the power to block a proposed takeover by FMC. In fact, FMC withdrew its offer after Scherer stockholders approved the 80% majority provision and the price of Scherer stock plummeted.

REPURCHASE STANDSTILL AGREEMENTS

Currently available evidence suggests that management's opposition to takeovers reduces shareholder wealth only when it eliminates potential takeover bids. In a privately negotiated or targeted repurchase, for example, a company buys a block of its common stock from a holder at a premium over market price – often to induce the holder, usually an active or a potential bidder, to cease takeover activity. Such repurchases, pejoratively labeled "greenmail" in the press, generate statistically significant abnormal stock price declines for shareholders of the repurchasing company and significantly positive returns for the sellers. These stock price declines contrast sharply with the statistically significant abnormal stock price increases associated with nontargeted stock repurchases found in six studies.

The managers of target companies also may obtain standstill agreements, in which one company agrees to limit its holdings in another. Announcements of such agreements are associated with statistically significant abnormal stock price declines for target companies. Because these agreements almost always lead to the termination of an acquisition attempt, the negative returns seem to represent the merger gains lost by shareholders.

Again, however, the issue is not clearcut because closer examination of the evidence indicates that these takeover forays by competing managers benefit target shareholders. Within ten days of an acquisition of 5% or more of a company's shares, the SEC requires the filing of information giving the identity of the purchaser, purpose of acquisition, and size of the holding. The significantly positive increase in stock price that occurs with the initial purchase announcement indicates that potential dissident activity is expected to benefit shareholders even given the chance that the venture will end in a targeted repurchase. Moreover, this is confirmed by the fact that on average during the period from the SEC filing through the targeted repurchase of the shares, target company shareholders earn statistically significant positive abnormal returns.

Thus, when you look at the whole process, repurchase agreements are clearly not "raiding" or "looting" but are profitable for the target shareholders – although not as profitable as a takeover. The stock price decline at repurchase seems due to the repurchase premium that is effectively paid by the nonselling shareholders of the target firm and to the unraveling of takeover expectations with consequent loss of the anticipated takeover premium.

Because, on average, target shareholders lose the anticipated takeover premiums shown in Exhibit 1 when a merger or takeover fails for any reason, we cannot easily tell whether they were hurt by a repurchase. If the takeover would have failed anyway and if the target company's stock price would have fallen even more without the repurchase, then the repurchase benefited target company shareholders. Such additional price declines might be caused, for example, by the costs of dealing with a disgruntled minority shareholder.

Although the issue requires further study, current evidence implies that prohibition of targeted large-block repurchases advocated by some may hurt target shareholders. Moreover, since shareholders can amend corporate charters to restrict targeted repurchases, there is little justification for regulatory interference by the state in the private contractual arrangements among shareholders. Such repurchase restrictions might well restrict the vast majority of stock repurchases that clearly benefit shareholders. In addition, by reducing the profitability of failed takeovers, such restrictions would strengthen the position of entrenched managers by reducing the frequency of takeover bids. Doing so would deprive shareholders of some of the stock price premiums associated with successful mergers.

GOING PRIVATE

The phrase going private means that publicly owned stock is replaced with full equity ownership by an incumbent management group and that the stock is delisted. On occasion, when going private is a leveraged buy out, management shares the equity with private investors. Some believe that incumbent managers as buyers are exploiting outside shareholders as sellers in these minority freeze outs.

Advocating restrictions on going-private transactions, in 1974 Securities and Exchange Commissioner A. A. Sommer, Jr. argued:

> What is happening is, in my estimation, serious, unfair, and sometimes disgraceful, a perversion of the whole process of public financing, and a course that inevitably is going to make the individual shareholder even more hostile to American corporate mores and the securities markets than he already is.

Study of stockholder returns in 72 going-private transactions, however, reveals that the average transaction offers a premium 56% over market price and that abnormal stock price increases on announcement of the offer average 30%. The gains apparently arise from savings of registration and other public ownership expenses, improved incentives for decision makers under private ownership, and increased interest and depreciation tax shields. Outside shareholders are not harmed in going-private transactions.

GOLDEN PARACHUTES

Some companies provide compensation in employment contracts for top-level managers in the event that a takeover occurs – that is, golden parachutes. Allied agreed, for example, to make up the difference for five years between Bendix CEO William Agee's salary in subsequent employment and his former annual $825,000 salary in the event of a change in control at Bendix. Much confusion exists about the propriety and desirability of golden parachutes, even among senior executives.

But the detractors fail to understand that the parachutes protect stockholders as well as managers. Think about the problem in the following way: top-level managers and the board of directors act as stockholders' agents in deals involving hundreds of millions of dollars. If the alternative providing the highest value to stockholders is sale to another company and the retirement of the current management team, stockholders do not want the managers to block a bid in fear of losing their own jobs. Stockholders may be asking managers to sacrifice position and wealth to negotiate the best deal for them.

Golden parachutes are clearly desirable when they protect stockholders' interests. Like anything else, however, they may be abused. For example, a stockholder doesn't want to pay managers so much for selling the company that they hurry to sell at a low price to the first bidder. But that is a problem with the details of the parachute's contractual provisions and not with the existence of the parachute itself. An analysis of 90 companies shows that adoption of golden parachutes on average has no negative effect on stock prices and provides some evidence of positive effects.

The thing that puzzles me about most golden parachute contracts is that they pay off only when the manager leaves his job and thus create an unnecessary conflict of interest between shareholders and executives. Current shareholders and the acquiring company will want to retain the services of a manager who has valuable knowledge and skills. But the officer can collect the golden parachute premium only by leaving; the contract rewards him or her for taking an action that may well hurt the business. As the bidder assimilates the knowledge that turnover among valuable top-level managers after the acquisition is highly likely, it will reduce its takeover bid. A company can eliminate this problem by making the award conditional on transfer of control and not on the manager's exit from the company.

SELLING THE "CROWN JEWELS"

Another often criticized defensive tactic is the sale of a major division by a company faced with a takeover threat. Some observers claim that such sales prove that managers will do anything to preserve their tenure, even to the extent of crippling or eliminating major parts of the business that appear attractive to outside bidders. Such actions have been labeled a "scorched earth policy.".

Studies of the effects of corporate spinoffs, however, indicate they generate significantly positive abnormal returns. Moreover, when target managers find a white knight to pay more for the entire company than the initial, hostile bidder, share-holders clearly benefit.

In the same way, when an acquirer is interested mainly in a division rather than the whole company, shareholders benefit when target management auctions off the unit at a higher price. Brunswick's sale of its Sherwood Medical Industries division to American Home Products shows how the sale of a crown jewel can benefit shareholders. Whittaker Corporation made a hostile takeover bid for Brunswick in early 1982. In defense, Brunswick sold a key division, Sherwood Medical, to American Home Products through a negotiated tender offer for 64% of Brunswick's shares. American Home Products then exchanged these shares with Brunswick for Sherwood's stock. Because its main interest lay in acquiring Sherwood, Whittaker withdrew its offer.

The value of the Whittaker offer to Brunswick shareholders ranged from $605 million to $618 million, depending on the value assigned to the convertible debentures that were part of the offer. The total value to Brunswick shareholders of the management strategy, selling off the Sherwood division, was $620 million. Moreover, because of the structure of the transaction, the cash proceeds went directly to the Brunswick shareholders through the negotiated tender offer. The $620 million value represents a gain of $205 million (49%) on the total equity value of Brunswick prior to the initial Whittaker offer. The Brunswick shareholders were $2 million to $15 million better off with the management strategy, hardly evidence of a scorched-earth policy.

TAKEOVER ARTISTS

Recently, criticism has been directed at corporate takeover specialists who are said to take advantage of a company's vulnerability in the market and thus ultimately harm shareholders. While acting in their own interests, however, these specialists also act as agents for shareholders of companies with entrenched managers. Returning to the Marshall Field story, for example, Carl Icahn launched a systematic campaign to acquire the chain after it had avoided takeover. When it looked as if he would achieve the goal, Marshall Field initiated a corporate auction and merged with BATUS (British American Tobacco Company, US) for $30 per share in 1982. After adjustment for inflation, that price was slightly less than the $20 price of Field's stock in 1977, when it defeated Carter Hawley's $42 offer.

Takeover specialists like Icahn risk their own fortunes to dislodge current managers and reap part of the value increases available from redeploying the assets or improving the management. Evidence from a study of 100 such instances indicates that when such specialists announce the purchase of 5% or more of a company's shares, the stockholders of that company on average earn significantly positive abnormal returns of about 6%.

THE EFFECTIVENESS OF THE MARKET

The corporation has contributed much to the enhancement of society's living standards. Yet the details of how and why this complex institution functions and survives are poorly understood, due in part to the complexity of the issues involved and in part to the political controversy that historically surrounds it. Much of this controversy reflects the actions of individuals and groups that wish to use the corporation's assets for their own purposes, without purchasing them.

One source of the controversy comes from the separation between managers and shareholders – a separation necessary to realize the large efficiencies in risk bearing that are the corporation's comparative advantage. The process by which internal control mechanisms work so that professional managers act in the shareholders' interest is subtle and difficult to observe. When internal control mechanisms are working well, the board of directors will replace top-level managers whose talents are no longer the best ones available for the job.

When these mechanisms break down, however, stockholders receive some protection from the takeover market, where alternative management teams compete for the rights to manage the corporation's assets. This competition can take the form of mergers, tender offers, or proxy fights. Other organizational forms such as non-profits, partnerships, or mutual insurance companies and savings banks do not benefit from the same kind of external market.

The takeover market also provides a unique, powerful, and impersonal mechanism to accomplish the major restructuring and redeployment of assets continually required by changes in technology and consumer preferences. Recent changes occurring in the oil industry provide a good example.

Scientific evidence indicates that activities in the market for corporate control almost uniformly increase efficiency and shareholders' wealth. Yet there is an almost continuous flow of unfavorable publicity and calls for regulation and restriction of unfriendly takeovers. Many of these appeals arise from managers who want protection from competition for their jobs and others who desire more controls on corporations. The result, in the long run, may be a further weakening of the corporation as an organizational form and a reduction in human welfare.

REFERENCES

Agency Problems and Residual Claims. *Journal of Law and Economics*. 1983/Jun. p. 327.

Asquith, Paul. Merger Bids, Uncertainty, and Stockholder Returns. *Journal of Financial Economics*. 1983/Apr. p. 207.

Asquith, Paul Bruner, Robert F. Mullins, David W., Jr. The Gains to Bidding Firms from Merger. *Journal of Financial Economics*. 1983/Apr. p. 121.

Bradley, Michael Desai, Anand Kim, E. Han. The Rationale Behind Interfirm Tender Offers: Information or Synergy? *Journal of Financial Economics*. 1983/Apr. p. 183.

Bradley, Michael Wakeman, L. MacDonald. The Wealth Effects of Targeted Share Repurchases. *Journal of Financial Economics*. 1983/Apr. p. 301.

Bradley, Michael. Interfirm Tender Offers and the Market for Corporate Control. *Journal of Business*. 1980/Oct. p. 345.

Brown, Stephen J. Warner, Jerold B. Measuring Security Price Performance. *Journal of Financial Economics*. 1980/Sep. p. 205.

Brown, Stephen J. Warner, Jerold B. Using Daily Stock Returns in Event Studies. *Journal of Financial Economics*. forthcoming.

Cary, William L. Federalism and Corporate Law: Reflections upon Delaware. *Yale Law Journal*. 1974/Mar. p. 663.

Coughlan, Anne Schmidt, Ronald. Executive Compensation, Management Turnover and Firm Performance: An Empirical Investigation. *Journal of Accounting and Economics*. forthcoming.

Dann, Larry. The Effect of Common Stock Repurchase on Stockholder Returns (unpublished dissertation). Los Angeles, CA: Univ. of California. 1980.

Dann, Larry. Common Stock Repurchases: An Analysis of Returns to Bondholders and Stockholders. *Journal of Financial Economics* 1981/Jun. p. 113.

Dann, Larry Y., DeAngelo, Harry. Standstill Agreements, Privately Negotiated Stock Repurchases, and the Market for Corporate Control. *Journal of Financial Economics*. 1983/Apr. p. 275.

DeAngelo, Harry Rice, Edward M. Antitakeover Charter Amendments and Stockholder Wealth. *Journal of Financial Economics*. 1983/Apr. p. 329.

DeAngelo, Harry DeAngelo, Linda Rice, Edward M. Going Private: The Effects of a Change in Corporate Ownership Structure. *Midland Corporate Finance Journal*. 1984/Jun.

DeAngelo, Harry DeAngelo, Linda Rice, Edward M. Going Private: Minority Freezeouts and Stockholder Wealth. *Journal of Law and Economics*. 1984/Oct.

Determinants of the Wealth Effects of Corporate Acquisitions Via Tender Offers: Theory and Evidence (working paper). Ann Arbor, MI: Univ. of Michigan. 1983/Dec.

Dodd, Peter. Merger Proposals, Management Discretion and Stockholder Wealth. *Journal of Financial Economics*. 1980/Jun. p. 1.

Dodd, Peter Leftwich, Richard. The Market for Corporate Charters: "Unhealthy Competition" Versus Federal Regulation. *Journal of Business*. 1980/Jul. p. 259.

Dodd, Peter Ruback, Richard S. Tender Offers and Stockholder Returns: An Empirical Analysis. *Journal of Financial Economics*. 1977/Dec. p. 351.

Dodd, Peter Warner, Jerold B. On Corporate Governance: A Study of Proxy Contests. *Journal of Financial Economics*. 1983/Apr. p. 401.

Easterbrook, Frank H. Jarrell, Gregg A. Do Targets Gain from Defeating Tender Offers? (unpublished manuscript). Chicago, IL: Univ. of Chicago. 1983.

Eckbo, B. Espen. Horizontal Mergers, Collusion, and Stockholder Wealth. *Journal of Financial Economics*. 1983/Apr. p. 241.

Eckbo, B. Espen. Horizontal Mergers, Industry Structure, and the Market Concentration Doctrine, Working Paper No. MERC 84-08. Rochester, NY: Univ. of Rochester. 1984/Mar.

Eckbo, B. Espen Wier, Peggy. Antimerger Policy and Stockholder Returns: A Reexamination of the Market Power Hypothesis, Working Paper No. MERC 84-09. Rochester, NY: Univ. of Rochester. 1984/Mar.

Elton, Edwin J. Gruber, Martin J. Modern Portfolio Theory and Investment Analysis. NY: Wiley. 1984. Chapter 15, p. 375; bibliography.

Fama, Eugene F. Fisher, Lawrence Jensen, Michael C. Roll, Richard. The Adjustment of Stock Prices to New Information. *International Economic Review*. 1969/Feb. p. 1.

Fama, Eugene F. Jensen, Michael C. Separation of Ownership and Control. *Journal of Law and Economics*, 1983/Jun. p. 301.

Grossman, S. Hart, O. Takeover Bids, the Free-Rider Problem, and the Theory of the Corporation. *Bell Journal of Economics*. 1980/Mar. p. 42.

Herzel, Leo Schmidt, John R. SEC Is Probing "Double Pac-Man" Takeover Defense. *Legal Times*. 1983/Apr/18. p.27.

Herzel, Leo Schmidt, John R. Shareholders Can Benefit from Sale of "Crown Jewels". *Legal Times*. 1983/Oct/24. p. 33.

Hite, Gailen Owers, James. Security Price Reactions Around Corporate Spin-off Announcements. *Journal of Financial Economics*. 1983/Dec. p. 409.

Hite, Gailen Owers, James E. The Restructuring of Corporate America: An Overview. *Midland Corporate Finance Journal*. 1984/Jun.

Holderness, Clifford G. Sheehan, Dennis. Evidence on Six Controversial Investors (Working Paper No. MERC 84-06). Rochester, NY: Univ. of Rochester. 1984/Aug.

Jarrell, Gregg A. The Wealth Effects of Litigation by Targets: Do Interests Diverge in a Merge? (unpublished manuscript). Chicago, IL: Univ. of Chicago. 1983.

Jensen, Michael C. Ruback, Richard S. The Market for Corporate Control: The Scientific Evidence. *Journal of Financial Economics*. 1983/Apr. p. 5.

Kummer, D. Hoffmeister, R. Valuation Consequences of Cash Tender Offers. *Journal of Finance*. 1978/May. p. 505.

Lambert, Richard A. Larcker, David F. Golden Parachutes, Executive Decision-Making and Shareholder Wealth. *Journal of Accounting and Economics*.

Linn, Scott C. McConnell, John J. An Empirical Investigation of the Impact of "Antitakeover" Amendments on Common Stock Prices. *Journal of Financial Economics*. 1983/Apr. p. 361.

Linn, Scott C. Rozeff, Michael. The Corporate Sell-off. *Midland Corporate Finance Journal*. 1984/Jun.

Linn, Scott C. Rozeff, Michael. The Effects of Voluntary Sell-offs on Stock Prices (unpublished manuscript). Univ. of Iowa. 1984.

Linn, Scott C. Rozeff, Michael. The Effects of Voluntary Spin-offs on Stock Prices: The Anergy Hypothesis. *Advances in Financial Planning and Forecasting*. 1984/Sep.

Malatesta, Paul H. The Wealth Effect of Merger Activity and the Objective Functions of Merging Firms. *Journal of Financial Economics*. 1983/Apr. p. 155.

Masulis, Ronald. Stock Repurchase by Tender Offer: An Analysis of the Causes of Common Stock Price Changes. *Journal of Finance*. 1980/May. p. 305.

McAnally, Claude W., III. The Bendix-Martin Marietta Takeover and Stockholder Returns (unpublished masters thesis). Cambridge, MA: MIT. 1983.

Miles, J. Rosenfeld, J. The Effect of Voluntary Spin-off Announcements on Shareholder Wealth. *Journal of Finance*. 1983/Dec. p. 1597.

Mullins, David W., Jr. Managerial Discretion and Corporate Financial Management (unpublished manuscript). Boston, MA: Harvard Business School. 1984. Chap. 7.

Rosenfeld, Ahron. Repurchase Offers: Information Adjusted Premiums and Shareholders' Response, Monograph and Thesis No. MERC MT-82-01. Rochester, NY: Univ. of Rochester. 1982.

Ruback, Richard S. The Conoco Takeover and Stockholder Returns. *Sloan Management Review*. 1982/Dec. p. 13.

Ruback, Richard S. Assessing Competition in the Market for Corporate Acquisitions. *Journal of Financial Economics*. 1983/Apr. p. 141.

Ruback, Richard S. The Cities Service Takeover: A Case Study. *Journal of Finance*. 1983/May. p. 319.

Ruback, Richard S. Mikkelson, Wayne H. Corporate Investments in Common Stock (Sloan School of Management Working Paper 1559-84). Cambridge, MA: MIT. 1984.

Schipper, Katherine Smith, Abbie. Effects of Recontracting on Shareholder Wealth: The Case of Voluntary Spin-offs. *Journal of Financial Economics*. 1983/Dec. p. 437.

Schipper, Katherine Thompson, Rex. The Impact of Merger-Related Regulations on the Shareholders of Acquiring Firms. *Journal of Accounting Research*. 1983/Mar. p. 184.

Schipper, Katherine Thompson, Rex. Evidence on the Capitalized Value of Merger Activity for Acquiring Firms. *Journal of Financial Economics*. 1983/Apr. p. 85.

Smith, Abbie Schipper, Katherine. Corporate Spin-offs. *Midland Corporate Finance Journal*. 1984/Jun.

Sommer, A. A., Jr. "Going Private". A Lesson in Corporate Responsibility, Law Advisory Council Lecture, Notre Dame Law School, reprinted in Federal Securities Law Report. Commerce Clearing House, Inc. 1974. p. 84.

Stillman, Robert. Examining Antitrust Policy Towards Horizontal Mergers. *Journal of Financial Economics*. 1983/Apr. p. 225.

Symposia. *Journal of Financial Economics*. 1978 Jun/Sep. p. 95.

Vermaelen, Theo. Common Stock Repurchases and Market Signalling. *Journal of Financial Economics*. 1981/Jun. p. 139.

Wier, Peggy. The Costs of Antimerger Lawsuits: Evidence from the Stock Market. *Journal of Financial Economics*. 1983/Apr. p. 207.

5 Cross-border mergers and acquisitions: global and regional perspectives

H. Donald Hopkins

INTRODUCTION

Two words capture the tenor of the times: Daimler-Chrysler. Others do as well: Exxon-Mobil, British Petroleum-Amoco, Ford-Volvo, Travelers-Citicorp, SBC-Ameritech, SBC-Pacific Telesis, Bell Atlantic-Nynex, Bell Atlantic-GTE, Bank-America-Nationsbank, World Com-MCI, AOL-Netscape. It sometimes seems like the urge to merge exists as some primitive driving force, which constantly marches forward immune to all obstacles, both real and imagined. It sometimes seems that anything that goes around eventually comes together in this constantly merging world.

And a plethora of ink has been spilled and a forest of trees leveled to chronicle these deals. Each one seems to rest on a story and a rationale that can not be told briefly. There seem to be a multitude of reasons and motives for these "reshufflings of the deck." For every case of successful cost reduction or R&D synergy, there are many other cases of outright failure and foolishness. Whereas some companies become so practiced that they establish ongoing "integration teams," others seem to be starting from ground zero.

Whereas stock market aficionados and gurus have developed a love affair with anything with the suffix "dot com," the real love affair that managers have is for joining together even in ill advised and questionable combinations. As important for investors as the Internet run-up and with huge significance for the economy, the 1990s have been a merger mania decade.

Since the start of 1994, marking the commencement of the decade's merger mania, over $7 trillion in deals have been announced on a global basis. Though these deals have been both domestic and international, American companies have shown a huge appetite for acquiring others. The 50 largest American companies have been involved in 4190 deals in the last five years. This comes to an average of 84 deals per company.

Included in this recent maniac period have been cross-border acquisitions such as Daimler-Chrysler. This has included a wealth of other foreign acquisitions of American companies. But unlike the 1980s, the response of Americans has been

Trillion dollars

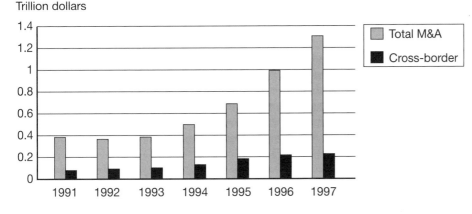

Figure 1 Foreign acquisitions in relation to total.

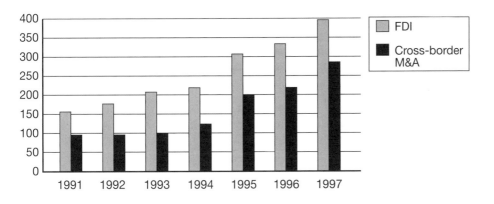

Figure 2 Cross-border M&A in relation to foreign direct investments.

muted with little discernable backlash given the robustness of the American economy.

Though cross-border mergers and acquisitions represent a small percentage of all mergers and acquisitions, they are a large and growing part of all direct foreign investment. For example, according to UN data, cross-border deals involved 236 billion dollars in 1997 compared with overall merger and acquisition activity of $1.6 trillion. But they represented approximately 60 percent of all foreign direct investment (FDI) inflows. This suggests that cross-border mergers and acquisition have become by far the single biggest means of integrating the world's economies. Figure 1 shows the relationship between the value of all M&A (i.e., merger and acquisition) activity and the value of cross-border M&As. Figure 2 shows the value of cross-border M&As in relation to total foreign direct investment.

The UN's "World Investment Report 1998" describes cross-border deals:

> Worldwide cross-border M&As, mostly in banking, insurance, chemicals, pharmaceuticals, and telecommunications, were aimed at the global restructuring or strategic positioning of

firms in these industries and experienced another surge in 1997. Valued at $236 billion, majority-owned M&As represented nearly three-fifths of global FDI inflows in 1997, increasing from almost half in 1996. Many of the 1997 M&A deals have been large, and 58 of them were each worth more than $1 billion. The United States, followed by the United Kingdom, France, and Germany, accounted for the biggest share of the large M&A deals. Together, developed countries accounted for approximately 90 percent of the worldwide majority-owned M&A purchases. These deals are not only a major driver of FDI flows for developed countries but also shed light on the prevailing strategies of TNCs (i.e., transnational corporations): divesting noncore activities and strengthening competitive advantages through acquisitions in core activities. These strategies have been made possible by liberalization and deregulation. One outcome is a greater industrial concentration in the hands of a few firms in each industry, usually TNCs.

In light of the growing role of cross-border M&As in integrating the world's economies, a conference was held at the Fox School of Business and Management of Temple University on April 21, 1999. The conference was titled, "Cross-Border Mergers and Acquisitions: Global and Regional Perspectives."

The purpose of this article is to present the highlights of this conference in the context of a broader examination of the important issues surrounding cross-border mergers and acquisitions. The conference program and brief biographical summaries for the presenters and discussants are presented in Appendix A. A very wide range of issues were discussed during the conference: M&A trends and regional patterns; the motives for domestic and cross-border M&As; the actual benefits that firms achieve; comparison of domestic and cross-border M&As; the special due diligence and negotiation problems and pitfalls of cross-border M&As; comparison of cross-border M&As and other modes of entry; types of cross-border M&A that seem to be the most successful; postacquisition integration and related issues on implementation.

Some of these topics have a section of this article devoted to them. Others topics are discussed at various points throughout the article.

M&A TRENDS AND REGIONAL PATTERNS

According to Christopher M. Foskett of Smith Barney, Salomon Brothers, "a little bit of the lemming theory" is at work in explaining the recent wave of mergers and acquisitions. "People are following each other off the cliff." The merger and acquisition trends depend on the industry. Some transactions make a lot of sense. They are strategic in nature. But in other cases, deal fever seems to catch on.

"In 1998, we saw a total of about 2.2 trillion. Already in the first quarter of 1999, there have been $775 billion worth of deals announced, a total of 976 deals, which would get you on course to reach about $3.1 trillion in deal volume in 1999. Once again, a record number.

"Interestingly enough, the first quarter results are approximately 86 percent higher than the first quarter of 1998 on 35 percent fewer deals. So the phenomenon here is you're moving towards the larger deal taking place and driving the market. We call those mega-mergers – defined as deals in excess of $10 billion.

"In 1998, three of the ten largest deals involved non-US parties. In the first quarter of 1999, seven of the ten largest deals involved non-US parties. So this mega deal phenomenon really has gone global. And these are numbers for the first quarter.

"In the first quarter of 1999, there were 14 mega deals totaling $384 billion in total volume. And four of these 14 mega deals were cross-border. There's the Trans-

America-Aegon transaction in financial services where TransAmerica was acquired by Aegon. Why were these deals done in one fell swoop? Aegon became the number three life insurer in the United States through the acquisition of TransAmerica. So there was a strategic reason for doing that.

"The AirTouch-Vodafone merger was approximately $66 billion. And again, that transaction allowed Vodafone, a UK cellular phone company, to acquire Airtouch and right away become one of the top three cellular providers in the United States. Again, a very strategic transaction.

"Frontier Corporation and Global Crossing. Frontier was a US company, and Global Crossing is a company in Bermuda. And then there was the Marconi Electronics-British Aerospace merger. So those were four large cross-border M&A transactions in the first quarter.

"Interestingly enough, the Euro was expected to lead to a tremendous amount of M&A activity within Europe. And it has, but it actually has been a fair amount of activity within the countries, each country trying to have in-market deals.

"So what we're seeing is within Europe in-country deals to position the surviving entity to be the survivor in the next wave of deals that will be the cross-border deals with-in Europe. So there will be some pressure to unify Europe, and the associated deals will take place after some intra, in-market mergers take place.

"It would seem quite obvious that the high stock market values in the United States and, to a lesser degree, around the world, give major companies, American companies, a currency that they can spend to do deals. Do European companies see those high stock market values here in the United States as a disincentive to invest? Has the pain threshold to make a purchase here gotten so high that deals that might otherwise have gotten done just aren't getting done?"

In response to the questions, Hans Black commented,

Partly because of the huge increase of passive investment and indexing here and, you know, if you throw $100 at the S & P, you're going to be spending over 90 percent of it on that top 100 companies. So that drives the biggest companies to higher and higher PE's. I don't think anybody in Europe or anyone else is going to buy out Microsoft or Intel or these very, very large-cap companies selling at huge multiples. Their high prices exclude them from mergers. On the other hand, smaller companies . . . the number three, number four in industries – TransAmerica is a good example in the insurance area – are very attractive. Interestingly, what's also driving some of the M&A activity domestically in the United States and driving some of the US players to go global is that there's a large disparity between the PE ratios of the top 100 companies in the Fortune 500 and the smallest 100 companies. Roughly the difference is about 11 multiple points difference. The top 100 companies are trading at about an average of 32 times earnings, whereas the smallest trade around 20. There is also a resurgence of Asia as an M&A market in the first quarter of this year. There was a steady decline on a quarterly basis through 1998, and already in the first quarter of this year there's been $33 billion of deals announced with eight deals exceeding a billion dollars, three of which were cross-border. These three include the Japan Tobacco acquisition of RJR's international business, GE Capital buying Japan Leasing, and the Renault-Nissan transaction. Looking ahead in 1999, according to Christopher Foskett, there will be some increased activity in Japan. Japan is going to offer a lot of opportunity for multinational firms in the coming months. There are lots of deals being talked about, particularly in financial services, insurance being one of the major ones. The eight or ten largest insurance companies globally have contingents of people in Japan now kicking the tires, looking at opportunities and there will be a fair amount of deal flow there. Going back ten years, of the 15 largest financial services companies by market cap in the world in 1988, all 15 of them were Japanese. Today, nine of the 15 are based in the United States, five of the 15 are European, and there's only one Japanese company. So Japan has really fallen far. But we believe that it's too big a market, too important an economy to stay down much longer and certainly if it does, there's going to be a lot of activity on the part of foreign buyers there. In Europe a second wave of deals will happen where inter-country transactions will take place. Latin America will continue as an active market, particularly with power and energy privatization continuing to lead the way. There was one last week in April 1999. British Gas and Shell bought Comgas in Brazil for just over a billion dollars. Brazil has scheduled a couple more privatizations. Argentina is always an active market with a number of multinationals, particularly some of the large retailers, like Carrefore. Wal-Mart is actually looking at Argentina as well. And in the United States the divergence in the equity markets is going to make for continued activity here. Interestingly, some Europeans are looking at the US market, particularly at those companies that are undervalued somewhat relative to the large players. The United States offers a fair amount of opportunity to the European buyers because the market here is certainly less regulated than Europe, has faster growth rates, better labor laws, and overall a more attractive economy than Europe in terms of its position.

MERGER AND ACQUISITION MOTIVES

One important aspect of understanding cross-border mergers and acquisitions is to examine the motives driving the deals. The discussion below examines four distinct but related motives: strategic, market, economic, and personal.

Strategic motives

Strategic motives involve acquisitions that improve the strength of a firm's strategy. Examples would include mergers intended to create synergy, capitalize on a firm's core competence, increase market power, provide the firm with complimentary resources/products/strengths, or finally to take advantage of a "parenting advantage." Ford's acquisition of Volvo could be called strategic. Ford has announced the acquisition of a firm whose products fill a gap in its product line both in terms of price, image, and geography. Ford plans to include Volvo as part of its newly formed Premier Automotive Group that will focus on the product segment, which, except for sport utility vehicles, has the greatest potential for profit.

Merging to create synergy is probably the most often cited justification for an acquirer to pay a premium for a target firm. The still cited classic case of this is the acquisition of Miller Beer by Philip Morris. Philip Morris applied their strengths in marketing cigarettes to the brewing industry, an industry that had previously emphasized production. They were very successful in improving Miller's position by using their already developed abilities in advertising, packaging, product development, and positioning of consumer branded products. In the process, they were able to improve Miller's market position from number seven to number two.

However, in a recent book by Mark Sirower, *The Synergy Trap: How Companies Lose the Acquisition Game* (Sirower, 1997), the author argues that synergy rarely justifies the premium paid. Sirower declares, "Many acquisition premiums require performance improvements that are virtually impossible to realize even for the best managers in the best of industry conditions" (p. 14). He further argues that the net present value of an acquisition can be modeled as:

NPV = Synergy − Premium,

And that firms that don't realize this and don't realize that synergy almost never justifies the premium paid are falling victim to the "synergy trap." He cites as a typical example the acquisition of WordPerfect for $1.4 billion by Novell.

> Did they ask what Novell, the parent, could do to make it more competitive against the office suite products of Microsoft or Lotus? If they asked, their answers apparently left something out. Novell lost $550 million of market value on announcement of the acquisition. Since then, Microsoft has continued to gain market share and Novell recently sold WordPerfect, less than two years later, to Corel for less than $200 million – a loss of over $1.2 billion (p. 10). For the past two decades, the premiums paid for acquisitions – measured as the additional price paid for an acquired company over its preacquisition value – have averaged between 40 and 50 percent, with many surpassing 100 percent. Yet, . . . the higher the premium is, the greater is the value destruction from the acquisition strategy (p. 14).

In exploiting a core competence a firm takes an intangible skill, expertise, or knowledge and leverages it by expanding its use to additional industries where it may create a competitive advantage. Thus, a company such as Honda may develop a core competence in engineering internal combustion engines and try to use it as a basis for competitive advantage in several different businesses. All of Honda's businesses involve internal combustion engines as a power source. Their businesses include automobiles, motorcycles, outdoor power equipment, generators, and lawnmowers.

One definition of market power rests on the value of having high market share. Another rests on the notion of increasing the firm's power in its relationship with customers by offering a broad rather than narrow product line. If we have high market power, this puts us in a stronger position to deal with buyers. So if we sell products to a buyer and then we go out and acquire several new product brands that the same customer buys, we become a more important and powerful suppler to that customer. We also may become a place where the customer may be able to do "one stop shopping."

One strategic reason to acquire is to gain complimentary products, resources or strengths. For example, the record company EMI, which became successful by selling Beatles records, planned in the 1970s to diversify based on their development of the CT scanner. The CT scanner allowed doctors to view three-dimensional X-rays of the human body. However, EMI had absolutely no resources to compete in the most important medical market, the United States. They had no sales or service network and no experience in the United States. When they entered the United States, they had temporary success based on being the only firm with the CT scanner. But shortly after their entry, the market was taken away by firms that copied their technology and had other strengths in the US medical equipment market. If EMI had acquired a firm in the US with an established service and sales force, established relationships with customers, and other related medical products, they would not have been as vulnerable to competitors.

Another example of this same idea focuses on the value of having complimentary products. A few years back, a young woman had an idea for a new product. It was gift boxes for CDs. Someone could buy a CD as a gift and then slip it into a CD gift box rather than having to buy wrapping paper and tape and wrapping it themselves. She sold it to record stores, and it sold well. But by the next holiday season, record store vendors who sold other products to the stores started to offer the same product. The stores almost immediately started to buy from these vendors with which they had established relationships. The stores could simplify their ordering process by buying this one new product at the same time that they ordered many other products from the same vendor. Again, sometimes there may be value in acquiring complimentary resources or products to support what a firm already has.

One last example of this same idea that applies specifically to cross-border acquisitions relates to the idea of "national differences." National differences between countries, such as having a national strength in working in groups (i.e., Japan) versus that of "rugged individualism" (i.e., United States), suggests that combining these differences may lead to a stronger company overall. And research shows that the greater the cultural distance of the countries in which merger partners are based the greater the benefit (Morosini et al., 1998).

Imagine a product being sold in two separate countries where both markets share the same critical success factors (CSFs). Imagine that in one of these markets, the parent firm has discovered and successfully utilized the CSFs. However, in the other market the competing firms have yet to discover what these key factors are. The potential increase in value from a firm that has the key information acquiring a firm in another country that does not have the key information should be readily apparent. This is an example of parenting advantage.

Parenting advantage, as discussed by Campbell et al. (1995) works according to a three-step process. First, a buyer attempts to identify the CSFs for a potential target firm. Second, the buyer next identifies the subset of CSFs that appear to have room for improvement. These represent parenting opportunities. Third, the buyer evaluates itself to determine if it has the resources needed to help the target firm improve. If there is a match between the parent's resources and the critical success factors with room for improvement, then the merger makes strategic sense.

Market motives

The most important market motive of a cross-border acquisition is to use it as a method to enter new markets in new countries. Increasingly, firms are acquiring already established firms as the fastest way to enter a new country. Previously cited figures from the UN, for example, show acquisitions to be the most important method of developing foreign direct investment. Often a market may be put into play (i.e., become the target of acquirers) because it has become deregulated. Firms from other countries may see acquisition of the formerly regulated or state-owned operation as the fastest way to gain a strong position in the new market.

In addition to being fast in acquiring a position in a particular market, it is a way to gain entry without adding additional capacity to a market that already may have excess capacity. This may be particularly important in mature markets. It may make much more sense in a mature market with established brands names to acquire a brand name and the company behind it instead of trying to grow a new brand name in a market where customer loyalty is hard to change.

To protect, maintain, defend, or grow a market position, companies may find it necessary to acquire instead of starting from "ground zero." For example, why would a strong and well-endowed competitor like Bridgestone find it useful to acquire a firm like Firestone? If you can buy a brand name, buy distribution, and buy customer relationships in a market that is important, this may be considered a market motive.

In thinking about acquisition as a mode of entry into a new market, it is useful to compare it with other modes of entry. Other modes of entry include exporting, licensing, franchising, joint ventures, or wholly owned subsidiaries. Exporting, licensing, and franchising all have in common that they offer a low degree of control/risk, low need for resource commitment, and fast implementation. Joint ventures, M&As, and wholly owned subsidiaries have in common a higher degree of control/risk and higher need for resource commitment. But M&As offer more control than a joint venture and are faster to implement than a wholly owned subsidiary. Furthermore, research shows that foreign buyers are more likely to use acquisition rather than establish a wholly owned subsidiary when they do not have clear advantages over their rivals and when they plan to manufacture a product that they do not manufacture at home (Hennart and Park, 1993). Thus, firms apparently are acquiring competitive advantage and experience.

Economic motives

Economic motives for acquiring include many important reasons to merge. One is to establish economies of scale. A second closely related reason is to be able to reduce costs due to redundant resources of two firms in the same or closely related industry. Thus, if we are acquiring a firm in the same or a closely related industry and there is substantial overlap between the two businesses, there may be ample opportunities to reduce costs. A third reason is the stock of the firms from a particular country may be undervalued. A final reason might be due to macroeconomic differences between countries.

The merits of using mergers to reduce costs are disputed by managers and by practitioners. For example, managers have been heard to comment that cost reductions are the merger benefit that is most likely to be achieved whereas the achievement of synergy is highly uncertain. On the other hand, Michael Porter argues that what passes for strategy today is simply improving operational effectiveness. Porter (1998) argues, "In many companies, leadership has degenerated into orchestrating operational improvements and making deals" (p. 70).

It is understandable how operational effectiveness may have come to be the driving motive for many mergers, however. Often at the same time a merger is announced, there will be an announcement of a cost reduction target. For example, when Mercedes acquired Chrysler, it was announced that the merger would lead to $1.3 billion of cost savings in the first year mainly through combined purchasing. Given that the 1980s and early 1990s was a period of re-engineering, restructuring, and downsizing, it is perhaps understandable why some mergers would seem to be driven by expected cost savings.

But of course, most mergers are driven by more than one motive. Thus, to argue the merits of operational effectiveness versus those of strategy is perhaps a false argument. For example, when the entertainment company Viacom acquired Paramount movie studios, cost savings were important because of the need to reduce the resulting debt. But more important was the theme set by CEO Sumner Redstone to use Paramount's entertainment content as the core of a strategy focused on the value of content over distribution.

Research shows that one important driver of cross-border mergers and acquisitions may be undervaluation (Gonzalez et al., 1998). This research shows that in cross-border mergers during the period of 1981 to 1990 US firms were more often targets than bidders. And the data suggest that is was related to differences in valuation.

Finally, a driver of cross-border mergers might be differences in the macro-economic conditions in two countries. That is, one country might have a higher growth rate and more opportunity than some other country. Thus, it would seem reasonable to expect the slower growth country to be more often home to acquirers whereas the faster growth country is likely to more often be home to target firms.

Personal motives

A final item worth mentioning is the personal motive of managers. Two specific variants are noted here: the agency problem and management hubris. The agency problem refers to the fact that any time you hire an agent to represent an owner, the two parties will have conflicting interests. In a sense, managers are the agents for stockholders. They are interested in the things that give them more power and more security, such as growth, size, and diversification. The owners, on the other hand, are interested in profitability and increases in the stock price. Thus, managers are more likely to be interested in mergers and acquisitions since they are likely to lead to the things managers care about. But since most mergers fail, stockholders are less likely to benefit.

Another reason managers continue to pursue mergers even when many of them fail is management hubris or ego. The argument here is that managers will think as follows: "I know that most mergers don't succeed. But I am an especially talented manager. And I know that I can make this merger work."

Motives for cross-border mergers and acquisitions

Most of the motives mentioned above do not specifically take into account cross-border mergers and acquisitions. One way to do that would be to consider for a moment the framework developed by Ghoshal (1987). This framework is shown in Table 1. The vertical axis shows the objectives pursued by the global firm, and the horizontal axis shows sources of competitive advantage.

Table 1 indicates that national differences within the firm due to across border acquisitions would give the firm greater ability to move operations to the lowest cost country, improve the firm's ability to cope with the risks from market changes or change in government policy, and improve the ability to learn and adapt because of the different strengths associated with the culture of different countries.

Table 1, column 2 suggests that scale economies created by the increase in market volume due to across border acquisitions would result in greater efficiency in each activity of the value chain, the need to balance scale and flexibility, and benefits from the experience curve. Table 1, column 3 suggests that scope economies created by the addition of new products, businesses, and markets due to across border acquisitions would result in sharing investments and costs, lower risk due to geographic, product, market, and business diversification, and the ability to share learning across units.

The advantages due to national differences probably would be increased with greater differences between culture. To benefit from scale economies would require a horizontal merger (i.e., two firms in the same industry). Scope economies are most likely where there is relatedness between products, markets, or business. For

Table 1 Global strategy: an organizing framework

	Sources of competitive advantage		
Strategic objectives	*National differences*	*Scale economies*	*Scope economies*
Achieving efficiency in current operations	Benefiting from differences in factor costs–wages and cost of capital	Expanding and exploiting potential scale economies in each activity	Sharing of investments and costs across products, markets, and businesses
Managing risks	Managing different kinds of risks arising from market or policy-induced changes in comparative advantages of different countries	Balancing scale with strategic and operational flexibility	Portfolio diversification of risks and creation of options and side-bets
Innovation learning and adaptation	Learning from societal differences in organizational and managerial processes and systems	Benefiting from experience–cost reduction and innovation	Shared learning across organizational components in different products, markets, or businesses

example, Ford's acquisition of Volvo is likely to benefit from all three sources of competitive advantage. For example, Sweden's culture is likely to be lower on the masculinity-femininity scale of culture (i.e., more feminine), and thus workers are better at communicating well and developing teamwork. Scale economies may be improved by higher volume requirements for certain components that can be shared. Scope economies of distribution might be developed by selling each companies' products by using the other companies' dealership network.

In response to the question of why these mergers and acquisitions are occurring at this time, Hans Black, President of Interinvest, a Canadian investment firm, offered the following comments:

Money is not always the driving force that will bring top management together. I think the importance of cultures and recognition for what people value in terms of how they view life is very important. We've seen a slowing growth, really, all over the world with the Asian crisis, we've seen large multinationals under pressure with respect to their ability to grow revenues, their ability to increase profits. In that context, how do firms grow revenues? By acquiring other firms and by pooling the interests of companies in similar fields. And this has given rise to enormous growth in terms of mergers over the last few years. Also, there are political pushes towards it. In North America, we now have NAFTA, so the impetus to have cross-border mergers that really emphasize political unions make a lot of sense. About six years ago, Wal-Mart took a major interest in a Mexican retailer, very successfully. They're now trying to do the same thing in Germany. In Europe, of course, effective January of this year [1999], we have the European Monetary Union. We also have a slightly larger European Union. There are some members of the European Union that did not take part in the Monetary Union. And the result, of course, is what we've heard over the last few days, the possible merger of telephone companies. It's not overly difficult to merge that kind of technology to bring it under a common roof for management. So the European Union will witness a lot of successful mergers. In South America with the devaluation problems in Brazil, the onset of a recession in Chile and certainly in Argentina, the more secure countries are going to have some mergers, and we will see them to a lesser extent, in Asia. As a global manager for quite a number of years on a cross-border basis, we don't just look at car companies. We don't just have an analyst who is going to follow car companies in the United States. We have somebody that's going to understand the car industry on a *global basis*. She's going to be able to talk about Daimler or talk about a Toyota or a General Motors. In many respects, the security industry has done this in automobiles, chemicals, oil companies, among others. This has been going on for about 10 or 15 years. So in many respects, these mergers simply reflect how a lot of people already look at industries. There is the worry that the mergers and acquisitions will become a fad. We saw such a fashionable wave in the late 60s and 70s in the semiconductor area. All of a sudden a lot of companies see the opportunities for growth in electronics, there's great growth in technology. They would like to be a part of the semiconductor industry. Schlumberger, for example, made a very ill-fated jump into the semiconductor industry. There were many others at the time. We now have a very new, hot industry – Internet-based industry in which price-earning multiples are sky high, but investors want to be part of this. If the Internet runs away, we've seen what Disney did with Infoseek last year. But in two, three, four years from now, there will be a reexamination of prices paid. Now, if a firm is going to do a merger and pay for it with overpriced stock, that's great isn't it? The question: how successful will be the merger?

Coming from a very different industry, viz., a public utility in New Jersey in the United States, Patrick Downes, Vice-President of PSE&G, described the reasons for his corporation to go international:

Very honestly, it's the word deregulation. It's a word that is going to change our business. It will change New Jersey at 10:00 o'clock this morning, about two hours ago, when our Board of Public Utility announced where we're going with the next step of deregulation. What does deregulation mean to most of us? It's going to mean a phone call at about 7:15 p.m., somewhere between mashed potatoes and hamburger that says, Hi, I want to help you buy energy and I want to link that energy to your phone, your gas, and your cat food, because that's how far and wide it will go. So as that changes here in the United States, we also start to look abroad, and we look at a word called privatization. The utility industry, communications, electric and gas predominately, are all state entities as we look around a lot of the world. Are there opportunities as those entities are privatized to take core competencies from the energy business here in New Jersey or in the United States and move it out both to grow the business and to learn because in those countries, some steps in regulation process are different and even more advanced than we have here.

Avi Eden, Vice-Chair of Vishay Intertechnology, a Pennsylvania-based high-tech enterprise, offered yet a different motive for the mergers and acquisitions:

We will not buy a company that we cannot improve. In other words, if a company is functioning well and doing a good job and we can't bring anything to it, or if we have to pay a premium to purchase it, we haven't accomplished anything for our shareholders. Our goal is to look at a company that's either in trouble or not doing as well as we think it can do and then take decisive steps very quickly to improve it. And that includes basically a two step approach: first, we look at the SG&A costs, the sales, general and administrative, and make immediate cuts. We expect an acquisition to be accretive within the quarter or within six months or it's not worth doing; the second step is to look for the manufacturing synergies. That involves taking the jobs from usually the highest paying region to the lowest paying region or to a lower paying region. These are steps that are important in cost cutting and providing the savings. But these, by definition, mean job losses and job cuts. You're either going to cut management jobs, the white-collar jobs, or you're going to cut the direct labor jobs, eliminate them, and transfer them. The decisions impact on the geographical region.

Christopher Foskett, Managing Director of Salomon Smith Barney echoed the faddish behavior in the merger and acquisition world:

> I'd say that there is a little bit of the lemming theory here with people following each other off the cliff. It depends on the industry. Some transactions make a lot of sense. They are strategic in nature. They are done for reasons, as Hans Black pointed out, growing market share, reaching new markets. In a number of other cases, the deal fever catches on. Some CEOs tend to do deals because they want to be bigger than their competitor or want to match their competitor for a deal in size and scope and not necessarily with the right long-term strategic desires in mind.

Finally, are the deals being done because the CEOs want to do them or because the investment bankers are coming to them and selling them on the need to have that deal done? Christopher Foskett replied:

> A little bit of both. I think our role, obviously, is to make money for our firms. And so we are, naturally, out pushing transactions on clients, trying to create deal opportunity. But at the end of the day, CEOs are the decision-makers of the organization along with the board of directors, and they will make a decision as to whether they want to pursue a deal.
>
> Certainly we will present the pros and the cons of an opportunity. We will present the strengths and weaknesses of a target in a particular situation and structure the deal. But at the end of the day, the board and the CEO makes the decision. So I would never say that investment bankers completely drive a deal.

FIRM PERFORMANCE

Given the discussion about motives, the next logical question is how well have mergers and acquisitions lived up to the intentions of managers. The answer: not very well. Acquisitions do not appear to result in an increase in value nor do they lead to strong financial performance. More specifically, the research shows that the value of the acquiring firm does not benefit from an acquisition. However, there is some evidence that related acquisitions and cross-border acquisitions do add value.

There seems to be clear evidence that mergers and acquisitions often fail. But this depends on how one defines failure. It failure is used in an extreme sense, such as the sale or liquidation of the business, then the rate of failure is relatively low. If failure is the lack of attainment of management's financial objectives, then the rate of failure is high.

Based on his experience, Joseph Miller, Senior Vice-President and Chief Technology Officer of DuPont, offered the following explanation for failure of some deals:

> In the case of [failure], it was an acquisition that was driven by the corporation and not supported by the business [strategic business unit] . . . and in the case of one that worked, there was total alignment and support from the corporation and from the business. The business has a tremendous immune system that it can put in the way of a deal. And, it's kind of like we will prove it to you that you were wrong. And that's what happens. Believe it or not, it happens in corporations where you think you have control over people and their behavior. You find out that you don't.

The conclusion on success and failure of a deal also depends on time horizon over which evaluation is done. Research which has examined short-term stock reaction to merger announcements, has found that the price of the target's stock rises while the stock of the acquirer stays about the same. Target share prices increase with the expectation that there will be a bid that is successful and involves a premium above the current market price of the stock. Acquirer prices stay the same, in general, as the market reacts conservatively, depending on the specifics of the deal. Though these short-term studies have come to dominate merger and acquisition research there is some question whether this is the best way to gauge the effect of mergers and acquisitions from a strategic perspective. The researchers who have judged mergers and acquisitions on a long-term basis have reported a more mixed outcome.

Short-term studies

Many researchers from the fields of strategic management have used "event study methodology" to isolate and study the reaction of the target and bidder's stock during a window of time ranging from a few days to several months. These studies were reviewed by Sirower (1997) and presented in a table that is reproduced in this article as Table 2. Table 2 shows that acquiring firms generally lost value as a result of their merger activity. Table 3 shows that the value going to the acquirer has declined over time.

Longer-term studies

Jensen and Ruback (1983) examined seven studies with a one-year event window and found an average stock loss of −5.5 percent. Magenhein and Mueller (1988) used a three-year postevent window and found returns ranging from −16 and −42 percent. Agrawal et al. (1992) found a decline of −10 percent by using a five-year postevent window for acquisitions made between 1955 and 1987 and −19 percent for those made between 1980 and 1987.

Table 2 Stock market reaction to acquirers in the 1980s

Study	Sample period	Sample size	Event window[a]	Average acquirer CAR[b] (%)
Sirower (1994)	1979–1990	168	(−1, +1)	−2.3
Byrd and Hickman (1992)	1980–1987	128	(−1, 0)	−1.2
Banerjee and Owens (1992)	1978–1987	57	(−1, 0)	−3.3
Jennings and Mazzeo (1991)	1979–1985	352	(day 0)	−0.8
Servaes (1991)	1981–1987	366	(day 0, closing)	−3.35
Morck et al. (1990)	1980–1987	172	(−1, +1)	−1.78
Bradley et al. (1988)	1981–1984	52	(−5, +5)	−2.9
Asquith et al. (1987)	1973–1983	342	(−1, 0)	−0.85
Varaiya and Ferris (1987)	1974–1983	96	(−1, 0)	−2.15
You et al. (1986)	1975–1984	133	(−1, +1)	−1.5

[a] days before and after announcement.
[b] CAR, cumulative abnormal return during the day(s) surrounding the announcement.
Source: Sirower (1997).

Table 3 Historical evidence of returns to acquirers

Study	Transaction type	1960s (%)	1970s (%)	1980s (%)
Loder and Martin (1990)	Tender offers and mergers	1.7	0.6	−0.07
Jarrell et al. (1988);	Tender offers	4.4	1.2	−1.10
Jarrell and Poulsen (1989)				
Bradley et al. (1988)	Tender offers	4.1	1.3	−2.93
Asquith et al. (1987)	Mergers	4.6	1.7	NA

Source: Mark L. Sirower, *The Synergy Trap*, Free Press, 1997, as sourced from Ronald Gilson and Bernard Black, *The Law and Finance of Corporate Acquisitions*, 2nd Edition.

In contrast, Bradley and Jarrel (1988) used the same sample as Magenheim and Mueller (1988) but different methods and yet did not find negative returns. Loder and Martin (1992) found negative returns after three years but not after five years. Lajoux and Weston (1998) conclude based on a broader review than presented here that, "Most of these [long-term] studies give rates of failure or success for mergers according to various definitions, with mixed results" (p. 35). A recent article from the *New York Times* (May 23, 1999) (Strom and Bradsher, 1999) reviewed Ford's investment in Mazda and concluded that it has taken 20 years for the companies to start to reap benefits from their relationship.

Non stock market-based studies

Other research has used measures like accounting-based measures of performance, change in market share, change in the attractiveness of the firm's portfolio of businesses, and the extent to which the merger meets management objectives and expectations. A number of these studies are mentioned below.

Ravenscraft and Scherer (1989) found significant decline in acquired businesses after being acquired based on a sample of 2732 lines of acquired businesses during 1975 to 1977. Porter found that 33 large companies involved in mergers during the period of 1950 to 1986 had a high failure rate for acquisitions. More specifically, he found that 55 percent of the acquisitions in new industries and 74 percent in unrelated industries were divested. A study by Hopkins (1987) examined unrelated acquisitions, as well as market- and technology-related acquisitions. These firms were compared in terms of the attractiveness of the industries in their portfolios as well as the market share in these industries. He found that though market related was the best performer, it did not perform better than nonacquisitive firms. Another author reviewing the wealth of studies showing divestiture of unrelated acquisitions says, "Taken together, the studies suggest that performance problems, excessive diversification, changes in ownership, and an emphasis on improving internal control and efficiency may be leading to divestitures of unrelated acquisitions" (Bergh, 1997:716).

A cover story in the March 21, 1998 issue of *Business Week* was titled, "Most Mergers Don't Work." After an extensive review, Morosini (1998) concludes that mergers fail approximately 50 percent of the time: "Overall, some researchers have maintained that at best, only about half of all M&As have lived up to their financial expectations, with failure rates typically falling within the 50–60 percent range" (p. 11). Later in the same publication, Morosini argues that the failure rate for joint ventures and strategic alliances is about the same as for mergers and acquisitions.

Performance of related and cross-border acquisitions

A number of studies have looked at the performance of related acquisitions, that is, acquisitions where there is a common link in market, product, or technology to already established businesses of the acquirer. For example, the Porter (1987) study showed a higher divestiture rate for unrelated over related acquisitions.

A number of studies have presented results indicating that relatedness between the acquiring and the acquired firm improves postmerger performance (Kitching, 1967; Elgers and Clark, 1980; Kusewitt, 1985; Singh and Montgomery, 1987; Shelton, 1988; Healy et al., 1997). For example, Singh and Montgomery (1987) examined a sample from the 1970s and found that based on total dollar gains related acquisitions performed better. There are a number of studies suggesting that relatedness is not an advantage (Chatterjee, 1986; Chatterjee and Lubatkin, 1990). Though there is a mix of studies on both sides of this question the weight of the evidence seems to support the value of relatedness. One recent study put it this way, "The general consensus arising from these studies, with a few exceptions, is that all things being equal, some product and market relatedness is better than none" (Ramaswamy, 1997).

Furthermore, a number of studies have gotten a positive performance result when looking at the match between acquirer and target in terms of managerial style or corporate culture (Datta et al., 1992; Chatterjee et al., 1992). Particularly interesting is research on horizontal mergers (i.e., a form of related merger that brings together two firms that are involved in the manufacture and/or sale of the same products and/ or services). A study from the banking industry showed that horizontal mergers with similar strategic characteristics had better performance compared with those involving strategically dissimilar banks (Ramaswamy, 1997). Haspeslagh and Jemison (1991), in their book titled, *Managing Acquisitions: Creating Value through Corporate Renewal*, present five years of research based on three separate projects. They conclude that the most successful acquirers have both strategic and operational fit.

It would be easy to extend the findings noted above. If two firms in related businesses, which had a common low cost strategy, where both believed in tight financial control, and both had cultures that were very disciplined merged, it would be likely to perform better than a merger where the two firms had little in common. According to one author, such a merger would be better because "The cost control emphasis would become accentuated and lead to greater efficiencies . . . Minimization of conflicts arising from disparities in core competencies would contribute to better performance" (Ramaswamy, 1997).

Finally, some studies present evidence suggesting that cross-border acquisitions outperform purely domestic ones. Though research on cross-border or international acquisitions has lagged behind its domestic counterpart (Gonzalez et al., 1998), there are theoretical reasons to believe that such mergers would outperform domestic ones. Earlier in this article, advantages available to global competitors but not purely domestic ones were discussed in terms of the matrix developed by Sumantra Ghosal and shown in Table 1. Furthermore, a study by Morosini et al. (1998) found a positive link between national cultural distance and cross-border acquisition performance. A study by Markides and Ittner (1994) shows that, in contrast to their domestic counterparts, 276 US international acquisitions created value for the acquiring firms.

MERGER AND ACQUISITION-RELATED PROBLEMS

What are the problems that might be responsible for such a high failure rate (i.e., 50–60 percent)? Three particular problems are worth noting. These are the inspection problem (due diligence), the negotiation problem, and the integration problem.

Inspection problem

A merger requires a transaction between a buyer and a seller. For the transaction to occur the bidder must place a higher value on the firm to be sold then the seller. Generally, it is the buyer who has less information about the firm to be sold than has the seller. In some cases, the main reason the buyer is willing to pay more than the value the seller places on the business is because the buyer lacks information. In other cases it may be that the buyer has special knowledge or resources that will increase the value of the target firm.

This asymmetry can create what is called the "lemons problem." This comes about because with buyers' lack of information, they are likely to offer a price that reflects the condition of an average quality business. For example, if you go to a business broker to buy a business there usually will be a "rule of thumb" as to the appropriate price for each type of business. So the price for an average restaurant might be two times annual cashflow.

But the seller is more likely to accept the average price if there is something wrong with the business. Thus with information asymmetry more lemons enter the market than do high-quality businesses. The implication would be that firms for sale are likely to be of lower than average quality. While with a takeover, where the target firm was not in the market, we might expect to be higher in quality.

Though a variety of motives might lead a target firm to be up for sale, the lemons problem points out the difficulty of getting adequate information before acquiring a firm. One reason related acquisitions may perform better and be divested less frequently than unrelated acquisitions is that the related buyer is likely to be more knowledgeable about the business.

An interesting example of the inspection problem is the acquisition by Renault of an equity interest in Nissan. The conference panelists offered the following comments:

Hans Black said:

> We have a merger now between two car companies (i.e., Renault and Nissan) that I can't figure out ... I think you've got some great car companies and you've got some car companies from our point of view that aren't going to be around in ten years. So now a couple of the ones that aren't going to be around in ten years are figuring out, you know, how do we pool our interests together? So I'm not sure that that merger is going to work.

In response to a question: how do acquiring firms make what may not be a transparent accounting system more transparent, Christopher Foskett replied:

> Due diligence is the driver. You really have to do more than adequate due diligence. You have to do incredibly in-depth due diligence. You need to use local firms to help you, firms that have capabilities locally and understand the local regulations, the local accounting. One way of managing the problem is illustrated by Renault. They did not buy 100 percent of the target. They are buying 35 percent. Ultimately maybe there'll be a merger between

the two companies but in the interim, Renault will get a chance to really get in the door and understand and make sure that everything they think is there is there. But, if you can't do the due diligence adequately, then my view has always been to recommend to a client walk away from the deal.

Elaborating on the suggestion that "get in the door and find out whether what's there is really there," Hans Black reminded that:

The problem in Japan has been that a lot of liabilities have been pushed on to affiliates. What's off the books on those affiliates, what transactions are off the balance sheet, and the whole issue of dealing with off balance sheet issues is the big stumbling block. Again, the answer is: due diligence, work hard, and a little bit of prayer helps.

Negotiation problem

Negotiating a cross-border merger is an extremely complex process. It is made even more difficult because of the lack of information and the difference in cultures. One author notes several guidelines (Sebenius, 1998). First, be prepared for a long process. Second, divide players into allies, potential allies, and opponents. Third, each of these groups should be handled differently and sequentially. Fourth, the negotiation does not stop even once the deal is done because you need to ensure the rationale for the deal remains viable and continues to create value.

Joseph Miller, Chief Technology Officer of DuPont, who had direct experience in cross-border merger and acquisition negotiations, commented that:

There's a very practical part to this. These (negotiations) are highly draining experiences. And so the composition of the team, their preparedness, their physical preparedness, and the support extended to that team to conduct a legitimate negotiation is most important. It's tough. It's draining. The importance of understanding human behavior and resourcing that team and supporting that team is a very important part so that the company gets the best with respect to the deal and inadvertently or consciously doesn't give away what might have been kept in the negotiation. So the negotiation is most important and the team that conducts it [is important].

On the issue of synergies and the need for realism around the synergies, Joseph Miller commented:

It's very difficult to evaluate the future potential of marketing and technological synergies. It's much easier to deal with the issue of what can be saved from the standpoint of administrative restructuring. Those costs are clear. Structures that deal with that are clearer. And the ability to consolidate production at plants are clear, and so the savings are clear. But that's not enough from our standpoint. The sustainability of that and how do you leverage technology and how do you leverage marketing and what's the true value of the enterprise are important aspects of the determination, and the importance of being realistic about that are critical. In some cases you get tied to the negotiation. And the negotiators look at it as win-lose. Negotiators must present the issues in a realistic way so that the corporate board can be convinced of the value. So realism, which then leads to the importance of the due diligence process, and getting one's hand on real information become very important.

On cross-border negotiations, Joseph Miller cautions that the acquiring firm must be prepared for lots of surprises. "You might understand what you're doing before you go in or think that you do, but you're going to get a lot of surprises in the process."

In response to the question on the special wrinkles that come up in the due diligence process, Joseph Miller commented:

Well the first thing is the quality of the information. The quality is variable. And one should be persistent with respect to getting the kind of information that you need to do as high a quality assessment as possible around the value of the acquisition. However, it's more difficult with cross-border because you have accounting conventions that might be different from the accounting conventions of an English company or a German company. And there is need to align those accounting conventions so that there's apples and apples comparison. Typically what we do in European acquisitions is to use European legal and accounting team to deal with that for us. The third thing is around regulatory requirements. They're different here than they are in Europe. [It is important to have] a better understanding of the timetable so that remediation efforts, at plants especially, are known. How much remediation must be done from an environmental standpoint, from a safety standpoint, and [in terms of] pending legislation in Europe? The answers will be helpful in determining the amount of money that should be reserved for the efforts and who's liable for those remediation efforts.

Integration problem

Integrating the merging firms is a process fraught with difficulty. The need for this has become more intense as mergers have increasingly moved away from unrelated conglomerate mergers to related and horizontal ones. And of course, cross-border acquisitions are more complex than purely domestic ones given differences of national culture between firms.

One survey found that one-third of all acquisition failures were because of integration problems (Shrivastava, 1986). One study suggests that cultural fit has a major effect on post-merger performance and that companies that allow multi-culturalism and prevent too much control perform better than less permissive firms (Chatterjee et al., 1992). The value of cross-border mergers noted earlier is based on research showing that the greater the cultural distance between merging firms the greater the benefit due to national differences. Furthermore, Porter (1991) has suggested that the origin of competitive advantage is the "local environment." Thus if we were a German firm interested in the computer software industry, we might want to acquire a firm in the best local environment (i.e., Silicon Valley) and try to help its expertise spread to the parent firm.

A recent book on cross-border mergers, acquisitions, joint-ventures, and alliances concludes, "The empirical evidence concerning the performance of cross-border M&As, JVs, and alliances so far presented suggests that, when handled effectively, a company actually can turn national cultural distance or initial deep-rooted cultural resistances into lasting practical advantages. Through executive oriented managerial approaches, a company's leaders and key managers can crystallize the potential upside associated with functioning global co-ordination mechanisms across national borders and local cultures" (Morosini, 1998:167).

The emphasis on execution in the integration process was a theme that was shared by Mark Feldman, Managing Director of PricewaterhouseCoopers. Mark Feldman offered the following comments in the opening address titled: "How to Beat the Odds." The following are excerpts from his address:

Of roughly 23 000 deals last year [1998] we can anticipate, based on past statistics, that approximately 4000 of them may return the cost of capital. Only about 15 percent of them will achieve the objectives that drove the deal. These are gambler's odds we're dealing with and it's important to know how to beat the odds. We did an interesting study and we've done that about five times, and we always come up with the same set of top five objectives in merger and acquisition deals. The top five objectives are access to new markets, growth and market share, access to new products, reduction in operating expense, and enhanced reputation. Those are the top five in the past five surveys that we've done over seven years. And what we've found is interesting. Just over half of the companies that targeted a particular objective actually achieved it. And in particular, if you look at reduction in operating expense, 38 percent of the companies targeted operating expense as a key objective in the deal, and only 15 percent were able to achieve that. Why do deals go wrong? Deals begin to lose value from the announcement. At the time of the announcement, they put the company into a holding pattern. They announce this with a lot of hype and speculation as the best deal that ever happened, and the first thing they do is say to the employees and management, "Keep cool. Don't call your counterparts in the other company. What we want you to do, essentially, is conduct business as usual. Don't change anything but, by the way we aren't going to be doing any new investments for a while. We're going to postpone the investments we planned until we can see what's going on." And what happens is everyone feels like they're running in place. They feel like they're not growing, they're not moving, they're frustrated, they're angry. And as a result of all that, we see the critics popping up. The critics are everywhere. Your internal critics are the worst critics. We call them molehill men. A molehill man is someone who comes in at 8:00 a.m. and finds a molehill on his desk, and has until 5:00 p.m. to turn it into a mountain. A really accomplished molehill man can get that done by noon and have the rest of the day to terrorize the organization. And of course, when this [merger] happens, there's a "competitors' free-for-all." You've just announced your strategy to the world. And all your competitors are executing countermeasures. They're contacting your clients, your customers, they're contacting your best employees to steal them. I've been doing this for 20 years, and I've seen a lot of merger models and no matter what they calculate as a drop in performance, they always underestimate. You can anticipate a loss of market share because people are focused internally instead of externally. People are making errors on accounts. Customers are complaining, customers are not getting their attention. You're going to see a reduction in productivity simply because there are more questions than answers. People do not know how to allocate time and priorities. What you find is they spend a lot of time speculating. And then, of course, there's dumbsizing. You know, we're paying substantial premiums on deals these days. In fact, they're unconscionable premiums. And one of the ways companies feel they can deal with these premiums is through downsizing. Rapid consolidation; pulling heads out of the organization. And I must tell you that what we find typically is that most companies have a net loss rather than a net gain from downsizing. Companies staff up to the capabilities of their systems. And if you take away heads before you change the systems and the procedures those heads are supporting, there will be, in fact, a burden on the remaining employees. There will be a further drop in productivity. When you add that drop in productivity to the severance costs, litigation costs, reputational costs, retraining costs, reengineering costs, you find that there is a net loss rather than a net gain. You don't cut an elephant in half and expect to get two elephants, you get one dead one! There will be, with all of this going on, a downturn in morale. At this time, key people begin to turn over. And who turns over? The best and the brightest people! All these things that I've been going through, loss of market share, reduced productivity, diminished margins, etcetera, this sounds like a gypsy curse. But it is not a gypsy curse. This is Murphy's law in full swing. The question is, do you want to go through this slowly, agonizingly, painstakingly or do you want to get through it quickly? The difference between a prolonged and an accelerated transition is nothing less than shareholder value.

The faster you capture the benefits in the deal, the faster you enjoy the returns. That's the time value of money. But there's another factor here. There's a time value of employee enthusiasm. It runs about three months. If you go three months after the announcement without, in fact, giving employees answers about the things that are going to affect their lives, you can expect them to become apathetic. We did another interesting survey. We looked at companies that executed transitions quickly versus slowly. What we found [was that] fast-transition companies outperform slow-transition companies. We had another interesting question. We asked them: If you had this to do over again, what would you do differently? Eighty-nine percent of the companies said they would execute the transition more quickly.

Mark Feldman continues by explaining what he sees as the keys to acquisition success:

SEVEN SINS THAT PRODUCE UNSUCCESSFUL DEALS

You want to have a successful deal anywhere in the world? This is what you need to do. You need to avoid these (seven) pitfalls: Obsessive list making, creating a planning circus, content-free communication, barnyard behavior, horse-trading, incenting inertia, and preaching platitudes.

The first one, obsessive list making, is interesting. This is one of my favorite sins. You know what happens when they announce a deal? The lords of infrastructure in every company get together and they make these long lists of things to do. Long, all-encompassing, encyclopedic lists of things to do. People don't know where to start. They try to do everything. As a result of this, what you find is basically efforts are diluted. Everything is undercapitalized. The redemption here is to focus on the 20 percent of actions likely to drive 80 percent of the value with the highest probability of success in the shortest time frame. I was with a client in Dallas recently and it was very interesting, and he handed me a book that was roughly three inches thick. And I said "What is this?" He said, "Those are our priorities." And I said, "How many are there?" And he said, "3100." I said, "My friend, you don't have priorities, you just have a list of things to do."

The second sin, creating a planning circus. We find that the really critical difference between those who are successful in deals and those who are not is that those who are successful execute and they execute quickly. Those who are not successful spend their lives planning . . . they try to put together lots and lots of transition teams. Transition teams everywhere to get people involved and get their buy in. They have too many teams. Usually the teams are too big. It becomes a nightmare. If you put together these small, short-term, fast-paced teams, you can, in fact, get all the planning done in about two days. By the time you're finished with those two days, you have all the baseline planning done for the merger going forward and you can begin to add as you go. The fact is, you can get through this and you can get through this quickly if you do it right.

The next item, sin number three, content-free communication. Most announcements of deals basically hype the deal and that's about it. They don't give anybody any answers on the real questions that they have. Now, you don't necessarily have those answers on the first day. But you can at least express the unasked questions on that first day and tell them what you're doing about getting those answers and when those answers will come. If not, what will happen is the longer you wait, the more people will speculate. And when people speculate, do you think they speculate on the positive side or the negative side? It's on the negative side because if it were positive, you'd be telling them. Sometimes it gets to the front page of the *Wall Street Journal*! What you [should] do is, in fact, conduct a sampling of focus groups with your employees throughout the organization. Find out basically what they think in terms of. How do you think it will affect customers? How do you think it's going to affect you? How do you think it's going to affect your co-workers? How do you perceive the other company? This raises a series of issues, and when you get those issues, you can array them on an interesting little matrix. Along the left side of that matrix, you see business issues, human resource issues, organizational issues, things that were derived from the focus groups. Across the top of the matrix, all your stakeholder groups, employees, managers, customers, vendors, distributors, shareholders. Everywhere where an issue and an audience intersect, in 25 words or less, what is the company's position on that issue? You fill in all the cells of that matrix and what do you have? You have a comprehensive communications plan. This is how you introduce stability. This is how you introduce support.

Sin number four is barnyard behavior. I don't know if your aware of this but sociologists since the late 1940s have been studying chicken behavior. You see, chickens have actually very well-defined social orders. We call them pecking orders. Some chickens can peck other chickens but not vice versa. If they do, there are fights. Guess what happens when you introduce a second flock to the first flock? Chaos erupts. You've disrupted the pecking order. There are fights. Feathers fly. Some birds are injured, some die. It's the same thing in mergers and acquisitions, and we see it every time. What most of these companies think they need to do is put together an organization chart, communicate it early, and that will solve their problem. It never solves their problem because an organization chart actually raises more questions than answers. It's entirely a halfway measure, and what these people are doing is ignoring a hundred years' worth of research on organization design. All of the research on organization design, if you go through it, you will find that it focuses on one thing. You can make any organization structure work if there is role clarity in terms of who's accountable for which results, who owns what decisions, and how they interrelate on that.

Sin number five is horse-trading. After the deal is done we find that the top managers are taking care of themselves. They have all the jobs. Now everybody feels guilty. So what they try to do is bend over backwards showing impartiality to everyone. Employees perceive that this is a process that is driven by politics and personality and nothing more. You want to avoid making decisions based on politics and personality. This is a time when the best and the worst comes to the surface. This is not the time to let politics and personality drive the selection and deployment process.

Sin number six, incentive inertia. Paying for anything except incremental value creation is a mistake. The redemption here is putting together what we call self-funding value creation incentives. These are incentive opportunities that are geared entirely to incremental value creation. You incent them over a three-year period on the creation of incremental value from the deal. You tie the incentives to the specific value drivers that will, in fact, create that value and you pay off on that value.

Sin number seven: preaching platitudes. A lot of companies get into this. They hire a consultant and the consultant says to the management team, well, we need a shared set of values. And so they take the management team out to some pastoral setting – lo and behold, they do have a shared set of values. And someone begins to chart these values on a chart pad, and when they're finished, everybody is pleased. Unfortunately, the set of values that they put on the chart pad usually reads like a list of universal platitudes that only Charles Manson could argue with. What you have is something that is thoroughly unexciting to the employees. And why? Because management typically has demonstrated in most companies that it is willing to engage in behavior that's inconsistent with their values. A deadly combination, standing up there and saying that we value quality, but what they do is reward quantity. It is not the values that drive culture, it is behavior that drives culture. Get them to engage in behavior, the values will follow. What this amounts to is a buyer's protection plan. Thus if you avoid the seven deadly sins you will have a successful merger. Now, the only way to do this, though, is to do this within about a hundred days. That is roughly a three-month period, and in that first three months you're going to have to do things simultaneously if you're going to do it all. And basically all these things overlap. But usually in about eight to ten weeks you've got it all done. It is finished.

CONCLUDING REMARKS

The worldwide merger and acquisition activities and the role that US corporations play in the deals, undoubtedly impact on the geographical regions of the country in which the corporations do business. Some of the impacts are positive whereas others are negative. How do regions compete? Who wins and who loses in terms of the regional impact? And how is it measured? These and related questions raise several larger social issues surrounding the deals.

According to Avi Eden, Vice Chair of Vishay Intertechnology,

> It's a buyer's market now for multinational corporations. When we do an acquisition, we're in the controlling seat. The region has to come to us and say we want these jobs to stay or we want this to be here. They have to enter into basically a bidding process. In a number of other countries we deal with the issues on a national level – for example, in Philippines, China, and Israel. But when you come to the United States, and specifically, Philadelphia or the region, it's very difficult to work because that region has to know what it wants. The region must decide if it must pursue jobs at a shipbuilding site, bring the CoreStates home office to the region, or keep the jobs that Vishay would normally transfer from here to the Czech Republic or to China. What is this region willing to do? And this is a tough question because politicians make the decision in the democratic arena. The decision is not going to be made quickly, it's not going to be made efficiently. Unless the region knows where it's heading, it's going to be very problematic. I know that as a manufacturer, it's almost impossible to think of opening a factory in the United States. Between the environmental laws, the labor cost, and all of the other restrictions, it's very hard to compete. And if there isn't a well-thought-out policy that anticipates this problem, the jobs will leave.

Continuing on, Avi Eden brings up a common problem that most multinationals face in doing business cross-border deals:

> But one of our problems is we're competing with countries that are not paying the same kind of labor rates that we're paying. And unless we can take advantage of efficiencies of facilities, we're going to have to transfer our jobs out of the region. And if we're competing with two or three American companies and 18 Asian companies for the region, it probably would make a lot more sense for us to merge the two or three American companies so that we can at least bring a solid front against the Asian challenge. But under federal law this is seen as harming the market and harming the competitive contribution to the market. And what it means is that we have to transfer the jobs offshore to remain competitive and that our competitors, domestic competitors, are transferring jobs. That's a very hard job to explain to our board or to our chairman, that one of the criteria that's not looked at by the FTC is job security in America. Because everywhere else in the world, whether it's France or Germany, when we talk about monopolies and mergers, you can be sure that one of the driving forces is really job preservation in that country. We don't have that in the States.

However, the response of John Parisi, Chief Counsel for European Community Affairs, US Federal Trade Commission, reminds us of the basic strength of the US economy in relation to other nations:

> One of the purposes of our antitrust laws is to help to move assets into more productive, more efficient uses. And one of the factors that has been driving our economy is its ability

to take these workers and put them back into useful employment. We've done a much better job of that in this economy than the Europeans have. And I don't want to shirk the responsibility for this, but I think that we should recognize that our economy is very attractive for investment and that it does result in more job creation.

In response to the continuing migration of jobs out of the country, following the mergers and acquisitions, state governments shifted focus away from relatively large to relatively small job creators. The comments of Sam McCullough, Secretary of Community and Economic Development, Commonwealth of Pennsylvania, illustrate the shift in focus:

> Clearly mergers and acquisitions hurt us. On the other hand, in the last four years, we've had a net gain in jobs in Pennsylvania of some 300 000. Guess where the gain occurred? It was in companies with five employees, ten employees, 20 employees. It was a lot of high-tech companies. We've got 10 000 technology jobs that are unfilled in the state.

In the context of cross-border mergers and acquisitions and the migration of jobs that follow, the multinationals frequently are charged of "shopping for the best environment for doing business," which in essence means looking for deals that would enable the parent to export accidents and pollution. However, businesses challenge the argument by pointing to the export of good business practices and right regulations that occurs in the deals. For example, Patrick Downes of PSE&G said:

> In Argentina, we measured safety by the OSHA standards here in this country. We benchmarked the performance of our employees against the employees in New Jersey. So we do not take safety as looking at a place to do the work less safe or to put more people in harm's risk. I think safety is a core of most businesses and you have to take that wherever you go or, very honestly, you're not very credible in the world. You're looking to sell yourself, market yourself internationally; you cannot say to people we care less about you in your country than we do about the people in our home country.

Echoing this view, Avi Eden said:

> One of the good influences of American business is that we have developed a code of ethics in the company that we apply worldwide. We have a set of standards that apply to environmental standards, information technology, among others. I mean across the board. As you become a unified global company, you have to apply the same sort of standards. But that's not to say that you're not often caught in very difficult dilemmas. When you look at a country like China, they can operate a fabrication plant without the regulations that we have here. For example, California, where we have one of our fabs, has extremely strict standards, and China has extremely lax standards. And the differential in cost, even if you only go halfway between those two, makes China completely more competitive than California. [With] an international business, you're stuck trying to find the balance between regulatory and business considerations.

What are the particular regulatory issues, specifically antitrust issues, that come up in these kinds of cross-border deals? According to John Parisi:

> There's really nothing different about a cross-border deal from a purely domestic deal. We are focused on markets that are affected by the merger. We focus in like a laser beam on the markets that are affected and try to determine what products are competing in those markets, whether the companies have products that are directly competing with one

another. So you could have a merger of multiples of billions of dollars with only a few markets that are affected by overlapping products that are offered by the merging parties. And what we attempt to do in those cases is focus the parties' attention on those particular markets and recommend that they suggest a way of solving the competitive problem because our purpose is to maintain competition in those markets that are affected. Our job is to umpire, referee the competition that goes on in the marketplace. And we can't very well allow the two sole suppliers of a particular product to merge to a monopoly. So we urge them to come up with a suggested solution of the problem which usually will involve a divestiture of one of the two companies' line of business. There's a recent case that illustrates a lot of what we do in the cross-border setting. It was a merger of two large auto component manufacturers, one based in the United States, one based in the United Kingdom. And there was one market in particular where these two companies were dominant as far as the auto industry was concerned. Ford, General Motors, Chrysler were enormously dependent upon these two companies for particular components. The parties were aware of this and they came in and they made an offer to divest what we would call an assortment of assets, some from company A's parts bin and some from company B's parts bin. And as we began to review the company's documents, we found in their planning documents that some of the assets that they were offering were assets that were generously referred to as under-performing, which meant clearly what the Europeans call slated for social dumping, closure with resulting job losses. Now, we weren't the only authority reviewing this. There were four authorities in Europe that were reviewing it. Believe it or not, the transaction was not big enough from a monetary standpoint to reach the merger review thresholds of the European Commission, the so-called one-stop shop in Brussels. As a result, the authorities in Berlin, in Rome, in London, and in Brussels, the Belgian agency, and in Paris, the French agency, were all involved in reviewing this merger. And of course, it's not good enough to get one or two approvals. You've got to get them from all of the authorities that have jurisdiction to review the merger. The French became very much aware of what the company was up to because some of the underperforming assets were located in France and it's within the ambit of the French competition authority to take that factor into consideration. It is not in our ambit. Based on our evaluation of the assets that were offered, these so-called underperforming assets, we did not believe that any company that acquired those assets would be able to maintain competition to supply the auto industry and keep competition for those products. We were fortunate to be able to persuade the companies to make a more generous offer, and they divested the entire line of business of one side of the merger. It also resolved another problem, another potential problem that arises in cross-border mergers, and that is a critical asset that is located in one jurisdiction. As we were reviewing the assets that were available, there was a research and development facility in the United Kingdom that was clearly a crown jewel of the British-based company. Under the original proposals that the parties made, they would retain that asset. Well, it was clear to us that both for the European-based makers, which included Ford and General Motors, as well as the American-based, there was a need to keep that research and development facility in competition with the other companies. Fortunately, in the end, that research and development facility went with the package of assets that was divested and there was a perfectly suitable buyer for it, and we are convinced that we have done the job of maintaining competition in that particular market.

In light of the previous comments about due diligence, due diligence should be expanded to include purely legal issues and scenarios as to possible behaviors abroad. Reflecting on his experiences in utility business in four countries in South America, Patrick Downes reiterated that:

Due diligence is probably the most complex part of the acquisition. Because it's not only looking at the country, it's not only looking at electricity, it's looking at economies, it's looking at politics, it's looking at financing. And very honestly, even if it's the best business but it's in the worst country, you better plan on walking away from the deal.

From a regulatory perspective, John Parisi offered another perspective on due diligence:

An argument we hear sometimes from companies when they come in to talk to us about their proposed merger is that their business is globalizing. And, as a result, there is little concentration in the market, the market is global, there's little concentration, there's little problem with this merger. Well, when you scratch below the surface and you look at the reality, that's seldom the case. We may live in a small world, but we don't live in one world. Consumer preferences, transportation costs, government regulations, all militate against global markets. There are very, very few products like airliners and computer software that really flow in a global market. As a result of that, what you find is that market structures differ, oftentimes from one country to another. When the European Commission and the Federal Trade Commission review a pharmaceutical merger, the EC reviews member state by member state, because a pharmaceutical maker needs a regulatory approval for their product to sell it in each EU member state. Also because of the health program, differences from member state to member state create a competitive difference. Due diligence is not to look at this deal as being in one global market, but in markets that are actually national or even regional. Corporations must look at the deals through the eyes of antitrust enforcers.

It is noteworthy that among the recent cross-border merger and acquisition deals, few are described as hostile deals. In the 1970s, the American government bailed out the Chrysler Corporation and for about 20 years after that Chrysler sort of marketed their cars as a buy American, as a patriotic duty, as "getting your investment back," etcetera. Now, of course, they've merged with Daimler and we're not sure if it's an American car or a German car. Is it surprising that the United States government didn't step in and protect its own investment and stop that merger?

John Parisi asked:

If Lee Iacocca were still the CEO of Chrysler, would he and Jurgen Schrempp have come to a merger deal? And another question to think about is whether eight or nine years ago, if Daimler-Benz had approached Chrysler with a merger, would there have been more of an outcry then than the lack of outcry now? If you go back and read newspapers from about ten years ago, in 1988, 1989, you found articles by Martin and Susan Tolshin in the New York Times raising clarion calls about foreign ownership, the buying of America. And I was a little surprised last summer when we had both the Daimler-Chrysler merger and the Bertelsmann-Random House merger because there you're talking about intellectual cultural goods, the Germans buying the English language. And there were some authors who were concerned about their royalty rights and so on, but there was no outcry. And I think it may be a measure of the economic prosperity that we're enjoying right now, that it's a little easier to tolerate these foreign investments because the economy is going good. I query whether that view would be different if economic times weren't so good right now.

APPENDIX A: Profiles of the panelists and discussants at the cross-border mergers and acquisitions: global and regional perspectives

A conference held on April 21, 1999 in Rock Hall of Temple University. Presented by the Institute of Global Management Studies (IGMS).

Opening address

Mark L. Feldman, PhD, Partner and Managing Director, Merger and Acquisition Consulting PricewaterhouseCoopers

Mark L. Feldman has 18 years international consulting experience. He has worked for clients in the United States, Asia, and Europe representing the electronics, information services, telecommunications, food process, healthcare, hotel, retail, software, and computer industries.

Prior to joining PricewaterhouseCoopers, Dr. Feldman was national director of mergers and acquisition consulting for two international consulting firms. He was also founder and managing director of The Rubicon Group International, specializing in acquisitions and joint ventures between United States and Asia/Pacific companies.

He has published numerous articles and co-authored a book with Mike Spratt titled *Five Frogs on a Log: A CEOs Field Guide to Accelerating the Transition in Mergers, Acquisitions and Gut Wrenching Change.*

Dr. Feldman holds MA and PhD degrees from Northwestern University.

First panel discussion: global perspectives

Moderator: Tyler Mathisen, Co-host, CNBC Business Center

Prior to joining CNBC, Tyler Mathisen worked for 14 years at *Money* magazine, rising to executive editor in 1993 and director of new media in 1994.

Mr. Mathisen has served as money editor of ABC's "Good Morning America" since April 1991, offering personal finance advice and news analysis on a weekly basis. From 1987 to 1994, he appeared regularly on WCBS-TV/New York's channel 2 "News at Noon" and other news broadcasts.

He also served for four years as a daily commentator on "This Morning's Business," a syndicated television program produced by the former Financial News Network, as well as on CNN's cable channel and radio network. In addition, he hosted *Money's* syndicated 1991 television special, "America's Best College Buys."

Mr. Mathisen began his career in 1976 as a writer and text editor for Time-Life Books. In 1976, he crafted biographies of American presidents for *Time* magazine's special US Bicentennial issue.

He has received numerous awards, including an Emmy from the New York Chapter of the National Academy of Television Arts and Sciences, ICI-American University Journalism Award, and Harry E. Fuller Award from the National Foundation for Consumer Credit.

Mr. Mathisen graduated with distinction from the University of Virginia, where he studied American government.

Hans P. Black, MD, President, Intervest

Hans P. Black organized Intervest in Montreal in the mid-1970s as a global money management firm affiliated with his family's investment business in Zurich. Today, Intervest manages accounts for private and institutional clients through offices in Boston, Montreal, Toronto, and its affiliates in Bermuda and Zurich.

Dr. Black has been featured in numerous publications, such as *Barron's, International Herald Tribune, Financial Times, Euromoney,* and *Wall Street Transcript.* In addition, he has appeared frequently as a special guest on PBS's *The Nightly Business Report.*

A native of Europe, Dr. Black received a BS (magna cum laude) from Union College in New York. He studied law in France and subsequently graduated from McGill University in Montreal with a Doctorate in Medicine.

Christopher M. Foskett, Managing Director, Mergers and Acquisitions, Salomon Smith Barney

Christopher M. Foskett has extensive experience in the banking, insurance, funds, electric power and retail industries.

Prior to joining Salomon Smith Barney, he served from 1996 to 1998 as global product head of Citicorp's mergers and acquisitions group where he managed 12 offices and 75 staff worldwide. In addition, Mr. Foskett served for five years as the vice president of the merger department at Goldman Sachs & Co., where he specialized in financial service companies. From 1984 to 1986, he worked at Merrill Lynch & Co., focusing on financial services mergers and acquisitions.

Mr. Foskett holds a BS (cum laude) from Providence College and an MBA (with distinction) from Babson College.

Joseph A. Miller, Jr., PhD, Senior Vice President and Chief Technology Officer, DuPont

Joseph A. Miller Jr. joined DuPont in 1966. Before becoming senior vice president in 1994 and chief technology officer in 1996, he held a variety of positions throughout DuPont in research and development, manufacturing, business and marketing. He also served in the US Army at the Jet Propulsion Laboratory in Pasadena, CA from 1967 to 1969, achieving the rank of captain.

Dr. Miller is president of the Delaware Science, Math and Technical Education Foundation and co-chair of the commission to reform science education in Delaware public schools. In addition, he is a fellow of the American Association for the Advancement of Science and of the Penn State Alumni.

He is a member of the American Chemical Society, American Institute of Chemical Engineers, Industrial Research Institute, National Academy of Engineering, Chemical Heritage Foundation, Council for Competitiveness, National Science and Technology Board International Advisory Panel of Singapore, University of Delaware Research Foundation, Delaware Public Policy Institute, Center for Science, and Mathematics and Engineering Education of the NRC. He is also a member of the advisory boards of the chemical engineering departments at the University of Delaware and Georgia Tech.

Dr. Miller received a BS from Virginia Military Institute and a PhD in chemistry from Penn State University.

Second panel discussion: regional perspectives

Moderators: Tyler Mathisen, Co-host, CNBC Business Center

Patrick J. Downes, PE, Vice President, PSE&G

Patrick J. Downes joined PSE&G in 1961. He was elected vice president in July 1998, after holding a variety of management positions, including vice president of electric distribution, manager of transportation and equipment, division manager of Trenton electric T&D, and division manager of metropolitan electric T&D.

Prior to his appointment as vice president, he served for one year as chief operating officer for two PSE&G Global International electric distribution companies serving approximately 400 000 customers in the Province of Buenos Aires, Argentina.

He has served as trustee of the Passaic County 200 Club, a group of business professionals who provide financial support and scholarships to families of public safety workers killed or hurt in the line of duty. He is also a member of IEEE and a participant of the University of Michigan Executive Program.

Mr. Downes received a BEE degree from Manhattan College and a MS degree from New Jersey Institute of Technology. He is also a professional engineer in the State of New Jersey.

Avi D. Eden, Vice Chairman, Vishay Intertechnology, Inc.
Avi Eden has been affiliated with Vishay since 1973. His responsibilities include all aspects of mergers and acquisitions and corporate legal matters.

Vishay, a Fortune 1000 company, is the largest US and European manufacturer of passive electronic components and a major producer of discrete semiconductors, IRDCs, and power integrated circuits. With headquarters in Malvern, PA, Vishay employs over 20 000 people in more than 60 facilities in the US, Mexico, Germany, Austria, the United Kingdom, France, Portugal, the Czech Republic, Hungary, Israel, Japan, Taiwan (ROC), China, and the Philippines.

Prior to joining Vishay Intertechnology, Mr. Eden practiced law from 1981 to 1993. He was also an attorney with the Office of the Legal Advisor to the Israel Income Tax Authority from 1972 to 1973.

He received a BA from the University of Cincinnati and a Doctorate of Law from Harvard University.

Samuel A. McCullough, Secretary of Community and Economic Development, Commonwealth of Pennsylvania
A business and community leader for 40 years, the Honorable Samuel A. McCullough was appointed Secretary of Community and Economic Development by Governor Tom Ridge in 1997.

Prior to this appointment, Mr. McCullough served as chairman, president and CEO of Meridan Bancorp, Inc. He was named CEO of Meridian when the holding company was founded in 1983, having previously served as CEO for American Bank and Trust Co., a predecessor to Meridian.

Mr. McCullough serves as board and executive committee member of Greater Philadelphia First, member of the executive committee of the Greater Philadelphia Chamber of Commerce, and vice chairman of the Board of Trustees of Albright College. He is also on the boards of the Commonwealth Foundation, Philadelphia Orchestra Association, University of Pittsburgh, Boy Scouts of America (Northeast Region), Reading Hospital and Medical Center, Wyomissing Foundation, and Brandywine Conservancy.

Mr. McCullough has received numerous awards, including the Builders of Israel Award, United Negro College Fund Golden Achievement Award, University of Pittsburgh Joseph M. Katz Graduate School of Business Distinguished Alumnus Award, Torch of Liberty Award of the Eastern Pennsylvania-Delaware Region of Anti-Defamation League, Boy Scouts of America Silver Antelop Award, and Boy Scouts of America Philadelphia Council Good Scout Award.

He received his BBA from the University of Pittsburgh.

John J. Parisi, Chief Counsel for European Community Affairs, US Federal Trade Commission

John J. Parisi joined the US Federal Trade Commission (FTC) in 1989, coordinating FTC antitrust enforcement activities with those of the European Commission and other European competition authorities. In 1991, upon the signing of the US–European Community antitrust cooperation agreement, he spent three months in the European Community's competition directorate, DGIV.

Previously, Mr. Parisi served 11 years as a counsel in both houses of the US Congress. In 1988–89, through a Robert Bosch Foundation fellowship, he worked in the German Federal Economics Ministry in Bonn and Federation of German Industry in Cologne.

Mr. Parisi received a BA in history from Kalamazoo College and a Doctorate of Law from Wayne State University. He is a member of the Michigan, District of Columbia, and American Bar associations.

REFERENCES

Agrawal, A. Jaffe, J. F., Mandelker, G. N., 1992. The post-merger performance of acquiring firms: a re-examination of an anomaly. *J Finance* 47, 1605–1671.

Asquith, P., Brunner, R. F., Mullins, Jr., D., 1987. The gains for bidding firms for merger. *J Financial Econ* 11, 121–139.

Banerjee, A., Owens, J. E., 1992. Wealth reduction in white knight bids. *Financial Manage* 21, 48–57.

Bergh, D. D., 1997. Predicting divestiture of unrelated acquisitions: an integrative model of ex ante conditions. *Strategic Manage J* 18 (9), 715–731.

Bradley, M., Desai, A., Kim, E. H., 1988. The rational behind interfirm tender offers: information of synergy? *J Financial Econ* 11, 183–206.

Bradley, M., Jarrel, G., 1988. Comment. In: Coffee Jr, J. C., Lowenstein, L., Rose-Ackerman, S. (Eds). *Knights, Raiders and Targets*. Oxford University Press, New York, pp. 252–259.

Byrd, J. W., Hickman, K. A., 1992. Do outside directors monitor managers? *J of Financial Econ* 32, 195–221.

Campbell, A., Goold, M., Alexander, M., 1995. Corporate strategy: the quest for parenting advantage. *Harvard Business Rev* March-April, 120–132.

Chatterjee, S., 1986. Type of synergy and economic value: the impact of acquisitions on merging and rival firms. *Strategic Manage J* 7, 119–139.

Chatterjee, S., Lubatkin, M., 1990. Corporate mergers, stockholder diversification, and changes in systematic risk. *Strategic Manage J* 11, 255–268.

Chatterjee, S., Lubatkin, M. H., Schweiger, D. M, Weher, Y., 1992. Cultural difference and stockholder value in related mergers. *Strategic Manage J* 13, 319–324.

Datta, D. K., Pinches, G. E., Narayanan, V. K., 1992. Factors influencing wealth creation from mergers and acquisitions: a meta-analysis. *Strategic Manage J* 13, 67–84.

Elgers, P., Clark, J., 1980. Merger types and stockholder returns: additional evidence. *Financial Manage* 9, 66–72.

Ghoshal, S., 1987. Global strategy: an organizing framework. *Strategic Manage J* 8, 425–440.

Gilson, R. J., Black, B. S., 1995. *The Law and Finance of Corporate Acquisitions*. 2nd Edition. Foundation Press, Westbury, NY.

Gonzalez, P., Vasconcellos, G. M., Kish, R. J., 1998. Cross-border mergers and acquisitions: the undervaluation hypothesis. *Q Rev Econ Finance* 38 (1), 25–45.

Haspeslagh, P. C., Jemison, D. B., 1991. *Managing Acquisitions: Creating Value through Corporate Renewal*. Free Press, New York.

Healy, P. M., Palepu, K. G., Ruback, R. G., 1997. Which takeovers are profitable? Strategic or financial? *Sloan Manage Rev* Summer, 45–57.

Hennart, J. F., Park, Y. R., 1993. Greenfield vs. acquisition: the strategy of Japanese investors in the United States. *Manage Sci* 39 (9), 1054–1070.

Hopkins, H. D., 1987. Acquisition strategy and the market position of acquiring firms. *Strategic Manage J* 8, 535–548.

Jarrell, G. A., Brickley, J. A., Netter, J. M., 1988. The market for corporate control: the empirical evidence since 1980. *J Econ Perspect* 2, 21–48.

Jarrell, G. A., Poulsen, A., 1989. Shark repellants and stockprices: the effects of antitakeover amendments since 1980. *J Financial Econ* 19, 127–168.

Jennings, R., Mazzeo, M., 1991. Stock price movements around acquisition announcements and management's response. *J of Business*, 64, 139–163.

Jensen, M. C., Ruback, R. S., 1983. The market for corporate control. *J Financial Econ* 11, 5–50.

Kitching, J., 1967. Why do mergers miscarry? *Harvard Business Rev* March-April, 84–101.

Kusewitt, J., 1985. An exploratory study of strategic acquisition factors relating to performance. *Strategic Manage J* 6, 151–169.

Lajoux, A., Weston, J. F., 1998. Do deals deliver on postmerger performance? *Mergers and Acquisitions* September/October, 34–37.

Loderer, C., Martin, K., 1992. Postacquisition performance of acquiring firms. *Financial Manage* Autumn, 69–79.

Magenheim, E. B., Mueller, D. C., 1988. Are acquiring firm shareholders better off after acquisition? In: Coffee, J. C., Lowenstein, L., and Rose-Ackerman, S. (Eds), *Knights, Raiders, and Targets: The Impact of Hostile Take-overs*. Oxford University Press, New York, pp. 171–193.

Markides, C. C., Ittner, C. D., 1994. Shareholder benefits from corporate international diversification: evidence from US international acquisitions. *J Int Business Stud* 25 (2), 343–366.

Morck, R., Shleifer, A., Vishny, R. W., 1990. Do managerial objectives drive bad acquisitions? *J Finance* 4, 31–48.

Morosini, P., 1998. *Managing Cultural Differences: Effective Strategy and Execution Across Cultures in Global Corporate Alliances*. Pergamon, New York.

Morosini, P., Scott, S., Singh, H., 1998. National cultural distance and cross-border acquisition performance. *J Int Business Stud* 29 (1), 137–158.

Porter, M. E., 1987. From competitive advantage to competitive strategy. *Harvard Business Rev* 65 (3), 43–59.

Porter, M. E., 1991. Towards a dynamic theory of strategy. *Strategic Manage J* 12, 95–117.

Porter, M. E., 1998. What is strategy? In: Collection of papers by M. Porter. *On Competition*. HBS Press, Boston, pp. 39–74.

Ramaswamy, K., 1997. The performance impact of strategic similarity in horizontal mergers: evidence from the US banking industry. *Acad Manage J* 40 (3), 697–715.

Ravenscraft, D., Scherer, F., 1989. The profitability of mergers. *Int J Ind Organ* 7, 101–116.

Sebenius, J. K., 1998. Case study: negotiating cross-border acquisitions. *Sloan Manage Rev* Winter, 27–41.

Servaes, H. 1991. Tobin's Q and the gains from takeover. *J Finance* 46, 409–419

Shelton, L., 1988. Strategic business fits and corporate acquisition: empirical evidence. *Strategic Manage J* May-June, 279–288.

Shrivastava, P., 1986. Post-merger integration. *J Business Strategy* 7, 65–76.

Singh, H., Montgomery, C., 1987. Corporate acquisition strategies and economic performance. *Strategic Manage J* 8, 377–386.

Sirower, M. L., 1994. Acquisition behavior, strategic resource commitments and the acquisition game. Ph.D. dissertation, Graduate School of Business. Columbia University.

Sirower, M. L., 1997. *The Synergy Trap*. Free Press, New York.

Strom, S., Bradsher, K., 1999. Wedding or Wipe-Out?, *New York Times*, May 23.

Varaiya, N. P., Ferris, K. R., 1987. Overpaying in corporate takeovers: The winner's curse. *Financial Analysts' J* May-June, 64–73.

You, V. L., Caves, R. E., Henry, J. S., Smith, M. M., 1986. Mergers and bidder's wealth: Managerial and strategic factors. In: Thomas, L. G. (Ed.), *The Economics of Strategic Planning*. Lexington Books, Lexington, MA, pp. 201–220.

Hopkins, H. D. (1999) "Cross-border mergers and acquisitions: Global and regional perspectives". Reprinted from *Journal of International Management*, 5, 207–239, with permission from Elsevier Science.

6 Joint ventures and the option to expand and acquire

Bruce Kogut

A fundamental problem facing the firm is the decision to invest and expand into new product markets characterized by uncertain demand. The problem is exacerbated when the new business is not related to current activities. In this sense, a firm's initial investments in new markets can be considered as buying the right to expand in the future.

In current parlance, the right to expand is an example of a "real option," real because it is an investment in operating as opposed to financial capital, and an option because it need never be exercised.[1] For many investments, such as the purchase of new capital equipment to reduce costs in ageing plants, the option value is insignificant. In industries where the current investment provides a window on future opportunities, the option to expand can represent a substantial proportion of the value of a project, if not of the firm.[2]

An analysis of joint ventures provides an interesting insight into investment decisions as real options. The task of building a market position and competitive capabilities requires lumpy and nontrivial investments. As a result, it is often beyond the resources of a single firm to buy the right to expand in all potential market opportunities. A partner, especially one which brings the requisite skills, may be sought to share the costs of placing the bet that the opportunity will be realized.

This perspective is related to the use of joint ventures to share risk. Pure risk-sharing arises in cases, such as bidding on oil lots, where firms have committed capital downstream (such as in refineries) but are dependent upon availability supplies of a finite resource. Multiple joint ventures among firms in the oil industry are analogous to collective insurance.[3]

In many industries, however, joint ventures not only share risks, but also decrease the total investment. Because the parties bring different capabilities, the venture no longer requires the full development costs. Due to its benefits of sharing risk and of reducing overall investment costs, joint ventures serve as an attractive mechanism to invest in an option to expand in risky markets.

However, in the event the investment is judged to be favorable, the parties to the joint venture face a difficult decision. To exercise the option to expand requires further commitment of capital, thus requiring renegotiation among the partners. One possible outcome is that the party placing a higher value on this new capital commitment buys out the other. Thus, the timing when it is desirable to exercise the option to expand is likely to be linked to the time when the venture will be acquired.

The exploration of the link in the timing of the acquisition of joint ventures and of the exercise of the option to expand is the focus of the following empirical investigation. The first two sections apply an option perspective to joint ventures. A distinction is made between acquisitions motivated by industry conditions and those stemming from the desire to expand in response to favorable growth opportunities. The third section develops the central hypothesis that the timing of the acquisition is related to a signal that the valuation of the venture has increased. This signal is proxied by two measures derived from the growth of shipments in the venture's industry. The effects of these industry signals on the likelihood of a venture terminating by an acquisition are tested by specifying and estimating a hazard model, while controlling for industry and other effects.

The same model is then tested on the likelihood of dissolution. If the option interpretation is correct, a signal that the venture's value has increased should lead to an acquisition; a signal that it has decreased, however, should not lead to dissolution, as long as further investment is not required and operating costs are modest. Strong support is found for the option argument.

These results run counter to prevailing presumptions in organizational theories that firms engage in cooperative ventures as buffers against uncertainty and that managerial discretion is severely limited by environmental volatility. In the view of Pfeffer and Nowak (1976), joint ventures are instruments to manage the dependency of the partner firms on the uncertainty of resources. Recent work in organizational mortality, as influenced by the seminal articles by Hannan and Freeman (1977) and McKelvey and Aldrich (1983), has advanced the proposition that managers are severely curtailed in their abilities to affect the prospects of survival of their firms.

To the contrary, an option perspective posits that joint ventures are designed as mechanisms to exploit, as well as buffer, uncertainty. Because firms have limited influence over the sources of uncertainty in the environment, it pays to invest in the option to respond to uncertain events. Joint ventures are investments providing firms with the discretion to expand in favorable environments, but avoid some of the losses from downside risk. In this regard, real option theory provides a way to ground the trial and learning aspect to joint ventures.

REAL OPTIONS

The assignment of the right to buy and sell equity in the joint venture is a common feature of many agreements. For example, in a recent announcement of a joint venture in the area of power generation equipment, Asea Brown Boverie received the option to buy the venture at some time in the future. Westinghouse, as the partner, has the right to sell its ownership interest. In the vernacular of financial markets, the terms of the venture provides a call option to Asea Brown Boverie and a put option to Westinghouse.

In drawing up a joint venture agreement, it is common practice to give first rights of refusal to the contracting parties to buy the equity of the partner who decides to withdraw. Sometimes, one party is given the priority to acquire in the case of termination. The legal clause serves to regulate the assignation of the rights to the underlying option. Such a clause may establish not only who has the first right to acquire, but also may set pricing rules.

The legal clause outlining acquisition rights should not be confused with the real option itself. Legal clauses serve simply as a way proactively to outline ownership rights in response to unspecified contingencies involving the failure of the cooperation. The termination of the venture by acquisition is not, therefore, necessarily equivalent to the creation and exercise of an option similar to those found in financial markets.

However, an economic option is often inherent in the decision to joint venture and the decision to exercise this option, as explained below, is likely to promote the divestment of the venture by one of the parties. Joint ventures are real options, not in terms of the legal assignation of contingent rights, but, like many investments, in terms of the economic opportunities to expand and grow in the future. The value of any investment can be broken into the cash flows stemming from assets as currently in place and those stemming from their redeployment or future expansion (Myers, 1977). Because these latter cash flows are only realized if the business is expanded, they represent, as Myers first recognized, the value of growth opportunities.

The intuition behind this argument can be explained by following the notation of Pindyck (1988). Given an investment of K, the value of the venture can be decomposed in terms of both assets in place and the embedded options:

$$V_j = F_j(K, \pi) + O_j(K, \pi), \tag{1}$$

where V is the value of the venture as estimated by the jth firm, $F_j(K, \pi)$ is the value of the assets in their current use, $O_j(K, \pi)$ is the valuation of the future growth opportunities, and π is the current value of an uncertain state variable. The difference between $F_j(K, \pi)$ and $O_j(K, \pi)$ is that the latter is not equivalent to the discounted cash flows of expected earnings, because the firm maintains the flexibility to choose among investment alternatives – including not to invest – in the future.

As both the value of the assets in place and the option can be potentially affected by current assets and opportunities of the partner firms, the valuations of the venture will differ among the parties. For example, the venture might source components from one partner and not the other, hence affecting the valuation of assets in place.[4] Differences in option valuation can arise if the potential spill-over effects of the venture's technology complement the product portfolio of one partner more than the other.

Changes in the value of these assets depend on the stochastic process determining the current value of the embedded option, where the state variables are prices, either of production or the inputs. In Figure 1, we illustrate the implications of this process by assuming that changes in a state variable (indicated as π) are normally distributed over time and depict a cross-section of the path. The expected value ($\bar{\pi}_{t+\Delta t}$) is the current value plus the expected increase; the variance is σ^2. If realization of $\pi_{t+\Delta t}$ is greater than some critical value π^*, the derived value of the venture is greater than its acquisition price and the option to acquire is exercised. If $\pi_{t+\Delta t}$ is less than π^*, no further investment is made. Nor is it necessary to divest the assets (if operating costs are low), for there is the possibility that future changes will be more favorable. It is for this reason that the downside risk is not consequential.

Below, we consider the conditions which generate the option value, as well as examine motives for acquisitions which are not driven by the underlying option value. We link the value of the option, and, thereby, the venture, to the market demand for new products and technologies. Then, the central issue of the timing of exercise is addressed.

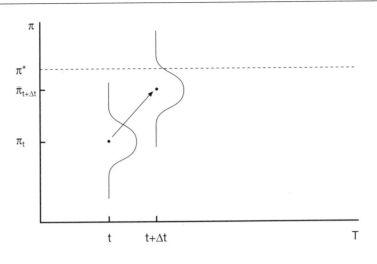

Figure 1 Expected change in π_t.

JOINT VENTURES AS REAL OPTIONS

In the following, we consider two options and examine qualitatively why joint ventures can be viewed as analogues. The first option is waiting to invest, whereby it pays to wait before committing resources. In the second option of expanding production, investment commitment is necessary in order to have the right to expand in the future. These two options, therefore, exemplify two polar types of real option strategies.[5]

It is often the case that an investment decision involves a comparison of both options. Committing engineers or product planners to a risky project incurs the possibility that the market does not develop; it also draws resources from other projects. Clearly, there is a value in waiting before the technology or market is proven. But if there is a benefit in investing today in order to gain experience with the technology or to establish a brand image with customers, then investing generates the valuable option to expand in the future.

A joint venture serves as a way to bridge these options through pooling resources of two or more firms. Because the value of the option to expand is greatest in new markets and technologies, any given firm is unlikely to possess the full repertoire of skills. A joint venture not only shares the investment burden, but sometimes reduces it, as the parties may bring different skills, thereby lowering the total investment cost. In this sense, a joint venture resolves partly the tradeoff between buying flexibility now and waiting to invest and focus later (Wernerfelt and Karnani, 1987).[6]

When the market for the technology or new product is proven, the option to acquire, as discussed later, is likely to be exercised. Through the joint venture, the buying party has acquired the skills of the partner firm and no longer needs to invest in the development of the requisite capability to expand into the targeted market. The divesting firm is willing to sell because, one, it realizes capital gains, and two, it may also not have the downstream assets to bring the technology to market (Teece, 1987; Shan, 1988). In this sense, the divestiture of joint ventures are the buyers' side to the argument and findings of Christensen and Montgomery (1981) that acquisitions are a way to buy into attractive industries.

For one of the partners to make the acquisition, the net value of purchasing the joint venture must be at least equal to the value of purchasing comparable assets on the market. This condition is likely to be satisfied due to the gain in experience in running the venture. If it does not hold, there was no advantage and, hence, no value to the option by investing early. But even if this condition does not hold *ex post*, a joint venture, as Balakrishnan and Koza (1988) point out, affords the possibility to learn the true value of the assets. As information is revealed, the acquisition is completed or withdrawn. From this perspective, regardless of other motives such as managerial experience, there is a bias to buy out the venture relative to other acquisition prospects simply due to better valuation information.

TIMING OF EXERCISE

As apparent from the above analysis, an acquisition or divestment is often a foreseen conclusion to the venture. The investing firms may be indifferent to whether a partner or a third firm purchases the venture. The reward is the capital gains return on the development efforts.

From this perspective, the timing of the acquisition is of critical significance. Simply stated, the acquisition is justified only when the perceived value to the buyer is greater than the exercise price. For a financial option, the terminal value is given by the stock price and the exercise price as set by the initial contract:

$$W = \max (S_t - E, 0), \tag{2}$$

where W is the value of the option, S is the price of the stock at time t, and E is the exercise price. (In this case, S_t is the state variable which we denoted earlier as π.) As the cost of purchasing the option is sunk, these two parameters determine, *ex post*, the value of the option when exercised.[7]

The joint venture analogue to equation (2) is

$$W_j = \text{Max} ((1 - \alpha) V_j - P, 0). \tag{3}$$

That is, the value of the option to acquire (W) is equal to the value to the *j*th firm of purchasing the remaining shares in the venture minus P, where $\alpha > 0$ and <1 and is the current share owned by firm j and P is the price of purchasing the remaining shares. (P is either negotiated between the parties or set according to a contractual clause.)[8]

For financial options, it is well established that an option should be usually held to full maturity (Hull 1989, pp. 105–129). Exceptions to this rule depend upon dividend policy on the underlying stock, where it may pay to exercise the option before payment to shareholders. Obviously, in the case of joint ventures, the acquisition is only carried out if $(1 - \alpha) V_j > P$.

But the exercise of the option to acquire the joint venture is likely to be immediate for two reasons. First, the value of the real option is *only* recognized by making the investment and realizing the incremental cash flows. If the investment in new capacity is not made in a period, the cash flows are lost. Second, the necessity to increase the capitalization of the venture invariably requires a renegotiation of the agreement, often leading to its termination.[9] The option to expand the investment is likely to coincide with exercising the option to acquire the joint venture.

Consider a pure research venture between two parties. Both parties provide initial funding and a pre-established contribution to costs. As long as the initial investment is sunk and additional capital commitments are not required, increased variance in the value of the technology raises the upside gain. (Of course, variable costs must be paid, but these "carrying" costs apply as well to some kinds of financial options.) Since the option need not be exercised, the downside is inconsequential. At any given time, whether it pays for one party to buy the venture is dependent upon the buy-out price and the valuation of the business as a wholly-owned operation.

But once it is profitable to exercise the option, there are sound reasons not to wait. The option value of the venture is realized by investing in expansion. The requirement to contribute further capital leads to a difficult renegotiation. By now, the partners have information to know that the original equity share may not reflect the division of benefits. This deviation can be expected to be compounded when the option to expand becomes economically viable, as the partners are likely to differ in their appraisal of these opportunities. Thus, the allocation of new capital burdens often forces a revaluation of the distribution of benefits. Buying out the partner is a common outcome.

The timing of the exercise of the option to terminate the venture by acquisition is, thus, influenced by two considerations: the initial base rate forecast underlying the valuation of the business and the value of the venture to each party (or third parties) as realized over time. For the acquisition to take place, the acquisition price P must be greater than the valuation placed on the assets by one of the partners. These considerations lead to the following hypothesis: *The venture will be acquired when its valuation exceeds the base rate forecast.*

SELECTIVE CUES AND MARKET VALUATION

Unlike the case for a contingent security, there are no written contracts and financial markets that indicate changes in the value of a real option. Testing this hypothesis is, clearly, difficult given the impossibility to collect data on changes over time of both partners' evaluations of the option to expand. Nor is it likely that managers possess clear base-rates and valuation signals by which to guide a decision to exercise the option to expand. Consequently, the specification of the above hypothesis raises important questions about what information and environment cues managers use to time the exercise of the option.

Despite theoretical interest and laboratory experiments, most of the research on environmental cues informing managerial decisions has been oriented to identifying biases in the interpretation of information rather than in the selection of the information itself. Of some guidance is the finding of Bowman (1963) that adherence to a consistent rule derived from previous decisions performs better than the decisions actually made, suggesting that the efficiency of decisionmaking is impaired due to biases in the selection cues.[10] More recent research has especially pointed to biases derived from base-rate errors and the salience, or availability, of information. Several studies have shown that individuals wrongly calculate probabilities by weighting recent information too heavily or failing to incorporate information on the marginal probabilities.[11] Base-rates are, thus, frequently ignored, especially when the causal relationships are not explicit.

Whereas experimental research has validated a number of heuristics used in selecting information, there is little guidance for establishing the base rates that might be used for irregular decisions, such as the acquisition of a joint venture. We would expect, as Camerer (1981) notes, that individuals rely upon only a few cues of those available. We experiment with two time-varying specifications of the market cues relevant to the acquisition decision: a short-term annual growth rate and an annual residual error from a long-term trend in shipments.

The short-term annual growth rate is calculated as

$$G_{t,j} = [PS_{t,j} - PS_{t-1,j}/PS_{t-1,j}], \tag{4}$$

where the growth rate is set equal to changes in the value of product shipments (PS) for the jth industry over an annual interval $[t - 1, t]$. The residual error is derived from the error from an estimated regression of the time trend in shipment growth:

$$R_{t,j} = PS_{t,j} - [a_j + b_j t], \tag{5}$$

where the residual error is the forecasting error from a linear time trend for the jth industry with intercept a and slope coefficient b. (The appropriateness of the linear specification is discussed below.)

It is essential to recognize that the above variables vary with time. Both specifications are derived from a constant dollar series of industry product shipments. The annual growth measure looks at year to year changes, always using the previous year as a benchmark. The residual error indicates that decision makers establish a long-term base-rate for each industry's historical growth and look at year to year departures from this trend. Unlike the growth measure, it assumes that managers act to acquire or divest when a market cue signals a rise in valuation relative to a long-term trend.

These two variables are, by our argument, proxies for changes in the unobserved state variable (given as π earlier) that determines the value of the joint venture. As our interest does not lie, however, in the pricing of the option but in the likelihood (or hazard) of acquisition, differences in the scales of the proxies are unimportant to the estimations, as described below. Positive movements in the value of industry shipments signal improved investment opportunities and an increase in the value of the real option embedded in the venture. Because the exercise of the option requires a decision to expand the investment and, hence, a renegotiation of the capital commitment of the parties to the venture, the likelihood of an acquisition should increase with positive movements of the proxy variables.

ACQUISITION AND VALUE OF ASSETS IN PLACE

Joint ventures can, of course, be acquired for reasons other than as the outcome to negotiations stemming from exercising the option to expand. In large part, the differences in the reasons to acquire are derived from differences in the original motivations to joint venture in the first place. The motivations to joint venture may sometimes have less to do with building an option to expand into new markets than with the benefits of sharing ownership of assets in their current use. Some ventures provide a mechanism to share scale economies and to coordinate the management of potentially excess capacity in mature and concentrated industries (Harrigan, 1986). The option proportion of the total value of these kinds of ventures is likely to be low, that is, the present value of the assets in their current use dominates the option to expand or redeploy.

There is, though, an interesting aspect to some ventures in concentrated industries which the terminology of the option literature illuminates, for many of these ventures are also partial divestments. A number of recent joint ventures fall in this category:

Firestone's sale of 50% of the equity of its tire business to Bridgestone, Honeywell's partnership with NEC and Bull in computers, and the above cited Asea Brown Boverie and Westinghouse agreement. In all of these ventures, the call option was given to the non-American firm.

The question of why do the parties not agree to an immediate acquisition underscores the critical roles of learning and pre-emption. Through the joint venture, the divesting party is contracted to pass on complex know-how on the running of the business, as well as to slow an erosion in customer confidence. Since this know-how may be essentially organizational – such as, the procedures by which an American firm are effectively managed, a joint venture serves as a vehicle of managerial and technological learning (Kogut, 1988; Lyles, 1988). In this case, a joint venture is a phased divestiture with a future exercise date.

The importance of this motivation is especially important in industries where there are few competitors. Tying up a potential acquisition target prevents other parties from making the acquisition, a threat which is particularly troubling in concentrated industries where there are few acquisition targets. Through the acquisition, full ownership is attained without adding further capacity to the industry by entering with a new plant.

DATA COLLECTION

In the above analysis, we related the likelihood of termination of a joint venture by acquisition to increases in the valuation of the embedded option and to industry conditions leading to divestment of existing assets. To test the effect of these two factors on the likelihood of acquisition, data were collected from both questionnaire and archival sources. Information on joint ventures was first acquired from the publication *Mergers and Acquisitions* for the years 1975 and 1983.[12] The sample included only ventures located in the United States in order to eliminate variance in political environments across countries. Moreover, all ventures had at least one American partner given the difficulty of gathering information on non-American firms. Of the 475 firms contacted in two mailings, 55.5% responded. However, due to a number of factors, such as misclassifying a contract as a joint venture or announcing a venture which never occurred, only 140 responses were useable. Of these, 92 are in manufacturing; it is this subsample which is used in this paper. Sources for the industry data are given below.

The questionnaire was designed to elicit factual information regarding the starting and, in the case of termination, ending dates for the venture, as well as its primary purpose. On the basis of this information, the percentage of ventures dissolved or acquired by one of the partners or a third party is 43%. A follow-up questionnaire was sent one-year later to those ventures reported still alive, which resulted in raising this percentage to 55%. A second follow-up was made the following year, with the percentage of terminations rising to 70%.

The questionnaire data makes it possible to construct life histories for the 92 manufacturing ventures. Of these 92, 27 terminated by dissolution, 37 by acquisition, and 28 are censored, that is, they are still in effect. In this study, we treat the ventures that terminated by dissolution as also censored. Such a treatment is reasonable as long as the individual hazards are independent. Given the low density of ventures in a particular industry, the assumption of independence is justified.

From the questionnaire data, we create three dummy variables (*R&D, Production and Marketing*) indicating whether the venture included any of these activities. These variables are used to control for differences in the contractual terms of the sampled joint ventures due to variations in their functional activities. Clearly, the expectations regarding the duration of the ventures may differ depending on whether they involve investments in production and capital equipment or in joint marketing or product development.

The other data are taken from secondary sources. Drawing on Bureau of Census data, we use the four-firm concentration ratio at the four-digit SIC level (*Concentration*) as a proxy for industry maturity that promotes the use of joint ventures as vehicles of planned divestment. Since concentration ratios are published for every fifth year, we employ the ratio nearest the midpoint of the venture's life. (As the ratios are highly correlated across years, there is little difference in results using this procedure or other alternatives.)

As discussed earlier, two different proxies are specified for the central hypothesis that the likelihood of an acquisition is related to the occurrence of a signal of an increase in the value of the venture. The two measures discussed earlier (*Annual Growth* and *Annual Residual Error*) are estimated from unpublished Department of Commerce data on annual shipments (i.e., goods sold) at the four-digit level in constant 1982 dollars for the years 1965 to 1986. Both of these variables are drawn from industry data.

The annual growth data is derived directly from the shipment series. To normalize the data, each industry time series was divided by the first year of the series; thus each series begins with 1965 set to 100. By first differencing the normalized series and dividing by the lagged year, growth in shipments were calculated for each year. This measure was then entered into the analysis as a time-varying covariate with a one-year lag.[13] The time-varying specification means that for a venture alive in 1978, the value of the growth variable is set equal to the annual growth of the venture's industry for 1977. If the venture survives to the next year, the growth covariate is updated to the realized growth rate in 1978.

The residual error is calculated in several steps. First, we again used the normalized series of shipments for each four-digit SIC industry. Second, a time trend was derived by a linear regression. The residual is calculated as the forecasting error for each year, using the estimated linear time trend as the base-rate predictor and the actual normalized shipment as the realized value. The residual error was also entered into the analysis as a time-varying covariate with a one-year lag.

The use of a linear fit for estimating the time trend is justified on a few grounds. With the exception of a few industries, the F-test indicated that the linear specification resulted in rather good fits. Thus, the simple linear model provides a good estimate of the long-term trend. Moreover, several studies have found that linear rules are commonly adopted by individuals to establish expectations (Hogarth, 1982). In some industries, a linear estimate is a poor one and unlikely to be widely maintained. Indeed, as we find below, the exclusion of outliers on the residual measure leads to much better results.

Descriptive statistics are provided for the variables in Table 1. The correlation of the variable *Acquisition* with the covariates is misleading, for the later regressions use time to acquisition as the basis of ordering the likelihoods. It, nevertheless, provides some insight into the underlying relationships. Evident from the table is the

Table 1 Descriptive statistics and correlation matrix

	Mean	Standard deviation	Lowest	Highest
A = Acquisition	0.4	0.49	0.0	1.0
B = Concentration	40.11	20.76	8.0	96.0
C = R&D	0.51	0.50	0.0	1.0
D = Production	0.57	0.50	0.0	1.0
E = Marketing/distribution	0.53	0.50	0.0	1.0

Spearman correlation matrix

	A	B	C	D	E
A	–				
B	0.19	–			
C	0.05	–0.08	–		
D	0.05	–0.04	–0.07	–	
E	0.10	–0.08	–0.05	–0.07	–

low degree of collinearity among these variables. We do not report the time-varying variables, since it would require reporting a covariate for each year of the sample.

STATISTICAL SPECIFICATION

To incorporate the effects of the unobserved stochastic process and the time-varying covariates, we use a partial likelihood specification to estimate the influence of these factors on termination by acquisition among a sample of joint ventures. Partial likelihood estimates the influence of explanatory variables (or covariates) on the hazard of termination without specifying a parametric form for the precise time to failure. Instead, it rank orders ventures in terms of the temporal sequence of terminations. For each event time, it specifies a likelihood that the observed terminated venture should have terminated, conditional on the covariates of the ventures at risk:

$$L_i(t_i) = h_0(t_i)(\exp(BX_i + BX_i(t_i)/h_0(t_i)))[\Sigma_j(\exp(BX_j + BX_j(t_i)))]. \tag{6}$$

For simplicity, the coefficients and covariates are given as vectors B and X, respectively, with i indexing the venture which failed at time t_i, j indexing the ventures at risk at time t_i, $h_0(t_i)$ is the baseline hazard, and L is the likelihood for the ith event. The time-varying covariates (*Annual Growth* and *Residual Error*) are indexed by the time of the event (t_i).

It should be noted that the partial likelihood is general in its specification. The parametric assumptions are the linearity imposed on the coefficients and the log-additivity of the baseline hazard and covariate terms. The distribution of the baseline hazard is nonparametric and entirely general. By leaving the baseline hazard unspecified, no bias is incurred by misspecifying the stochastic process by which unobserved variables influence the observed hazard rate. While efficiency is lost by ignoring the exact termination times, the estimates are consistent; the efficiency loss has been shown to be modest (Efron, 1977; Kalbfleisch and Prentice, 1980).

This generality is achieved by restricting the baseline hazard to be the same for all the ventures. By this assumption, $h_0(t_i)$ cancels out. As shown first by Cox (1972), this likelihood is equivalent to allowing only the conditional probabilities to contribute to the statistical inferences. No information on the precise timing of, or the elapsed time to termination is required; hence it provides a partial, rather than full maximum, likelihood estimate. Consequently, we do not need to know the functional form of the baseline hazard and, implicitly, the underlying process generating changes in the valuation of the venture or the boundary condition giving the point of exercise of the option.

The partial likelihood is calculated as the product of the individual likelihoods. Estimation proceeds by maximizing jointly the likelihoods that the ith venture should terminate conditionally on the characteristics of the other ventures at risk at the time of termination. We use the Newton-Raphson algorithm by which to estimate numerically the coefficients and standard errors. There is no constant or error term. A positive coefficient indicates that increases in the covariate tend to increase the likelihood of termination; a negative coefficient indicates the reverse.[14]

STATISTICAL RESULTS

The statistical results are given in Table 2. As can be seen from the Student T scores, the principal hypotheses are confirmed under a two-tail significance test. Concentration is significant at .002. In concentrated industries, joint ventures appear to be used as an intermediary step towards a complete acquisition. A complementary but more speculative interpretation is that joint ventures are also often part of the restructuring of mature industries, either due to new, and perhaps foreign, competition or to efforts to stabilize the degree of rivalry. By acquiring the assets, a shifting of ownership occurs without an increase in industry capacity.

Table 2 Partial likelihood estimate of covariates' effects on log likelihood of acquisition

Variable name	Full sample (1)	Without computer industry (2)	Without computer industry (3)	Without computer industry (4)
Concentration	0.26	0.02	0.03	0.02
	(3.16[a])	(2.84[a])	(3.08[a])	(2.59[b])
R&D	0.58	0.70	0.57	0.70
	(1.67[c])	(1.88[c])	(1.58)	(1.91[c])
Production	0.16	0.10	0.20	0.06
	(0.44)	(0.26)	(0.56)	(0.16)
Marketing/distribution	0.61	0.66	0.59	0.62
	(1.75[c])	(1.76[c])	(1.63)	(1.66[c])
Annual growth	0.03	0.22	0.03	–
	(2.25[b])	(1.28)	(1.89[c])	–
Residual error	0.0001	0.006	–	0.01
	(0.45)	(2.88[a])	–	(3.48[a])
$N =$	92	88	88	88

Significance under two-tail T-test: (T-statistics in parentheses).
[a] $P < .01$.
[b] $P < .05$.
[c] $P < .10$.

Ventures with R&D activities or marketing and distribution activities are more likely to be acquired at .1 significance under a two-tail test and at .05 under a one-tail. The production variable is positive, though insignificant.

The most interesting comparison is between the growth and residual error variables. The growth variable has a positive effect on acquisitions and is significant at .05. The residual error coefficient, on the other hand, is indistinguishable from a null effect.

Given the sample size, it is important to look at the effect of possible outliers. Large residuals might be generated by a poor fit of the linear trend line. The trend lines for ten industries (in which there are twelve ventures) have significance levels worse than .05. Of these twelve ventures, six terminated by acquisition. Their elimination from the sample changed the results only mildly.

A more direct way to identify outliers is to plot the residual errors and growth rates for each industry. The electronic computing machinery industry (SIC 3573) stands out dramatically from the rest. For 1986, for example, the residual error for computers was 30 times greater than the next highest industry. The remarkable trait of the industry is that since these growth rates have been sustained for two decades and more, negative residual errors are generated even when the growth rate is still substantially above the mean and median for the whole sample. As three of the four ventures in this industry terminated in an acquisition, the estimates are strongly affected.

Reestimating the regression equation without these four ventures gives strikingly different results. Significance levels for the other variables stay largely the same. The most striking change is in the positions of the residual error and growth variable. Both are now positively signed, but the residual error variable is significant at .01. The coefficient on the growth variable is indistinguishable from the null hypothesis. These results are much kinder to the proposition that managers are sensitive to a long-term intra-industry base rate which serves as a standard by which to evaluate annual changes.

The decline in significance of the growth variable is partially the result of the collinearity with the measure of the residual error. Unusually high (low) growth is likely to result in larger (smaller) residual errors. The correlations for *Annual Growth* and *Residual Error* ranged as high as .85 for one year, though often were much lower. Since collinearity tends to raise the standard errors, the loss in significance for *Annual Growth* should be interpreted with some caution.

To address this confounding, *Annual Growth* and *Residual Error* were entered separately into the regression analysis. The results are given in equations (3) and (4) of Table 2. Whereas *Annual Growth* is only significant at .1, *Residual Error* is significant at .001. It is reasonable to conclude that the decision by managers whether to acquire or divest the joint venture is more significantly sensitive to annual departures from a long-term trend than to short-term indices of industry growth.[15]

DISCUSSION OF MARKET SIGNALS

The above findings indicate that increases in excess of the long-term trend in shipment growth are significantly related to the timing of the acquisitions of ventures. Such a relationship suggests that managerial decisions are cued by market signals that the venture's value has increased. Because of the level of aggregation of our sample, the cue may be indirectly related, that is, there are intervening variables (e.g., revenues to the venture) between the variables we chose and the direct cues bearing on managerial choice.

In turn, it could be argued that the take-off in growth signals industry consolidation, thus forcing exits. Conceptually, this objection is weak, for a shake-out should occur when the market does poorer than its historical record. The relationship between *Residual Error* and the likelihood of acquisition suggests the opposite, namely, acquisitions tend to occur when the market does better than its historical record.

To test whether consolidation leads to divestment, we calculate a new variable *Change in Concentration* which indicates the percentage change in the four-firm concentration at the 4-digit SIC level during the life of the venture.[16] The results given in equations (1) and (2) of Table 3 show no support that consolidation leads to an increase in acquisition.

Another interpretation of the findings is that managers are myopic and fail to consider that short-term deviations may be outliers. Frequently, this error is referred to as ignoring regression to the mean or the law of small numbers (Hogarth, 1982; Tversky and Kahneman, 1971). Incidences of annual growth rates and residual errors, in other words, may reflect extreme values of a random process.

That managers do not simply react to any short-term change can also be addressed empirically. If short-term myopia leads to a divest and acquire decision, then it should lead to a dissolve decision when the market turns down. We can test this proposition by estimating the same model for the likelihood of termination by dissolution.

Table 3 Partial likelihood estimates of covariates' effects on log likelihood of termination

	Acquisition		Dissolution	
Variable name	Full sample (1)	Without computer industry (2)	Without computer industry (3)	Without computer industry (4)
Concentration	0.03 (3.14^a)	0.03 (2.90^a)	0.01 (1.16)	0.01 (1.16)
R&D	0.59 (1.66^c)	0.75 (1.96^c)	0.53 (1.30)	0.53 (1.30)
Production	0.16 (0.45)	0.10 (0.27)	−0.18 (−0.43)	−0.17 (−0.43)
Marketing/distribution	0.62 (1.75^c)	0.69 (1.83^c)	0.30 (0.73)	0.30 (0.74)
Annual growth	0.03 (2.23^b)	0.02 (1.22)	−0.01 (−0.77)	−0.01 (−0.77)
Residual error	0.0001 (0.39)	0.007 (2.93^a)	0.003 (0.72)	0.003 (0.72)
Change in concentration	0.143 (0.14)	0.59 (0.60)	– –	– –
N =	92	88	92	88

Significance under two-tail T-test: (T-statistics in parentheses).
^{a} $P < .01$.
^{b} $P < .05$.
^{c} $P < .10$.

This test is especially important if the argument that joint ventures frequently serve as real options is correct. The nature of an option should be kept in mind. Once the capital is committed, the downside risk is low, especially if there is a market for the acquisition of the assets and operating costs are not high. The selling of the venture means that one firm puts a higher value on the assets; it does not mean the venture is unprofitable.

Though it should not be expected that the same covariates should be theoretically related to dissolution, we include them in order to make the results comparable.[17] These results are given in columns 3 and 4 of Table 3. As can be seen, there is no significant relationship between dissolution and the growth and residual error measures.

The insignificance of the *Annual Growth* and *Residual Error* variables lends further support to the options argument. For if joint ventures are designed as options, then as long as the investment is sunk and the operating costs are moderate, downward movements should not lead to dissolution. Rather, it pays to wait and see if the process generates more favorable outcomes. The asymmetry in the acquisition and dissolution results supports strongly the interpretation that joint ventures are designed as options.

CONCLUSION

This article has investigated the proposition that joint ventures are designed as options that are exercised through a divestment and acquisition decision. The statistical investigation analyzes what factors increase the likelihood of an acquisition. These factors have been shown to be unexpected increases in the value of the venture and the degree of concentration in the industry.

There is a wider implication of this study for theories of organizational behavior. At least since Knight's (1921) observations, it has been widely claimed that risk reduction can be achieved through organizational mechanisms, or what Cyert and March (1963) labelled "uncertainty reduction." But firms, if not other organizations, may also profit from uncertainty.[18] Such profit taking might be achieved through a more flexible production process or organizational design, as described by Piore and Sabel (1984). It might also be achieved by investments in joint ventures which serve as platforms for possible future development. After decades of research on the mechanisms of reducing risk, a look focusing at the way which organizations benefit from uncertainty appears promising.[19,20]

NOTES

1   See Myers (1984) for an interesting qualitative discussion of real options and Mason and Merton (1985) for an extensive analytical treatment.

2   See Kester (1984) for an interesting tabulation of the option value of many large firms.

3   For a study of joint ventures in the oil industry, see Mead (1967). Note, however, that the decision whether to pump the oil can be viewed analytically as an option to wait. See McDonald and Siegel (1986).

4   See Contractor (1985) for an analysis of joint ventures with resulting side payments.

5   Variations on the waiting to invest option are given in McDonald and Siegel (1986), Majd and Pindyck (1987), and Pindyck (1988). Kulatilaka (1988) provides a general formulation, allowing for switching between active and wait modes.

6 This explanation is incomplete without a consideration why a joint venture is favored over alternatives. For a discussion, see Kogut (1988).

7 *Ex ante*, the value of the option is determined not only by the known parameters, but also the stochastic process determining the value of the venture.

8 As the acquisition price is likely to be state dependent, it is important to note that McDonald and Siegel (1986) provide a solution for an option where the value of the underlying asset and exercise price are both stochastic.

9 The comments of one of the referees helped clarify the necessity of both conditions. See also Doz and Schuen (1988) for a discussion of negotiating problems stemming from different evaluations of the venture's growth potential.

10 See also Kunreuther (1969) and the analysis of similar "bootstrapping" models in psychology by Camerer (1981).

11 See Tversky and Kahneman (1982) and the discussion in Hogarth (1982, pp. 38–42).

12 In the sampling process, some of the joint ventures were reported as starting up later and, in a few cases, earlier than the initial time span.

13 The lag is motivated by pragmatic and design concerns. Since the shipment data ends in 1986, a lag would have been necessary for the ventures surviving to 1987. Also, as the ventures can terminate at any time during a given year and as the termination date usually follows by several months the decision, it is more conservative to take the lag value.

14 See Allison (1984) and Kalbfleisch and Prentice (1980) for the treatment of tied data.

15 Though the coefficient to *Annual Growth* is larger, they are not comparable due to the differences in their measurement.

16 As concentration is only published for every fourth year, we took the starting year closest to the year of birth of the venture and the closing year closest to the year of termination or censorship.

17 For an analysis of the dissolution of joint ventures, see Kogut (1989).

18 In some cases, they may even seek higher risk (Myers, 1977; Bowman, 1980).

19 One of the more interesting directions of population ecology is the comparison between strategies which differ by their ability to survive under varying conditions of risk. See, for example, Brittain and Freeman (1980).

20 The author would like to acknowledge the research assistance and suggestions of Kristiaan Helsen and the comments of Ned Bowman, Colin Camerer, Weijian Shan, Gordon Walker, and the anonymous referees. The research has been funded under a grant from AT&T under the auspices of the Reginald H. Jones Center.

REFERENCES

Allison, P. D., *Event History Analysis: Regression for Longitudinal Event Data*, Sage Publications, Beverly Hills, 1984.

Balakrishnan, S. and M. Koza, "Information Asymmetry, Market Failure and Joint Ventures," mimeo, UCLA, 1988.

Bowman, E. H., "Consistency and Optimality in Managerial Decision Making," *Management Sci.*, 9 (1963), 310–321.

——, "A Risk/Return Paradox for Strategic Management," *Sloan Management Rev.*, 21 (1980), 17–31.

Brittain, J. W. and J. H. Freeman, "Organizational Proliferation and Density-Dependent Selection: Organizational Evolution in the Semiconductor Industry," in J. R. Kimberly and R. M. Miles (Eds.), *The Organizational Life Cycle*, Jossey Bass, San Francisco, CA, 1980.

Camerer, C., "General Conditions for the Success of Bootstrapping Models," *Organizational Behavior and Human Performance*, 27 (1981), 411–422.

Christensen, H. K. and C. A. Montgomery, "Corporate Economic Performance: Diversification Strategy Versus Market Structure," *Strategic Management J.*, 2 (1981), 327–343.

Contractor, F., "A Generalized Theorem for Joint Ventures and Licensing Negotiations," *J. International Business Studies*, 16 (1985), 23–50.

Cox, D. R., "Regression Models and Life Data," *J. Royal Statistical Society*, (B) 34 (1972), 187–202.

Cyert, R. M. and J. G. March, *A Behavioral Theory of the Firm*, Prentice-Hall, Englewood Cliffs, NJ, 1963.

Doz, Y. and A. Shuen, "From Intent to Outcome: A Process Framework for Partnerships," INSEAD, working papers, 1988.

Efron, B., "The Efficiency of Cox's Likelihood for Censored Data," *J. Amer. Statistical Assoc.*, 72 (1977), 557–564.

Hannan, M. and J. Freeman, "The Population Ecology of Organizations," *Amer. J. Sociology*, 82 (1977), 929–964.

Harrigan, K., *Managing for Joint Venture Success*, Lexington Books, Lexington, MA, 1986.

Hogarth, R. M., *Judgment and Choice*, Wiley, New York, 1982.

Hull, J., *Options, Futures, and Other Derivative Securities*, Englewood Cliffs, Prentice-Hall, NJ, 1989.

Kalbfleisch, J. D. and R. L. Prentice, *The Statistical Analysis of Failure Time Data*, Wiley, New York, 1980.

Kester, W., "Today's Options for Tomorrow's Growth," *Harvard Business Rev.*, (March–April 1984).

Knight, F. H., *Risk, Uncertainty, and Profit*, University of Chicago, Chicago, IL, 1971; originally published, Houghton-Mifflin, Boston, MA, 1921.

Kogut, B., "Joint Ventures: Theoretical and Empirical Perspectives," *Strategic Management J.*, 9 (1988), 319–332.

—, "The Stability of Joint Ventures: Reciprocity and Competitive Rivalry," *J. Industrial Economics*, 38 (1989).

Kulatilaka, N., "The Value of Real Options," unpublished manuscript, Boston University, 1988.

Kunreuther, H., "Extensions of Bowman's Theory on Managerial Decision Making," *Management Sci.*, 15 (1969), 415–439.

Lyles, M. A., "Learning among Joint Venture Firms," *Management Internat. Rev.*, 28 (1988), 85–97.

McDonald, and D. Siegel, "The Value of Waiting to Invest," *Quart. J. Economics*, 101 (1986), 707–728.

McKelvey, B. and H. Aldrich, "Populations, Natural Selection and Applied Organizational Science," *Administration Sci. Quart.*, 20 (1983), 509–525.

Majd, S. and R. Pindyck, "Time to Build, Option Value, and Investment Decisions," *J. Financial Economics*, 18 (1987), 7–27.

Mason, S. and R. Merton, "The Role of Contingent Claims Analysis in Corporate Finance," in *Recent Advances in Corporate Finance* (E. Altman and M. Subrahmanyam, Eds.), Irwin, New York, 1985.

Mitchell, G. R. and W. F. Hamilton, "Managing R&D as a Strategic Option," *Research-Technology*, 31 (1988), 15–22.

Mead, W., "Competitive Significance of Joint Ventures," *Antitrust Bull.*, 12 (1967).

Myers, S. C., "Determinants of Corporate Borrowing," *J. Financial Economics*, 5 (1977), 147–176.

——, "Finance Theory and Financial Strategy," *Interfaces*, 14 (1984), 126–137.

Nelson, R. R. and S. G. Winter, *An Evolutionary Theory of Economic Change*, Harvard University Press, Cambridge, MA, 1982.

Pfeffer, J. and P. Nowak, "Joint Ventures and Interorganizational Interdependence," *Administrative Sci. Quart.*, 21 (1976), 315–339.

Pindyck, R., "Irreversible Commitment, Capacity Choice, and the Value of the Firm," *American Economic Rev.*, 78 (1988), 967–985.

Piore, M. and C. Sabel, *The Second Industrial Divide*, Basic Books, New York, 1984.

Shan, W., "An Analysis of Organizational Strategies by Enterpreneurial High-Technology Firms," working paper, Sol C. Snider Enterpreneurial Center, Wharton School, 1988.

Teece, D., "Profiting from Technological Innovation: Implications for Integration, Collaboration, Licensing, and Public Policy," in *The Competitive Challenge, Strategies for Industrial Innovation and Renewal*, Ballinger, Cambridge, MA, 1987.

Tversky, A. and D. Kahneman, "Belief in the Law of Small Numbers," *Psychological Bull.*, 2 (1971), 105–110.

—— and ——, "Evidential Impact of Base Rates," in *Judgement under Uncertainty: Heuristics and Biases* (D. Kahneman, P. Slovic, and A. Tversky, Eds.), Cambridge University Press, Cambridge, UK, 1982.

Wernerfelt, B. and A. Karnani, "Competitive Strategy under Uncertainty," *Strategic Management J.*, 8 (1987), 187–194.

Kohut, B. (1991) "Joint ventures and the option to expand and acquire". *Management Science*, 37, 19–33. Reprinted with permission.

International expansion through start-up or acquisition: a learning perspective

7

Harry G. Barkema and Freek Vermeulen

Firms can internationalize in a number of ways, including through exports, licensing, and foreign direct investments (e.g., Dunning, 1980, 1988). Foreign direct investments (FDIs) have increased dramatically over the last few decades, both in relative and absolute terms, reaching annual growth rates of nearly 30 percent and a worldwide total of about $1.5 trillion in the late 1980s (United Nations, 1991, 1993). An extensive literature examines ownership of FDIs – whether firms expand alone or with one or more partners (e.g., Gatignon and Anderson, 1988; Gomes-Casseres, 1989; Hennart, 1988, 1991). A second literature, which has attracted less research so far, focuses on another dimension of FDIs: whether ventures are set up from scratch (i.e., start-ups or greenfield investments) or whether they are acquired (i.e., acquisitions). Various scholars have recently emphasized that the latter dimension of foreign direct investment is underresearched (Chang, 1995; Melin, 1992). We sought to extend this tradition and to shed light on what motivates the strategic choice to expand internationally through either start-ups (wholly owned or partly owned) or acquisitions.

Previous studies in this tradition have examined the influence of a variety of factors (for instance, cultural distance, multinational experience, firm size, and gross national product of the host country) on this strategic choice (Caves and Mehra, 1986; Cho and Padmanabhan, 1995; Hennart and Park, 1993; Zejan, 1990) but have offered no coherent theoretical framework for explanatory variables. The present study used a fresh approach – an organizational learning perspective (Fiol and Lyles, 1985; Huber, 1991) – to develop hypotheses regarding how multinational diversity and multiproduct diversity influence the decision to expand abroad through start-ups or acquisitions. A key insight was that a firm which operates in diverse national settings and product settings can develop a rich knowledge structure and strong technological capabilities. These capabilities in turn increase the firm's propensity to set up a new venture in a foreign country rather than acquire an existing local company. In sum, a firm's strategic posture, in terms of its multinational diversity and multiproduct diversity, influences whether it expands abroad through start-ups or acquisitions. We also explored interaction effects between multinational diversity and product diversity (cf. Hitt, Hoskisson, and Ireland, 1994; Tallman and Li, 1996).

Hypotheses were tested on data about the foreign start-ups and acquisitions of 25 large Dutch firms over a period spanning almost three decades (1966–94). These firms began to increase their FDIs in the late 1960s or later, starting almost from scratch. The sample contained data on 829 start-ups and acquisitions in 72 countries. The Netherlands is currently the sixth largest foreign investor, after the United States, Japan, Germany, the United Kingdom, and France.

BACKGROUND

Learning from diversity

Experience is a prime source of learning in organizations (Penrose, 1959). Learning is fostered by diversity in experience. Operating in diverse circumstances increases the variety of events and ideas to which a firm is exposed (Huber, 1991), leading to a more extensive knowledge base and stronger technological capabilities (cf. Hedberg, 1981; March, 1991). Learning different ways of doing things fosters innovation (Mezias and Glyn, 1993). Managers and workers with experience in a variety of environments are more productive than workers without such experience (Walsh, 1995). CEOs of internationally diversified firms have richer knowledge structures than CEOs of domestic firms (Calori, Johnson, and Sarnin, 1994). The greater diversity in the knowledge of managers and other workers aggregates to richer knowledge structures at the level of the firm (Walsh, 1995), and stronger technological capabilities (Cohen and Levinthal, 1989, 1990, 1994).

Firms that remain within one industry in one particular country, with familiar opportunities and threats and familiar routines with which to handle them (cf. Huff, 1982; Reger and Huff, 1993), may perform well in the short run (Miller, 1993, 1994). However, repeated spirals of competition and cooperation within the familiar setting lead to blindness to opportunities and threats that transcend the specific setting (Abrahamson and Fombrun, 1994; Leonard-Barton, 1992; Levinthal and March, 1993; Levitt and March, 1988). Companies that deal with relatively few competitors and customers have a narrower range of experience and narrower mental models because they confront a more limited range of challenges. This narrowness hurts performance in the long run if conditions change (Miller and Chen, 1994, 1996). Case studies have indeed shown that blind spots or holes in knowledge structures cause failures (Walsh, 1995).

In contrast, managers who receive a wide range of information can spot problems they would have missed if their vision were narrower (Kiesler and Sproull, 1982). An organization that operates in diverse national and/or product markets has a wider range of organizations that managers can imitate. The infusion of new ideas and new practices sparks innovations and boosts technological capabilities (cf. Abrahamson and Fombrun, 1994; Miller and Chen, 1994, 1996). New markets confront the firm with new consumer needs and new testing grounds for its (core) technology, which triggers new solutions and stronger technological skills (Argyres, 1996a). Moreover, operating in national and product markets that are initially unfamiliar – in terms of customers, suppliers, rivals, and partners – triggers failures, incentives for search (Simon, 1955), and new solutions that further enhance the firm's technological capabilities (Levitt and March, 1988; Miller and Chen, 1994, 1996).

In sum, operating in diverse national markets, product markets, or both enhances a firm's technological capabilities. Firms operating in diverse markets can learn something from each of them (Miller and Chen, 1996). However, learning from market diversity is subject to organizational constraints.

Organizational constraints

When a group of individuals is brought together, each with his or her own knowledge about particular information environments, some kind of collective knowledge structure is likely to emerge (Walsh, 1995). However, an important difference between individual learning and organizational learning is that organizational learning depends on information sharing between individuals (Cohen and Levinthal, 1990). Only through communication will individual insights become accessible to others, making cross-fertilization between ideas and knowledge possible (Huber, 1991; Jelinek, 1979). Thus, the learning capacity of an organization is constrained by the flow of information between the individuals in the firm (Brown and Duguid, 1991; Cohen and Levinthal, 1990).

In multidivisional firms, for instance, organizational learning (triggering innovations) depends on links between divisions (Drazin and Schoonhoven, 1996). The greater the number of divisions, the more costly it will be to achieve coordination between them (Argyres, 1996a). If a firm is engaged in many businesses, interrelations between the various businesses fostering mutual learning and capability building are no longer feasible; the amount of information to be processed and assimilated exceeds the individuals' and organization's cognitive limits (cf. Hedberg, 1981; Hill and Hoskisson, 1987; Huber, 1991; Jones and Hill, 1988). The organization becomes too complex, and learning is hampered by information overload. In reaction, highly diversified firms often adopt M-form structures (Chandler, 1962; Fligstein, 1985; Rumelt, 1974, 1982; Williamson, 1975, 1985), employing financial rather than strategic control of divisions by headquarters (Baysinger and Hoskisson, 1989; Hoskisson and Hitt, 1988; Hoskisson, Hitt, and Hill, 1993) and little communication between highly independent divisions. In sum, learning and capability building based on a presence in a variety of product markets is constrained by organizational limits on information sharing.

Start-up or acquisition?

When a firm expands into a foreign market by establishing a local subsidiary, it has to decide whether to start a new venture or acquire an existing local company. Foreign start ups (or greenfield investments, or de novo entries) entail building an entirely new organization in a foreign country from scratch. Companies often establish start-ups by sending over expatriates who carefully select and hire employees from the local population (Hofstede, 1991) and gradually build up the business (Simmonds, 1990; Teece, 1982), alone or with a local partner with knowledge of local institutions, local business practices, and so on. Companies often use start-ups to exploit firm-specific advantages that are difficult to separate from the organizations and that are embedded in their labor forces (Hennart and Park, 1993). Japanese firms, for instance, have displayed a clear tendency to establish startups in foreign markets (Cho and Padmanabhan, 1995; Wilson, 1980). Producing clones of the Japanese parents has been the most efficient way to transfer Japanese competitive advantages to the foreign market (Florida and Kenney, 1991; Hennart and Park, 1993). Start-ups allow a parent firm to hire and train a new labor force, which makes it possible to incorporate firm-specific advantages from the outset.

In the case of an acquisition, the expanding firm buys at least part of the equity of an existing firm in a foreign country. The acquisition allows the firm to acquire new technological resources (Prahalad and Hamel, 1990), which substitute for the internal development of technological skills (Hitt, Hoskisson, and Ireland, 1990; Hitt, Hoskisson, Johnson, and Moesel, 1996; Lei and Hitt, 1995; Wernerfelt, 1984). A firm's stock of resources and capabilities at the time of an expansion influences whether it expands through start-ups or through acquisitions (Hoskisson and Hitt, 1990; Wernerfelt, 1984). Firms with few technological capabilities are inclined to obtain technology by acquiring innovative firms (Granstrand and Sjölander, 1990). Alternatively, firms with strong technological abilities have less need to buy existing firms and the technological capabilities they embody and are more likely to enter foreign markets through start-ups (Hennart and Park, 1993).

Organizational inertia. There is also a second reason why firms with strong technological capabilities will be less inclined to acquire existing firms than to set up new ventures in foreign countries. If a firm with strong technological capabilities acquires a local firm with weaker technological capabilities, it will probably need to install its own technology in the acquired company. However, strong inertial forces within organizations prevent even adaptations that appear technologically rational (Nelson and Winter, 1982). "Simply" adopting new technological routines from a parent may not be sufficient. The new technology may require the acquired firm to learn new rules, procedures, conventions, and organizational strategies (cf. Levitt and March, 1988). This is particularly difficult if these new rules, procedures, conventions, and strategies do not match the beliefs, codes, knowledge, and culture of the acquired firm.

Moreover, being acquired by a firm with a different culture may cause tensions and hostility, and the acquired firm may be reluctant to implement the required changes. Indeed, many studies have found that cultural differences increase the probability that acquisitions will fail (Buono and Bowditch, 1989; Cartwright and Cooper, 1993; Chatterjee, Lubatkin, Schweiger, and Weber, 1992; Datta, 1991; Haspeslagh and Jemison, 1991; Jemison and Sitkin, 1986), particularly if the two firms are rooted in different national cultures (Barkema, Bell, and Pennings, 1996; Calori, Lubatkin, and Very, 1994; Hofstede, 1980, 1983; Schneider and DeMeyer, 1991; Weber, Shenkar, and Raveh, 1996).

Bringing about fundamental change, or higher-level learning (Argyris and Schön, 1978; Fiol and Lyles, 1985; Lant and Mezias, 1992), is very difficult for organizations (Romanelli and Tushman, 1994; Tushman and Romanelli, 1985; Tushman and O'Reilly, 1996). The acquired firm needs to unlearn (cf. Bettis and Prahalad, 1995; Hedberg, 1981; Prahalad and Bettis, 1986) old routines in the areas of technology, rules, procedures, conventions, and strategies and perhaps needs to unlearn beliefs, codes, culture, and knowledge as well before new routines can be learned. Hofstede (1980, 1991) defined culture as "programming of the mind" (1991: 5). Unlearning a culture, or reprogramming minds, may be difficult or impossible. If the technology of an acquiring firm is vastly superior and does not relate to the existing knowledge structure of the acquired company, the latter will be unable to assimilate the new technology and apply it to commercial ends (Cohen and Levinthal, 1989, 1990; Greenwood and Hinings, 1996; Herriott, Levinthal, and March, 1985).

Conclusion. In sum, firms with strong technological capabilities are less inclined to undertake acquisitions than start-ups for two reasons. First, existing firms have relatively little to offer them in terms of technological skills. Second, if acquiring firms have superior technological capabilities, it may be difficult or impossible to bring these capabilities into the acquired companies because of organizational inertia. Hence, it may be easier to set up a new venture that is not entrenched in old routines (Bettis and Prahalad, 1995; Prahalad and Bettis, 1986; Leonard-Barton, 1992; Miller, 1993; Miller and Chen, 1994, 1996). New ventures are starting with a clean slate and "do not have the problem of having to run down an unlearning curve in order to be able to run up a learning curve" (Bettis and Prahalad, 1995: 10). Parent firms can send over employees to select, hire, and train workers from the local population and implement firm-specific advantages (technology and embedding rules, procedures, conventions, beliefs, knowledge, etc.) from the outset in a start-up but cannot do so in an acquisition. Consistent with this view, various studies have found that a parent's R&D level increases the likelihood that foreign expansions are start-ups rather than acquisitions (Anderson and Svensson, 1994; Cho and Padmanabhan, 1995; Hennart and Park, 1993).

HYPOTHESES

The theory in the background section suggests that a firm's multinational diversity and multiproduct diversity influence its technological capabilities. These capabilities in turn influence its propensity to set up a new venture in a foreign country rather than to acquire an existing local company. Below, we develop hypotheses on how a firm's strategic posture, in terms of its multinational diversity and product diversity, affect its propensity to expand internationally through start-ups or acquisitions.

Multinational diversity

Geographical diversity exposes a firm to a rich array of environments, which leads to higher innovation levels (Ghoshal, 1987; Kim, Hwang, and Burgers, 1993). The diversity of the national markets in which the firm operates confronts it with a broad array of demand characteristics and a large variety of rivals, suppliers, and partners (cf. Abrahamson and Fombrun, 1994; Miller and Chen, 1994, 1996). The additional information – combined with incentives for search triggered by failures in unfamiliar environments – leads to a richer knowledge structure and stronger technological capabilities than purely domestic firms will enjoy. A multinational presence may foster technological capabilities in other ways as well. Foreign sales increase the returns from innovations (Galbraith and Kay, 1986; Hitt et al., 1994; Hymer, 1960; Kim et al., 1993) and allow firms to recoup investments in large-scale R&D operations (Franko, 1989; Kobrin, 1991). Multinational diversity also lowers the risk of innovation, providing a firm with a greater number of national markets from which it can retaliate against competitors (Kogut, 1985) and allowing it to hedge against local fluctuations in supply and demand. The anticipated increased returns and lower risks from R&D projects in multinational firms (cf. Kim et al., 1993) may further boost R&D levels and innovation.

The higher technological capabilities of multinational firms in turn influence their propensity to set up new ventures in foreign countries rather than to take over existing companies. As we argued in the background section, existing firms have relatively little to offer them in terms of technological skills. Furthermore, a multi-national that wants to apply superior technology in a foreign company may need to change existing companies' inappropriate (inert) organizational knowledge structures. Thus,

> **Hypothesis 1**. Multinational diversity increases the propensity of a firm to set up a new venture in a foreign country rather than to acquire an existing company.

Caves and Mehra (1986) and Kogut and Singh (1988) provided previous evidence on the statistical relationship between multinationality and the propensity to expand abroad through start-ups or acquisitions. Kogut and Singh (1988) found a non-significant effect of multinationality on the propensity to set up a new company rather than to acquire one; Caves and Mehra (1986) found a negative effect.[1] However, these studies ignored firms' product diversity (both as a control variable and as a moderating factor) when estimating the influence of multinationality on the choice of foreign entry mode. Furthermore, they examined entries into a single host country (the United States) during a relatively short period of time. These characteristics may have influenced the empirical results of these studies. In the present study, we controlled for product diversity as well as many other factors, and the data on expansions into a large number of countries covered almost three decades.

Product diversity

Like a firm operating in multiple countries, a firm that leverages its technological capabilities into multiple businesses will be exposed to a richer set of demand characteristics (cf. Argyres, 1996a), rivals, suppliers, and partners than a firm operating in a single business. Leveraging technological capabilities into multiple businesses may also lead to economies of scale and scope, which may increase the returns from innovation while spreading the risks (Peteraf, 1993; Teece, 1982). Hence, product diversity also fosters innovation.

However, as previous researchers have argued (see "Background"), if the number of a firm's product lines becomes too large, the cognitive limits of its management team will prevent their comprehending all opportunities and stimuli (cf. Bettis and Prahalad, 1995; Prahalad and Bettis, 1986). Firms that enter many businesses therefore typically adopt M-form structures with rather independent divisions and financial control of divisions by headquarters. This arrangement reduces information sharing between divisions and between divisions and headquarters (Williamson, 1975, 1985), which in turn constrains learning and innovation. Financial controls, furthermore, promote short-term orientations and risk-averse behavior by division managers (Hoskisson, Hitt, and Hill, 1993), which further reduces innovation levels. Consistent with these views, various studies have found that highly diversified firms invest less in R&D (Baysinger and Hoskisson, 1989; Hoskisson and Hitt, 1988).

In sum, we expect product diversity to have a curvilinear relationship to techno-logical capabilities, which will first increase and then decrease when product diversity increases; a plot of the relationship would have an inverted U-shape. We argued earlier that the level of a firm's technological capabilities is related to its propensity to expand through start-ups rather than through acquisitions. Hence, we also expect a curvilinear (an inverted U-shaped) relationship between firms' product diversity and their propensity to expand through start-ups. Furthermore, since highly diversified firms often use financial controls rather than strategic control of divisions (Hoskisson, Hitt, and Hill, 1993), it may be relatively easy for these firms to integrate foreign companies into themselves as, for instance, additional divisions (Chatterjee et al., 1992; Keats and Hitt, 1988; Williamson, 1975). This further increases the probability that highly diversified firms will expand through acquisitions. Formally,

Hypothesis 2. The relationship between a firm's product diversity and its propensity to expand through start-ups rather than acquisitions is curvilinear (an inverted U-shape).

Previous evidence on the linear relationship between product diversity and the choice of a foreign entry mode has been mixed. Some studies have reported that product diversity diminishes a firm's propensity to expand through start-ups (Caves and Mehra, 1986; Zejan, 1990); others have found non-significant effects (Cho and Padmanabhan, 1995; Hennart and Park, 1993; Kogut and Singh, 1988). Our study is the first to explore a nonlinear relationship between product diversity and the propensity to expand through start-ups rather than acquisitions.

Interaction between multinational diversity and multiproduct diversity

The above theory implies that intermediately product-diversified firms have relatively strong technological capabilities because they benefit from multiple learning opportunities while staying within cognitive and organizational limits on information sharing between divisions and between divisions and headquarters (cf. Hitt et al., 1994; Tallman and Li, 1996). Such firms are thus more likely than both single-business firms and highly product-diversified firms to set up new ventures in foreign countries.

However, our reasoning also suggests that intermediately product-diversified firms have relatively little cognitive capacity left with which to handle the further complexities of increasing multinational diversity. In contrast, single-business firms and the rather independent divisions of highly product-diversified firms (Hitt et al., 1994) are less complex and can thus better benefit from expansions into a number of countries (cf. Kim, Hwang, and Burgers, 1989; Tallman and Li, 1996): their specific organizational configuration makes them more likely to benefit from the learning opportunities that multinational diversity offers. In sum, firms with either very low or very high product diversity may reap learning benefits beyond the point where they occur for intermediately diversified firms that already combine several divisions and therefore reach their organizational limits more quickly.

Consequently, we expected multinational diversity to have a relatively strong positive effect on the technological capabilities of single-business firms and on highly product-diversified firms and, thus, on their propensity to set up new ventures in foreign countries. That is, we expected the curvilinear relationship between product diversity and the propensity to start new ventures (an inverted U-shape) to become weaker (cf. Tallman and Li, 1996) at higher levels of multinational diversity. Formally,

Hypothesis 3. The curvilinear (inverted U-shaped) relationship between product diversity and the propensity to set up new ventures in foreign countries becomes weaker at higher levels of multinational diversity.

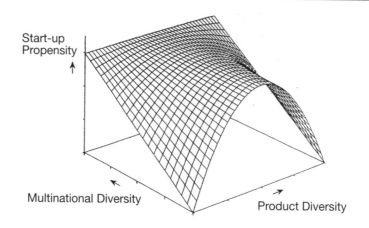

Figure 1 Hypothesized relationships.

The hypothesized relationships between multinational diversity, product diversity, and the propensity to expand through start-ups rather than acquisitions (cf. Hypotheses 1–3) are depicted in Figure 1.

Product relatedness

Firms adapt their routines incrementally to experience, which leads to idiosyncratic technological paradigms and trajectories (Nelson and Winter, 1982). Such growth also implies that the firms' current knowledge bases limit the steps they can take (Cohen and Levinthal, 1990). Individuals (Ellis, 1965; Singley and Anderson, 1989) as well as organizations (Anderson, Farrell, and Sauers, 1984; Barkema, Shenkar, Vermeulen, and Bell, 1997; Cohen, 1991; Cohen and Bacdayan, 1994; Nelson and Winter, 1982) can apply and build on existing organizational routines if new production environments are related to those in which the routines were developed. In contrast, a transfer of routines may be impossible if a new environment is predominantly novel (Cohen and Bacdayan, 1994; Ellis, 1965; Singley and Anderson, 1989).

If a firm expands abroad in its own core business (Prahalad and Hamel, 1990), pursuing a horizontal expansion, it can transfer existing organizational routines to the new venture: the firm may replicate itself on foreign soil (Florida and Kenney, 1991; Hennart and Park, 1993; Nelson, 1991). If the firm expands into another business that is proximate to its core business, pursuing a related expansion, existing routines can be fairly easily modified to fit the new situation. Similarly, in the case of a vertical expansion, the firm may be able to apply its knowledge up or down the value chain (Argyres, 1996b; d'Aveni and Ravenscraft, 1994; Pennings, Barkema, and Douma, 1994). In contrast, a firm pursuing an unrelated expansion (e.g., Ramanujam and Varadarajan, 1989) may find it difficult or impossible to build on existing routines, and the firm may have to take over an existing firm and acquire the needed technological capabilities.

This formulation suggests that if a firm expands into a familiar business, through horizontal, related, or vertical expansion, it may transfer existing technological skills and routines to the new venture and set the latter up from scratch. In contrast, if the firm expands into an unfamiliar business, it is less likely to be able to build on existing routines, and it is more likely that it will have to buy the needed capabilities – that is, to take over an existing firm (Caves and Mehra, 1986; Harrison, Hitt, Hoskisson, and Ireland, 1991; Wernerfelt, 1984). Furthermore, the bureaucratic costs of integrating related acquisitions (horizontal, related, and vertical) into a firm are typically higher than the costs of implementing unrelated acquisitions (cf. Jones and Hill, 1988), particularly if the parent firm and the acquired company are rooted in different national cultures (cf. Calori et al., 1994), which further increases the probability that related expansions into foreign countries will be start-ups. Moreover, research by Harrison and colleagues (1991) has suggested that differences rather than similarities between the resources of acquiring and target firms produce synergies. Therefore, unrelated acquisitions might be attractive. This discussion suggests the following hypothesis:

> **Hypothesis 4**. Horizontal, related, and vertical expansions into foreign countries are more likely to be start-ups, and unrelated expansions are more likely to be acquisitions.

METHODS

Sample and analysis

The sample contained data on the foreign ventures of 25 large nonfinancial Dutch firms. These firms were active in a wide variety of industries: in the manufacture of office equipment, precision machinery, paper and packaging, food products, and pharmaceutical and chemical products and in brewing, publishing and printing, retailing, trading, tank storage, and many other industries. The firms were selected in the following way: We selected all nonfinancial firms listed on the Amsterdam Stock Exchange in 1993.[2] No data were gathered about the four largest firms (Royal Dutch, Unilever, Philips, Akzo) since they differed considerably from other firms in terms of breadth of activities, international experience, scope, and size. The average number of employees in the remaining 25 firms was 13,907, with a median of 10,327. Their average sales amounted to $2,566 million (US) in 1993, with a median of $1,898 million. The average percentage of sales abroad was 63 percent, with a median of 63 percent.

The database contained information on all start-ups and acquisitions reported in the annual reports of these firms between 1966 and 1994. This window was chosen because the FDIs of these firms began to increase around the mid-1960s or later, starting almost from scratch. The total number of these firms' foreign expansions in this period was 829; 595 were acquisitions and 234 were start-ups. Of these ventures, 441 acquisitions and 148 start-ups were fully owned by the Dutch firm; 154 acquisitions were partly owned, and 86 start-ups were initiated with a local partner in the foreign country. The entries were distributed across 72 countries. Table 1 gives the geographical distribution of these start-ups and acquisitions.

We tested the hypotheses using binomial "logit" models regarding the choice to start a new venture in a foreign country rather than to acquire an existing company. Using binomial choice models is the conventional method of analysis in the foreign entry mode literature (e.g., Caves and Mehra, 1986; Hennart and Park, 1993; Zejan, 1990).

Table 1 Geographical distribution of the observations

Expansion type	Europe	North America	Latin and South America	Asia	Africa	Australia	Total
Start-up	104	34	34	44	12	6	234
Acquisition	343	168	26	20	18	20	595

Variables

Mode of foreign entry. A venture was called an acquisition if it entailed the takeover of another company (or one of its business units) in which the Dutch firm did not previously have an ownership stake; it was called a start-up if it was a subsidiary newly established by the Dutch firm, alone or with one or more partners.

Multinational diversity. Multinational diversity – the number of different national settings in which a firm operated at the time of an expansion – was measured by the number of countries in which the firm had established subsidiaries at the time of the expansion (cf. Caves and Mehra, 1986; Kogut and Singh, 1988).

Product diversity. Product diversity was measured by the number of three-digit Standaard Bedrijfs Indeling (SBI) codes[3] in which the firm was active at the time of the expansion (cf. Lubatkin, Merchant, and Srinivasan, 1993).

Product relatedness. An expansion was coded as horizontal if it took place within the same three-digit SBI category as the core activities of the firm, as related if it took place within the same two-digit SBI category but not in the same three-digit category, as vertical if it took place within the firm's value-added chain, and as unrelated if none of the other three categories applied (cf. Pennings et al., 1994). Summary statistics for this and other variables are presented in Table 2.

Control variables

Ownership. This dummy had a value of 1 if the expansion was wholly owned by the Dutch multinational; if not, it was coded 0.

Return on equity. Managers of highly profitable firms may use the firms' "free cash flow" for outright acquisitions of other companies to increase their power, prestige, and salary, even if these acquisitions do not enhance firm value (Finkelstein and Hambrick, 1989; Jensen, 1986). We used return on equity (ROE) as a proxy for firm profitability.

Firm size. In general, larger firms have more resources. Previous evidence on the influence of firm size on the propensity to acquire is mixed (cf. Kogut and Singh, 1988). We nevertheless controlled for the size of the multinational, using the logarithm of its assets as our measure.

Cultural distance. Cultural differences between the home country of the expanding firm and the host country may increase the probability that firms expand through start-ups rather than through acquisitions (Cho and Padmanabhan, 1995; Kogut and Singh, 1988). We measured the cultural distance between the host country and the home country (i.e., the Netherlands) using Kogut and Singh's (1988) index. This index is based on Hofstede's four cultural dimensions (Hofstede, 1980).[4] The index has been used in many other studies of foreign entry (e.g., Agarwal and Ramaswami, 1992; Barkema et al., 1996; Benito and Gripsrud, 1992). The scores for individual countries were obtained from Hofstede (1980, 1991). The scores of the few countries

Table 2 Means, standard deviations, and correlations[a]

Variable	Mean	SD	1	2	3	4	5	6	7	8	9	10	11	12	13	14	15	16	17	18	19
1. Start-up	0.28	0.45																			
2. Multinational diversity	9.04	5.99	.02																		
3. Product diversity	8.83	5.15	.11	.21																	
4. Horizontal expansion	0.64	0.48	.02	.08	−12																
5. Related expansion	0.13	0.33	−.00	−.10	.14	−.50															
6. Vertical expansion	0.15	0.36	−.01	−.01	−.10	−.55	−.15														
7. Unrelated expansion	0.08	0.28	−.00	−.02	.17	−.40	−.11	−.13													
8. Cultural distance	2.27	0.79	.22	.08	.12	.02	−.02	−.03	.03												
9. Local experience	2.84	4.17	−.28	.24	−.01	−.07	−.04	−.09	−.04	−.20											
10. Return on equity	0.15	0.14	−.23	.05	−.27	−.09	−.15	.09	−.09	−.09	−.27										
11. Time[b]	2.66	0.69	−.28	.51	.04	−.06	.04	.08	−.05	−.10	.38	.30									
12. Legal restrictions	0.17	0.38	.26	−.13	.03	.03	−.02	−.03	.03	.15	−.21	−.15	−.34								
13. Low country risk	0.75	0.43	−.31	−.13	−.16	−.10	.06	.03	.07	−.33	.31	.12	.15	−.32							
14. Medium country risk	0.18	0.38	.27	.03	.03	.08	−.02	−.02	−.08	.27	−.25	−.08	−.04	.30	−.80						
15. High country risk	0.08	0.26	.12	.16	.22	.06	−.07	−.02	−.00	.13	−.14	−.08	−.18	.09	−.49	−.13					
16. Real GNP	1.15	1.48	−.22	.10	−.01	−.06	−.03	.12	−.02	−.32	.57	.17	.29	−.28	.38	−.31	−.18				
17. GNP growth	0.06	0.22	−.01	−.07	−.07	.03	.02	−.04	−.02	−.01	−.06	−.05	−.07	−.02	.02	.04	−.09	−.06			
18. GNP per capita	1.22	3.35	.02	.13	.09	−.08	−.01	.13	−.01	−.03	.04	.04	.08	−.08	.04	−.11	.09	.28	.01		
19. Wholly owned subsidiary	0.71	0.45	−.11	−.01	.00	.01	.02	.00	−.05	−.22	.17	.17	.11	−.18	.22	−.12	−.18	.19	−.05	.07	
20. Size	13.4	1.13	−.17	.24	.24	−.11	.14	−.02	.06	−.06	.18	−.12	.47	−.20	.11	−.01	−.17	.11	−.06	−.01	−.14

[a] $N = 829$. Correlations with absolute value greater than .06 are significant at the 5 percent level.
[b] Variable is a logarithm.

not listed in these sources were determined through personal communication with Hofstede.

Local experience. Firms may learn how to handle acquisitions from their previous experience in a host country, which makes acquisitions in that country more likely. Previous evidence on the influence of local experience is mixed (cf. Hennart and Park, 1993; Hennart and Reddy, 1977; Kogut and Singh, 1988). We nevertheless controlled for a firm's local experience, using the number of its previous entries into the host country as our measure (cf. Kogut and Singh, 1988).

Gross national product (GNP). Both the size and the growth of a local market may influence the mode of foreign entry (Gomes-Casseres, 1989, 1990; Larimo, 1993; Shane, 1993; Zejan, 1990). Three control variables were used: the size of the host country market, measured as real GNP in the year of entry; the growth of the market, measured as the growth in GNP in the year of entry (Gomes-Casseres, 1990; Zejan, 1990); and the level of development of the host country, measured as GNP per capita in the year of entry (cf. Wilson, 1980; Zejan, 1990).

Legal restrictions. Numerous countries are known to impose, or to have imposed, legal restrictions on foreign ownership of local enterprises (Contractor, 1990; Gomes-Casseres, 1990). Many countries relaxed those restrictions around the 1980s; others did so at other times, or did not do so at all during our window of analysis. Using various publications from the United Nations, we defined a dummy variable measuring whether or not the host country imposed such legislation at the time of an expansion. A score of 1 indicated legal restrictions on foreign ownership; 0 indicated the absence of such restrictions.

Country risk. We used the three clusters of country risk developed by Goodnow and Hansz (1972). They classified countries as presenting either low, medium, or high risk to investment on the basis of pre-1970 data. For a few countries, this classification did not seem representative for our window of analysis (1966–94). Therefore, we compared Goodnow and Hansz's classification with more recent data published by *Euromoney*, which has been publishing a consistent measure of country risk since 1982. If an individual country's average score differed from its cluster's average by more than one standard deviation, we assigned it to the next cluster.

Time dummy variables. Since the 1980s, there has been a general tendency to acquire companies – a takeover wave – for reasons that may not be captured by our hypotheses. In the United States, prime triggers of the takeover wave were relaxation of antitrust regulations under the Reagan administration (Shleifer and Vishny, 1991) and tax policy changes (Hoskisson and Hitt, 1990). This takeover wave may have triggered similar developments in other countries, perhaps because of mimetic behavior (cf. DiMaggio and Powell, 1983; Haveman, 1993). Zejan (1990) used a linear time variable on data about Swedish firms and found that acquisitions increased during his window of analysis. A take-over wave motivated by reasons other than those captured by our hypotheses may have occurred in the Netherlands as well.

The importance of controlling for such an autonomous trend is illustrated in Figure 2, which contains *hypothetical* data points about the propensity of firms to set up new ventures and about their multinational diversity, in 1970 and 1990. If the time component is ignored, the dotted line emerges when the effect of multinational diversity on the propensity to set up new ventures is estimated. In contrast, explicitly modeling the time component through a time dummy reveals the expected relationship. Since we do not know the exact relationship between time and reasons for entry

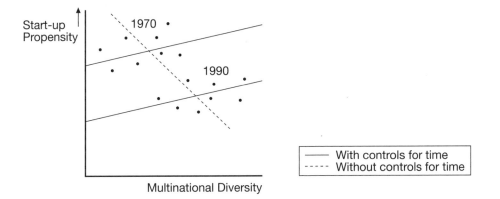

Figure 2 Start-up propensity and multinational diversity with and without controls for time.

mode choices during our window (1966–94) other than the ones captured by our hypotheses, we began our analysis by using $(T - 1)$ time dummy controls.

Firm dummy variables. Pitts (1977, 1980) argued that expansion through internal development and expansion through acquisitions are two pure strategies: firms either choose one strategy or the other (cf. Amburgey and Miner, 1992). Lamont and Anderson (1985) could not confirm this prediction for highly diversified US firms. We nevertheless controlled for firm-specific propensities to expand through start-ups or through acquisitions, using dummy variables for firm.

RESULTS

Hypotheses

The estimation results are presented in Table 3. Model 1 provides some first evidence on the hypotheses (the effects of the time and firm dummy variables are not shown in the table).[5] Hypothesis 1 predicts that multinational diversity increases preference for start-ups. The parameter estimate of the effect of multinational diversity is highly significant ($p < .001$) and in the expected direction, which offers strong support for Hypothesis 1. Hypothesis 2 predicts a curvilinear (inverted U-shaped) relationship between a firm's product diversity and its propensity to expand through start-ups rather than acquisitions. Consistent with Hypothesis 2, the coefficient of product diversity is positive and significant ($p < .05$), and the coefficient of product diversity squared is negative and significant ($p < .01$), indicating that an initial preference for start-ups changes toward a preference for acquisitions at higher levels of product diversity.

Hypothesis 3 predicts that the curvilinear relationship becomes weaker at higher levels of multinational diversity. We therefore expected that both the effect of product diversity (which captures initial increase in a preference for start-ups) and the effect of product diversity squared (which captures the change in favor of acquisitions) diminish at higher levels of multinational diversity. Thus, we expected that the signs of the interactions between multinational diversity and product diversity and between multinational diversity and product diversity squared (cf. Tallman and Li, 1996) would be opposite to those of the main effects of product diversity and of product diversity squared. Consistent with our predictions, the first interactive effect is negative and significant ($p < .001$), and the second is positive and significant ($p < .001$).

Figure 3 shows the *estimated* relationships between multinational diversity, product diversity, and a firm's relative preference for start-ups over acquisitions (keeping other variables constant).

Figure 3 shows a curvilinear relationship between product diversity and the propensity for start-ups at low levels of multinational diversity. The inverted U-shape disappears at higher levels of multinational diversity. Figure 3 furthermore suggests that intermediately product-diversified firms are hardly affected by multinational diversity in terms of their propensity for start-ups in foreign countries. Figure 3 even suggests that the inverted U-shape turns into a U-shape at high levels of multinational diversity. However, careful inspection of the data reveals that there are hardly any data points (start-ups or acquisitions of multinationals in our sample) that combine high levels of multinational diversity with either very high or very low

Table 3 Results of logit models: start-up versus acquisition[a]

Variable	Model 1		Model 2		Model 3	
Intercept	–4.482**	(1.712)	–2.701[†]	(1.635)	–5.800**	(1.924)
Multinational diversity	0.267***	(0.065)	0.272***	(0.067)	0.298***	(0.070)
Product diversity	0.332*	(0.132)	0.459***	(0.137)	0.515***	(0.141)
Product diversity squared	–0.016**	(0.005)	–0.020***	(0.006)	–0.022***	(0.006)
Multinational diversity × product diversity	–0.049***	(0.015)	–0.062***	(0.015)	-0.069***	(0.016)
Multinational diversity × product diversity squared	0.002***	(0.001)	0.002***	(0.001)	0.003***	(0.001)
Horizontal expansion	–0.209	(0.371)	–0.196	(0.365)	3.372**	(1.134)
Related expansion	0.256	(0.442)	–0.031	(0.441)	3.561*	(1.587)
Vertical expansion	0.249	(0.448)	0.338	(0.437)	3.376*	(1.580)
Cultural distance	0.244*	(0.099)	0.248**	(0.096)	0.257**	(0.097)
Local experience	–0.251***	(0.062)	–0.218***	(0.059)	–0.223***	(0.059)
Return on equity	–3.412***	(1.046)	–3.430**	(1.104)	–3.479**	(1.118)
Time[b]			–0.730**	(0.235)		
Horizontal expansion × time					–0.766**	(0.262)
Related expansion × time					–0.771[†]	(0.481)
Vertical expansion × time					–0.559	(0.464)
Unrelated expansion × time					0.704[†]	(0.409)
Legal restrictions	0.511*	(0.259)	0.512*	(0.248)	0.539*	(0.250)
Medium country risk	1.209***	(0.293)	1.108***	(0.305)	1.139***	(0.287)
High country risk	0.370	(0.441)	–0.022	(0.441)	–0.010	(0.427)
Real GNP	–0.002	(0.102)	–0.003	(0.102)	–0.019	(0.102)
GNP growth	0.538	(0.447)	–0.095	(0.459)	–0.172	(0.470)
GNP per capita	0.005	(0.013)	0.007	(0.019)	0.005	(0.013)
Wholly owned subsidiary	0.096	(0.235)	–0.056	(0.220)	–0.002	(0.220)
Size[b]	0.054	(0.121)	–0.047	(0.120)	–0.001	(0.121)
Log likelihood	–332		–355		–351	
Percentage correct	80.0		78.5		79.0	

[a] $N = 829$; start-up = 1. In model 1, dummy variables for time are not shown. In models 1, 2, and 3, dummy variables for firm are not shown. Numbers in parentheses are standard deviations.
[b] Variable is a logarithm.
[†] $p < .10$; * $p < .05$; ** $p < .01$; *** $p < .001$.
All two-tailed tests.

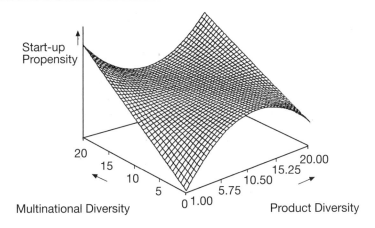

Figure 3 Estimated relationships.

levels of product diversity. Thus, the U-shape at high levels of multinational diversity appears to be driven by the extrapolation of patterns existing at lower levels of multinational diversity rather than by actual observations.

Hypothesis 4 predicts that horizontal, related, and vertical expansions into foreign countries are more likely to be start-ups and that unrelated expansions are more likely to be acquisitions. However, the coefficients of the three dummy variables for product relatedness (unrelated was the omitted category) are nonsignificant and do not support the hypothesis.

Results for the dummy variables for time (not shown here) showed a gradual tendency toward acquisitions over the study period. We therefore tested a version of the model with the time dummies replaced by one single variable: the logarithm of time (1966 = 1 to 1993 = 27). The results, displayed under model 2, show that the time variable is highly significant ($p < .01$) and that other effects in the model do not change much. Hence, it appears that modeling the effect of time through one linear variable rather than through dummy variables was an appropriate research strategy in this study.

Product relatedness moderated by time

The effect of the logarithm of time was significant, consistent with the idea of an autonomous trend toward acquisitions during our window of analysis (cf. Andersson and Svensson, 1994; Shleifer and Vishny, 1991; Zejan, 1990). However, our time variable may not fully control for autonomous developments during our window. Shleifer and Vishny (1991) observed not only a trend in the number of takeovers (i.e., an increase from the 1980s onward) but also a trend in the *type* of take-overs. The relaxation of antitrust laws by the Reagan administration triggered a wave of US acquisitions in industries related to the parents' core businesses (cf. Palmer et al., 1995; Simmonds, 1990), reversing the trend toward conglomeration in the 1960s and 1970s (Bhagat, Shleifer, and Vishny, 1990; Davis, Diekmann, and Tinsley, 1994; Hoskisson and Johnson, 1992; Hoskisson and Turk, 1990; Markides, 1992, 1995;

Porter, 1987). This type of restructuring may have been imitated by firms in other countries (cf. DiMaggio and Powell, 1983; Fligstein, 1985, 1991; Haveman, 1993). Indeed, Pennings and colleagues (1994) observed that in the 1980s Dutch firms shed unrelated activities that they had initiated during the 1960s and 1970s. Thus, the trend in the United States in the 1980s toward related acquisitions – perhaps incited by more liberal legislation (cf. Hoskisson, Johnson, and Moesel, 1994) – may have caused similar trends in other countries, such as the Netherlands. Furthermore, firms in many industries compete increasingly in global markets, leading to an increased propensity worldwide to acquire other firms in their own industries (i.e., to make horizontal acquisitions) to increase their global market power. In conclusion, a trend toward related acquisitions for reasons other than the ones suggested by our hypotheses may also have influenced the choice of foreign entry mode of the Dutch firms in our sample.

We therefore reestimated our model with the time variable divided into four components, by means of interactions, for horizontal, related, vertical, and unrelated expansions. The results are shown in model 3 of Table 3. Consistent with the conjectures, the results associated with the interactions show increased preferences over time for acquisitions in horizontal and related businesses. With this finer-tuned modeling of the takeover wave, horizontal, related, and vertical expansions all have positive, significant ($p < .05$) relationships with a preference for start-ups, which is consistent with Hypothesis 4.

Further analysis

Alternative measures of diversity. We also tested whether our results were robust by using entropy measures of diversity (e.g., Jacquemin and Berry, 1979; Hoskisson et al., 1993) instead of product and country count measures. The entropy measure captured the number of geographical markets in which a firm operated at the time of an expansion as well as the relative importance of each market. Relative importance is usually measured by the share of the foreign sales realized in a particular market (e.g., Hitt, Hoskisson, and Kim, 1997). However, for most of the Dutch firms in our sample, data on foreign sales per global market area were not available for every year in the period under consideration. We therefore used the number of expansions present in the particular geographical market, instead of sales, to construct the weight for each market. As geographical markets, we used the country clusters identified by Ronen and Shenkar (1985): Nordic, Germanic, Anglo, Latin European, Latin American, Near Eastern, Arab, Far Eastern, and African.[6] Models estimated with the entropy measure instead of the country count measure yielded results similar to the ones reported in Table 3. Finally, we constructed an entropy measure based on sales per global market area following Hitt, Hoskisson, and Kim (1997). We were able to obtain the necessary data for 295 observations. In the models estimated with this variable, the effects of multinational diversity and multiproduct diversity (linear and squared) as well as the interaction effects remained significant ($p < .05$) and in the expected direction.

An entropy measure with weights based on shares of sales was also constructed for product diversity. Data could be obtained for 458 observations.[7] Logit models using this entropy measure confirmed the hypothesized inverted U-shape for product diversity ($p < .01$) as well as the hypothesized relationships between multinational diversity and entry mode choice ($p < .10$). Hypothesized interactions between product and multinational diversity were significant at the $p < .05$ level. In sum, the results using entropy measures were similar to those obtained using product and country count measures.

Mode and ownership. In our models we controlled for differences in ownership using a dummy variable that captured whether start-ups and acquisitions were wholly or partly owned by the Dutch firm. However, the *degree* of ownership may also be important. Therefore, we also ran a model with three dummy variables: majority, half, and minority ownership (with fully owned ventures as the omitted category). The results showed that majority-owned ventures were significantly ($p < .05$) more often acquisitions and half-owned ventures were significantly more often start-ups ($p < .01$). No significant effect was found for minority-owned ventures. The more detailed modeling of the control variable ownership did not decrease the support for our hypotheses.

Finally, we cannot *a priori* exclude the idea that modeling ownership by a control variable confounds interactions between ownership and other effects in our model. For instance, firms may prefer joint ventures in culturally remote countries, because joint ventures allow them to use the knowledge of the local partners about local business practices, local institutions, and so on (e.g., Kogut and Singh, 1988). Thus, cultural distance may affect preferences for joint ventures and for wholly owned subsidiaries differently. Ignoring such differences (as in Table 3) might lead to biased support for our hypotheses.[8] Alternatively, analyzing a model that distinguishes between wholly owned start-ups, start-up joint ventures, jointly owned acquisitions, and wholly owned acquisitions in the dependent variable would avoid this problem.

We therefore estimated a multinomial logit model with a fourfold dependent variable (wholly owned start-up, jointly owned start-up, jointly owned acquisition, and wholly owned acquisition). We could not use dummy variables for firm in this model because of multicollinearity problems. Hence, the results in Table 4 should be interpreted with some care. Wholly owned acquisitions served as the omitted category. Thus, a positive coefficient on one of the other categories stands for a preference for that category over wholly owned acquisitions.

The results shown in Table 4 show that firms indeed favor partial ownership of ventures, both start-ups and acquisitions, when they expand into countries that are culturally remote. Partial ownership is also favored in high-risk countries and in countries that impose legal restrictions on foreign ownership. Table 4 also shows, however, that the effects of the diversity variables are quite similar for jointly owned start-ups and wholly owned start-ups. In both cases, the effects differ significantly from those for wholly owned acquisitions. These results further support Hypotheses 1–3. Hypothesis 4, which states that related expansions are more often start-ups, is also supported, although it appears that the support is largely driven by the wholly owned ventures. In conclusion, the results from the multinomial logit model, which avoids potential biases stemming from ignoring differential effects across ownership structures, generally support our hypotheses. The results in Table 4 suggest that the diversity variables in our study primarily distinguish start-ups from acquisitions rather than jointly owned ventures from wholly owned ventures.

DISCUSSION

This study offers a new approach to studying the strategic choice to expand internationally through start-ups or through acquisitions: a learning perspective. The perspective implies that a firm's strategic posture at the time of an expansion, in terms of its multinational diversity and its multiproduct diversity, influences this strategic choice. This diversity – which reflects the different consumer needs, rivals, suppliers, and partners to which the firm is exposed – offers opportunities for learning and for strengthening technological capabilities. These capabilities in turn increase the propensity of the firm to set up new ventures in foreign countries rather than to acquire existing companies. Predictions from this theory were strongly corroborated using data on the 829 foreign expansions of 25 Dutch firms over a period spanning almost three decades (1966–94).

The results also supported the idea that learning from diversity is subject to organizational constraints. We found a curvilinear relationship between product diversity and the propensity to expand through start-ups rather than acquisitions. This was consistent with the idea that learning and capability building increase as firms expand into a variety of businesses (cf. Argyres, 1996a), until they meet organizational (cognitive) constraints on information sharing and adopt M-form structures with relatively autonomous businesses, little information sharing between businesses,

Table 4 Results of multinomial logit analysis: jointly and wholly owned ventures[a]

Variable	Start-up wholly owned venture		Start-up joint venture		Acquired joint venture	
Intercept	−3.337	(2.325)	−10.298***	(2.300)	−10.332***	(1.885)
Multinational diversity	0.291***	(0.078)	0.202*	(0.100)	0.082	(0.071)
Product diversity	0.474**	(0.163)	0.470*	(0.198)	0.086	(0.154)
Product diversity squared	−0.022**	(0.007)	−0.026**	(0.009)	−0.010	(0.007)
Multinational diversity × product diversity	−0.050**	(0.017)	−0.052*	(0.022)	−0.025	(0.016)
Multinational diversity × product diversity squared	0.002**	(0.001)	0.003**	(0.001)	0.001[†]	(0.001)
Horizontal expansion	4.775**	(1.695)	0.106	(1.364)	0.104	(1.052)
Related expansion	6.527**	(2.355)	3.677[†]	(2.210)	2.566	(1.964)
Vertical expansion	0.449	(2.733)	1.689	(1.974)	−3.310	(2.171)
Cultural distance	0.229[†]	(0.123)	0.649***	(0.135)	0.426***	(0.123)
Local experience	−0.222**	(0.068)	−0.251**	(0.091)	−0.019	(0.038)
Return on equity	−5.619***	(1.289)	−5.120**	(1.586)	−3.035**	(1.072)
Horizontal expansion × time	−0.930***	(0.277)	−0.578[†]	(0.346)	−0.387	(0.283)
Related expansion × time	−1.458*	(0.668)	−1.625*	(0.749)	−1.441*	(0.656)
Vertical expansion × time	0.574	(0.787)	−0.616	(0.609)	0.781	(0.698)
Unrelated expansion × time	0.927	(0.604)	0.035	(0.478)	−0.147	(0.314)
Legal restrictions	0.460	(0.314)	1.380***	(0.365)	0.937**	(0.326)
Medium country risk	1.369***	(0.340)	1.196***	(0.406)	0.592	(0.431)
High country risk	−0.342	(0.544)	1.409*	(0.580)	1.485**	(0.577)
Real GNP	−0.166	(0.122)	0.160	(0.153)	−0.144	(0.116)
GNP growth	−0.627	(0.644)	0.092[†]	(0.518)	0.690	(0.476)
GNP per capita	0.006	(0.009)	−0.011	(0.016)	−0.024	(0.035)
Size[b]	−0.181	(0.121)	0.445**	(0.156)	0.732***	(0.130)

[a] $N = 829$. Acquired wholly owned subsidiary is the omitted category. Numbers in parentheses are standard deviations.
[b] Variable is a logarithm.
[†] $p < .10$; * $p < .05$; ** $p < .01$; *** $p < .001$.
All two-tailed tests.

and lower levels of learning and capability building. We also found that intermediately product-diversified firms benefited relatively little from increases in multinational diversity, which further supports the idea that these firms approached organizational limits on information sharing and learning.

Our research is consistent with the idea that traditional boundaries between strategic management and international business are at least partly artificial (Tallman and Li, 1996). We used learning theory to develop hypotheses regarding both product diversity (traditionally the domain of strategic management) and multinational diversity (traditionally studied in international business). Furthermore, our theory and evidence suggest that multinational diversity and product diversity interact to influence choices of foreign entry mode. Thus, a good understanding of the effect of multinational diversity requires insight into the effect of product diversity, and vice versa (cf. Hitt et al., 1994, 1997). We believe that future studies examining the effects of both multinational diversity and product diversity using a coherent framework (for instance, learning theory) will provide better insights into firms' innovation levels, foreign entry mode choices, and profitability than studies that stay within traditional research boundaries.

Links with other literature

Our research adds to the scant literature on whether firms expand abroad through start-ups or through acquisitions. Some of these studies have examined the linear effects of multinationality (Caves and Mehra, 1986; Kogut and Singh, 1988) and of product diversity (Caves and Mehra, 1986; Cho and Padmanabhan, 1995; Hennart and Park, 1993; Kogut and Singh, 1988; Zejan, 1990). The results have been mixed, and nonsignificant effects have often been found. The present study found, congruent with an organizational learning perspective, that both a firm's multinational diversity and its product diversity influence whether it expands abroad through start-ups or through acquisitions, that product diversity has a nonlinear effect, and that the two types of diversity interact to influence the foreign entry mode choice. We also found that firms that expanded abroad into related industries (horizontal, related, and vertical expansions) were more likely to build on their existing technological routines (i.e., to set up new ventures) than firms expanding into unrelated businesses, which were more likely to buy the needed capabilities (i.e., to acquire existing firms).

Pitts (1977, 1980) argued that expansion through internal development and expansion through acquisition are two pure strategies: firms choose either one or the other. However, Lamont and Anderson (1985) found that US firms often used both expansion forms. In our most complete model, 2 of the 24 firm dummy variables were significant (results are not shown), which signals that the choice to expand through start-ups or acquisitions may indeed have a firm-specific component (cf. Hitt, Hoskisson, and Ireland, 1990). At the same time, our theory and evidence suggest that firms may use both forms (cf. Lamont and Anderson, 1985) and that, moreover, the propensity to expand through start-ups rather than acquisitions varies with the strategic posture at the time of an expansion.

Cultural differences magnify the problems of implementing acquisitions (e.g., Weber et al., 1996). However, organizations can be remarkably successful in replicating their capabilities on foreign soil using new ventures (cf. Florida and Kenney, 1991; Zaheer, 1995). Barkema and colleagues (1996) found that the failure rate of acquisitions increased more sharply with cultural distance than did the failure rate of start-ups. Kogut and Singh (1988) and Cho and Padmanabhan (1995) found that Japanese firms were more likely to set up new ventures in culturally remote countries. The present study confirms the latter finding for Dutch multinationals. The combined evidence corroborates the idea that cultural differences hurt acquisitions more than they do start-ups and that start-ups are therefore more likely in culturally remote countries.

Local experience may help a firm to learn the peculiarities of a local culture (e.g., Li, 1995) and to reduce implementation problems in future trials. The firm may learn how to communicate and negotiate with the local workforce, and so on, which will facilitate the transfer of technology (Kedia and Bhagat, 1988) to the foreign subsidiary. Experience with local circumstances will also increase a multinational's ability to spot and evaluate local companies that are potential acquisition candidates. In conformity with these views, Barkema and colleagues (1996) found that local experience more strongly enhanced the success of acquisitions than that of start-ups. The present study adds to these findings by showing that acquisitions become more *likely* as a firm gains experience in a host country[9]. The combined evidence suggests that local experience reduces the problems of making acquisitions in a given host country, thus increasing the likelihood of such acquisitions. This evidence adds to previous studies that found insignificant support for the prediction that local experience triggers acquisitions (Hennart and Park, 1993; Kogut and Singh, 1988).

Limitations and suggestions for further research

Our findings may have been influenced by idiosyncratic features of our sample. The firms in our sample were based in a single country, the Netherlands. The Netherlands has a small home market and has been intensively engaged in international trade for more than 400 years. Furthermore, organizational learning may be moderated by the culture in which a firm is rooted (cf. Hickson, 1996; Hofstede, 1983). Future studies may provide more insight into whether the results from this study also apply in other settings.

We argued, drawing on previous research (e.g., Howkisson, Hitt and Hill, 1993; Tallman and Li, 1996), that firms that diversify into a variety of businesses will eventually meet organizational constraints, which leads to the adoption of M-form structures with relatively independent divisions, little information sharing, and lower levels of learning and capability building than are present in intermediately diversified firms. However, firms may also encounter organizational constraints if they expand into many countries. Although various authors have suggested that internationalizing firms mitigate such problems through horizontal and/or informal links between subsidiaries and headquarters (Bartlett, 1981; Malnight, 1995, 1996), using task forces, project teams, and so on (Bartlett and Ghoshal, 1989; Hedlund, 1986, 1994), Hitt and colleagues (1997) suggested that innovation levels decrease at high levels of multinational diversity. Therefore, we also tested a model that included the variable multinational diversity squared (results not shown). The effect turned out to be negative but statistically insignificant. However, the firms in our sample began to increase their FDIs around the late 1960s or later, starting almost from scratch; thus, they were not in advanced stages of internationalization during our window of analysis. Future studies using samples that include highly multinationally diversified firms can provide more insight into whether multinationals eventually encounter organizational constraints when they enter many countries.

Like previous studies in this literature (e.g., Caves and Mehra, 1986; Cho and Padmanabhan, 1995; Hennart and Park, 1993), this study emphasized the strategic choice between foreign start-ups and acquisitions. Future research may examine the impact of the strategic posture of a firm (in terms of its multinational diversity and product diversity, interactions between these variables, and nonlinearities) on a wider range of strategic options. First, it is possible to make a finer distinction within the subset of start-ups, separating wholly owned start-ups from start-ups with local partners (i.e., joint ventures). International joint ventures are often marketing ventures that combine a multinational's technological skills with a local partner's knowledge of local circumstances, business practices, and so on (e.g., Inkpen and Beamish, 1997; Gomes-Casseres, 1989). However, joint ventures may also serve to combine the technological knowledge of a firm with the technological knowledge of a partner (e.g., Mowery, Oxley and Silverman, 1997). Actually, some of the joint ventures in our data set may have been technology joint ventures (the annual reports did not provide sufficient information here), in which case joint ventures would be closer to acquisitions than to wholly owned start-ups (although Table 4 showed similar effects of multinational diversity and of product diversity for wholly owned start-ups and for start-up joint ventures, as opposed to acquisitions). Future studies that explicitly distinguish, both theoretically and empirically, between wholly owned ventures and start-up joint ventures will supplement the present study. Second, this study restricted the foreign entry mode choice to foreign direct investment; other expansion forms were not considered. Future studies that consider a wider range of strategic options, such as export, licensing, franchising, and nonequity alliances and other expansion forms, will also add to the present study.

Our research examined the choice between start-up and acquisition in a foreign country at the time a venture is established; we did not study the evolution of individual ventures over time. Jointly owned ventures may, for instance, eventually be acquired by one of the parents. Acquisitions (or start-ups) may be preceded by some kind of corporate alliance between companies (although research by Hagedoorn and Sadowksi [1996] suggested that transitions from alliances to acquisitions rarely take place). Future studies may provide more insight into the influence of a firm's strategic posture on such dynamic aspects of foreign entry.

Future studies should also examine the influence of different *types* of experience on the entry mode choice; whether the learning varies with the form of previous expansions (e.g., export, licensing, franchising, acquisitions or start-ups, alone or with partners). Multinationals may also learn through regional knowledge networks of their foreign subsidiaries (cf. Cohen and Levinthal, 1989; Johanson and Mattsson, 1988; Kogut, 1989) or by hiring engineers and other employees through their foreign subsidiaries who formerly worked for competitors in the same region (Almeida, 1996). Further research could provide more insight into these issues.

Finally, the findings of this study point to the need for more research on the relation between a firm's financial performance and its foreign entry mode choice. Some studies have reported that international start-ups outperformed acquisitions (Li and Guisinger, 1991; Woodcock, Beamish and Makino, 1994). However, such findings do not necessarily imply that start-ups are a superior expansion mode *per se*. Various studies have found that technological capabilities correlate positively with financial performance (Franko, 1989; cf. Hitt et al., 1994). Others have concluded that technological capabilities lead to international start-ups rather than to acquisitions (Anderson and Svensson, 1994; Cho and Padmanabhan, 1995; Hennart and

Park, 1993; the present study). Thus, the positive correlation between international start-ups and a firm's financial performance may be caused by a third variable, strong technological capability; it does not necessarily mean that start-ups are a superior expansion mode *per se*. Future studies may provide more insight into this issue.

Conclusion

A key notion of the organizational learning perspective developed here and strongly corroborated by our evidence is that multinational diversity and product diversity provide alternative opportunities for learning and capability building, until a firm reaches organizational limits on information sharing and learning. The implication, both from a research point of view and from a managerial perspective, is that the influence of both diversity variables characterizing a firm's strategic posture should be studied simultaneously rather than in isolation (cf. Hitt et al., 1994, 1997; Tallman and Li, 1996). We studied the influence of both diversity variables on the strategic choice of whether to expand internationally through start-ups or through acquisitions. We hope that our perspective regarding learning from diversity, technological capability building, and organizational constraints will prove useful for future investigation of the influence of firm diversity on the choice of start-up or acquisition and perhaps on other strategic choices as well.

NOTES

1 Caves and Mehra did not provide an explicit theory regarding this relationship but suggested (1986: 461) that acquisitions provide foreign experience and are therefore less likely when firms have much international experience. Their findings are, however, inconsistent with this conjecture. Kogut and Singh (1988) used multinationality as a control variable when testing the hypothesis that the cultural distance between the home country of the expanding firm and the host country influenced the choice of foreign entry mode.

2 The firms on the Amsterdam Stock Exchange are divided into two segments – "main funds," large firms that are frequently traded – and less traded funds: smaller firms that are infrequently traded. The first segment contains about 35 firms, the second around 230 firms. We selected our firms from the main funds segment.

3 The SBI codes are the Dutch equivalent of the Standard Industrial Classification codes.

4 The Kogut and Singh (1988) index of cultural distance is an arithmetic average of the deviations of each country from the index of the Netherlands along Hofstede's (1980) four cultural dimensions. Algebraically, it is calculated as $CD_j = \Sigma_{i=1,2,3,4} [(I_{ij} - I_{in})^2/V_i]/4$, where CD_j is the cultural distance of the jth country from the Netherlands, I_{ij} is the index for the ith cultural dimension and jth country, n is the Netherlands, and V_i is the variance of the index of the ith dimension.

5 We also estimated versions of the models in Table 3 with industry dummies, which captured overlap in the core activities of different firms, measured by three-digit SBI codes, instead of firm dummies. The estimation results were very similar to the results in Table 3.

6 The correlation between this entropy measure and our original country count measure of multinational diversity was .74 ($p < .0001$).

7 The correlation between the original product count measure and the entropy measure of product diversity was .48 ($p < .0001$).

8 We are grateful to an anonymous reviewer for suggesting this line of thought.

9 We also tested a version of the model that included experience in other countries in the same cultural block (cf. Ronen and Shenkar, 1985). This experience triggered a weak preference for acquisitions ($p < .10$).

REFERENCES

Abrahamson, E., & Fombrun, C. J. 1994. Macrocultures: Determinants and consequences. *Academy of Management Review,* 19: 728–755.

Agarwal, S., & Ramaswami, S. N. 1992. *Choice of organizational form in foreign markets: A transaction cost perspective.* Paper presented at the annual meeting of the Academy of International Business, Brussels.

Almeida, P. 1996. Knowledge sourcing by foreign multinationals: Patent citation analysis in the US semiconductor industry. *Strategic Management Journal,* 17 (winter special issue): 155–165.

Amburgey, T. L., & Miner, A. S. 1992. Strategic momentum: The effects of repetitive, positional, and contextual momentum on merger activity. *Strategic Management Journal,* 13: 335–348.

Anderson, J. R., Farrell, R., & Sauers, R. 1984. Learning to program in LISP. *Cognitive Science,* 8: 87–129.

Andersson, T., & Svensson, R. 1994. Entry modes for direct investment determined by the composition of firm-specific skills. *Scandinavian Journal of Economics,* 96: 551–560.

Argyres, N. 1996a. Capabilities, technological diversification and divisionalization. *Strategic Management Journal,* 17: 395–410.

Argyres, N. 1996b. Evidence on the role of firm capabilities in vertical integration decisions. *Strategic Management Journal,* 17: 129–150.

Argyris, C., & Schön, D. 1978. *Organizational learning.* London: Addison-Wesley.

Barkema, H. G., Bell, J. H. J., & Pennings, J. M. 1996. Foreign entry, cultural barriers, and learning. *Strategic Management Journal,* 17: 151–166.

Barkema, H. G., Shenkar, O., Vermeulen, F., & Bell, J. H. J. 1997. Working abroad, working with others: How firms learn to operate international joint ventures. *Academy of Management Journal,* 40: 426–442.

Bartlett, C. A. 1981. Multinational structural change: Evolution versus reorganization. In L. Otterbeck (Ed.), *The management of headquarters subsidiary relationships in multinational corporations:* 121–145. London: Gower.

Bartlett, C. A., & Ghoshal, S. 1989. *Managing across borders: The transnational solution.* Cambridge, MA: Harvard Business School Press.

Baysinger, B., & Hoskisson, R. E. 1989. Diversification strategy and R&D intensity in large multiproduct firms. *Academy of Management Journal,* 32: 310–332.

Benito, G. R. G., & Gripsrud, G. 1992. The expansion of foreign direct investments: Discrete rational location choices or a cultural learning process? *Journal of International Business Studies,* 23: 461–476.

Bettis, R. A., & Prahalad, C. K. 1995. The dominant logic: Retrospective and extension. *Strategic Management Journal,* 16: 5–14.

Bhagat, S., Shleifer, A., & Vishny, R. W. 1990. Hostile takeovers in the 1980s: The return to corporate specialization. *Brookings Papers on Economic Activity* (special issue): 1–84.

Brown, J. S., & Duguid, P. 1991. Organizational learning and communities of practice: Toward a unified view of working, learning, and innovation. *Organization Science,* 2 (special issue): 40–57.

Buono, A., & Bowditch, J. 1989. *The human side of mergers and acquisitions. Managing collisions between people, cultures, and organizations.* San Francisco: Jossey-Bass.

Calori, R., Johnson, G., & Sarnin, P. 1994. CEOs' cognitive maps and the scope of the organization. *Strategic Management Journal,* 15: 437–457.

Calori, R., Lubatkin, M., & Very, P. 1994. Control mechanisms in cross-border acquisitions: An international comparison. *Organization Studies,* 15: 361–379.

Cartwright, S., & Cooper, C. L. 1993. The role of culture compatibility in successful organizational marriage. *Academy of Management Executive,* 7(2): 57–70.

Caves, R. E., & Mehra, S. K. 1986. Entry of foreign multinationals into US manufacturing industries. In M. E. Porter (Ed.), *Competition in global industries,* pp. 449–481. Boston: Harvard Business School Press.

Chandler, A. 1962. *Strategy and structure: Chapters in the history of American industrial enterprise.* Cambridge, MA: MIT Press.

Chang, S. J. 1995. International expansion strategy of Japanese firms: Capability building through sequential entry. *Academy of Management Journal,* 38: 383–407.

Chatterjee, S., Lubatkin, M. H., Schweiger, D. M., & Weber, Y. 1992. Cultural differences and shareholder value in related mergers: Linking equity and human capital. *Strategic Management Journal,* 13: 319–334.

Cho, K. R., & Padmanabhan, P. 1995. Acquisition versus new venture: The choice of foreign establishment mode by Japanese firms. *Journal of International Management,* 1: 255–285.

Cohen, M. D. 1991. Individual learning and organizational routine: Emerging connections. *Organization Science*, 2(special issue): 135–139.

Cohen, M. D., & Bacdayan, P. 1994. Organizational routines are stored as procedural memory: Evidence from a laboratory study. *Organization Science*, 5: 554–568.

Cohen, W. M., & Levinthal, D. A. 1989. Innovation and learning: The two faces of R&D. *Economic Journal*, 99: 569–596.

Cohen, W. M., & Levinthal, D. A. 1990. Absorptive capacity: A new perspective on learning and innovation. *Administrative Science Quarterly*, 35: 128–152.

Cohen, W. M., & Levinthal, D. A. 1994. Fortune favors the prepared firm. *Management Science*, 40: 227–251.

Contractor, F. J. 1990. Ownership patterns of US joint ventures abroad and the liberalization of foreign government regulations in the 1980s: Evidence from the benchmark surveys. *Journal of International Business Studies*, 21: 55–73.

Datta, D. K. 1991. Organizational fit and acquisition performance: Effects of post-acquisition integration. *Strategic Management Journal*, 12: 281–297.

d'Aveni, R. A., & Ravenscraft, D. J. 1994. Economies of integration versus bureaucracy costs: Does vertical integration improve performance? *Academy of Management Journal*, 37: 1167–1206.

Davis, G. F., Diekmann, K. A., & Tinsley, C. H. 1994. The decline and fall of the conglomerate firm in the 1980s: The deinstitutionalization of an organizational form. *American Sociological Review*, 59: 547–570.

DiMaggio, P. J., & Powell, W. W. 1983. The iron cage revisited: Institutional isomorphism and collective rationality in organizational fields. *American Sociological Review*, 48: 147–160.

Drazin, R., & Shoonhoven, C. B. 1996. Community, population, and organization effects on innovation: A multilevel perspective. *Academy of Management Journal*, 39: 1065–1083.

Dunning, J. H. 1980. Toward an eclectic paradigm of international production: Some empirical tests. *Journal of International Business Studies*, 11: 9–31.

Dunning, J. H. 1988. The eclectic paradigm of international production: A restatement and some possible extensions. *Journal of International Business Studies*, 19: 1–31.

Ellis, H. C. 1965. *The transfer of learning.* New York: Macmillan.

Finkelstein, S., & Hambrick, D. C. 1989. Chief executive compensation: A study of the intersection of markets and political processes. *Strategic Management Journal*, 10: 121–134.

Fiol, C. M., & Lyles, M. A. 1985. Organizational learning. *Academy of Management Review*, 10: 803–813.

Fligstein, N. 1985. The spread of the multidivisional form among large firms, 1919–1979. *American Sociological Review*, 59: 377–391.

Fligstein, N. 1991. The structural transformation of American industry: The causes of diversification in the largest firms, 1919–1979. In W. W. Powell & P. J. DiMaggio (Eds.), *New institutionalism in organizational analysis*: 311–336. Chicago: University of Chicago Press.

Florida, R., & Kenney, M. 1991. Transplanted organizations: The transfer of Japanese industrial organization to the US *American Sociological Review*, 56: 381–398.

Franko, L. G. 1989. Global corporate competition: Who's winning, who's losing, and the R&D factor as one reason why. *Strategic Management Journal*, 10: 449–474.

Galbraith, C. S., & Kay, N. M. 1986. Towards a theory of multinational enterprise. *Journal of Economic Behavior and Organization*, 7: 3–19.

Gatignon, H., & Anderson, E. 1988. The multinational corporation's degree of control over foreign subsidiaries: An empirical test of a transaction cost explanation. *Journal of Law, Economics, and Organization*, 4: 305–336.

Ghoshal, S. 1987. Global strategy: An organizing framework. *Strategic Management Journal*, 8: 425–440.

Gomes-Casseres, B. 1989. Ownership structures of foreign subsidiaries. *Journal of Economic Behavior and Organization*, 11: 1–25.

Gomes-Casseres, B. 1990. Firm ownership preferences and host government restrictions: An integrated approach. *Journal of International Business Studies*, 21: 1–22.

Goodnow, J. D., & Hansz, J. E. 1972. Environmental determinants of overseas market entry strategies. *Journal of International Business Studies*, 3: 33–50.

Granstrand, O., & Sjölander, S. 1990. The acquisition of technology and small firms by large firms. *Journal of Economic Behavior and Organization*, 13: 367–386.

Greenwood, R., & Hinings, C. R. 1996. Understanding radical organizational change: Bringing together the old and the new institutionalism. *Academy of Management Review*, 21: 1022–1054.

Hagedoorn, J., & Sadowksi, B. 1996. *Exploring the potential transition from strategic technology partnering to mergers and acquisitions*. Working paper no. 2/96–010, Maastricht Economic Research Institute on Innovation and Technology, Maastricht University, the Netherlands.

Harrison, J. S., Hitt, M. A., Hoskisson, R. E., & Ireland, R. D. 1991. Synergies and post-acquisition performance: Differences versus similarities in resource allocations. *Journal of Management*, 17: 173–190.

Haspeslagh, P. C., & Jemison, D. B. 1991. *Managing acquisitions: Creating value through corporate renewal*. New York: Free Press.

Haveman, H. A. 1993. Follow the leader: Mimetic isomorphism and entry into new markets. *Administrative Science Quarterly*, 38: 593–627.

Hedberg, B. 1981. How organizations learn and unlearn. In P. Nystrom & W. Starbuck (Eds.), *Handbook of organizational design*, vol. 1: 3–27. Oxford: Oxford University Press.

Hedlund, G. 1986. The hypermodern MNC – A heterarchy? *Human Resource Management*, 25: 9–25.

Hedlund, G. 1994. A model of knowledge management and the n-form corporation. *Strategic Management Journal*, 15: 73–90.

Hennart, J. F. 1988. A transaction costs theory of equity joint ventures. *Strategic Management Journal*, 9: 361–374.

Hennart, J. F. 1991. The transaction costs theory of joint ventures: An empirical study of Japanese subsidiaries in the United States. *Management Science*, 37: 483–497.

Hennart, J. F., & Park, Y. R. 1993. Greenfield versus acquisition: The strategy of Japanese investors in the United States. *Management Science*, 39: 1054–1070.

Hennart, J. F., & Reddy, S. 1997. The choice between mergers/ acquisitions and joint ventures: The case of Japanese investors in the United States. *Strategic Management Journal*, 18: 1–12.

Herriot, S. R., Levinthal, D., & March, J. G. 1985. Learning from experience in organizations. *American Economic Review*, 75: 298–302.

Hickson, D. J. 1996. The *ASQ* years then and now through the eyes of a Euro-Brit. *Administrative Science Quarterly*, 41: 217–228.

Hill, C. W. L., & Hoskisson, R. E. 1987. Strategy and structure in the multiproduct firm. *Academy of Management Review*, 12: 331–341.

Hitt, M. A., Hoskisson, R. E., & Ireland, R. D. 1990. Mergers and acquisitions and managerial commitment to innovation in M-form firms. *Strategic Management Journal*, 11: 29–47.

Hitt, M. A., Hoskisson, R. E., & Ireland, R. D. 1994. A mid-range theory of the interactive effects of international and product diversification on innovation and performance. *Journal of Management*, 20: 297–326.

Hitt, M. A., Hoskisson, R. E., Johnson, R. A., & Moesel, D. D. 1996. The market for corporate control and firm innovation. *Academy of Management Journal*, 39: 1084–1119.

Hitt, M. A., Hoskisson, R. E., & Kim, H. 1997. International diversification: Effects on innovation and firm performance in product-diversified firms. *Academy of Management Journal*, 40: 767–798.

Hofstede, G. 1980. *Culture's consequences. International differences in work-related values*. Beverly Hills, CA: Sage.

Hofstede, G. 1983. The cultural relativity of organizational practices and theories. *Journal of International Business Studies*, 14: 75–89.

Hofstede, G. 1991. *Cultures and organizations: Software of the mind*. Berkshire, England: McGraw-Hill.

Hoskisson, R. E., & Hitt, M. A. 1988. Strategic control systems and relative R&D investment in large multiproduct firms. *Strategic Management Journal*, 9: 605–621.

Hoskisson, R. E., & Hitt, M. A. 1990. Antecedents and performance outcomes of diversification: A review and critique of theoretical perspectives. *Journal of Management*, 16: 461–509.

Hoskisson, R. E., Hitt, M. A., & Hill, C. W. L. 1993. Managerial incentives and investment in R&D in large multiproduct firms. *Organization Science*, 4: 325–341.

Hoskisson, R. E., Hitt, M. A., Johnson, R. A., & Moesel, D. D. 1993. Construct validity of an objective (entropy) categorical measure of diversification strategy. *Strategic Management Journal*, 14: 215–235.

Hoskisson, R. E., & Johnson, R. A. 1992. Corporate restructuring and strategic change: The effect on diversification strategy and R&D intensity. *Strategic Management Journal*, 13: 625–634.

Hoskisson, R. E., Johnson, R. A., & Moesel, D. D. 1994. Corporate divestiture intensity in restructuring firms: Effects of governance, strategy, and performance. *Academy of Management Journal*, 37: 1207–1251.

Hoskisson, R. E., & Turk, T. A. 1990. Corporate restructuring: Governance and control limits of the internal capital market. *Academy of Management Review*, 15: 459–477.

Huber, G. P. 1991. Organizational learning: The contributing processes and literatures. *Organization Science*, 2 (special issue): 88–115.

Huff, A. S. 1982. Industry influences on strategy formulation. *Strategic Management Journal*, 3: 119–131.

Hymer, S. H. 1960. *The international operations of national firms: A study of direct foreign investment.* Cambridge, MA: MIT Press.

Inkpen, A. C., & Beamish, P. W. 1997. Knowledge, bargaining power, and the instability of international joint ventures. *Academy of Management Review*, 22: 177–202.

Jacquemin, A. P., & Berry, C. H. 1979. Entropy measure of diversification and corporate growth. *Journal of Industrial Economics*, 27: 359–369.

Jelinek, M. 1979. *Institutionalizing innovation: A study of organizational learning systems.* New York: Praeger.

Jemison, D. B., & Sitkin, S. B. 1986. Corporate acquisitions: A process perspective. *Academy of Management Review*, 11: 145–163.

Jensen, M. C. 1986. Agency costs of free cash flow, corporate finance, and takeovers. *American Economic Review*, 76: 323–329.

Johanson, J., & Mattsson, L. G. 1988. Internationalization in industrial systems – A network approach. In N. Hood & J. E. Vahlne (Eds.), *Strategies in global competition*, pp. 287–314. New York: Croom Helm.

Jones, G. R., & Hill, C. W. L. 1988. Transaction cost analysis of strategy-structure choice. *Strategic Management Journal*, 9: 159–172.

Keats, B. W., & Hitt, M. A. 1988. A causal model of linkages among environmental dimensions, macro organizational characteristics, and performance. *Academy of Management Journal*, 31: 570–598.

Kedia, B. L., & Bhagat, R. S. 1988. Cultural constraints on transfers of technology across nations: Implications for research in international comparative management. *Academy of Management Review*, 13: 559–571.

Kiesler, S., & Sproull, L. 1982. Managerial response to changing environments: Perspectives on problem solving from social cognition. *Administrative Science Quarterly*, 27: 548–570.

Kim, W. C., Hwang, P., & Burgers, W. P. 1989. Global diversification strategy and corporate profit performance. *Strategic Management Journal*, 10: 45–57.

Kim, W. C., Hwang, P., & Burgers, W. P. 1993. Multinationals' diversification and the risk-return trade-off, *Strategic Management Journal*, 14: 275–286.

Kobrin, S. J. 1991. An empirical analysis of the determinants of global integration. *Strategic Management Journal*, 12 (summer special issue): 17–37.

Kogut, B. 1985. Designing global strategies: Profiting from operational flexibility, part 1. *Sloan Management Review*, 27(1): 27–38.

Kogut, B. 1989. A note on global strategies. *Strategic Management Journal*, 10: 383–389.

Kogut, B., & Singh, H. 1988. The effect of national culture on the choice of entry mode. *Journal of International Business Studies*, 19: 411–432.

Lamont, B. T., & Anderson, C. R. 1985. Mode of corporate diversification and economic performance. *Academy of Management Journal*, 28: 926–934.

Lant, T. K., & Mezias, S. J. 1992. An organizational learning model of convergence and reorientation. *Organization Science*, 3 (special issue): 47–71.

Larimo, J. 1993. *Foreign direct investment behaviour and performance: An analysis of Finnish direct investments in OECD countries.* Working paper, Acta Wasaensia, no. 32. Vaasa, Finland: University of Vaasa.

Lei, D., & Hitt, M. A. 1995. Strategic restructuring and outsourcing: The effect of mergers and acquisitions and LBOs on building firm skills and capabilities. *Journal of Management*, 21: 835–859.

Leonard-Barton, D. 1992. Core capabilities and core rigidities: A paradox in managing new product development. *Strategic Management Journal*, 13: 11–125.

Levinthal, D. A., & March, J. G. 1993. The myopia of learning. *Strategic Management Journal*, 14: 95–112.

Levitt, B., & March, J. G. 1988. Organizational learning. In W. R. Scott (Ed.), *Annual review of sociology*, vol. 14: 319–340. Palo Alto, CA: Annual Reviews.

Li, J., & Guisinger, S. 1991. Comparative business failures of foreign-controlled firms in the United States. *Journal of International Business Studies*, 2: 209–224.

Li, J. T. 1995. Foreign entry and survival: Effects of strategic choices on performance in international markets. *Strategic Management Journal*, 16: 333–351.

Lubatkin, M., Merchant, H., & Srinivasan, N. 1993. Construct validity of some unweighted product-count diversification measures. *Strategic Management Journal*, 14: 433–449.

Malnight, T. M. 1995. Globalization of an ethnocentric firm: An evolutionary perspective. *Strategic Management Journal*, 16: 119–141.

Malnight, T. M. 1996. The transition from decentralized to network-based MNC structures: An evolutionary perspective. *Journal of International Business Studies*, 27: 43–65.

March, J. G. 1991. Exploration and exploitation in organizational learning. *Organization Science*, 2 (special issue): 71–87.

Markides, C. C. 1992. Consequences of corporate refocusing: Ex ante evidence. *Academy of Management Journal*, 35: 398–412.

Markides, C. C. 1995. Diversification, restructuring and economic performance. *Strategic Management Journal*, 16: 101–118.

Melin, L. 1992. Internationalization as a strategy process. *Strategic Management Journal*, 13: 99–118.

Mezias, S. J., & Glyn, M. A. 1993. The three faces of corporate renewal: Institution, revolution, and evolution. *Strategic Management Journal*, 14: 77–101.

Miller, D. 1993. The architecture of simplicity. *Academy of Management Review*, 18: 116–138.

Miller, D. 1994. What happens after success: The perils of excellence. *Journal of Management Studies*, 31: 325–358.

Miller, D., & Chen, M-J. 1994. Sources and consequences of competitive inertia: A study of the US airline industry. *Administrative Science Quarterly*, 39: 1–23.

Miller, D., & Chen, M-J. 1996. The simplicity of competitive repertoires: An empirical analysis. *Strategic Management Journal*, 17: 419–439.

Mowery, D. C., Oxley, J. E., & Silverman, B. S. 1996. Strategic alliances and interfirm knowledge transfer. *Strategic Management Journal*, 17: 77–91.

Nelson, R. R. 1991. Why do firms differ, and how does it matter? *Strategic Management Journal*, 12: 61–74.

Nelson, R. R., & Winter, S. E. 1982. *An evolutionary theory of economic change*. Cambridge, MA: Harvard University Press.

Palmer, D., Barber, B. M., Zhou, X., & Soysal, Y. 1995. The friendly and predatory acquisition of large US corporations in the 1960s: The other contested terrain. *American Sociological Review*, 60: 469–499.

Pennings, J. M., Barkema, H. G., & Douma, S. W. 1994. Organizational learning and diversification. *Academy of Management Journal*, 37: 608–640.

Penrose, E. T. 1959. *The theory of the growth of the firm*. London: Basil Blackwell.

Peteraf, M. A. 1993. The cornerstones of competitive advantage: A resource-based view. *Strategic Management Journal*, 14: 179–191.

Pitts, R. A. 1977. Strategies and structures for diversification. *Academy of Management Journal*, 20: 197–208.

Pitts, R. A. 1980. Towards a contingency theory of multibusiness organization design. *Academy of Management Review*, 5: 203–210.

Porter, M. E. 1987. From competitive advantage to corporate strategy. *Harvard Business Review*, 65(3): 43–59.

Prahalad, C. K., & Bettis, R. A. 1986. The dominant logic: A new linkage between diversity and performance. *Strategic Management Journal*, 7: 485–501.

Prahalad, C. K., & Hamel, G. 1990. The core competence of the corporation. *Harvard Business Review*, 68(3): 79–91.

Ramanujam, V., & Varadarajan, P. 1989. Research on corporate diversification: A synthesis. *Strategic Management Journal*, 10: 523–552.

Reger, R. K., & Huff, A. S. 1993. Strategic groups: A cognitive perspective. *Strategic Management Journal*, 14: 103–123.

Romanelli, E., & Tushman, M. L. 1994. Organizational transformation as punctuated equilibrium: An empirical test. *Academy of Management Journal*, 37: 1141–1166.

Ronen, S., & Shenkar, O. 1985. Clustering countries on attitudinal dimensions: A review and synthesis. *Academy of Management Review*, 10: 435–454.

Rumelt, R. P. 1974. *Strategy, structure, and economic performance*, Cambridge, MA: Harvard University Press.

Rumelt, R. P. 1982. Diversification strategy and profitability. *Strategic Management Journal*, 3: 359–369.

Schneider, S. C., & DeMeyer, A. 1991. Interpreting and responding to strategic issues: The impact of national culture. *Strategic Management Journal*, 12: 307–320.

Shane, S. A. 1993. The effect of cultural differences in perceptions of transactions costs on national differences in the preference for international joint ventures. *Asia Pacific Journal of Management*, 10: 57-69.

Shleifer, A., & Vishny, R. W. 1991. Takeovers in the '60s and the '80s: Evidence and implications. *Strategic Management Journal*, 12: 51–59.

Simmonds, P. G. 1990. The combined diversification breadth and mode dimensions and the performance of large diversified firms. *Strategic Management Journal*, 11: 399–410.

Simon, H. A. 1955. A behavioral model of rational choice. *Quarterly Journal of Economics*, 69: 99–118.

Singley, M. K., & Anderson, J. R. 1989. *The transfer of cognitive skill*. Cambridge, MA: Harvard University Press.

Tallman, S., & Li, J. 1996. Effects of international diversity and product diversity on the performance of multinational firms. *Academy of Management Journal*, 39: 179–196.

Teece, D. J. 1982. Towards an economic theory of the multiproduct firm. *Journal of Economic Behavior and Organization*, 3: 39–63.

Tushman, M. L., & O'Reilly, C. A., III. 1996. Ambidextrous organizations. *California Management Review*, 38(4): 8–30.

Tushman, M. L., & Romanelli, E. 1985. Organizational evolution: A metamorphosis model of convergence and reorientation. In L. L. Cummings & B. M. Staw (Eds.), *Research in organizational behavior*, vol. 7: 171–222. Greenwich, CT: JAI Press.

United Nations. 1991. *World investment report. The triad in foreign direct investment*. New York: United Nations.

United Nations. 1993. *Explaining and forecasting regional flows of foreign direct investment*. New York: United Nations.

Walsh, J. P. 1995. Managerial and organizational cognition: Notes from a trip down memory lane. *Organization Science*, 6: 280–321.

Weber, Y., Shenkar, O., & Raveh, A. 1996. National and corporate cultural fit in mergers and acquisitions: An exploratory study. *Management Science*, 42: 1215–1227.

Wernerfelt, B. 1984. A resource-based view of the firm. *Strategic Management Journal*, 5: 171–180.

Williamson, O. E. 1975. *Markets and hierarchies*. New York: Free Press.

Williamson, O. E. 1985. *The economic institutions of capitalism: Firms, markets, relational contracting*. New York: Free Press.

Wilson, B. D. 1980. The propensity of multinational companies to expand through acquisitions. *Journal of International Business Studies*, 11: 59–64.

Woodcock, C. P., Beamish, P. W., & Makino, S. 1994. Ownership-based entry mode strategies and international performance. *Journal of International Business Studies*, 25: 253–273.

Zaheer, S. 1995. Overcoming the liability of foreignness. *Academy of Management Journal*, 38: 341–363.

Zejan, M. 1990. New ventures or acquisitions: The choice of Swedish multinational enterprises. *Journal of Industrial Economics*, 38: 349–355.

Barkema, H. G. and Vermeulen F. (1998) "International expansion through start-up or acquisition: A learning perspective". *Academy of Management Journal*, 41(1), 7–26. Reprinted with permission.

Section 2
Motives and Targets

Merger theory, property rights and the pattern of US direct investment in Canada

8

H. G. Baumann

I INTRODUCTION

The issue of foreign direct investment, and specifically US foreign direct investment, has received increased attention in the last few years. There have been a number of studies on the industrial and geographical pattern of foreign direct investment, the trends in foreign investment over time as well as the costs and benefits of foreign direct investment.[1] The present paper is concerned with the determinants of inter-industry variations in the pattern of US direct investment in Canadian manufacturing industries. This is a subject which is of interest in its own right, but it becomes of crucial importance when policies to control foreign direct investment are being considered.[2]

The current pattern of US ownership of Canadian industries or any other country's industries is the result of the following phenomena: (a) the takeover of existing Canadian owned enterprises, (b) the establishment of subsidiaries of parent US firms and (c) the growth of these entities relative to the remaining Canadian owned firms or new domestically owned firms, either through further takeovers or a better growth performance.

This taxonomy immediately suggests two alternative theoretical foundations for research on the pattern of foreign direct investment (FDI), i.e., the theory of mergers[3] as developed by industrial organization specialists and the theory of investment whether neoclassical, accelerator, profitability, liquidity or some eclectic version.

However, the traditional theory of investment is not directly applicable to the problem of the pattern of foreign direct investment.[4] Thus, FDI does not include only plant and equipment expenditures but also inventories and financial capital. More-over, no new capital formation is involved in takeovers which form a major part in foreign direct investment. Unfortunately, little information exists on the relative importance of takeovers and investment in newly established subsidiaries in Canada. Nevertheless, a recent study shows that there were 352 foreign acquisitions (take-overs) in manufacturing in the 1945 to 1961 period, and the value of assets of these acquired firms represents 12% of the total value of assets of manufacturing firms controlled by non-residents in the year 1962.[5] The 12% figure represents an underestimate of the importance of takeovers in foreign direct investment because (a) takeovers which occurred before 1945 or after 1961 were not included; (b) information on takeovers in this study was obtained from trade journals, newspapers and financial magazines which raises the possibility of omissions; (c) a strict definition of foreign acquisition or takeover involving the purchase of 50% of the acquired Canadian firms is employed.[6] Moreover certain dynamic effects should be noted since empirical research has demonstrated that the number of foreign takeovers is positively related to the number of foreign controlled firms already in the industry.[7]

In the case of expansion investment which may play an important role in some Canadian industries where foreign direct investment has been of longstanding significance, explanations for the relatively greater growth rate of foreign owned subsidiaries are required, but again the traditional theory of investment is not readily applicable.[8] In other words, relative advantages not possessed by domestically owned firms play the key role both in the initial investment decision, and the relatively higher rate of expansion of subsidiaries.

In order to explain more fully those advantages which encourage a firm to seek out foreign investments through takeovers or establishing new enterprises and to prosper subsequently, a theory of the international firm based on property rights concepts is presented in Section III of the paper i.e. after merger theory has been applied to FDI in Section II.[9] This is an appropriate inclusion for two reasons. First, takeovers are not the only source of foreign direct investment as already shown above. Second, the property rights theory when applied to FDI supplants the view that tariffs and relative cost differences play an important role as determinants of the pattern of FDI.[10]

After discussing the theoretical underpinning of this study some empirical work is presented in Section IV, and the conclusions which emerge from this exercise are presented in Section V.

II THE THEORY OF MERGERS APPLIED TO FOREIGN DIRECT INVESTMENT

The theory of mergers remains as one possible foundation for the analysis of the pattern of foreign direct investment. Several versions of merger theory classified basically according to different merger motives exist.[11] Moreover, in a recent article, one economist has advanced an economic disturbance theory of mergers.[12] However, the theory of conglomerate mergers will not be discussed in the present article because most US foreign direct investment in Canada occurs in the same industry as that of the parent acquiring firm.[13]

Why do takeovers or mergers (the terms are used interchangeably in this paper because no ambiguity results) occur ? A necessary condition is the existence of a valuation or an appraisal gap between the managers (stockholders) of the one firm and the managers (stockholders) of another.[14] More specifically, the managers of the acquiring firm may place a higher valuation on the acquired firm than the latter's own management, or the managers of the acquiring firm may recognize that the combined firm after the takeover has a higher present value than the two independent firms.

In a more rigorous form, one may note that the demand price of firm A for firm B will be the present value of the difference between the expected profits of the combined firm C and the existing firm A, or in symbols.

$$D_A = \sum_{t=0}^{\infty} \frac{[(\Pi_C^A)_t - (\Pi_A^A)_t]}{(1 + R_A)^t}$$

where D_A = the demand price of firm A, Π_C^A = the expected profits of the combined firm according to A's managers and Π_A^A = the expected profits of firm A alone, and R_A = the discount rate of A's managers. On the other hand, the supply price of B (S_B) is the present value of its expected future profits or

$$S_B = \sum_{t=0}^{\infty} \frac{(\Pi_B^B)_t}{(1 + R_B)^t}$$

where Π_B^B = B's expected future profits according to B's managers and R_B = the discount rate of B's managers. In the absence of transaction costs, A will takeover B if $D_A > S_B$, and this condition may occur under a variety of circumstances.

Merger motives: Monopoly power, economics of scale, synergistic effects

On a purely technical level, it is apparent that $D_A > S_B$ when $[(\Pi_C^A)_t - (\Pi_A^A)_t > (\Pi_B^B)_t$ or the combined expected profits of the merged firm exceed the sum of the profits of the two independent firms with $R_A = R_B$. This situation may occur when the combined firm has market power or power over price which neither A nor B have independently. Although this reason or motive for a takeover may have some validity on the domestic scene, it has limited relevance in the takeover of a foreign firm unless the formation of an international oligopoly (monopoly) is involved where the potential for price fixing on a global scale is feasible. Moreover, the takeover of a Canadian firm by a US corporation could hardly make a substantial contribution in this direction. It must be noted that the foreign investment decision in the form of a takeover or the establishment of a subsidiary is discrete in nature, and hence, a marginal improvement in monopoly power on a global scale is not directly relevant.

Conceivably, American firms might acquire Canadian firms as a hedge against a movement toward free trade between the two countries since this might assure price tranquility if not market dominance. However, this version of the monopoly motive for takeovers would only be relevant in those few manufacturing industries where Canadian owned firms had a large potential impact. Nevertheless, one must admit that it is extremely difficult to evaluate the monopoly motive for takeovers because of the obvious reluctance by businessmen to discuss this issue, and also, on occasion, their lack of knowledge about hidden effects of mergers. If merger motives can be judged by the effects achieved (keeping in mind the gap between intent and performance), the results of recent research indicate that mergers or takeovers have become a less important factor in increasing concentration over time within the United States and Canada.[15]

More important than potential monopoly power is that the combined firm will achieve economies of scale which neither firm A nor B can achieve independently.[16] The scale economies in question must arise at the firm rather than plant level since the latter type of economics would encourage production at a central location for both the domestic and foreign markets, all other things including transportation costs being equal. More fundamentally, plant level economies cannot be readily realized through a takeover. Firm level economies may occur in all management or head office functions, but especially in research and development (R&D), marketing of output, purchasing of inputs and risk bearing. This is a mixed bag of technical (real) economies of scale (parent firm and subsidiary sharing a common pool of scientists and engineers, market researchers, etc.) and pecuniary economies of scale (quantity discounts from suppliers of inputs), but the ultimate effect is a reduction in costs for the combined firm. The differential importance of firm level economies in one industry as compared with another can explain industry differences in the extent of foreign direct investment. Moreover, the takeover activity of foreign owned subsidiaries can be rationalized in terms of quantity discounts which are not available across frontiers. An interesting outcome of the economies of scale (or market structure) hypothesis is the implicit suggestion that the pattern of US direct investment in Canada should be similar to the pattern of Canadian investment in the United States.

However, the literature on synergistic effects[17] which provides a third reason for the higher present value of the combined firm indicates why the pattern of US direct investment in Canada may take on a specific form. Thus, firm B may have available underutilized resources which cannot be rented or are nonmarketable because of indivisibilities, transaction costs, etc. and firm A may be able to utilize this excess capacity thus increasing the present value of the combined firm. Note that no synergistic effects will occur if all of firm B's resources are fully employed or if both firms use the same resources to the fullest extent before the merger. Thus, complementarity of resources between firms and the existence of market imperfections are required for the presence of synergistic effects.

In the United States–Canada situation, it appears likely that the parent US firm has or potentially[18] will have underutilized resources in research and development as well as the marketing of new products while Canadian firms may have underutilized production and financial resources.[19] This complementarity can explain the takeover of Canadian rather than other US firms although institutional factors such as antitrust also play a role.

Both the economies of scale argument and the underutilized resources argument indicate that research and development intensity provides an explanation of the pattern of foreign direct investment. The lumpiness of research and development expenditures suggests that the marginal cost of additional R&D output would lie below average costs while the appropriability problem points to a nonmarket solution in the R&D services market, i.e., a takeover or subsidiary operations.[20] Although a domestically owned firm can forego the costs of adaptation to local factor price ratios, the existence of economies of scale is likely to dominate in the Canada–US environment. This is the view implicit in Caves' analysis when he notes that the cheap services from the stock of intangible capital built up by US firms overcomes the advantages domestic firms have in their local market.[21]

In this analysis, intangible capital refers to the technical and marketing know how, as well as the goodwill and connections which a firm has acquired in the process of designing, modifying and promoting products. Therefore, the key issue from the viewpoint of FDI is the optimal use of these resources controlled by the parent firm although Caves relates his notion of intangible capital to the static concept of product differentiation.[22] However, licensing of domestically controlled firms would be a feasible alternative in industries with an unchanging product mix since quality changes, brand changes, etc. pose no difficulties for agreements. All of these arguments suggest that the R&D intensity of industries as well as the extent of product changes (average product age) are, more relevant for foreign direct investment than any measure of product differentiation (e.g. advertising intensity) *per se* although empirically a positive correlation between these measures may exist.[23]

It should be noted that research and development activities are viewed here as being firm or industry specific. In other words, the output of research and development can be used by other firms in the industry although imperfections may prevent a competitive market from arising. In a recent paper McManus argues that a "general" factor such as research and development can play no role in determining the pattern of foreign direct investment.[24] Presumably, he means that any underutilized R&D resources could be employed equally well in new product or process developments anywhere in the economy. Thus, there would be no reason to expect a greater potential discrepancy in discounted profits between two separate firms and a combined firm in technology intensive industries. However, this assumption of general applicability of research and development resources is questionable.

Additional merger motives: Non-profit maximizing behaviour, differences in attitudes toward risk

A second reason for $D_A > S_B$ is that A's discount rate is smaller than B's discount rate or $R_A < R_B$. This situation can occur when B's management values future profits less than the market does (possibly because of a wish to retire from control of the corporation) or A's management uses a discount rate which is relatively low for internal projects such as takeovers. The most frequent reason given for the use of a low discount rate by firm A, leading to a high present value of firm B, and therefore a takeover, is the desire for expansion of sales and the realization of dreams of empire. This is not necessarily inconsistent with long-run profit maximization, but growth can also be an autonomous goal in situations where there is an absence of stockholder control over management.

In order for these factors to determine the pattern of FDI, further assumptions are required. For example, one might be able to show that managers in one country put more weight on growth maximization than managers in another country, and that there are interindustry differences or variations in this factor. At a minimum, one would have to show that there is greater stockholder control in one country as compared with the next, or that owner-managers are more prevalent, or that management is older and that these characteristics affect firm behaviour. No conclusive studies have been undertaken in this area, possibly because of a lack of data although it has been shown that merger prone firms have inferior earnings performance, but this may be due to factors other than the goals of the entrepreneurs.[25]

Alternatively, one can view differences in the discount rate as being caused by different attitudes toward risk. In this connection, $R = a + w \, Var \, (\mu)$ where "a" is a constant representing the riskless rate of discount or the yield on risk-free securities while "μ" is a random disturbance term summarizing effects which are not covered by expected net earnings or Π. The argument suggests that $w_B > w_A$, and therefore, $R_B > R_A$ leading to a higher estimated present value of firm B by managers of firm A as compared to firm B's own management. In present circumstances, firm A's managers should be thought of as foreign (US) entrepreneurs and firm B's as domestic (Canadian) entrepreneurs. At least, this has been the long-standing opinion on the subject of United States–Canada differences in attitudes toward risk. It can be shown that the above risk adjusted discount rate follows from a utility function in which profits (net earnings) enter as a positive and risk enters as a negative argument, but this exercise is superfluous for present purposes.[26]

The economic disturbance theory

Even though the managements of firms A and B have the same discount rate ($R_A = R_B$) and firm A expects no additional profits from a combined firm i.e., $(\Pi_C^A)_t = (\Pi_A^A)_t + (\Pi_B^A)_t$, firm A may still decide to take over B if it expects greater profits from B than B's own management. This divergence of expectations which provides the third possibility for $D_A > S_B$ is seen by Gort[27] as the immediate determinant of variations in the frequency of mergers among industries over time. He argues that economic disturbances (shocks, drastic economic changes) alter expectations about future income streams so that non-owners move to the right of owners on a value scale of firms, and in addition, the variance of valuations of firms increases because the future becomes less predictable. These are the necessary conditions for a takeover.

What are the economic disturbances which bring about the discrepancies in the valuations of firms? Foremost among them is technological change because the demand for new products is difficult to predict and so are production costs – the latter point also applies with respect to process innovations. Other sources of economic disturbances might be variations in industry growth patterns and barriers to entry, but the empirical evidence and theoretical justification for these factors are less clearcut.

In his article, Gort rejects the importance of non-growth maximizing behaviour and economies of scale as determinants of takeovers because the former cannot readily explain the pattern of acquisitions across industries unless additional information on the industrial distribution of these factors is introduced while the latter cannot explain the variations in merger activity over time. While agreeing with the first point, a healthy skepticism is called for with regard to the second since technology and scale changes are often interlinked. Moreover, the purpose of the present paper is the explanation of the industrial pattern as opposed to the volume or changes in the volume of FDI. Nevertheless, the attempt by Gort to develop a more "general" theory is laudatory. In any case, some of the variables which the economic disturbance theory suggests can also be derived from the economies of scale theory, the most obvious example being the technological intensity of the industry.

III PROPERTY RIGHTS THEORY APPLIED TO FOREIGN DIRECT INVESTMENT

At this point, it may be useful to discuss the theory of the international firm as developed by McManus from the earlier discussion of the theory of the firm found in Coase.[28] This theory can be interpreted as providing an explanation for the greater present value of the combined firm compared with the constituent parts, but it offers some important additional insights by suggesting that tariffs and cost differences from one country to the next may have a very limited role in determining the pattern of FDI. Moreover, property rights theory explains why firms seek out foreign investments not only through takeover activity, but through subsidiary operations in general.

McManus is seeking the fundamental determinants of foreign direct investment, and he begins (correctly in my opinion) by noting that the international transfer of capital is not the essence of the problem since the existence of equity ownership or control and not debt capital must be explained. Rather the key to the analysis is the recognition of interdependence between the parent firm and the subsidiary, or the interconnectedness of ownership rights between the two. If such interdependence exists, then there are potential efficiency gains from taking over or merging with a foreign firm. In other words, a process of internalizing externalities is involved. For example, the advertising of American products on US television spills over into Canada and the benefits therefrom can be captured by the American firm through subsidiary sales. However, the American firm could also pursue a policy of export sales or manufacture under licensing arrangements in order to capture the spillover effect. The choice among these three methods depends on the costs of coordination. In other words, the efficiency gains which possibly lead to a higher present value for the combined firms are only one side of the equation while the coordination costs determine which method (subsidiary production, export sales, licensing) will be used to exploit the externalities.

McManus compares three methods of coordination, i.e., the price system (market), the contract (license) and fiat (within the firm). The costs of coordination may be identified with transaction costs and these have two components: (i) the costs of measurement of services from a stock of assets and (ii) costs of enforcement of property rights. Given this outline, one can readily rationalize why General Motors insisted on complete *control* of the McLaughlin Company and why Holiday Inns *licenses* Commonwealth Holiday Inns. As it becomes more difficult to define what services will be exchanged and what actions will fulfil an agreement, a contract (license, franchise) becomes a less appropriate means of exchanging property rights. Therefore, on the subject of interindustry differences in foreign direct investment McManus concludes that, "the international firm will be chosen as the means of organizing production internationally in those industries in which both the inter-dependence among producers in various countries and the costs of coordinating their actions are relatively high".[29]

McManus illustrates his theory by giving examples, but one must be careful to avoid falling into a tautological argument, e.g., foreign ownership is high in the computer industry, therefore interdependence and the costs of coordinating through the price system or by contract must be high. However, the theory is not empty since it implies that the inter-county, interstate and international firms arise from similar conditions, i. e interdependence and coordinating costs, and this proposition can be readily tested. Moreover, interdependence is more likely to be recognized and exists on a broader scale *vis-á-vis* the larger foreign firms, and these would be the main targets for takeover.

Nevertheless, the issue of tautology remains bothersome, and one should establish whether the theory is capable of suggesting *a priori* the industries where the costs of coordinating are high and interdependence is widespread. Industries with rapidly changing technology, and industries with high selling costs would appear to be the most obvious candidates. Thus, a new type of steelmaking furnace might be built under licence, but not a new computer system which will go through many modifications and involve rigid quality control and servicing standards. As already noted, McManus rejects the idea that a "general" factor such as technology can affect the interindustry variation in foreign ownership, but his conclusion appears to be based on the unwarranted assumption of no firm or industry specific technological know how.

The notion that tariffs can stimulate foreign direct investment and that Canadian tariff policy is a major cause of US ownership of Canadian industries has been part of the conventional wisdom for a long time. More recently, Horst[30] has provided a theoretical basis and empirical support for the proposition that, given foreign penetration, tariffs imposed by the foreign country (Canada) encourage US firms to substitute subsidiary production for exporting. However, neither Orr nor Caves[31] who worked on a more disaggregated industry level were able to confirm a positive relationship between tariffs and subsidiary sales. Generally these inconclusive empirical results have been explained by the following factors: (i) investment patterns reflect much more than tariffs; (ii) current behaviour of firms reflect past decisions or there is a problem of lags; (iii) tariff setters give protection to local producers threatened by import competition and this leads to perverse results; (iv) in disaggregating to a finer industry breakdown extreme cases (high tariff, low exports, high subsidiary sales) were decomposed into very few industries while intermediate cases (medium tariff, medium exports and subsidiary sales) were decomposed into many industries.

However, there may be theoretical objections to the hypothesis of a positive relationship between tariffs and subsidiary sales because, while a tariff will undoubtedly stimulate domestic production in a particular industry, it is not clear why foreign owned firms should take advantage of it to a greater extent than indigenous entrepreneurs. In other words, some of the arguments on merger motives or spillover effects made above should be looked on as the more fundamental causes of FDI or introduced in conjunction with the tariff.[32] The tariff can, of course, play a primary role with respect to FDI if it is less costly to avoid the tariff within an international firm through manipulating transfer prices than achieving the same end with two separate firms. Moreover, the tariff can affect the economy wide level of foreign direct investment in an upward direction if it tends to stimulate the output of industries which are interdependent.

The argument with respect to tariffs can be extended to cover the role of a number of additional factors. For example, some researchers contend that lower raw material costs, wage costs, and possibly capital costs in other countries will stimulate foreign direct investment.[33] However, these advantages also accrue to domestically owned firms, and as long as one can assume the existence of indigenous entrepreneurs, and no differences or changes in the goals of entrepreneurs (profit maximizing versus growth maximizing) it is difficult to see why foreign owned firms will grow relatively to domestically owned firms.

IV THE EMPIRICAL ANALYSIS

The theoretical analysis of the last two sections suggests the following model:[34]

$$\overset{(+)\quad(+)\quad(+)\quad(+)\quad(+)}{SUS_i = f\,(PROT_i,\ FTD_i,\ CONC_i,\ MULTI_i,\ SIZUC_i,\ Z_i,)}$$

where

SUS_i = shipments (sales) of US controlled[35] subsidiaries over total shipments in Canada. This is a measure of the level of FDI in the industry;

$PROT_i$ $\equiv$ a measure of the technological intensity of the industry;

FTD_i $\equiv$ the average age of products of the industry measured on the basis of their year of appearance in international trade, i.e., 1947, 1950 and so on;

$CONC_i$ $\equiv$ a concentration measure to serve as a proxy for firm level economies of scale;

$MULTI_i$ $\equiv$ shipments originating in multi-plant firms over total shipments;

$SIZUC_i$ $\equiv$ a ratio of the average size of American firms in the US relative to Canadian owned firms in Canada;

Z_i $\equiv$ other factors such as risk, advertising intensity, etc;

i $\equiv$ industry where i = 1, 2, . . ., 67.

With a few exceptions the data are based on US information since Canadian data for explanatory variables may be biased because of foreign controlled operations. For example, research and development expenditures in Canada may be relatively low in industries where considerable foreign direct investment exists, but there is little evidence to support this hypothesis.[36] Nevertheless, where Canadian data sources were used, simple correlations were first performed on the more limited sample of industries for which data from both countries were available in order to determine whether no distortions were likely to result from the use of Canadian data.

The inclusion of the explanatory variables has been considered in the previous section, but the rationale can be summarized in the following manner. The technological intensity variable (PROT) is included to reflect the existence of firm level economies of scale in the research and development function, and specifically the possibility of excess capacity on the part of US firms in their R&D resources. With the average age of products variable one can argue that economies of scale in marketing new products are also being captured. Moreover, in industries with a rapid turnover of products the costs of coordination would tend to be high, and this encourages foreign subsidiary operations as we have indicated. The likely divergence of opinion on the valuation of firms in industries where product innovations are common provides additional support for the inclusion of FTD. The concentration (CONC) measure is intended to reflect all economies of scale both technological and pecuniary.

One would expect that the variables CONC and MULTI (multi-plant shipments) would be correlated, and this is indeed the case with the correlation coefficient being 0.66. Nevertheless, MULTI would appear to be a more accurate proxy for McManus' theory of the international firm since he argues that there is no fundamental difference between the inter-county, interregional and international firm.

The SIZUC variable is intended to reflect the prediction that the larger Canadian firms would be taken over because the potential efficiency gains are higher where the interdependence is greater.[37] Therefore, a high level of FDI would be positively related to a large size difference between firms in the US and Canadian controlled firms in Canada for the same industry.[38]

The empirical results for the model based on OLS regression are presented in the table. It has been possible to explain approximately 50% of the variation in the dependent variable, and this compares favorably with previous work in this area.[39] All of the variables in equations (1) and (2) have the expected sign and are significant. Unfortunately, it is impossible to distinguish the degree of validity of the various theories (market structure, economic disturbance and property rights). As

Empirical Results

(1) $SUS = -0.338 + 1.758 \text{ PROT} + 0.716 \text{ FTD} + 0.341 \text{ MULTI} + 0.018 \text{ SIZUC}$
     (-1.823) (3.007) (1.888) (2.288) (3.146)
                $\overline{R}^2 = 0.476$ $F = 16.102$

(2) $SUS = -0.270 + 2.121 \text{ PROT} + 0.849 \text{ FTD} + 0.416 \text{ CONC} + 0.015 \text{ SIZUC}$
     (-1.582) (4.074) (2.236) (2.504) (2.516)
                $\overline{R}^2 = 0.485$ $F = 16.523$

(3) $SUS = -0.339 + 1.766 \text{ PROT} + 0.711 \text{ FTD} + 0.342 \text{ MULTI} + 0.018 \text{ SIZUC} - 0.035 \text{ CRU}$
     (-1.811) (2.981) (1.848) (2.274) (3.106) (0.135)
                $\overline{R}^2 = 0.468$ $F = 12.603$

(4) $SUS = -0.346 + 1.730 \text{ PROT} + 0.745 \text{ FTD} + 0.321 \text{ MULTI} + 0.018 \text{ SIZUC} + 0.329 \text{ K/O}$
     (-1.842) (2.917) (1.912) (2.025) (3.136) (0.379)
                $\overline{R}^2 = 0.469$ $F = 12.651$

(5) $SUS = -0.399 + 1.756 \text{ PROT} + 0.723 \text{ FTD} + 0.343 \text{ MULTI} + 0.018 \text{ SIZUC} + 0.42 \text{ WA}$
     (-1.148) (2.979) (1.884) (2.279) (3.119) (0.206)
                $\overline{R}^2 = 0.468$ $F = 12.603$

(6) $SUS = -0.305 + 1.795 \text{ PROT} + 0.449 \text{ FTD} + 0.494 \text{ MULTI} + 0.021 \text{ SIZUC} - 0.743 \text{ SIZUS}$
     (-1.697) (3.180) (1.170) (3.130) (3.717) (-2.361)
                $\overline{R}^2 = 0.512$ $F = 14.847$

(7) $SUS = -0.338 + 1.764 \text{ PROT} + 0.720 \text{ FTD} + 0.337 \text{ MULTI} + 0.018 \text{ SIZUC} + 0.193 \text{ SCA}$
     (-1.805) (2.949) (1.857) (2.028) (3.011) (0.060)
                $\overline{R}^2 = 0.508$ $F = 12.597$

(8) $SUS = -0.319 + 1.760 \text{ PROT} + 0.687 \text{ FTD} + 0.341 \text{ MULTI} + 0.027 \text{ SIZUC} - 0.107 \text{ TRAN}$
     (-1.633) (2.989) (1.753) (2.271) (3.060) (-0.330)
                $\overline{R}^2 = 0.469$ $F = 12.651$

(9) $SUS = -0.227 + 1.744 \text{ PROT} + 0.733 \text{ FTD} + 0.319 \text{ MULTI} + 0.017 \text{ SIZUC} - 0.081 \text{ ETC}$
     (-0.847) (2.965) (1.916) (2.059) (3.098) (-0.582)
                $\overline{R}^2 = 0.470$ $F = 12.749$

(10) $SUS = -0.420 + 1.777 \text{ PROT} + 0.915 \text{ FTD} + 0.301 \text{ MULTI} + 0.017 \text{ SIZUC} + 1.355 \text{ ADV}$
     (-2.169) (3.060) (2.268) (1.994) (2.967) (1.373)
                $\overline{R}^2 = 0.484$ $F = 13.371$

(11) $SUS = -0.260 + 1.666 \text{ PROT} + 0.605 \text{ FTD} + 0.346 \text{ MULTI} + 0.018 \text{ SIZUC} - 0.063 \text{ CONS}$
     (-1.242) (2.792) (1.497) (2.310) (3.204) (-0.820)
                $\overline{R}^2 = 0.494$ $F = 12.847$

(12) $SUS = -0.331 + 1.838 \text{ PROT} + 0.781 \text{ FTD} + 0.325 \text{ MULTI} + 0.017 \text{ SIZUC} - 0.800 \text{ RISK}$
     (1.768) (3.024) (1.947) (2.121) (2.978) (-0.524)
                $\overline{R}^2 = 0.470$ $F = 12.700$

(13) $SUS = -0.302 + 1.760 \text{ PROT} + 0.734 \text{ FTD} + 0.337 \text{ MULTI} + 0.018 \text{ SIZUC} - 0.034 \text{ GROCU}$
     (1.405) (2.988) (1.903) (2.236) (3.141) (-1.405)
                $\overline{R}^2 = 0.469$ $F = 12.651$

Note: $t > 1.670$ significant at the 5% level, one tail test.

already noted some of the explanatory variables refer to more than one theory and while the concentration measure leads to marginally better results than the multi-plant shipments variable we are unable to reject either the market structure or property rights theory as applied to the problem of foreign direct investment. The obvious conclusion is that an eclectic approach is desirable, and a combination of factors is involved which speaks against McManus' univariate explanation.

However, equations (3), (4), and (5) clearly show that cost factors probably play no role in determining the industry level of foreign direct investment. One might hypothesize that the abundance of mining, forestry and fishing resources as represented by the CRU variable would lead to low costs for these materials in Canada, and hence, according to some economists to increased FDI, but this is apparently not the case. A similar argument applies with respect to the wage variable (WA) and the capital variable (K/O) both of which have the wrong sign, but they are not significant. Thus, the view that cost factors should be introduced into the analysis only insofar as they affect subsidiaries of foreign firms and domestically owned firms in a differential manner is confirmed.

Nevertheless, one must keep in mind that the relatively unimpeded flow of industrial materials and capital in North America complicates the empirical analysis. Moreover, a high level of FDI based on improved technology would tend to raise the level of wages in an industry and even though the wage variable was lagged, the simultaneity problem could probably not be entirely removed. More fundamentally, given that US firms have a competitive advantage over Canadian firms because of economies of scale captured in a larger domestic market etc. the differences in costs may affect their ratio of export sales versus subsidiary production, but the underlying cause for subsidiary production is not the difference in factor costs.[40] Therefore, when these other variables are introduced with SUS as the dependent variable the cost factors become irrelevant. The same arguments as already suggested in Section III, apply with respect to the result for the Canadian effective tariff rate presented in equation (9) since it is apparently *not* significantly related to the extent of subsidiary production.

A surprising result is apparent in equation (6) which indicates that the average size of firms (SIZUS) has a negative influence on the industry level of FDI. This apparently contradicts results of other studies which indicate that FDI is the preserve of large firms. However, the hypothesis here is merely concerned with whether FDI is related to larger or smaller mean firm size at the industry level. Moreover, when MULTI is dropped as an explanatory variable the significance of SIZUS (correlation coefficient with MULTI is 0.49) is impaired although the sign remains negative. These results call for caution in suggesting that larger firm size is the answer to limiting FDI since there may be significant discontinuities.[41] and firms might have to be of very large size indeed before the proposition holds true. Thus, it is relative size of firms which is important as well as a number of other factors.

Both plant level economies of scale and transportation costs are not significant variables, and their contribution to the explanatory power of equations (7) and (8) is insignificant. One might hypothesize that plant level economies of scale would lower the level of FDI, but these are correlated with firm level economies which pull in the other direction. High transportation costs should increase FDI, if the same traditional argument which was discussed with respect to tariffs applies. However there are the following complicating features: (i) in the North American context interregional transport costs are often lower than international costs; and (ii) a fully integrated production process encompassing various stages may be taking place within the multinational firm. An interaction variable which combined plant level scale economies and transportation costs was also included on the assumption that these two factors determine multi-plant production, but the results were not encouraging.

Contrary to expectation the advertising variable (equation (10)) was not significant although it has the correct sign. In this connection, it is interesting to note that the correlation coefficient between the age of products and advertising is (-0.31) i.e., industries with newer products tend to advertise less. This suggests that the advertising variable may be a poor proxy for the kind of product differentiation, i.e., product innovation, modification and style change which can be readily connected with the theories of mergers discussed in Section II.[42] Moreover, the spillover effects from advertising may be minimal when local tastes differ, and/or government regulations over the media intervene. Finally, older differentiated products can probably be more readily produced under licence, i.e., the costs of coordination through a contract are low.

The result for the risk variable in equation (12) runs contrary to traditional expectations. Thus, there is no support for the contention that Canadians are more risk averse in the sense of seeking out less risky industries, but it has been assumed that the returns of firms in the two countries are similarly distributed and that US firms are limited in their ability to minimize risk through diversification in the Canadian market.[43] The latter two assumptions may not hold and further research is indicated.

The last equation of the table indicates that FDI is not concentrated in industries where growth in Canada has been relatively more rapid than in the United States. Some may find this result surprising since it would appear to contradict the growth maximization hypothesis. However, US firms which are growth maximizers have the option of conglomerate mergers.[44] Moreover, it was impossible at this stage to develop industry growth data which go back to the immediate postwar period when a lot of US investment occurred because of classification problems.

V CONCLUSIONS AND AGENDA FOR FUTURE RESEARCH

It has been possible to show that the theories of mergers and takeovers originally developed in the context of a closed economy can be usefully applied to the problem of FDI. A multi-factor model based on market structure, economic disturbance and property rights concepts is capable of explaining approximately one half of the interindustry variation of US controlled subsidiary sales in Canada. There is some indication that further improvements in explanatory power of the model are feasible if more accurate proxies for sales effort could be introduced and a more sophisticated treatment of risk and industry growth patterns was undertaken.[45] This last variable brings up the point that the present model was built exclusively on the assumption of joint profit maximization between parent firm and subsidiary and this may not be entirely adequate. Certainly, several economists have pointed to a bandwagon effect or the reaction of rivals to the FDI initiatives of other firms in a particular industry as additional explanations for the industry level of FDI.[46] One would also hope that the determinants of the level of US investment in other countries, and especially, the EEC would receive additional attention. Moreover, the pattern of direct investment of countries other than the United States should also be studied because one of the implications of McManus' theory of the international firms is that this pattern would not differ from that of the United States. Finally, the pattern of FDI in the service industries on the one hand, and the primary industries on the other may involve a somewhat different set of motivations.

APPENDIX

SUS_i $\equiv$ The ratio of sales by US controlled firms divided by total sales of industry i in 1968. Data provided by Dale Orr from *Corporations and Labour Unions Returns Act* (CALURA), data, unpubl.

K_i/L_i $\equiv$ The dollar value of net fixed assets per man for 1969 in industry i. *Source*: Statistics Canada: *Corporation Financial Statistics*, Ottawa, Information Canada, 1972; *Review of Manufacturing Industries of*

K_i/O_i ≡ Canada, 1969, Ottawa, Information Canada, 1972. – Data on the same variable based on US sources are from Hufbauer, *op. cit.*, Appendix, Table A–2.

K_i/O_i ≡ The dollar value of net fixed assets per million dollars of shipments for industry i in 1969. Along with K_i/L_i serves as a measure of capital intensity.

CRU_i ≡ Direct requirements of crude materials per dollar value of gross output for 1961 in industry i. *Source*: Statistics Canada: *The Input-Output Structure of the Canadian Economy, 1961*, Ottawa, Information Canada, 1969. Crude materials are defined to include all shipments arising from the primary sector (agriculture, fishing, forestry, mining, coal, oil, gas) of the Canadian economy. Various alternative measures which included only *some* of the industries of the primary sector were also derived.

$PROT_i$ ≡ The proportion of professional and technical workers for 1961 in industry i. *Source*: Statistics Canada, *Census of Canada, 1961*, Vol. 3, Part 3, Ottawa, Information Canada n.d.

$CONC_i$ ≡ The four firm concentration ratio for industry i. *Source*: US Bureau of the Census, *Census of Manufactures, 1967*, Washington, DC.

$MULTI_i$ ≡ The ratio of shipments from multi-plant enterprises to total shipments of industry i. *Source: Ibid.*

$SIZUS_i$ ≡ The total assets divided by the number of firms in industry i. This is a measure of average firm size. *Source*: Department of the Treasury, Internal Revenue Service, *Statistics of Income, 1968*, Washington, DC.

$SIZUC_i$ ≡ $SIZUS_i$ divided by the equivalent figure for Canadian owned firms in industry i. *Source for Canada: Corporations and Labour Unions Returns Act* (CALURA), Report for 1967, Ottawa, Information Canada, 1970.

ETC_i ≡ The Canadian effective rate of protection, 1963. *Source*: James R. Melvin and Bruce W. Wilkinson, *Effective Protection in the Canadian Economy*, The Economic Council of Canada, Special Study, No. 9, Ottawa, 1968, Table 1.

ADV_i ≡ Advertising expenditures over sales for industry i. *Source*: Statistics Canada, *Market Research Handbook, 1969*, Ottawa.

$TRAN_i$ ≡ The shipping cost of a dollar of product value in the 1960s over a specified distance (Chicago-Cleveland in this case). It is derived from the formula [(1)/\$1/W] (R) where R = freight per pound over a specified distance and W = shipping weight of \$ 1 of product in question. *Source*: R. Murphy, *The Determinants of the Extent of Multi-Plant Operations in United States Manufacturing Industries*, University of Michigan, 1972, unpubl. dissertation.

WA_i ≡ US wages per man-hour divided by Canadian wages per man-hour for industry i. *Source*: Department of Industry, Trade and Commerce, *Comparative Tables of Principal Statistics and Ratios for 1967*, Ottawa, 1971.

$GROCU_i$ ≡ The ratio of the value of shipments in Canada divided by the US shipments in 1967 over the same figure for 1963 in industry i. *Source: Ibid.*

$RISK_i$ ≡ The variance of the return of firms in industry i divided by the mean of the return. *Source*: Gordon R. Conrad and Irving H. Plotkin, "Risk/

Return: US Industry Patterns", *Harvard Business Review*, Vol. 46, Boston, Mass., 1968, p. 94.

The following variables are based on US data alone, and were obtained from Hufbauer, *op. cit.*, Appendix Table A–2.

SCA_i $\equiv$ An estimate of "α" or the scale elasticity parameter in the equation $v = kn^\alpha$ where "v" represents the ratio between value added per man for a given size class of plant and the average value added per man for all establishments in the industry; "n" represents the average number of men employed per establishment in the given size class; "k" is a constant. The measure is based on 1963 US *Census of Manufactures* data.

FTD_i $\equiv$ The average first trade date for the commodities produced by industry i. This variable was obtained by examining the detailed [1958] schedule of exportable goods of the United States for the first appearance of specific commodities.

$CONS_i$ $\equiv$ The ratio of consumer goods to producer goods produced by industry i. Consumer goods are defined as products which are sold to households or government acting as a consumer. The data are derived from the 1958 US input-output table and both the proportion of products sold by an industry directly to final consumers and indirectly through another industry are taken into account up to the second round. Thus, producer goods are commodities which do not reach the consumer very quickly.

Note: The variables FTD and TRAN were multiplied by 10^{-2}, KOC and RISK by 10^{-3} and SIZUS by 10^{-5} before being introduced into the regression.

NOTES

1 For a survey of the literature and additional references see John H. Dunning, "The Determinants of International Production", *Oxford Economic Papers*, N. S., Vol. 25, 1973, pp. 289 sqq.

2 Recently, the Canadian government has established a screening agency for foreign takeovers, and other countries have various mechanisms for controlling foreign direct investment.

3 The terms merger and takeover are used interchangeably in this paper, but strictly speaking we are interested in the latter. On the distinction consult Ajit Singh, *Take-Overs: Their Relevance to the Stock Market and the Theory of the Firm*, Cambridge, 1971, p. xi.

4 For a similar view see J. David Richardson, "Theoretical Considerations in the Analysis of Foreign Direct Investment", *Western Economic Journal*, Vol. 9, Los Angeles, 1971, esp. pp. 88 sq., and Yair Aharoni, *The Foreign Investment Decision Process*, Boston, 1966, who argues that the existence of uncertainty as opposed to risk, high information costs and organization attitudes make traditional investment theory inoperable for the foreign investment decision.

5 G. L. Reuber and F. Roseman, *The Take-Over of Canadian Firms, 1945–61: An Empirical Analysis*, Economic Council of Canada, Special Study, No. 10, Ottawa, 1969, pp. 3sqq. – The role of foreign firms in merger activity is discussed in detail by G. Rosenbluth, "The Relation between Foreign Control and Concentration in Canadian Industry", *The Canadian Journal of Economics*, Vol. 3, Toronto, 1970, pp. 14 sqq. who argues that US firms were not responsible for an exceptionally high proportion of mergers relative to Canadian firms in the 1945 to 1961 period, but overseas firms were.

6 This raises the possibility that control might have been acquired after 1962 while before that date less than 50% of the voting shares were obtained.

7 Reuber and Roseman, *op. cit.*, p. 26. Unfortunately, there is a scarcity of data on the relative growth rates of foreign versus domestically owned firms which have been involved in merger activity nor are there data on this variable for foreign and domestic firms in general.

8 Insofar as the foreign owned subsidiaries are more profitable, one would like to examine the causes for this performance which can subsequently be related to relative growth and expansion.

9   The theory of portfolio balance and specifically the mean/variance approach is also of limited applicability for the pattern of foreign direct investment since takeover of foreign firms would appear to be a costly method of diversification to minimize risk on the part of stockholders. Moreover, one must assume the absence of a strong correlation between the returns of firms in the countries involved, and this assumption requires careful empirical substantiation for two integrated economies such as the US and Canada. Admittedly, the return might be higher in the foreign market, but it is important to discover why this is the case, and why domestic entrepreneurs are less responsive to these opportunities than foreign entrepreneurs.

10 The role of the tariff in FDI has been studied by Eastman and Stykolt among others. See H. C. Eastman and S. Stykolt, *The Tariff and Competition in Canada*, Toronto, 1967.

11 For a concise and accurate discussion of these versions of merger theory consult F. M. Scherer, *Industrial Market Structure and Economic Performance*, Rand McNally Economics Series, Chicago, 1970, pp. 112 sqq.

12 For a detailed discussion and application of this theory see Michael Gort, "An Economic Disturbance Theory of Mergers", *The Quarterly Journal of Economics*, Vol. 83, Cambridge, Mass., 1969, pp. 624 sqq.

13 For the theory of conglomerate mergers consult Dennis C. Mueller, "A Theory of Conglomerate Mergers", *ibid.*, pp. 643 sqq. – As Rosenbluth notes, horizontal mergers constitute by far the most important class both in terms of numbers and in terms of sales of acquired firms in Canada. Moreover, US firms would appear to be responsible for a *high* share of horizontal mergers and a *low* share of forward integration, conglomerate and especially backward integration mergers. See Rosenbluth, *op. cit.*, p. 37.

14 A sufficient condition is that the cost of building the assets must be higher than acquisition by merger.

15 Scherer *op. cit.*, p. 113. – Rosenbluth, *op. cit.*, observes that there is no evidence for foreign firms to seek out the more concentrated industries, but our results in Section IV do not disprove this connection. Note that the Rosenbluth study is concerned with the effect of foreign control on concentration while the present study involves the reverse.

16 The market structure or economies of scale theory has been used to explain the variation in mergers over *time* in a number of countries, e.g. Bengt Ryden, *Mergers in Swedish Industry*, Stockholm, 1972. It has been applied to the United States–Canada situation by Reuber and Roseman, *op. cit.*

17 For a concise discussion of this concept see Dennis E. Logue and Philippe A. Naert, "A Theory of Conglomerate Mergers: Comment and Extension", *The Quarterly Journal of Economics*, Vol. 84, 1970, pp. 663 sqq.

18 The distinction between economies of scale and synergistic effects partly revolves around the difference between static and dynamic analysis. Thus, a US firm may foresee excess capacity in its research or marketing resources in the future. The takeover of a Canadian firm will give the combined firm greater flexibility in reallocating resources.

19 Canadian production facilities may be underutilized in the sense of producing too many product lines and so on. Readers may wonder about the excess financial resources given the arguments in support of capital scarcity in Canada.. However, at least one Canadian subsidiary of a US auto company has been a major source of funds for the parent firm through its relationship with a large Canadian bank.

20 For a rigorous analysis of the lumpiness and appropriability problems see William D. Nordhaus, *Invention, Growth and Welfare: A Theoretical Treatment of Technological Change*, Massachusetts Institute of Technology, 10, Cambridge, Mass., London, 1969.

21 See Richard E. Caves, "Causes of Direct Investment: Foreign Firms' Shares in Canadian and United Kingdom Manufacturing Industries", *The Review of Economics and Statistics*, Vol. 56, Cambridge, Mass., 1974, pp. 279 sqq.

22 There is a discernible shift in emphasis away from product differentiation as the underlying cause of foreign direct investment between Richard E. Caves "International Corporations: The Industrial Economics of Foreign Investment", *Economica*, NS, Vol. 38, London, 1971, pp. 1 sqq., and *idem*, "Causes of Direct Investment", *op. cit.*

23 In fact, there is a significant negative correlation between product age (FTD) and advertising intensity (ADV) but a positive correlation between the latter and R&D for a cross section of sixty-seven industries.

24 J. C. McManus, "The Theory of the International Firm", in: *The Multinational Firm and the Nation State*, Ed. by C. Paquet, Toronto, 1972, p. 70.

25 Scherer, *op. cit.*, p. 121.

26 Douglas Vickers, *The Theory of the Firm: Production, Capital and Finance*, New York, 1968, pp. 33 sqq.

27 Michael Gort, "An Economic Disturbance Theory of Mergers", *The Quarterly Journal of Economics*, Vol. 83, 1969, pp. 624 sqq.

28 To my knowledge, the only person who has examined the theoretical implications of this theory in the context of foreign direct investment is McManus, *op. cit.* – See also R. H. Coase, "The Nature of the Firm", *Economica*, NS., Vol. 4, 1937, pp. 386 sqq., and the recent survey by Eirik Furubotn and Svetozar Pejovich, "Property Rights and Economic Theory: A Survey of Recent Literature", *Journal of Economic Literature*, Vol. 10, Menasha, Wisc., 1972, pp. 1137 sqq., for the basic theory.

29 McManus, *op. cit.*, p. 85.

30 Thomas Horst, "The Industrial Composition of US Exports and Subsidiary Sales to the Canadian Market", *The American Economic Review*, Vol. 62, Menasha, Wisc., 1972, pp. 37 sqq. – *Idem*, "Firm and Industry Determinants of the Decision to Invest Abroad: An Empirical Study", *The Review of Economics and Statistics*, Vol. 54, 1972, pp. 258 sqq.

31 Dale Orr, "The Industrial Composition of US Exports and Subsidiary Sales to the Canadian Market: Comment", *The American Economic Review*, Vol. 65, 1975, pp. 230 sqq. – Caves, "Causes of Direct Investment", *op. cit.*

32 This point has been made by McManus, *op. cit.*, p. 88, who does not, however, extend it to other cost factors.

33 Endel Kolde, *International Business Enterprise*, 2nd Ed., Englewood Cliffs, 1973, pp. 161 sqq.

34 Precise definitions and sources of data are found in the Appendix.

35 US controlled subsidiaries are those which are 50% US owned either directly or indirectly. In other words, the US parent firm may own 50% of the equity of subsidiary A operating in Canada outright, or it may own at least 50% of subsidiary B which in turn owns 50% of subsidiary A.

36 The effect of using US coefficients is analyzed by H. G. Baumann, *Structural Characteristics of Canada's Pattern of Trade*, University of British Columbia, 1974, unpubl., and G. C. Hufbauer, "The Impact of National Characteristics and Technology on the Commodity Composition of Trade in Manufactured Goods", in: *The Technology Factor in International Trade*, Ed. by Raymond Vernon, New York, London, 1970, pp. 145 sqq.

37 On the relationship between size and takeover activity see Singh, *op. cit.* He finds that larger firms take over smaller firms (of less than median size), and many Canadian firms would fall into the latter category relative to UK or US firms.

38 The positive relationship between SIZUC and FDI in the table confirms the earlier result of Rosenbluth who writes that "there is a clear tendency for foreign capital to seek out (establish or buy into) the larger firms of each industry". Rosenbluth, *op. cit.*, p. 19.

39 Compare for example Horst, "The Industrial Composition of US Exports", *op. cit.* – *Idem*, "Firm and Industry Determinants", *op. cit.* – H. G. Baumann, "The Industrial Composition of US Exports and Subsidiary Sales to the Canadian Market: Note", *The American Economic Review*, Vol. 63, 1973, pp. 1009 sqq. – Dale Orr, *Foreign Control and Foreign Penetration in the Canadian Manufacturing Industries*, University of British Columbia, 1973, unpubl. – Bernard Wolf, *Underutilized Resources, Domestic Industrial Diversification and Internationalization: Some Empirical Evidence*, York University, Toronto, 1973, unpubl. – Caves, "Causes of Direct Investment", *op. cit.* – Only Caves surpasses our empirical results, but only when he stratifies his sample into producer-good versus consumer-goods industries and so on. We have preferred to keep the model general. Previous studies use a more limited or different set of explanatory variables, nor are these motivated in the same manner as in the current study.

40 For empirical support on this point consult Horst, "The Industrial Composition of US Exports", *op. cit.*; idem, "Firm and Industry Determinants", *op.cit.*; Baumann, "The Industrial Composition of US Exports, Note", *op. cit.* These studies are based on more aggregated data and Orr, "Foreign Control", *op. cit.*, was unable to show that cost factors significantly affect the ratio of US export sales to subsidiary production.

41 Caves, "Causes of Direct Investment", *op. cit.*, found that there was a significant relationship between US subsidiary sales in Canada and the proportion of industry output in the United States accounted for by firms with over $ 100 million in assets. This suggests a discontinuity, but no variable for multi-plant shipments was included in these regressions.

42 One economist who finds paradoxically that advertising intensity and FDI are positively correlated for producer goods industries suggests that advertising expenditures although small may be a good proxy for "structural" differentiation in these industries. In our view, this proxy serves as a useful measure of the total sales effort including product modification and information thereof for the producer goods sectors. See Caves, "Causes of Direct Investment", *op. cit.*, p. 286.

43 One example which casts doubt on the supposed risk aversion of Canadian entrepreneurs is provided by the oil and gas industry where Canadian owned firms are concentrated on the exploration and wildcatting stage and not the more stable refining and distribution end.

44 On this point see Mueller, *op. cit.*

45 Additional cost factors such as taxes can also be introduced, but only if they affect foreign and indigenous firms in a differential manner.

46 The original firm undertaking FDI may be following profit maximizing rules, but subsequent followers may be placing a premium on avoiding errors, minimizing losses and so on.

Baumann, H. G. (1975) "Merger theory, property rights and the pattern of US direct investment in Canada". *Weltwirtschaftlices Archiv*, 111(4), 676–697. Reprinted with permission.

9 How buyers cope with uncertainty when acquiring firms in knowledge-intensive industries: caveat emptor

Russell W. Coff

The acquisition of knowledge often underlies merger and acquisition strategies. But knowledge, as a strategic asset, creates special problems for an acquiring firm. This paper examines the impact of knowledge on merger and acquisition strategies both theoretically and empirically.

Jay B. Barney

Though knowledge may be a key factor in explaining firm performance (Prahalad and Hamel, 1990), it also poses serious management challenges (Coff, 1997; Szulanski, 1996). For example, since knowledge may be maintained at the group, organization, and network levels, it is often "bundled" with other resources (Nonaka, 1994). This bundling, along with tacitness, makes knowledge difficult to acquire in traditional factor markets or even through strategic alliances (Kogut and Zander, 1992; Liebeskind, 1996; Mowery et al., 1996).

It is therefore not surprising that knowledge-based assets are often the key motivation behind corporate acquisitions (Barney, 1988; Chi, 1994; Haspeslagh and Jemison, 1991). Indeed, recent acquisition activity seems to focus on knowledge-intensive industries such as business services, health services, software, and precision medical equipment (*Mergers & Acquisitions Journal*, 1999).

However, knowledge-based assets are harder to assess than tangible assets (Chi, 1994). First, it is difficult to observe asset quality. For example, financial statements rarely provide meaningful information about such assets. Second, buyers cannot be certain about what will be transferred due to turnover and tacitness (Flamholtz and Coff, 1994; Zander and Kogut, 1995).

The amount of asymmetric information may also depend on whether the buyer and target draw on similar knowledge bases. Related buyers are probably better able to assess targets since they are steeped in the knowledge base. Asymmetric information,

Figure 1 Coping with knowledge intensity in acquisitions.

in turn, is linked to the buyer's risk of overpaying or buying a "lemon" (Akerlof, 1970; Giammarino and Heinkel, 1986; Hirshleifer and Titman, 1991). Unfortunately, while there is ample reason to believe that knowledge-based assets pose hazards, there is little research exploring these problems or how buyers cope.

This study proposes steps that buyers may take to cope with the information problems and tests whether they take these steps. The following section elaborates on the uncertainty associated with acquiring targets in knowledge-intensive industries (see Figure 1). This analysis is followed by hypotheses about how buyers cope – especially when they are in unrelated industries. I then present the research methods, results, and implications for future research.

KNOWLEDGE-INTENSIVE INDUSTRIES AND INFORMATION DILEMMAS

Industry-level variation in knowledge-intensity

This study focuses specifically on knowledge that resides in people – in other words, *human capital*. That is, although knowledge may be embedded in routines, information systems, or networks (Nelson and Winter, 1982), I will focus specifically on knowledge that employees carry home with them each day. Of course, the individual-level knowledge at issue here is an essential building block for knowledge at the group, network, and organization levels as well (Nonaka, 1994).

Like physical capital, knowledge is an input in the production process for all industries. Also like physical capital, industries vary greatly in the amount and type of the resource used (Farjoun, 1994; Foss and Eriksen, 1995). For example, although a motel chain and a pharmaceutical firm might both rely on knowledge, the amount and type of knowledge are vastly different.

Of course, knowledge also varies among firms within industries. This is a fundamental assumption underlying the resource-based view. Nevertheless, systematic industry-level variation in knowledge may be even more substantial due to fundamental differences in markets, technologies, and the expertise deployed.

Some industries – particularly those that employ professionals – rely heavily on general knowledge or education (Raelin, 1991). External educational institutions or professional associations develop and maintain much of the knowledge deployed in these industries (Freidson, 1988). Where industries draw extensively on such outside sources, then, the knowledge is relatively general and explicit. That is, knowledge gained from universities is general because it is applicable in more than one setting or firm (Becker, 1983). Education is also explicit in the sense that it is both codifiable and teachable (Polanyi, 1966). As we shall see, industries like computer software, pharmaceuticals, and management consulting draw heavily on this form of knowledge. Of course these are merely the building blocks for knowledge that ultimately becomes cospecialized with other firm resources.

Other industries develop and maintain knowledge through firm-sponsored formal or informal training (US Department of Labor, 1996). Informal training especially tends to be industry- or firm-specific (Arrow, 1974; Lynch, 1991). For example, employees may have to learn industry-specific language to describe the competitive environment or production processes (Spender, 1989; Tsoukas, 1996). In addition, informal training may be relatively tacit in that workers must learn through direct experience or apprenticeship with co-workers (Polanyi, 1966). The measures used in this study suggest that mining, chemical manufacturing, and market research rely on informal training and mentoring to maintain employee knowledge.

Note that these types of knowledge are not mutually exclusive and may be correlated. General knowledge is often a starting point from which to generate specific knowledge (Arrow, 1974). For example, Helfat (1994) describes firm-specific knowledge in corporate R&D. Here, firms typically hire highly educated employees who then acquire and/or create firm-specific knowledge. Thus, general knowledge may serve as a signal to identify high-aptitude employees who are essential in creating specific knowledge (Spence, 1973).

Industry knowledge intensity and uncertainty about the target's value

In general, markets have much less information about the quality of a firm's knowledge base (whether general or specific) than its physical capital. It is almost as if balance sheets are provided for some industries but not for others (since the primary assets of knowledge-intensive industries are systematically excluded). While physical assets are adequately measured in financial statements, knowledge is excluded – particularly when embodied in people (Flamholtz and Coff, 1994). Thus, for more knowledge-intensive industries, publicly available financial information is less useful.

This difference in available information about firms in knowledge-intensive industries is a central theme of this article: it is more difficult for buyers to assess the value of targets in such industries. The value of knowledge-based assets is less certain than that of tangible assets for three fundamental reasons: 1) quality is more difficult to observe or measure; 2) the buyer cannot be certain what can be transferred; and 3) the prospects for synergy are difficult to assess.

Uncertain Quality of Knowledge-Based Assets. Quality refers to an assessment of the target's "stand alone" value independent of the buyer. On this issue, the failure of financial statements to provide accurate information is only part of the dilemma. Presumably, targets could provide any additional information required. However, targets may not always cooperate wholeheartedly. It may be in their interest to provide inflated assessments of knowledge-based assets, particularly if they own stock and would benefit from overpayment. Alternatively, if they don't like the prospect of being acquired, they may withhold important information. In any event, the information provided might be suspect and would be harder to verify than, say, historical cash flows.

For example, short product life cycles may mean that the value of a software manufacturer depends greatly on the promise of new products. Future success, then, depends largely on the quality of the software designers. To some extent, past success may serve as an indicator. However, the buyer is more interested in the capability of software development than in the existing product line. If turnover or depreciating skills mean that the software team is not high quality, the product pipeline may not be promising, and the target would be worth less to the buyer. A target, in this case, may hide information that suggests limitations in its capabilities from the buyer.

However, even if targets cooperate enthusiastically, knowledge may be hard and/ or costly to convey (Haspeslagh and Jemison, 1991; Teece, 1982). If knowledge is tacit, there may be no way to convey it in the time required to negotiate an acquisition (Polanyi, 1966; Zander and Kogut, 1995). Furthermore, even explicit knowledge may be sufficiently complex that (especially compared to tangible assets) it is hard to convey in negotiations.

Uncertainty About What Can Be Transferred. The stand-alone value is not a complete representation of the uncertainty that buyers face. An acquisition is a major organizational change, and it is not clear that all of the organization's capabilities would be retained through such an event. Even if buyers could fully evaluate the *going concern* value of a target's knowledge-based assets, there would still be uncertainty about what assets could be transferred through an acquisition.

While buyers can be fairly certain about whether tangible assets can be transferred, human capital is much less certain. Since acquisitions can be used to break "inefficient" implicit contracts, some buyers may consider turnover desirable (Shleifer and Summers, 1988). Discipline of this type is most strongly associated with poorly performing targets (Walsh and Kosnik, 1993). However, the changes associated with friendly acquisitions (e.g., well-performing targets) may also push employees to initiate job searches since such changes may also break implicit contracts (Lee et al., 1996; Walsh and Ellwood, 1991). The IBM/Lotus transaction is illustrative because the creator of Lotus Notes, Raymond Ozzie, threatened to quit unless IBM retained the CEO of Lotus (*Wall Street Journal*, June 13, 1995).

Uncertain Synergy. Synergy is the additional value that the buyer hopes to achieve by integrating the two firms' unique capabilities (Barney, 1988). The prospect of synergy injects even more uncertainty into a buyer's valuation since the combined capabilities cannot be observed *a priori* in assessing the synergy. Since it is speculative, buyers may tend to overestimate their own ability to generate synergy (Hayward and Hambrick, 1997; Roll, 1986).

While estimating synergy might be difficult in many acquisitions, it may be relatively easier for physical assets than for human capital. In the case of tangible assets, it may be as simple as checking whether a machine is tooled in metric or English increments. This can be accomplished with reasonable certainty before the acquisition is consummated.

In contrast, synergy with a human capital intensive firm may require knowledge transfers that are difficult to predict. It may be hard to specify, *a priori*, how much knowledge will be transferred and whether the knowledge can be deployed in a new setting – even if targets cooperate enthusiastically (Haspeslagh and Jemison, 1991;

Polanyi, 1966; Teece, 1982). There simply may be no way to convey tacit knowledge in the time required to negotiate an acquisition (Zander and Kogut, 1995). Furthermore, even explicit or general knowledge may be sufficiently complex that it is hard to convey in negotiations (especially compared to tangible assets).

Avoiding overbidding: dilemmas created by uncertainty and asymmetric information

The uncertainty associated with targets in knowledge-intensive industries may create several types of dilemmas for buyers. If information about knowledge-based assets is scarce and the transferability of assets is uncertain, buyers may have a hard time determining the target's value. This uncertainty may mean that the risks of winner's curse and of adverse selection are greater for targets in knowledge-intensive industries.

The Winner's Curse. The winner's curse occurs when buyers bid based on imperfect information. Even if all bidders have unbiased estimates of a target's value, the highest estimate is, by definition, above the true value (Giliberto and Varaiya, 1989). If bidders fail to adjust their offers down from their estimates, the highest bid will always exceed the value of the target – the winner will be cursed.

Given that this problem arises from uncertainty about the asset's value, knowledge-based assets might exacerbate the risk. That is, if firm-level variation in the quality of knowledge-based assets is hard to assess, the risk of winner's curse may be more severe in knowledge-intensive industries. Bidders' assessments of the target's value may be more widely dispersed when there are knowledge-based assets, and the winner faces an even greater risk of bidding above the target's true value.

Adverse Selection. Adverse selection is a related problem associated with uncertainty in valuations. Akerlof (1970) described how used car buyers respond to imperfect information. Specifically, buyers formulate offers based on the expected value of a given car – accounting for the possibility that it will turn out to be a lemon. As a result, owners of high quality cars are unable to get what they feel are fair offers. While they might provide buyers with signals of quality, these are suspect because sellers have an incentive to overstate the value. Accordingly, these "discounted" offers are lower than the true value, and high quality cars are kept from the market. Thus, the used car market may contain a disproportionate number of lemons.

If buyers face more uncertainty for targets in knowledge-intensive industries, these industries may operate like markets for lemons. Targets with strong knowledge-based assets may get lower bids (smaller premia) than the owners feel are appropriate since it is harder for buyers to assess such assets. This might lead to a disproportionate number of "lemons" seeking to be acquired in knowledge-intensive industries.

BUYER COPING STRATEGIES FOR TARGETS IN KNOWLEDGE-INTENSIVE INDUSTRIES

A given buyer should take steps to cope with uncertainty in its estimate of a target's value. Figure 1 lists the coping strategies that are the focus here. Buyers may (1) offer lower bid premia, (2) offer contingent (noncash) forms of payment, and (3) seek better information from the target. The overarching proposition is that buyers apply these strategies when acquiring targets in knowledge-intensive industries.

Reduce the bid premium offered

The information and uncertainty dilemmas put buyers at risk of overpaying. If an adverse selection problem arises, the firms that want to be acquired may be of a disproportionately lower quality than those that do not. The classic response to the threat of adverse selection is to reduce the offer price (Akerlof, 1970). That is, where buyers have imperfect information, they may discount their offers to reflect the probability that the target will turn out to be a lemon. The winner's curse problem requires a similar response. That is, if the buyer is aware of uncertainty in its valuation of the target, it should reduce the offer price. If all buyers reduce their offers in this way for targets in knowledge-intensive industries, bids may be systematically lower, and the winner may not be "cursed" (Thaler, 1992). However, some discounting may already be present in the stock price – that is, the price should reflect uncertainty about a target's future.

Typically, a premium above the target's pre-announcement stock price is ascribed to expected synergy or preemptive bidding (Fishman, 1989, Hayward and Hambrick, 1997). However, if it is hard to determine whether knowledge can be applied, buyers may be conservative in predicting synergy from knowledge-based assets. Also, while the stock price reflects all assets, the premium only includes assets the buyer expects to transfer (i.e., after turnover).

Preemptive bidding is the use of a high premium to preempt other bidders from emerging (Fishman, 1989). However, competing bidders might not get the benefit of a fair auction for targets in knowledge-intensive industries. If the first bidder secures the target's cooperation, subsequent bidders may be viewed as hostile. Information asymmetries and the threat of turnover make enthusiastic cooperation essential for knowledge-based assets, and additional bidders would in this case find it harder to create value. Buyers may therefore be able to offer lower premia without attracting other bidders into the arena. If target shareholders only compare the offer with other transactions within that industry, they may consider lower premia to be acceptable. Therefore:

> **H1.** As target industry knowledge intensity increases, the bid premia offered by buyers decreases.

Offer noncash/contingent consideration

Another strategy that may reduce the risk of overpaying is to use a medium of exchange that is contingent upon the value created (Chi, 1994). In this way, buyers may use noncash consideration when they are less certain about the actual value that will be created (Eckbo et al., 1990). Whereas cash has a fixed value that does not depend on the outcome, stock, securities, or earnouts are more flexible. In contrast, when there is great confidence, buyers may use cash to preempt other bidders (Fishman, 1989). Contingent consideration performs two important functions: it limits the buyer's risk of overpaying; and if the target is closely held, it provides an incentive for the seller to help manage the transition process. Thus:

> **H2.** As target industry knowledge intensity increases, the portion of the offer in cash (as a percent of the total consideration) decreases.

Seek better information from the target

Lower offers and noncash payment focus primarily on how buyers can reduce the risk of overpaying assuming a given amount of asymmetric information. A different way of approaching the problem would be to try to secure better information. Accordingly, when the target is in a knowledge-intensive industry, there should be differences in the length of negotiations and the use of tender offers.

Negotiation Time. If publicly available information is less useful for targets in knowledge-intensive industries, buyers might need to obtain more information through negotiations. This need for information may mean that such targets require lengthier negotiations.

Lengthy negotiations may be especially necessary if the buyer wants to integrate the target's knowledge, since the two management teams must establish an ongoing working relationship. Lengthy integrative negotiations may be needed to work out the details of the relationship (Pruitt, 1983). Typically, the acquisition literature assumes that bid premia are the focal point of negotiation (Haunschild, 1994; Walkling and Edmister, 1985). However, the premium is relatively simple compared to the complexity of establishing the parameters of an ongoing relationship. Thus:

> **H3.** As target industry knowledge intensity increases, negotiation time increases.

Tender Offers. Tender offers also affect the amount of information available from the target. These arms-length transactions provide relatively limited opportunities for information exchange. While they are not necessarily hostile, tender offers are more likely to be resisted – increasing the required bid premium (Huang and Walkling, 1987; Walkling and Edmister, 1985).

However, even where a tender offer is friendly, negotiating directly with the shareholders implies that there may be a relatively restricted information flow. For the reasons stated above, this restriction can be a serious problem if the target is in a knowledge-intensive industry. Since the strategic assets must often be integrated to generate synergy (Chatterjee, 1986; Haspeslagh and Jemison, 1991), this type of distance may prevent the buyer from gaining access to key information. Thus, tender offers may be a relatively undesirable method for acquiring targets in knowledge-intensive industries.

> **H4.** As target industry knowledge intensity increases, tender offers are less likely (controlling for hostile transactions).

KNOWLEDGE AND DIVERSIFICATION STRATEGY: HOW DO UNRELATED BUYERS COPE?

The hypotheses presented above are based on the assumption that buyers have less complete information about targets in knowledge-intensive industries than they do in other industries. *Relatedness*, however, is another factor that may influence and moderate the degree of asymmetric information. Relatedness is the extent to which the buyer and target industries draw on similar forms of expertise. One possibility is that unrelated buyers face more severe information problems because they lack key expertise. If so, such buyers should be more likely to apply coping strategies. This scenario assumes that related and unrelated buyers have comparable information requirements.

However, relatedness may also serve as a proxy for diversification strategy and, as such, would have implications for the intended postacquisition integration. The diversification strategy, in turn, impacts the nature and quantity of information needed to assess the target's value to the buyer. The following discussion examines whether unrelated buyers are more or less likely to apply the coping strategies described above.

Are unrelated buyers more at risk of dilemmas arising from asymmetric information?

Different buyers do not necessarily face the same risk of information-based dilemmas. When a buyer and target are in unrelated industries, the buyer may lack access to the target's industry knowledge base and may be at greater risk of falling prey to the dilemmas described above. For example, one might require years to absorb even the explicit portion of a biochemist's knowledge-base (e.g., that which is codified in textbooks). Thus, a buyer without that knowledge (compared to a buyer with that knowledge) may face difficulties acquiring a biotechnology firm. Though the buyer might absorb such information over time from the target or from other sources, tacit or technical knowledge is harder to convey in negotiations than information about tangible assets. A buyer with related expertise, on the other hand, would be in a better position to assess the value and potential of ongoing research.

Indeed, the concept of core competence in the diversification literature implies related expertise (Kim and Kogut, 1996; Prahalad and Hamel, 1990). That is, a corporation should be more adept at managing businesses that rely on similar knowledge bases. Otherwise, management may lack expertise to add value (Williamson, 1975). Based on this, it is not surprising to find that knowledge-based resources are associated with related diversification (Chatterjee and Wernerfelt, 1991).

The information dilemmas and governance problems in managing diverse business units may be very much like those that unrelated buyers face. If so, relatedness may moderate the extent of information problems. While it may be especially important for targets in knowledge-intensive industries, relatedness may not be particularly useful in evaluating tangible assets. Thus, the most serious information dilemmas should occur for unrelated buyers and targets in knowledge-intensive industries. If so, the interaction of these two attributes should predict an even greater reliance on the coping strategies described above.

Unrelated diversification may require less information

An alternative may be that unrelated buyers of targets in knowledge-intensive industries do not intend to integrate the two firms. This scenario, in turn, would reduce the buyer's information needs. That is, tacit information is primarily required to assess the value that could be created through integration (Nahavandi and Malekzadeh, 1988; Zander and Kogut, 1995). Datta and Grant (1990) support this proposed difference in acquisition objectives in their finding that unrelated acquisitions result in less postacquisition integration.

If unrelated buyers do not seek synergy through knowledge transfers, they may have many other objectives for the acquisition. Rational explanations include the buyer's intentions to create value through internal capital markets, through entering new markets, or by facilitating market discipline (Trautwein, 1990). Nonrational explanations include managerialism or hubris.

Whatever the objective, if the target is not to be integrated, buyers primarily seek financial information (Walter and Barney, 1990). Specifically, such buyers are often most concerned about the target's cash flows. Although financial information may not fully represent the target's assets, information about cash flow is available, and these buyers may be less at risk for information dilemmas than related buyers who intend to fully integrate the firms.

If buyers are able to obtain the financial information they seek, they may not need to discount the bid premia or offer contingent consideration (e.g., stock). In addition, information-seeking strategies might not be necessary because cash flow is relatively easy to confirm. This implies that an alternative would be that unrelated buyers are actually less likely to rely on the coping strategies.

Whether unrelated diversification actually requires less information or puts buyers at a greater risk of overbidding, the proposed relationship focuses on how related expertise may moderate the need for the coping strategies described above. Thus:

> **H5.** The relationship between target industry knowledge intensity and the coping strategies (premia, noncash payment, negotiation time, and tender offers) is moderated by the extent to which the buyer and target industries draw on related expertise.

DATA AND METHODS

The hypotheses above suggest that coping strategies should vary with target industry knowledge-intensity and relatedness. These hypotheses were tested using OLS, Poisson, and logistic regression on key transaction parameters. The following is a description of the data and measures along with a brief discussion of their limitations.

Sample

The sample for this study was drawn from ADP's mergers and acquisitions database, which contains all publicly announced transactions totaling over $1 million. The database provides descriptive data for the buyer and target along with basic transaction parameters. I have selected all full acquisitions (218) that closed in the years 1988–1989 which could be cross referenced in COMPUSTAT or Compact Disclosure to obtain control variables.

In general, this eliminated transactions involving small private firms for which such information was not public. In the case of the buyers, many of the private firms were partnerships assembled to conduct a single transaction. Here, the industry coding was not sufficiently reliable to measure relatedness. Also, most of these partnerships were found to involve members of the target's management team and thus were management buyouts rather than corporate acquisitions.

Primary measures

Dependent Variables. The hypotheses predict that coping strategies will be used for targets in knowledge-intensive industries. Variables indicating these strategies were compiled by ADP from SEC filings, news reports, and, in some cases, interviews with management. The BID PREMIUM is the extent to which the offer exceeds the target's market value two months before announcement (log transformed). The PERCENT CASH is the portion of the offer that is in cash. NEGOTIATION TIME is the number of days from the announcement of the buyer's interest to the date that the transaction closed. Finally, TENDER OFFER indicates whether the transaction was a tender offer.

Target Industry Knowledge Intensity. I used two measures of industry-level knowledge intensity that were based on measures of human capital from the US Census and the Bureau of Labor Statistics National Longitudinal Survey of Youth (NLSY). The NLSY survey tracks a panel of 12 000 people from 1979 forward. All respondents are reinterviewed each year and have reported their work histories, education, and the informal training required to come up to speed at their current jobs. For this study, the 1989 survey was used to match the time period of the acquisitions. Industry averages were calculated using the respondent's three-digit industry code. These variables, education and informal training, are described below.

General Knowledge/Education. Years of schooling is the most common measure of human capital (Becker, 1983; Mincer, 1974). Average industry education was calculated from US census data and ranges from the high school level (12 years of school) to some graduate school (17 years). While some firms in each industry are above and some are below the average, the measure still helps to indicate which industries rely heavily on educated employees. Though it reflects explicit or codified knowledge, the complexity may make it hard to convey to those who do not have the same educational background. The potential mobility of such assets may pose a greater risk of turnover, which should introduce uncertainty into the target's estimated value.

Specific Knowledge/Informal Training. NLSY respondents were asked about the number of hours of training required in the last year to maintain their skills. This number of hours of training was used as an indicator of firm-specific knowledge. The hours of training were then aggregated at the respondent's industry level (3 digit). This measure reflects the average hours of informal training required to upgrade or maintain knowledge in each industry and ranges from 0 hours to 55 hours of training.

Table 1 shows examples of high and low human-capital-intensive industries based on the two measures. Some industries (e.g., software) seem to import more knowledge from educational institutions while others (e.g., mining) rely on informal

Table 1 Examples of human capital intensive industries by measure

Measure of human capital	High human capital intensity	Low human capital intensity
Education (years of schooling)	• Computer software • Pharmaceuticals • Advertising • Management consulting • Economic and market research	• Knife/blade manufacturing • Waste/garbage disposal • Glass manufacturing (bowls, blocks, etc.) • Hand tool manufacturing • Carpet/floor coverings
Informal training (hours with supervisor)	• Guided missile manufacturing • Acids and chemical manufacturing • Furniture manufacturing • Aircraft parts manufacturing • Retail home improvement stores	• Advertising • Vending machine operators • Carpet/floor coverings • Economic and market research • Gypsum/plaster manufacturing

training to bring employees up to speed. Furthermore, these measures are not mutually exclusive. Some industries (e.g., economic and marketing research) rely on highly educated individuals and still require a great deal of informal training. Still other industries (e.g., hotels and motels) rely on neither form of human capital.

Table 2 presents a correlation matrix for all of the variables. While general and industry-specific knowledge are related, the modest (.11) association is far from 1.0 and suggests that these variables capture different types of knowledge. Most of the correlations (75%) between target industry knowledge and the coping strategies are significant. This significance is notable since knowledge has not been carefully studied in the context of corporate acquisitions. Associations among dependent variables are generally significant but vary widely. These correlations are consistent with relationships reported in other research. For example, bid premia are higher for noncash offers, for tender offers, for hostile transactions and when there are multiple bidders (Morck et al., 1988; Walkling and Edmister, 1985).

Unrelated Industries. Buyers in unrelated industries are identified by comparing the expertise profiles for the buyer and target industries. The measure used here draws from Farjoun's (1994) expertise-based industry profiles and from Klavens' (1990) expertise-based relatedness measure. Farjoun (1994) used industry expertise profiles to identify industry groups. He compared industries using 41 two-digit occupational categories as clustering variables from the Occupational Employment Survey. Klavens (1990) used the top two occupational categories for an industry to predict diversification patterns.

The Occupational Employment Survey, used by both Klavens (1990) and Farjoun (1994), is conducted annually by the Bureau of Labor Statistics. It contains detailed occupational breakdowns by 3-digit SIC code. Specifically, for each industry, it provides the percent distribution of employees in 823 occupational categories.

In contrast to past research that has used this data source, this study draws on 823 five-digit codes to calculate the same basic Euclidean distance criterion.[1] The finer delineation of expertise may make this measure sensitive to the buyer's core competence. For example, agricultural engineering and nuclear engineering cannot be differentiated using 41 categories. The Euclidean distance between industry expertise profiles ranges from 0 to 1 and is expressed as follows:

$$UNRELATED_{EXP} = \sum_{o=1}^{823} \sqrt{(EB_o - ET_o)^2}$$

where EB_o is the percent of the employees in the buyer's primary industry in occupation o; and ET_o is the percent of the employees in the target's primary industry in occupation o.

Control Variables. A number of important contextual factors were controlled in the regression analyses. These controls fall into four categories: (1) the context under which the transaction took place; (2) transaction parameters that are not the subject of hypotheses; (3) characteristics of the buyer; and (4) characteristics of the target firm. The specific controls are as follows:

- *Change in S&P 500 Index.* The change in the Standard & Poors Composite 500 Index indicates market volatility prior to the announcement. During the period studied, the S&P ranged from about 2900 to 3800, suggesting a great deal of

Table 2 Means, standard deviations and correlations

	$\bar{x}$	σ	1	2	3	4	5	6	7	8	9	10	11	12
1. General knowledge	13.27	1.00	1.000											
2. Specific knowledge	4.39	5.30	0.111***	1.000										
3. UNRELATED$_{\text{EXP}}$	0.59	0.31	-0.203***	0.002	1.000									
4. Bid premium	0.42	0.61	-0.063†	-0.074*	-0.116***	1.000								
5. Percent cash	88.11	29.66	-0.118***	-0.072*	0.250***	0.081**	1.000							
6. Negotiation time	127.00	123.22	0.014	-0.027	-0.271***	0.293***	-0.229***	1.000						
7. Tender offer	0.28	0.45	-0.160***	-0.084**	-0.070*	0.395***	0.1000***	0.170***	1.000					
Control variables														
8. Change in S&P500	0.01	0.04	-0.026	0.018	-0.064*	0.075**	0.116***	-0.119***	-0.005	1.000				
9. Multiple bidders	0.12	0.32	-0.113***	0.018	-0.038	0.309***	0.033	0.173***	0.311***	0.068**	1.000			
10. Hostile	0.04	0.16	-0.036	0.030	-0.043	0.147***	0.045†	-0.063*	0.262***	-0.009	0.232***	1.000		
11. Buyer market value	6,699.18	6,342.72	0.138***	-0.026	0.263***	-0.156***	0.106***	-0.134***	-0.116***	0.080**	-0.104***	-0.187***	1.000	
12. Target sales	833.60	2331.30	-0.212***	0.039	0.129***	0.208***	0.049	0.060	0.310***	0.101***	0.265***	0.193***	0.223***	1.000
13. Target sales growth	3.67	9.68	0.041	-0.003	0.101***	-0.196***	0.071**	-0.068**	-0.191***	0.026	-0.069***	-0.097***	0.155***	-0.044

Significance is as follows: *** = .001; ** = .01; * = .05; † = .1.

change. Volatility might impact estimates of value creation and might make stock a less desirable medium of exchange from the target's perspective.

- *Multiple bidders*. This binary variable indicates whether there were competing bidders (about 12% of the time). Not surprisingly, this variable is associated with higher bid premia, tender offers, and hostile transactions. It is relatively rare to have multiple bidders for targets in knowledge-intensive industries.
- *Hostile*. ADP records the target's response to the offer with special focus on whether the offer is contested (about 4% of the sample). Here a 1 indicates that the offer was resisted. Hostile transactions are associated with higher bid premia, tender offers, and cash payment. Interestingly, there is no clear association with target industry knowledge-intensity.
- *Buyer Market Value*. This is the buyer's market value prior to the acquisition (obtained from COMPUSTAT). The buyer's size is an indication of the resources at the buyer's disposal and thus of their ability to conduct an acquisition. Among other things, large buyers are more likely to be unrelated (.26) and tend to offer more cash (.11).
- *Target sales*. Sales reflect the target's size (obtained from COMPUSTAT). Size is an indicator of how complex the transaction will be. Prior to the 1980s, size alone was considered to be a sufficient takeover defense. While innovations in financing have reduced this effect dramatically (Jensen, 1988), it remains an important contextual factor.
- *Target sales growth*. This is the target's growth in sales over the 5 years prior to the acquisition. This was calculated using COMPUSTAT data and indicates whether the target has a proven track record before the announcement. It is important to note that unrelated buyers seem to rely more heavily on this track record (r = .10).

Some dependent variables are correlated (see Table 2) and might reasonably be used as controls in predicting other dependent variables (e.g., bid premia and the percent cash are clearly intertwined). However, since there is no consensus about causality among these variables and some are dichotomous, they were not modeled simultaneously. A single grand model of takeovers is beyond the scope of this study.

Limitations of data and measures

While the data are relatively unique and are well suited to studying the implications of industry-level knowledge, there are some limitations with respect to the sample and the measures. Like most studies of acquisitions, this sample is made up of relatively large publicly held firms – partnerships and service firms are underrepresented. In spite of this, there are enough service firms (34%) to provide variation in knowledge intensity and thus to test the hypotheses. Still, the total population of acquisitions is probably somewhat more knowledge-intensive than this sample (e.g., 47% of the acquisitions in full ADP database were in service industries). In a more representative sample, then, knowledge may play an even greater role. While this limitation is a concern, it should mean that the results actually understate the impact of knowledge intensity.

In addition, knowledge is measured at the industry- rather than at the firm-level. The 54 three-digit industries represented in this sample do provide variance in

Table 3 Regressions on bid premium[a]

	A Education (main effects)	B Education (interaction)	C Training (main effects)	D Training (interactions)
Model fit				
Adjusted R-square	0.21	0.22	0.21	0.20
F	6.37***	6.08***	6.41***	5.72***
N	165	165	165	165
Hypotheses				
General knowledge	−0.354*	−0.825**		
	(0.196)	(0.331)		
Specific knowledge			−0.039*	−0.060[†]
			(0.021)	(0.040)
General K* UNRELATED$_{EXP}$		1.008*		
		(0.574)		
Specific K* UNRELATED$_{EXP}$				0.041
				(0.068)
Controls				
UNRELATED$_{EXP}$	0.023	−2.682[†]	0.031	−0.030
	(0.040)	(1.542)	(0.040)	(0.109)
Change in S&P 500 index	1.273***	1.252***	1.317***	1.302***
	(0.308)	(0.306)	(0.309)	(0.310)
Multiple bidders	0.049	0.057[†]	0.053[†]	0.052
	(0.033)	(0.033)	(0.033)	(0.033)
Hostile	−0.077	−0.077	−0.090	−0.086
	(0.084)	(0.083)	(0.084)	(0.084)
Buyer market value	0.014	0.015	0.010	0.011
	(0.010)	(0.010)	(0.010)	(0.010)
Target sales	0.016*	0.016[†]	0.020**	0.021*
	(0.008)	(0.008)	(0.008)	(0.008)
Target sales growth (5 yr)	−0.026	−0.027	−0.033[†]	−0.032
	(0.021)	(0.021)	(0.021)	(0.021)

[a] Standard errors are shown below each coefficient. Significance as follows: *** = .001; ** = .01; * = .05, [†] = .1. One-tailed tests are used for main effects since the sign was hypothesized, while two-tailed tests are used in other cases.

knowledge. For example, average industry education ranges from the high school level (12 years of school) to some graduate school (17 years). However, firms within an industry may differ greatly in their ability to create and apply knowledge (Conner and Prahalad, 1996). The measures do not indicate a given target's knowledge intensity relative to other firms in that industry.

RESULTS

The over-arching proposition in this study is that buyers apply a pattern of coping strategies when acquiring targets in knowledge-intensive industries. While the correlations in Table 2 suggest that knowledge intensity is associated with most of the coping strategies as predicted, it is possible that other factors might account for the relationships. Tables 3–6 present regressions (OLS, Poisson, and logistic) that control for many of these factors to test how robust the associations are. Note that the summary of results in Table 7 is particularly useful for evaluating whether a pattern of coping strategies was observed.

Table 4 Regressions on medium of exchange (% of offer in cash)[a]

	E Education (main effects)	F Education (interaction)	G Training (main effects)	H Training (interactions)
Model fit				
Adjusted R-square	0.10	0.13	0.10	0.11
F	4.02***	4.65***	3.90***	4.03***
N	216	216	216	216
Hypotheses				
General knowledge	−114.553***	−286.636***		
	(43,452)	(72,834)		
Specific knowledge			−10.571**	−25.143**
			(4.304)	(8.044)
General K* UNRELATED$_{EXP}$		359.617***		
		(123.324)		
Specific K* UNRELATED$_{EXP}$				28.127*
				(13.162)
Controls				
UNRELATED$_{EXP}$	24.844**	−939.565**	29.045***	−13.570
	(8.735)	(330.837)	(8.511)	(21.654)
Change in S&P 500 index	37.041	39.902	50.981	44.787
	(64.696)	(63.567)	(65.109)	(64.623)
Multiple bidders	14.266*	16.482*	16.835*	16.101*
	(7.490)	(7.398)	(7.496)	(7.440)
Hostile	13.346	7.587	6.875	9.675
	(16.271)	(16.107)	(16.551)	(16.463)
Buyer market value	−1.483	−1.075	−2.348	−2.470
	(2.033)	(2.002)	(2.021)	(2.005)
Target sales	−0.920	−1.230	0.122	0.224
	(1.850)	(1.821)	(1.818)	(1.804)
Target sales growth (5 yr)	3.767	4.240	1.610	2.926
	(4.939)	(4.855)	(4.911)	(4.908)

[a] Standard errors are shown below each coefficient. Significance as follows: *** = .001; ** = .01; * = .05, [†] = .1. One-tailed tests are used for main effects since the sign was hypothesized, while two-tailed tests are used in other cases.

Do buyers offer lower bid premia for targets in knowledge-intensive industries?

Models A through D in Table 3 predict the bid premium. Models A and B test hypotheses using general knowledge (e.g., education), while Models C and D use specific knowledge (e.g., informal training) to test the same hypotheses. Model A and Model C both provide some support for H1 – buyers offer lower premia for targets in knowledge-intensive industries. The R-Square (.21) suggests that the model fits about as well as other studies of bid premia (Hayward and Hambrick, 1997; Walkling and Edmister, 1985).

As Model B illustrates, general knowledge has a greater impact on bid premia once we include the interaction with UNRELATED$_{EXP}$. This is consistent with H5, which suggests that relatedness moderates the relationship between knowledge intensity and the coping strategies. This finding indicates that unrelated buyers do not reduce their offers when the target's industry relies on general knowledge. One explanation advanced earlier was that information needs are less critical when buyers don't intend to integrate the two firms or to make major changes in the target. This interaction was not supported in Model D for specific knowledge.

Table 5 Poisson regressions on negotiation time (days)[a]

	I Education (main effects)	J Education (interaction)	K Training (main effects)	L Training (interactions)
Model fit				
Chi square/df ratio	88.97***	84.57***	87.46***	85.72***
N	218	218	218	218
Hypotheses				
General knowledge	0.950***	3.611***		
	(0.080)	(0.134)		
Specific knowledge			0.149**	0.309***
			(0.008)	(0.014)
General K* UNRELATED$_{EXP}$		−5.986***		
		(0.235)		
Specific K* UNRELATED$_{EXP}$				−0.340***
				(0.025)
Controls				
UNRELATED$_{EXP}$	−0.420***	15.647***	−0.447***	0.095*
	(0.017)	(0.631)	(0.016)	(0.042)
Change in S&P 500 index	−1.816***	−1.883***	−2.014***	−1.955***
	(0.115)	(0.114)	(0.116)	(0.116)
Multiple bidders	0.203***	0.184***	0.170***	0.168***
	(0.014)	(0.014)	(0.014)	(0.014)
Hostile	−0.086**	0.003	0.012	−0.030
	(0.037)	(0.037)	(0.037)	(0.037)
Buyer market value	0.004	−0.008*	0.016***	0.017***
	(0.004)	(0.004)	(0.004)	(0.004)
Target sales	0.069***	0.074***	0.060***	0.060***
	(0.004)	(0.004)	(0.004)	(0.004)
Target sales growth (5 yr)	0.232***	0.226***	0.257***	0.246***
	(0.011)	(0.011)	(0.010)	(0.010)

[a] Standard errors are shown below each coefficient. Significance as follows: *** = .001; ** = .01; * = .05, † = .1. One-tailed tests are used for main effects since the sign was hypothesized, while two-tailed tests are used in other cases.

Do buyers offer less cash for targets in knowledge-intensive industries?

H2 predicted that buyers of targets in knowledge-intensive industries would offer noncash payment to shift risk to the target and provide incentives to help make the transaction successful. In Models E and G (Table 4), the coefficients for both general and specific knowledge are significant and negative as predicted. This suggests consistent support for H2 regardless of which measure of knowledge intensity is used.

Models F and H present the interactions with relatedness. Here, both general and specific knowledge have greater impacts on PERCENT CASH once the interaction with UNRELATED$_{EXP}$ is included. The sign on the interaction indicates that unrelated buyers are actually more likely to use cash. This result provides further support for H5 and is consistent with the reasoning that unrelated buyers may actually have more modest information needs – unrelated buyers certainly do not appear to mitigate their risk by offering stock.

Do buyers seek information from targets in knowledge-intensive industries?

There are also numerous significant findings with respect to information-seeking strategies. Table 5 presents results for models of negotiation time, and Table 6

Table 6 Logistic regressions on tender offer[a]

	M Education (main effects)	N Education (interaction)	O Training (main effects)	P Training (interactions)
Model fit				
Adjusted pseudo R-square	0.37	0.43	0.35	0.38
Chi square/df	69.77/10***	84.98/11***	65.94/10***	72.55/11***
N	218	218	218	218
Hypotheses				
General knowledge	−6.788***	−21.815***		
	(2.457)	(5.094)		
Specific knowledge			−0.488*	−1.498***
			(0.246)	(0.491)
General K* UNRELATED$_{EXP}$		30.090***		
		(8.220)		
Specific K* UNRELATED$_{EXP}$				2.004**
				(0.812)
Controls				
UNRELATED$_{EXP}$	1.114*	−79.439***	1.347**	−1.635
	(0.490)	(21.989)	(0.477)	(1.275)
Change in S&P 500 index	6.708†	8.617†	6.559†	6.310
	(4.160)	(4.590)	(4.075)	(4.110)
Multiple bidders	1.185**	1.276**	1.345**	1.364**
	(0.458)	(0.473)	(0.456)	(0.472)
Hostile	1.304	0.855	1.223	1.149
	(1.180)	(1.196)	(1.244)	(1.188)
Buyer market value	0.169	0.212†	0.112	0.088
	(0.116)	(0.124)	(0.114)	(0.117)
Target sales	0.323**	0.318**	0.372***	0.382***
	(0.109)	(0.114)	(0.109)	(0.110)
Target sales growth (5 yr)	−0.066	0.040	−0.209	−0.140
	(0.280)	(0.285)	(0.273)	(0.281)

[a] Standard errors are shown below each coefficient. Significance as follows: *** = .001; ** = .01; * = .05, † = .1. One-tailed tests are used for main effects since the sign was hypothesized, while two-tailed tests are used in other cases.

presents models predicting tender offers. All models are highly significant and seem to explain a reasonable portion of the variance. In addition, there is support for both H3 and H4 – when the target is in a knowledge-intensive industry, negotiations are more lengthy and tender offers are less likely. The finding is not sensitive to the measure of knowledge intensity.

Negotiation Time. Models I and K in Table 5 present regressions on NEGOTIATION TIME (the number of days between the announcement date and the deal closing). Poisson regression is used to predict NEGOTIATION TIME since it is essentially a count of days. The models are both significant and seem to fit the data. OLS regressions (not presented) indicated that the R-Square was approximately .24. H3 was supported because both general and specific knowledge have positive main effects. That is, as target industry knowledge-intensity increases, the length of negotiations also increases.

In addition, the interaction between knowledge-intensity and UNRELATED$_{EXP}$ is significant and negative for both measures of knowledge (Models J and K). This provides additional support for H5. Furthermore the pattern remains consistent with

Table 7 Summary of regression coefficients for knowledge intensity[a]

	Main effects		Interactions	
	General knowledge	*Specific knowledge*	*General* UNRELATED$_{EXP}$*	*Specific* UNRELATED$_{EXP}$*
Bid premium	−	−	+	
	H1 supported. Buyers offer lower premia for targets in knowledge-intensive industries.		H5 supported for general: Unrelated buyers do not offer lower premia for targets in industries that rely on general knowledge.	
Percent cash	−	−	+	+
	H2 supported: Buyers use less cash in offers for targets in knowledge-intensive industries.		H5 supported: Unrelated buyers do not offer contingent payment (non-cash) for targets in knowledge-intensive industries.	
Negotiation time	+	+	−	−
	H3 supported: Lengthier negotiations are required for targets in knowledge-intensive industries.		H5 supported: Unrelated buyers do not use lengthy negotiations for targets in knowledge-intensive industries.	
Tender offer	−	−	+	+
	H4 supported: Buyers avoid tender offers of targets in knowledge-intensive industries.		H5 supported: Unrelated buyers do not avoid tender offers of targets in knowledge-intensive industries.	

[a] A "−" indicates a significant negative coefficient while a "+" denotes a positive coefficient.

the idea that buyers with unrelated diversification strategies have more modest information requirements.

Tender Offers. Models M and P in Table 6 are logistic regressions predicting the probability of tender offers. The fit is reasonably good, with adjusted Pseudo R-Squares of .37 and .35 (respectively) and significant Chi-square statistics.[2] There is support for H4 since tender offers are less likely when the target is in a knowledge-intensive industry.

The interaction terms are added in Models N and P. Again, the interactions are significant, providing further support for H5. The positive signs on the interactions suggest again that unrelated buyers do not avoid tender offers that might exacerbate information dilemmas. This result is also consistent with the pattern of findings in the other interactions. That is, unrelated buyers may need less information if they don't seek to build synergy.

DISCUSSION AND IMPLICATIONS

The hypotheses concerned two related questions. First, are buyers more likely to adopt coping strategies for targets in knowledge-intensive industries? Second, are unrelated buyers more or less likely to adopt coping strategies for such targets? Table 7 summarizes the findings and helps to make the overall patterns more salient. The following discussion examines what we can conclude and identifies directions for future research.

Do buyers adopt coping strategies for targets in knowledge-intensive industries?

There is evidence that buyers adopt the proposed coping strategies for targets in knowledge-intensive industries. First, all of the raw correlations were in the predicted directions and, with the exception of negotiation time, all were significant. Second, these relationships were robust when controls were added. In all cases, the main effects were significant in the predicted directions.

Therefore, there seems to be a pattern consistent with the predicted coping strategies for both general and specific knowledge. As shown in Table 7, buyers do offer lower bid premia and less cash for targets in knowledge-intensive industries. In addition, buyers appear to initiate information-seeking strategies through more lengthy negotiations and by avoiding tender offers for such targets.

Are unrelated buyers more or less likely to adopt coping strategies?

Almost all of the interactions between knowledge and relatedness were significant and indicated that unrelated buyers are less likely to adopt coping strategies. There was no support for the idea that unrelated buyers are more likely to apply coping strategies when purchasing a firm in a knowledge-intensive industry. As discussed, this may reflect the distinct information requirements of different diversification strategies. In other words, if the buyer does not intend to integrate the two firms, the information requirements may be much more modest and the coping strategies might not be needed. For example, if the buyer intended to create value through internal capital markets, the information requirements prior to the transaction would be primarily issues of cash flow and might be relatively easy to convey (Hill, 1988).

Of course, this study does not attempt to observe the buyer's acquisition objectives or whether they actually create value. Therefore, we cannot draw unambiguous conclusions. Other objectives, such as managerialism or hubris (Roll, 1986), cannot be ruled out. Asymmetric information may make unrelated buyers more prone to hubris when the target is in a knowledge-intensive industry.

Nevertheless, discipline is probably not a motive for unrelated buyers. The pattern of transaction parameters raises this question because it is similar to that observed for hostile transactions (higher premia, more cash, tender offers, etc.). However, additional analysis revealed that unrelated buyers typically pursue targets that have a strong record of growth.[3] Because the targets were performing well, discipline seems unlikely. In fact, the strong record of growth may even suggest that the buyers are signaling their resolve to preempt other bidders from emerging (Fishman, 1989).

Implications for theory

The findings suggest that industry knowledge intensity affects acquisition processes and may be linked to information problems as hypothesized. Since the strategy and organizational theory literatures address issues of tacitness, specificity, and asymmetric information, this study has implications for future research.

Strategic Management. Within the strategy literature, this study implies new directions for resource-based theory and for diversification research. First, knowledge is a key component of resource-based theory because it is hard to imitate (Barney, 1991;

Conner and Prahalad, 1996). Although this study examines knowledge at the industry level, the findings might be similar, or even amplified, if firm-level knowledge could be measured and included. This suggests that additional research should study knowledge-intensity using firm-level measures of the construct.

Also, most of the resource-based literature has focused on what resources have potential for a sustainable advantage and not on the management dilemmas that such resources create (Amit and Schoemaker, 1993; Reed and DeFillippi, 1990). These findings suggest that firms may need to develop competencies that allow them to acquire strategic assets. Further inquiries might focus on how firms develop such competencies (Zollo and Singh, 1998).

The second strategy research area, diversification, may also be informed by this study. There are many anomalous findings regarding the relationship between diversification and performance (Ramanujam and Varadarajan, 1989). The interaction between relatedness and knowledge was important in this study and may also be critical in the diversification literature. For example, relatedness may be important for some types of knowledge but not for others. Possibly, some of the inconclusive findings in the diversification literature may be untangled if additional studies conclude that the type of knowledge determines what type of diversification is efficient. Future research should test whether knowledge moderates the relationship between diversification and performance.

This study has also raised the possibility that unrelated buyers may have different objectives. However, the data do not allow us to discern whether unrelated buyers intend to create internal capital markets or enter new markets. For example, it would be interesting if such buyers were systematically more prone to hubris. While this study cannot address this question, the observation that unrelated buyers do not adopt coping strategies suggests that acquisition objectives and value creation are key areas for future research.

Along these lines, internal capital markets may offer a particularly fruitful area of inquiry (Hill, 1988). Theoretically, a buyer might be able to take advantage of asymmetric information about firms in knowledge-intensive industries to offer a lower cost of capital than the market (Chatterjee, 1986). That is, even if the market reflects all publicly available information (semi-strong efficiency), there may be greater asymmetric information about the primary assets for firms in knowledge-intensive industries (Gertner et al., 1994). Over time, the buyer may come to have better information about the acquired unit than is easily available to the market. Additional work might explore whether firms can create value in this way.

Organizational Theory. These findings also underscore the importance of knowledge intensity in market transactions. Much of the knowledge literature has been process-oriented in the sense that it has focused on how knowledge is transmitted and on the role of tacitness (Zander and Kogut, 1995; Nonaka, 1994). However, the strategic management and finance literatures tend to focus more on the impact of information imbalances on transactions (Chi, 1994; Myers and Majluf, 1984). This study integrates these perspectives in that it starts with a process-oriented context in which knowledge is the most important asset to be acquired. This study also includes the strategy perspective by focusing on the impact of asymmetric information. Additional research should explore how different types of knowledge impact both market and nonmarket transactions.

Implications for research methods

Future research should also identify improved measures of knowledge intensity, relatedness, and coping strategies. The industry-level measures of general and specific knowledge appear to add relevant information, but they are far from perfect. For example, though the interactions seem more important for general knowledge, we cannot determine whether the result is attributable to the knowledge type or to the quality of the measure. Also, while this study was crafted to examine the impact of industry-level differences in knowledge-intensity, it ignored the rich anecdotal evidence about key contributors and firm-level variation in knowledge intensity. The fact that these measures appear to yield interesting findings highlights the need to develop better operationalizations and study the construct at the firm level as well.

Innovations in measuring relatedness might also be applied in the diversification literature. Most relatedness measures have been based on SIC codes (e.g., product-based relatedness). Current diversification research compares various measures of relatedness and develops new measures based on resources (Hoskisson et al., 1993; Lubatkin et al., 1993; Robins and Weirsema, 1995). The expertise-based measure is relatively new and seems to add important information. Future refinements might help to clarify the diversification literature.

The measures and theory surrounding the coping strategies should also be examined further. This study identified a few observable coping strategies, but this is clearly not an exhaustive list. New measures are needed to explore other ways that buyers cope with uncertainty in acquisitions. In addition, while the coping strategies are clearly linked, this study did not attempt to untangle the interrelationships. Future work might develop a simultaneous model of coping strategies.

Implications for managers

Finally, this inquiry has important practical implications. It builds on Haspeslagh and Jemison's (1991) work by placing the acquisition process in the context of creating a competitive advantage. Increasingly, differences in firm performance are attributed to knowledge because it is hard to acquire and to imitate (Barney, 1991; Peteraf, 1993; Reed and DeFillippi, 1990; Wernerfelt, 1984). Dynamic capabilities that allow firms to adapt are also fundamentally knowledge-based (Teece and Pisano, 1994). While much of the literature focuses on identifying such resources (Amit and Schoemaker, 1993; Peteraf, 1993), this study sheds some light on the management dilemmas associated with knowledge acquisition.

ACKNOWLEDGMENTS

The author owes special thanks to Don Hatfield, Bob Hoskisson, Kevin Laverty, Julia Liebeskind, Michael Lubatkin, Jackson Nickerson, Laura Poppo, and Todd Zenger for their comments and suggestions on previous drafts. In addition, Jay Barney and three anonymous reviewers provided excellent guidance. This research was conducted while the author was at the John M. Olin School of Business, Washington University.

NOTES

1   This can also be expressed as: $\Sigma_o^{823}|EB_o - ET_o|$ However, Euclidean distance is usually represented as a squared term.

2   Chi-square compares the fit of the intercept only model with the specified model ($\Delta X^2 = 2\log(L_1) - 2\log(L_2)$). See Nagelkerke (1991) for a discussion of the adjusted R-Square for logistic models. The unadjusted R-Square is a function of the likelihood of the intercept only model (L_1) and the specified model (L_β). Specifically, $R^2 = 1 - [L_1/L_\beta]^{2/n}$. This ratio is then adjusted so that the maximum is 1 to simplify interpretation.

3   See the correlation between growth and UNRELATED$_{EXP}$ in Table 2. In addition, the analyses were run with a three way interaction that included growth and these were also significant (Knowledge $\times$ UNRELATED$_{EXP}$ $\times$ growth).

REFERENCES

Akerlof, G. A. 1970. The market for lemons: Quality uncertainty and the market mechanism. *Quart. J. Econom.* **84** 488–500.

Amit, R., P. J. H. Schoemaker. 1993. Strategic assets and organizational rent. *Strategic Management J.* **14** 33–46.

——. 1994. Methodological individualism and social knowledge. *Amer. Econom. Rev* **84**(2) 1–9.

Arrow, K. J. 1974. *The Limits of Organization*, Norton, New York.

Barney, J. B. 1988. Returns to bidding firms in mergers and acquisitions: Reconsidering the relatedness hypothesis. *Strategic Management J.* **9** 71–78.

——. 1991. Firm resources and sustained competitive advantage: A comment. *J. Management* **17**(1) 99–120.

Becker, G. 1983. *Human Capital: A Theoretical and Empirical Analysis with Special Reference to Education*, University of Chicago Press, Chicago, IL.

Bock, R. D., E. G. Moore. 1986. *Advantage and Disadvantage: A Profile of American Youth*, Lawrence Erlbaum Associates, Hillsdale, NJ.

Chatterjee, S. 1986. Types of synergy and economic value: The impact of acquisitions on merging and rival firms. *Strategic Management J.* **7** 119–139.

——, B. Wernerfelt. 1991. The link between resources and type of diversification: Theory and evidence. *Strategic Management J.* **12**(1) 33–48.

Chi, T. 1994. Trading in strategic resources: Necessary conditions, transaction cost problems, and choice of exchange structure. *Strategic Management J.* **15**(4) 271–290.

Coff, R. 1997. Human assets and management dilemmas: Coping with hazards on the road to resource-based theory. *Acad. Management Rev.* **22**(2) 374–402.

Conner, K. R., C. K. Prahalad. 1996. A resource-based theory of the firm: Knowledge versus opportunism. *Organ. Sci.* **7**(5) 477–501.

Datta, D., J. Grant. 1990. Relationships between type of acquisition, the autonomy given to the acquired firm, and acquisition process: An empirical analysis. *J. Management* **16**(1) 29–44.

Eckbo, B. E., R. M. Giammarino, R. L. Heinkel. 1990. Asymmetric information and the medium of exchange in takeovers: Theory and tests. *Rev. Financial Studies* **3**(4) 651–675.

Farjoun, M. 1994. Beyond industry boundaries: Human expertise diversification, and resource-related industry groups. *Organ. Sci.* **5**(2) 185–199.

Fishman, M. J. 1989. Preemptive bidding and the role of the medium of exchange in acquisitions. *J. Finance* **XLIV** March 41–57.

Flamholtz, E. G., R. Coff. 1994. Human resource valuation and amortization in corporate acquisitions: A case study. *Advances in Management Accounting* **3** 55–83.

Foss, N. J., B. Eriksen. 1995. Competitive advantage and industry capabilities. In Cynthia A. Montgomery (Ed.), *Resource-Based and Evolutionary Theories of the Firm*, Kluwer Academic Press, Boston.

Freidson, E. 1988. *Professional Powers: A Study of the Institutionalization of Formal Knowledge*, University of Chicago Press, Chicago.

Gertner, R. H., D. S. Scharfstein, J. C. Stein. 1994. Internal versus external capital markets. *Quart. J. Econom.* **109**(4) 1211–1230.

Giammarino, R. R. Heinkel. 1986. A model of dynamic takeover behavior. *J. Finance* **41**(2) 465–480.

Giliberto, M. S., N. P. Varaiya. 1989. The winner's curse and bidder competition in acquisitions: Evidence from failed bank auctions: *J. Finance* **44**(1) 59–75.

Haspeslagh P., D. Jemison. 1991. *Managing Acquisitions: Creating Value through Corporate Renewal*, The Free Press, New York, NY.

Haunschild, P. 1994. How much is that company worth?: Interorganizational relationships, uncertainty, and acquisition premiums. *Admin. Sci. Quart.* **39**(3) 391–411.

Hayward, M. L., D. C. Hambrick. 1997. Explaining premiums paid for large acquisitions: Evidence of CEO hubris. *Admin. Sci. Quart.* **42**(1) 103–127.

Helfat, C. 1994. Firm-specificity in corporate applied R&D. *Organ. Sci.* **5**(2) 173–184.

Hill, C. W. 1988. Internal capital market controls and financial performance in multidivisional firms. *J Indust. Econom.* **37**(1) 67–83.

Hirshleifer, D., S. Titman. 1991. Share tendering strategies and the success of hostile takeover bids. *J Political Econom.* (December).

Hoskisson, R., M. Hitt, R. Johnson, D. Moesel. 1993. Construct validity of an objective (entropy), categorical measure of diversification strategy. *Strategic Management J.* **14**(3) 215–235.

Huang, Y., R. A. Walkling. 1987. Target abnormal returns associated with acquisition announcements: Payment, acquisition form, and managerial resistance. *J. Financial Econom.* **19** 329–349.

Jensen, M. C. 1988. Takeovers: Their causes and consequences. *J. Econom. Perspectives* **2**(1) 21–48.

Kim, D. J., B. Kogut. 1996. Technological platforms and diversification. *Organ. Sci.* **7**(3) 283–301.

Kim, J. O., C. W. Mueller. 1978. *Factor Analysis: Statistical Methods and Practical Issues*, Sage Publications, Beverly Hills, CA.

Klavens, R. 1990. Acquisitions: Resource dependency vs. human resource perspectives. *Acad. Management Best Papers Proceedings 1990.* 170–174.

Kogut, B., U. Zander. 1992. Knowledge of the firm, combinative capabilities, and the replication of technology. *Organ. Sci.* **3**(3) 383–397.

Lee, T., T. R. Mitchell, L. Wise, S. Fireman. 1996. An unfolding model of voluntary turnover. *Acad. Management J.* **39**(1) 5–36.

Liebeskind, J. P. 1996. Knowledge, strategy and the theory of the firm. *Strategic Management J.* **17** (Winter special issue) 93–108.

Lubatkin, M., H. Merchant, N. Srinivasan. 1993. Construct validity of some unweighted product count diversification measures. *Strategic Management J.* **14**(6) 433–478.

Lynch, L. M. 1991. The role of off-the-job vs. on-the-job training for the mobility of women workers. *Amer. Econom. Rev.* **81**(2) 151–156.

Mergers & Acquisitions Journal. 1999. M&A Scoreboard. **33**(4), 57–68.

Mincer, J. 1974. *Schooling, Experience, and Earnings*, NBER, Columbia University Press, New York, NY.

Morck, R., A. Shleifer, R. Vishny. 1988. Characteristics of targets of hostile and friendly takeovers. In Alan Auerbach (Ed.), *Corporate Takeovers: Causes and Consequences*, University of Chicago Press, Chicago.

Mowery, D. C., J. E. Oxley, B. S. Silverman. 1996. Strategic alliances and interfirm knowledge transfer. *Strategic Management J.* **17** (Winter special issue) 77–92.

Myers, S., N. Majluf. 1984. Corporate financing and investment decisions When Firms Have Information That Investors Do Not Have. *J. Financial Econom.* (June) 187–221.

Nagelkerke, N. J. D. 1991. A note on the general definition of the coefficient of determination. *Biometrica* **78** 691–692.

Nahavandi, A., A. Malekzadeh. 1988. Acculturation in mergers and acquisitions. *Acad. Management Rev.* **13**(1) 79–90.

Nelson, R. R., S. G. Winter. 1982. *An Evolutionary Theory of Economic Change*, Belknap, Cambridge MA.

Nonaka, I. 1994. A dynamic theory of knowledge creation. *Organ. Sci.* **5**(1) 14–37.

Peteraf, M. A. 1993. The cornerstone of competitive advantage: A resource-based view. *Strategic Management J.* **14** 179–191.

Polanyi, M. 1966. *The Tacit Dimension*, Anchor Day Books, New York.

Prahalad, C. K., G. Hamel. 1990. The core competence of the corporation. *Harvard Bus. Rev.* (May-June) 79–91.

Pruitt, D. G. 1983. Integrative agreements: Nature and consequences. In M. H. Bazerman and R. J. Lewicki (Eds), *Negotiating in Organizations*, Sage Publishing, Beverly Hills, CA.

Raelin, J. A. 1991. *The Clash of Cultures: Managers Managing Professionals*, Harvard Business School Press, Boston, MA.

Ramanujam, V., P. Varadarajan. 1989. Research in corporate diversification: A synthesis. *Strategic Management J.* **10** 523–551.

Reed, R., R. J. DeFillippi. 1990. Causal ambiguity, barriers to imitation, and sustainable competitive advantage. *Acad. Management Rev.* **15**(1) 88–102.

Robins, J., M. F. Weirsema. 1995. A resource-based approach to the multi-business firm: Empirical analysis of portfolio inter-relationships and corporate financial performance. *Strategic Management J.* **16**(4) 277–300.

Roll, R. 1986. The hubris hypothesis of corporate takeovers. *J. Bus.* **59** 197–216.

Schleifer, A. and L. Summers. 1988. Breach of Trust in Hostile Take-overs. Alan Auerbach, Ed. *Corporate Takeovers: Causes and Consequences.* The University of Chicago Press, Chicago.

Spence, M. 1973. Job market signaling. *Quart. J. Econom.* **87** 355–374.

Spender, J. C. 1989. *Industry Recipes*, Blackwell, Oxford.

Szulanski, G. 1996. Exploring internal stickiness: Impediments to the transfer of best practice within the firm. *Strategic Management J.* **17** (Winter special issue) 27–44.

Teece, D. 1982. Towards an economic theory of the multiproduct firm. *J. Econom. Behavior Organ.* **3**(1) 38–63.

——, G. Pisano. 1994. The dynamic capabilities of firms: An introduction. *Indust. Corporate Change* **3**(3) 537–556.

Thaler, R. H. 1992. *The Winner's Curse: Paradoxes and Anomalies of Economic Life*, The Free Press, New York.

Trautwein, F. 1990. Merger motives and merger prescriptions. *Strategic Management J.* **11** 283–295.

Tsoukas, H. 1996. The firm as a distributed knowledge system: A constructionist approach. *Strategic Management J.* **17** (Winter special issue) 11–26.

US Department of Labor, Bureau of Labor Statistics. 1996. *BLS Reports on the Amount of Formal and Informal Training Received by Employees.* December 19, 1996. USDL 96–515.

Walkling, R. A., R. O. Edmister. 1985. Determinants of tender offer premiums. *Financial Analysts J.* (January-February) 27–37.

Wall Street Journal. (1995). Industry soothsayers wonder: How long will Lou woo Jim. June 13, A3.

Walsh, J. P., J. W. Ellwood. 1991. Mergers, acquisitions and the pruning of managerial deadwood. *Strategic Management J.* **12**(3) 201–217.

——. R. D. Kosnik. 1993. Corporate raiders and their disciplinary role in the market for corporate control. *Acad. Management J.* **36**(4) 671–700.

Walter, G. A., J. B. Barney. 1990. Management objectives in mergers and acquisitions. *Strategic Management J.* **11** 79–86.

Wernerfelt, B. 1984. A resource-based view of the firm. *Strategic Management J.* **5** 171–180.

Williamson, O. 1975. *Markets and Hierarchies Analysis and Antitrust Implications: A Study in the Economics of Internal Organization*, Free Press, New York.

Zander, U., B. Kogut. 1995. Knowledge and the speed of the transfer and limitation of organizational capabilities. *Organ. Sci.* **6**(1) 76–92.

Zollo, M., H. Singh. 1998. The impact of knowledge codification, experience trajectories and integration strategies on the performance of corporate acquisitions. *Acad. Management Best Paper Proceedings* BPS L1–L10.

Coff, R. W. (1999) "How buyers cope with uncertainty when acquiring firms in knowledge-intensive industries: Caveat emptor". *Organization Science*, 10(2), 144–161. Reprinted with permission.

10 Option nature of company acquisitions motivated by competence acquisition

Tomi Laamanen

INTRODUCTION

Small technology-based companies can be regarded as growth options. Growth options and real options, in general, represent an expanding stream of research (Trigeorgis, 1993; Dixit and Pindyck, 1994). Concurrently with the research carried out in the field of finance, growth options and option platforms have become an important object of study in management research. Management research has increasingly moved towards evolutionary resource and options views of the firm (Rumelt, 1984; Bowman and Hurry, 1993; Sanchez, 1993). Presently, applications of option theory are also being found in several other research areas. Examining small companies and decisions that are being made in small companies as options (see e.g. Calcagnini and Iacobucci, 1997) makes the option theory a relevant element in the research carried out in the field of small business economics.

Despite the concurrent methodological development in the field of finance and conceptual development in the field of management, the two streams of research on real options do not yet form a cohesive theory. There is also lack of empirical evidence. There are only few studies that empirically examine the existence of option characteristics of real life phenomena. Company acquisitions and collaborative arrangements are among the situations where the options analogy has been claimed to be applicable (see e.g. Trigeorgis, 1993). Kogut (1991) is one of the few researchers that has empirically addressed the option nature of collaborative arrangements. There is no published research that would empirically examine the option nature of company acquisitions.

The aim of this paper is to contribute to the understanding of growth options provided by collaborative arrangements and company acquisitions. A special emphasis is placed on empirical analysis. Studying small, technology-based company acquisitions makes it possible to test the validity of the conception of "small businesses as options". The purpose of the analysis is to find out whether competence-motivated small business acquisitions could, in fact, be considered as acquisitions of growth options into the acquiring companies. Assuming this is the case, a further objective of the paper is to examine factors contributing to the option nature of acquisitions and factors contributing to option upside. It is argued that factors contributing to option upside should be taken into account in option-type of company acquisitions when the companies are valued. These factors should be taken into account when determining the uncertainty structure affecting the option value of the company.

The plan of this paper is as follows: Section 2 presents the theoretical background and the hypotheses. Section 3 provides a general description of the sample and describes the principles underlying the sample selection. Section 4 reports the results of data analysis. Finally, Section 5 provides the conclusions and summary.

HYPOTHESES

Collaborative arrangements as options to acquire

In line with the reasoning of the evolutionary economics' path-dependent view of technology (Nelson and Winter, 1982; Dosi, 1982), technology-motivated joint ventures and other collaborative arrangements can be regarded as options to buy technology. Mutual history, joint projects, and asset specific investments lead into increasing levels of commitment. Initial investments in collaborative arrangements can be modeled as call options (Kogut, 1991; Folta, 1994). If a joint venture arrangement proves to be successful, it can be bought by one of the partners. In a study of 148 joint ventures, Kogut (1988) found that the industries that were the most active acquirers of joint ventures were chemicals, primary metal industries, communications, machinery, and other manufacturing industries. In a follow-up study of a subsample of 92 manufacturing joint ventures, Kogut (1991) found that 27 joint ventures had been terminated by dissolution, 37 by acquisition, and 28 were still operational. Hypothesizing that joint ventures are options to acquire, Kogut studied factors increasing the likelihood of acquisition. In line with the option hypothesis, the main relationships were found between the unexpected increases in the value of the venture, the degree of concentration of the industry, and the propensity to acquire the joint venture. Similarly in line with the option hypothesis, it was found that market decline did not correlate statistically significantly with the dissolution of joint ventures (Kogut, 1991).

The successive option nature of the transition process has also been evidenced in studies focusing on the gradual transition from contractual collaborative arrangements to more integrated equity-based collaborative arrangements and to company acquisitions. For example, Harrigan (1988) found that contractual arrangement were replaced by other arrangements of more permanent nature. In general, contractual collaboration is assumed to lead into decreasing uncertainty and, in successful cases, into increasing levels of integration. The increasing levels of integration in a network can typically take place along many different dimensions including institutional integration, integration of decision making, and integration of execution (Herz, 1992). Demonstrating a similar gradually increasing involvement, Gulati (1995) discusses the effect of social structure in alliance formation.

Hagedoorn and Sadowski (1996) have studied the transition from collaborative arrangements to acquisitions on the basis of two extensive databases of collaborative arrangements and acquisitions. In addition, they studied whether contractual technology alliances are transformed into joint ventures. The results were contrary to expectations. Out of the total of 6060 alliances in the database only 143 or 2.4% had been transformed to joint ventures. Hagedoorn and Sadowski (1996) found that if the transition to an acquisition took place, it took place in 64% of the cases within a period of five years after the establishment of the partnership. It is interesting to note that over 70% of the companies in the transformed alliances had over 5000 employees. Only 19% of the companies in the transformed alliances had below 500 employees. The distribution of the transformed companies differs statistically significantly from the distribution of all the companies in the database. In the whole database, nearly 70% of the companies had below 5000 employees.

The empirical findings of Hagedoorn and Sadowski (1996) concerning the unexpectedly insignificant role of the transition would seem to contradict the findings of Kogut and the notion of gradual evolution. One explanatory factor for the differing findings may be that Kogut studied joint ventures, not collaboration in general. Another explanatory factor for the differing findings may be the size of the acquired companies. It may be that the large acquiring companies do not use much equity collaboration in the pre-acquisition process when acquiring small companies. In the case of larger acquisitions, the importance of the gradual approach may be better acknowledged. Acknowledging the earlier results, it is interesting to study the existence of option-type of collaborative arrangements when acquiring small technology-based companies. It is hypothesized that

Hypothesis 1

> Previous option-type of collaborative arrangements *do not* play a significant role in the acquisition of small, technology-based companies by large companies

Company acquisitions as options

Following a similar logic than with collaborative arrangements, company acquisitions can be regarded as options to acquire a new technology or business area. In particular, small, technology-based company acquisitions can be expected to play an important option role. Small, technology-based companies are defined in this paper to be companies: (1) whose business idea is essentially based on technology; (2) that are established and owned by entrepreneurs or entrepreneurs together with financiers; (3) and that have below 500 employees. The companies are not required to be new, but the technologies that the companies are developing should be *situationally* new. Situational newness means that the technologies of the small, technology-based companies should be new to the acquiring companies. Technologies possessed by the small, technology-based companies may in some cases have already reached a mature stage of the technology life cycle from the perspective of the small company. The word "small" refers to the requirement that the company size is under 500 employees.

The small, technology-based companies are interesting objects of study since they typically have one major area of specialization. Acquiring such a technology-based company could be regarded as an acquisition of an option to the technology possessed by the small company. By regarding technology-based company acquisitions as option acquisitions, it is hypothesized that the acquiring companies in fact assume that the technology possessed by a small, technology-based company develops or can be developed favorably making the technology option valuable in the future. Other motivations to carry out the acquisition could be, for example, elimination of potential competition, acquisition of extra capacity, or other behavioral reasons.

The main purpose of the second hypothesis is to empirically test whether the acquisition of small, technology-based companies is regarded as option acquisition.

Hypothesis 2

> Large companies acquire small, technology-based companies as options to enter business or technology areas that they do not already have

Assuming that the main hypothesis is supported, it is necessary to go deeper in the analysis of the option nature of the small, technology-based company acquisitions. In order to deepen the understanding of the phenomenon, it is important to understand factors contributing to the option nature of the acquisitions. The following hypotheses concerning the age and size of the acquired companies, the role of technology maturity, the possibility to patent technology, the role of industry trend, and the characteristics of the acquiring company, are grounded in the resource-based and evolutionary economics views of technology (Penrose, 1959; Nelson and Winter, 1982; Dosi, 1982).

Hypothesis 2a

> The option-nature of small, technology-based company acquisitions is more apparent
> - the less mature the acquired technological competencies are
> - the younger the acquired companies are
> - the smaller, in terms of sales revenue and personnel, the acquired companies are

The first three-part sub-hypothesis tests the small, technology-based company related population variables that are associated with option-type of company acquisitions: small, young companies possessing new technologies. The option nature of the acquisitions is expected to be more apparent, the newer the technological competencies possessed by the small, technology companies. When the technologies are mature, many of the possible application areas that can be expected to emerge are already known. This can be seen to decrease the option nature of the acquisition. With less mature competencies, the co-evolution of markets and technology may not yet have proceeded as far. In addition to the maturity of technology and the size of the acquired companies, the age of the acquired company is another dimension describing the yet unfulfilled option nature of the small, technology-based companies. The younger the companies are, the less time there commonly has been for realizing the options inherent in the technological competencies. The age of the acquired company and the maturity of technological competencies are two commonly related dimensions describing the position of the company and its technological competencies in their evolutionary cycle.

The option nature of acquisitions is also expected to be more important the smaller the acquired companies are at the time of acquisition. The small size of the acquired company could indicate that the technology has not yet created significant growth for the company. Even though all the acquired companies under study in this paper can be regarded small, the smallest companies could be assumed to be the clearest cases of option acquisitions. As the age of the company and the maturity of competencies reflect the time dimension, the small size reflects the outcome dimension in terms of non-realized growth. The maturity of technological competencies, the size of the acquired company, and the age of the acquired company are assumed to correlate with each other.

Hypothesis 2b

> The option-nature of small, technology-based company acquisitions is more apparent
> * the more patentable the acquired technological competencies are

The second sub-hypothesis examines the appropriability of technological competencies bought through option-type of company acquisitions. Being able to patent the acquired technological competencies is used as an indicator of the possibility to protect the acquired technology. It is expected that option acquisitions represent acquisition of technological competencies that can be protected, allowing for the maximum value of the acquired options.

Hypothesis 2c

> The option-nature of small, technology-based company acquisitions is more apparent
> * the more research and development intensive the acquiring company

The third sub-hypothesis addresses the ability of the acquiring company to participate in the evolution of the acquired technology. It is acknowledged that several characteristics of the acquiring companies are linked to the eventual decision to carry out option acquisitions. In line with the evolutionary economics view of technology evolution, the research and development intensity of the acquiring company is chosen here as a variable characterizing the acquiring companies. The more research and development intensive acquiring companies are assumed to be better able to notice and link the potential technology options to their existing technologies providing for path dependencies with their own technology evolution (Cohen and Levinthal, 1990).

Hypothesis 2d

> The option-nature of small, technology-based company acquisitions is more apparent
> * the more favorable the industry trend at the time of acquisition

The fourth sub-hypothesis addresses the influence of external factors on the decision to carry out option-type of acquisitions. Factors outside the acquiring and the acquired company can be assumed to play a role. The industry trend at the time of the acquisition is chosen as such an external variable. If the industry, where the small, technology-based company is positioned, is growing, even though the small, technology-based company itself would not be growing, the potential for growth is assumed to affect the option nature of the acquisition. The more favorable the industry trend at the time of the acquisition, the more likely an acquisition is regarded as an option to participate in the evolution.

Factors contributing to option upside realization

In addition to the behavioral aspects of small, technology-based company acquisitions, it is useful to study the option upside realization in option acquisitions. Factors related to option upside in company acquisitions are studied in order to get a deeper insight into the uncertainty structure of the option-type of company acquisitions. An analysis of the option upside realization is related to the research on the company acquisition success factors in general. The performance of company acquisitions has been the topic of a large number of both conceptual and empirical studies. It has attracted the interest of a large number of disciplines. The performance of acquisitions has been studied from the perspectives of financial economics, different schools of strategy, and organizational behavior. So far there are no studies, however, that would report results of the performance of specifically option-type of small, technology-based company acquisitions.

Studies in the field of financial economics have focused on stock market responses to company acquisitions. The focus of the studies has been on relatively large acquiring and acquired companies. In these studies, the companies have been clustered according to several variables. The clustering has been done mainly into related and unrelated companies according to the similarity of the acquired company and the acquiring company. The studies have empirically attempted to find out whether the acquisitions lead into above average cumulative abnormal returns for the shareholders of the acquiring and acquired companies. A typical finding has been that the announcements of acquisitions have created positive or no changes in the combined wealth. The gains have occurred mainly for the shareholders of the acquired companies while the gains for the shareholders of the acquiring companies have commonly been insignificant, see, for example, Jensen and Ruback (1983).

In parallel with the stock market studies, more in-depth conceptual work has been carried out in the management literature (Kitching, 1967; Rumelt, 1974). Earlier, the concept of relatedness between the acquired and the acquiring company played a major role also in the management literature. The main focus was on the relationships between different acquisition strategies and company performance. Due to the dissatisfaction in the dominating relatedness focus of both the management and the financial economics schools of acquisition research, there has been an increasing shift in the focus towards postacquisition integration issues. Combining the organization theoretical approach to acquisition integration with the traditional management approach has resulted in a process perspective on acquisitions (Jemison and Sitkin, 1986; Haspeslagh and Jemison, 1991).

A handful of studies have been carried out with the main focus on success of small, technology-based company acquisitions. These studies include the studies carried out by the Ghalmers University of Technology research team (Granstrand and Sjölander, 1990; Lindholm, 1994), the studies carried out by Chakrabarti (Chakrabarti and Burton, 1983; Chakrabarti et al., 1994), and the study of Laamanen (1997). Based on the research on small, technology-based company acquisition success factors, a number of factors can be expected to contribute to the option upside in option-type of acquisitions. The factors examined in this paper are based on this research. The main emphasis is on co-evolution of the technological competencies of the acquired and the acquiring company in line with the thinking of evolutionary economics. The continuing favorable industry trend is used as an external control variable. Other variables chosen for the analysis include (1) the relatedness of the acquiring and the acquired company (Granstrand and Sjölander, 1990); (2) technology; (3) finance; (4) distribution complementarity of the acquiring and the acquired company (Laamanen, 1997); and (5) the atmosphere for collaboration measured as the proactive sales motive of the entrepreneur wanting to sell the company (Granstrand and Sjölander, 1990; Laamanen, 1997).

Hypothesis 3

> In option-type of acquisitions of small, technology-based companies, the option upside is positively linked
> - to the industry relatedness of the acquiring and the acquired company
> - to the existence of technological complementarity
> - to the existence of distribution complementarity
> - to the existence of finance complementarity
> - to the existence of cooperative atmosphere
>
> and as a control variable
> - to the continuing existence of a favorable industry trend

According to the evolutionary economics and resource-based views, technological evolution is path dependent. Technologies tend to evolve to related directions. Resources provide the highest rents in uses that are most closely related to the original intended use of the resources (Penrose, 1959). Accordingly, certain industry relatedness is expected to contribute to the upside realization in the option-type of company acquisitions. The concept of industry relatedness is understood here as the closeness of the main areas of operation of the acquiring and the acquired company. Resources of the acquiring and the acquired company are combined in a dynamic manner continuously after the acquisition. Sometimes, complementing technological resources are needed from the large company to enhance the technological evolution of the acquired small company. Sometimes, complementing marketing and distribution is needed to commercialize the technology developed by the small, technology-based company. Sometimes, complementing financial resources from the large company may be needed to realize the option upside. To avoid sacrificing the knowledge and willingness of the personnel of the acquired company to collaborate after the acquisition, it can be expected that the probability for option upside realization is further enhanced by the existence of cooperative atmosphere after the acquisition. A simple measure of the cooperative atmosphere is the proactive sales motive of the entrepreneurs that sold the company (Granstrand and Sjölander, 1990). A construct summarizing the behavioral hypotheses 2a, b, c, and d, related to the option acquisition decision, and the normative hypothesis 3, related to option upside realization, is shown in Figure 1.

EMPIRICAL SAMPLE

The empirical sample of this paper consists of 111 small, technology-based company acquisitions. The focus was set intentionally on small, technology-based companies. These companies can be seen to represent bundles of technological competencies. Accordingly, the valuation of these companies can be seen to represent the valuation of bundles of technological competencies. The technological competence component can be seen to dominate the company acquisitions. Due to the small sizes of the acquired companies, it would seem improbable that many of the companies would have been acquired for other reasons. In the case of larger companies, there are often also several other assets and resources that could be regarded as targets in

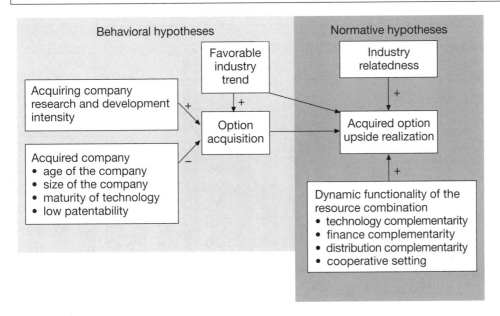

Figure 1 Construct summarizing the research setting and hypotheses of this paper.

acquisitions. For example, in larger companies the existing customer base or brand name could be considered as such desirable assets. Examining acquisitions involving diverse assets as option acquisitions is beyond the scope of this paper. In such acquisition situations, clarity would be compromised by the increasing importance of several diverse acquisition motives. From the option perspective, ambiguity would be caused also by the existence of interrelationships between the different option values.

The sample of small, technology-based company acquisitions was selected from among the total of 4531 company acquisitions, during the period 1987–1995, where a Finnish company was either the acquiring or the acquired company. The company acquisition volumes in Finland have varied over the years. The number of closed company acquisition deals has followed the economic cycles. The overall volume of company acquisitions has increased since 1980. Before the 1980s, relatively few company acquisitions took place in Finland. The development of the company acquisition volumes is shown in Figure 2. The time focus of this paper is on the most recent economic half-cycle. The half-cycle can be seen to start in 1987 and it would seem to end in 1994. The whole half-cycle has been selected as the total population to be studied. This has been done to control, if possible, the effect of systemic economic fluctuations on acquisition behavior. The nature of competence acquisition through the acquisition of companies may be influenced by the stage of the economic cycle.

Out of the total of 4531 acquisitions, 109 acquisitions were initially selected for a more detailed study. The initial case selection resulted from a process of examining the information of all the 4531 company acquisitions in the database. The database information was supplemented with more detailed descriptions of the acquisitions in the Finnish press. There were four selection criteria for the selection of the company acquisition cases. The first selection criterion, in accordance with the definition of the

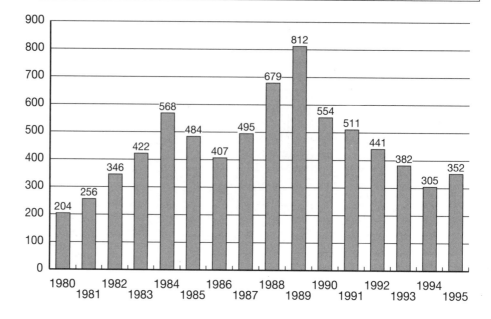

Figure 2 The development of the company acquisition volumes in Finland during the period of 1980–1995. The data on the acquisition volumes during the period 1980–1986 is based on Talouselämä 1, 1990. The data on the acquisition volumes during the period 1987–1989 is based on the Talouselämä database.

small, technology-based companies, was to select companies that had been sold by entrepreneurs. The companies needed to be majority owned by entrepreneurs before the acquisition transaction. If there was a group of entrepreneurs or entrepreneurs and a venture capitalist or entrepreneurs and a bank as the majority owner, the company was included in the sample. In some cases, the companies were sold through holding companies, for example, due to tax reasons. These company acquisitions were included in the sample if such holding company structure was recognized.

The second selection criterion was to select companies that would base their business on the exploitation of technological competencies. This was determined on the basis of the description of the acquired company. If there was uncertainty whether the acquired company based its business on the exploitation of technological competencies, the company acquisition case was included in the sample. The third selection criterion was to select only companies that were bought by other companies. Companies bought by private persons were excluded. The fourth selection criterion was to select companies that would not only be capacity expansions for the acquiring company. To be included in the sample, it was required that, in addition to possessing technological competencies, the acquired companies possessed *new* technological competencies for the acquiring companies. The fourth criterion was difficult to determine on the basis of the database. In some cases, the description of the background of the acquisition in the Talouselämä magazine or other press provided more information to decide on the criterion. Otherwise, the fourth criterion was used comparatively loosely in the selection of acquisition cases. All the acquisition cases that fulfilled the other criteria and that *could* have provided new competencies for the acquiring company were included. Carrying out a more detailed screen in the first interviews improved the validity of the sample. This was feasible in Finland where there are not many large companies in technology-based industries.

The case selection was adjusted after the first interviews. There were altogether 10 cases that were excluded from the initial sample due to discovered non-conformance of the predetermined criteria. There were 20 cases that were added to the sample after the preliminary discussions in the acquiring companies. There were 8 acquisitions that could not be analyzed due to the inability to reach the appropriate persons or due to refusals. There were 5 refusals and 3 cases where the companies or the necessary persons could not be located. Four of these eight missing cases can be considered to have been failures as acquisitions. One was continued but it was confidential due to military reasons. Two were so new that they had no history. Concerning the eighth missing case there is no data.

As a result, the total number of cases included in the study became 111. The response rate of the study was 111/119 = 93%. The missing cases are not considered to cause any significant bias. Even though the 111 acquisitions represent only 2.4% of all the 4531 acquisitions in Finland during 1987–1995, the sample can be regarded to cover well the population where (1) the seller was an entrepreneur; (2) the acquired company based its business idea on technological competencies; (3) the company was acquired by another company; and (4) the acquisition was not capacity expansion. Since the population fulfilling the predetermined criteria was relatively small, a survey of the whole population was possible. Technology-motivated business unit transfers between companies were not included.

The time-industry distribution of the 111 acquisitions is shown in Table 1. One third of the acquisition cases, 29%, took place in the electronics industry. One fourth, 25%, of the acquisition cases took place in the field of information technology. Around 18% of the acquisition cases represented the metals and machinery industry. The studied industries represent a relatively small proportion of all the acquisitions that have taken place during the chosen time period. On the other hand, in some of the industries included in the study, the studied acquisition cases are relatively representative. For example, the electronics acquisitions studied in this paper represent 19% of all the acquisitions in the electronics industry in Finland during the period. The information technology acquisitions represent 19% of all the acquisitions in the field of information technology during the period. In the metal and machinery industry, the proportion is smaller constituting only 4% of all the acquisitions in the metal and machinery industry. In consulting and engineering, the studied acquisitions account for 11% of all the acquisitions during the period. In the chemicals industry, the acquisitions account for 6% of all the chemicals acquisitions during the period.

Due to the technological competence focus of this paper, the industry distribution of the sample does not correspond to the industry distribution of the total population of company acquisitions carried out in Finland during the period. All the acquisitions in all the industries were screened, but in many of the industries, there were no companies that would have fulfilled the predetermined criteria. The studied population of 111 company acquisition cases is not representative of the whole 4531 population of company acquisitions in the database. In addition to the different industry distributions, there are also systemic differences. For example, the acquired companies are on average smaller in the studied population than in the whole

Table 1 Company acquisition cases selected for the analysis

	Selected acquisition cases	1987	1988	1989	1990	1991	1992	1993	1994	1995	Total
1	Food and beverages										0
2	Printing and publishing		1								1
3	Furniture and wood items production										0
4	Chemicals	1	1		2	1	1			1	7
5	Plastics			1				1			2
6	Metal and machinery	3	6	7	2	1			1		20
7	Forestry										0
8	Construction										0
9	Electronics	4	8	3	3	4		5	1	4	32
10	Textile and clothing		1								1
11	Conglomerate companies										0
12	Other industrial production		1	1		3			1		6
13	Construction services										0
14	Wholesale										0
15	Retail										0
16	Financial services										0
17	Hotels and restaurants										0
18	Transportation										0
19	Information technology	3	9	6	1	5			2	2	28
20	Consulting and engineering	2	1	7	3	1					14
21	Marketing services										0
22	Information services										0
23	Other services										0
	Total	13	28	25	11	15	1	6	5	7	111

population. The average sales revenue of the total population of acquired companies was 130 MFIM. The average sales revenue of the companies in the sample was 24.6 MFIM. The average number of people employed in the total population of acquired companies was 163 persons. The average number of people employed by the acquired companies in the sample was 47. Both differences in means are statistically significant.

Interviews were carried out with the managers responsible for the acquisitions and with the entrepreneurs that had sold their companies. The persons interviewed in the acquiring companies were typically presidents, vice presidents, or division managers. The persons interviewed in the acquired companies were typically founders or presidents. Altogether 128 interviews were carried out. In total there were 62 companies that were responsible for the 111 acquisitions. In many of the large companies, the same person had been responsible for all the acquisitions carried out by the company. In all the cases, it was not possible to reach the entrepreneur. This is, however, not seen to reduce the reliability of the findings significantly. The focus of the study was on relatively concrete issues that could also be verified from second sources in case there was any reason to doubt the quality of the data received. Such verification was in fact carried out in some of the cases. The interviews were complemented with internal material, for example, internal audits available in some of the acquiring companies. All interviews were carried out as personal interviews. Variable operationalization and variable distributions are shown in Appendix 1.

DATA ANALYSIS

Collaborative arrangements as options

To study if pre-acquisition collaborative arrangements had an option-role in the 111 small, technology-based company acquisition sample, it was necessary to analyze in how many cases there were collaborative arrangements. The motives for the establishment of these collaborative arrangements were examined. Based on the analysis, an evaluation of the option role of collaborative arrangements in small, technology-based companies was made. The previous collaboration was divided into previous equity collaboration and previous non-equity collaboration. Out of the 111 acquisitions, there were 14 acquisitions where there was previous equity collaboration. In addition, there were 25 acquisitions with previous non-equity collaboration.

The previous equity collaboration does not differ in volume in the studied sample and the total sample of acquisitions carried out during the period of 1987–1995 in Finland. Out of all the 4531 company acquisitions carried out in Finland, there were 430 company acquisitions where there was previous equity collaboration. The relative proportions, 12.6% and 10.1% respectively, do not differ statistically significantly. The motives for the collaboration, as stated in the interviews by the representatives of the acquiring companies, are shown in Table 2. In only relatively few of the contractual collaboration cases, the option to acquire the collaborative partner played an important role when establishing the collaboration. Fourteen cases can be seen to represent collaboration in business terms, for example, engineering, marketing, or installation collaboration. Six cases can be seen to represent collaboration in terms of sub-contracting. Only two of the contractual collaboration cases can be seen to represent option type of collaboration from the perspective of the larger company. In the previous equity collaboration, the initiation of collaboration would seem to have been more influenced by the options thinking. Eight cases represent investments into an option to acquire. Four cases were pure financial investments without any option considerations.

In addition to previous equity and non-equity collaboration, previous contacts between the companies were mentioned in 20 other cases. On the whole, the equity participation, non-equity collaboration, and previous contacts are represented in 59

Table 2 Motives for collaboration in the 39 cases with previous collaboration

Primary motive for collaboration	Number of cases with previous contractual collaboration (N = 25)
Collaboration in business terms, e.g. engineering	14
Subcontracting relationship	6
Joint establishment background	3
Option-type of collaboration	2
Primary motive for collaboration	Number of cases with previous equity investment (N = 14)
Option-type of equity investment	8
Financial investment	4
Earlier established by the acquirer	1
Acquisition techique: earn-out formula	1
Total occurrences of collaboration	39

cases. The previous contacts do not seem to provide much exposure alone. They would seem to act more as a mechanism to attract attention. Altogether, the option-role would seem to be present in the previous collaboration of 10 of the studied 111 small, technology-based company acquisition cases. This is such a small proportion, 9%, that it cannot be considered sufficient for rejecting hypothesis 1. Hypothesis 1 would seem to get support from the 111 small, technology-based company acquisition sample.

Company acquisitions as options

In the analysis of whether acquisitions of small, technology-based companies could be regarded as options to enter a new business or technology area, the 111 company acquisition cases were grouped into two categories. The first category consisted of company acquisition cases where there were no explicit option elements in the acquisition. The second category consisted of company acquisition cases where there was regarded to be an explicit option element in the acquisition. As expected, the option element was present in relatively many of the studied acquisition cases. Altogether 58 companies could clearly be classified as option acquisitions. In contrast to the lack of evidence concerning the role of collaborative arrangements as options to acquire small, technology-based companies, the acquisitions of small, technology-based companies would seem to have a more established option role. The first part of hypothesis 2 would seem to get support from the studied sample. To test the sub-hypotheses of hypothesis 2, correlation analysis is applied. The variables hypothesized to contribute to the option role of the small, technology-based company acquisitions are correlated with the dichotomous variable indicating whether the acquisition was an option acquisition or not. The Kendall correlation coefficients are shown in Table 3.

The correlation analysis indicates that four of the hypothesized variables correlate statistically significantly with the option nature of the acquisition: the maturity of the acquired competencies, the research and development intensity, the patentability of the acquired competencies, and the age of the acquired company. No statistically significant correlations were found between the option nature of the acquisition and the sales revenue of the acquired company, the personnel of the acquired company, and the industry trend at the time of acquisition.

Table 3 The correlation coefficients of the hypothesized variables and the option nature of the acquisition; N = 111. The logarithm of the personnel variable is used in the analysis to avoid bias due to large maximum values.

Correlation coefficients of the variables hypothesized to correlate with the option nature of the acquisition	Expected sign	Kendall correlation coefficient	p-valued	Statistical significance
Age of the acquired company	−	−0.26	0.001	significant
Sales revenue of the acquired company	−	−0.04	0.657	n.s.
Ln (Personnel of the acquired company)	−	−0.07	0.390	n.s.
Maturity of the acquired competencies	−	−0.52	0.000	significant
Patentability of the acquired competencies	+	0.48	0.000	significant
Research and development intensity	+	0.45	0.000	significant
Industry trend at the time of acquisition	+	0.01	0.953	n.s.

The maturity of the acquired technological competencies correlates statistically significantly negatively with the option nature of the acquisition. The more mature the technological competencies are the less they typically are associated with uncertainly and, consequently, the less they seem to contain option elements. The research and development intensity of the acquiring company correlates positively with the option nature of the acquisition. The more research and development intensive the acquiring companies are, the more likely they seem to carry out option type of acquisitions. The patentability correlates positively with the option nature of the acquisition. It would seem that the acquiring companies acquire small, technology-based companies as options when the technology can be patented. One reason for this may be that the large companies are in fact buying the rights for an attractive technology. Similarly to the maturity of the acquired competencies, the age of the acquired company correlates negatively with the option nature of the acquisition.

The variables correlating statistically significantly with the option nature of the acquisition can further be analyzed with the aid of logistic multiple regression analysis. The variables are regressed against the dependent variable indicating the option nature of the acquisition. It is necessary to use the logistic multiple regression instead of the normal multiple regression since the dependent variable is dichotomous. To first determine that there is no collinearity among the four non-dependent variables, a correlation matrix is constructed. The correlation matrix is shown in Appendix 2. The correlation matrix shows that many of the independent variables correlate with each other. This would seem to indicate some degree of collinearity among the variables. Particularly, the age of the acquired company and the maturity of the acquired competencies correlate strongly positively, as expected. The patentability of the acquired competencies and the maturity of the acquired competencies correlate negatively. The patentability correlates also statistically significantly negatively with the research and development intensity. The collinearity is attempted to take into account in the logistic multiple regression analysis by carrying out the regression analysis both normally and by using the standard backward elimination procedure with the likelihood-ratio elimination criterion. The results of the regression analyses are shown in Table 4.

Table 4 Regression equations of two regression analyses: 1 with all the variables that correlated statistically significantly with the option nature of the acquisition, 2 with same variables as in 1 but with a backward elimination procedure that applies the likelihood-ratio (LR) test in eliminating the variables; N = 111.

Regression analysis with the option nature of the acquisition as the dependent variable	All variables B	Significance	Backward elimination B	Significance
Maturity of the acquired competencies	−1.47	$p= 0.00$	−1.32	$p= 0.00$
Research and development intensity	0.90	$p= 0.01$	0.97	$p= 0.01$
Patentability of the acquired competencies	1.18	$p= 0.03$	1.18	$p= 0.03$
Age of the acquired company	0.02	$p= 0.34$	Eliminated	Eliminated
Constant coefficient	2.55	$p= 0.03$	2.30	$p= 0.04$
Goodness of fit statistic	97.0		93.9	
Chi-Square test value	63.2	$p= 0.00$	62.3	$p= 0.00$
Level of prediction (prediction table)	75.7%		77.5%	

After the elimination procedures, three variables seem to remain to predict the dependent variable with a high level of prediction. These are the maturity of the acquired competencies, the research and development intensity of the acquiring company, and the patentability of the acquired competencies. The regression results do not show the relative importance of the different variables since the variables represent categorical data that is coded differently in different variables. Coding the maturity of the acquired competencies and the research and development intensity further according to the indicator-variable coding scheme, the relative importance of the variables can be discovered. The results are relatively similar to the ones shown in Table 4. The influence of the competence maturity variable is the strongest. The research and development intensity of the acquiring company and the patentability of the acquired competencies are of relatively equal importance.

On the whole, the three explanatory variables are as expected. The younger companies with the less developed technological competencies are easily perceived and acquired as options. The importance of patentability would seem to indicate that the acquiring companies acquired the small, technology-based companies in a relatively high appropriability regime. Most of the acquisitions were also carried out without any pressure from competition. The acquisitions would predominantly seem to be have taken place in the high appropriability–low competition regime. The hypothesis concerning the option role of small, technology-based company acquisitions would seem to get additional support.

The third hypothesis addressed the value drivers in option upside realization. In real option valuation, these value drivers are elements of the uncertainty structure underlying the valuation situation. In company acquisition literature, the value drivers coincide with the company acquisition success factors. To analyze the value drivers in option acquisitions, the 58 option acquisitions are taken as a basis for the analysis. In the sample of these 58 option acquisitions, the chosen company acquisition variables are correlated against the option upside realization. The option upside was realized in 28 of the 58 acquisitions. The correlation coefficients of the different acquisition variables and the option upside realization are shown in Table 5.

The correlation analysis shows that five of the hypothesized variables correlate statistically significantly with the upside realization of the acquisition: technological complementarity, distribution complementarity, favorable industry trend after the acquisition, relatedness of the companies, and the proactive sales motive of the seller. Being able to provide funds for the acquired company does not correlate statistically significantly with the option upside in the acquisitions. The strongest correlations

Table 5 The correlation coefficients of the hypothesized variables and the option upside realization; N = 58.

Correlation coefficients of the variables hypothesized to correlate with the option upside of the acquisition	Expected sign	Kendall correlation coefficient	p-value	Statistical significance
Relatedness of the companies	+	0.45	0.00	significant
Technological complementarity	+	0.26	0.05	significant
Distribution complementarity	+	0.34	0.01	significant
Finance complementarity	+	−0.15	0.26	n.s.
Proactive sales motive of the seller	+	0.28	0.03	significant
Industry trend after the acquisition	+	0.41	0.00	significant

with the option upside seem to be the correlations with the industry relatedness and the industry trend after the acquisition. The closer the acquired company is to the acquiring company's core business area, the more successful the acquisitions seem to be. The importance of the favorable industry trend could mean that the acquiring companies were able to project the industry development and acquire the small, technology-based companies as options at the right time. From the complementarities, the distribution complementarity seems to have the highest statistically significant correlation with the option upside. Technological complementarity rates somewhat lower. Both are elements of fit between the companies. Similarly as in earlier studies (Granstrand and Sjölander, 1990; Lindholm, 1994), the proactive sales motive of the seller seems to stand out as a success factor.

The variables correlating statistically significantly with the option upside can further be analyzed with the aid of logistic multiple regression analysis. The variables are regressed against the dependent variable indicating the option upside. It is necessary to use the logistic multiple regression instead of the normal multiple regression since the dependent variable, option upside, is dichotomous. To first examine the collinearity among the five non-dependent variables, a correlation matrix is constructed. The correlation matrix is shown in Appendix 2.

The correlation matrix shows that some of the independent variables correlate with each other. Again, there would seem to be some degree of collinearity among the variables. Particularly, the distribution complementarity, the technological complementarity, and the relatedness of the acquiring and the acquired company correlate statistically significantly with each other. This is as expected. The technological complementarity correlates also with the proactive sales motive of the seller. The collinearity is taken into account in the logistic multiple regression analysis by carrying out the regression analysis both normally and by using the standard backward elimination procedure with the likelihood-ratio elimination criterion. The results of the regression analyses are shown in Table 6.

After the elimination procedure, three variables seem to stand out. These are the relatedness of the companies, the industry trend, and the creation of a positive setting

Table 6 Regression equations of two regression analyses: 1 with all the variables that correlated statistically significantly with the option upside of the acquisition, 2 with same variables as in 1 but with a backward elimination procedure that applies the likelihood-ratio (LR) test in eliminating the variables; N = 58. Time from the acquisition time to year 1996 is included to control for the bias of the different acquisition times.

Regression analysis with the option nature of the acquisition as the dependent variable	All variables B	Significance	Backward elimination B	Significance
Technological complementarity	1.06	$p = 0.26$	Eliminated	Eliminated
Distribution complementarity	−0.35	$p = 0.72$	Eliminated	Eliminated
Industry trend after the acquisition	2.07	$p = 0.01$	1.90	$p = 0.01$
Industry relatedness of the companies	5.73	$p = 0.05$	5.25	$p = 0.00$
Proactive sales motive of the seller	1.59	$p = 0.07$	1.69	$p = 0.05$
Time from the acquisition to year 1996	−0.16	$p = 0.48$	Eliminated	Eliminated
Constant coefficient	−5.99	$p = 0.02$	−6.22	$p = 0.00$
Goodness of fit statistic	36.6		43.9	
Chi-Square test value	32.1	$p = 0.00$	30.2	$p = 0.00$
Level of prediction (prediction table)	78.4%		84.3%	

for cooperation measured by the seller's proactive sales motive. Again, the regression results do not show the relative importance of the different variables since the variables represent categorical data that is coded differently in different variables. Coding the relatedness and the industry trend further according to the indicator-variable coding scheme, the relative importance of the variables can be assessed. The results are relatively similar to the ones shown in Table 6. The influence of relatedness is the strongest. With the coding scheme, the goodness of fit of the logistic multiple regression model can be increased to 56.1 and the level of prediction up to 90.2%.

The fact that the acquisitions did not take place at the same time may bias the results of the regression analysis. The more recent option acquisitions have a lower probability of a realized upside since less time has passed after these acquisitions. If the time for each option realization could be determined exactly, the Cox proportional hazard regression model could be used to eliminate the basis. Unfortunately, the exact times of option exercise and option realization are difficult to determine in connection with company acquisitions. Fortunately, based on the regression analysis in Table 6, the different acquisition times do not seem to bias the regression analysis. The time variable is non-significant. To further analyze the time bias, sensitivity analysis can be carried out. Eliminating the acquisitions that have taken place from 1993 to 1995 would leave in the sample acquisitions where at least four years has passed. In the remaining acquisitions, the time bias can be seen to play already a less significant role with respect to option upside realization. The elimination removes 11 acquisitions from the sample. Replicating the regression analysis with the remaining 47 acquisitions can be used to assess the magnitude of the bias caused by the different acquisition times. The results of the new regression analysis do not change much from the previous regression analysis. A further analysis that eliminates all the acquisitions younger than six years would seem to reconfirm this.

In a more elaborate analysis, also the magnitude of option upside realization could be taken into account. Such an analysis could be carried out by running the Tobit regression. The main problem in running the tobit regression would be the actual measurement of the magnitude of the option realization. Sales revenue growth could be used as one measure. It would be, however, a biased measure since different companies had significantly different cost structures. Same sales revenue growth would mean different magnitudes of option realization in different companies. Furthermore, it is difficult to determine the point in time at which to measure the sales revenue growth. The real option realization does not take place instantaneously. A better measure would be the net earnings growth. The problem with the net earnings growth is that it is difficult to determine which net earnings can be attributed to the acquiring company and which net earnings can be attributed to the acquired company. For example, the integration of distribution channels, production, marketing, and management functions makes the measurement difficult. The measurement becomes even more difficult the longer the time from the acquisition transaction.

DISCUSSION AND CONCLUSIONS

The relatedness of the acquiring and the acquired company seems to be an important explanatory variable in the option upside realization. One possible explanation for the importance of relatedness for the option upside is the need for complementary resources. Acquiring a totally unrelated small, technology-based company may provide an option for a new technology area, but it may not be a realizable option even if the technology area would eventually start to grow. The importance of relatedness would seem to support the basic argument of the resource-based view: A related use of specialized resources provides the highest rent for the resources (Penrose, 1959). Interestingly, Barney and Turk (1994) contradict this basic proposition of the resource-based view in their study on company acquisitions. They point out that in efficient competitive markets, the acquisition of related resources should not provide any additional value creation potential. The value creation potential is already taken into account in the acquisition price. Barney and Turk argue that the main value creation potential is in the combination of unrelated resources into the operation of the company. This was clearly not the case in the present study. One reason for this may be that the markets for small, technology-based companies are not efficient. Valuation is necessarily based to some degree on imperfect, incomplete information, and incomplete methods. Based on the findings of this study, it would seem that higher value creation potential could be achieved by acquiring companies possessing options into related, instead of clearly unrelated, technological competencies. These findings would seem to be corroborated by the findings of Capron et al. (1995) and Capron (1996).

The evolutionary explanation does not seem to hold in connection with the option role of collaboration. Collaboration does not seem to be extensively used as option creation when considering if a small, technology-based company should be acquired. Based on the acquiring company representatives' comments, it would appear that the small technology-based companies typically require relatively large investments for further development compared to the company size. For the large companies, it would not seem to be rational to make large investments in collaboration with small companies owned by entrepreneurs. It is more rational to acquire the companies immediately and start investing after the companies have been bought. This explanation would seem to provide support for the agency theoretical explanation instead of the evolutionary options theoretical explanation. To avoid post-acquisition incentive problems, the acquisition contract can be drawn with the entrepreneur so that the acquired companies are not integrated fully and that the entrepreneurs can also benefit from the option upside.

The evolutionary and option explanations would seem to apply better in explaining the role of small, technology-based company acquisitions. The option acquisitions, in addition to providing new technologies for the acquiring companies, seem to represent relatively new technologies in general. Companies that carry out option-type of company acquisitions seem to be more research and development intensive than companies that acquire small, technology-based companies in general. The research and development intensity can be seen to increase the ability of the acquiring companies to identify and to further develop the acquired technology options. The acquired technologies also seem to represent predominantly the high appropriability–low competition regime (classification by Kester, 1984). Options in this regime allow for long times to expiration. It seems logical that companies prefer to acquire and develop options that can be protected and have long times to expiration. The long time to expiration may be one of the reasons why the industry trend at the time of acquisition transaction does not seem to be linked to the decision to carry out the option acquisition.

In an analysis of the option upside realization, the industry trend seems to play an important role. In conjunction with the industry trend, the relatedness between the acquiring and the acquired company and the collaborative atmosphere, measured by the proactive sales motive of the entrepreneur, were found important. The importance of relatedness has to be contrasted back to the definition of relatedness. Relatedness or "industry relatedness" was defined in terms of *operational* links to the core business of the acquiring company. It was examined whether the acquiring companies could connect the acquired company operationally to the core business or to an emerging new business area, see Appendix 2. Relatedness was not only measured in terms of technology, market, product or production relatedness, but as an aggregate structural combination of these. Technology and distribution complementarities did not correlate as strongly when looked at separately. In a way, relatedness, as defined in this paper, can be regarded to represent the complementing overall resource support system for the acquired small, technology-based company. The collaborative atmosphere was also found important. Creation of a collaborative atmosphere facilitated joint work, gradually integrating the two companies. Capability to develop the existing competencies further was not lost.

On the whole, this study would seem to support the conception of "small businesses as growth options". This study would seem to confirm the applicability on the acquisition level. Expanding the discussion to the level of an economy, an interesting analogy can be made. In acquisitions, the option upside could be realized when a complementing resource support system existed in the acquiring company. On the level of an economy, a similar requirement for a complementing resource support system would mean that accelerating the creation of small businesses to create growth options is not sufficient. Attention has to be paid also to the complementing resource support system. The small businesses need complementing technological, distribution, and structural resource support systems to be able to realize the option upside. One interesting area for future research would be the search for the option characteristics of such systems in small economies. Other interesting future research areas would be the valuation of systemic resource platforms, option valuation of absorptive capacity, and the influence of pre-acquisition collaborative arrangements on the value of subsequent acquisitions.

APPENDIX 1   VARIABLE OPERATIONALIZATION

To test the hypotheses, the dependent and independent variables were operationalized. Both equity or non-equity collaboration can be considered to qualify as previous collaboration. Both can be measured on a binary scale indicating if there was equity or non-equity collaboration or not. The option nature of acquisitions can be determined on a binary scale. The option upside realization can be measured on a binary scale. The operationalization is shown in Exhibit 1 below.

Exhibit 1   Operationalization of variables necessary for the hypothesis testing

Name of the variable	Variable operationalization
Equity collaboration before the acquisition	Measured on a binary scale whether one of the companies owned shares of the other company before the acquisition
Non-equity collaboration before the acquisition	Measured on a binary scale whether the companies collaborated before the acquisition in business issues
Dependent variables Option nature of the acquisition	Measured on a binary scale whether there was in the acquisition an expectation of long term growth to be

	realized at a later point in time or whether the acquisition was motivated by short term objectives
Option upside realization	Measured on a binary scale whether the combined business of the acquiring and the acquired company started growing in terms of sales revenue or whether the growth was not realized

Independent variables

Maturity of the acquired competencies	Measured on a four-level scale from technological competencies that have not been introduced to mature declining competencies [1, 4]
Sales of the acquired company	Measured in absolute terms in Finnish marks as the sales revenue of the acquired company at the time of the acquisition
Personnel of the acquired company	Measured in absolute terms as the number of persons employed by the acquired company at the time of the acquisition
The industry trend at the time of acquisition	Measured on a three-level scale whether the industry was declining, stable, or growing at the time of the acquisition [−1, 0, 1]
Acquirer research and development intensity	Measured on a three-level scale: Acquiring companies or acquiring divisions having no or only insignificant explicit research and development investment are categorized into category 0. Companies or divisions having significant volumes of explicit investment in research and development are categorized into category 2. The remaining companies are categorized into category 1 [0, 1, 2]
Patentability of the acquired competencies	Measured on a binary scale whether the competencies cannot be patented at all [0] or whether the competencies of the acquired company had been patented before the acquisition [1] or whether the competencies could have been patented before the acquisition [1]
Age of the acquired company	Measured in absolute terms in full years as the age of the acquired company at the time of the acquisition
The existence of technological complementarity	Measured on a binary scale whether the acquiring company could support the acquired company technologically after the acquisition
The existence of distribution complementarity	Measured on a binary scale whether the acquiring company could provide the acquired company new customers after the acquisition through its existing distribution system
The existence of finance complementarity	Measured on a binary scale whether the acquiring company could provide funds for the acquired company after the acquisition
The industry trend after the acquisition	Measured on a three-level scale whether the industry has been in general declining, stable, or growing after the acquisition [−1, 0, 1]

| The [industry] relatedness of the companies | Measured on a scale of [0%, 25%, 50%, 75%, 100%]. The relatedness between the acquiring and the acquired company is rated 100% if the acquired company can be operatively connected to the core business area of the acquirer. The relatedness is rated 75% if the acquired company cannot be operatively connected to the core business area of the acquiring company, but there is some direct link between the core business areas. The relatedness is rated 50% if the acquired company can be connected operatively to a new emerging non-core business area. The relatedness is rated 25% if the acquired company has some distant links to a new, non-core business area. The relatedness is rated 0% if there are no pre-existing links |
| The proactive sales motive of the seller | Measured on a binary scale whether the seller wanted to sell the company for further growth in contrast to cashing out |

The numerical values for the variables were assigned based on interviews. For example, the variable indicating the option nature of the acquisition was determined based on the acquisition motivation of the acquiring company, as stated by the interviewed persons. If the acquisition was motivated by long-term growth possibly realizable in the future in contrast to short-term motivations, the acquisition was considered to have the option nature. The option upside realization was determined based on the sales growth of the acquired company. If the sales of the acquired business area started growing significantly, the option upside variable was assigned a value indicating option upside realization. The distributions of the variables used in hypothesis testing are shown in Exhibit 2 below.

Exhibit 2 Distribution of variables used in hypothesis testing: total: 111, option acquisitions: 58

Name of the variable	Variable operationalization	
Equity collaboration before the acquisition	Equity collaboration No equity collaboration	14 (13%) acquisitions 97 (87%) acquisitions
Non-equity collaboration before the acquisition	Non-equity collaboration No non-equity collaboration	25 (23%) acquisitions 86 (77%) acquisitions
Dependent variables		
Option nature of the acquisition	Option nature of the acquisition No option nature	58 (52%) acquisitions 53 (48%) acquisitions
Option upside realization	Option upside was realized Option upside not realized	28 (48%) option acquisitions 30 (52%) option acquisitions
Independent variables		
Maturity of the acquired competencies	1: Competencies not introduced 2: Introduction to the markets 3: Growth in the markets 4: Mature declining competencies	17 (15%) acquisitions 20 (18%) acquisitions 30 (27%) acquisitions 44 (44%) acquisitions
Sales of the acquired company	Sales revenue 0–5 MFIM Sales revenue 6–10 MFIM Sales revenue 11–20 MFIM Sales revenue 21– MFIM	41 (37%) acquisitions 21 (19%) acquisitions 19 (17%) acquisitions 30 (27%) acquisitions
The industry trend at the time of acquisition	−1: Industry declining 0: Industry stable +1: Industry growing	5 (5%) acquisitions 70 (63%) acquisitions 36 (32%) acquisitions

Acquirer research and development intensity	0: No or insignificant R&D 1: Moderate levels of R&D 2: Significant volumes of R&D	30 (27%) acquisitions 30 (27%) acquisitions 51 (46%) acquisitions
Patentability of the acquired competencies	Patentable competencies Non-patentable competencies	61 (55%) acquisitions 50 (45%) acquisitions
The existence of technological complementarity	Technological complementarity No technological complementarity	36 (62%) option acquisitions 33 (57%) option acquisitions
The existence of distribution complementarity	Distribution complementarity No distribution complementarity	25 (43%) option acquisitions 33 (57%) option acquisitions
The existence of finance complementarity	Finance complementarity No finance complementarity	47 (81%) option acquisitions 11 (19%) option acquisitions
The industry trend after the acquisition	−1: Industry declining 0: Industry stable +1: Industry growing	10 (17%) option acquisitions 33 (57%) option acquisitions 15 (26%) option acquisitions
The relatedness of the companies	No pre-existing relatedness Distant links to new non-core area Related to new non-core area Distant links to core business area Related to core business area	5 (9%) option acquisitions 8 (14%) option acquisitions 18 (31%) option acquisitions 12 (21%) option acquisitions 15 (26%) option acquisitions
The proactive sales motive of the seller	Proactive sales motive No proactive sales motive	25 (43%) option acquisitions 33 (57%) option acquisitions

APPENDIX 2 CORRELATION MATRICES

Exhibit 1 Correlation matrix 1; $N = 111$; variables used as independent variables when the option nature of the acquisition is used as the dependent variable

Research and development intensity	−0.31 $p = 0.00$		
Patentability of the acquired competencies	−0.36 $p = 0.00$	−0.36 $p = 0.00$	
Age of the acquired company	0.48 $p = 0.00$	−0.09 $p = 0.22$	−0.18 $p = 0.02$
	Maturity of the acquired competencies	Research and development intensity	Patentability of the acquired competencies

Exhibit 2 Correlation matrix 2; $N = 58$; variables used as independent variables when the option upside realization is used as the dependent variable

Technological complementarity	0.32 $p = 0.01$			
Distribution complementarity	0.12 $p = 0.35$	0.39 $p = 0.00$		
Industry trend after the acquisition	0.28 $p = 0.04$	0.22 $p = 0.11$	0.20 $p = 0.13$	
Relatedness of the companies	0.07 $p = 0.58$	0.20 $p = 0.09$	0.47 $p = 0.00$	0.01 $p = 0.95$
	Proactive sales motive of the seller	Technological complementarity	Distribution complementarity	Industry trend after the acquisition

APPENDIX 3   EMPIRICAL SUMMARY

This paper set out to analyze the option nature of collaborative arrangements and small, technology-based company acquisitions. To summarize, a number of specific findings can be pointed out:

- Small, technology-based company acquisitions could be seen more as option acquisition than as option exercise. An analysis of the previous equity and non-equity collaboration shows that in only ten small, technology-based company acquisition cases, the previous collaboration was initiated with the purpose to get an option to acquire the collaborative partner. Most of the cases where the collaboration had the option role were initiated as equity collaboration. Only 2 of the 25 non-equity collaborative arrangements could be regarded to have had the option role.

- Contrasting to collaborative arrangements, the option analogy would seem to be more relevant in acquisitions. Altogether 58 of the 111 small, technology-based company acquisitions were found to have explicit option elements. This would seem to favor the use of real option valuation methods in the valuation of technology-motivated company acquisitions.

- Using the logistic multiple regression analysis to analyze the variables contributing to the option nature of the acquisitions, four variables stand out. These are the age of the acquired company, the maturity of the acquired competencies, the research and development intensity of the acquiring company, and the patentability of the acquired competencies. The level of prediction with these four variables is 75.7%. Backward elimination procedure is used to remove the age of the acquired company as a variable causing collinearity. This increases the level of prediction to 77.5%.

- The patentability of the acquired competencies correlates with the option nature of the small, technology-based company acquisitions. The option nature of the acquisitions seems to coincide with high appropriability and low competition regimes. According to Kester's classification of real options (Kester, 1984), it is more optimal to defer the exercise of this kind of options than to exercise them early. The option to defer can be considered to create additional value-added when combined with the growth option.

- From logistic multiple regression analysis, three variables stand out to explain the realization of the option upside in the sample of 58 option acquisitions. These variables are: the industry relatedness of the acquiring and the acquired company, the industry trend after the acquisition, and the proactive sales motive of the seller. Technology, distribution, and finance complementarity were eliminated. The level of explanation with the three variables is 84.3%. The level of prediction can further be enhanced to 90.2% by coding the independent variables of the regression equations according to the variable-indicator coding scheme.

REFERENCES

Barney, J. B. and T. A. Turk, 1994, "Superior Performance from Implementing Merger and Acquisition Strategies: A Resource-based Analysis", in G. von Krogh, A. Sinatra and H. Singh (eds), *The Management of Corporate Acquisitions: International Perspectives*, Macmillan Press.

Bowman, E. H. and D. Hurry, 1993, "Strategy through the Option Lens: An Integrated View of Resource Investments and the Incremental-Choice Process", *Academy of Management Review* **18**(4), 760–782.

Calcagnini, G. and D. Iacobucci, 1997, "Small Firm Investment Decisions: An Option Value Approach", *Small Business Economics* **9**, 491–502.

Capron, L., P. Dussauge and W. Mitchell, 1995, *Appropriation of Resources within Horizontal Mergers and Acquisitions: An International Empirical Study*, HEC Working Papers: CR 542/1995.

Capron, L., 1996, *Mechanisms of Value Creation Through Mergers and Acquisitions: A Revision of the Traditional Explanations*. Conference paper. The 16th Annual International Conference of the Strategic Management Society (November).

Caves, R., 1980, "Industrial Organization, Corporate Strategy, and Structure", *Journal of Economic Literature* **18**, 64–92.

Chakrabarti, A. K. and J. Burton, 1983, "Technological Characteristics of Mergers and Acquisitions in the 1970s in Manufacturing Industries in the US", *The Quarterly Review of Economics and Business* **23** (Autumn), 81–90.

Chakrabarti, A. K., J. Hauschildt and C. Süverkrüp, 1994, "Does it Pay to Acquire Technological Firms?", *R&D Management* **24**(1) (January), 47–54.

Cohen, W. M. and D. A. Levinthal, 1990, "Absorptive Capacity: A New Perspective on Learning and Innovation", *Administrative Science Quarterly* **35**, 128–152.

Dixit, A. K. and R. S. Pindyck, 1994, *Investment Under Uncertainty*, Princeton, NJ: Princeton University Press.

Dosi, G., 1982, "Technological Paradigms and Technological Trajectories", *Research Policy* **11**, 147–162.

Folta, T. B., 1994, *Innovation through Quasi-integration: An Application of Option Theory to Governance Decisions in the Biotechnology Industry*, Doctoral dissertation, Purdue University.

Granstrand, O. and S. Sjölander, 1990, "The Acquisition of Technology and Small Firms by Large Firms", *Journal of Economic Behavior and Organization* **13**, 367–386.

Gulati, R., 1995, "Social Structure and Alliance Formation Patterns: A Longitudinal Analysis", *Administrative Science Quarterly* **40**, 619–652.

Hagedoorn, J. and B. Sadowski, 1996, *Exploring the Potential Transition from Strategic Technology Partnering to Mergers and Acquisitions*, MERIT, The Netherlands: University of Limburg.

Harrigan, K. R., 1988, "Joint Ventures and Competitive Strategy", *Strategic Management Journal* **9**, 141–158.

Herz, S., 1992, "Towards More Integrated Industrial Systems", in B. Axelsson and G. Easton (eds), *Industrial Networks: A New View of Reality*, Routledge.

Jemison, D. and S. B. Sitkin, 1986, "Corporate Acquisitions: A Process Perspective", *Academy of Management Review* **11**, 145–163.

Jensen, M. C. and R. Ruback, 1983, "The Market for Corporation Control: The Scientific Evidence", *Journal of Financial Economics* **11** (April), 3–50.

Kester, W. C., 1984, "Today's Options for Tomorrow's Growth", *Harvard Business Review* (March–April), 153–160.

Kitching, J., 1967, "Why Do Mergers Miscarry?", *Harvard Business Review* **45** (November–December), 84–101.

Kogut, B., 1988, "A Study of the Life Cycle of Joint Ventures", *MIR* (Special Issue), 39–52.

Kogut, B., 1991, "Joint Ventures and the Option to Expand and Acquire", *Management Science* **37**, 19–33.

Laamanen, T., 1997, *The Acquisition of Technological Competencies Through the Acquisition of New, Technology-Based Companies*, Helsinki University of Technology, Research Report 1997/1.

Lindholm, Å., 1994, *The Economics of Technology-Related Ownership Changes*, Doctoral dissertation, Chalmers University of Technology.

Penrose, E., 1959, *The Theory of the Growth of the Firm*, London: Basil Blackwell.

Rumelt, R., 1974, *Strategy, Structure, and Economic Performance*, Cambridge, Massachusetts: Harvard University Press.

Rumelt, R. P., 1984, "Towards a Strategic Theory of the Firm", in R. B. Lamb (eds), *Competitive Strategic Management*, Englewood Cliffs: Prentice Hall, pp. 566–570.

Sanchez, R., 1993, "Strategic Flexibility, Firm Organization, and Managerial Work in Dynamic Markets: A Strategic-Options Perspective", *Advances in Strategic Management* **9**, 251–291.

Teece, D. J., G. Pisano and A. Shuen, 1992, *Dynamic Capabilities and Strategic Management*, Working paper, Berkeley: University of California.

Trigeorgis, L., 1993, "Real Options and Interactions with Financial Flexibility", *Financial Management* **22**, 202–224.

Laamanen, T. (1999) "Option nature of company acquisitions motivated by competence acquisition". *Small Business Economics*, 12, 148–168. Reprinted with kind permission from Kluwer Academic Publishers.

11 Cross-border acquisitions of US technology assets

Andrew C. Inkpen, Anant K. Sundaram
and Kristin Rockwood

There has been a boom in mergers and acquisitions (M&A) activity in Silicon-Valley-type technology sectors of the US economy.[1] Analysis of the Securities Data Corporation (SDC) M&A database reveals that during the 1990s there were over 11 500 such acquisitions in the US, for a total value exceeding $1.75 trillion. To put these numbers into perspective, consider that such technology acquisitions accounted for over one-fifth of all M&A activity in the United States by number and, even more impressive, two-fifths of all US M&A activity by value. Moreover, the trend toward such acquisitions has accelerated dramatically in recent years. The year-and-a-half since January 1998 accounted for nearly 57% of the $1.75 trillion in assets acquired (a more detailed analysis of M&A activity in US technology sectors is presented later).

Although still predominantly a US game – since nearly nine out of ten technology acquisitions in the United States are made by US acquirers – the proportion of cross-border acquisitions has been growing significantly. During the 1990s, non-US firms acquired nearly $250 billion worth of technology acquisitions in the US, and three-quarters of this occurred during the year-and-a-half since January 1998.

To gain more insight into this important trend, this article examines non-US acquisitions of technology-based companies in the United States. We focus on European acquisitions of Silicon-Valley-type target firms and conclude that European firms have struggled with their acquisitions and, in particular, with the integration and governance of the acquired firms. Our emphasis on European acquirers is driven by two primary considerations. One, out of the $250 billion in non US acquisitions of technology companies, 60% were done by acquirers from the European Union (EU). Two, we believe that the issues raised in this article apply to the Asian context. Asia is closer to the EU than to the US in governance and management styles with respect to issues involving the acquisition of US technology assets.

MOTIVATION FOR THE STUDY

Potential acquirers in any industry must keep in mind the following. One of the most compelling pieces of both domestic and international business research evidence is that, based on accounting and stock market performance measures, acquisitions do not, on average, create value for acquiring firms.[2] In other words, acquiring firms' shareholders do not get more than they pay for, and often get less. In contrast, the shareholders of acquired firms walk away with stock price gains of anywhere from 20% to 30%.[3] When acquisitions are made using shares as the medium of exchange (rather than cash), this evidence holds up even stronger. In addition to not creating value for the acquiring firm, acquisitions often have negative impacts on the employees and managers of acquired firms.[4] Consider, for example, the network communications industry, an industry with a major presence in Silicon Valley. This industry consists of the firms that provide the backbone of telecommunications and, more importantly, data communications. When Nortel of Canada, seeking a stronger position in internet and data communications, announced its $9.1 billion stock-based acquisition of the Silicon Valley firm Bay Networks in June 1998, Nortel's share price dropped by about 15% upon the announcement. There was a similar negative stock price reaction of about 10%, again in June 1998, when Alcatel of France announced the purchase of DSC Communications for $4.4 billion.

Managers cannot ignore such evidence: value creation through acquisitions, measured by long-term gains in excess of the price paid, is extremely difficult. Target firms' shareholders are adept at extracting synergy-related acquisition gains up-front. Notwithstanding the evidence that value creation through M&A is extremely difficult, we live in an era in which M&A activity dominates the competitive landscape. The year 1998 alone witnessed more than $1.8 trillion of M&A of 14 000 assets in just the United States, with another $900 billion or so in such activity abroad. Going forward, virtually all major firms anticipate more acquisitions rather than less and many of the acquisitions will be cross-border transactions.

Given the importance of M&A in today's economic environment and the poor track record of many firms in the M&A area, there is clearly a need for more research into its key success factors. This need is amplified when one considers the history of research on M&As. Although there have been many studies of acquisitions in the finance and economics literatures, there is limited understanding of the complex organizational implications of acquisitions. For instance, Larsson and Finkelstein reported that the various streams of research in the M&A area are only marginally informed by one another. In particular, strategic, economic, and financial M&A research tends to disregard the organizational and governance issues that are central to the acquisition process. These, in turn, are issues that play a large role in determining the success or failure of M&As.[5]

Toward that end, this study examines cross-border technology acquisitions with a focus on post-acquisition integration and corporate governance issues. With the movement towards global technological convergence, non-US companies are becoming more active in acquiring computer- and communications-related companies, especially in the Silicon Valley area. However, many of these acquisitions have encountered significant challenges, particularly with post-merger integration. In this study we examine the following questions:

- What is the nature and extent of M&A activity in Silicon-Valley-type technology sectors in the US?
- What are the key factors in acquisition integration success in Silicon Valley?
- What are the critical corporate governance factors that non-US firms must address when acquiring Silicon-Valley-type assets?
- Do non-US firms have an inherent disadvantage when it comes to chances of success in Silicon-Valley-type acquisitions?

The two most commonly cited reasons for acquisition failure are differences in management styles and practices and inadequate planning for post-acquisition integration.[6] These issues are exacerbated in the cross-border setting. In cross-border acquisitions, differences in management styles and practices incorporate questions of corporate culture, national culture, and corporate governance. Non-US culture and corporate governance are different from American culture and corporate governance; American organizational culture, in turn, is different from technology culture; and technology culture is different from Silicon Valley technology culture.

METHODOLOGY

We examined all the technology-based M&A activity involving US targets that were the closest approximation to Silicon-Valley-type firms: firms in the communications- and computers-related industries (but excluding media companies and telecommunications service providers; for the specific industries included see note 15) for the period January 1990 to July 1999. We used the comprehensive Mergers & Acquisitions databases published by SDC. This list included approximately 11,600 acquisitions completed by both US and non-US firms.

The initial list of 11,600 acquisitions was narrowed to include only targets in California and then to those acquired by non-US firms. From this larger pool of Silicon-Valley-type M&As by non-US acquirers, several firms were selected for detailed clinical study and interviews. Six case studies of Silicon-Valley-type companies acquired by non-US firms (all from the EU) were conducted. In addition, interviews were conducted with various individuals and analysts associated with Silicon Valley M&As, including consultants, entrepreneurs, and journalists. The majority of interviews were conducted on-site in Silicon Valley, although several were conducted via e-mail.

Finally, as a basis of comparison and in order to benchmark against best practices, the M&A integration process of Cisco Systems was examined. Cisco is widely recognized as one of the most successful Silicon Valley acquirers and offers a stunning counter-example to years of M&A research. Cisco, the leading provider of network communications equipment (called routers) for the internet-based economy, went public in 1990 at a market value of $226 million. In less than a decade, Cisco grew to a market value of nearly $230 billion by end of July 1999, an astounding stock price growth of over 100,000% during this period. As of the time of writing, Cisco had become the 4th most valuable company in the United States and had announced its eighth stock split in nine years.

What makes this stock price growth and financial performance truly impressive is the fact that Cisco has used "growth by acquisition and partnership" as the centerpiece of its strategy. During the seven-year period 1993–October 1999, the company grew through 42 carefully executed, related and strategic acquisitions of often unknown and usually small firms, almost always using its own shares as the medium of exchange. Only two acquisitions were for more than $1 billion.[7] Cisco also made various minority equity investments during this time. Although it may be a cliché in the M&A world to say that "if the assets walk out the door every evening, the acquirer had better make sure that they want to come back the next morning," Cisco's assets do appear to come back the next morning. In fact, Cisco management claims that employee turnover in acquired companies is lower than Cisco's average employee turnover.[8]

THE SILICON VALLEY ENVIRONMENT

As Cohen and Fields point out, it is difficult to imagine an example of regional economic development that is more successful, or more famous, than Silicon Valley.[9] It is an economic area dominated by rapid innovation and commercialization in many new technologies. However, Silicon Valley (and, to a lesser degree, other technology-driven geographical clusters such as Route 128 in Boston) is more than a random cluster of technology firms located geographically close to one another.[10] In much the same idea as a natural ecosystem, Silicon Valley's growth can be attributed to a constant formation of diverse companies that support and interact with one another. Constituents of this ecosystem include venture capitalists, a pool of knowledge-workers from around the world, universities and research institutes, and a sophisticated service infrastructure, as well as many customers, lead-users, and early adopters of new technologies.[11] Although one must be careful in generalizing about a region as diverse as Silicon Valley, several key cultural characteristics do exist.

First and most important, there is an entrepreneurial culture driven by innovation and commercialization of new ideas.[12] Innovation is largely the result of collaboration between the various constituents of the ecosystem. The close proximity of companies, the fast-moving nature of high-technology industries, the high mobility rate of engineers and other professionals, and the frequent formation of alliances support the cross-pollination of knowledge and ideas. Together with short product cycles and market windows, this implies that the competitive challenge is not just in knowing what new products existing markets are looking for but also in developing new products which can then look for or create new markets.

A second characteristic is learning through failure. In Silicon Valley, there is little stigma attached to honest failure, although there is a stigma associated with resting on laurels. Entrepreneurs are measured by what they are currently doing, not by whether their previous venture was a success or a failure. A third characteristic is the nature of the labor market. Aspiring entrepreneurs from around the United States and the world flock to Silicon Valley, creating an internationally diverse group of highly educated and motivated people. These people work under exceedingly high levels of pressure and are perhaps more loyal to technology and innovation than to employers and firms.[13] The result is an extraordinarily high level of labor mobility.

Given these unique cultural characteristics, our research proposition was that firms from outside Silicon Valley would have difficulty in successfully managing and integrating acquisitions of Silicon Valley-based firms. As we heard early in the study from a Silicon Valley HR director, "It's not just Europeans who experience difficulties in Silicon Valley acquisitions, but everybody in the technology industry." The problem is not that Silicon Valley is closed to new ideas or outsiders. Quite the contrary: new ideas and outsiders are the lifeblood of the region. However, it was expected that firms from outside the United States without experience in Silicon Valley would struggle with their acquisitions. As we were told by Alex Gove, a journalist with *Red Herring* magazine:[14]

> Foreign companies have had problems dealing with issues involving control and compensation. Startups in Silicon Valley flourish because they are free agents; because of distance and culture, foreign companies often restrict this freedom. Also, foreign companies are not accustomed to granting large amounts of stock to key employees or creating financial structures such as spinouts that reward high-powered teams.

Table 1 Mergers and acquisitions of Silicon-Valley-type assets in the United States: January 1990–July 1999

Attribute	All acquisitions	US acquisitions	European acquisitions
Number	11,639	10,309	446
Value (US$ billion)	1,760	1,510	145
Average size (US$ million)	151	155	326
Deal value ≤ $200 mn (%)	94.2%	95.0%	89.9%
Four-week premium[a]	–	14.2%	43.4%
One-week premium[a]	–	13.7%	34.4%
One-day premium[a]	–	11.8%	31.8%
Extent of information leakage[b] (%)	–	2.1%	8.8%
% Using cash only[c]	54.5%	53.2%	66.9%
% Using some or all stock[c]	45.5%	46.8%	30.1%

Source: Securities Data Corporation
Notes:
[a] 'Premium' is the excess of price paid as a percentage of pre-bid price as of relevant time. Not available for the whole sample.
[b] Measured as the percentage increase in pre-bid price during the period spanning four weeks prior to the acquisition announcement to one day before; not available for the whole sample.
[c] Medium of exchange data are not available for the whole sample.

EVIDENCE ON SILICON-VALLEY-TYPE ACQUISITIONS IN THE UNITED STATES

During the decade of the 1990s, there were over 11,500 acquisitions of Silicon-Valley-type assets in the US, for a total value slightly exceeding $1.75 trillion (see Table 1).[15] These numbers are quite impressive given that during this period, the sum total of *all* mergers and acquisitions involving a US company (as either an acquirer or a target) amounted to 54,500 deals for a value total of approximately $4.52 trillion. In other words, Silicon-Valley-type assets in the United States as acquisition targets accounted for about 21% of *all* US M&A activity by number and, even more impressive, 39% by value.

Acquisitions of such assets are predominantly a US domestic activity. As shown in Table 1, US acquirers accounted for 88.5% of all such acquisitions by number, followed by 3.8% from the European Union.[16] Asia accounted for only 2.4% and Latin American acquirers accounted for less than one-quarter of one percentage point. The breakdown by value is roughly similar: US acquirers accounted for 86% by value, while European acquirers accounted for 8.3%, a slightly higher share of value relative to number of acquisitions. European buyers are, on average, buying assets that are more than twice as large as those of US acquirers ($325.5 million versus $155 million). Two possible reasons could explain this difference: one, Europeans are buying assets that are twice as large by paying about the same premium as a US company does; or two, Europeans are buying a less-than-twice as large asset by paying a much higher premium.

Table 1 reveals that the latter is true. The average premium paid by a European acquirer of a Silicon-Valley-type asset in the United States (measured by the price paid relative to the target firm's stock price one month prior to the acquisition announcement date) is over 43%, compared to just 14.23% for US acquirers. In other words, European acquirers appear to be paying about three times the premium that

US acquirers are paying.[17] An ancillary piece of evidence is that there appears to be much more "information leakage" with acquisitions made by European companies, compared to that made by US companies. The premium paid by European firms relative to the target's price one day prior to the acquisition announcement is 31.8%, implying an 8.8% pre-bid run-up in the target's prices during the month prior to the announcement. The one-day premium paid by US acquirers is 11.8%, implying a smaller 2.1% pre-bid run-up.

There is also tremendous size-related skewness in the data, in that the typical acquisition of a Silicon-Valley-type asset is a small acquisition. We see that of the 11,637 deals reported by the SDC database, 94.2% were acquisitions valued at $200 million or less. This proportion is 95% for US firms and 90% for European firms.

As we might expect, given that European companies are less likely to be listed on US stock exchanges and hence less able to use stock as a medium of exchange in acquisitions, there is a marked difference in the medium of exchange used. Approximately 47% of all acquisitions by US acquirers involved some or all stock as a medium of exchange (26% used all stock), compared to 30% for European firms (less than 10% used all stock).

Table 2 replicates the same analysis as in Table 1, but for the more recent year-and-a-half period January 1998 to July 1999. Basically, the table makes the evidence above even more compelling. This recent year-and-a-half period accounted for 33% of all the activity during the 1990s by number and 57% of the activity by value. While the proportion of deals made by US companies remains about the same (90%), there is an increase in the share of European activity (from 3.8% to 4.8%).

Deal sizes have become larger (average deal size of $537 million for Europeans versus $237 million for US firms), the premiums being paid have become higher (one-month premium of 53.4% for Europeans compared to 19.5% for US firms), the extent of information leakage continues to be higher for European firms, and most of

Table 2 Mergers and acquisitions of Silicon-Valley-type assets in the United States: January 1998–July 1999

Attribute	All acquisitions	US acquisitions	European acquisitions
Number	3,871	3,477	185
Value (US$ billion)	1,008	825	99
Average size (US$ million)	281	237	537
Deal value ≤ $200 mn (%)	92.5%	92.9%	84.8%
Four-week premium[a]	–	19.5%	53.4%
One-week premium[a]	–	18.0%	40.8%
One-day premium[a]	–	15.1%	34.8%
Extent of information leakage[b] (%)	–	3.8%	13.8%
% Using cash only[c]	42.6%	40.4%	64.6%
% Using some or all stock[c]	57.4%	59.6%	35.4%

Source: Securities Data Corporation
Notes:
[a] 'Premium' is the excess of price paid as a percentage of pre-bid price as of relevant time. Not available for the whole sample.
[b] Measured as the percentage increase in pre-bid price during the period spanning four weeks prior to the acquisition announcement to one day before; not available for the whole sample.
[c] Medium of exchange data are not available for the whole sample.

the deals still continue to be smaller deals (of size less than or equal to $200 million). The proportion of deals involving stock as a medium of exchange is nearly 60% for US companies, while it remains a much lower 35% for European companies.

In summary, Silicon-Valley-type assets are being acquired in impressive numbers but non-US companies are still minor players. Non-US companies tend to buy larger assets, pay a much higher premium, and appear less able to hide their acquisition intentions from the financial markets. Finally, non-US companies are more likely to use cash rather than stock as the medium of exchange.

ACQUISITION INTEGRATION: FINDINGS FROM THE CASE STUDIES

In our case study research, key issues surfaced in interviews and, in particular, around the areas where the European firms struggled to adapt. European firms' acquisitions of technology companies in Silicon Valley tended to be for two reasons: to enhance an existing product line and/or to access the target's technology and existing customer relationships. The primary reasons why targets accepted acquisition offers were equally straightforward: a need for a stronger brand name, a need for expanded marketing and distribution capability, and a need for more operating and investment capital.

Four organizational factors emerged as important drivers of successful post-merger integration: speed in integration and the nature of decision making, acquirer communication styles and vision creation, networking and socialization, and the target employees' sense of "who is in charge?"

Integration speed and decision making

The speed with which acquired firms are integrated – i.e., melded with the acquirer's culture and systems – is a vital issue in any acquisition. GE Capital, for example, tries to create a 100-day plan for acquisition integration on the basis that since change is inevitable when firms are acquired, it is best to create the change as quickly as possible.[18] We found little consistency in how acquiring companies integrated their acquisitions. In one case, the target company retained almost total autonomy in its daily operations and the European acquirer's view was strictly "hands off." At the opposite end of the integration continuum, an acquirer and target firm were combined into one company with a fully vertical functional structure, which was the third structure tried in the span of a year.

A particularly problematic area for European acquirer firms was in adjusting to the style of Silicon Valley decision making. Given the nature of technology products and the culture of innovation in Silicon Valley, decision making must happen quickly, particularly if it involves technological issues. The target firms reported that:

- The European decision making process is slower than that in Silicon Valley, often relying on a consensus method of decision making that was viewed by target firms as inappropriate in Silicon Valley.
- European acquirers exhibit an excessive dependence on data and information. The result is that the newly acquired organizations often lost market opportunities.
- A general lack of personal accountability on the part of acquirer management was reported, with "nobody willing to be the decision maker." In one case, the existing target management team was left in place far too long, even though it was

acknowledged to be one of the worst in Silicon Valley. However, the European acquirer was unable to move quickly to make the changes.

- Change is regarded as positive in Silicon Valley, whereas European acquirers think that change is often negative.
- European acquirers' development teams "are not fast enough" and, as a result, market opportunities have been lost.
- European acquirers are considered too risk averse. Consider the following comments from target management:

> They [European acquirer management] should be more concerned with getting a product out the door than with making sure it is 100 percent perfect.

> They [the Europeans] want to make sure the market is great for a product, and they want sales projections and marketing plans. But startups [in the Valley] just introduce a product to market and see how the market reacts.

> The Europeans always want a 5-year plan and projection. Start-ups laugh because they have 3-year plans. Three-year plans are common in the Valley. Most venture-backed companies have three year plans.

In summary, the findings suggest that because European acquirers are unaccustomed to the nature of Silicon Valley decision making and cultural norms, acquisition integration processes are often poorly implemented. In turn, this jeopardizes product development and market opportunities because of inattention to the need for very fast response times.

Communication and vision

In any acquisition, communication is essential, particularly to ensure that target employees understand the rationale and objectives of the acquisition. In virtually all acquisitions there will be uncertainty about job status. The high level of labor mobility in Silicon Valley means that uncertainty about jobs will translate into even greater turnover than for acquisitions in other industries and geographic regions. Thus, any acquirer in Silicon Valley is faced with the strong probability that key employees will leave if they are uncomfortable with the acquisition.[19]

An overwhelming conclusion that emerged from our interviews was that the European acquirers did not do well in communicating a vision for the acquired organization. Each target firm in the study reported a lack of clarity as to its role in the combined organization even though having a "story" for the newly acquired firm is a basic integration element. The most immediate downside of a failure to communicate expectations and an atmosphere of uncertainty is that employees will leave. In one target company there was a 50% turnover in R&D and 35% in the company as a whole. As we heard from one acquired company:

> The combined company is a company without soul. People are leaving because there is no vision and no direction. The president is not getting enough buy-in from senior management [in the European acquirer] to be able to execute. There is a gap between understanding and doing.

And from another company:

> Good news and bad news can spread very quickly. You need vision to spread good news. In this industry, you only have the technology and the people. If the combined company

doesn't clean up quickly, it will only get the B players ... There is a great job market in the Valley and it is not difficult for qualified people to be hired into another exciting company that has a vision.

In addition to the nature of communication, we found that target firm and European acquirers preferred and used different tools for communication:

* European companies preferred personal contact, then telephone, then fax, then e-mail.
* The Silicon Valley targets used e-mail as a primary method of communication.
* Silicon Valley targets rarely used fax as a method of outgoing communication.

From this we can again surmise that European acquirers move too slowly relative to the firms acquired.

Networking and socialization

As Cohen and Fields argued, trust is a critical asset in Silicon Valley and it is tied to performance and reputation.[20] This is consistent with observations from a European manager:

> In the Silicon Valley, the social network is important. Networking builds trust, and Silicon Valley and the software industry are built on trust ... If you don't socialize, why are you even here? Both your customer and your competitor are next door ... It is important to never burn bridges in Silicon Valley because your customer today could be your employer tomorrow.

Saxenian describes how the Silicon Valley social structure was created.[21] Young engineers and entrepreneurs came to Silicon Valley from distant places, often from outside the United States and without friends or family. Anonymity resulted in a willingness to take chances and risk failure. Loyalty to an employer was secondary to doing excellent work and building a reputation by association with exciting projects. Frequent job-hopping became a way of life in Silicon Valley and workers quickly created interlocking networks of former colleagues and personal friends. Trust is willingly extended to outsiders as long as there is a commercial reason for doing so. When individuals or companies experience difficulties, the informal social networks make it easier for companies to help each other in new markets and avoid duplication of effort through joint ventures, special licensing agreements, and common technical standards.

Clearly, networking is critical to the success of Silicon Valley firms. However, based on our case studies, there was a tendency for Europeans to socialize with each other to the exclusion of the target firm employees.[22] While this may be typical behavior in France or Germany or wherever the European firm is based,[23] it is atypical in Silicon Valley and, from a business perspective, very unwise given that networks provide a key source of information about employment, work in progress, new technologies, and so on.

Who is in charge?

In all of the cases, the target firms were much smaller than the acquirers. When a small company is acquired by a large one, there is often confusion as to which acquirer managers are responsible for the acquisition and subsequent integration. A typical problem is that acquirer managers appear and then disappear. This problem of managerial continuity was evident in this study. Consider the following examples provided by target managers:

> About two weeks after the acquisition, a high level manager from the acquirer walked in the door, spent a week meeting with people, assured them that no changes would occur and that he would be back in two weeks to assist with the acquisition. He never returned.

> In the Valley, you lend credibility to a manager's statement that something is broken. In the Valley, managers have a higher ability to listen to employees. In Europe, there is still a class system.

> There is no planning, no vision for the future, and no energy. Our CEO is not even coming to work every day [Because he gets no direction from the acquirer and is extremely demotivated]. As a matter of fact, in mid-March, his secretary sent a company-wide e-mail informing employees that he would be available from 10–5 on Tuesday through Thursday, and on Friday by appointment only. There is no longer any leadership. He is taking dancing lessons and making pottery these days.

A related issue involves information flows and the acquirer responsibility to answer questions. As we heard from the former CEO of an acquired firm:

> People kept asking me what would happen to their medical plan. Could they still go to the same doctor? I did not have any answers so all I could say was that I don't know. The company that bought us was not providing any information, which was very frustrating to the employees.

CORPORATE GOVERNANCE-RELATED FACTORS

Clearly, integration issues were problematic for the European firms studied. In addition to integration challenges, four corporate governance-related issues create impediments for European, Asian, and other non-US firms acquiring Silicon Valley assets: differences in compensation structures between Silicon Valley and acquiring companies, the nature of the acquirer's ownership structure, the role of M&A in the acquirer's strategy process, and the roles played by some of the key acquirer stakeholders, especially bankers.

Compensation systems

Incentive compensation structures and the political climate of established firms can create a chasm between individual motivations and organizational goals. In a start-up, much of an individual's compensation is in the form of stock options, which align individual and organizational goals and generate intense commitment on the part of the employee for the success of the venture. Since technology industries are knowledge-intensive and knowledge resides in people, individual attitudes and motivation levels can make or break a firm and affect its position in an industry.

In Silicon Valley, stock options are taken for granted. This has created a major problem since few non-Anglo-American firms have stock option plans. There are various legal, tax, and cultural reasons why European and Asian firms do not use stock options. For example, Daimler-Benz (now part of DaimlerChrysler) did not introduce a stock option program until 1996 (and it was not finally approved by the board until 1998). In 1998, Deutsche Bank AG was the first German bank (and among the first non-UK European firms) to introduce a management stock option plan. In 1998, the District Court of Braunschweig rejected the management share option scheme proposed by the Volkswagen AG board adopted in the 1997 general meeting by VW's shareholders. Among other concerns, the court was of the opinion that, given the present compensation plus bonus for members of the board, additional incentives through share options were hardly justifiable. In Sweden, until recently, the benefits of granted stock options were included in taxable income in the year when the options become available to be exercised as opposed to when they actually were exercised. Similarly, in Japan, only a few firms (for example, Sony) have introduced employee stock option plans, and only in the last two or three years. Indeed, outside of the Anglo-American system of corporate governance, management and employee (even CEO) salaries are almost entirely based on a fixed salary plus a bonus, something unthinkable in the United States. According to a manager we interviewed in a European firm that has made acquisitions:

> Europeans don't get it. For retention and attraction, options can be compared to a company car in Europe. The only difference is that the company car is a special perk and options are almost an expected norm.

In our study, the European acquirers that maintained options plans had difficulties with the structure of the plans. For example, in one company, existing target options were converted to options on the European company's stock, which was worth less per share and growing at a much slower rate than the target company's stock had been growing. In another case, the stock option plan was replaced by a phantom option plan, which created dissatisfaction because it did not share ownership. As well, the calculations leading to the valuations of such phantom options are often opaque, compounding the information flow problems referred to earlier. The larger issue that looms for many non-US acquirers is the problem that if they were to introduce such plans in one part of the organization (such as a recently acquired firm), they face the prospect of compensation upheaval in the rest of the organization. This can be a daunting problem. As one acquiring firm's manager put it:

> We are over 100 years old, in more than a 100 countries worldwide, and have more than 100 000 employees. We have been extremely successful without stock options. If we were to introduce stock options over an acquisition worth a couple of hundred million dollars, we would be creating a compensation nightmare in the rest of the multi-billion dollar company. We feel like we are in a bind.

Ownership structure

In the US system of governance, the concept of one share-one vote and the belief in shareholder democracy are taken for granted. In much of the rest of the world, especially Europe and Asia, this is not the case. There is often substantial asymmetry between ownership and control proportions. Multiple classes of stock are common and some classes (often called A class stock) have multiple voting rights relative to those of other classes. For instance, in one of the acquiring companies in our case study data, the majority owners of the company have a class of shares that have 1000 times the voting rights as those traded on the NASDAQ; as a result, although US stockholders *own* 49% of the company, they *control* less than 2% of the shareholder vote. A related problem is that the by-laws of many European and Asian companies impose the condition that regardless of the proportion owned, non-controlling shareholders cannot exercise more than, say, 5% or 10% of the shareholder votes.

Compounding ownership versus control asymmetry is that majority owners in many non-US companies are often old, patriarchal families that have owned the company for decades (often having founded them as well). Not only are such owners unwilling to cede control to managers (since managers with stocks and stock options would dilute their own ownership stakes), their vintage does not often lend itself to understanding or comfort with the norms and nuances of a fast-moving Silicon-Valley-type culture. To quote an acquiring firm manager:

> [Our owners] don't wake up every morning worrying about Cisco or the Silicon Valley. We, unfortunately, do. But, we are just another holding in a vast multi-billion dollar family empire of everything from A to Z.

This unwillingness to cede control also constrains the ability of non-US acquirers to use their stock as the medium of exchange in acquisitions. To use stocks for acquisitions in the United States requires non-US companies to be listed on one of the major US stock exchanges. However, that also means greater required disclosure since they have to report under US GAAP accounting standards and fall under the purview of oversight by the SEC, just as any US company would, giving up ownership stakes to a new group of outside investors and, perhaps most unappealing, increased and incessant scrutiny by analysts, Wall Street, institutional investors and the like. Indeed, as noted earlier, this was reflected in the fact that, compared to US acquirers, European firms were substantially less likely to use stock as the medium of exchange.

The role of M&A in the strategy process

The market for M&A – and, more generally, the market for corporate control – is extremely well-developed, mature, and ingrained in the US corporate culture. For instance, during the period 1981–1998, there were over 82 000 mergers and acquisitions in the United States, for a total value exceeding $6 trillion (in other words, more than eight deals on average per listed company). During the same period, the rest of the world had perhaps $4 trillion worth. Thus, the United States alone has accounted for about 60% of the world's market share in M&A. Equally important, the market for M&A is closely related to the market for corporate restructuring. Firms are continuously revamping themselves through asset sales, spin-offs, equity carve-outs, divestitures, and so forth. As has been well-documented by numerous strategy researchers, the United States has been witness to an unprecedented era of return to focus in industry after industry.

In the 1990s, M&A activity in the United States has increasingly shifted from a corporate, CEO-level, investment banker-driven activity to one that is being conducted by managers at the divisional level, as firms have (arguably) used M&As as an important means of implement strategies. Consider that in 1998, the peak year of M&A activity thus far (and the year of dozens of mega-mergers), over 93% of all acquisitions in the United States were for assets valued at less than $200 million. In fact, while headline-grabbing mergers such as Exxon-Mobil and Citibank-Travellers got much of the attention in the press, the 93% that were less than $200 million in size collectively accounted for only about one-eighth of the total value of acquisitions in 1998. Paralleling this shift in M&A from corporate to divisional levels, dozens of successful organizations such as Cisco, GE Capital, Lucent, and Textron have set up their own internal M&A units that are responsible for everything from merger valuation, to due diligence, to managing post-merger integration. It is not uncommon for many US companies to have an M&A budget whereby managers are encouraged to seek out and acquire strategically attractive firms, and then be evaluated on the performance of the acquisitions.

The strategic role of M&A activity in Europe, although changing, is very different. Much of the M&A activity is still done at the corporate level and is CEO-driven, rather like the activity in the United States during the 1960s through the 1980s. The market for restructuring activity – especially if it involves downsizing, divestitures, spin-offs, and so forth – still has a long way to go, given the dominant roles that stakeholders such as labor unions, suppliers, and even the government play in the governance process. Many large companies are still a grab-bag of widely diversified businesses that are cobbled together only because the same family group or holding company owns – or, more aptly, controls – those assets. In other words, European firms must go a long way to achieve the kind of de-conglomeration and focus that US companies have achieved during the late 1980s and the 1990s. Moreover, unlike the United States where less than 2% of stock is held by other corporations, inter-corporate shareholdings are extremely common in Europe. For instance, 40% of the shares of German companies and 25% of the shares in Japanese companies are held as inter-corporate holdings.

These attributes of European governance structures play a negative role in successfully executing Silicon-Valley-type acquisitions. Recall that over 95% of such acquisitions are small and valued at less than $200 million. It is unlikely that a CEO of a multi-billion dollar company will devote the same energy or attention to a million dollar deal as he or she would to a billion dollar one; yet M&A activity and related incentives are thin at the divisional level, the level at which such deals should be executed. This situation is worsened by the diversified nature of the acquirer's businesses, since the technology acquisition simply becomes another "small fish in a large pond" of various divisions, products, and technologies scattered all over the world. Furthermore, this is despite the fact that, as some managers we interviewed suggested, their Silicon Valley assets may hold the key to their technological futures. The ownership problems addressed previously get exacerbated because of the complicated holding company and inter-corporate ownership structures. Further, even if an employee of a target firm does get stocks or options in the acquiring company he or she may be left wondering what exactly is the asset that the stock represents and how it relates to the Silicon-Valley-type company's cash flows and valuations.

The role of other major stakeholders, especially banks

In non-US governance systems, stakeholders other than shareholders play significant roles in the governance of the corporation; e.g., employees in Germany, suppliers and presidents of affiliated ("keiretsu") companies in Japan, the government in France, and so forth. One of the most important such stakeholders worldwide, outside of the Anglo-American system, is banks. Banks play an active role in the governance process and have major board representation in most countries in Continental Europe, Asia, and Latin America. In contrast, bankers are far less common on US boards.

As Bradley, Schipani, Sundaram, and Walsh argue, the active role of banks in the boardroom creates many adverse incentives in the governance and M&A process, especially when it comes to high-technology, human-capital-intensive assets.[24] They argue that the very nature of the banking business – the business of loaning money – dictates focus on the total risk (i.e., systematic plus unsystematic risks), since lenders must always be concerned about the bankruptcy risk of their assets (which, in turn, is driven by the asset's total risk). Shareholders, on the other hand, are driven by the systematic risks of an asset relative to a well-diversified portfolio. A focus on total risks creates a fundamental kind of investment distortion: under-investment in assets with a great deal of cash flow volatility and assets that are seen as non-collateralizable.

Silicon-Valley-type assets are an example of extreme combinations of cash flow volatility and non-collateralizable assets. These assets have a great deal of cash flow risk resulting from competitive and technological uncertainty and from their rapid growth and investment needs. Their primary assets are human capital, which is fundamentally non-collateralizable, and what is more, as we observed earlier, the assets have the habit of walking out the door every evening. A banker interested in cash flow predictability and traditional valuation yardsticks would tend to view a Silicon Valley firm with no bricks and mortar, negative cash flow, and high labor turnover as very high risk. In contrast, a company like Cisco Systems might look at the same firm and see a valuable technology, long-term cash flow expectations, and a workforce that, suitably motivated, will not leave.

COMPARISON OF THE NON-US EXPERIENCE WITH CISCO SYSTEMS

Cisco management believes there are two keys to a successful acquisition: doing the necessary homework to select the right company and applying an effective and replicable integration process once the deal is struck. Cisco has created acquisition rules for itself and nearly every acquisition is completed according to these rules. In order to be considered a potential target by Cisco, a company must be fast-growing, focused, entrepreneurial, culturally similar to Cisco, and geographically desirable. In general, Cisco limits its searches to three geographic areas: the Silicon Valley, the Research Triangle in North Carolina and the Route 128 corridor outside Boston – with a preference for Silicon Valley. According to Cisco, geographic proximity is critical because when targets are too far from headquarters, cultural fit is less likely and the speed of integration is slowed.[25] As Cisco CEO John Chambers has stated:

> The cultures have to be alike and they've got to be complementary. When you're geographically close you can look the employees in the eye and say, "You know, we're not going to lay anybody off." And the key is, do you have a common vision of where the industry's going and do your product strategies complement each other as opposed to compete? ... You've got to create some short-term wins. We refer to this industry in dog years. One calendar year is equivalent to seven years of normal growth, and so you have to move at an unbelievable pace.... There has to be a long-term win for all those constituencies [customers, share-holders, and employees] that are strategic.[26]

In Cisco's industry, acquisitions are primarily about people. Cisco adheres to a rule whereby no employees in the acquired firm will be terminated until Chambers and the former CEO of the acquired firm give their consent. Cisco strives to ensure that top people in the target firm are given key positions in the new organization.[27] About half of the CEOs of companies acquired by Cisco have stayed with the combined company. Cisco also believes in fast integration and tries to present the acquired company to its customers as part of Cisco as soon as possible, usually within 100 days (similar to the GE Capital model). Similarly, Cisco uses integration teams, something that was not observed in the case studies. Cisco has a department of 12 people dedicated to acquisition integration. The day after a deal closes, the integration team begins an orientation to Cisco that involves Cisco's hiring, sales, and engineering practices.[28] The process takes about 30 days. The acquired company is quickly integrated with Cisco's computer and payroll systems. In contrast, in one of the cases we studied it took four months to link the target company with the acquiring company's network and e-mail system, which generated an inordinate number of complaints in the target firm.

Table 3 shows the significant differences between Cisco and the European acquirers. Obviously, some of the Cisco factors, such as geographic proximity, cannot be implemented by European acquirers. However, given Cisco's acquisition success, Cisco should be viewed as an industry benchmark. Cisco has established an acquisition and integration process that works and creates value for multiple stakeholders.

CAN NON-US ACQUIRERS SUCCEED IN SILICON VALLEY?

Though the findings and analysis presented here seem to indicate that non-US acquirers will experience difficulties in acquiring Silicon Valley targets, the positive news is that many of these issues are solvable. With respect to integrating acquired firms, and with the exception of geographic proximity, we do not believe that non-US firms are *innately* disadvantaged relative to American firms (although in many cases they behave as if they were operating at a disadvantage). To be more successful with Silicon Valley acquisitions, non-US acquirers do not have to radically invent new management processes. What they must do is understand the realities of Silicon Valley and realize that, for better or worse, it is important to do business the "Valley way." Matters of corporate governance present more challenging problems, particularly those associated with stock ownership, cross-shareholdings, and bank involvement. Clearly, changing corporate governance practices is not something that can happen in a vacuum, since they are often intricately woven into (and derive from) the nature of law, politics, and culture in the various countries. In other words, the evolution of corporate governance structures is characterized by "path dependency."

Some of the corporate culture and merger integration issues – such as speed of integration and decision making, communication of a vision for the acquired firm, and the problem of who is in charge – should be relatively easy to manage by non-US firms. One of the European firms we studied has significantly improved its integration process as the result of experience and familiarity with Silicon Valley business norms. Developing networking and socialization skills that are comparable to leading firms like Cisco will be more difficult to attain, given the implicit or explicit lifetime employment culture in many non-US firms. In this culture, there is the notion that you are employed by the firm rather than the profession, which means the absence of an active managerial labor market along US lines. Even here, however, some acquirers are making the effort. For example, a non-US acquiring company we studied created a Silicon Valley office (ironically, in space formerly used by Cisco) populated by younger, non-traditional managers. These managers have been given a

Table 3 Comparison of Cisco and Non-US acquirers

Acquisition issues	Cisco systems	Non-US acquirers in Silicon Valley
Integration speed and decision making	Uses integration teams to integrate everything, usually within 100 days Thinks in internet years and plans quarterly Acquires close to home, simplifying various integration issues	Usually do not use integration teams Slow to make decisions By default, do not acquire close to home
Communication and vision	Immediately lets the new employees know what their roles and titles will be Has a strong vision for the future of the company(ies) acquired	Need to improve both the quantity and quality of their communication with the target. Do not communicate a vision to the target
Networking and socialization	Finds new markets and acquisition opportunities through socializing and word-of-mouth	Seem reluctant to socialize
Who is in charge?	Prefers to keep a target's senior managers, if they fit in with Cisco's culture. Otherwise, they are asked to leave Retains the majority of an acquired company's employees by understanding what is important to them and what motivates them	Prefer to keep a target's senior managers Attempt to retain senior management through golden handcuffs Seem to have no clear plan for retaining other employees
Stock options	Continues to give stock options to an acquired company	Usually discontinue stock option plans
Integration approach	Integrates the target as a business unit in charge of its own product development and marketing, but centralizes the target's manufacturing, finance, sales, and distribution Focuses on the people first, and then on how to drive the business Is not arrogant. Instead, the company is 'paranoid'.	Each acquirer created a different, unique structure Not consistent in focus Suffer from a stereotype of arrogance

relatively unstructured agenda with the key goal being to understand and assimilate the Silicon Valley culture and bring it into the larger firm (one employee has a business card that reads "Chief Evangelist, Internet and New Media").

The governance issues appear, on the surface, more daunting. However, with the exception of one issue (stocks and options for target firm employees will continue to be difficult for non-US firms unless they change their world-wide compensation practices), it appears that dramatic changes are under way in non-US governance practices. Non-US governance systems, especially those in Europe, are transforming themselves along Anglo-American lines.[29] Traditional ownership structures, including bank ownership, are slowly being dismantled. The result is that an active market for corporate control has taken shape to the point where, by the time all the data are in, the aggregate value of M&A activity in the EU in 1999 may equal or exceed that in the United States. Substantial restructuring activity is under way; hundreds of non-US firms are listing their shares on the New York and NASDAQ stock exchanges; boards and board guidelines are being reconstituted; and, more generally, corporate governance has become important for top management agendas.[30] The Asia crisis of 1997–1998 and its aftermath are leading to similar changes in countries such as Japan, Korea, Taiwan, and Thailand.

Finally, although there are areas where European firms are lacking, there are some specific areas and situations where European firms could actually add value in acquiring technology firms:

- Many small Silicon Valley firms are characterized by an environment managed by intimidation and tenacity rather than by cooperation and strong leadership. To succeed in the long term, management in the target firms must be professionalized and strengthened. A European acquirer may be able to add these qualities, assuming that issues such as speed of decision making and communication can be properly dealt with.
- Managers and employees below the founder/top management level may welcome a more cooperative, employee- (rather than shareholder-) centered style of management that is found in many European organizations.
- If a company has not yet had an IPO, a large acquirer may be viewed as the next best thing to achieving financial goals for founders and key employees (this also applies for large American acquirers).
- European acquirers may be able to provide access to global markets much faster than US acquirers.

CONCLUSION

As pressures for globalization and convergence brought about by the computer- and communications-related industries continue, the number of technology-based acquisitions by non-US firms of United States targets will continue to grow. European (and by implication, other similar non-US) firms face some unique challenges with their acquisitions and, in particular, with the integration and governance of the acquired firms. As noted, much of the research in the M&A area ignores or downplays the organizational and governance issues that are central to the acquisition integration process, despite the fact that practitioners are increasingly coming to realize that these issues are the critical determinants of acquisition success. As revealed in this study, a failure to deal with integration properly can lead to demoralized staff and employee defections. In technology-based industries where the main assets are the people, such an outcome can be disastrous. In fact, in one of the cases studied, turnover escalated to the point that in a few months, the acquired firm bore little resemblance to the original firm acquired and the acquisition was subsequently formally dissolved with its remaining employees absorbed into the various divisions of the larger firm.

Understanding the Silicon-Valley-type business culture and attention to integration will help mitigate the kinds of problems documented here. The various areas critical to M&A integration success are: communication, decisionmaking, integration speed, networking and socialization, and clearly delineated structures of authority and responsibility. In the area of corporate governance, stock and option-based compensation, alignment between ownership and control, enhancing the role of M&A in the strategy process (especially at the divisional level) and limiting the role of stakeholding constituencies (such as bankers) are key factors for non-US companies to address.

NOTES

1 For what we mean by Silicon-Valley-type technology assets, see note 15 below.
2 Robert G. Eccles, Kersten L. Lanes, and Thomas C. Wilson, "Are You Paying Too Much For That Acquisition?" *Harvard Business Review*, 77/4 (1999): 136–146.
3 The earliest evidence in this regard was pointed out more than fifteen years ago by Michael Jensen and Richard Ruback in their famous article, "The Market for Corporate Control: The Scientific Evidence," *Journal of Financial Economics*, 11/1 (1983): 5–50. Subsequently, finance scholars have re-examined this evidence in the context of various types of acquisition activities (e.g., mergers, tender offers, proxy fights, leveraged buyouts, cash versus stock-based offers, and contested versus uncontested bids) and in the context of other countries (e.g., the UK, France, Germany, and Australia). The Jensen and Ruback evidence has held up remarkably well.
4 Amy L. Pablo, "Determinants of Acquisition Integration Level: A Decision Making Perspective," *Academy of Management Journal*, 37 (1994): 803–836.
5 Rikard Larsson and Sydney Finkelstein, "Integrating Strategic, Organizational, and Human Resource Perspectives on Mergers and Acquisitions: A Case Study of Synergy Realization," *Organization Science*, 10 (1999): 1–26.
6 For detailed discussions of the M&A process, see Philippe C. Haspeslagh and David B. Jemison, *Managing Acquisitions: Creating Value Through Corporate Renewal* (New York, NY: Free Press, 1991); Mitchell Lee Marks and Philip H. Mirvis, *Joining Forces: Making One Plus One Equal Three In Mergers, Acquisitions, And Alliances* (San Francisco, CA: Jossey-Bass, 1998).
7 In 1996, Cisco acquired StrataCom Inc. for $4.6 in stock. At the time StrataCom had $330 million in sales and 1,000 employees. In August 1999, Cisco acquired Cerent Corporation for $6.9 billion in stock. When acquired, Cerent had 210 employees and less than $10 million in sales.
8 Glenn Drexhage, "How Cisco Bought its Way to the Top," *Corporate Finance*, 163 (June 1998): 21–25.
9 Stephen S. Cohen and Gary Fields, "Social Capital and Capital Gains in Silicon Valley," *California Management Review*, 41/2 (Winter 1999): 108–130.
10 Annalee Saxenian provides clear evidence as to how the cultures of Route 128 and Silicon Valley differ. For example, Saxenian characterizes Route 128 as a continued part of the Puritan culture, where well-defined social hierarchies are important. In contrast, Silicon Valley consists of newer firms with a collegiate atmosphere that emphasized the exchange of information and ideas and also friendly competition. See Annalee Saxenian, *Regional Advantage: Culture and Competition in Silicon Valley and Route 128* (Cambridge, MA: Harvard University Press, 1994).
11 Homa Bahrami and Stuart Evans, "Flexible Re-cycling and High-technology Entrepreneurship," *California Management Review*, 37/3 (Spring 1995): 62–89.
12 Cohen and Fields, op. cit., p. 120.
13 Saxenian, op. cit.
14 *Red Herring* is a monthly magazine based in San Francisco focused on technology issues.
15 The analysis in this section is based on the online Mergers and Acquisitions database of the Securities Data Corporation (SDC), which is now part of Thomson Financial Securities Data. The following SDC-defined sectors represent Silicon-Valley-type assets: all computer and computer-related industries (such as mainframes, workstations, PCs, portables, all computer peripherals, modems, CAD-CAM systems, networking systems such as LANs, software, and computer-related services) and communications-related industries (such as telecommunications equipment, cellular/satellite/mobile communications systems, modems, data communications equipment, internet services, and internet software). The list excludes telecommunications service providers and media companies. If those two were added the numbers would be even more impressive, given that there has been almost $1 trillion in M&A activity in just the US telecommunications service sector in the 1990s.

16 Given that acquirers from the EU are the largest group other than those from the United States, the tables break out the data for this group of countries separately.

17 Note, however, that we are generalizing here based on a subsample of acquisitions: those of target firms whose stocks were publicly traded prior to the acquisitions.

18 Ronald N. Askkenas, Lawrence J. DeMonaco, and Suzanne C. Francis, "Making the Deal Real: How GE Capital Integrates Acquisitions," *Harvard Business Review*, 76/1 (1998): 165–178.

19 In Silicon Valley, if a young engineer or programmer has been in a job for more than two years, he or she risks being considered stale. Along Route 128, an individual with a succession of 2-year positions is seen as having a poor employment history and as posing a risk.

20 Cohen and Fields, op. cit., p. 127.

21 Saxenian, op. cit.

22 This is a common phenomenon in all expatriate communities.

23 Saxenian (op. cit.) reports that the traditional conservatism of Boston society made it harder for the management and staff of Route 128-area firms to risk dramatic innovations in personal lifestyle or company policy. As a result, New England employees tended to be more family- and community-oriented than their Silicon Valley counterparts and they spent less time socializing with fellow workers. A parallel could be drawn with the employees of European firms and their resistance to networking in Silicon Valley.

24 Michael Bradley, Cindy Schipani, Anant Sundaram, and James Walsh, "The Purposes and Accountability of the Corporation: Corporate Governance at a Cross-roads," *Law and Contemporary Problems*, 62/4 (Fall 1999).

25 John A. Byrne, "The Corporation of the Future," *Business Week*, August 31, 1998, pp. 102–106.

26 Eric Nee, "Interview with John Chambers of Cisco," www.upside.com, June 30, 1996.

27 *Business Week*, op. cit., p. 106.

28 H. Goldblatt, "Forty-Two Acquisitions and Counting: Cisco's Secrets," *Fortune*, November 8, 1999, pp. 177–181.

29 Bradley et al., op cit.

30 Indeed, the English words corporate governance and shareholder value have made their way into the French and German lexicons, respectively. There was no prior German language equivalent for the term shareholder value.

Section 3
Strategic Planning, Tactics and Valuation

Valuation problems in service-sector mergers 12

Michael Keenan

Modern analysis of the financial impact of a merger between two firms has focused almost exclusively on the risk-redistribution impact of a conglomerate-type merger, having zero synergistic benefits, in equilibrium capital markets. This chapter examines the other, and we believe more pervasive, situation in which real economic adjustments evolve from the merger.

Our focus is on the valuation problem associated with real synergistic benefits arising from the acquisition of a service-sector firm. Of particular interest is the value of labor in an acquired firm in which the alternative mechanism for the acquiring firm is entry into the industry by starting a new firm. It would appear, particularly in service-sector acquisitions, that the value of labor is being capitalized. Since the capital markets are not assumed to capitalize the inherent value of the labor force (only its marginal product), this poses a number of questions for the financial manager.

Some might argue that, since mergers are a particularization of the capital-budgeting process, there is really no issue to consider. At least two answers are offered to such assertions. First, capital-budgeting theory has not been very well developed for the typical multiperiod problem where risk levels are shifting and where project-tied financing considerations exist (and these are the typical parameters of a merger decision). Despite its cavalier use in some textbooks and even some professional journals, it is usually recognized that CAPM cannot easily be applied to many capital-budgeting projects without violating critical one-period-horizon, full-equilibrium assumptions. Second, to the extent existing theory is applicable, it remains uncomfortably generalized for application at the firm level – for example, telling a firm its product prices can be best determined by solving the simultaneous system of equations for all demand, supply, and budget constraints in the economy. In the merger area the analogous statement suggests that if the capital markets are strongly efficient and all investors hold their desired (leveraged where necessary) portion of the market portfolio, then the valuation impact of merger and the amount of securities exchanged between firms is a matter of indifference to investors.[1] However, some evidence shows that the real economic markets for labor and capital are not strongly efficient, which complicates matters even if the financial-securities markets should appear to be highly efficient.

In the rest of this chapter, we look first at the drift of current research in the mergers and acquisitions area and why that research has limited applicability to the question at hand. The following section reviews general valuation alternatives and how they relate to synergistic merger opportunities. In the last section we look at some simple examples of the acquisition of a firm in which current wages may understate the value of labor. Throughout, the focus is on the expected value of cash flows and not their distributions. We leave for another book the further complication of what happens if disequilibrium exists in the price of risk in addition to the disequilibrium in the factor prices.

DRIFT OF RESEARCH ON MERGERS AND ACQUISITIONS

Most of the research on mergers and acquisitions since the early 1960s has focused on two questions: (1) Are there any real benefits to conglomerate-type mergers, and (2) what are the portfolio implications of a merger between two firms? Even in this latter question the analysis has tended to focus on portfolio implications of a merger between two firms for which no positive or negative economic benefits accrue. For example, Bierman and Hass (1970) argue that merger-created growth in per-share earnings should be a valuation fiction; the value of a merged firm (with zero net benefits) is the sum of the economic values of the two premerged firms so that two firms with different price-earnings ratios merging through share exchange must have an intermediate price-earnings ratio after the merger. Levy and Sarnat (1970) suggest that, under standard Markowitz portfolio theory, there may be no risk-reducing benefits in such mergers, and Myers (1976) and Mossin (1968) suggest that, under standard equilibrium conditions for CAPM, there are no valuation or risk-reducing benefits to mergers. Lewellen (1971) argues that while stockholders cannot gain, creditors may benefit from this type of merger, but Higgins (1971) Stapleton (1975), and Elton, Gruber, and Lightstone (1977), all suggest in different ways that the bankruptcy-creditor risks are not as simple as suggested and come entirely at the expense of stockholder returns.

As to the question of whether there have been any real benefits to conglomerate mergers, Reid (1968); Steiner (1975); Franks, Broyles, and Hecht (1977); and others argue that statistically there are few apparent valuation benefits to mergers observed and that much merger activity may actually be to the detriment of standard profit-maximizing goals. Mandelker (1974) and Dodd and Ruback (1977) reinforce this conclusion with short-run efficient market tests of abnormal stock returns associated with mergers; while the stockholders of acquired firms appear to reap some benefits (and hence violate equilibrium-CAPM assumptions used to make the tests), the shareholders of acquiring firms basically do not.

One can easily get the impression from this research that a merger or acquisition decision makes little difference, except perhaps to the employment of antitrust lawyers. From a valuation viewpoint, or a cost-of-capital evaluation, or a financial-structure consideration, merger appears to be a mere detail of currently received theory. Unfortunately, as Myers (1976) and other researchers have indicated, existing theory can explain very few of the facts of real merger activity: for example, why there have been great merger waves in the United States rather than continuous random activity; why some merger financial strategies are preferred to others and how these are related to business-cycle conditions; and most important, when there are real economic increments (positive or negative) associated with consolidation, what the relevant financial theory and industrial organization implications are. Part of this last issue is what concerns us in this chapter.

Unfortunately, as Table 1 indicates, there is not even a clear picture of overall merger activity in the United States. The most widely quoted series is one released by the Federal Trade Commission (FTC), but this series focuses primarily on the mining and manufacturing firms over which the FTC has jurisdiction. Most finance-

Table 1 Overall merger activity in the United States

Year	Total transactions[a]	Total transactions[b]
1965	1893	2125
1966	1746	2377
1967	2384	2975
1968	3932	4462
1969	4542	6107
1970	3089	5152
1971	2633	4608
1972	2839	4801
1973	2359	4040
1974	1474	2861
1975	1047	2297
1976	1171	2276
1977	1183	2244
1978	1245	2106

[a] Series of completed mergers and acquisitions from the Bureau of Economics, Federal Trade Commission, 1980.
[b] Series of total publicly announced transactions, including the acquisitions of divisions of other firms with a value of more than one-half million dollars as reported by W.T. Grimm & Company (data from Joseph M. Sheer, "Divestitures and Spin-Offs', MBA thesis, New York University, 1978).

sector industries – banking, securities firms, and some insurance – most regulated industries, and many small service-sector firms, are apparently omitted. While many of these acquisitions are small in dollar value, they may portend trends in an increasingly service-sector-oriented economy.

SOME MERGER-VALUATION POSSIBILITIES

Before looking at a simple example of what might happen in a merger in which the cost of the labor factor is not in equilibrium, it may be useful to consider some of the possible valuation outcomes in the merger process. In this way the reader may get some feel for the scope of the whole process and for what a very small piece of it we are actually addressing here (and what a small piece most research in the 1960s and 1970s has addressed). To keep the situation as simple as possible, we will assume firm A acquires firm B for a payment vector that might include cash, securities, or future considerations of some sort. Each firm generates cash flows that are the basis of valuation.[2] The *expected value* of a firm is assumed to be a properly discounted sum of the cash flows being distributed directly or indirectly to the various suppliers of capital. The discount rates applied to the streams of each firm are a function of risk-free-interest-rate term structures and risk premiums applied for things like capital structure, market covariance, inflation, extreme value potential, and so forth.

The *market value* of either firm may be higher, lower, or equal to the rational-expectations-equilibrium value described as the expected value in the previous paragraph. Existing studies suggest that premiums of more than 30 percent may be commonly paid to acquire another firm. Since related studies suggest that for conglomerate mergers there may be few real economic benefits, the implication is that short-run market-value disequilibrium exists either before the merger (if the

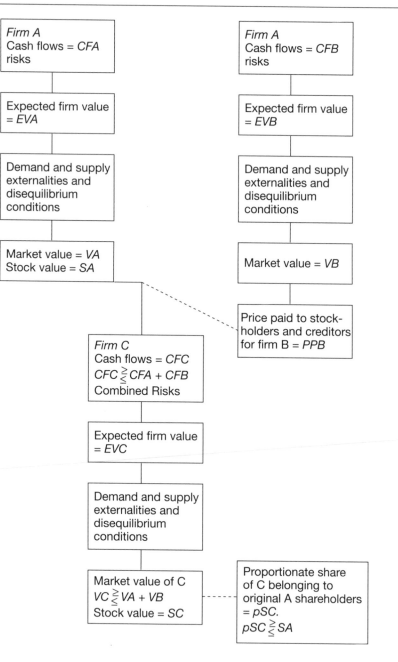

Figure 1   Valuation factors in mergers.

market value of B is less than the expected value) or after the merger (if A paid too much for B) for at least some types of mergers. One of the assumptions of this chapter is that short-run demand, supply conditions, or noneconomic psychological pressures may cause the market value of individual firms (or even the market as a whole) to deviate from the full-horizon expected values. That is, the market provides real merger opportunities from time to time in addition to the real opportunities always present if there are positive synergistic benefits.

After the merger, the new firm C has a cash-flow vector that has its own risk characteristics. There is an expected value for this stream and a market value for firm C that at any point in time may again be higher or lower than the expected value determined from marketwide parameters (the expected value calculated from the discounting of the cash flows at rates set by the prices of the various risk premiums). Since the cash-flow vector of firm C may be (less than, equal to, greater than) the sum of the premerger vectors, and the same is true for the market value of C relative to the premerger values of A and B, there are already nine possible states to analyze. A summary of the stages of this decision process is described in Figure 1.

Mergers and acquisitions research has customarily stated null hypotheses in terms of premerger and postmerger cash flows ($CFC = CFA + CFB$ – that is, there are no real economic benefits), or in terms of similar market-value conditions ($VC = VA + VB$ – that is, there are no financial markets benefits). Research findings seem to support the cash-flow null hypotheses for pure conglomerate mergers between firms already having adequate access to the capital markets. The hypothesis has never been adequately tested for other types of acquisitions and, as we shall argue later, probably not even for conglomerates since the process of merging two disparate flows is more complex than the simple valuation models have made it out to be. For the market-value hypothesis, the evidence is mixed. On the one hand, the acquiring firms seem to be paying significant premiums for the firms acquired. On the other hand, there seem to be no significant negative returns for the firm As or firm Cs around the merger date, even for pure conglomerate mergers. Yet the consensus seems to be that the null valuation hypothesis cannot be rejected.

Actually, if the goal of maximizing shareholder wealth is taken as the prime objective [and Reid (1968) and other provide ample evidence that this is not the case in many mergers], the situation becomes even more complex, for the null hypothesis becomes: "The proportionate share of firm A's stockholders' market value in firm C is equal to their premerger value in firm A." It is entirely possible that the stockholders of firm A would be better off after a merger with firm B even though the cash flows of firm C are less than $CFA + CFB$ and the market value of firm C is less than $VA + VB$. Somebody will be a loser – the stockholders of B or the creditors – but exactly who depends on the terms offered or securities used in the acquisition.[3]

Even the simplest cases have complications. Suppose firms A and B are simple Gordon-model firms – that is, all equity firms whose cash flows are growing at different constant rates, where each has an established dividend policy and a constant marginal rate of return on its investment opportunities (see Gordon, 1962). Thus we might have for the expected prices of these firms:

$$E(P_A) = \frac{dv_A}{k_A - g_A} \qquad E(P_B) = \frac{dv_B}{k_B - g_B},$$

where $E(P)$ = expected stock price,
dv = expected per-share dividends,
k = return required by stockholders,
g = long-run growth rate in dividends.

If these two firms are merged, one does not get a simple Gordon-model firm. The merger of two firms with different constant growth rates yields a firm that *does not* have a constant growth rate. Thus,

$$E(P_C) = f(dv_C, k_C),$$

where dV_C = full vector of specified dividends,

$$k_C = f(i^*, \beta_A, \beta_B, \text{capital structure, and so on}).$$

Since these complications seem to have been ignored in empirical studies to date, it is not surprising that we have trouble discerning whether or not real economic benefits accrue in mergers, let alone market-value benefits.

ACQUISITION OF LABOR-INTENSIVE FIRMS

The objective of the previous section was to suggest how difficult it is to trace through a reasonable number of states in the merger decision process. However, such a trace is necessary if macro market inferences are to be drawn. In this section we do not attempt such a complete trace, but we use some simple examples to illustrate what may be an increasingly serious problem in the merger and acquisition of service-sector firms. Without the full trace, we cannot make inferences about market-equilibrium states, but we may be able to draw inferences about individual firms.

The problem that must be faced in acquiring a labor-intensive firm can be described by a simple scenario: Firm A has decided to acquire firm B, which happens to be a baseball team. Firm B could just as easily be a brokerage firm, an advertising agency, a law firm, a hospital-management company, a computer-software firm, a bank, or any of a host of other service-sector firms in which management or key labor is the critical input factor. Firm A has excess cash at the moment and has decided to make the acquisition for cash. Thus it will go through as a purchase type of merger accounting treatment. If the acquisition had been a simple exchange of stock, and if other conditions were met, it would be possible for the acquisition to be treated as a pooling-of-interest type of accounting treatment. The problems described later would still exist under a pooling treatment, though they would appear on the surface to be slightly less dramatic. In order to make the point more sharply, and because there is some probability that pooling accounting will be completely banished within the next five years, we restrict the example to the purchase accounting treatment.

Summary balance-sheet data and income-statement data for firm B are indicated in Table 2. Although B has only a book-value net worth of $100 000, it is currently generating $500 000 in net income. The public market for the firm's stock is limited, and the current market value of that stock is about $3 million. Thus, the total value of firm B at the moment is slightly under $4 million.[4]

Firm A believes that, with some help in the public relations department and with computerized scouting reports that A can help B generate, firm B could be made even more profitable. As it stands, B is not perceived by A to be a high-risk investment so A is willing to capitalize cash flows at 10 percent. We also assume that in the long run this in fact might be a reasonable rate at which to capitalize flows for this baseball team. Thus the current expected value of this team is about $5.5 million and, with positive synergy, firm A believes an expected value of $7 million is reasonable (given the expanded cash flows).[5]

Table 2 Financial statements for a service-sector, labor-intensive firm B (thousands of dollars)

Income statement	Scenario 1[a]	Scenario 2[b]	Scenario 3[c]
Total revenues	2,000	2,000	1,500
Labour costs	600	1,200	600
Depreciation	50	50	50
Interest	50	50	50
Other costs	300	300	300
Operating income	1,000	400	500
Taxes	500	200	250
Preliminary net income	500	200	250
Goodwill expense	150	150	150
Reported net income	350	50	100
Cash flow	550	250	300
Expected market value	5,500	2,500	3,000

Balance sheet			
Current assets	800	Current liabilities	600
Net fixed income	200	Long-term debt	300
		Net worth	100
Total	1,000		1,000

[a] Firm B as it exists at the time of its acquisition.
[b] Firm B if labor captures all of its real value.
[c] Firm B if existing employees are replaced by other labor.

Though firm B seems to be currently undervalued by the market, the owners drive a hard bargain and receive an offer of $6 million cash for their firm – which works out to be twelve times the current reported net income of $500 000. At this point our scenario branches into three possible directions. In the best of all worlds (scenario 1), we assume that no positive synergy develops but that firm B continues operating as a division as it has in the past as a firm; thus cash flows remain the same. Since it is not usually possible to capitalize the true value of labor, firm A must write off almost the whole $6 million as a goodwill expense so reported earnings from division B (or firm A% as a whole) would decline by about $150 000 to $350 000 even though actual earnings are the same. (In the real world it turns out to be possible to capitalize part of the value of players' current contracts for professional sport teams; in general, even this is not possible for management or key employees of most firms acquired).

It is entirely possible the world will not turn out to be so nice. In our second scenario (2), key players and managers decide that the sale of the team is a good time to renegotiate their contracts. The price paid for the firm acts as a trigger – if the firm is really worth that much to stockholders, why should they not get salaries that more closely reflect the value of their contribution? Because firm A believes these key managers and players are critical to the success of the team, labor contracts are altered so that the current wage bill doubles. The results are summarized in scenario 2 of Table 2. Real cash flows drop substantially; reported earnings are now, in effect, reflecting the fact that the firm is paying twice for the value of the labor in firm B – once as part of the capitalized value of the goodwill deduction and again in the increased labor expenses. In addition, the tax status of the two deductions is not even the same. Any new firm that came along and offered to purchase division B would now see a division with expected cash flows of $250 000 and hence an expected stock value of about $2 million. At this point, firm A may in fact have a positive incentive to sell division B, take the real capital loss, and reinvest the remaining funds elsewhere.

Of course firm A might refuse to negotiate salaries, saying the players are already well paid and that other players can be found for similar wages. The key managers and players quit, and firm A does hire new employees at comparable wages, but things are not the same. The combination of new players does not work as well for the existing team so that revenues drop substantially; see scenario 3 of Table 2. Firm A is again faced with a lower cash-flow and reported-earnings situation and now must deduct the capitalized value of an incremental labor product that it no longer owns and for which it received no payment when the labor departed. Further, under current accounting standards, it is not permitted to write off all the goodwill created by the purchase of this departed labor capital immediately against the firm's capital account.

The scenarios described in this section suggest to us that there may be serious problems in the expected-value determination, negotiated-price determination, and accounting standards applied to the acquisition of a service-sector firm where the value of the labor product is greater than the wage rate paid. We believe this type of market disequilibrium may be fairly pervasive among key personnel of service-sector firms. There are suggestive data in the brokerage industry, for example, to indicate that the pattern described in scenarios 2 or 3 is happening in some of the acquisitions being made. Key partner salaries and bonuses are altered, and the best salesmen renegotiate their cuts or are bid away by other firms. For the reasons outlined in the merger-valuation section, it will not be easy to develop empirical tests to validate this trend or its impact, but it may be possible to do something with a firm-by-firm analysis.

CONCLUSION

It is not obvious how to resolve these problems. The goodwill accounting requirements seem to be even more misleading here than in the typical acquisition, so some new accounting procedure should be designed that reflects the noncapitalization of labor product and the mobility of labor despite firm contractual agreements. The valuation problems are more difficult. Some researchers might argue that the original $3 million market value for firm B was a more correct value since it reflected the anticipated wage increase or labor transfer that happened in scenarios 2 and 3. A firm selling at six times earnings in the long run, however, will always turn out to be an attractive takeover target. Some might argue that some intermediate value that reflected the probabilities of key labor shifts might be appropriate (ending up with an expected value of, say, $4.5 million). Something is disturbing in a macro sense in this resolution, for it would seem to imply that, while on average all firms were correctly valued, in fact every individual firm would be incorrectly valued depending on whether the labor product was captured by the stockholders or the workers. Finally, some might argue that, as part of the acquisition process and final price, negotiations should go on simultaneously with the executives of firm B as representatives of the stockholders and with the executives and other key personnel as representatives of the wage bill. This of course would create a whole new vector of possibilities in the valuation framework described in that section when we are not yet able to handle fully even that limited framework.

NOTES

1　It is interesting to note that some have argued that the principal reason for increased merger activity in recent years is that many firms are undervalued – that is, the capital markets are not efficient in pricing real resources controlled by corporate securities. For comments by selected professionals, see Boucher (1980).

2　Even this assertion is debatable. While received-capital-budgeting theory focuses on the valuation of a cash-flow vector (excluding financing costs), much of the professional approach in equity valuation is focused on the valuation of a net-income stream.

3　An increasing part of mergers and acquisitions business involves reversing the process – divestitures, spin-offs, leveraged buy-outs, and similar activities. Analogous valuation procedures (in a reverse order) to Table 1 can be developed for such activities. Very little research has been devoted to this side of the merger process.

4　Our numbers in the illustration are obviously somewhat exaggerated for effect, but they are really combinations from two types of firms that exist: (1) a highly leveraged (and profitable) brokerage firm, and (2) a very profitable advertising agency.

5　To keep the illustration simple, we refer to these valuations as the value of the equity for firm B. Thus, the 10 percent capitalization rate should not be considered the cost of capital for A but a kind of modified equity-capitalization parameter appropriate for the cash flows as defined in the example.

REFERENCES

Bierman, H., and J. Hass. "The Use and Misuse of the P/E Ratio in Acquisition and Merger Decisions." *Financial Executive* (October 1970):62–68.

Boucher, Wayne I. *The Process of Conglomerate Merger.* Prepared for Federal Trade Commission, Bureau of Competition, Washington, DC June 1980.

Dodd, Peter, and Richard Ruback. "Tender Offers and Stockholder Returns." *Journal of Financial Economics*, December 1977, pp. 351–374.

Elton, E.; M. Gruber; and J. Lightstone. "The Impact of Bankruptcy on the Firm's Capital Structure, the Reasonableness of Mergers, and the Risk Independence of Projects." New York University Graduate School of Business Working Paper 134, December 1977.

Federal Trade Commission. *Statistical Report on Mergers and Acquisitions.* Washington, DC: Bureau of Economics, August 1980.

Financial Accounting Standards Board. *Financial Accounting Standards.* rev. (July 1978) Stamford, Conn.

Franks, J. R.; J. E. Broyles; and M. J. Hecht. "An Industry Study of the Profitability of Mergers in the United Kingdom." *Journal of Finance*, December 1977, pp. 1513–1525.

Gordon, Myron J. *The Investment, Financing, and Valuation of the Corporation.* Homewood, Ill.: Richard O. Irwin, 1962.

Halpern, P. J. "Empirical Estimates of the Amount and Distribution of Gains to Companies in Mergers." *Journal of Business*, October 1973, pp. 554–575.

Higgins, R. "Reply to Lewellen." *Journal of Finance* (May 1971):543–545.

Kummer, D., and J. Haffmeister. "Valuation Consequences of Cash Tender Offers." *Journal of Finance*, May 1978, pp. 505–516.

Levy, H., and M. Sarnat. "Diversification, Portfolio Analysis, and the Uneasy Case of Conglomerate Mergers." *Journal of Finance*, September 1970, pp. 795–802.

Lewellen, W. G., "A Pure Financial Rationale for the Conglomerate Merger." *Journal of Finance*, May 1971, pp. 521–537.

Mandelker, G. "Risk and Return: the Case of Merging Firms." *Journal of Financial Economics* (December 1974):303–335.

Mossin, J. "Merger Agreements: Some Game Theoretic Considerations." *Journal of Business*, October 1968, pp. 460–477.

Myers, S. "Introduction to Mergers. In *Modern Developments in Financial Management*, ed. S. Myers, pp. 633–645. New York: Praeger Publishers, 1976.

—. "Procedures for Capital Budgeting under Certainty." *Industrial Management Review*, Spring 1968, pp. 1–20.

Rappaport, A. "Financial Analysis for Mergers and Acquisitions." *Mergers and Acquisitions Journal* (Winter, 1976): 18–36.

Reid, S. R. *Mergers, Managers, and the Economy.* New York: McGraw-Hill, 1968.

Stapleton, R. "The Acquisition Decision as a Capital Budgeting Problem." *Journal of Business, Finance, and Accounting* (Summer 1975): 187–199.

Steiner, Peter O. *Mergers: Motives, Effects, Policies.* Ann Arbor: University of Michigan Press, 1975.

Keenan, M. (1980) "Valuation problems in service sector mergers". In *Mergers and Acquisitions: Current Problems in Perspective*, pp. 29–40. Reprinted with permission from Lexington Books.

Corporate acquisition strategies and economic performance 13

Harbir Singh and Cynthia A. Montgomery

Research on corporate diversification is an important area in the strategic management literature. As this research has developed, some appealing operationalizations of diversification have emerged (Rumelt, 1974). These have resulted in generalizations about the linkage between diversification strategy and profitability.

As the specificity of research on diversification has increased, corporate acquisitions have been researched as an exclusive focus. Notable among this research is Salter and Weinhold's (1979) work on the strategic relationships between acquiring firms and target firms. These authors classified acquisitions into the broad groups of related and unrelated transactions. Their overall criterion for relatedness lay in the key success factor of the acquiring and acquired firms. Relatedness was reflected in the transfer of functional skills between businesses (functional skills could be subdivided into research and development, production, marketing and distribution).[1]

The Salter–Weinhold typology was developed as an integrative device designed to be consistent with strategic concepts. In his research on diversification strategy, Rumelt considered businesses to be related if they (1) served similar markets using similar distribution channels; (2) used similar production technologies; or (3) exploited similar scientific research. There is a clear consistency between Salter and Weinhold's criteria for relatedness and Rumelt's criteria. Additionally, by operating at the level of skills and resources, the typology is consistent with Andrews' (1980) concept of developing and effectively exploiting a distinctive competence.

An important contribution of the Salter and Weinhold work was a linkage drawn between the acquisition of key skills or product market positions and the potential for value creation. These authors asserted that value would be created through the reinforcement of skills or positions critical to the success of the combined businesses – i.e. through related acquisitions. Value in this context should be reflected in the stock price of the firms (and specifically in the change in stock prices as the market adjusts its expectation of future earnings from the businesses). This concept of economic value is consistent with that of financial economists.

Though it may be conceptually appealing, Salter and Weinhold's work only proposes how value is created – it suggests a hypothesis; it does not empirically test a hypothesis.

Parallel, but independent to the conceptual work noted above, several researchers in the area of financial economics have examined the stock market's responses to corporate acquisitions. In this work, researchers have aggregated related and unrelated acquisitions and have treated them as homogeneous. Within this framework it has generally been found that the announcements of acquisitions are accompanied by positive and significant changes in the combined wealth of the firms (Halpern, 1973; Mandelker, 1974; Langetieg, 1978; Dodd, 1980; Asquith, 1983; Bradley, Desai and Kim, 1983). In these studies the partitioning of gains has consistently favored the acquired firms, and gains to acquirers have often been non-significant (see Jensen and Ruback, 1983 and Halpern, 1983 for comprehensive reviews of these financial studies).

These two research streams suggest a natural overlap. The strategy view embodied in Salter and Weinhold's typologies could be tested via the theory and methodology of financial economics. The combination would not only benefit the policy area, but would simultaneously address Halpern's (1983) criticism that the finance work has not addressed the issue of how value is created through acquisitions.[2] The present research addresses this empirical question. We will first present theoretical arguments for expecting differences between related and unrelated acquisitions, state the hypotheses and discuss the methodology and results of the research.

THE FIRM AS A COLLECTION OF RESOURCES

A resource-based perspective of the multiproduct firm was first advanced by Penrose (1959). In Penrose's view a firm is a "collection of productive resources". Products made by a firm represent outcomes of its chosen activities and its internal resource positions. Penrose defined a resource as a fixed input which when combined with the choice of activities (processes) resulted in a product. Rubin (1973), who advanced a theory of corporate expansion, defines a resource as "a fixed input which allows a firm to perform a particular task". The definition of an input is broad enough to include a combination of human capital (specialized) and physical assets. For instance, in an automatic assembly plant the metal-stamping section (a stage in production) would be a resource comprising managers, specialized labor *and* equipment. There are strong analogies between Rubin's (1973) and Penrose's (1959) perspective on resources.

Penrose made an important observation when she noted that a balance in the usage of a firm's resources is never wholly achieved (1959: 70). The indivisibility of a firm's various inputs, each of which may be capable of rendering not only different amounts but different kinds of services, suggests that underutilized resources of one kind or another will always exist in a firm. The next question to consider is what a firm will do with a given bundle of such resources. The following alternatives exist:

1. status quo operation,
2. sales of resources in factor markets,
3. contractual sharing of resources with another firm,
4. expansion in present product markets,
5. diversification.

If status quo operation in a firm's present markets causes the firm to forgo significant profit opportunities, the firm may consider selling or contracting-out some portion of its resources, expanding its presence in its existing product markets, or diversifying into new products or services. To the extent that the resources involved are specialized and transactions costs in the factor markets are significant, expansion or diversification may be the most attractive alternatives (Teece, 1980; Williamson, 1975).

THE INCENTIVES/DISINCENTIVES TO ACQUIRE

Considering or having decided to expand or diversify, a firm can choose between two available modes – internal growth or development requires a long time for the accrual of returns (8 years in the 1979 Biggadike study). This is primarily due to the high needs for investment and business development in the early years after new entry into a market. Apart from the issue of timing, the incremental nature of the internal development process can be more expensive than the purchase of an ongoing business.

Another argument for acquisition rather than internal growth or development pertains to entry into concentrated product markets. In such markets incumbents may be earning supernormal profits and the markets themselves may be characterized by substantial barriers to entry (Bain, 1956; Caves, 1981). Under these circumstances entry or expansion in the market may be more expensive than acquisition of an incumbent (for example, see Yip, 1980).

Disincentives to acquire relate to (1) the unavailability of potential acquisition candidates; (2) the size of the premium that an acquirer may need to pay to the shareholders of the target firm; and (3) the transactions costs that will be incurred in the purchase.

In evaluating its expansion and diversification options a firm would be expected to weigh the relative impact of these sets of factors.

POTENTIAL GAINS THROUGH ACQUISITION

Having reviewed the process through which a firm reaches expansion or diversification decisions, and then the decision to acquire rather than to grow internally, we now address potential gains through acquisition. In this discussion we differentiate between related and unrelated acquisitions.

Related acquisitions

In a related acquisition, value creation can arise from three sources: economies of scale, economies of scope, and market power.

Economies of scale are present when efficiencies arise from the expanded production of a *specific product*. In a resource framework this would mean that a given bundle of resources is being more fully utilized. Scale economies can occur in specific functional areas, i.e. manufacturing, research and development, selling and distribution – the traditional areas used to identify related acquisitions (Salter and Weinhold, 1979; Rumelt, 1974), as well as in the more general areas of administration and financial management.

Economies of scope arise when a given bundle of resources are used in the *joint production of two or more products*. For example, when some of the assembly facilities in an automobile plant (body manufacture) are used both for cars and light trucks, scope economies may be operating. Note that the indivisibility of the resource provides *scale* economies when capacity utilization is increased through increased production of a single product. When capacity utilization is increased through the production of two or more products, *scope* economies are provided through the utilization of the indivisible shared resource.

It is important to note that scope economies can occur outside of the production area. Distribution systems and intangible assets like brand names can be the source of scope economies if they are used for more than one product. The sharing of specialized know-how is another important source of scope economies (Teece, 1982; Williamson, 1979). Due to market imperfections this know-how may be unavailable at the same cost to other firms in the market place. This idea is similar in spirit to Rumelt's (1974) concept of diversifying around a core science-based resource.

Market power effects, in the traditional framework of industrial organization economies, are operating when a market participant has the ability to influence price, quantity, and the nature of the product in the market place (Shepherd, 1970: 3). In turn, market power may lead to excess returns. In related acquisitions a firm's market power may be increased through horizontal acquisitions (where the acquiring and the acquired firm are operating in the same product market) or through product or market extension acquisitions where a firm's effective size is increased relative to its competitors.

Overall, we can argue that in related acquisitions there are several mechanisms available for the combination of the two firms to be potentially more valuable than the sum of their preacquisition values. We will now examine the mechanisms for potential gain in unrelated acquisitions.

Unrelated acquisitions

In related acquisitions, by definition technological or product market relationships between target and bidder are not apparent. If we assume rationality on the part of the bidder, we would expect that the management of that firm would pay a premium over the market value of the target that would be less than or equal to the bidding firm's expected gains from the acquisition.

The gains available in unrelated acquisitions would, *ceteris paribus*, be lower than those for related acquisitions. While the specialized resources in related acquisitions may result in increased efficiencies in technological or product markets activities, or increased market-specific market power, the efficiency and power gains in unrelated acquisitions are of a much more general variety. Gains in unrelated acquisitions may result from reduced financing costs (due to lowered bankruptcy risk or internal financing arrangements), increased administrative efficiencies, or superior human capital not specific to products or businesses. In unrelated acquisitions, increases in market power may arise from increases in the absolute size and breadth of the firm. This view suggests that unrelated acquisitions may increase the opportunities for predatory pricing and reciprocal buying, and reduce intra-industry rivalry through the presence of several large firms facing each other in many markets (Caves, 1981; Miller, 1973).

In summary, the value changes in unrelated acquisitions are expected to be positive. However, we note that the benefits from these transactions should also be available in related acquisitions. In contrast, the specific gains in related acquisitions are not expected to be present in unrelated acquisitions. On average, therefore, the gains in related acquisitions should be greater than the gains in unrelated acquisitions.

HYPOTHESES

I: The abnormal dollar value changes associated with the event of acquisition are expected to be positive.

This expectation is consistent with the view that management's actions should be undertaken in the interests of their shareholders. When treated as a homogeneous group the event of acquisition can be expected to increase the value of the combined firms.

II: Total dollar value changes associated with related acquisitions are expected to be higher than those of unrelated acquisitions.

III: Acquiring firms making related acquisitions are expected to have higher gains than acquiring firms making unrelated acquisitions.

IV: Acquired firms that are related to their acquirers are expected to have higher gains than acquired firms that are unrelated to their acquirers.

Hypotheses II, III, and IV reflect the expectations that related acquisitions signal to the market that synergies leading to higher income streams will result from the combination of previously separate sets of resources.

METHODOLOGY

The methodology used in the study involves the computation of the risk-adjusted returns on the stock of acquired and acquiring firms. The adjustment for risk is done using the market model

$$R_{it} = \alpha_i + \beta_i R_{mit} + \epsilon_{it} \tag{1}$$

where:

R_{it} = daily stock return for stock i on day t;
R_{mit} = daily return on market portfolio (equally weighted) at day t;
α_i, β_i = coefficients in the model for stock i
ϵ_{it} = disturbance term in the model for security i at time t – this is normally distributed with mean 0 and variance σ^2.
i.e. $\epsilon_{it} \sim N(0, \sigma^2)$

The model[3] specified above controls for market-wide variations through the independent variable R_{mit}. Any variation due to factors not present in the market portfolio will be captured in the disturbance term ϵ_{it}.

The model is estimated for each security on relative day[4] (day relative to the critical event of acquisition) -800 to -551. This period was chosen to ensure that the time frame for plotting the residuals would include the precursors of the event, if any systematic ones exist.

The procedure for capturing performance differences of the firms is to estimate *abnormal returns*. An abnormal return of a firm i at time t is the deviation between its realized return at day t and the expected return as per model (1).

$$AR_{it} = \tilde{R}_{it} - (\hat{\alpha}_i + \hat{\beta}_i R_{mit}) \tag{2}$$

where:

R_{it} = realized return for security i at day t;
$\hat{\alpha}, \hat{\beta}$ = estimated values of coefficients in equation (1).

Computing abnormal returns for a portfolio

Firm-level abnormal returns must be aggregated to a portfolio in order to study generalizable performance differences. This will be done by taking an equal-weighted portfolio:

$$AR_{pt} = \frac{1}{N_{pt}} \sum_{j=1}^{N_{pt}} AR_{jt}$$

(3)

where:

N_{pt} = number of securities on the portfolio;
AR_{pt} = average residual for the portfolio at day t.

The effect on the portfolio over time will then be obtained by cumulating these portfolio residuals.

Tests of significance of event-related performance

In this kind of analysis the procedure used to study abnormal performance is two-fold. The first part is to test the statistical significance of cumulative abnormal returns associated with the acquisition. The second is to examine the time series plots of the cumulative abnormal returns. This section deals with the specific tests used to establish the significance of cumulative average residuals.

The first step is to standardize the abnormal returns on the firms' securities. This is done by computing

$$SR_{it} = \frac{AR_{it}}{\sigma(AR_i)}$$

(4)

where:

SR_{it} = standardized abnormal return on security i on day t;
$\sigma(AR_i)$ = standard deviation of abnormal return on security i on day t.

This is then computed for an equally weighted portfolio of the securities, as required in the study. This is computed using

$$SR_{pt} = \frac{1}{N_{pt}} \sum_{t_i=1}^{N_{pt}} SR_{it}$$

(5)

If cross-sectional independence is assumed it can be shown that the variance of standardized returns on the portfolio would be $1/N_{pt}$. The Z-statistic necessary to test for significance is then computed by

$$Z_E = \frac{SR_{pt}}{\sigma(SR_{pt})} = \frac{SR_{PT}}{1/(\sqrt{N_{pt}})} \qquad (6)$$
$$= \sqrt{N_{pt}} SR_{pt}$$

This is distributed $\sim N(0, 1/N_{pt})$

Next, the test statistics for measuring changes in dollar value of the security associated with the event of acquisition are computed as follows.

If $V_{i,t-1}$ = market value of firm i on day t $-$ 1, then

$$\Delta V_{it} = AR_{it} \cdot V_{i,t-1} \qquad (7)$$

where

ΔV_{it} = abnormal change in dollar value of the firm i as the result of the acquisition announcement.

To compute the standardized abnormal dollar value change, the standard deviation of the abnormal dollar change must be estimated. From equation (1),

$$\sigma^2 \sqrt{(\Delta V_{iv})} = \sigma^2(AR_i) V^2_{i,t-1} \qquad (8)$$

This value of $\sigma(\Delta V_{iv})$ can be estimated for periods between two events, e.g. announcement and completion. Then $\sigma(\Delta V_{it})$ would be the value computed in this period $t = 0, T$.

It is necessary to compute the abnormal dollar value changes associated with the event, to determine whether there are significant value gains available to successful bidders and acquired firms. However, to estimate the synergistic gains as a result of the transaction, it would be necessary to compute

$\Delta V = \Delta V_A + V_B;$
ΔV_A = abnormal for the dollar value change acquired firm as a result of acquisition event;
ΔV_B = abnormal dollar value change of the bidding firm as a result of the acquisition event.

THE DATA

The data included 105 acquisitions of market value greater than \$100million in the period 1975–80. This is the same period as used by Salter and Weinhold, and enabled the use of their classifications of related and unrelated acquisitions. Acquisitions were classified as related[5] if the bidding firm and the acquired firm shared at least one of the following characteristics:

similar production technologies,
similar science-based research,
similar products and/or markets.

The starting sample corresponding to Salter and Weinhold's study had 165 acquisitions. Of these 60 acquisitions were dropped from the sample due to incomplete return data on the CRSP (Center for Research on Security Prices) files. The starting sample size was 165, of which 105 pairs of targets and bidders had complete vectors[6] of returns for the study period on the CRSP tapes. This sample of 105 was used to examine the wealth effects of related and unrelated acquisitions (Hypotheses I and II).

Information regarding competitive bids (before the event of acquisition) was also collected and included in the data base. This information indicated that 77 of the 105 acquisitions were single-bidder events. These 77 single-bidder events were then used to estimate the effect on acquiring and acquired firms (Hypotheses III and IV). Multiple bids could influence the distribution of gains between bidders and targets, and therefore are not reported in this analysis – see Singh, 1984, for results on the multiple-bid events.)

Data on security returns (cum dividend) were collected for each firm in the sample from the CRSP (Center for Research on Security Prices, University of Chicago) files. These data were collected from day -800 to day $+400$ (with the announcement day being defined as day 0). This means that the daily stock returns have been collected for a period of 1200 days, beginning from 800 days before the first announcement of the acquisition and ending with 400 daily returns after the event.

The database then contains the vector of daily stock returns for targets and bidders during the study period, and the corresponding equal-weighted market portfolio returns.

RESULTS

Table 1 provides the results on dollar gains of related and unrelated acquisitions, along with their standard errors. Both dollar gains are significantly higher than 0 at the 0.025 level but are not significantly different from each other. Table 2 presents total dollar gains standardized on the value of acquired assets. With the measure of standardized gain, the difference between means is significant at the 0.05 level.

Table 1 Dollar gains in different types of acquisitions

	Mean dollar gain[a]	Standard deviation of mean gain
Related acquisitions ($n = 40$)	10.745[b]	5.255
Unrelated acquisitions ($n = 37$)	8.643[b]	3.139

[a] All figures in millions of dollars.
[b] Significant difference from 0 at the 0.025 level.

Table 2 Dollar gains (standardized) for different types of acquisitions

	Standardized gains[a]	Standard deviation of mean
Related acquisitions ($n = 40$)	0.2382[b]	0.051
Unrelated acquisitions ($n = 37$)	0.1648[b]	0.042

[a] This will range from 0 to 1.
[b] Significant difference of means (related vs unrelated acquisitions) at the 0.05 level.

Table 3 Cumulative abnormal returns of acquired firms

	Period I[a] (day −5 to +25)	Period II (day +25 to +100)
Related single-bid acquisitions (n = 40)	0.359[b,d]	0.065
Unrelated single-bid acquisitions (n = 37)	0.219[c,d]	0.016

[a] These results are not sensitive in their direction to the location of window chosen. The choice of window is determined by examining the target CARs and selecting the time period which most suitably captures plots of the effect of announcement. This time window is consistent with other event studies.
[b] Significant difference from zero at the 0.001 level.
[c] Significant difference from zero at the 0.005 level.
[d] Significant difference of returns at the 0.01 level.

These results confirm our hypotheses regarding the differences between the total dollar gains from related and unrelated acquisitions.

The abnormal returns for acquired firms are positive and significant for related and unrelated targets (Table 3). For related firms there is a rise of 0.29 in the CAR (cumulative abnormal returns) from 2 days before to 2 days after the event. The reassessment of firm returns from 5 days before to 25 days after the event is 0.359 (35.9 percent) significant at the 0.001 level (see Figure 1). This indicates that the announcement of the acquisition by the bidder causes a revaluation of the earnings potential of the target. This is sustained over time, as seen in the period from 25 days to 100 days after the event (CAR = 0.065).

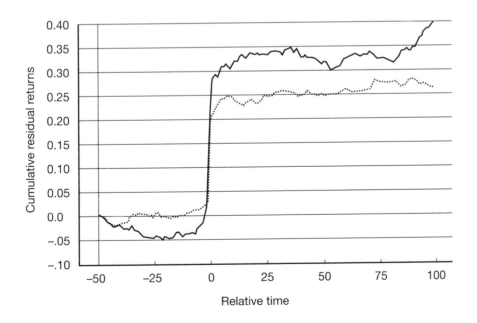

Figure 1 Cumulative residual returns to acquired firms. Solid lines are related targets; broken lines are unrelated targets.

Table 4 Cumulative abnormal returns of acquiring firms

	Period I (day −5 to +25)	Period II (day +25 to +100)
Related single-bid acquirers (n = 40)	−0.006	+0.0182
Unrelated single-bid acquirers (n = 37)	−0.019	+0.068

For unrelated targets there is also a positive and significant announcement effect. The change in CAR from day −5 to day +25 is 0.219 (21.9 percent) (see Figure 1). This change is positive and statistically significant at the 0.001 level, indicating that a substantial revaluation of the earnings potential of the acquired firm has taken place. The sustenance of this CAR from 25 days to 100 days after the event (+0.099), indicates that there are no significant downward revaluations within the time frame of the study. The results reported in Table 3 further indicate that related acquired firms obtain significantly higher returns than unrelated acquired firms (35.9 percent versus 26.9 percent, significantly different from each other at $p < 0.01$). This indicates that the announcement of the acquisition is viewed as a value-increasing event for the acquired firm, when acquired by an unrelated acquirer. We therefore observe positive and significantly higher returns to related target firms, as compared to unrelated targets.

The abnormal returns for acquiring firms are not significant in related or unrelated acquisitions (see Table 4). These results are consistent with other studies, which were done on aggregated samples of acquisitions, and also did not find significant announcement effects for bidders (Asquith, 1983; Dodd and Ruback, 1977). Comparing our results with those obtained by Lubatkin (1984), we observe overall consistency with his findings on conglomerate vs. horizontal and product-market extension mergers. Our sample differs to the extent that we chose larger acquisitions of greater than $100million in value, while Lubatkin's (1984) sample includes acquisitions greater than $10million in value. It was anticipated that the disaggregation into related and unrelated categories would help overcome some of the measurement problems found in bidder firms, but this was not the case. The measurement problems referred to above relate to what may be termed a "size-effect" problem. While acquisition involves all the assets of the target firms the event is usually a subset of the acquirer's operations. When only a moderate fraction of the acquirer's assets are directly related to the acquisition, the returns to the acquirer will also be influenced by events that are not related to the acquisition. Jarrel (1983) showed that when the acquirer is more than five times the size of the target it would need a "true" t-statistic of 4.50 (on the merging portions of its businesses) to provide an obtained t-statistic of 2.0. To investigate the possible dilution effects of the high relative size of targets to acquirers, we selected a subsample consisting of the upper quartile of relative size of targets to acquirers. In this subsample we found that related acquirers had a significant positive announcement effect of 0.01434 while unrelated acquirers had a negative announcement effect of −0.0061 over a 2-day window. These results support the existence of a dilution effect on acquirers.

CONCLUSION

This research investigates whether corporate acquisitions with shared technological resources or participation in similar product markets realize superior economic returns in comparison with unrelated acquisitions. The rationale for superior economic performance in related acquisitions derives from the synergies that are expected through a combination of supplementary or complementary resources.

It is clear from the results of this research that acquired firms in related acquisitions have higher returns than acquired firms in unrelated acquisitions. This implies that the related acquired firm benefits more from the acquirer than the unrelated acquired firm. The higher returns for the related acquired firms suggest that the combination with the acquirer's resources has higher value implications than the combination of two unrelated firms. This is supported by the higher total wealth gains which were observed in related acquisitions.

We do, however, in the case of acquiring firms, find that the abnormal returns directly attributable to the acquisition transaction are not significant. As discussed earlier, there are reasons to believe that the announcement effects of the transaction on the returns to acquirers are less easily detected than for target firms. First, an acquisition by a firm affects only part of its businesses, while affecting all the assets (in control-oriented acquisitions) of the target firm. Thus the measurability of effects on acquirers is attenuated. Second, if an acquisition is one event in a series of implicit moves constituting a diversification program, its individual effect as a market signal would be mitigated. However, in this instance the market's response is expected to be diffuse and difficult to measure precisely (see Schipper and Thompson, 1983, for a discussion of this issue).

It is also likely that the theoretical argument which postulates that related acquisitions create wealth for acquirers may be underspecified. Relatedness is often multifaceted, suggesting that the resources of the target firm may be of value to many firms, thus increasing the relative bargaining power of the target *vis-à-vis* the potential buyers. Even in the absence of explicit competition for the target (multiple bidding), the premiums paid for control are a substantial fraction of the total gains available from the transaction.

For managers, some implications from the research can be offered. First, it seems quite clear from the data that a firm seeking to be acquired will realize higher returns if it is sold to a related rather than an unrelated firm. This counsel is consistent with the view that the market recognizes synergistic combinations and values them accordingly.

Second, managers in acquiring firms may be advised to scrutinize carefully the expected gains in related and unrelated acquisitions. For managers the issue of concern is not whether or not a given kind of acquisition creates a significant total amount of wealth, but what percentage of that wealth they can expect to accrue to their firms. Thus, although acquisitions involving related technologies or product market yield higher total gains, pricing mechanisms in the market for corporate acquisitions reflect the gains primarily on the target company. Interpreting these results conservatively, one may offer the argument that expected gains for acquiring firms are competed away in the bidding process, with stockholders of target firms obtaining high proportions of the gains.

On a pragmatic level this research underscores the need to combine what may be called the theoretical with the practical. In the case of acquisitions, pragmatic issues like implicit and explicit competition for a target firm alter the theoretical expectations of gains from an acquisition transaction. Further efforts to clarify these issues theoretically and empirically will increase our understanding of these important phenomena.

ACKNOWLEDGEMENTS

We wish to thank Professors Birger Wernerfelt and Ann Thomas for their helpful comments and encouragement during various stages of this research. We also thank Professor Edward Bowman for his comments on an earlier draft of this paper.

NOTES

1 Salter and Weinhold further divided relatedness acquisitions into related-complementary and related-supplementary classification. That level of distinction is not used in the present analysis.
2 Some researchers have begun to address these issues – see for instance, Rappaport (1981), Bettis, (1983) and Peavy (1984).
3 See Brown and Warner (1980) for further information on the measurement of stock returns, and Halpern (1983) for a review of studies using the Market Model.
4 In studies using the Market Model for measuring returns there is a choice of using daily returns or monthly returns. This issue has been extensively addressed by Brown and Warner (1980). The principal benefit in using daily returns for such studies is the added precision in measuring the effects of acquisition announcement on stock returns. The use of daily returns also minimizes the likelihood of other uncorrelated events influencing the returns at the time of acquisition transactions. This had been addressed by Jensen and Ruback (1983).
5 See Salter and Weinhold, 1979, 1982.
6 Given the amount of data necessary for each observation, this is not an unusually high number of incomplete records. Further, there was no indication that the acquisitions dropped from the sample were systematically unusual.

REFERENCES

Andrews, Kenneth. *The Concept of Corporate Strategy.* Richard D. Irwin, Homewood, IL: 1980.
Asquith Paul. "Merger bids, uncertainty and stockholder returns", *Journal of Financial Economics*, **11**, April 1983, pp. 51–83.
Bain, Joseph S. *Barriers to New Competition*, Harvard University Press, Cambridge, MA, 1956.
Bettis, Richard A. "Modern financial theory, corporate strategy and public policy: three conundrums", *Academy of Management Review*, 1983, pp. 406–415.
Biggadike, Ralph. "The risky business of diversification", *Harvard Business Review*, May–June 1979, pp. 103–111.
Bradley, Michael, Anand Desai and E. Han Kim. "The rationale behind interfirm tender offers", *Journal of Financial Economics*, **11**, April 1983, pp. 183–206.
Brown, S. J. and J. B. Warner. "Measuring security price performance", *Journal of Financial Economics*, **8**, 1980, pp. 205–258.
Caves, Richard D. "Diversification and seller concentration: evidence from change, 1963–1972", *Review of Economics and Statistics*, **63**, 1981, pp. 289–293.
Dodd, Peter. "Merger, proposals, management discretion, and stockholder's wealth", *Journal of Financial Economics*, **8**, 1980, pp. 105–138.
Dodd, Peter and Richard Ruback. "Tender offers and stockholder returns: an empirical analysis", *Journal of Financial Economics*, **5**, December 1977, pp. 351–373.
Elgers, P. and J. Clark. "Merger types and shareholder returns: additional evidence", *Financial Management*, Summer 1980, pp. 66–72.
Halpern, Paul J. "Empirical estimates of the amount and distribution of gains to companies in mergers", *Journal of Business*, October 1973, pp. 554–575.
Halpern Paul J. "Corporate acquisitions: a theory of special cases? A review of event studies applied to acquisitions", *Journal of Finance*, May 1983, pp. 297–317.
Jarrel, G. "Do acquirers benefit from corporate acquisitions?", University of Chicago Working Paper, 1983.
Jensen, Michael C. and Richard Ruback. "The market for corporate control: the scientific evidence", *Journal of Financial Economics*, **11**, April 1983, pp. 3–50.
Langetieg, Terence. "A three-factor performance index to measure gains from merger", *Journal of Financial Economics*, **6**, December 1978, pp. 365–383.

Lubatkin, Michael. "Merger and the performance of the acquiring firm", *Academy of Management Review*, **8**(2), 1983, pp. 218–225.

Lubatkin, Michael. "Merger strategies and shareholder returns: a test for merger synergy", Working Paper, University of Connecticut, 1984.

Malatesta, Paul H. "The wealth effects of merger activity and the objective functions of merging firms", *Journal of Financial Economics*, **11**, April 1983, pp. 155–181.

Mandelker, G. "Risk and return: the case of merging firms", *Journal of Financial Economics*, **1**, 1974, pp. 303–335.

Miller, R. A. "Concentration and marginal concentration advertising and diversity: three issues in structure-performance tests", *Industrial Organization Review*, **1**(1), 1973, pp. 15–24.

Peavy, J. W. "Modern financial theory, corporate strategy and public policy: another perspective", *Academy of Management Review*, 1984, pp. 152–157.

Penrose, Edith T. *The Theory of Growth of the Firm*. Oxford, Blackwell, 1959.

Rappaport, Alfred. "Selecting strategies that create shareholder value", *Harvard Business Review* May–June 1981, pp. 139–149.

Rubin, Paul H. "The expansion of firms", *Journal of Political Economy*, July–August 1973, pp. 936–949.

Rumelt, Richard P. *Strategy, Structure and Economic Performance*. Division of Research, Harvard University, Boston, MA, 1974.

Salter, Malcom S. and Wolf A. Weinhold. "Diversification via acquisition: creating value". *Harvard Business Review*, July–August 1978, pp. 166–176.

Salter, Malcom S. and Wolf A. Weinhold. *Diversification Through Acquisition: Strategies for Creating Economic Value*, The Free Press, New York, 1979.

Salter, Malcom S. and Wolf A. Weinhold. "What lies ahead for merger activities in the 1980s?" *Journal of Business Strategy*, Spring 1982, pp. 66–99.

Schipper, K. and R. Thompson. "Evidence in the capitalized value of merger activity of acquired firms", *Journal of Financial Economics*, **11**, April 1983, pp. 85–119.

Shepherd, William G. *Market Power and Economic Welfare*. Random House, New York, 1970.

Singh, Harbir. "Corporate acquisitions and economic performance", Doctoral dissertation, University of Michigan, Ann Arbor, 1984.

Teece, David J. "Economies of scope and the scope of the enterprise", *Journal of Economic Behavior and Organization*, **3**, 1980, pp. 223–247.

Teece, David J. "Towards an economic theory of the multiproduct firm", *Journal of Economic Behavior and Organization*, **3**, 1982, pp. 39–63.

Wernerfelt, Birger. "A resource-based view of the firm", Working Paper, University of Michigan Graduate School of Business Administration, 1983.

Williamson, O. E. *Markets and Hierarchies: Analysis and Antitrust Implications'*, Free Press, New York 1975.

Williamson, O. E. "Transactions cost economics: the governance of contractual relations", *Journal of Law and Economics*, **22**, 1979, pp. 233–267.

Yip, George S. "Barriers to entry", Unpublished doctoral dissertation, *Harvard Business School*, 1980.

Singh, H. and Montgomery, C. A. (1987) "Corporate acquisition strategies and economic performance'. *Strategic Management Journal*, 8, 377–386. Reproduced by permission of John Wiley & Sons Limited.

14 Control mechanisms in cross-border acquisitions: an international comparison

Roland Calori, Michael Lubatkin and Philippe Very

INTRODUCTION

This research investigates the extent to which firms differ in the control mechanisms they exercise over firms acquired abroad, in line with the administrative systems in place in that country; systems which, in turn, are rooted in the national culture.

The issue of the technical, political and cultural integration process following mergers and acquisitions is crucial (Shrivastava, 1985; Buono and Bowditch, 1989; Haspeslagh and Jemison, 1991). Differences in organizational culture and management practices between merging firms may be sources of conflicts (Buono and Bowditch, 1989) and may impede the implementation of synergies and limit the benefits of the merger (Haspeslagh and Jemison, 1991; Chatterjee et al., 1992). Differences in management values and practices have been found between nations (Hofstede, 1980; Chandler, 1986). Consequently, in the case of international acquisitions, the incompatibility between the buyer and the acquired firm may be enhanced (Very, Calori and Lubatkin 1993: 323–346). This could occur when the buying firm does not adapt its practice to the local practice, when it is "ethnocentric" (Perlmutter, 1969), or when it does not question its national "administrative heritage" (Bartlett and Ghoshal, 1989). The control mechanisms (formal and informal) are at the heart of the relationship between the buyer and the acquired firm. It may seem obvious that a firm needs to adjust its control structures in order to effectively manage across borders, yet firms are prone to carry their home practice with them as they move into foreign markets (Kogut, 1991).

There is abundant research on the relationships between headquarters and foreign subsidiaries in multinational corporations (see, for instance, Gupta and Govindarajan, 1991). However, only a few studies have addressed the issue of the influence of the country of origin on the control mechanisms in MNCs (Gates and Egelhoff, 1986; Bartlett and Ghoshal, 1989). Moreover, these include greenfield affiliates as well as acquired affiliates, and among acquired affiliates no control is built into the studies to account for the time that has elapsed since the acquisition. Actually, little research has focused on integration practices following international acquisitions – most was in the form of case studies (Ghoshal and Haspeslagh, 1990; Kester, 1991). For this reason our work cross-fertilizes previous research on headquarters-subsidiaries relationships, research on integration mechanisms in acquisitions, and research on cultural contingencies in international management, in order to formulate and test hypotheses on the influence of the national administrative heritage on the control mechanisms exercised by buyers engaging in international acquisitions. Then the paper explores the relationships between the control mechanisms and the improvement in attitudinal and economic performance of the acquired firms, so as to provide a foundation for more prescriptive research in future on the management of international acquisitions.

In order to make statistical comparisons, target firms in two countries were selected: France and the United Kingdom. In France we compared US buyers with British buyers; in the United Kingdom we compared US buyers with French buyers. In 1989, France, the United Kingdom and the United States were the first three countries (according to the Translink data base) from which firms bidding for European companies originated. Moreover, the literature had already shown differences in management between the British and the American systems (Chandler, 1986; Gates and Egelhoff, 1986), and between the American and the French systems (Hofstede, 1980; Laurent, 1983; d'Iribarne, 1989) on which hypotheses could be built.

LITERATURE AND HYPOTHESES

In studying the structure of control within multinational corporations, Gupta and Govindarajan (1991) make a distinction between formal organizational structures and control systems (such as the design of decision processes and control systems) and informal coordination mechanisms (such as emergent patterns of communication and socialization). Formal structures and control systems combine into two dimensions of control strategies: centralization and formalization (Child, 1972; 1973). Centralization can be defined as "the division of decision-making authority between the headquarters and the various operational units" (Garnier, 1982). Formalization is an attempt to control behaviour indirectly by relying upon procedures and records as methods for limiting discretion and for monitoring activities. Informal coordination mechanisms, also referred to as socialization (Edstrom and Galbraith, 1977; Ouchi, 1980) complement formal mechanisms and are based on informal communication patterns and emergent behaviour.

The dimensions describing integration mechanisms following acquisitions may vary between authors (see, for instance, Shrivastava, 1985; Haspeslagh and Jemison, 1991), but they all share the same above-mentioned foundations. It is important to understand formal and informal mechanisms as they provide a measure of integration vs differentiation processes. Formal systems are the "anatomy" of the organization and informal mechanisms are its "physiology" and "psychology", to use the terms adopted by Bartlett and Ghoshal (1989).

The beliefs about effective control structures become embedded into the ways things are done at a firm; they become a firm's administrative heritage (Bartlett and Ghoshal, 1989). Part of the administrative heritage is idiosyncratic (linked to the history of the firm and to the style of its leaders), and part of the administrative heritage is rooted in the national culture of the home country (Bartlett and Ghoshal, 1989). The beliefs and behaviour of the local managers, who grew up within this national context, are influenced by it (Schneider and de Meyer, 1991; Smith, 1992). A national context is defined by specific cultural characteristics (Hofstede, 1980;

Laurent, 1986) as well as by economical and political characteristics (Dore, 1973; Rohlen, 1974) formed during the history of the country. Other researchers have argued in favour of culture-free factors influencing organizational structure (Hickson et al., 1974), or for the increasing universality of management practices (Levitt 1983). Nevertheless, a whole body of research has shown the influence of the national context on management: work-related values (Hofstede, 1980), cognitive frames and attitudes (Haire et al., 1966; Laurent, 1983), human resource management policies (Pascale and Maguire, 1980; Child, 1981), negotiation practices, leadership styles (Smith et al., 1992), organizational structures (Chandler, 1986), and control mechanisms (Redding and Pugh, 1986; Bartlett and Ghoshal, 1989; Child, 1990). We share the view that cultural contingencies have to be considered in management theories (Hofstede, 1993), and that some characteristics of the administrative heritage of firms are rooted in their original national context. In order to illustrate this point, we turn our discussion to three specific national cultures, those of Great Britain, the United States and France, compared by pairs as indicated earlier. Our analysis of the literature in this domain will be focused on a few earlier studies, selected because of their approach to the issue of control mechanisms.

COMPARISON OF THE FRENCH AND THE AMERICAN SYSTEMS

The study of work-related values (and associated management practices) achieved by Hofstede (1980) is still the most complete empirical research comparing nations. On the basis of Hofstede's cultural dimensions, the French appear to be stronger than the Americans on "uncertainty avoidance" and "power distance", and the Americans higher than the French on "masculinity" (performance orientation). Combining high uncertainty avoidance and high power distance should lead to a relatively high centralization of decision-making in French companies, compared with the American, but there may be an exception to the French tendency towards centralization: Gates and Egelhoff (1986) found that firms from continental Europe have more decentralized financial decision-making (compared with American and British firms). Also the higher masculinity factor in the United States may lead to a tighter control of the performance of individual managers. Chandler (1986) suggests that the integration processes in North American companies are characterized by higher formalization (i.e. control by procedures and management systems) than in European and Japanese companies, in line with Child's findings (1990) concerning the management of international joint ventures. D'Iribarne (1989) also found that US companies exercise more control over procedures and contracts than the French firms, where a "logique de l'honneur" governs social relationships. Finally, as demonstrated by Laurent (1983), Anglo-Saxons view the organization primarily as a network of relationships between individuals who get things done by influencing each other through communication and negotiating. The French, on the other hand, view the organization as a hierarchical structure. Consequently, it may be that US companies rely more than the French on team-work as an informal control mechanism over their foreign subsidiaries.

This brief review of the literature comparing the administrative heritages of the French and the Americans leads to the following hypothesis concerning the control mechanisms exercised over foreign acquired firms:

H1: In line with their national administrative heritage:

(a) The French will exercise higher formal control by centralization than the Americans with the exception of formal control over individual managers and financial resources;

(b) Americans will exercise higher formal control over individual managers and financial resources than the French;

(c) Americans will exercise higher formal control through procedures than the French;

(d) Americans will exercise higher informal control through team-work than the French.

A COMPARISON OF THE AMERICAN AND BRITISH SYSTEMS

According to Hofstede's study of work-related values (1980) the Americans and the British are relatively close to each other within the Anglo-Saxon group, so at first sight, there should not be much difference between the two groups of buying firms in our study. However, Gates and Egelhoff (1986) found that, compared with the United States and continental Europe, British multinationals have more decentralized decision-making practices in the domains of marketing and manufacturing. Chandler (1986) also noted that the British prefer broad-gauged financial controls to the coordination of technical or operational details. Moreover, Chandler (1986) strongly differentiated the British "family capitalism" from the American "managerial capitalism". British firms sent "family members" or "hand-picked trusted company servants" to manage off-shore operations, while US companies had a tendency to coordinate and control through sophisticated management systems and procedures.

This brief review of the literature comparing the administrative heritages of the American and the British leads to the following hypothesis concerning the control mechanisms exercised over foreign acquired firms:

H2: In line with their national administrative heritage:

(a) Americans will exercise higher formal control by the centralization of marketing and manufacturing decisions, than the British;

(b) Americans will exercise higher formal control through procedures than the British.

Previous research identified several other factors related to control mechanisms in multinational corporations or to integration mechanisms following acquisitions. Controls for these factors are built into our study.

CONTROLS FOR OTHER VARIABLES

The larger the subsidiary compared to the parent company, the lower is the degree of centralization by the headquarters (Hedlund, 1981; Garnier, 1982), in particular as far as manufacturing decisions are concerned (Gates and Egelhoff, 1986). In the case of acquisitions Hunt (1990) suggests the same relationship, and Haspeslagh and Jemison (1991) mention the impact of relative size as a secondary factor in the integration process. The "health" of the acquired firm prior to the merger (profitability, growth, functional capabilities) is a contextual variable related to the degree of control exercised by the buyer in the implementation phase (Hunt, 1990): the more healthy the acquired firm, the more autonomy it gets. Haspeslagh and Jemison (1991) consider a slightly different concept – the "quality" of the acquired company – as a secondary factor in the integration process. For Haspeslagh and Jemison (1991), one of the two main factors which determine the integration process in M&As is the "need for strategic interdependence". By interdependence, they mean resource sharing between related businesses and transfers of functional skills or general management capability. The higher the need for interdependence, the higher the level of control ("absorption" and "symbiosis" acquisitions). In related mergers, considerable pressure is often put on the acquired firm to conform to the goals, control systems and values of the buyer (Walter, 1985).

The degree of environmental change may also affect the level of centralization (Burns and Stalker, 1961; Lawrence and Lorsch, 1967). The higher the degree of environmental uncertainty of the subsidiary, the lower the degree of centralization by the headquarters (Bartlett and Ghoshal, 1986; Egelhoff, 1988; Ghoshal and Nohria, 1989).

Prahalad and Doz (1987) argued that when subsidiaries depend less on the parent for strategic resources, the level of centralization is reduced. In the same way, Bartlett and Ghoshal (1986) argued, and Ghoshal and Nohria (1989) demonstrated that the "level of local resources" of the subsidiary is negatively related to the degree of centralization. The concepts of "local resources" and "specific strategic capabilities" of the acquired firm (Haspeslagh and Jemison, 1991) are similar.

Garnier (1982) found that the "older" the subsidiary, the lower the level of centralization by the headquarters. Gates and Egelhoff (1986) confirmed this relationship as far as financial centralization is concerned. In the case of acquisitions, after a period of a few months following the merger, when the buyer tends to keep his "hands off" (Buono and Bowditch, 1989), control is likely to increase and then decrease again slowly as trust develops.

The industrial sector to which the company belongs may also influence the level of control by the parent or buyer (Gates and Egelhoff, 1986), at least for marketing decisions. Such differences can be explained by the structural characteristics of different industries (global vs locally responsive in the terms used by Prahalad and Doz, 1987).

Finally, the strategies of the parent and of the subsidiaries may affect the level and nature of control, "prospectors" and "defenders" may have different control practices (Golden, 1992).

CONTROL AND PERFORMANCE IN INTERNATIONAL ACQUISITIONS

Considering the relatively high failure rate of acquisitions (Buono and Bowditch, 1989), it is tempting to test the relationships between control mechanisms exercised by the buyer and the performance of acquired firms, both in terms of attitudes in the work place and in economic performance. For years, researchers studied the influence of the level of relatedness between merging companies and performance and the findings were mixed. More recently, socio-cultural issues were put forward to explain successes and failures (Shrivastava, 1985; Buono and Bowditch, 1989). Finally, from the cases they studied, Haspeslagh and Jemison (1991) showed that performance may depend on the adequacy of the integration process, given a certain level of strategic interdependence and a certain level of need for autonomy. Strategic interdependence can be approached by the level of shared resources and transfer of skills. The need for autonomy can be approached by the level of specific strategic capabilities embedded in the culture of the acquired firm.

In the perspective of our research, given such contingencies, the question is: are there any relationships between the control mechanisms and the performance of the acquired firm in the particular cases of international acquisitions? The literature on "managing across borders" (Bartlett and Ghoshal, 1989) suggests that informal emergent communication and coordination is positively related to performance in "transnational companies", and that a relatively decentralized form of "integrated network" is more effective to combine integration, differentiation and innovation. Moreover, according to Bartlett and Ghoshal (1989), "transnational" companies should moderate their administrative heritage and converge towards similar best international practices.

However, given the limited indications from previous research, we formulate our third hypothesis in the null form:

> **H3:** In international acquisitions the control mechanisms exercised by the buyer are not related to the performance of the acquired firm (when the level of shared resources and the level of strategic capabilities of the acquired firm are kept constant).

METHODOLOGY

Sample

A random sample of 155 French and 191 British acquired firms was drawn from a list of European mergers published in the *Acquisition Monthly* during three recent years (1987, 1988, 1989). The sample met the following criteria; the acquiring firms were either from France, Britain or the United States; the selling firm was valued at over $10 million; the buying firm gained controlling interest in the acquired firm; and the names and addresses of at least two (and as many as five) top managers who were affiliated with the acquired firm before the time of the merger were available in Kompass France, Kompass Great Britain, and Dun and Bradstreet Europe. A questionnaire was mailed in Spring 1991, directly to all of the identified top managers (chairman, managing director, general manager, personnel manager, and financial manager); i.e. to 392 French managers and 612 British managers (from two to five managers per firm). Only top managers were surveyed because the likelihood of contact between the merging organizations is greatest at the top management level (Schweiger and Walsh, 1990). Moreover, because of their position, top managers probably have a more comprehensive (if not more accurate) view of the integration process. The French managers received the version of the questionnaire that had been translated into French (and then translated back into English by a second translator to ensure reliability).

After two mailings, responses were received from 70 French managers and 109 British managers (a response rate of about 18 per cent). Of those, 18 contained inaccurate or incomplete information and were removed from further analysis. Although the response rate is relatively low, we consider it acceptable given the sensitive nature of the questionnaire and the fact that an unknown percentage of our mailings went to managers who, due to voluntary or unvoluntary reasons left their firm after the merger.

The final sample included 161 top managers and 117 firms; from these we retained 75 firms:[1] 25 British firms acquired by French firms, 21 British firms acquired by US firms (for the purpose of the comparison between the French and the Americans buying abroad); 16 French firms acquired by British firms, 13 French firms acquired by US firms (for the purpose of the comparison between the British and the Americans buying abroad).

In this study we took the perspective of the acquired firms (perceptions of the acquisition from the managers of the acquired firm, improvement of the performance of the acquired firm) in the belief that the perceptions of the managers at the acquired firm will determine these firms' behaviour (Schneider, 1975). This aspect of the research differs from most of the studies on acquisitions where the perspective of the buyer was taken. We acknowledge the inherent limitations of both perspectives. In our case, a complementary study of the perceptions at the buying firm could have usefully complemented information on the integration process. To check for a non-response bias we compared the "late" and "early" respondents in our survey as suggested by Oppenheim (1966). No evidence of a non-response bias was found.

We received multiple answers from 25 firms. As most of the measures were perceptual, the multiple answers from a given firm were used to test the validity of our questionnaire according to the consistency of the answers. Then aggregated scores were computed at the firm level. A perceived organizational phenomenon may be ambiguous if "one cannot be sure whether it implies an attribute of the organization or of the perceiving individual" (Guion, 1973: 120). This is particularly important if the individual's perceptions are used to represent a group of people. Multiple respondents per unit of analysis are therefore desirable to check for consensus (James and Jones, 1974). We tested for the consistency of multiple responses within firms using methods suggested by Finkelstein (1992). We computed two-tailed correlations between multiple responses when there were two responses from the same firm, and Cronbach Alphas when there were more than two responses from the same firm. Both series of tests showed high consistency between multiple responses:

- in the case of two responses, 18 cases out of 21 showed correlations with a probability of the null hypothesis lower than 0.05;
- in the case of more than two responses, all the 4 cases showed Cronbach Alphas higher than 0.70.

In order to improve reliability, we deleted the variables on which the level of agreement was not high enough, it was the case for the 6 variables which described the type of strategy of the buying firm and of the acquired firm. Bowman (1991) also found high inconsistencies between members of top management teams in their assessment of the current strategy of their company. For this reason we could not control for the firm's strategies as planned in the initial research design.

Measures

Two dimensions of formal control were measured: decision-making authority and control through procedures. In line with previous research on centralization a list of typical decisions concerning the acquired firm was elaborated based on items developed by Lorange and Vancil (1977), and Larsson (1989). The original list included 11 items. The managers were asked to respond on a five-point scale ranging from "your firm (the acquired) decides" (1) to "the buying firm decides" (5), with an intermediary position "consensus, both firms decide" (3). The responses on the 11 items were factor analyzed in order to find consistent orthogonal dimensions of control in acquisitions (principal component, varimax rotation). Three factors emerged (with an eigenvalue > 1) and explained 69.5 percent of the variance.

The first factor was mainly loaded by four items describing what we called "the control of operations" – administrative, marketing, R&D, production – (similar to Larsson's "operational control" 1989).

The second factor was mainly loaded by four items describing what we called "the control of resources" – investment decisions, reward systems, recruitment policies and social policies – (similar to what Golden 1992 called "centralization of operational activities").

The third factor was mainly loaded by three items describing what we called "strategic control" – goals, portfolio of businesses, business strategies – (similar to what Golden 1992 called "centralization of the strategic planning process").

The level of control through procedures was measured by an index combining three variables: the alignment on headquarters' strategic planning systems, financial and budget control systems, and accounting and analysis procedures (Cronbach Alpha = 0.79), measured on five-point scales. These variables correspond to "procedural integration" as defined by Shrivastava (1985) and "data management" as defined by Prahalad and Doz (1987).

Two dimensions of informal control were measured: informal communication and cooperation, and personal efforts from the managers of the buying firm. Most of the studies on integration processes suggest that the intensity of informal communication and personal behaviour is at the core of socialization processes (Edstrom and Galbraith, 1977; Shrivastava, 1985; Bartlett and Ghoshal, 1989; Buono and Bowditch, 1989; Gupta and Govindarajan, 1991; Haspeslagh and Jemison, 1991). The intensity of informal communication was measured by a set of three variables describing informal behaviours implemented by the buying firm, in the field of communication between individuals and groups. The three items were measured on five-point scales and combined into an index "informal communication and cooperation" (Cronbach Alpha = 0.80). A last variable measured the personal efforts of the managers from the buying company "beyond what is normally expected", as perceived by the managers at the acquired firm (five-point scale). It captured the informal personal behaviour of people at the interface, which seems to influence the integration process in M&As (Buono and Bowditch, 1989). Informal control is sometimes approached by measuring the rotation of managers between units or between headquarters and subsidiaries (Edstrom and Galbraith, 1977). We did not use this measure because, in the case of acquisitions the transfer of managers from the buying firm to the acquired firm may also be interpreted as formal control by taking power (Buono and Bowditch, 1989; Haspeslagh and Jemison, 1991).

The performance of the acquired firms was measured by two dimensions: improvements in attitudinal performance, and improvements in economic performance. The acquired firms' performance was assessed by asking the managers of the acquired firm to report their perceptions as to the performance of their firm "since, and because of, the merger", the items were constructed to elicit responses on five-point scales, ranging from "greatly deteriorated" (1) to "greatly improved" (5). Three items captured the economic performance – earnings, sales, and market share (Cronbach Alpha = 0.72); three items captured the attitudinal performance – "the attitude towards the job", "enthusiasm", and "willingness to help others" (Cronbach Alpha = 0.85). We used self-reported performance measures, rather than objective accounting and/or market-based measures in assessing post merger performance because secondary data about acquired businesses is rarely available. Fortunately, there is evidence supporting the general reliability of self-reported performance measure (see, for example, Dess and Robinson, 1984; Venkatraman and Ramanujam, 986).

The measurement of the six other variables that we controlled for is briefly presented in the Appendix – relative size, prior performance, level of environmental uncertainty, level of shared resources, level of local resources, and elapsed time since the acquisition.

The core businesses of the firms in our sample spanned twenty of the possible twenty-five, 2-digit SIC industries, with no one 2-digit industry representing more than 11 percent of the sample. As such, the study covered a wide variety of industries and our sample is not likely to reflect an industry bias. The pairs of acquiring/acquired firms included companies involved in the same industry (57 cases), and companies from different industries (18 cases). The answers concerning the level of shared resources between the merging firms (an important variable to control for) gave an average of 2.44 and a standard deviation of 0.73. Considering the measurement on a five-point scale from "total independence" (1) to "total combination" (5) (see the Appendix for further details), these figures show the variety of degrees of physical integration in the sample. The sample consists of twelve acquisitions performed in 1987, twenty-eight performed in 1988, and thirty-five in 1989.

DATA ANALYSIS

The analysis of data was done on the SPSS PC + software. The tests of differences in control mechanisms between (i) the French and the American, and (ii) the American and the British were done by stepwise discriminant analysis (Wilk's lambda); the country of the buyer was the dependent variable, six independent variables measured control mechanisms and six were covariates. Considering the high number of variables and the limited theoretical basis of our research we used a stepwise procedure in order to select variables, recognizing that stepwise procedures are controversial as they may cause data to be overfitted. The test of the relationships between (i) attitudinal performance, and (ii) economic performance and control mechanisms was done by multiple regressions (method enter) including the six independent variables measuring control and the six covariates, on the whole sample of seventy-five firms. We did not find collinearity between the independent variables (all coefficients < 0.50, all but three coefficients < 0.30).

RESULTS AND DISCUSSION

Table 1 contains the results that compare the responses from the sample of British companies acquired by French firms and the sample of British companies acquired by US firms. The model's overall chi square statistic of 23.13 is significant at the 0.001 level, suggesting that differences between the two home countries of the buyers are being explained by the discriminant function. Three variables measuring control mechanisms appear to be important discriminators even after accounting for extraneous influences.

Specifically, the French acquiring firms relied more on formal control of strategy and formal control of operations than the American firms, at least as perceived by the respondents from the respective acquired firms.

Table 1 Differences between French and American buyers in the United Kingdom

Variables	Step entered	Coefficient	Wilk's lambda
Elapsed time	1	−0.55	0.85**
Environmental uncertainty	2	0.57	0.76**
Control of resources	3		0.71**
Strategic control	4	0.69	0.68**
Shared resources	5	−1.05	0.66**
Control of operations	6	0.97	0.57**
Control of resources (removed)	7		0.57***
Cooperation/communication	8	−0.29	0.55***

Model's chi square = 23.13; p = 0.0008***

Canonical discriminant function evaluated at group means	
Group	No. of cases
French buy British: 0.80	24
Americans buy British: −0.96	20

Note: Levels of significance: * p = < 0.05; ** p = 0.01; *** p = < 0.001.

This finding is consistent with Hypothesis 1a: the French exercise higher formal control by centralization, with the exception of formal control over human resources and financial resources.

The factor measuring the level of control of resources entered in the discriminant function at Step 3 and then was removed at Step 7 so, after controlling for other variables, the difference between the French and the American firms did not prove to be significant (Hypothesis 1b is not supported). However the Americans seem to exercise higher control over resources than the French, in the predicted direction (French average: −0.47, SD: 0.83; American average: 0.14, SD: 1.05).

Hypothesis 1c is not supported: the Americans do not exercise more formal control by procedures than the French. Although the averages are in the expected direction, the differences are not significant, at least as perceived by British managers at the acquired firm.

The American acquiring firms relied more on informal communication and cooperation (teamwork) than the French. This finding supports Hypothesis d.

Taken together, these results show that French and American buyers do differ in some of the control mechanisms they exercise over acquired firms in line with their respective national administrative heritage.

Table 2 contains the results that compare the responses from the sample of French companies acquired by British firms and the sample of French companies acquired by US firms. The model's overall chi square statistic of 11.65 is significant at the 0.01 level, suggesting differences between the two home countries of the buyers are being explained by the discriminant function. Two variables measuring control mechanisms appear to be important discriminators, even after accounting for extraneous influences.

Specifically, the US acquiring firms relied more on formal control by procedures than the British, at least as perceived by the respondents from the respective acquired firms. This finding supports Hypothesis 2b.

On the other hand, Hypothesis 2a is not supported: the Americans do not seem to exercise more formal control of operations (marketing and manufacturing) than the

Table 2 Differences between British and American buyers in France

Variables	Step entered	Coefficient	Wilk's lambda
Personal efforts from the buyer	1	0.98	0.76*
Prior performance	2	−0.55	0.63**
Control by procedures	3	0.41	0.60*

Model's chi square = 11.65; p = 0.009**

Canonical discriminant function evaluated at group means

Group	No. of cases
British buy French: −0.62	16
Americans buy French: −1.00	10

Note: Levels of significance: * p = < 0.05; ** p = 0.01; *** p = < 0.001.

British. The difference found by Gates and Egelhoff (1986), who studied headquarters-subsidiaries relationships, is not confirmed in the case of acquisitions. Also the geographical distance between the countries of the merging firms (over the Atlantic vs over the Channel) may moderate the level of control of operations.

Another dimension of control seems to discriminate between the Americans and the British: the level of personal efforts of the managers at the buying firm to ensure that the merger is successful. At least as perceived by the French managers at the acquired firm, American managers become more personally involved than the British. The relationship between this aspect of informal control and the country of the acquired firm was not hypothesized, and, as far as we know, it was not commented upon in previous research comparing the North American culture with that of the British. This variable did not discriminate between the French and the Americans in the first analysis, so it seems that this "hands off" attitude from the managers of the buying firm is typically British.

Taken together, these results show that British and American buyers do differ in some of the control mechanisms they exercise over acquired firms, some of these practices being in line with their respective administrative heritage.

Considering the two comparisons and the four sub-samples, we conclude that, as far as international acquisitions are concerned, there are some national biases in the way buyers exercise both formal and informal control over the foreign acquired firms. Then, towards more prescriptive findings the question is: "do these differences in control mechanisms matter?" or, in terms of this research, are there any relationships between control mechanisms and the performance (attitudinal and economic) of the acquired firms? Table 3 presents the results of the two multiple regression models explaining the improvements in attitudinal performance and in economic performance.

The twelve variables of the model explain 44 percent of the variance of the attitudinal performance at the acquired firm (F = 3.79 significant at the 0.001 level). More precisely three variables showed significant multiple correlation coefficients (Betas). The "health" of the acquired firm prior to the merger is negatively correlated to the improvements in attitudinal performance. The lower the prior performance of the acquired firm, the higher the improvements in attitudes. More interestingly both informal communication and cooperation (teamwork), and informal personal efforts from the managers of the buying firm are positively correlated with the improvements in attitudinal performance of the acquired firm. This result is not surprising; it

Table 3 Control mechanisms and performance of the acquired firm in international acquisitions

Dependent variable:	Attitudinal performance	Economic performance
Independent variables:	*Betas*	*Betas*
Shared resources and transfers	0.12	0.25+
– Control of resources	−0.03	−0.12
Environmental uncertainty	−0.12	−0.06
Local resources/strategic capabilities	0.07	−0.09
– Personal efforts from the buyer	0.24*	0.33*
Elapsed time since the acquisition	−0.02	0.37**
Relative size	−0.01	−0.01
– Informal communication/cooperation	0.34**	−0.14
– Control of strategy	−0.18	−0.12
– Control through procedures	−0.02	0.16
Prior performance of the acquired firm	−0.39**	0.03
– Control of operations	−0.17	−0.30*
$R^2 =$	0.44	0.30
Adj. $R^2 =$	0.33	0.15
$F =$	3.79***	2.00*

Note: Levels of significance: * $p = <0.05$; ** $p = 0.01$; *** $p = <0.001$.

confirms the view that socialization is a key factor in reducing the risks of conflicts and demotivation (Buono and Bowditch, 1989; Haspeslagh and Jemison, 1991).

The twelve variables of the model explain 30 percent of the variance of the economic performance of the acquired firm ($F = 2.00$ significant at the 0.05 level). Two extraneous variables are positively correlated with the improvements in economic performance: the elapsed time since the acquisition and the level of shared resources and transfers. The implementation of synergies between the merging firms contributes to economic performance (cf. Haspeslagh and Jemison, 1991), and there seems to be a delay before economic performance improves at the acquired firm. More interestingly, two variables measuring control mechanisms are correlated with the improvements in economic performance. The higher the informal personal efforts of the managers of the buying firm, the higher the economic performance of the acquired firm. It seems that the positive effects of such behaviour on the attitudes of the managers of the acquired firm indirectly affects economic performance. Finally, the level of control of operations exercised by the buyer over the acquired firm is negatively correlated with economic performance, and as far as international acquisitions are concerned (and keeping other extraneous variables constant) operational decisions should not be centralized.

Taken together, these results show that some control mechanisms (formal and informal) are related to the improvements of the performance of the acquired firms (attitudinal, economic or both). Hypothesis 3, formulated in the null form, is not supported. The message for practitioners would be the following: the buying firms should develop informal control and coordination, and reduce formal control of operational decisions in order to make their foreign acquisitions more successful (at least from the perspective of the acquired firm). These findings are consistent with the arguments developed by Bartlett and Ghoshal (1989) in the "transnational solution": groups are managed as "integrated networks" (the relative decentralization of operational decisions), and coordinated through informal processes of socialization which are the "physiology" and the "psychology" of the transnational organization.

However, such universal conclusions could be moderated. The relationship between the performance of the acquired firm and the control mechanisms exercised by the buying firm may well be mediated by the preferred modes of control in the country of the acquired firm. Our sample was too small to be split between two sub-samples (British acquired firms and French acquired firms) and to allow multiple regressions in each so as to test such a moderating effect. Also, buyers may well demonstrate superior skills in implementing the forms of control with which they are most familiar. Consequently the relationship between success and control mechanisms may be moderated by both the national administrative heritage of the acquired firm and the national administrative heritage of the buyer.

Nevertheless, the confrontation between these results and the findings of the first part of our study is striking. Differences were found between French and US buying firms in the level of operational control and in the level of the informal communication that they develop in foreign acquisitions. Differences were found between British and US buying firms in the level of personal involvement. The three variables above appear to be related to the performance of the acquired firm after the acquisition. Taken together, these results show how important the issue of administrative rigidity vs flexibility is in the integration process following international acquisitions.

The first and main part of this research provided the first empirical test of the influences of the home country administrative heritage on the control mechanisms exercised by buying firms in international acquisitions. The knowledge of such influences should help anticipate some of the problems of incompatibility between merging organizations from different national cultures.

APPENDIX: MEASUREMENT OF EXTRANEOUS VARIABLES

- The relative size of the buying firm compared to the acquired firm was measured by six-point scale variable, from "smaller" to "more than 10 times the size".
- The prior performance ("health") of the acquired firm prior to the merger was measured by a composite of two five-point scale variables: growth and financial situation (Cronbach Alpha = 0.60).
- The level of environmental uncertainty was measured by a five-point scale variable from "market conditions very predictable" to "market conditions very unpredictable".
- The level of shared resources and transfers of capabilities between the buying firm and the acquired firm was measured by a composite of seven five-point scale variables from "total independence" to "total combination", in the following domains of the value chain: production, supply sources, research and development, distribution, sales and after sales services, marketing, and personnel management (Cronbach Alpha = 0.83).
- The level of local resources/strategic capabilities of the acquired firm was measured by a composite of three five-point scale variables: the brand image, the access to a superior technological know-how, and the access to skilled workforce (Cronbach Alpha = 0.58).
- The elapsed time since the acquisition was measured by the number of years since the acquisition. The study took place in Spring 1991 and the more recent mergers

of the sample were achieved in 1989, so as to avoid the turbulent transitory period which may follow the acquisition and to allow measures of post-acquisition performance.

- The industry: responses came from 20 industries (among the 25 SIC codes used in *Acquisitions Monthly*). The small number of cases in each industry did not allow directly controlling for the industry by splitting the sample. We assume that controlling for shared resources and transfers between the buyer and the acquired firm indirectly controls for the industry (i.e. the balance between forces of global integration and forces of local adaptation).

NOTE

1 The rest were domestic acquisitions: British firms buying British firms and French firms buying French firms.

REFERENCES

Bartlett, Christopher A., and Sumantra Ghoshal (1986) "Tap your subsidiaries for global reach". *Harvard Business Review* (Nov.–Dec.): 87–94.

Bartlett, Christopher A., and Sumantra Ghoshal (1989) *Managing Across Borders, the Transnational Solution*. Boston: Harvard Business School Press.

Bowman, Cliff (1991) *Managerial Perceptions of Porter's Generic Strategies*. Cranfield, UK: Cranfield School of Management, SWP 53/91.

Buono, Anthony F., and James L. Bowditch (1989) *The Human Side of Mergers and Acquisitions: Managing Collisions Between People and Organizations*. San Francisco: Jossey Bass.

Burns, Tom, and Georges M. Stalker (1961) The Management of Innovation. London: Tavistock.

Chandler, Alfred D. (1986) "The evolution of modern global competition" in *Competition in Global Industries*. M. E. Porter (ed.), 405–448. Boston: Harvard Business School Press.

Chatterjee, Sayan, Michael H. Lubatkin, David M. Schweiger, and Yaakov Weber (1992) "Cultural differences and shareholder value in related mergers: linking equity and human capital". *Strategic Management Journal* 13: 319–334.

Child, John (1972) "Organization structure and strategies of control: a replication of the Aston study". *Administrative Science Quarterly* 17: 163–177.

Child, John (1973) "Strategies of control and organizational behaviour". *Administrative Science Quarterly* 18: 1–17.

Child, John (1981) "Culture, contingency and capitalism in the cross-national study of organizations" in *Research in Organizational Behavior*, Vol. 3. B. M. Staw and L. L. Cummings (eds.), 303–356. Greenwich, CT. JAI Press.

Child, John (1990) *The Management of Equity Joint Ventures in China*. Beijing: China-EC Management Institute.

Dess, Gregory C., and Richard B. Robinson (1984) "Measuring organizational performance in the absence of objective measures: the case of the privately held firm and conglomerate business unit". *Strategic Management Journal* 5: 265–273.

D'Iribarne, Philippe (1989) *La Logique de L'honneur, Gestion des Entreprises et Traditions Nationales*. Paris: Editions du Seuil.

Dore, Ronald P. (1973) *British Factory–Japanese Factory*. Berkeley: University of California Press.

Edstrom, Anders, and Jay R. Galbraith (1977) "Transfer of managers as a coordination and control strategy in multinational organizations". *Administrative Science Quarterly* 22: 248–263.

Egelhoff, William G. (1988) *Organizing the Multinational Enterprise*: An Information-processing Perspective. Cambridge, MA: Ballinger.

Finkelstein, Sydney (1992) "Power in top management teams: dimensions, measurement, and validation". *Academy of Management Journal* 35/3: 505–538.

Garnier, G. (1982) "Context and decision making autonomy in the foreign affiliates of US multinational corporations". *Academy of Management Journal* 25: 893–908.

Gates, Stephen R., and William G. Egelhoff (1986) "Centralization in parent headquarters-subsidiary relationships". *Journal of International Business Studies* 17/2: 71–92.

Ghoshal, Sumantra, and Nitin Nohria (1989) "Internal differentiation within multinational corporations". *Strategic Management Journal* 10: 323–337.

Ghoshal, Sumantra, and Philippe C. Haspeslagh (1990) "The acquisition and integration of Zanussi by Electrolux: a case study". *European Management Journal* 8/4: 414–433.

Golden, Brian R. (1992) "SBU strategy and performance: the moderating effects of the corporate-SBU relationship". *Strategic Management Journal* 13: 145–158.

Guion, R. M. (1973) "A note on organizational climate". *Organizational Behavior and Human Performance* 9: 120–125.

Gupta, Amil K., and Vijay Govindarajan (1991) "Knowledge flows and the structure of control within multinational corporations". *Academy of Management Review* 16/4: 768–792.

Haire, Mason, Edwin F. Ghiselli, and Lyman W. Porter (1966) *Managerial Thinking: An International Study.* New York: Wiley.

Haspeslagh, Philippe C., and David B. Jemison (1991) *Managing Acquisitions, Creating Value Through Corporate Renewal.* New York: The Free Press.

Hedlund, Gunnar (1981) "Autonomy of subsidiaries and formalization of headquarters sub-sidiary relationships in multinational corporations" in *The Management of Headquarters–Subsidiary Relationships in Multinational Corporations.* L. Otterbeck (ed.), 25–78. New York: St Martin's Press.

Hickson, David J., C. R. Hinings, C. McMillan, and J. P. Schwitter (1974) "The culture-free context of organization structure". *Sociology* 8: 59–80.

Hofstede, Geert (1980) *Culture's Consequences: International Differences in Work-related Values.* Beverly Hills: Sage.

Hofstede, Geert (1993) "Cultural constraints in management theories". *Academy of Management Executive* 7/1: 81–94.

Hunt, John W. (1990) "Changing pattern of acquisition behaviour in takeovers and the consequences for acquisition processes". *Strategic Management Journal* 11: 69–77.

James, L. R., and A. P. Jones (1974) "Organizational climate: a review of theory and research". *Psychological Bulletin* 81: 1096–1112.

Kester, W. Carl (1991) *Japanese Takeovers, the Global Contest for Corporate Control.* Boston: Harvard Business School Press.

Kogut, Bruce (1991) "Country capabilities and the permeability of borders". *Strategic Management Journal* 12 (Special Issue): 33–48.

Larsson, Rikard (1989) *Organizational Integration of Mergers and Acquisitions.* Lund SWE: Lund University Press.

Laurent, Andre (1983) "The cultural diversity of Western conceptions of management". *International Studies of Management and Organization* 13/1–2: 75–96.

Laurent, Andre (1986) "The cross-cultural puzzle of international human resource management". *Human Resource Management* 25/1: 91–102.

Lawrence, Paul R., and Jay W. Lorsch (1967) *Organization and Environment.* Boston: Harvard Business School, Division of Research.

Levitt, Theodore (1983) "The globalization of markets". *Harvard Business Review* (May–June): 92–102.

Lorange, Peter, and Richard F. Vancil (1977) *Strategic Planning Systems.* Englewood Cliffs, NJ: Prentice Hall.

Oppenheim, A. N. (1966) *Questionnaire Design and Attitude Measurement.* New York: Basic Books.

Ouchi, William G. (1980) "Markets, bureaucracies and clans". *Administrative Science Quarterly* 25: 129–141.

Pascale, Richard T., and M. A. Maguire (1980) "Comparison of selected work factors in Japan and the United States". *Human Relations* 33: 433–455.

Perlmutter, Howard (1969) "The tortuous evolution of the multinational corporation". *Columbia Journal of World Business* 4: 9–8.

Prahalad, C. K., and Yves L. Doz (1987) *The Multinational Mission, Balancing Local Demand and Global Vision.* New York: The Free Press.

Redding, S. G., and David S. Pugh (1986) "The formal and the informal: Japanese and Chinese organization structures" in *The Enterprise and Management in East Asia.* S. R. Clegg, D. C. Dunphy and S. G. Redding (eds) 153–167. Centre for Asian Studies, University of Hong Kong.

Rohlen, Thomas P. (1974) *For harmony and strength: Japanese White Collar Organization in Anthropo-logical Perspective.* Berkeley: University of California Press.

Schneider, B. (1975) "Organizational climates: an essay". *Personnel Psychology* 28: 447–479.

Schneider, Suzan C. and Arnoud de Meyer (1991) "Interpreting and responding to strategic issues: the impact of national culture". *Strategic Management Journal* 12: 307–320.

Schweiger, David M., and James P. Walsh (1990) "Mergers and acquisitions: an interdisciplinary view" in *Research in Personal and Human Resources Management*. K. Rowlands and G. Ferris (eds), 41–107. Greenwich, CT: JAI Press.

Shrivastava, Paul (1985) "Postmerger integration". *Journal of Business Strategy* 7/1: 65–76.

Smith, Peter B. (1992) "Organizational behaviour and national cultures". *British Journal of Management* 3: 39–51.

Smith, Peter B., M. F. Peterson, J. Misumi, and M. H. Bond (1992) "A cross-cultural test of the Japanese PM leadership theory". *Applied Psychology: An International Review* 41/1: 5–19.

Venkatraman, N., and V. Ramanujam (1986) "Measurement of business performance in strategy research: a comparison of approaches". *Academy of Management Review* 11: 801–814.

Very, Philippe, Roland Calori, and Michael Lubatkin (1993) "Linking organizational and cross cultural differences in recent European mergers". *Advances in Strategic Management*, Vol. 9. Greenwich, CT: JAI Press.

Walter, G. A. (1985) "Culture collisions in mergers and acquisitions" in *Organizational Culture*. P. J. Frost, L. F. Moore, M. R. Louis and C. C. Lundberg (eds), 301–314. Beverly Hills: Sage.

Calori, R., Lubatkin, M. and Very, P. (1994) "Control mechanisms in cross-border acquisitions". *Organisation Studies*, 15(3), 361–379. Reprinted with permission.

15 Cross-border mergers and acquisitions: the undervaluation hypothesis

Pedro Gonzalez, Geraldo M. Vasconcellos and Richard J. Kish

INTRODUCTION

The growing web of interdependencies in the global economy has developed new relationships between economic agents of different countries. In the last decade, an interesting phenomenon surfaced in the international market for corporate control. The number of foreign firms acquiring US firms, in aggregate terms, has been larger than the number of US firms taking over foreign companies. For instance, during the 1981–1990 period the average number of transactions per year involving a foreign bidder for a US company was 218 and the yearly average dollar amount for the same period was \$23.4 billion. We can contrast with this the average number of transactions and dollar amounts involving US bidders for a foreign company which were 147 and \$8.5 billion respectively. Thus, as Table 1 shows, US companies have played mainly a target role in the cross-border market for corporate control. The exact motivations for observing US firms as targets outnumbering bidders are many

Table 1 Cross-border merger and acquisition activity involving US companies

| Year | US target | | US bidder | |
	Transactions	Billions (\$)	Transactions	Billions (\$)
1981	243	18.1	10	11.1
1982	153	5.1	121	0.8
1983	125	5.9	146	2.5
1984	151	15.5	147	2.6
1985	197	10.9	175	1.4
1986	264	24.5	180	5.2
1987	220	40.4	142	11.0
1988	307	55.5	151	14.5
1989	285	40.4	220	22.2
1990	266	33.0	266	18.0
Average	218	23.4	147	8.5

Source: *Mergerstat Review*.

(e.g., macroeconomic factors, firm-specific financial characteristics, corporate strategic moves, political motives, and/or the possibility of a "good buy"). The focus of our study is on this final factor, management's quest for undervalued assets.

International mergers and acquisitions research focuses primarily on wealth transfers. For instance, Doukas and Travlos (1988), besides offering an excellent review of this literature, contrasts the returns to shareholders from US and non-US based firms expanding into foreign markets. Conn and Connell (1990) also include an extensive literature review of merger and acquisitions within their empirical study of wealth transfers between US and British firms expansion into each other's markets. Outside of the wealth transfer research, empirical international merger and acquisition research is lagging behind its domestic (e.g., US) counterpart which is rich in studies from the perspective of both sides of the negotiation table. In this tradition, Harris and Ravenscraft's (1991) linkage of the undervaluation, management inefficiency, and market imperfections hypotheses provides the theoretical foundation for our empirical testing. Thus, our contribution to the merger literature is the empirical validation of undervaluation as one of the key financial motivations underlying acquisitions in the international arena.

Under our hypotheses, we postulate that the existence of product and service market imperfections that cause frictions in the global market (such as transaction costs and costs associated with barriers to entry) contributes to favor the acquisition of a company already operating. This is because the amount paid for an existing company, as compared to the replacement cost of its assets, more than compensates for the costs that could have been incurred had the foreign firm started with brand new facilities. Thus, in order to minimize the acquisition costs, foreign firms should follow the same pattern of analysis as their domestic counterparts and search for undervalued and/or mismanaged companies as targets for their acquisitions.[1] The results of our undervaluation hypotheses testing, within the Tobin's q framework utilized by Servaes (1991) for the study of domestic mergers, support this viewpoint.[2] To our knowledge, there are no other studies on cross-border merger and acquisitions that validate the theoretical undervaluation hypothesis within an international setting.

Other domestic M&A studies, such as Palepu (1986) and Dietrich and Sorensen (1984), provide the foundation for our use of the logit methodology for predicting acquisition targets. Palepu (1986) also stresses the need to take into account the fact that the targets and bidders are oversampled and therefore the Maximum Likelihood estimators might be biased. We attempt to compensate for this problem by using a choice-based sample based on a Weighted Maximum Likelihood Estimator (hereafter WMLE) as explained in Appendix II and outlined by Manski and McFadden (1981).

Consistent with previous studies applied to the domestic market for corporate control (see for example Chappel and Cheng, 1984), we hypothesize that undervalued US companies are more likely to be targets of foreign companies. Thus, our first hypothesis, **Undervaluation-Target Hypothesis**, is described as:

    H1: The likelihood of a US firm becoming a target increases when the firm is perceived as being undervalued.

Within the empirical analysis, we proxy this undervaluation with Tobin's q (i.e., the ratio of market value to replacement cost of assets of the US firm), which is a continuation of the approach pioneered by Tobin (1969). Since then many other researchers have used Tobin's q as both a theoretical and an empirical tool to establish a relationship between the product or service markets and the capital markets. For instance, Chirinko (1987) concludes that the theoretical usefulness of Tobin's q stems from the fact that it incorporates forward-looking behavior, reflects optimal choices, and contains estimated coefficients that are readily identified.

Under this hypothesized relationship, investment (i.e. the addition to the stock of capital) is determined by the marginal "q", defined as the ratio of the discounted future revenues from an additional unit of capital to its net-of-tax purchase price. However, due to difficulties of empirically valuing a marginal "q", our study relies on an average "q." This proxy is supported by Tobin and Brainard (1977), who emphasized that the forces of continuity in the economy are strong and that we can expect that the same factors which raise or lower "q" on the margin will likewise raise or lower "q" on the average.

Assuming that the takeover decision is motivated by the same stimuli that encourage firms to grow internally, Chappell and Cheng (1984) were among the first to study the "q" ratio as a predictor of takeover targets. They found that the high abnormal returns experienced by acquirers before the merger are consistent with a high "q" ratio, signaling to the companies that it is time to expand. Nevertheless, they concluded that the effect of the "q" ratio is not always significant and that these effects vary. Holly and Longbottom (1988), using the same framework followed by Chappell and Cheng (1984), analyzed UK firms and found that if the average "q" ratio is more than one, the takeover (i.e., investment) is desirable. If it is less than one, it is not.

Lang, Stulz and Walking (1989) studied tender offers and their relationship to Tobin's q. Under the assumption that the financial market rewards well-managed firms, Lang et. el. interpret a "q" greater than one as a measure of good management. Conversely, a ratio less than one is viewed as evidence of poor management. They conclude that, to the extent that Tobin's q measures managerial performance, the results of their research may be interpreted as follows: (a) Well-managed bidders benefit substantially from tender offers, but more so when they take over poorly managed targets; (b) Well-managed targets benefit less from tender offers than poorly managed targets; (c) The total takeover gain is highest for tender offers by well managed bidders which acquire poorly managed targets.[3] This is consistent with Jensen's (1988) contention that highly valued firms are likely to be bidders in the market for corporate control. Therefore, we test the following hypothesis, which we called the **Undervaluation-Bidder Hypothesis:**

> **H2**: The likelihood of a foreign firm bidding for a US company increases when the firm is perceived as being overvalued.

We proxy this strength component by using the ratio of market value to replacement cost of the overseas company, i.e., we imply that the ratio would be greater than one. Since this hypothesis expands the research into the international marketplace, the role of the exchange rate must be accounted for. Several alternative (and not mutually exclusive) explanations for the importance attributed to the exchange rate have been offered in previous studies. For example, Vasconcellos, Madura, and Kish (1990) and Vasconcellos and Kish (1993), examining the difference between the number of US acquisitions of foreign companies and the number of foreign acquisitions of US firms, found that the exchange rate could affect the timing of the acquisition more than the acquisition decision itself. In order to control for exchange rate variations, we follow the approach of Harris and Ravenscraft (1991) and proxy exchange rate effects with the quotient of the exchange rate differences (current exchange rate less the three-year moving average) and the three-year moving average exchange rate.

Prior studies have also documented the gains made from taking over an under-valued company.[4] This undervaluation could be observed in a company whose stock price does not reflect the replacement cost of the company's assets or, in a related fashion, it could be due to inefficient management not operating the company to its true potential. Therefore as a complement to our set of undervaluation hypotheses, we also tested the **Management Inefficiency Hypothesis**. Lang et. al. (1989) have argued that undervalued companies (those with Tobin's $q < 1$) are an indication of management inefficiency. This interpretation is based on the premise that management fails to use the resources of the company up to their full potential. Thus, our Management Inefficiency Hypothesis can be stated as:

> **H3**: The more inefficient a firm's management, the greater the probability of the firm becoming a target.

Examples of variables that have been used before (in addition to the Tobin's q) to gauge management efficiency are the return on equity and sales growth. If management is inefficient, then we might expect both variables to be negatively related with the probability of an acquisition.

THE DATA

The compilation of the data started by identifying US firms that have been acquired by foreign companies during the 1981–1990 period. This information was gathered from two sources: *Mergers and Acquisitions* and *Mergerstat Review*. At the same time, the name and country of origin of the foreign bidder were also gathered. Relevant information for each target was extracted from COMPUSTAT (Research and Industrial Files). Information regarding the foreign bidders were obtained from COMPUSTAT global vantage, an international data base compiled by Standard and Poor's.

Moody's Industrial Manuals were used to obtain the information on yields (bonds and preferred stock) in the United States. Information on macroeconomic aggregates was gathered from the *Survey of Current Business*. The sources for the relevant data on yields and macroeconomic aggregates of foreign countries included the following publications: the *Monthly Bulletin of Statistics* published by the United Nations, *International Financial Statistics* prepared by the International Monetary Fund, and *Financial Statistics* issued by the Statistical Office of the European Communities.

In order to include a firm in our sample, the following criteria had to be met: the merger or acquisition took place in the 1981–1990 period; the merger or acquisition transaction was reported by *Mergers and Acquisitions*; and the necessary company data for testing the hypotheses of interest was available from COMPUSTAT. A total of 242 US companies that were acquired by foreign companies met the necessary requirements to be included in the sample. A total of 216 US bidders meeting the same set of requirements were also included in the sample. In the case of foreign bidders for US firms, a total of 76 companies were sampled.

In order to test the Undervaluation-Target and Management Inefficiency Hypotheses pertaining to US companies, a control sample of 2000 companies was used. The targets and bidders were classified by their SIC industrial code. Within each SIC code, companies in the same sub-sector were ordered alphabetically. Each company was then matched with a randomly selected firm from within the control group, using SIC codes up to a 4 digit level. A total of 700 foreign companies formed the control sample for testing of the Undervaluation-Bidder Hypothesis. Matching within this sector was also controlled by the country of origin of the bidder.[5]

The incidence of US companies as targets was observed throughout the period of analysis. The US industrial sector most actively involved in the international cross-border merger and acquisition activity was Retail, with 9% of the targets. Other significant sectors included Conglomerates (*Mergerstat* defines a conglomerate as a company diversified in 3 or more areas) accounting for 6% of the US companies acquired by foreign companies, Wholesale/ Distribution and Oil/Gas both with 5.6%, and Drugs/Medical Supplies with 5%.

In the case of US companies bidding for foreign companies, 6.5% were from Conglomerates and Instruments/Photographic Equipment. The other leading sectors were Aerospace/Aircraft, Industrial/Farm Equipment, Insurance, and Office Equipment/Computer Hardware (5.5% each). From the 76 foreign bidders sampled, 32% were Conglomerates, 12% were classified as Oil/Gas, and 8% were from both the Banking/Finance and Retail sectors. Although both the US target firms and the US bidders range across a number of similar industries, we do not observe the same proportions. The foreign bidders cover a more limited range of industries than their American counterparts. Table 2 shows a summary of successful foreign bidders, desegregated by country of origin. Companies from Great Britain were the most active bidders for US companies over the period 1982 through 1990 (53%). The second most active country was Japan with 17% of the companies involved as buyers of American enterprises.

In order to test the hypotheses using the ratio of market value to replacement cost of assets (Tobin's q ratio), we employed the proxy used by Lindenberg and Ross (1981) and by Smirlock, Gilligan and Marshall (1984). We define the market value of a company as the sum of the market value of common stock, the market value of the preferred stock, and the market value of the debt. The market value of the common stock is the product of the year-end price times the number of outstanding shares at the end of the year prior to the acquisition.[6] The preferred stock was assumed to be a perpetuity valued at the average yield reported by Moody's for the year preceding the acquisition.[7]

Due to the difficulty of readily observing the market value of the components of debt, we follow the proxy methodology employed by Smirlock et al. (1984) and

Table 2 Foreign bidders by country of origin

Country	1982	1983	1984	1985	1986	1987	1988	1989	1990	Total
UK	2	2	4	6	4	10	4	3	5	40
Japan	1	1	2	0	0	1	2	3	3	13
Canada	0	0	2	0	1	1	2	0	1	7
France	1	0	1	1	0	0	0	3	0	6
Germany	0	0	0	1	0	0	0	3	0	4
Australia	0	0	1	2	0	1	0	0	0	4
Netherlands	0	0	0	0	2	0	0	0	0	2
Total	4	3	10	10	7	13	8	12	9	76

Fabozzi (1990). Thus, the market value of the debt was computed by discounting the balances of the debt maturing in two, three, four, and five years, assuming that the debt was originally issued with a maturity of 20 years, using the Moody's Composite Average yield on industrial bonds for the year of the issue.[8] The use of the debt maturing in these periods is ad-hoc but the lack of a better approximation to the actual distribution of long-term debt and the availability of the data (i.e., COMPU-STAT reports these items) make this proxy a reasonable one. For the case of foreign countries, we could not obtain the distribution of the maturities of the long-term debt. Thus, we employed the book value of the long term debt. The probable impact of using the book value is to underestimate the market value of debt, making it easier to disprove the Undervaluation-Bidder Hypothesis.[9] Unlike the case of long-term debt, we assume that the information given in the financial statements regarding short-term debt reflects the market value of this debt. Deferred Taxes were subtracted from the value of the debt under the assumption that equity investors never expect to pay these non-interest bearing amounts.[10]

Given the significance and valuation problems for Property, Plant and Equipment, and Inventory, special computations were necessary for these items in order to calculate their replacement cost. In other words, in order to compute the replacement cost of assets we had to use a proxy for Property, Plant and Equipment and Inventory, as shown in Appendix I. All the other assets were assumed to have a market value similar to their book value.

METHODOLOGY

In order to test our hypotheses, we use a logit model whose parameters were estimated using the Weighted Maximum Likelihood Method (WMLM) under choice-based sampling. The logit model is defined as:[11]

$$p(i,t) = \frac{1}{[1 + e^{-\beta x(i,t)}]} \tag{1}$$

where, $p(i,t)$ is the probability that firm i will be acquired in period t, $\mathbf{x}(i,t)$ is the vector of measured attributes, and β is the vector of unknown parameters to be estimated.

Thus, the bias caused by the characteristics of the sampling procedure can be eliminated by modifying the simple Maximum Likelihood Estimator (MLE). In our analysis we use WMLE as computed by the econometrics package LIMDEP. This estimation procedure was complemented by performing paired t-tests (see Appendix II) on the different variables for the targets and non-targets and for the bidders and non-bidders.

RESULTS AND ANALYSIS

Our hypothesis testing is partitioned into three subsets: the Undervaluation-Target Hypothesis, the Undervaluation-Bidder Hypothesis, and Management Inefficiency Hypothesis.[12]

The Undervaluation-Target Hypothesis

The Undervaluation-Target Hypothesis states that the likelihood of a firm being a target increases when the firm is perceived as being undervalued, which we proxy by the ratio of the market value to replacement cost of its assets being less than one. Thus, the Undervaluation-Target Hypothesis can be expressed as:

H4: The ratio of market value to replacement cost (Q) of a US firm's assets has no affect on the likelihood of the firm becoming a target of foreign firms.

H5: The likelihood of a US firm becoming a target increases when the ratio of market value to replacement cost of its assets is less than one.

The Undervaluation-Target Hypothesis implies that there is an inverse relationship between the probability of a US company being acquired and the Tobin's q. Table 3 shows the results of the Logit model that has as the dependent variable acquisition ($Y=1$) or no acquisition ($Y=0$) and as the independent variable Tobin's q (Q). The coefficient for q is statistically significant and supports the inverse relationship between Tobin's q and the probability of a US company being acquired by a foreign firm. Thus, at least for the decade under analysis, the data provide support for the Undervaluation-Target Hypothesis.[13]

The Undervaluation-Bidder Hypothesis

The Undervaluation-Bidder Hypothesis states that the likelihood of a foreign firm bidding for a US company increases when the firm is perceived as being overvalued. Therefore, the relationship between the ratio of market value to replacement cost of

Table 3 Undervaluation-Target Hypothesis

H(0): The ratio of market value to replacement cost of a US firm's assets has no effect on the likelihood of a firm becoming a target of foreign firms.

$$Y = a + b\,Q$$

where:

$Y = 1$ (acquisition)
$\quad = 0$ (no acquisition)
$Q = $ Tobin's q

Variable	Coefficient	t-ratio
Constant	−1.51	−7.812[a]
Q	−1.63	−8.434[a]

Likelihood ratio index:	0.72[b]
Chi-squared:	75.249[c]
Significance level:	0.0000032

Notes
[a] Significant at a 0.05 level two-tailed test – supports the Undervaluation Target Hypothesis.
[b] The log likelihood ratio index is defined as $1 - ($log likelihood at convergence/log likelihood at zero). It plays the same role as the R^2 regression analysis, providing an indication of the model's explanatory power.
[c] Tests the hypothesis that all the parameters in the model are simultaneously equal to zero.

assets of foreign firms (QF) to the likelihood of these companies acquiring US companies is analyzed. Within the context of cross-border merger and acquisition activity, our Undervaluation-Bidder Hypothesis can be stated as:

H6: The ratio of market value to replacement cost of a foreign firm's assets (QF) does not affect the probability of this firm becoming a bidder for a US firm.

H7: There is a positive relationship between the likelihood of a foreign firm bidding for a US company and the ratio of market value to replacement cost of the foreign firm.

The independent variables in this case include Tobin's q of foreign bidders (QF) and a control variable for the exchange rate (EXRA). In this case, $Y=1$ if the foreign firm bid for a US company and $Y=0$ if the overseas company did not. In order to construct the exchange rate variable based on the home country of each buyer, we took the currency's three-year moving average exchange rate for the sample period 1981–1990 and subtracted the currency's exchange rate for the year of the takeover. The exchange rate variable (EXRA) was defined as this difference divided by the three-year moving average exchange rate. As a result, positive (negative) values will indicate the currency is strong (weak) relative to the US dollar.[14] For example, if the $/£ exchange rate was on average 2.0 for the sample period and the 1988 $/£ exchange rate was 1.5, then the exchange rate figure is −0.25 (i.e., (1.5 − 2) / 2).

The results show that there was a direct relation between the possibility of a foreign firm bidding for a US firm and the Tobin's q of the overseas firm. The coefficient of our "Tobin's q" (QF) variable is 1.93 and it is significant at a 5% level, using a two-tailed test. On the other hand, the exchange rate variable, EXRA,

Table 4 Undervaluation-Bidder Hypothesis

H(0): The ratio of market value to replacement cost of a foreign firm's assets has no effect on the probability of this firm becoming a bidder of a US firm.

$$Y = a + b_1 \ QF + b_2 \ EXRA$$

where:

Y	= 1 (acquisition)
	= 0 (no acquisition)
QF	= Tobin's q for foreign firm
EXRA	= Exchange rate variable

Variable	Coefficient	t-ratio
Constant	−1.632	−3.52[a]
Q	−1.932	−5.55[a]
EXRA	+0.380	+0.54

Likelihood ratio index:	0.38
Chi-squared:	38.03
Significance level:	0.000001387

Note
[a] Significant at a 0.05 level two-tailed test – supports the Under-valuation Bidder Hypothesis.

although with the expected sign (+), is not significantly different from zero. The model appears to explain well the relationship between the independent variables and the dependent variable, as shown by the Chi-Square test of the overall model.[15]

The Management Inefficiency Hypothesis

As a complement to the Undervaluation Hypotheses, we test the Management Inefficiency Hypothesis. Previous studies (see for example Lang et. al. 1989) argue that undervalued companies (those with Tobin's $q < 1$) are an indication of management inefficiency. This interpretation is based on the premise that management fails to use the resources of the company up to their full potential. Examples of variables that have been used before (in addition to the Tobin's q) to gauge management efficiency are the return on equity (ROE) and sales growth (GROWTH). If management is inefficient, then we might expect both variables to be negatively related with the probability of an acquisition. Thus, our Management Inefficiency Hypothesis, which tests whether more inefficient management increases the probability of that firm becoming a target, is stated for testing purposes as:

H8: The ratio Return on Equity (ROE) and the Growth (GROWTH) of a US firm has no impact on the probability of this firm becoming a target of a foreign acquirer.

H9: There exists an inverse relationship between the ratio Return on Equity and Growth and the probability of the US company becoming a target of foreign firm.

Therefore, we hypothesize that low ROE and/or GROWTH are manifestations of low quality management. Table 5 presents the results of a Logit model where both

Table 5 Management Inefficiency Hypothesis

H(0): Return on equity and growth of a US firm has no impact on the probability of this firm becoming a target of a foreign acquirer.

$$Y = a + b_1 \ ROE + b_2 \ GROWTH$$

where:

Y	= 1 (acquisition)	
	= 0 (no acquisition)	
ROE	= Return on equity	
GROWTH	= Sales growth	

Variable	Coefficient	t-ratio
Constant	+0.66	+2.28[a]
ROE	−3.07	−5.93[a]
GROWTH	−2.66	−5.33[a]
Likelihood ratio index:	0.50	
Chi-squared:	134.00	
Significance level:	0.0000031	

Note
[a] Significant at a 0.05 level two-tailed test – supports the Management Inefficiency Hypothesis.

variables (ROE and GROWTH) are employed as predictors of the probability of US companies becoming targets of foreign firms.

Both the ROE and GROWTH coefficients are negative and significant at a 5% level, implying that the probability that a US company will be taken over by a foreign firm is higher the more inefficient the management of the domestic company. Paired *t*-tests, not shown, are also significant at a 5% level, offering additional support. These results are consistent with the management inefficiency interpretation of the Tobin's *q*.

CONCLUSION

The increasing importance of foreign firms in the US market for corporate control motivated us to take a closer look at the financial characteristics of the companies involved in international mergers and acquisitions. The financial characteristics of a total of 533 foreign and US firms involved in cross-border mergers and acquisitions are analyzed.

This study empirically validates the Undervaluation Hypothesis within the international setting using a Logit analysis. The results support the existence of an inverse relationship between the probability of a US firm becoming a target of a foreign company and the Tobin's *q* ratio. In other words, undervalued US companies are more likely to be targets of foreign companies. This result is consistent with previous studies applied to the domestic market for corporate control (see for example Chappel and Cheng, 1984), but never tested empirically within the international merger and acquisition market.

It is also argued that undervalued companies are the result of a lack of managerial capabilities. Using a Tobin's *q* < 1 as a proxy for management inefficiency, we test this interpretation for the case of US targets. Our findings show that firms with low return on equity and low growth are more likely to be acquired by foreign companies.

Using the financial characteristics of 76 foreign bidders from 7 industrialized nations, we find that the exchange rate does not have a strong impact on the probability of acquisition of a US company when measured with the valuation of the firm. We observed a very strong dollar during the first half of the 1980s and a weaker dollar in the second half; however, the number of US companies acquired is on average the same. We also find that the foreign firms have a relatively high return on equity (ROE) when compared to the industry average. Since we employ ROE as a proxy for management efficiency, we may conclude that foreign companies with above average efficiency in their countries have a higher likelihood of acquiring US firms.

If we relate these findings to Lang's et al. (1989) conclusions from the domestic marketplace, then one should observe positive abnormal returns for foreign companies upon the announcement of the foreign firms taking over poorly managed US firms. A firm's overvaluation is proxied by a Tobin's *q* > 1. Recall that Lang et al. (1989) found positive abnormal returns when a firm with a Tobin's *q* > 1 (well-managed firm) acquired an undervalued company. If this is the case then this study extends Lang et al's (1989) conclusions to the takeover market across countries. We also found that the foreign acquirers and US targets belong to the same industrial sectors. This can be interpreted as foreign companies reducing acquisition costs by acquiring undervalued firms or, as previously said, as foreign firms trying to use their business know-how to enhance the efficiency of the US targets.

As pointed out within the introduction, there are many factors that influence a management's decision under both international and domestic mergers. Therefore, future research endeavors should not only isolate the impact of the various merger factors (e.g., industry characteristics, competitiveness, timing of capitalization, etc.), but also try to capture within a single model or a multi-staged model the total merger decision process. Of course, as with all research endeavors, the researcher has to overcome the data gathering problem, which in the international setting usually is more formidable.

APPENDIX I:
VALUING NET PROPERTY PLANT & EQUIPMENT AND INVENTORY

The replacement cost of **Net Property, Plant and Equipment** can vary over time due to price level changes, technological change, real economic depreciation, and investment in new plant. Following Lindenberg and Ross (1981) we compute the Replacement cost for Net Property, Plant and Equipment at time $t(\text{RNP}_t)$ as:

$$R\hat{N}P_t = R\hat{N}P_{t-1} \left[\frac{1 + \phi_t}{(1 + \delta_t)(1 + \theta_t)} \right] + I_t, \, t \geq 1 \tag{A1}$$

where RNP_{t-1} for the reporting period $t = 0$ is the same as the book value of the net plant in year 0. Year 0 is defined as the first year of a 10 year period before the acquisition. I_t represents the investment in new plant equipment, ϕ_t is the rate of growth of capital goods prices, δ_t is the rate of (real) depreciation, and θ_t is the rate of cost-reducing technical progress.

In order to obtain an estimate of the rate of growth of capital goods prices (ϕ_t), we also follow the methodology outlined by Lindenberg and Ross (1981) by using the GNP deflator for nonresidential fixed investment. The real depreciation rate (δ_t) was computed using equation (A2)

$$\delta_t = \frac{DEP_t}{HNP_{t-1}} \tag{A2}$$

where DEP_t is book depreciation and HNP_t is the historical value of net property, plant, and equipment. The rate of cost-reducing technical progress (θ_t) was computed by the ratio of the firm's annual growth of Research and Development Costs to Total Assets.

In the case of **Inventory**, its book value was adjusted according to the valuation method employed by the firm. Under LIFO (Last in-First out), ending inventory is valued at old prices. Thus, in inflationary times the book value of inventory will be underestimated. This adjustment gives more weight and accounts for large under-valuations of old inventory (first term) and smaller weight to recent increments (second term). It was assumed that this iterative computation begins at year 0 with the Replacement Value of Inventory (RINV_t) equal to the Historical (Book) Value of Inventory (HINV_t)

$$RINV_t = RINV_{t-1} * \frac{P_t}{P_{t-1}} + (HINV_t - HINV_{t-1}) * \frac{0.5 * (P_t + P_{t-1})}{P_{t-1}} \tag{A3}$$

where P_t equals the Inventory Price Index and the subscript is used to designate the year.

Adjustments are also undertaken for the other inventory methods. Under FIFO (First in-First out), inventories at the end of the year reflect current costs:

$$RINV_t = HINV_t \qquad\qquad\qquad (A4)$$

Under the AVERAGE COST METHOD, inventory is reported at time t at roughly an average of the prices at t–1 and t. In equation form, the Average Cost Method is:

$$RINV_t = HINV_t * \frac{2P_t}{(P_t + P_{t-1})} \qquad\qquad\qquad (A5)$$

Finally under the RETAIL COST METHOD, inventory quantities are priced at the expected retail prices. Since producers normally sell at wholesale it is necessary to do the following adjustment,

$$RINV_t = HINV_t * \frac{WPI}{RPI} \qquad\qquad\qquad (A6)$$

where WPI equals the Wholesale Price Index and RPI equals the Retail Price Index. $RINV_t$ and $HINV_t$ are as defined previously.

APPENDIX II:
LOGIT, CHOICE-BASED SAMPLING, WMLE, AND PAIRED T-TESTING

The **logit** model is derived from assuming that the random error u_i follows a Logistic distribution. The Logistic distribution is the cumulative distribution of the hyperbolic-secant-square (sech^2) distribution whose density function is given by:

$$f(u) = \frac{e^u}{(1 + e^u)^2} \, du \qquad -\infty < u < +\infty \qquad\qquad (A7)$$

where u is an underlying random variable, and e is the exponential function. The cumulative distribution is

$$F(Z) = \frac{e^Z}{1 + e^Z} \qquad\qquad\qquad (A8)$$

where Z is the variable of interest. One of the advantages of this distribution is that it has a closed form solution.

In the case of the logit model, the realizations of the dependent variable y $(0,1)$ will be the realization of a binomial process with a likelihood function given by:

$$L = \Pi_{y_i = 0} F(-\beta' x_i) \, \Pi_{y_i = 1} [1 - (F - \beta' x_i)] \qquad\qquad (A9)$$

where $F(-\beta' x_i)$ is the cumulative distribution function for u. In the logit model, the x's represent the attributes of the target firm and the bidder (i.e., "q" ratios, financial ratios, etc.) that influence the probability of being acquired. We assume that these attributes are quantitatively measured. However, we are not able to observe or quantify all the characteristics that could play a role in the takeover decision. Accordingly, we assume that these unobservable characteristics are random and follow a Type I extreme value distribution. This is consistent with Palepu (1986).

The cumulative density function of the standard Type I extreme value distribution has the form: $1 - \exp(-(\exp(\mathbf{x}))$. The probability density function of a standard Type I extreme value distribution is very close to that of a log-normal distribution. This approach is similar to McFadden's (1974) consumer utility analysis within the context of conditional logit analysis. McFadden (1974) argues that the consumer utility function can be written in the form

$$U = V(s,\mathbf{x}) + \varepsilon(s,\mathbf{x}) \qquad (A10)$$

where V is nonstochastic and reflects the "representative" tastes of the population, and ε is stochastic and reflects the idiosyncracies of this individual in tastes for the alternative with attributes x. The individual will choose the alternative that maximizes utility.

The sampling procedure used is known as **choice-based sampling** (other names are hold-out sampling or state-based sampling). Since the number of targets and bidders in the population is limited, the use of a random sampling procedure could exclude many of the companies whose attributes are of interest. Hence, in order to gain efficiency we have to oversample both the targets and the bidders. If the sample was random, the information provided by this sample would be very small since the majority of the firms would be non-targets or non-bidders.

The practice in previous studies dealing with prediction of targets and/or bidders has been to choose a target or a bidder and a non-target or a non-bidder from a control sample. Imbens (1992) concludes that the equal share sample is significantly better than random sampling to the extent that controlling with an equal share sample gives more relevant information. Coslett (1981) argues that the choice-based sample of equal proportions is usually a close-to-optimum design. However, if we use estimators that assume random sampling, the estimates of the model parameters could be inconsistent and asymptotically biased. The bias caused by the use of simple maximum likelihood (MLE) procedure that assumes random sampling is described by Palepu (1986) as follows:

Consider a firm i in the *population* with a probability p of being a target. Let p' be the probability that the firm i in the *sample* is a target. Using Bayes' formula for conditional probability,[16]

$$p' = probability \left(\frac{i \text{ is target}}{i \text{ is sampled}} \right) \qquad (A11)$$

In the case of random sampling, the probability of the firm being sampled is the same whether it is a target or not. Hence, the above expression is equal to p. However, under choice-based sampling if N_1 and N_2 are the number of targets and non-targets in the population and n_1 and n_2 are the corresponding numbers in the sample, then

$$p' \frac{p\,(n_1 / N_1)}{p(n_1 / N_1) + (1 - p)\,(n_2 / N_2)} \neq p \qquad (A12)$$

Thus, the bias is:

$$p' - p = \frac{(n_1 / N_1)p(1 - p)}{p(n_1 / N_1) + (1 - p)\,(n_2 / N_2)} \qquad (A13)$$

since in most of the cases $N_1 < N_2$ and $n_1 < n_2$, $(p' - p) > 0$.

Imbens (1992) presents the following example to describe the **Weighted Maximum Likelihood** estimator. Consider a model with two choices, $i = 1,2$ and two strata, $s = 1,2$. With probability $H_1 = h$ an observation is drawn from strata 1, $\mathscr{F}(1)=1\}$, and with probability $H_2 = 1-h$ it is drawn from $\mathscr{F}(2)=2\}$. The population probability of choice 1 is $Q_1 = q$, and that of choice 2 is $Q_2 = 1 - q$. The joint density function of (s,i,x) is

$$g(s, i, x) = \left[\frac{h}{q}P(1 \,/\, x,\theta)\right]^{I[i=1]} * \left[\frac{1-h}{1-q}(1 - P(1\,/\,x,\theta))\right]^{I[i=2]} * r(x) \qquad (A14)$$

where $r(x)$ is a unknown function; compared to

$$P(1/x, \theta)^{I[i=1]} * (1 - P(1/x, \theta))^{I[i=2]} * r(x) \qquad (A15)$$

when the sampling is random.

A proper analysis of **paired data** could be supplemented by taking into account the absolute value of the difference of the observations ($Y=1$ and $Y=0$) for each variable, to test the null hypothesis that the mean difference, μ_d is D_0. This hypothesis is equivalent to $H_0: \mu_1 - \mu_2 = D_0$. In this study H_0 is $D_0=0$, and the test statistic is:

$$t = \frac{\bar{d} - D_0}{\dfrac{s_d}{n}} \qquad (A16)$$

where d and s_d are the sample mean and standard deviation of the n differences with n-1 degrees of freedom. We divided the units into two groups for each hypothesis (US targets–US nontargets, foreign bidders–foreign nonbidders, and US bidders–US nonbidders) based on the SIC codes.

According to the hypothesis under test, corresponding observations are assumed to have approximately the same value apart from random variations, from which it follows that the differences all have the true value of 0. Further, the differences are assumed to be normally distributed with variance v_d^2, so that the mean difference,

$$\bar{d} = \frac{1}{n}\sum_{i=1}^{n} d_i \qquad (A17)$$

is normally distributed with parameters $(0, v_d^2 \,/\, nt)$ and

$$u = \frac{\bar{d}}{(\sigma_d \,/\ n)} \qquad (A18)$$

is normally distributed with parameters $(0,1)$. As an estimate of v_d^2 we compute the sample variance as

$$s_d^2 = \frac{1}{n-1}\sum_{i=1}^{n}(d_i - \hat{d})^2 \qquad (A19)$$

Hence, it follows that

$$t = \frac{\hat{d}}{(s_d /\ n} \qquad (A20)$$

has a *t*-distribution with *n*-1 degrees of freedom.

By choosing the pairs so that the properties of the units within each pair are similar and the properties of the units differ widely from one pair to another, we may investigate the differences or similarities of the firms involved in cross-border mergers and acquisitions. Another good property of this test is that it is not affected by measurement errors. In this sense it represents a robust test statistic. Furthermore, the variables between the pairs will not influence the variance of the mean difference, because this variance only depends on the variations of the differences between the units within the pairs.

ACKNOWLEDGMENT

This paper is based in part on Gonzalez's doctoral dissertation at Lehigh University. We thank the participants of the doctoral workshops at Lehigh for their comments and suggestions. Special thanks go to the two anonymous referees and the editor, Joe Finnerty, for their helpful feedback. Remaining errors are our own.

NOTES

1 It would be simplistic to believe that the primary motivation for M&A activity internationally is simply the random search for undervalued assets. For instance, Doukas and Travlos (1988: pp 1161–1162) point out the underlying valuation of international assets stems from "(a) the firm's ability to arbitrage institutional restrictions (e.g., tax codes, antitrust provisions, and financial limitations), (b) the informational externalities captured by the firm in the conduct of international business (e.g., learning cost externalities), and (c) the cost saving gained by joint production in marketing and in manufacturing." We thank an anonymous referee for bringing this to our attention.

2 "Tobin's *q*" is defined as the market value of assets divided by the replacement cost of assets.

3 If we identify a high "*q*" ratio with good managerial performance, this conclusion is consistent with the free cash flow theory advanced by Jensen (1988). According to this theory, firms with free cash flow (i.e., a high "*q*" ratio) may waste resources on unprofitable investments rather than make higher cash payments to shareholders; acquisitions that force a bidder to make better use of these cash flows benefit both target and bidder shareholders.

4 See for example Lang et al. (1989), Holly and Longbottom (1988), Chappell and Cheng (1984).

5 *Mergerstat* classifies the companies in 50 major industrial groups based on SIC codes.

6 We recognize the possibility of the existence of the anomalies known as the "January Effect" or "Small Firm" effect. This would mean that the end of the year prices could be depressed, not reflecting the price of the stock for the rest of the year. However, we do not know *a priori* how large are the US targets.

7 For example, if the firm pays x dollars of preferred stock dividends, and the average yield for preferred stock was 10%, the market value would be x divided by 10%. In the case of the foreign companies we will look into the possibility of using country specific preferred stock yields.

8 Here again, we will be using each country's average yield for industrial bonds. For instance, let's assume we are computing the market value of the debt for 1990. In this case, the debt maturating in 5 years is supposed to have been issued in 1975. Thus, the balance that appears in the financial statement will be discounted using the country's average yield for industrial bonds of 1975.

9 Since the book value of debt will almost always be greater than the market value of debt in real terms (i.e., after adjusting for changes in purchasing power over the life of the debt contract), the numerator of the Tobin's q ratio will be overstated in real terms making it harder to reject the null hypothesis. Thus, a significant QF builds a better case for strong firms becoming bidders in the cross-border M&A market.

10 Deferred Tax Liabilities are recorded when there is a timing difference that causes a difference between the Tax Expense and the Tax Liability. Thus, it is an accounting treatment that does not affect the equity investors. In the worst case, if the company goes bankrupt, the timing differences never will be reversed.

11 See G. S. Maddala, 1983, *Limited-Dependent and Qualitative Variables in Econometrics*, Econometric Society Monographs.

12 Our test results would be strengthened by a test on unsuccessful attempts and unsuccessful bidders. Unfortunately, to the best of our knowledge, this data is unavailable. Also since our data set of foreign firms as bidders is limited, we did not think that segmenting it into new acquisitions and follow-on acquisitions would have an adequate critical mass. We thank an anonymous referee for making this point.

13 A paired t-test was also performed, and there was significant difference between the Tobin's q of the targets and non-targets at a .05 level.

14 For example: if the \$/DM exchange rate was on average 0.5 (i.e., DM 2.0/\$) for the 1980–1990 period, and the 1988 \$/DM exchange rate was 0.67 (i.e., DM 1.5/\$), then the exchange rate figure to be used will be $(0.67-0.5)/0.5 = .33$.

15 The paired t-test shows that there was a statistically significant difference between the QF of bidders and non-bidders.

16 p' is further defined as

$$\frac{P(i\text{:target}) * P(i\text{:sampled} \mid i\text{:target})}{P(i\text{:target}) * P(i\text{:sampled} \mid \text{:target}) + P(i\text{:non-target}) * P(i\text{:sampled} \mid i\text{:non-target})}$$

REFERENCES

Chappell, H., and D. Cheng. 1984. "Firms' Acquisition Decisions and Tobin's q Ratio," *Journal of Economics and Business,* 36: 29–42.

Chirinko, R. S. 1987. "Tobin's q and Financial Policy," *Journal of Monetary Economics,* 19(1): 69–87.

Conn, R. I. and F. Connell. 1990. "International Mergers: Returns to US and British Firms," *Journal of Business, Finance, and Accounting,* 17(5): 689–710.

Coslett, S. R. 1981. "Maximum Likelihood Estimation for Choice-based samples," *Econometrica,* 49(5): 1289–1316.

Dietrich, J. K. and E. Sorensen. 1984. "An Application of Logit Analysis to Prediction of Merger Targets," *Journal of Business Research,* 12: 392–402.

Doukas, J. and N. G. Travlos. 1988. "The Effects of Corporate Multinationalism on Shareholders' Wealth: Evidence from International Acquisitions," *Journal of Finance,* 43(5): 1161–1175.

Fabozzi, F. 1990. "Corporate Bonds." Pp. 253–287 in *The Handbook of Fixed Income Securities,* edited by Frank Fabozzi. Homewood, IL: Business One Irwin.

Harris, R. S. and D. Ravenscraft. 1991. "The Role of Acquisitions in Foreign Direct Investment: Evidence from the US Stock Market," *The Journal of Finance,* 46(3): 825–844.

Holly, S. and A. Longbottom. 1988. "Company Acquisitions, Investment and Tobin's Q: Evidence from the UK," *Journal of Economics and Business,* 40(2): 103–115.

Imbens, W. 1992. "An Efficient Method of Moments Estimator for Discrete Choice Models with Choice-based Sampling," *Econometrica,* 60(5): 1187–1214.

Jensen, M. 1988. "Takeovers: Their Causes and Consequences," *Journal of Economics Perspectives,* 2(1): 21–48.

Lang, L. H., R. M. Stulz, and R. A. Walking. 1989. "Managerial Performance, Tobin's Q, and the Gain from Successful tender Offers," *Journal of Financial Economics,* 24(1): 137–154.

Lindenberg, E. B. and S. A. Ross. 1981. "Tobin's q Ratio and Industrial Organization," *Journal of Business,* 54(1): 1–32.

Maddala, G. S. 1983. *Limited-dependent and Qualitative Variables in Econometrics.* Cambridge, MA: Cambridge University Press.

Manski, C. F. and D. McFadden. 1981. "Alternative Estimators and Sample Designs for Discrete Choice Analysis." Pp. 51–111 in *Structural Analysis of Discrete Data with Econometric Applications*, edited by C. F. Manksi and D. McFadden. Cambridge, MA: MIT Press.

McFadden, D., 1974, "Conditional Logit Analysis of Qualitative Choice Behavior." Pp. 113–118 in *Frontiers in Econometrics*, edited by Paul Zarembka. New York: Academic Press.

Palepu, K. G. 1986. "Predicting takeover targets: A Methodological and Empirical Analysis," *Journal of Accounting and Economics,* 8(1): 3–36.

Servaes, H. 1991. "Tobin's q and the Gains from Takeovers," *The Journal of Finance,* 46(1): 409–419.

Smirlock, M., T. Gilligan, and W. Marshall. 1984. "Tobin's q and the Structure-Performance Relationship," *The American Economic Review,* 74(5): 1051–1060.

Tobin, J. 1969. "A General Equilibrium Approach to Monetary Theory," *Journal of Money, Credit and Banking,* 1: 15–29.

Tobin, J. and W. Brainard. 1977. "Asset Markets and the Cost of Capital." Pp. 235–262 in *Economic Progress, Private Values and Public Policies: Essays in Honor of William Fellner*, edited by B. Belassa and R. Nelson. Amsterdam: North-Holland.

Vasconcellos, G., J. Madura, and R. Kish. 1990. "An Empirical Investigation of Factors Affecting Cross-Border Acquisitions: the United States vs United Kingdom Experience," *Global Finance Journal,* 1(3): 173–189.

Vasconcellos, G. M. and R. J. Kish. 1993. "Cross-Border Mergers and Acquisitions and International Capital Flows: US–Japan." Pp. 85–120 in *Competitiveness and American Society*, edited by Steven L. Goldman. Bethlehem, PA: Lehigh University Press.

Section 4
Merger Processes

When cultures collide: the anatomy of a merger[1] 16

**Anthony F. Buono, James L. Bowditch
and John W. Lewis, III**

INTRODUCTION

Mergers and takeovers have rapidly become significant factors in US industry as numerous companies have used such strategies to achieve corporate growth, economies of scale, vertical integration, and diversification. Yet, despite this trend, the projected increase in mergers and acquisitions (Bleakely, 1984; *Business Week*, 1982; Hertzberg, 1984), and the emerging public policy debate over such activity (Behr, 1984; Salter and Weinhold, 1982), our understanding of the full effects of mergers on organizations and their human resources is limited. Indeed, the existing literature is largely concerned with the strategic, financial, and operational consequences of merger activity (Allen, Oliver, and Schwallie, 1981; Bradley and Korn, 1982; Davidson, 1981). While there is a focus on the "human side" of mergers (Birch, 1983; *Business Week*, 1979; Carter, 1983; Hayes, 1979; Ingrassia, 1982; Sinetar, 1981, Uttal, 1983), this literature is largely pragmatic in nature and concerned with either surviving the "aftermath" or maintaining organizational morale and productivity. What has been less fully documented are (1) the perceptions of the merger partners toward their old and the newly formed organization; (2) attitudes toward the job and other facets of organizational life; and (3) the process through which these perceptions and attitudes are formed.

One approach toward a conceptual understanding of the dynamics which occur during and after a merger is to view the process as an attempt to combine different organizational cultures. Within anthropology and sociology, of course, culture has long been recognized as a significant determinant of beliefs, attitudes, and behaviors. As such, it has been a central variable in the study of different societies and their "natural" spheres of action. The importance of culture for organizational research, however, has only recently been emphasized through the recognition of the potency of culture at the organizational as well as societal level. Several researchers, for example, have argued that strategy formulation, preferred leadership style, and accepted ways of accomplishing tasks among other central facets of organizational life are actually reflections of a particular organization's culture (Deal and Kennedy, 1982, 1983; Harris and Moran, 1979; Peters and Waterman, 1982; Pettigrew, 1979; Schein, 1983; Schwartz and Davis, 1981; Smircich, 1983).

This paper attempts to clarify our understanding of organizational culture and its consequences for the merger process by examining (1) the cultures of two banking organizations prior to a merger between the two institutions; (2) the attitudes and perceptions of organizational members before and after the merger; and (3) the emerging culture of the newly formed organization. After briefly discussing the foundations of societal and organizational culture and related methodological concerns, data on pre-merger conditions, the merger process, and the post-merger experience are presented. Finally, the cultural implications of mergers and their effects on organizational members are examined.

TOWARD A GENERAL UNDERSTANDING OF CULTURE

Most definitions of culture used currently in the social sciences are modifications of E. B. Tylor's (1871, p. 1) delineation of the concept as "that complex whole which includes knowledge, belief, art, morals, law, custom, and any other capabilities and habits acquired by man as a member of society." In its broadest sense, culture can be thought of as that part of the entire repertoire of human action and its products which are socially as opposed to genetically transmitted. The term, however, has been criticized as being conceptually difficult since it has been defined in a number of different ways and no consensus has clearly emerged (see Bhagat and McQuaid, 1982). Moreover, the concept has also been viewed as an excuse for "intellectual laziness" since researchers often use culture as a synonym for nation without any theoretical underpinnings (Child, 1981).

Part of this conceptual confusion can be clarified by briefly noting the differences between the sociological and anthropological uses of the term. Sociologists, for the most part, use culture to describe the *ideational aspects* of social life in order to distinguish culture from society or social structure. The anthropological approach, by contrast, more often takes its entire subject matter as culture. Thus, the sociological orientation stresses the process through which behavior is learned (Linton, 1936, 1945), the symbolic and evaluative aspects of tradition, ideas or beliefs (Parsons, 1951), and culture as a set of rules governing behavior (Radcliffe-Brown, 1957). On the other hand, while anthropologists like Kroeber and Kluckhohn (1952) focus on the ideational aspects of "social heredity," i.e., patterns of behavior acquired and transmitted by symbols, they also see culture as "constituting the distinctive achievement of human groups, including their embodiment in artifacts." This orientation, thus, adds a material dimension to the concept of culture.

Based on this comparison, two basic aspects of culture can be delineated. First, central to both the anthropological and sociological uses of the term is the integrative concept of *custom*, i.e., traditional and regularized ways of doing things. Second, a distinction can be made between material or objective culture and ideational or subjective culture. *Objective culture* refers to the artifacts and material products of a society (Barnouw, 1979; Mitchell, 1973). *Subjective culture*, by contrast, is a "cultural group's characteristic way of perceiving the man-made part of its environment," the rules and the group's norms, roles, and values (Triandis, Vassilou et al., 1972, p. 4).

Organizational culture

Just as culture is a central factor which influences the ways in which people act and interact in a given society, indigenous cultures evolve over time in organizations which affect individual and group behavior in predictable though subtle ways. In fact, many conceptual similarities can be drawn between the concepts of societal and organizational culture. While culture at the organizational levels is also implicitly diffused, it is a pervasive and powerful force in shaping behavior (Miles, 1980;

Whorton and Worthley, 1981). Moreover, although there are multiple definitions and uses of the concept at the organizational level as well (Harris and Moran, 1979; Miles, 1980; Pettigrew, 1979; Schwartz and Davis, 1981; Schein, 1983; Siehl, 1982), there is still the integrative theme of *custom*. This "normative glue" holds an organization together through traditional ways of carrying out organizational responsibilities, unique patterns of beliefs and expectations which emerge over time, and the resultant shared understandings of reality at given points in time.

For analytic purposes and a fuller understanding of the subtleties of organizational culture, three conceptual issues should be examined. First, although recent use of the concept (Deal and Kennedy, 1982) suggests that differences between organizational cultures exist primarily across industries rather than between organizations within the same industry, this focus seems too restrictive. In their research, for example, Deal and Kennedy (1982) formulate four general corporate culture types which range from the "tough guy/macho" culture characterized by high risks and quick feedback as found in advertising, construction, and entertainment industries to the "process" culture characterized by low risks, slow feedback, and a focus on process rather than content as found in insurance and utility companies and the public sector. The broader social and business environment on which Deal and Kennedy focus *is* an important influence on the development of a corporate culture. However, while such global differences do exist and are useful as a guide for empirical research, the present study suggests that cultural differences between organizations in the same industry can be just as great as cultural differences across industries. In terms of mergers and acquisitions, although it may be easier to accomodate intra-industry differences over the long term as compared with inter-industry differences, divergent cultures between organizations in the same industry can still present many difficulties.

Second, organizations have both subjective and objective cultures. *Subjective organizational culture* refers to the shared pattern of beliefs, assumptions, and expectations held by organizational members, and the group's characteristic way of perceiving the organization's environment and its norms, roles, and values as they exist outside the individual (Schwartz and Davis, 1981; Triandis et al., 1972; Triandis, 1977). This includes such things as corporate heroes, i.e., those people who personify the culture's values and provide tangible role models for others, myths and stories about the organization, taboos, organizational rites and rituals, and perceptions of "Mecca" (those important symbolic locations and prideful extensions of the organization; Deal and Kennedy, 1982, 1983; Pettigrew, 1979; Smircich, 1983; Wilkins, 1984). Subjective organizational culture also encompasses what may be termed a *managerial culture*, the leadership styles and orientations, mental frameworks, and ways of behaving and solving problems that are influenced by the values supported by the organization (Litterer, 1978; Peters, 1980). While some aspects of managerial culture are, of course, shared across organizations, crucial but subtle facets are indigenous to particular organizations.

Objective organizational culture refers to the artifacts created by an organization. For instance, Digital Equipment Corporation's modular, open-office configuration, the comfortable restbreak areas on the assembly line of the Solihull plant of British Leyland, and the chassis assembly team bays with sauna, coffee room, and entrance at Volvo's Kalmar plant are objective (material) reflections of each organization's culture. Such physical settings, office locations and decor, and even the fleet of cars an organization leases for its executives can reflect things that are valued by the organization. BankAmerica Corporation, for example, is well known for its ponderous bureaucracy, and the corporate hierarchy rigidly determines who receives what kind of car: the president uses a Lincoln Continental, an executive vice president a Buick LeSabre, while lower level executives must make do with Pontiac Phoenixes and Chevrolet Citations. When the corporation acquired the discount broker Charles Schwab & Co., known for its innovative, entrepreneurial style, a clash emerged over Schwab's fleet which included BMWs, Porsches, Saabs, Mercedes, and Jaguars. The norm at Schwab was "You go out and pick a car, and the company leases it for you." While those at Schwab did not want to change their fleet, arguing that they didn't want to "squelch individuals' initiative," many of Bank of America's executives expressed dissatisfaction and frustration with the situation since it did not follow their hierarchical norms (Zonana, 1983).

Although both aspects of culture are important for a full understanding of a particular organization, subjective organizational culture can provide a more distinctive basis for the characterization and interpretation of similarities and differences among people in different groups. While objective culture may contain similarities across organizations, subjective organizational culture by definition is unique to a particular enterprise. At times, however, something that is part of the objective culture of an organization can begin to take on a "life" of its own. When this occurs, there is a distorted magnification of the importance of the artifact which then becomes part of the subjective culture of the organization. As will be illustrated later in the article, this is part of the process by which myths concerning organization life are created.

Finally, there are differences between subjective organizational culture and *organizational climate*. Climate is defined as a "measure of whether people's expectations about what it should be like to work in an organization are being met" (Schwartz and Davis, 1981, p. 33). Thus, subjective organizational culture is concerned with the *nature* of beliefs and expectations about organizational life, while climate is an indicator of the extent to which these employee beliefs and expectations are being fulfilled. Climate is frequently measured by surveys on a favorable-unfavorable dimension. Widely different organizational cultures, however, may produce rather similar climate profiles. Respondents perceive themselves as being satisfied or unsatisfied with their organizational situation compared to their expectations of what "should be." These expectations are based on the type of psychological contract formed at organizational entry and early socialization experiences, in addition to individuals' own prior experiences and perceptions of the larger environment. To illustrate, one organization may have a relatively autocratic managerial culture where managers' styles are perceived as autocratic, while another may be more democratic in nature and perceived as such. Yet, responses to the survey statement "My manager involves me in decisions which affect me whenever appropriate" can produce a similar *favorability* rating in the two organizations. Even though the actual situations may be very different, if they are congruent with the nature of employee expectations about what life in the organization should be like, climate profiles can be similar.

In summary, organizational culture tends to be unique to a particular organization, composed of an objective and subjective dimension, and concerned with tradition and the nature of shared beliefs and expectations about organizational life. It is a powerful determinant of individual and group behavior. Organizational culture affects practically all aspects of organizational life from the way in which people interact with each other, perform their work and dress, to the types of decisions made in a firm, its organizational policies and procedures, and strategy considerations.

The full potency of organizational culture can be seen during a merger or acquisition when two divergent cultures are forced to become one. Since organizational members are so embedded in their own culture, they rarely realize fully its influence on their behavior. During the cultural "collision" which occurs during a merger, however, the shock for organizational members created by living in a different organizational world can disrupt the entire workings of the newly formed firm.

In an attempt to understand these dynamics, this paper examines a merger between two medium-sized savings banks. By comparing (1) each bank's objective and subjective culture and organizational climate prior to the merger with (2) the resultant culture, each merger partner's perception of the new culture, and climate surveys after the merger, we can begin to clarify the influence of organizational culture on job and organizational satisfaction, individual behavior, and the process underlying organizational mergers.

METHODOLOGY

A multimethod approach employed in a longitudinal framework was used to gather data about the two pre-merger banks (1979–1980), the merger process itself (1981) and the post-merger experience (1982). Information on the organizational cultures of the merger partners was collected through in-depth interviews with a cross-section of organizational members, and observations and archival data gathered throughout the study period. The physical settings, e.g., office location and decor, and consistency of decor across departments and levels, of both banks were studied as were each institution's own statements about itself, e.g., annual reports, copies of the house organ, and internal memos. Lengthy discussions with the Chief Executive Officers (CEO), upper level managers, and employees throughout both organizations were also undertaken. The interviews focused on such items as (1) personal descriptions of the organization, (2) organizational history, (3) types of people working in the firm, (4) type of place the bank is to work at, and (5) other facets of organizational life. These individual perceptions were then tested in discussions with other organizational members to develop shared perceptions of each organization's culture.

Pre-merger data on organizational climate were collected through survey questionnaires with the populations of the two banks during late 1979 and early 1980. The survey used in Bank A ($N = 325$) was part of an internally developed quality of work life and organization development program (see Bowditch and Buono, 1982), while Bank B ($N = 188$) used a nationally developed survey form. Both surveys focused on employee perceptions about various facets of organizational life including compensation, organizational commitment, interpersonal relations, job security and advancement, job satisfaction, and management and supervisory behavior. Although the data-gathering process for information on organizational climate differed in that Bank A relied on a more participatory approach with small groups of employees providing input to the formulation of the survey and Bank B provided a standardized questionnaire for its employees to complete, clear climate profiles of the two pre-merger institutions were obtained. Since organizational climate data reflect the extent to which people's expectations about what it *should* be like to work in an organization are being met, these profiles can provide an indicator of the satisfaction with and acceptance of a particular organization's culture.

Information concerning the merged bank was obtained through a similar process. Data on the "new" or emerging organizational culture were obtained through a study of the physical setting of the newly formed institution, its self-reports, and in-depth interviews with a stratified random sample of organizational members (the two former chief executive officers of the merger partners, ten members of former Bank A, ten members of former Bank B, and six new employees who joined the institution following the merger). The interviews covered such areas as the types of management style before and after the merger, policy and procedural changes, working conditions and atmosphere, general organizational change, the merger process itself, and outcomes of the merger.

Due to the contrast between the "old" and the "new" cultures of the organizations, members of the merged bank freely discussed sharp recollections about salient aspects of the culture of their former bank and of the merged institution. Although a criticism of such data is that they become less accurate with the passage of time between a given situation and the subsequent interview, evidence indicates that if the information is collected within a couple of years of the studied event there does not appear to be an accuracy or bias problem (see Gutek, 1978). Moreover, within the context of the present study, research suggests that any threat to an organization's existing culture can readily make it clearer and more significant to organizational members (Mirvis and Sonka, 1983).

Data on the organizational climate of the merged bank were collected through a survey questionnaire administered in 1982. The instrument was developed to reflect the earlier climate items covered by the 1979 and 1980 surveys and was given to a stratified random sample of post-merger bank employees (former Bank A = 45, former Bank B = 45, new employees = 10).

Overall, uniformity of data collection efforts was attempted throughout the study period. Although a limitation of the data concerns differences in the method used to obtain organizational climate data for Bank A and Bank B during the pre-merger period, the information generated still provides a basis for comparative analysis. Combined with qualitative interview and observation data, and archival information, this material provides a clear picture of the objective and subjective organizational cultures and organizational climate profiles of each bank prior to the merger and the new institution following the merger.

THE PRE-MERGER PERIOD

Prior to the fall of 1980, Bank A was the fourth largest savings bank in the state, with approximately $600 million in assets and 325 full-time employees. The institution served a largely blue-collar clientele, which was a function of its urban setting and the location of its branches. It operated with a divisional structure, and was rather bureaucratic in nature, with clearly defined and bounded jobs at all levels.

Bank B was the fifth largest ($500 million in assets) mutual savings bank in the state, with approximately 275 employees. In contrast to Bank A, the merger partner had both its headquarters and all branches in suburban areas and served largely white-collar and professional customers. The institution operated with a centrally controlled functional organization, but with individual jobs more loosely defined, particularly at the professional and managerial levels. For instance, there was a more complete file of job descriptions for all employees at Bank A, while at Bank B, the expressed "policy" was that employees should do what was needed, especially at the professional level, for the success of the bank.

The subjective cultures

Although these two institutions were approximately equal-sized mutual savings banks operating in the same Standard Metropolitan Statistical Area (SMSA), each bank employee group saw itself as being quite different from the other. As suggested earlier, such differences can be seen by comparing various facets of the subjective cultures of organizations along such lines as managerial culture, perceptions of Mecca, and organizational heroes, myths, and stories. As discussed in the methodology section, these comparisons, which are summarized in Table 1, are based on widely held and shared perceptions obtained through interviews with organizational members at all levels of each institution's hierarchy.

Managerial culture

Since leaders are often perceived as embodying the core values and beliefs of a group and exemplifying the group's pivotal norms, the way in which people characterize their leaders can reveal much about how they see themselves as a group. Moreover, the accuracy of these views in the present study is reflected in that self-characterizations by both CEOs confirmed the perceptions held by other organizational members. In

Table 1 Subjective and objective organizational cultures of Banks A and B

	Bank A	Bank B
Subjective culture		
Managerial culture		
CEO style	Participative	Authoritarian
	Egalitarian	Elitist
	"Good guy"	"Bad guy"
	"Buddha"	"Dennis the menace"
	Externally oriented	Internally oriented
Locus of power	Bureaucratic	Personal
Management style	Anticipatory	"Management by crisis"
General orientation	People oriented	Task oriented
Heroes	V.P. human resources, first woman bank officer	Prior CEO, treasurer
Mecca	Branches	"CEO's office"
Myths	"Fat cats/lazy personnel"	"Lean and Mean", "Hell hole"
When new job duties emerge	New people are hired, highly specialized employees	Responsibility is delegated, "jack of all trades"
Community involvement	High	Low
Objective culture		
Employee eating facility (main office)	Plush, restaurant-like	Spartan, cafeteria-like
Branches	High-quality appearance (spare no expense)	Functional appearance (avoid embellishment)
CEO's office	Isolated, view of external environment	Centralized, view of internal working environment

Bank A, the *CEO's style* was reported by senior officers and other administrators as being participative and concerned with creating an egalitarian atmosphere. Employees referred to him as a "good guy" and a "Buddha," a person who delegated many internal decisions and focused his attention more on the external environment than on the internal workings of the bank. In sharp contrast, the CEO of Bank B, who even referred to himself as a "Calvinist," was seen by his employees as a "bad guy" and an "elitist." His style was regarded as authoritarian, and he paid such close attention to internal bank affairs even at the detail level that he was continuously referred to as "Dennis the Menace." Within this context, the organizational *locus of power* was seen as more bureaucratically dispersed in Bank A, while consolidated in the hands of the president of Bank B.

The orientation at the "top" of the organization was also a significant factor in the way in which individual managers behaved in each bank. *Management style and tone* in Bank B was reported by its employees to be "management by crisis," while in Bank A, actions and decisions were perceived by its members to be more planned and deliberate, and based on widely gathered and shared information. A Bank A manager, for example, said a common way to propose something was "to run it up the flagpole and see if anyone salutes it." Other organizational members added, however, that decisions from the president's office were often slow in coming. In Bank B, employees remarked about the unambiguous way in which decisions came from their CEO.

With respect to the relative orientation toward *people vs task*, in Bank A there seemed to be a much stronger emphasis on the "human side" of business than in Bank B. Social events such as the annual picnic, Christmas party, and retirement activities were spontaneously mentioned by Bank A members when asked about life in their organization. There was a strong consensus among managers that employee job and organizational satisfaction was important, and that the bank should do all it could to ensure that employee needs were met. The relative emphasis in Bank B appeared to be more strongly task focused, with employees, especially officers, expected to continue working beyond "quitting time" until the job was finished. A post-merger story told by Bank B's CEO recalled an incident when he returned from a trip late in the day to find a number of prior Bank A officers leaving "on time" which angered him. His postscript to the researchers was that "old habits die hard." There were virtually no stories spontaneously mentioned about social events in interviews with Bank B personnel, and the consensus among managers was that organizational needs and responsibilities "came first."

Heroes, myths, and stories

Interviews with members of both institutions provided further insight into what was viewed as important in each organization. *Heroes*, i.e., those individuals who personify the culture's values and provide tangible role models for others in Bank A, were the Vice President for Human Resources and the first woman bank officer. In contrast, Bank B employees identified a former CEO and the treasurer as two heroes in their organization. Other cultural differences surfaced when employees were asked where *Mecca*, i.e., the most important symbolic location, was in their organization. Bank A members pointed to the branches, since that was where one "established a reputation" in order to move up in the bank. In Bank B, Mecca was the CEO's office. Interestingly, none of the respondents asked what was meant by Mecca, but responded without hesitation. Thus, the CEO's office and two top-line officers were of central importance in Bank B, while a "people specialist," a minority, and the branches were mentioned in Bank A. These perceptions provide a reflection of what is valued in each organization and present a significant part of the mosaic of the different cultures.

A number of *myths*, i.e., narratives which organize beliefs about the organization and its value system, also characterized life in these organizations. As mentioned earlier, such perceptions can develop when something that is part of the objective situation begins to take on a life of its own and becomes a distorted magnification of the actual situation. Both groups of employees, for example, perceived Bank A personnel as "fat cats," specialists to the degree that when new job duties evolved it was not uncommon for a new person to be hired. Sharply in contrast was the image of Bank B as a "hell hole" where new duties were generally distributed to existing organizational members, many of whom saw themselves as "jacks of all trades." While these perceptions did not reflect the actual policies for organizational hiring and work delegation, Bank A did have a larger employee population than Bank B despite the relatively equal size of other aspects of the organizations.

Another myth about the two organizations focused on institutional commitment to the Community Reinvestment Act (CRA).[2] Based on CRA guidelines and the discussion sessions Bank A initiated with local groups, it appeared that the organization was more concerned with meeting community needs than was Bank B. Bank A, however, received a considerable amount of favorable press for the rehabilitation of an urban three-decker structure which was sold (with mortgage assistance) as condominiums to three moderate-income families in the local community. Over time, the highly favorable perceptions of Bank A which emerged from this venture and the relatively unfavorable image which developed concerning Bank B's community reinvestment activities exceeded the actual performance differences between the two organizations. A story told by several employees, for example, was that when a community group would approach the banks with a request, Bank A's CEO would respond "Let's sit down and talk about it," while Bank B's CEO would simply say "(expletive deleted) them!" Thus, although the actual CRA performance of the two banks did not differ that significantly, the image of each institution and the beliefs which that image represents in the story reflects the values of each culture. Especially when such stories are about the actions of influential people or organizationally important programs, they provide ample clues about how things are "supposed to be done." The clearer and more concrete the story, the more powerful it is as both a symbol and as a guide for action (Wilkins, 1984).

The objective cultures

As suggested earlier, there are various material products or artifacts created by organizations which are symbolic elements of their cultural traditions, beliefs, and value patterns. In Bank A many of its artifacts reflected its strong commitment to its personnel, while similar types of artifacts in Bank B reflected quite different values. In Bank A, for example, the employee eating facility in the main office was quite plush and decorated like a fine restaurant, expensive wood paneling, numerous plants throughout the room, cushioned booths, and so forth. In Bank B, by contrast, the same type of facility in the main office was much more like a tranditional cafeteria, relatively spartan in nature, simple chairs and tables, and a small refrigerator in one of the corners. This distinction is a reflection of the values and orientations of each bank, the importance of a comfortable physical setting for Bank A (people orientation) compared to the "lean and mean," competitive aura of Bank B (task orientation). The differences in physical setting were further reflected in the branches. Bank A was so particular about the quality of the physical setting of the branches that it established its own subsidiary corporation to oversee and control any construction or upgrading of facilities. Bank B's policy was that its branches avoid expensive embellishments and take on a simple, functional appearance. Interestingly, these policies were in direct contrast to the populations served by these banks, the largely blue-collar population of Bank A and the professional, white-collar clientele served by Bank B.

Another material symbol of the different cultures is reflected by the location and nature of the offices of the two CEOs. The office of Bank A's CEO was located in a prime corner of the third floor of the main office building, isolated from the day-to-day workings of the organization. Richly decorated, the office was framed by a panoramic window looking out over the city. The office of Bank B's CEO, in contrast, was much simpler in nature, with two glass enclosed walls facing inside the bank overlooking the teller cages and officer's platform. The offices, in effect, were physical symbols of the style of each CEO (see McCaskey, 1979), the external focus and preference for delegation of Bank A's CEO, and the more internally focused concern for detail style of Bank B's CEO.

Culture and climate comparison

While the above discussion suggests significant differences in the cultures of these two institutions, organizational climate data (gathered through the pre-merger surveys) indicate that members of both banks readily accepted their own cultures (see Table 2). As argued in the earlier description of the subtle aspects of organizational culture, while culture is concerned with the *nature* of beliefs and expectations about organizational life, climate is an indicator of *whether* those beliefs and expectations are being *fulfilled*. Even though there were definite differences across the managerial and organizational culture between the two banks prior to the merger, similar portions of employees reported pride in working for their respective organization, and satisfaction with their systems of compensation and advancement, the context of their work, and interpersonal relations. As shown in Table 2, the similarity of favorable response, i.e., strongly agree and agree to positive statements, on like items of the pre-merger climate surveys suggests that expectations about what it *should* be like to work in each organization were being met. In fact, despite the image held by members of both organizations that Bank B was more authoritarian in nature while Bank A was more democratic in its orientation, the management and supervisory questions on the pre-merger surveys elicited a slightly higher level of favorable response in Bank B than in Bank A. Moreover, each group of employees took pride in their organizational image, Bank A as a "good" place to work with a "happy" atmosphere and Bank B with its image of being "lean and mean" and a "hell hole," while at the same time deriding the image of the other.

Thus, given the employee acceptance of and satisfaction with these different cultures, and the attachments that organizational members develop to their own traditions, heroes, and other symbols of the workplace, it is predictable that any change which threatens these cultures will result in feelings of confusion, insecurity, resistance, and even anger.

Table 2 Pre- and post-merger climate profiles

	Percent favourable				
	Pre-merger		Post-merger 1982 survey		
	1980 survey	1979 survey		Prior affiliation	
Selected questions	Bank A	Bank B	Merged bank	Bank A	Bank B
Organizational commitment					
Sense of pride	90	86	46	34	50
Management and supervisory					
Bank is effective in training people	50	73	44	39	41
Positive action will come from survey	55	60	49	44	45
Top management cares about employee feelings	67	74	38	32	36
Supervisor is fair	83	90	79	78	81
Supervisor sees that employees are trained	64	73	66	61	62
Compensation					
Paid fairly	43	39	48	53	42
Benefits are good	86	86	88	90	89
Job security and advancement					
I can say what I think without fear	58	61	54	36	63
Job is secure if performed well	91	89	58	47	64
Opportunity for those who want to get ahead	71	72	41	37	37
Work context					
Work hours satisfactory	84	86	93	90	89
Amount of work reasonable	72	60	77	72	81
Interpersonal					
Co-workers do their share	73	74	77	76	73
Good-department/branch cooperation	57	48	31	28	26
Employees have opportunity to meet with upper management and other staff	47	61	36	29	38

THE MERGER

The merger between these two banks began as part of an informal discussion between the two CEOs during the return trip from an industry association meeting in mid-1980. During their talk, the two presidents agreed that industry and general economic conditions were making it very difficult for even medium-sized savings banks to survive. They continued their discussion over the next several months and finally agreed that a merger between the two organizations was a good idea. Since the banks were not in immediate competition with each other either by territory or clientele, and they were roughly the same size with similar goals, the CEOs reasoned that a merger would not only create a stronger, more competitive institution but in the long run could significantly expand their sphere of influence as well.

In early 1981, the employees of both banks were informed about the merger plans at meetings held at each institution. Initially, employees of Bank A were quite favorable toward the merger since they felt it would give them (an urban bank) the opportunity to expand into the more prosperous surburban communities. They even spontaneously applauded the announcement. Members of Bank B, by contrast, were less enthusiastic about the proposed venture since they felt that their organization had less to gain. A number of employees from both banks, however, thought that the merger would provide a more solid base of operations in the increasingly turbulent economic and competitive environment.

During this period, a number of joint committees were formed to resolve any operating and procedural differences between the two organizations. These meetings continued over several months, but little was resolved. Experimental transfers of employees between the banks prior to the merger was attempted, but individuals were reluctant to go to the "other" bank allegedly because of an increase in commuting time. Although these groups focused on specific concerns such as which computer system, forms, and operating procedures the merged bank would use, the discussions were largely characterized by defensiveness on the part of each group about why "their way" was better. Thus, while a series of meetings and a transfer program were attempted as a way of preparing employees and the organizations for the pending merger, nothing of substance emerged from them.

A content analysis of all memos relating to the merger during this period and interviews with organizational members indicated that despite these difficulties, no problems or potential problems were publicly anticipated. Moreover, while the initial acceptance of the merger had not waned, it was apparent that few people in either bank openly discussed the possibility of staff reductions, particularly in the head-quarters group, or specific changes within departments and branches which were likely to occur. Although some job security concerns were expressed, the issue was largely defused by statements made by both CEOs to their organizations that no one would lose their jobs because of the merger if they were conscientious about their work, and that minimal changes would take place.

The actual merger occurred during August, 1981. As employees from each of the banks began to interact with each other on a consistent basis, the disparate nature of the cultures between the two organizations became more and more apparent. It was also clear that, despite feelings expressed by the two CEOs that "we over-met" about the merger, organizational members felt that communication concerning the merger was too infrequent, the exchanges between the two groups prior to the merger raised more issues than it resolved, and that the process did not involve enough representatives from each bank.

THE POST-MERGER EXPERIENCE

Soon after the merger actually took place, each parent organization was seen by the employees of the other bank as an "invading enemy," rather than as a co-equal partner (despite the relatively equal size of the banks). Although one might expect a type of "honeymoon period" between the two organizations, especially considering the initial acceptance of the merger, the differences in organizational cultures led to almost immediate competition between the employee groups. As would be predicted by Schein's (1980) characterization of what happens between competing groups, there were distorted perceptions about and feelings of hostility toward this "enemy."

Members of both organizations reported that "they (the other bank) took us over." Employees from the two firms told about negative stories regarding the merger partner that circulated in each of the banks prior to the official date of coming together. Responsibility for why things were not going as well as they should, why communications were so poor, or why "I" or "my boss" was not fairly treated were routinely attributed to the other bank. Moreover, people tended to become nostalgic about their prior bank affiliation very early in this process. Frequently mentioned by *both* merger partners were the loss of family atmosphere, freedom, camaraderie, and accessibility to management.

After this "negative stereotyping" stage came what might be described as the "arm wrestling" phase. In the functional units which had supervisors from each partner bank, there appeared to be a period when top management allowed for ambiguity as to who would be named to head a combined function. The competitors from each bank "jockeyed for position" to take over a particular role, but without clear signals from top management as to who was favored. While this might have been a useful managerial selection mechanism from top management's perspective, it had the unintentional dysfunctional effect of contributing to the friction at operating levels between merged departments. Indeed, the influence of this process and the refusal to give up the culture of the previous institution manifested themselves in that identity with one's prior department and supervisor and persisted long after functions were formally merged. It also became increasingly clear that this selection procedure compounded the problem of having too many middle managers.

Concomitant with the arm wrestling period, members felt betrayed by their top leaders, each of whom publicly assured his employees that they would be secure in their membership in the new organization. The new CEO (former Bank A CEO) repeated earlier public statements that there would be no merger-related layoffs as long as people did their jobs well. Subsequent management decisions to lay off organizational members, even though nonperformance factors in the situation supported such action, resulted in a profound and widespread general distrust of the new leadership and the organization. People interpret such events as symbols of what is important to an organization and, as a result, such events can significantly affect the shared beliefs about the organization and its leadership (Nystrom and Starbuck, 1984). The layoff, which occurred in mid-December, quickly became known as the "Christmas massacre."[3] The chief operating officer's (former Bank B's CEO) office was subsequently referred to as "murderer's row" since most employees, especially those from Bank A, attributed the layoffs to his influence on the new institution.

Both CEOs expressed concern that the merged institution reflect a true blend of the two banks. As indicated in Table 3, however, while the logo and location of its headquarters were a hybrid of the two original banks, the merged institution retained the name of Bank B, as well as many of its systems and orientations, important symbols of organizational identity. Moreover, as the new chief operating officer of the merged bank, the former president of Bank B was given control over internal decisions and was substantially more visible than his Bank A counterpart. The former president of Bank A assumed the role of chief executive officer and focused predominantly on external industry and environment concerns. Although this was his preferred set of activities, extending back to his presidency of former Bank A, many of the employees of that institution felt that he had "sold them out."

As indicated by the post-merger climate survey data in Table 2 and the responses to the merger-related survey questions in Table 4, the perceived influence of the

Table 3 Origin of solution to merger-related issues and problems

Issue	Bank A	Hybrid	Bank B
Logo		X	
Name			X
Charter	X		
Location of headquarters		X	
Chief executive officer	X		
Chief operating officer			X
Computer system			X
Computer procedures	X		
Management style			X
Telephone system		X	
Pay and benefits	X		
Perquisites			X
Planning procedures	X		
Community involvement			X
Organization structure		X	

former Bank B CEO on the emerging culture of the new institution is reflected in the fact that former Bank B employees felt significantly less alienated and less negative after the merger than did former Bank A members. It was becoming increasingly clear that although this was to be a "merger of equals," the culture of the new institution, in terms of its subjective interpretations and its objective artifacts and symbols, more closely resembled Bank B than Bank A.

Table 4 T tests on merger-related survey questions by former bank of employment: 1982 post-merger survey

Question	Percent favorable	
	Bank A	Bank B
All things considered, the merger should not have taken place.	47	28[a]
My former bank's philosophy is the dominant one since the merger.	26	37[b]
There has been an improvement of policies and procedures in the new (merged bank) compared to those in my pre-merger bank.	20	38[a]
There is a lingering feeling of resentment between the employees of the merger partners.	78	57[b]
There is a a lot of friction between former Bank A and former Bank B employees.	64	36[a]
The atmosphere at the bank is becoming similar to the "good old days".	10	22[a]
My department has been strengthened by the merger.	24	53[b]
I feel that employee benefits have improved as a result of the merger.	66	83[b]
A majority of the employees have come to accept the merger as a necessary and worthwhile step.	36	58[a]
Most people are afraid to open up with their feelings about the merger.	74	37[a]

[a] $p > .01$.
[b] $p > .05$.

DISCUSSION

Although the lack of communication about the merger and the way in which layoffs were handled obviously influenced how people responded to the merger, the "culture shock" experienced by the employees, especially the members of former Bank A, contributed greatly to these feelings. Taken together, (1) the comparison of climate profiles from before and after the merger (Table 2); (2) the contrast between climate ratings of former Bank A and former Bank B employees following the merger (Table 2); (3) the differences between perceptions of the merger from the perspective of former Bank A and former Bank B employees (Table 4); and (4) the interview data suggest several points to consider about the potency of organizational culture and the acceptance of mergers.

First, there was significant discomfort when the merger took place. Since the cultures of Banks A and B were different (despite being in the same industry) and as revealed by climate data, employees accepted their respective cultures, their frames of reference and expectation levels were influenced by their prior experiences, their shared understanding of what organizational life should be like. When the merger took place, these two sets of shared understandings were undermined as the new bank attempted to establish its own policies, procedures, and operating systems. The resultant "culture shock" helps explain some of the reasons why a "before–after" analysis reveals uneasy feelings about the merger.

Second, the fact that in virtually all instances the employees from Bank A were less favorable in their responses on the post-merger climate survey than the employees from Bank B suggests that the new bank was perceived to be more similar to Bank B than to Bank A. Put another way, even though the merger was between the fourth and fifth largest mutual savings banks in the state, the perception by the majority of employees was that the relatively smaller bank had more significant influence in determining the destiny of the new enterprise. Moreover, the greater internal visibility of former Bank B's president as chief operating officer appeared to influence employee perceptions of what life in the new organization would be like to a significant degree (see Schein, 1983). Thus, the fact that the most visible aspects of the new institution were either taken from Bank B or a hybrid of the two organizations further reinforced the dominance of former Bank B over Bank A, and operated as symbols of the dominant belief system and values held by the merged institution (see Nystrom and Starbuck, 1984).

As indicated by the merger-related questions on the post-merger climate survey (Table 4), *all* of the items pointed to lower satisfaction among former Bank A employees compared to members of former Bank B. It seems that in the emergent culture, managerial and organizational behavior and activities contradicted many of the professed values of Bank A employees. Thus, despite feelings of being better paid, having better benefits, and so forth (Table 2), there were significantly lower feelings of satisfaction and commitment on the part of these former Bank A managers and employees compared to the members of former Bank B. This reflects the influence of custom and tradition. Since the culture of the merged organization was more similar to that of Bank B than Bank A, the familiarity of Bank B's employees with its traditions and customary ways of carrying out organizational responsibilities and behaviors facilitated their "entry" into the new organization. In contrast, the "shock" of merging was much more pronounced for Bank A members, despite the fact that they were initially more favorable about the merger than Bank B's employees.

Finally, when comparing the nature of items on the post-merger climate survey that produced greater differences in favorability between the employees from former Banks A and B with those items that produced little difference, it appears that statements reflecting "hard" organizational factors and characteristics, e.g., compensation, hours and amount of work, and training policies, had no significant differences, while items reflecting subjective culture, e.g., organizational commitment and attitudes toward top management style produced more significant differences. This indicates the strong influence and subtlety of organizational culture. Paradoxically, during a merger most attention is usually focused on the procedural and material aspects of the organizations in question, while the more subjective, cultural aspects of organizational life are overlooked.

CONCLUSION

Obviously, a merger of two previously autonomous organizations involves an enormous amount of adjustment to change in a relatively compressed period of time. While people generally resist such change, the literature suggests that most people will support the change effort if they can understand the need for it. Our data indicate that a majority of members of both banks were aware of the problems in the thrift industry, and understood and even acknowledged the fact (intellectually, at least) that mergers were inevitable. There are limits, however, to the amount and rate of change people are able to assimilate. Culture change is among the most difficult for human beings, since culture provides the foundation for one's life. Familiar symbols of objective culture and the shared meaning of subjective culture become important components of organizational identity as they are assimilated over time by organizational members.

It is not surprising then, that seemingly rational requirements for effecting organizational, procedural, and other merger-related changes are resisted or even "sabotaged" because of threats to the pre-existing cultures. Indeed, in this study, initial attempts to resolve potential operating difficulties and to facilitate interaction between employees from both banks *before* the merger were undermined by the attachments to the respective cultures and the resulting ethnocentric attitudes concerning the "right" ways of fulfilling member and organizational needs. Yet, rarely does the literature report attempts to study the culture of merger partners ahead of time as a means for diagnosing potential problems that could interfere with the healthy birth and growth of the new organization.

In this case study, we have focused on the dominant cultures of two banks prior to their merger and the emerging dominant culture following the merger. Culture, however, is multifaceted and complex. There is the possibility (and even probability) that *subcultures*, i.e., groups of people who share common systems of beliefs that distinguish them from the majority of organizational members, and *countercultures*, i.e., groups of people whose behavior rejects that of the dominant culture, exist in organizations, or evolve out of mergers and acquisitions. Although it is beyond the scope of this paper to address these concerns, managerial efforts to ensure the acceptance and influence of what has been referred to as "strong" organizational cultures and unified belief systems (Deal and Kennedy, 1982; Nystrom and Starbuck, 1984) can be an important determinant of organizational success.

This paper has attempted to outline some of the issues involved in the study of organizational cultures and the problems that emerge when two cultures are forced together by a merger. The objective and subjective aspects of a given culture greatly influence the behaviors, satisfactions, and expectations of organizational members. Although individuals may not fully realize this influence during "normal" organizational functioning, when the culture is threatened it becomes quite salient in people's minds. Since subjective culture evolves over time as a product of shared experience, when attempting to merge two firms, the greater the number of these shared experiences that can be reproduced within a period of time, the faster a repertoire of symbols and shared meanings will develop with which the merged group of members can begin to identify, and a new culture can begin to take hold. There is a clear need for those involved with mergers or acquisitions to explicitly consider the central facet of organizational culture much more fully.

NOTES

1 Portions of this paper were presented at the 1983 meeting of the Academy of Management.
2 The CRA, which was passed in 1977, calls for banks to play a central role in the community renewal process by working toward the revitalization of declining neighborhoods through an affirmative action program of local housing and small business lending. Since success in these efforts is thought to depend primarily upon improved communication between banks and their local communities, the CRA requires financial institutions to take the initiative to ensure that the bank serves the "legitimate credit needs" and "convenience" of its community.
3 Ironically this became one of the incipient stories now being handed down in the emerging culture.

REFERENCES

Allen, M. G., Oliver, A. R., and Schwallie, E. H. The key to successful acquisitions. *The Journal of Business Strategy*, 1981, *2*(2), 14–23.

Barnouw, V. *Culture and personality*. Homewood: Dorsey Press, 1979.

Behr, E. A. Corporate takeover maneuvers prod congress to defend investors. *Wall Street Journal*, June 22, 1984, 1.

Bhagat, R. S., and McQuaid, S. J. Role of subjective culture in organizations: A review and directions for future research. *Journal of Applied Psychology*, 1982, *67*(5), 653–685.

Birch, W. J. A human resource perspective on mergers. *Personnel Journal*, 1983 (March), 244–246.

Bleakley, F. R. The merger makers' spiraling fees. *New York Times*, September 30, 1984, F1, F24.

Bowditch, J. L., and Buono, A. F. *Quality of work life assessment: A survey based approach*. Boston: Auburn House, 1982.

Bradley, J. W., and Korn, D. H. The changing role of acquisitions. *Journal of Business Strategy*, 1982, *2*(4), 30–42.

Business Week. How to survive your company's Merger. *Business Week*, September 17, 1979, 146–148.

Business Week. Holding on in a Takeover. *Business Week*, September 27, 1982, 118–120.

Carter, R. A. The human factor: When companies are sold, merged or conglomerated, what happens to the people who work for them? *Publishers Weekly*, January 21, 1983, 41–46.

Child, J. Culture, contingency, and capitalism in the cross national study of organizations. In L. L., Cummings, and B. M., Staw (Eds), *Research in organizational behavior* (Vol. 3), Greenwich, Connecticut: JA1 Press, 1981.

Davidson, K. M. Looking at the strategic impact of mergers. *The Journal of Business Strategy*, 1981, *2*(1), 13–22.

Deal, T. E., and Kennedy, A. A. *Corporate cultures: The rites and rituals of corporate life*. Reading, Massachusetts: Addison-Wesley, 1982.

Deal, T. E., and Kennedy, A. A. Culture: A new look through old lenses. *Journal of Applied Behavioral Science*, 1983, *19*(4), 498–505.

Gutek, B. A. On the accuracy of retrospective attitudinal data. *Public Opinion Quarterly*, 1978, 42, 390–401.

Harris, P. R., and Moran, R. T. *Managing cultural differences*. Houston: Gulf Publishing Co., 1979.

Hayes, R. H. The human side of acquisition. *Management Review*, November 1979, 6, 41–46.

Hertzberg, D. Competition spurs mergers of US banks. *Wall Street Journal*, October 22, 1984, 33.

Ingrassia, L. Employees at acquired firms find white knights often unfriendly. *Wall Street Journal*, July 7, 1982, 23.

Kroeber, A. L., and Kluckhohn, C. Culture: A critical review of concepts and definitions. *Papers of the Peabody Museum of American Archeology and Ethnology*, 1952, 47(1), 36–47.

Linton, R. *The study of man*. New York: Appleton-Century-Crofts, 1936.

Linton, R. *The cultural background of personality*. New York: Appleton-Century-Crofts, 1945.

Litterer, J. A. *An introduction to management*. New York: John Wiley, 1978.

McCaskey, M. B. The hidden messages managers send. *Harvard Business Review*, 1979, 57(6), 135–148.

Miles, R. *Macro organizational behavior*. Santa Monica: Goodyear, 1980.

Mirvis, P. H., and Sonka, A. L. When cultures collide: The case study of a corporate culture. Paper presented at 43rd Annual Meeting of the Academy of Management, Dallas, Texas, August 16, 1983.

Mitchell, G. D. *A dictionary of sociology*. London: Routledge and Kegan Paul, 1973.

Nystrom, P. C., and Starbuck, W. H. Managing beliefs in organizations. *Journal of Applied Behavioral Science*, 1984, 20(3), 277–287.

Parsons, T. *The social system*. Glencoe: Free Press, 1951.

Peters, T. Management systems: The language of organizational character and competence. *Organizational Dynamics*, 1980 (Summer), 3–27.

Peters, T., and Waterman, R. H. *In search of excellence*. New York: Simon and Schuster, 1982.

Pettigrew, A. M. On studying organizational cultures. *Administrative Science Quarterly*, 1979, 24(4), 570–581.

Radcliffe-Brown, A. R. *A natural science of society*: Glencoe: Free Press, 1957.

Salter, M., and Weinhold, W. What lies ahead for merger activities in the 1980s. *The Journal of Business Strategies*, 1982, 2(4), 66–99.

Schein, E. *Organizational psychology (3rd edition)*. Englewood Cliffs: Prentice Hall, 1980.

Schein, E. *The role of the founder in creating organizational culture*. Organizational Dynamics, 1983 (Summer), 13–28.

Schwartz, H., and Davis, S. M. Matching corporate culture and business strategy. *Organizational Dynamics*, 1981 (Summer), 30–48.

Siehl, C. Management or culture: The need for consistency and redundance among organizational components. Presentation delivered at the Symposium on Organizational Culture, Academy of Management, National Meeting, New York, August 16, 1982.

Sinetar, M. Merger, morale and productivity. *Personnel Management*, (November) 1981, 863–867.

Smircich, L. Concepts of culture and organizational analysis. *Administrative Science Quarterly*, 1983, 28(3), 339–358.

Triandis, H. D. Cross-cultural social and personality psychology. *Personality and Social Psychology Bulletin*, 1977, 3, 143–158.

Triandis, H. D., Vassilou, V., Vassilou, G., Tanka, Y., and Shanmugan, A. V. *The analysis of subjective culture*. New York: Wiley-Interscience, 1972.

Taylor, E. B. *Primitive culture: Researches into the development of mythology, philosophy, religion, language, art and custom* (Vol. 1). New York: Henry Holt, 1871.

Uttal, B. The corporate culture vultures. *Fortune*, October 17, 1983, 108(8), 66–72.

Whorton, J. W., and Worthley, J. A. A perspective on the challenge of public management: Environmental paradox and organizational culture. *Academy of Management Review*, 1981, 6(3), 357–361.

Wilkins, A. L. The creation of company cultures: The role of stories and human resource systems. *Human Resource Management*, 1984, 23(1), 41–60.

Zonana, V. F. The Porsches and Saabs at Schwab aggravate some at Bank-America. *Wall Street Journal*, January 20, 1983, 27.

A. F. Buono, Bowditch, J. L. and Lewis J. W., III (1985) "When cultures collide: The anatomy of a merger". *Human Relations*, 38(5), 477–500. Reprinted by permission of Sage Publications Ltd from A. F. Buono, J.L. Bowditch and J.W. Lewis, III, "When cultures collide: The anatomy of a merger". Copyright © The Tavistock Institute, 1985.

National cultural distance and cross-border acquisition performance

17

Piero Morosini, Scott Shane and Harbir Singh

Cross-border merger and acquisition (M&A) activity has continued to increase at a torrid pace during the past decade and a half, to the point that it has become a major strategic tool for growth of multinational corporations (Cartwright and Cooper, 1993). Throughout the 1980s, the number of cross-border acquisitions occurring each year had more than tripled, accounting for a significant proportion of total M&A activity by the early 1990s – 95 percent in the case of Japanese companies and 50 percent for European Union companies (Morosini and Singh, 1994). After a temporary slowdown during the recessionary global economy of the early 1990s, the value of cross-border M&A reached a record high of US$181.7 billion within the first nine months of 1996 (*The Economist*, 1997).

Recent research findings suggest that national cultural distance is relevant to cross-border acquisition performance (Morosini, 1998). In the context of a cross-border acquisition, national cultural distance represents distance in the norms, routines and repertoires for organizational design, new product development, and other aspects of management that are found in the acquirer's and the target's countries of origin (Kogut and Singh, 1988). In particular, specific routines and repertoires have been shown to be critical to post-acquisition performance, *and* to vary significantly across countries in direct association with the national cultural distance between them (Jemison and Sitkin, 1986; Hofstede, 1980). This is the case with routines and repertoires related to innovation effectiveness (Shane, 1993), degree of entrepreneurship (McGrath et al., 1992), decision-making practices (Kreacic and Marsh, 1986; Bourgoin, 1989), and the power and control structures of an organization (Brossard and Maurice, 1974).

Multinational corporations may need to possess a diverse set of routines and repertoires if they are to compete in a diverse world. Routines and repertoires are often dependent on the multinational corporation's unique institutional and cultural environment, and are therefore not imitated easily by other firms (Barney, 1986). Given uncertainty as to the routines and repertoires that will be valuable in the future, a multinational corporation may increase the probability of possessing a greater variety of potentially valuable routines and repertoires by acquiring a firm in a culturally distant country.

Against this background, we attempt to address an issue which has received very little attention in the literature, namely, the effects of national cultural distance on cross-border acquisition performance. As multinational companies increasingly acquire targets in more culturally distant countries, they face new challenges in managing their external environment (Moran, 1980). Such considerations have motivated the central question of this article: How does national cultural distance between the acquirers' and targets' countries of origin influence cross-border acquisition performance?

This article tests the relationship between national cultural distance and cross-border acquisition performance, while controlling for firm- and industry-level variables. The findings suggest that researchers and practitioners should incorporate national cultural distance into cross-border acquisition decision-making and research. The article is structured in the following manner: In the next section, we outline the terminology used to define national cultural distance. We then develop the theoretical explanation for the effects of national cultural distance on cross-border post-acquisition performance. We go on to describe the methodology and empirical model designed to test this explanation, and to present the results. We also present the results of field interviews of four multinational companies that complement the findings of the empirical model. In the final section, we draw the conclusions.

TERMINOLOGY

It is important to establish a clear terminology at the outset. National cultural distance is defined as the degree to which the cultural norms in one country are different from those in another country (Kogut and Singh, 1988). In their article on national culture and choice of entry modes, Kogut and Singh (1988) estimated national cultural distance as a composite index based on the deviation from each of Hofstede's (1980) national culture scales: Power distance, uncertainty avoidance, masculinity/femininity, and individualism. Following this approach, we measure national cultural distance between the countries of origin of the acquiring and target firms following Hofstede's (1980) four cultural dimensions. We employ Hofstede's (1980) national culture scores because they are consistent with our empirical approach to measure national cultural distance. Our measure is discussed in detail in the methodology section, along with a justification for selecting Hofstede's (1980) quantitative scores to measure national culture.

In the context of this article, we define routines and repertoires as the ways in which a firm typically addresses aspects of organizing its business activities. These routines and repertoires include such elements as R&D procedures, policies for supervising subordinates, and procedures for scanning the competitive environment. As previously mentioned, critical routines and repertoires within organizations in different countries have been shown to vary significantly and in direct association with the national cultural distance between them (Shane, 1993; McGrath et al., 1992; Hofstede, 1980; Brossard and Maurice, 1974). They have also been shown to affect post-acquisition performance through learning and specialization that take place between the acquiring and the target firms following the acquisition (Haspeslagh and Jemison, 1991; Jemison and Sitkin, 1986; Lincoln et al., 1981).

THEORY DEVELOPMENT

Research within the perspective of the resource-based view of the firm has indicated that sustainable competitive advantage results from valuable, rare and inimitable resources that can be physical, financial or human (Barney, 1986; Barney, 1991). Human capital-based resource advantages often lie in the administrative routines and repertoires that firms develop to make decisions, to govern the allocation of resources, to formulate strategy, to interact with stakeholders, or to make use of assets (Fiol, 1991).

For administrative routines and repertoires to create a sustainable competitive advantage, they must not be easily imitated by other firms. This is the case for organizational routines developed in interaction with a firm's history and institutional environment (Collis, 1991). Indeed, such interaction leads to the development of a unique set of routines and repertoires within the organization. Even though these unique routines and repertoires are often seen by managers of other firms as valuable, they may not be easily replicated by companies other than the advantaged firm if they have not followed a similar path of historical development, or if they have not been present in the same institutional environment (Barney, 1991).

The institutional environment of a firm and the historical path of development of the routines and repertoires that generate a firm's competitive advantage appear to be embedded in national culture (Barney, 1986). Routines and repertoires are shaped by the national cultures of firm founders and the national circumstances of their foundation (Pettigrew, 1979). Some routines, such as the process of innovating and inventing, decision-making practices, stakeholder relationships, strategies, structure and training, are more common in some national cultures than in others because of the institutional environment in which firms operate (Shane, 1992; Schneider and DeMeyer, 1991; Kreacic and Marsh, 1986; Barney, 1986; Hofstede, 1980). As a result, the organizational routines and repertoires that lead to a firm's sustainable competitive advantage tend to be constrained by national culture (Hofstede et al., 1990; Lincoln et al., 1981; Kogut and Singh, 1988), which makes them difficult to replicate in other national cultures (Barney, 1986).

However, firms that operate on a multinational scale may need to possess a diverse set of routines and repertoires if they are to compete in a diverse world. In an uncertain environment, it is difficult for managers to know *ex ante* what routines and repertoires will provide sustainable competitive advantage and performance over time. Given the difficulty of forecasting valuable future routines and repertoires, it may be in a multinational firm's best interest to access a relatively large and diverse pool of routines and repertoires, thus increasing the probability that it will possess those that prove to be valuable in the future. Cross-border acquisitions provide a mechanism for accessing valuable routines and repertoires embedded in other national cultures without having to follow the developmental path that leads to them (Jemison and Sitkin, 1986). Acquisitions across national cultures could enhance firm performance by providing access to a valuable pool of critical routines and repertoires previously not available to the firm (Ghoshal, 1987).

Access to routines and repertoires via acquisition of a firm in another national culture could enhance the performance of the combined organization in two different ways. The first way is through learning (Ghoshal, 1987). Firms in some national cultures are unable or unwilling to develop certain routines because they lack a tradition of a particular "way of doing things" (Barney, 1991). Following a cross-border acquisition, the two firms interact and learn from each other at various operating levels, pooling their organizational routines (Haspeslagh and Jemison, 1991). The second way is through specialization. Acquisition of a firm in another national culture enables access to routines specialized to that firm's local context (Lincoln et al., 1981). National culture leads and contributes to the adoption of country-specific routines for accomplishing certain tasks (Fiol, 1991). It is less costly to have employees perform tasks in ways that are consistent with their national cultural values than to have them carry out tasks in ways that are not compatible with their cultural beliefs (Shane, 1993). For example, the acceptability of freedom from organizational control varies across national cultures (Hofstede, 1980). Consequently, it has been shown that it is less costly to innovate in the context of some national cultures than in others (Shane, 1992).

However, it has been argued that a relatively high level of cultural distance between firms is likely to lead to "cultural ambiguity" and process losses when different cultures "collide" during the post-acquisition period (Jemison and Sitkin, 1986; Buono et al., 1985). Higher levels of cultural distance between firms have been associated with a higher degree of conflict during the day-to-day post-acquisition integration period (Jemison and Sitkin, 1986). While cultural distance is often seen as a potential source of difficulty, the eventual outcome of an acquisition is dependent upon steps taken during the post-acquisition phase (Haspeslagh and Jemison, 1991). Moreover, many of the concerns about cultural distance that have been put forward in the literature on post-acquisition performance are based on corporate culture differences (Datta, 1991). In the context of a cross-border acquisition, however, benefits of national cultural distance between the acquirer and the target firm may offset the potentially disruptive impact of other sources of difficulty related to corporate cultural distance during the post-acquisition period (Ghoshal, 1987), or even during the pre-acquisition phase, for example, through learning.

Extensive empirical research has shown that, on average, the greater the national cultural distance between two countries, the greater the differences between them in terms of routines and repertoires (Hofstede, 1980; Lincoln et al., 1981). For example, routines and repertoires related to innovation and inventiveness, as well as the degree of entrepreneurship, have been found to vary significantly across countries along Hofstede's (1980) "individualism-collectivism" polarity (Shane, 1993; McGrath et al., 1992). It has also been shown that firms in countries which are significantly distant along Hofstede's (1980) "uncertainty-avoidance" and "power-distance" national cultural dimensions present specific differences in their decision-making practices and in their power and control structures (Bourgoin, 1989; Kreacic and Marsh, 1986; Hofstede, 1980; Brossard and Maurice, 1974). National cultural distance between countries has also been associated with significant differences in their legal systems, incentive routines, administrative practices and working styles (Hofstede, 1980; Shane, 1992; Ouchi, 1980).

If, as we argued earlier, the ability to develop certain routines and repertoires is partly dependent on the national cultural environment in which firms operate, multinational firms will find that cross-border acquisitions in culturally distant countries tend to be more valuable, because a greater national cultural distance makes it more likely that the target will provide a set of routines and repertoires that are significantly different from the bidding firm's own set, and which cannot be easily replicated in the acquirer's country of origin – or vice versa (Barney, 1991). Since these different routines and repertoires can be utilized to significantly transform a firm's business strategy, structure and operations in order to improve performance (Hofstede, 1980; Ghoshal, 1987), a cross-border acquisition might be interpreted as a mechanism for the acquiring (or the target) firm to access different routines and repertoires that are missing in its own national culture, and which have the potential to enhance the combined firm's competitive advantage and performance over time (Jemison and Sitkin, 1986).

These arguments lead to the following hypothesis tested in this study:

The greater the national cultural distance between the acquirer's country and the target's country, the greater will be the post-acquisition performance of the combined firm.

METHODOLOGY

A survey of firms involved in cross-border acquisition activity was undertaken, complemented by in-depth interviews of individuals involved in cross-border acquisitions in four multinational companies.

Survey of firms

The sample

A detailed questionnaire was designed in both Italian and English, and 400 companies that had engaged in cross-border acquisition activity in Italy between 1987 and 1992 were invited to participate in the survey. These 400 companies were identified from a database put together by KPMG Peat Marwick Consultants, which, in Italy, is commonly regarded by researchers and practitioners as one of the most comprehensive databases. A total of 73 companies responded positively to the invitation, and were sent the detailed questionnaire designed to gather information on cross-border acquisitions in which one of the partners – either the acquirer or the target company – was Italian. Out of these 73 companies, a total of 64 responded to the questionnaire. To ensure data reliability, only information on companies for which performance data could be independently verified from archival sources was used. Only responses of 52 companies could be verified in this way, and therefore the statistical analysis is based on the 52 companies, which is sufficient for the multivariate analysis performed here (Mazen et al., 1987). Country frequencies for these 52 responses are shown in Table 1.

The data was checked for non-response bias, by comparing the respondents and non-respondents on the publicly accountable variables in our model: Size, country of origin and relatedness. These tests showed that the differences between the two groups were not significant at the $p < .10$ level, indicating no problem of non-response bias.

The variables

Dependent variable: Performance was measured as the percentage rate of growth in sales (denominated in US dollars) over the two-year period following the acquisition. The measure of sales growth was calculated based on data gathered in the questionnaires distributed to the sample, and was checked against archival sources to ensure accuracy.

Table 1 Number of acquisitions by the acquirer's country of origin

Acquirer's country of origin	Number of acquisitions
Italy	17
United States	7
United Kingdom	6
France	6
Belgium	3
Germany	3
Sweden	3
Switzerland	3
Finland	2
Netherlands	2
Total	52

Note: The target countries of the Italian acquirers abroad were: France (7), United States (5), Germany, United Kingdom, Switzerland, Austria and Spain (1 in each country).

Market-based measures have been suggested as superior alternatives for performance measurements (Woo et al., 1992), and have been used frequently to measure post-acquisition performance in the literature (Chatterjee et al., 1992; Singh and Montgomery, 1987). However, the applicability of this type of approach in the largely European and Italian context of the present research was rather limited for two reasons. First, the Italian stock market is considerably small relative to other developed economies, both in terms of the number of companies quoted and as a proportion of the total size of the economy (Marelli, 1994; Morosini, 1994). As a consequence, the acquisition activity taking place through the Italian stock market is not always representative of the total level of activity (*Acquisizioni*, 1994). Second, a number of the stock markets of countries well represented in our sample (e.g., Italy, France, Germany) have been, until recently, notorious for their lack of market efficiency, hindering the usefulness of stock price measures.

Growth in sales has been used as a measure of performance in strategic management research (Woo et al., 1992; Morrison and Roth, 1992), including studies of post-acquisition performance (Datta, 1991; Haspeslagh and Jemison, 1991). Moreover, sales growth is an appropriate performance measure for such process-based operating phenomena as M&As (Haspeslagh and Jemison, 1991; Pursche, 1990). The usefulness of sales growth as a measure of post-acquisition performance allows us to capture the effects of our hypothesized relationship effectively.

We measured performance for two years following the acquisition based on two justifications. First, a wide body of literature suggests that the first two years after an acquisition are critical to its overall performance (Jemison and Sitkin, 1986; Balloun and Gridley, 1990). Second, by the end of a two-year period after the acquisition, the process of combining the firms usually has been completed, and the results of the underlying integration effort can be measured effectively (Jemison and Sitkin, 1986).

Independent variable: The key independent variable in this study, national cultural distance, was measured following Kogut and Singh's (1988) measures, based on Hofstede's (1980) national culture scores. Kogut and Singh (1988) defined national cultural distance as the degree to which the cultural norms in one country differ from those in another country. Based on this definition, a number of authors have shown that critical routines and repertoires within firms in different countries vary significantly in direct association with the national cultural distance between them (Shane, 1993; McGrath et al., 1992; Kreacic and Marsh, 1986; Hofstede, 1980; Brossard and Maurice, 1974). Using Kogut and Singh's (1988) formula for national cultural distance, we created a multidimensional measure that estimated the distance between Italy and the other countries along Hofstede's (1980) power distance, uncertainty avoidance, masculinity/femininity and individualism scores:

$$CD_j = \sqrt{\sum_{i=1}^{4} (I_{ij} - I_{il})^2}$$

where:

CD_j: Is the cultural difference for the jth country.
I_{ij}: Hofstede's score: ith cultural dimension and jth country.
I_l: Indicates Italy.

We selected this measure of cultural distance because of the extensive evidence of the validity and reliability of the underlying Hofstede's (1980) national cultural scores (Morosini and Singh, 1994; Shane, 1992; Kogut and Singh, 1988). Moreover, there are significant advantages to using Hofstede's scores as a measure of national cultural distance over administering a questionnaire on national culture to the managers of the companies in the sample. First, the use of Hofstede's scores avoids the problem of common method variance in which the same individuals answer questions about firm performance in the same way as answering questions about national culture (see Shane, 1995 for a discussion of the problem). Second, the use of Hofstede's scores avoids the problem of retrospective evaluation of national culture. Since people tend to be ethnocentric and prefer similarity (Hofstede, 1980), if surveyed after the acquisition, members of the acquiring firms might "remember" the national culture of target firms as being more similar than they really were. The design of this study avoids the problem of retrospective rationalization by using national culture scores from a source external to the sample and not dependent on the memory of the respondents.

Control variables

Relatedness: Relatedness was defined according to the industries of the acquiring and acquired firms. Research on post-acquisition performance has argued that relatedness of the acquisition should enhance post-acquisition performance (Salter and Weinhold, 1979; Lubatkin, 1983; Datta, 1991). A number of explanations for this relationship have been given, including economies of scale and scope (Salter and Weinhold, 1979; Lubatkin, 1983; Datta, 1991; Williamson, 1981; Porter, 1980) and market power (Eckbo, 1983; Stillman, 1983). Singh and Montgomery (1987) demonstrated that gains to shareholders were higher in related acquisitions than in unrelated ones. Shelton (1988) has shown that related acquisitions create more shareholder value than unrelated acquisitions. For this reason, we control for relatedness of the acquisition in this study.

Relatedness was measured based on the industry of the acquirer and the target firms. If archival data indicated that the two companies were in the same industry, the acquisition received a relatedness score of one. If archival data indicated that the two companies were in different industries, the acquisition received a relatedness score of zero.

Size: A number of scholars have shown that the size of an acquisition influences post-acquisition performance (Kusewitt, 1985; Kitching, 1967). Therefore, we also controlled for size in this study. This variable was measured as the dollar value of the target's net sales in the year of the acquisition. These data were taken from the survey, and a reliability check was made based on archival sources.

Post-acquisition strategy: The post-acquisition strategies implemented by the acquiring firms can be thought of as following "integration" or "execution" modes (Morosini, 1998; Morosini and Singh, 1994), and are commonly regarded as critical for the strategic and financial success of the acquisition. Research on the post-acquisition process has shown that effective integration of operations enhances post-acquisition performance as the combined firm lowers costs by increasing scale economies in production, marketing, distribution and advertising (Rappaport, 1987; Datta, 1991). Therefore, we control for the inherent degree of integration in the post-acquisition strategies implemented by the acquiring firms in this study.

Following Pursche (1990) and Morosini and Singh (1994), we broadly characterize the different post-acquisition strategies implemented by the acquirer on the basis of the degree of post-acquisition integration between the target and the acquiring firm (Shrivastava, 1986), and on whether the source of value of the acquisition resides in the combination of the merging firm's resources or only in the target firm's resources (Chatterjee, 1992). Based on those criteria, the post-acquisition strategies were defined as: "Integration" (i.e., significant changes in both firms' businesses and functions; the source of value resides in combining both firms' resources); "restructuring" (i.e., significant changes in the target's businesses and functions; the source of value resides predominantly in the target firm); and "independence" (i.e., very limited or no business or functional changes in any of the merging companies following the acquisition).

The post-acquisition strategy implemented by the acquiring firm was measured by a questionnaire item asking if the acquiring company was following an "integration" strategy, a "restructuring" strategy, or an "independence" strategy. Explanations for each of these strategies were provided in the questionnaire so that respondents had a consistent definition of each strategy. A dummy variable received a score of minus one if the post-acquisition strategy implemented was "independence," zero if it was "restructuring," and one if it was "integration," respectively

Uncertainty Avoidance: Uncertainty avoidance on the part of the acquirer can influence post-acquisition performance and is therefore controlled for in this study. Uncertainty avoidance has been associated with a preference for organizational rules and procedures favoring monitoring, planning and control (Hofstede, 1980), which in turn have been shown to influence post-acquisition performance (Achtmeyer and Daniell, 1988). It has also been observed that countries where there is uncertainty avoidance favor short-term feedback (Hofstede, 1980), leading to top-down types of post-merger management approaches that are generally fast to implement and lead to quick sales growth (Pursche, 1990). Because of this, we argue that uncertainty avoidance could have a beneficial impact on post-acquisition performance. In order to control for uncertainty avoidance in our model, we use Hofstede's (1980) national culture scores for the uncertainty avoidance of the acquiring firm's country of origin.

Year: Controlling for the year of the acquisition was necessary because national and international economic and financial conditions vary year by year, and have a clear impact on the performance of all acquisitions. Moreover, important political, economic and financial changes took place in Italy during the period under consideration in this research; particularly in 1991 and 1992, a large scale devaluation forced the Italian government to temporarily withdraw the Lira from the European Monetary System of minimal exchange rate fluctuations between the main European currencies. These events may have affected the performance of the acquisitions under study, as many of the Italian companies acquired were export oriented (e.g., in the textiles and apparel industry). We used dummy variables for the years 1987, 1988, 1989, 1990 and 1991.

Industry: Research has documented industry differences in the preference of acquisitions as an entry mode (Caves, 1982). Moreover, strong patterns are present in the preference for acquisitions across services and manufacturing industries (Kogut and Singh, 1988). Industry differences in the preference of acquisitions as an entry mode suggest that industry might have an effect on post-acquisition performance. Therefore, through the use of dummy variables, we controlled for acquisitions in four key industries in which there was significant acquisition activity during the period under study: Banking, textiles and apparel, waste management, and pharmaceuticals.

The model

We tested our hypothesis on the sample of acquisitions using ordinary least squares regression analysis. The regression model was of the following form:

Performance $\quad = f(\text{CD, UA, RE, SI, IN, 87, 88, 89, 90, 91, TE, WA, BA, PH})$

where:

Performance	= Percentage growth in sales for the two years following the acquisition.
CD	= Cultural distance score between Italy and the counterpart firm's country of origin.
UA	= Hofstede's uncertainty avoidance score for the acquiring firm's country of origin.
RE	= Dummy variable for relatedness of the acquisition.
SI	= Dollar value of the target's net sales in the year of acquisition.
IN	= Post-acquisition strategy implemented by the acquiring firm.
87, 88, 89, 90, 91	= Dummy variables for acquisitions that took place in 1987, 1988, 1989, 1990 and 1991, respectively.
TE, WA, BA, PH	= Dummy variables for the textiles and apparel, waste management, banking, and pharmaceutical industries, respectively.

Field-based interviews

Field based interviews of 16 senior executives in four companies engaged in cross-border acquisitions were also employed to provide a more fine-grained understanding of the mechanisms by which national cultural distance was addressed in the corporations. Indeed, it is questionable whether exclusively quantitative approaches are appropriate to characterize the multiform and highly diverse contextual aspects in which cross-cultural mechanisms are carried out in practice within multinational companies (Lane and Beamish, 1990). Thus, our expectation was that by combining quantitative and qualitative analysis we could gain a deeper understanding of the phenomenon under investigation (Parkhe, 1993).

The field work consisted of interviews of CEOs, other high ranking executives and line managers with deep knowledge of their companies' international M&A activity. These executives were selected on the basis of their direct decision-making and long-term involvement in their companies' M&A activities throughout the assessment, negotiation and implementation phases. The varied managerial levels and specific experiences sought after intended to avoid potential problems of hindsight rationalization or partial knowledge of the business situations examined (Regnér, 1996). Detailed research of these companies, particularly focusing on their cross-border M&A activities, preceded every interview. The interviews themselves were highly structured, and focused on the companies' M&A activities in culturally distant countries.

An interview protocol was designed and used throughout the field interviewing process. A letter was sent to the company executives chosen asking them to answer a few questions during a one hour personal meeting. An interview guide was attached to the letter in order to illustrate the types of issues being investigated, but without describing the hypothesis, theoretical basis, or quantitative results of the research. The interview guide had several open-ended questions and consisted of two parts. The first part included several questions related to whether, in the context of their companies' cross-border acquisition activity, decision makers had been significantly motivated by the value they saw in national cultural distance; what specific kind of benefit was provided by culturally distant acquisitions; and how was this benefit transferred to the acquiring firm. The second part of the questionnaire was tailored to investigate in more depth each company's specific instances of culturally distant acquisitions, characterizing the benefits provided by nationally embedded factors, and providing concrete examples of the mechanisms through which these benefits were effectively transferred to the acquirer.

There was a high degree of consensus among respondents on benefits provided by national cultural distance (e.g., acquisition of diverse routines and repertoires in areas such as R&D procedures, executive compensation systems, international project management and financing), and on the mechanisms through which these benefits were transferred to the acquirer (e.g., the international rotation of key personnel between the acquiring and the target firms), but these tended to present some variety depending on the type of industry and the specific competitive context of each company. Following the initial contacts with the executives, multiple interviews were conducted at each company's location during 1995 and 1996. Typically, there were initially individual meetings with highly ranked executives, such as CEOs or board members. After these initial meetings, additional interviews were arranged and carried out with lower level executives and line managers at each company following the same interviewing approach. Every interview was recorded, and subsequently transcribed and analyzed in a structured way, establishing in the context of every executive's cross-border acquisition experiences:

- whether his/her company had been significantly motivated by the value they saw in national cultural distance;
- what kind of value and/or benefits were specifically provided by national cultural distance; and

• how were nationally embedded benefits transferred to the acquirer or to the combined firm's operations.

Multiple interviewing sessions and follow-up meetings were carried out during 1995 through 1996.

The companies were chosen to be representative of different geographic locations, variation in degree of internationalization, industry differences and level of M&A activity. Thus, the sample included companies that were "globalized" and companies that had only recently begun to expand overseas. We also ensured that Swedish-Italian acquisitions were included, given that the national cultural distance between Sweden and Italy was found to be the highest in the empirical sample utilized in the first part of our research.

RESULTS

Statistical analysis

Table 2 shows the means, standard deviations and correlation coefficients for the variables. The Table shows that the highest correlation between the independent

Table 2 Descriptive statistics

	Mean	SD	SA	CD	UA	RE	SI	IN	87	88	89	90	91	TE	WA	PA	PH
SA	−0.17	0.39	1.00														
CD	37.34	12.29	0.31	1.00													
UA	61.36	18.88	0.12	−0.38	1.00												
RE	0.88	0.32	0.06	0.04	0.04	1.00											
SI	538.87	913.62	−0.05	−0.03	0.18	0.15	1.00										
IN	0.06	0.80	0.21	0.22	−0.03	−0.05	0.11	1.00									
87	0.17	0.38	−0.34	−0.07	−0.02	0.17	−0.00	−0.10	1.00								
88	0.15	0.36	−0.05	−0.02	−0.33	−0.18	−0.04	−0.10	−0.20	1.00							
89	0.42	0.50	−0.05	0.12	0.08	−0.06	−0.27	0.09	−0.39	−0.37	1.00						
90	0.15	0.36	0.25	−0.06	0.14	−0.01	0.33	−0.03	−0.20	−0.18	−0.37	1.00					
91	0.04	0.19	0.33	−0.07	−0.01	0.07	−0.05	0.11	−0.09	−0.09	−0.17	−0.09	1.00				
TE	0.04	0.19	0.50	−0.10	0.15	0.07	0.33	0.11	−0.09	−0.09	−0.17	0.47	−0.04	1.00			
WA	0.02	0.14	−0.12	−0.05	−0.12	0.05	−0.08	−0.01	−0.06	0.33	−0.12	−0.06	−0.03	−0.03	1.00		
BA	0.04	0.19	−0.11	−0.00	0.15	0.07	−0.11	0.11	0.17	0.19	−0.17	−0.09	−0.04	−0.04	−0.03	1.00	
PH	0.04	0.19	−0.13	−0.07	0.31	−0.24	−0.11	−0.02	−0.09	−0.09	0.23	−0.09	−0.04	−0.04	−0.03	−0.04	1.00

Key:
SA = Percentage growth in sales for the two years following the acquisition.
CD = Kogut and Singh's (1988) cultural distance score between Italy and the counterpart company's country.
UA = Hofstede's uncertainty avoidance score for the acquirer's country.
RE = Dummy variable for relatedness of the acquisition.
SI = Dollar value of the target's net sales in the year of the acquisition.
IN = Post-acquisition strategy.
87 = Dummy variable for acquisitions that took place in 1987.
88 = Dummy variable for acquisitions that took place in 1988.
89 = Dummy variable for acquisitions that took place in 1989.
90 = Dummy variable for acquisitions that took place in 1990.
91 = Dummy variable for acquisitions that took place in 1991.
TE = Dummy variable for the textiles and apparel industry.
WA = Dummy variable for the waste management industry.
BA = Dummy variable for the banking industry.
PH = Dummy variable for the pharmaceuticals industy.

variables (r = 0.47) is that between the dummy variable for the textiles and apparel industry and the dummy variable for 1990. This modest overall level of correlation indicates that multicollinearity is not a problem in this study.

We also conducted tests to ensure the robustness of the regression model. Tests of heteroskedasticity and autocorrelation of errors showed that neither of these problems were present in the data. Plots of the independent variable against the dependent variable indicated that a linear model was the best model to fit the data. Plots of the residuals also indicated the robustness of the regression model.

The results of the regression analyses are shown in Table 3. The ordinary least squares form of regression on the dependent variable produces results that support our hypothesis. As Table 3 shows, the regression coefficient associated with the cultural distance variable was 0.13 (t = 2.04; p < .05), indicating that cultural distance had a positive effect on post-acquisition performance. In other words, after controlling for year, industry, size, relatedness, post-acquisition strategy and uncertainty avoidance of the acquirer, the greater the national cultural distance between the acquirer and the target, the greater the sales growth rate over the two-year period following the acquisition.

Table 3 also shows that the regression coefficient associated with the acquirer's national cultural value of uncertainty avoidance was 0.01 (t = 2.23; p < .05), indicating that the national cultural value of uncertainty avoidance had a slight, but significant effect on post-acquisition performance. The results suggest that this effect is positive, but very small.

One of the empirical findings on post-acquisition performance in the literature has been that integration of operations increases efficiencies and economies of scale and

Table 3 Results of the ordinary least squares regression analyses

Variable	Coefficient	t-Value
Cultural distance	0.13	2.04*
Uncertainty avoidance	0.01	2.23*
Post-acquisition strategy	0.06	1.17
Relatedness	0.08	0.58
Size	−0.00	−3.14*
1987	−0.30	−1.52
1988	0.08	0.37
1989	−0.14	−0.76
1990	−0.03	−0.14
1991	0.51	−1.95
Banking	−0.37	−1.61
Waste management	−0.44	−1.46
Textiles/apparel	1.05	4.45*
Pharmaceuticals	−0.38	−1.69
Constant	−0.57	−1.85
Adjusted R-squared	0.479	
df	37.14	
F-value	4.35*	
N	52	

* Significant at the p < .05 level or better in a two-tailed test.

thereby enhances performance (Porter, 1980; Salter and Weinhold, 1979; Datta, 1991). However, our findings show that the regression coefficient associated with post-acquisition strategy implemented by the acquirer, which is akin to the integration mode of the acquisition, was non-significant. This indicates that, in our model, the post-acquisition strategy for target integration did not seem to affect post-acquisition performance.

Table 3 also shows that the regression coefficient associated with the relatedness variable was positive and non-significant, indicating that the degree of relatedness of the acquirer and the target firms did not influence sales growth of the combined firm during the two-year period following the acquisition.

The results show that the regression coefficient associated with the size variable was negative and significant, although the magnitude of this effect is very small. We therefore cautiously observe that, in our sample, acquiring larger targets resulted in lower sales growth in the two-year period after the acquisition than did acquiring smaller targets, but the amount of this difference was very slight.

Among the regression coefficients controlling for year, the variable for 1991 was positive and approached significance. This result indicated that the year of the acquisition had an almost significant, but large, effect on post-acquisition sales growth. Interestingly, as mentioned earlier, 1991 was characterized by momentous political, fiscal and monetary policy events with few precedents in the Italian post-war history. It may be argued that these factors, particularly the large devaluation of the Lira, affected both the level of activity and the relative performance of cross-border acquisitions in Italy during the years around 1991.

One of the regression coefficients controlling for industry, namely the dummy variable for the textiles and apparel industry, had a significant and positive effect on post-acquisition sales growth. As mentioned earlier, this positive effect can be related to the fact that acquisitions in the Italian textiles and apparel industry, which were mostly export oriented, may have benefited from the large devaluation of the Lira during 1992. This result also indicates the importance of controlling for industry in studies on cross-border acquisition performance. Acquisitions in the textile and apparel industry had significantly faster revenue growth in the two years after the acquisitions compared with other industries.

Field-based interviews

To provide a richer understanding of the mechanisms by which national cultural distance enhanced post-acquisition performance and to confirm the survey results, we outline below the major results of our interviews conducted in four multinational firms engaged in cross-border acquisitions.

All of the interviews indicated that senior executives considered cultural traits less prevalent in their home national culture necessary to capture. For example, in Pharmacia's acquisition of Farmitalia Carlo Erba, and Electrolux's acquisition of Zanussi, senior executives sought to gain access to Italian cultural characteristics that were generally difficult to find in Sweden. As Gianmario Rossignolo, the former Chairman of Electrolux-Zanussi, formed from a Swedish acquisition of an Italian firm, observed, "One fundamental reason for Electrolux to acquire Zanussi is that people skills were sufficiently complementary in marketing and product design. Our [Italian] people were more creative, more aggressive and much more flexible. This flexibility is part of the Italian culture, and you see many examples of this in

Zanussi." While the company's cross-border acquisitions occurred across a variety of industries and at different points in time, all of the executives interviewed highlighted the value of national cultural distance as a significant motive for cross-border acquisition. As Gianmario Rossignolo explained: "You don't buy just machine tools here in this company [Zanussi], you get access to the people's [Italian] culture, which is an asset to be preserved." Specifically, Electrolux executives explained that the acquisition of Italian Zanussi provided access by researchers and product designers to innovative routines and repertoires different from those of Electrolux.

Similarly, senior executives at Sweden's Pharmacia pointed out that ensuring access to different innovative routines and repertoires in critical pharmaceutical research areas was a significant motive for acquiring Italian Farmitalia Carlo Erba. As Lars Lindegren, a former CEO of Pharmacia-Farmitalia Carlo Erba, remarked, "We Swedes are very different from the Italians. This is a big cultural difference between the countries. One could notice this diversity reflected in the very different research approaches and working methods that Farmitalia Carlo Erba had developed here in Italy *vis-à-vis* our own ways of doing research in Pharmacia."

The beneficial effect of country-specific routines and repertoires stemming from acquisitions across culturally distant locations were described as bi-directional. Thus, in the case of Pharmacia, the concern for social inter-dependence and welfare of others also provided routines valuable to the Italian target firm. The acquirers were able to transfer routines and repertoires for team-based and non-hierarchical ways of working in which Italian creativity and innovativeness could fully develop its potential. As Lars Lindegren explained, "Italians had a big problem. They lacked an understanding of the conditions under which research works. See, creativity and innovation cannot flourish in a place where control and hierarchy are more important than delegation. Research means to innovate, to invent and create new things, and that needs freedom, delegation and team-work. So, the acquired company's way of working, hierarchical, individualist and not cross-functional, was counterproductive in this context."

Senior executives at Swedish/Swiss ASEA Brown Boveri (ABB) also pointed to the acquisition of Italian companies as providing access to specific and valuable skills embedded in that country's particular cultural environment, which could then be internationally transferred across other ABB country operations. Through their purchase of SACE, a Bergamo-based electrical components producer, ABB gained access to, and know-how of, flexible financing instruments available in Italy to finance large-scale infrastructure projects. Such flexible financing instruments have been historically developed within Italy's specific business context and traditionally uncertain political milieu, which have been closely linked with the country's particular national cultural traits (Putnam, 1993). Following its acquisition of SACE, ABB was able to absorb and transfer the Italian target's flexible financing mechanisms and know-how to fund large-scale electrical engineering projects, particularly across transitional economies and developing countries that were perceived as being culturally distant *vis-à-vis* the Swedish/Swiss parent company.

High-ranked executives at Deutsche Bank's headquarters stressed that their acquisitions of major Italian financial institutions, such as Banca d'America e d'Italia (BAI), Banca Popolare di Lecco and Finanza e Futuro, also provided their company with valuable country-specific organizational routines, such as flexible and aggressive sales approaches. However, these executives added that Deutsche Bank's absorption of nationally embedded and valuable organizational routines through acquisition was also characteristic of other cross-border operations carried out in locations perceived as culturally distant *vis-à-vis* Germany. A significant example of that was Deutsche Bank's acquisition of Britain's Morgan Grenfell, a merchant and investment banking operation based in London. Deutsche Bank's executives repeatedly referred to the value of this acquisition as injecting the aggressive culture of the acquired firm into the acquirer's more conservative banking style. When asked to give a concrete example of these cultural benefits to Deutsche Bank, the executives interviewed described the organizational and incentives routines typical of British merchant banks, but highly uncommon in the German financial sector by the time of the Morgan Grenfell acquisition in 1989. After acquiring Morgan Grenfell, Deutsche Bank transformed its previously conservative executive salary and incentives structure towards a performance-based system learned from the acquired firm. Deutsche Bank executives explained that performance-based executive compensation mechanisms, such as stock options and bonuses, had been unprecedented in their more conservative business environment. Corporate policies and know-how developed by Morgan Grenfell within the British cultural context of higher individualism and lower uncertainty avoidance were stressed by Deutsche Bank executives as crucial to drive the rapid transformation of the German bank's incentives and compensation systems.

We also examined the mechanisms through which new routines and repertoires were incorporated by the acquiring companies. At Pharmacia and Electrolux, autonomy was important. By providing the Italian research teams with a great deal of autonomy, the acquirers were able to use the target companies as a template for learning new skills in team-based research. The Swedish acquirers established a limited presence in the target company (only a few Swedes were present in Italy in either case, their purposes being to set up goals, train and develop key local managers, and ensure that targets were met). Similarly, Deutsche Bank's executives explained that national cultural distance did not hinder their acquisition of Morgan Grenfell because of the flexible approach used in integrating both firms. Additionally, the acquirer showed an open mind in maintaining the target's incentives and salary schemes and other organizational practices as a model to learn from, and transfer to other parts of Deutsche Bank.

Given the reliance on autonomy, communication links were important for the firms in the survey. A strong effort was made to ensure a high level of communications between the two firms, with objectives and progress being communicated at all levels. Regular communication meetings were employed to transfer information. As one executive explained: "The organization and systems set up by us have been useful for improving communication between people."

Policies to provide long-term and temporary international assignments and incentives for internationalizing subordinates were also important in making cross-border transfer of routines and repertoires work. In many of the companies, business line managers were given opportunities to transfer what they had learned from others to different parts of the organizations around the world. ABB's executives explained that national cultural differences do not undermine learning from this variation because of a heavy reliance on rotation, training and internal communications to effectively integrate their cross-border acquisitions. To capture the value of national cultural distance, ABB created "multidomestic" organizational routines and repertoires that allowed it to absorb rapidly companies in culturally distant countries. These also stimulated considerable increases in productivity, through global transfer of knowledge embedded in national culture, but made proprietary through ABB acquisitions. ABB executives explained that the extensive use of rotation programs, company parenting schemes, and the development of global management skills and communications made ABB able to absorb varied national cultures at a relatively low organizational cost.

The interviews confirm that executives of firms undertaking cross-border acquisitions see value in national cultural distance. The executives of the companies in which we conducted the interviews repeatedly echoed the theme that these acquisitions provided access to valuable organizational routines that were embedded in other national cultures, and which would have been difficult to develop in the home country despite their value. In order to transfer the benefits stemming from acquisitions in culturally distant countries, the firms rely on specific absorptive mechanisms. Executives of the companies surveyed explained that valuable organizational routines embedded in the targets' national cultures are learned and transferred back to the acquirer through human-resource management practices, such as job rotation, communication, incentive mechanisms, internal reporting systems, and through global co-ordination functions involving people from different national cultural backgrounds sharing a strong corporate culture. The executives remarked that the resulting availability and timely deployment of line managers capable of effectively executing company-specific routines for assimilation which have been learned over time, and the existence of a strong global corporate culture and global coordinating mechanisms lowered the cost and increased the likelihood of new routines being absorbed from distant national cultures.

CONCLUSIONS

This article provided empirical support for the notion that national cultural distance enhances cross-border acquisition performance. Because national cultural distance between countries has, in turn, been linked to significant differences between these countries' norms, routines and repertoires (Hofstede, 1980; Kogut and Singh, 1988), our findings highlight the fact that the cross-border acquisitions that tended to perform better were those in which the routines and repertoires of the target's country of origin were, on average, more distant than those of the acquirer's. Some of these routines and repertoires, such as those related to inventiveness, innovation, entrepreneurship, and decision-making practices, have been found to be relevant to performance, and also difficult to develop and imitate across different national cultures (Shane, 1993; McGrath et al., 1992; Bourgoin, 1984; Kreacic and Marsh, 1986; Barney, 1991). Thus, cross-border acquisitions in more culturally distant countries might provide a mechanism for multinational companies to access diverse routines and repertoires, which have the potential to enhance the combined firm's performance over time.

The empirical relationship between national cultural distance and cross-border post-acquisition performance was supported by interviews of executives in firms making cross-border acquisitions. Executives at these companies explained why the acquisition of nationally embedded routines and repertoires was important, how the value of these routines was transferred to the rest of the firm, and why national cultural differences did not impede this transfer.

Our findings provide evidence that might contrast with the "gradual" pattern of internationalization proposed by some theorists, suggesting that companies start by entering locations that are culturally close to their own in order to learn and perform well when expanding into more distant countries (Johanson and Vahlne, 1977). However, our results show that if companies do enter culturally distant countries through acquisition, they can perform well relative to acquisitions in culturally close countries.

The results of this study also indicate that national cultural distance appears to have a significant effect on cross-border acquisition performance *vis-à-vis* relatedness, or post-acquisition strategy. This finding has some implications for future research on acquisitions. It suggests that research related to cross-border acquisitions should take a broader look at the factors that influence post-acquisition performance. In this context, researchers may choose to follow the route of Morosini (1998), Chatterjee et al. (1992), Datta (1991), and others who have examined both strategic and cultural factors when explaining acquisition performance.

This study also has implications for managers of multinational companies with responsibility for newly acquired affiliates abroad. Various scholars have argued that the failure rate of acquisitions can be reduced through increased strategic planning for the acquisition (Datta, 1991; Achtmeyer and Daniell, 1988; Rappaport, 1979). Our study suggests that managers of parent firms making acquisitions in culturally distant countries should not underestimate the value of specific firm routines and repertoires embedded in the target's national culture, which can have a beneficial impact on the performance of the combined firm.

This study presents a number of limitations and suggests some avenues for future research. Paramount amongst the former is the fact that our sample consisted of cross-border acquisitions in which one of the partners was an Italian corporation, and the other corporation was headquartered in either Europe or the United States. From that perspective, the empirical findings should be evaluated with care as regards their applicability beyond the predominantly Western context of this study. Another limitation of this study is that, as a course-grained analysis, it looked at the effect of national cultural distance on cross-border acquisition performance, rather than at the process by which managers of multinational corporations make decisions about acquisitions to take advantage of national cultural distance. Our findings suggest that firms acquiring companies in culturally distant countries might be accessing diverse routines and repertoires which are beneficial to their performance. We believe that these empirical results justify future process research on the value of acquisitions in culturally distant countries. Our study provides a contribution by suggesting that scholars investigate an alternative line of reasoning, namely, the value of cultural distance to acquisition performance. Future research should also consider the impact of other variables, such as corporate culture, which could be influencing cross-border acquisition performance as well. Such studies could serve to separate the effects of corporate cultural differences and national cultural differences on post-acquisition performance. Finally, further studies in the areas of national cultural distance and post-acquisition performance could explore the specific mechanisms through which cultural factors influence performance.

In short, this study has examined a previously unexplored topic – the effect of national cultural distance on cross-border acquisition performance. Our empirical findings suggest that national cultural distance is an important factor for researchers and managers to consider when deciding about, and carrying out, a cross-border acquisition. In a business milieu increasingly dominated by such trends as globalization and greater interaction between firms in culturally distant countries, this type of finding is expected to be of particular value to internationally oriented companies facing the pressing need of managing effectively in an uncertain external environment.

REFERENCES

Achtmeyer, W. and M. Daniell. 1988. How advanced planning widens acquisition rewards. *Mergers and Acquisitions*, 23(1): 37–42.

Acquisizioni. Rapporto M&A Italia. 1993. January 1994. English editors: Philip Healey and Susan Healey (co-publisher), Acquisitions Monthly, Lonsdale House, Kent, UK.

Balloun, James and Richard Gridley. 1990. Post-merger management – Understanding the challenges. *The McKinsey Quarterly*, 4: 90–102.

Barney, Jay B. 1986. Organizational culture: Can it be a source of sustained competitive advantage?. *Academy of Management Review*, 11(3): 656–65.

Barney, Jay B. 1991. Firm resources and sustained competitive advantage. *Journal of Management*, 17(1): 99–120.

Bourgoin, Henry 1989. *L'Afrique malade du management*. Paris: Jean Picollec.

Brossard, M. and M. Maurice. 1974. Existe-t-il un modele universel des structures d'organization?. *Sociologie du Travail*, 4:402–26.

Buono, Anthony F., James L. Bowditch and J. Lewis, J. 1985. When cultures collide: The anatomy of a merger. *Human Relations*, 38: 477–500.

Cartwright, S. and C. L. Cooper. 1993. The role of cultural compatibility in successful organizational marriage. *Management Executive*, 7: 57–70.

Caves, Richard E. 1982. *Multinational enterprise and economic analysis*. Cambridge, UK: Cambridge University Press.

Chatterjee, Sayan 1992. Sources of value in take-overs: synergy or restructuring – implications for target and bidder firms. *Strategic Management Journal*, 13: 267–86.

——, Michael H. Lubatkin, David M. Schweiger and Yaakov Weber, Y. 1992. Cultural differences and shareholder value in related mergers: Linking equity and human capital. *Strategic Management Journal*, 13: 319–34.

Collis, D. 1991. A resource-based analysis of global competition: The case of the bearings industry. *Strategic Management Journal*, 12 (Summer): 49–68.

Datta, Deepak K. 1991. Organizational fit and acquisition performance: effects of post-acquisition integration. *Strategic Management Journal*, 12: 281–97.

Eckbo, B. 1983. Horizontal mergers, collusion and stockholder wealth. *Journal of Financial Economics*, 11(1): 241–73.

Fiol, M. 1991. Managing culture as a competitive resource: An identity-based view of sustainable competitive advantage. *Journal of Management*, 17(1): 191–211.

Ghoshal, Sumantra 1987. Global strategy: an organizing framework. *Strategic Management Journal*, 8: 425–40.

Haspeslagh, P. and David Jemison. 1991. *Managing acquisitions: Creating value through corporate renewal*. New York: Free Press.

Hofstede, Geert 1980. *Culture's consequences: International differences in work-related values*. Beverley Hills: Sage Publications.

——, Bram Neuijen, Denise D. Ohayv and Geert Sanders. 1990. Measuring organizational cultures: A qualitative and quantitative study across twenty cases. *Administrative Science Quarterly*, 35: 286–316.

Jemison, David B. and Sim B. Sitkin. 1986. Corporate acquisitions: A process perspective. *Academy of Management Review*, 11(1): 145–63.

Johanson, J. and J. Vahlne. 1977. The internationalization process of the firm: A model of knowledge development and increasing foreign market commitments. *Journal of International Business Studies*, 8 (Spring-Summer): 23–32.

Kitching, John 1967. Why do mergers miscarry?. *Harvard Business Review*, 45(6): 84–101.

Kogut, Bruce and Harbir Singh. 1988. The effect of national culture on the choice of entry mode. *Journal of International Business Studies*, 19(3): 411–32.

Kreacic, Vladimir and Philip Marsh. 1986. Organisation development and national culture in four countries. *Public Enterprise*, 6: 121–34.

Kusewitt, John R. 1985. An exploratory study of strategic acquisition factors relating to performance. *Strategic Management Journal*, 6: 151–69.

Lane, Henry W. and Paul W. Beamish. 1990. Cross-cultural cooperative behavior in joint ventures in LDCs. *Management International Review*, Special Issue: 87–102.

Lincoln, James R., Mitsuyo Hanada and Jon Olson. 1981. Cultural orientations and individual reactions to organizations: A study of employees of Japanese-owned firms. *Administrative Science Quarterly*, 26: 93–114.

Lubatkin, Michael. 1983. Merger and the performance of the acquiring firm. *Academy of Management Review*, 8(2): 218–25.

Marelli, Maurizio. 1994. Struttura di correlazione dei rendimenti e applicazioni della moderna teoria del portafoglio. *Finanza, Imprese e Mercati*, 3: 113–23.

Mazen, A., M. Hemmasi and M. Lewis. 1987. Assessment of statistical power in contemporary strategy research. *Strategic Management Journal*, 8(4): 403–10.

McGrath, Rita, Ian MacMillan, Elena Ai-Yuan Yang and William Tsai. 1992. Does culture endure or is it *malleable*? Issues for entrepreneurial economic development. *Journal of Business Venturing*, 7: 441–58.

Moran, Robert. 1980. Cross-cultural dimensions of doing business in Latin America. In D. R. Shea, F. W. Swacker, R. J. Radway and S. T. Stairs, editors, *Reference manual of doing business in Latin America*. Milwaukee: University of Wisconsin, Center for Latin America.

Morosini, Piero. 1998. *Managing cultural differences: Effective strategy and execution across cultures in global corporate alliances*. Oxford, UK: Pergamon Press.

——. 1994. Effects of national culture differences on post-cross-border acquisition performance in Italy. PhD Dissertation. Management Department, The Wharton School, University of Pennsylvania, Philadelphia, Pennsylvania.

—— and Harbir Singh. 1994. Post-cross-border acquisitions: Implementing "national culture compatible" strategies to improve performance. *European Management Journal*, 12(4): 390–400.

Morrison, Alan and Kendall Roth. 1992. A taxonomy of business-level strategies in global industries. *Strategic Management Journal*, 13: 399–418.

Ouchi, William G. 1980. Markets, bureaucracies and clans. *Administrative Science Quarterly*, 25: 129–42.

Parkhe, Arvind. 1993 "Messy" research, methodological predispositions, and theory development in international joint ventures. *Academy of Management Review*. 18(2): 227–68.

Pettigrew, Andrew M. 1979. On studying organizational cultures. *Administrative Science Quarterly*, 24: 570–81.

Porter, Michael. 1980. *Competitive strategy*. New York: Free Press.

Pursche, William. 1990. Post-merger management – The project stage: Focusing the best approach. *The McKinsey Quarterly*, 4: 103–11.

Putnam, Robert D., Robert Leonardi and Raffaella Y. Nanetti. 1993. *Making democracy work: Civic Traditions in Modern Italy*. Princeton, NJ: Princeton University Press.

Rappaport, A. 1979. Strategic analysis for more profitable acquisitions. *Harvard Business Review*, 57: 99–110.

Regnér, Patrick 1996. Swedish mergers and acquisitions in the US – Acquisition performance and strategic acquisition factors. Discussion paper. Institute of International Business, Stockholm School of Economics.

Salter, Malcom S. and Wolf A. Weinhold. 1979. *Diversification through acquisitions: Strategies for creating economic value*. New York: Free Press.

Schneider, Susan C. and Arnoud De Meyer. 1991. Interpreting and responding to strategic issues: The impact of national culture. *Strategic Management Journal*, 12: 307–20.

Shane, Scott 1992. Why do some societies invent more than others?. *Journal of Business Venturing*, 7: 29–46.

——. 1993. Cultural influences on national differences in rate of innovation. *Journal of Business Venturing*, 8(1): 59–74.

——. 1995. Uncertainty avoidance and the preference for innovation championing roles. *Journal of International Business Studies*, 26(1): 47–68.

Shelton, Lois M. 1988. Strategic business fits and corporate acquisition: Empirical evidence. *Strategic Management Journal*, 9: 279–88.

Shrivastava, Paul 1986. Post-merger integration. *Journal of Business Strategy*, 7: 65–76.

Singh, Harbir and Cynthia A. Montgomery. 1987. Corporate acquisition strategies and economic performance. *Strategic Management Journal*, 8: 377–86.

Stillman, R. 1983. Examining antitrust policy towards horizontal mergers. *Journal of Financial Economics*, 11(1–4): 225–40.

The Economist, 1997. January 4: 21.

Williamson, Oliver E. 1981. The modern corporation: Origins, evolution and attributes. *Journal of Economic Literature*, 19: 1537–68.

Woo, Carolyn Y., Gary E. Willard and Urs. S. Daellenbach. 1992. Spin-off performance: a case of overstated expectations? *Strategic Management Journal*, 13: 433–47.

Morosini, P., Shane, S. and Singh, H. (1998) "National cultural distance and cross-border acquisition performance". *Journal of International Business Studies*, 29(1), 137–158. Reprinted with permission.

Section 5

Managerial and Social Consequences of Mergers

The social and political consequences of conglomerate mergers

18

John J. Siegfried and M. Jane Barr Sweeney

Conglomerate mergers may have significant economic, political, and social consequences. In order to gain some appreciation for the welfare effects of conglomerate mergers, the Bureau of Economics of the Federal Trade Commission published major reports in 1969 and 1980. The underlying theme of *Economic Report on Corporate Mergers*, published in 1969, was that conglomerate firms reduce economic efficiency by hampering competition through engaging in reciprocal dealing with their customers, reducing potential entry, and cross-subsidizing predatory efforts that increase market concentration in the long run.[1] These hypotheses were debated extensively during the 1970s.[2] The recently published volume, *The Economics of Firm Size, Market Structure and Social Performance*, explores how the economic characteristics of conglomerates affect the income distribution, worker satisfaction, political power, and welfare of local communities.[3] The themes of the book are that social goals other than efficiency also matter and that economists have useful insights to contribute to debates about them.

In this chapter we attempt to summarize the contributions of economists regarding the effects of conglomerates on the nonefficiency dimensions of performance. We review the hypotheses relating the fundamental economic characteristics of conglomerates (market concentration, large size, and product and geographic dispersion) to various nonefficiency social goals. Then we briefly summarize the available empirical evidence on the hypotheses.

The issues surveyed in this chapter are of considerable significance for public policy. The vast majority of testimony at the Spring 1979 hearings on S. 600, the Small and Independent Business Protection Act of 1979, sponsored by Senator Edward Kennedy, concentrated on the effects that conglomerate mergers may have on social goals other than economic efficiency.[4] In addition, there have been many specific proposals to limit the discretion of firms to move or close plants and to control the extent of business influence on the political process.

The concept of social property rights may help to explain the rising interest in nonefficiency goals of the economy. If individuals or firms believe that they deserve some right to constancy of the rules that define behavior, changes in such rules are likely to arouse resistance since they would effectively constitute redistributions of wealth. Both individuals and firms may feel threatened by changes in social property rights. People who have moved into a community, voted in elections, and gone to work for a small firm that contributed generously to local charities may feel that they have been treated unjustly if the firm grows large, discontinues its contributions to local charities, contributes heavily to local political campaigns, or perhaps, ultimately moves to another location.

Business firms depend on social property rights as well. If, for example, it becomes very difficult for companies to reverse decisions (for example, about where to locate production facilities), then the expected returns from investments will decline (since a negative return stream cannot be truncated) and certain investments may never be undertaken in the first place. Businesses often make decisions under the belief that they can change them in the future if things do not work out as planned. They may feel that they have been treated unjustly if they later discover that their decisions are irrevocable because the social property rights of consumers, employees, or local community residents are invoked.

Presumably such conflicts over social property rights might be handled efficiently by private transactions. There are some examples of employees' purchasing plants or exerting such social pressure on firms that the firms find it preferable to remain with their initial plant locations or policies. In cases in which transactions costs are very high, however, private markets do not function well. In such cases we may depend on the judicial system to resolve the conflict. Unfortunately, courts are not well equipped to weigh the values of competing claims. They have no method of determining the true values adversaries place on different states of nature since the adversary system creates incentives to exaggerate values and the participants do not have to stand behind their claims with a willingness and ability to pay.

The problem of valuing social property rights is particularly acute in the areas of political power, local community welfare, income redistribution, and worker welfare because individuals' values depend on their *perceptions* of reality, which may deviate significantly from reality itself. If business size really has no effect on political power, yet people continue to think that it does, and if people value dispersion of power greatly, how should we value their dissatisfaction? Shall it be valued at zero because, in fact, we know that there is no influence of business on political outcomes? Or should we recognize the value of reducing perceived business political power, even though in reality actual business political power is unaffected?

The valuation problem reduces to the issue of consumer sovereignty in social issues. Should we respect people's views regardless of how wrong-headed we think they are? If one argues that advertising should not be regulated since consumers are intelligent enough to understand their values and are in the best position to know what is best for themselves, are we not obliged also to accept the notion that people are intelligent enough and understand their values enough so that if they want to dismantle corporate giants for factually unsound reasons, we should urge them to do so?

The main difference between these noneconomic social goals and economic efficiency is that there is no consensus regarding the value of the noneconomic goals analogous to the general agreement that more efficiency is always preferred to less efficiency (if there are no associated negative by-products in achieving it). Whether more business political power is better or worse depends on the view one has of how social values should be determined. Whether a redistribution of wealth is desirable or not depends on who is identified as more deserving and one's view of the effect that redistributive policies have on the total output of goods and services available for redistribution. Whether workers should enjoy their job more or less depends on how individuals value the monetary and nonmonetary elements of compensation packages and whether one believes that wages should be or actually are adjusted to reflect different characteristics of jobs. Whether a plant should be moved from one community to another is likely to depend on the residence of workers who are asked.

There is, no doubt, an optimal level of such things as political power of business firms, dissatisfaction from working in large, impersonal firms, income redistribution, and local community welfare. However, the values placed on the marginal benefits and the marginal costs of various levels of achievement of these goals determine whether or not the effects that accompany conglomeration move us toward this optimal level. To value such things as an increased or diminished quantity of business political power requires knowledge of a social-demand curve that is very elusive. Because considerable disagreement exists regarding the value of such things, it is difficult to determine if more or less political power, worker dissatisfaction with job conditions, income redistribution, or welfare of certain communities are net benefits or costs to society. In this chapter we do not attempt to deal with such issues. Indeed, they seem to us to be solidly grounded in value judgments. Our purpose in this chapter is simply to chronicle the effects of conglomeration on various types of noneconomic social goals without passing judgment on the net welfare implications of these effects.

EFFECTS ON POLITICAL DEMOCRACY

There is no shortage of proclamations regarding the importance of the connection between economic structure and the political influence of business. Unfortunately, careful theoretical and empirical analyses of the intertwined relationships between business and politics are in short supply. The greatest confusion probably arises from the failure to distinguish among the multiplicity of attributes possessed by conglomerate firms, each of which may affect the firms' intensity of effort and effectiveness in influencing policy. The essential structural characteristics of conglomerates are: (1) market concentration, (2) firm size, (3) product diversification, and (4) geographic dispersion. It has been argued that each of these elements of market structure is a characteristic of conglomerates.[5]

For business successfully to influence political outcomes, there must be sufficient incentives to make such efforts, adequate resources to mount the effort, enough knowledge of the production process for political influence to apply those resources to the objectives effectively, and finally, a response from the political decision makers that achieves the desired goals. We believe that much of the ignorance surrounding the debate on political influence of conglomerate firms emanates from the failure to recognize that individual market-structure elements (for example, market concentration) principally determine the incentives to influence government policy, while firm-size characteristics primarily dictate the efficiency with which such efforts are transformed into results – that is, the theoretical reasons to expect firms in more concentrated industries to have a greater effect on political decisions arise from the larger effort that firms in concentrated industries are likely to muster. The reasons to expect large firms to have more effect on political outcomes are based on the greater efficiency with which they apply their resources to achieving the objectives, holding constant the intensity of their effort.[6] If this characterization of the political-influence process is accurate, measures of market concentration should be most successful in explaining the intensity of efforts to influence policy – for example, lobbying efforts and campaign contributions. Absolute firm size should be most successful in explaining differences in political outcomes holding the effort variables constant.

Market concentration

Market concentration affects the incentives of individual firms to contribute to group efforts designed to influence industrywide political decisions. The nature of the political decision-making process creates a divergence between firm and industry incentives to invest in these activities. Because the costs of excluding noncontributors from the benefits are prohibitive, each individual firm in a competitive industry will reap some of the benefits of any successful efforts to influence policy regardless of whether it assumes part of the costs. Indeed, in order to collect sufficiently broad support for a policy initiative or position, proponents will likely find it in their interest to broaden their appeal beyond a single firm to an industry or sector of the economy. This increases the opportunity for free riders.

The standard theory of collective action yields the prediction that, as a public good, political influence will be supplied at less than the efficient level.[7] Olson identified the number and size distribution of individuals (here, firms) constituting a group (here, industry) as the primary factor determining the effectiveness of group efforts to produce public goods.[8] There are several reasons for this logic. First, the fewer the firms in an industry, the better is the chance that their values and objectives will coincide, thus reducing the bargaining and organizational costs of forming a collective-action group. Second, the fewer the firms in an industry, the greater will be the relative share of benefits accruing to each individual firm (other things, such as size distribution, held constant). This increases the expected dollar value of benefits to a firm undertaking the investment on its own. Third, the fewer the firms in an industry, the easier it is for the collective-action group to enforce any voluntary agreements among the firms. For example, because the impact of noncompliance by one firm on the remaining firms increases inversely with the number of firms, it is easier for three firms, each of which has pledged $10 000 to a certain lobbying effort, to evaluate compliance with the pledge than it is for each of 100 firms pledging $300 each to determine the level of compliance with their agreement. Finally, as the size distribution of firms becomes more unequal, the chance of any one firm's finding it in its interest to pursue the public policy alone increases because the share of benefits from a successful effort to influence policy accruing to the largest firm usually rises with its relative share of the market. Since these factors minimize the possibility that any one firm will attempt to be a free rider if the market is more concentrated, we expect efforts at political influence to increase with market concentration. If results are related to efforts, we should observe that the achievement of political goals is more frequent in more concentrated industries than in competitive industries.

If industry profits and market concentration are positively related, there may be another reason to expect greater political efforts from concentrated industries. On the one hand, if economic rents accrue to firms with market power, they may be used to further political objectives. On the other hand, if investments in political influence were better than the alternative investment opportunities of a firm, why would they have to be financed out of economic rents? One answer is that it may be difficult to obtain a bank loan to finance political activities. In that case, capital-market imperfections create an advantage for firms that can finance such investments out of retained earnings.

The impact of market concentration on political influence might be negative if the visibility that usually accompanies high levels of market concentration tends to attract adverse public attention and to increase opposition to political efforts by firms in highly concentrated industries. If opposing efforts are encouraged, the projected marginal benefit of investments in political influence would fall, thus reducing the optimal level of such efforts.

A major problem with the interpretation of statistical results correlating political outcomes with market concentration is that the direction of causation is not clear. Perhaps certain political outcomes affect concentration. For example, tariffs and tax reductions increase the after-tax profitability of domestic producers, thereby tending to increase the number of firms and decrease the level of concentration. For this reason, a negative correlation might be observed even though concentration is causing more political influence.

Firm size

The relationship between absolute firm size and political power seems to be the basis for much of the US concern about conglomerates and aggregate concentration. Presumably the hypothesis is that one large firm would have more political influence than ten firms, each one-tenth of the size of the larger firms. Thus, aggregation of economic power yields disproportionately greater political power.

The reasons for expecting absolute firm size to create disproportionate amounts of political power fall into three main categories. First, large firms have a greater incentive to participate in politics because larger firms usually (although certainly not always) have greater market shares. Thus, even if other firms in their industry choose to ride free, large firms would be more likely to enjoy benefits from their efforts that exceed the expected costs. This argument for expecting more concentrated industries to participate more intensively in political influence is similar to that based on collective-choice theory.

Second, larger firms may have greater access to the critical resources necessary for producing political influence because they are more likely to have acquired these resources already for their production of nonpolitical goods and services. There may be important elements of joint cost in performing economic and political activities. For example, the larger firms already have the public-relations experts, attorneys, Washington law firms, and executives with personal contacts throughout the political system needed to make a political-influence effort possible at reasonable marginal cost.

Third, what makes the absolute size of available resources, and, hence, firm size so important politically is the fact that political involvement has certain fixed costs associated with it. The larger firms will be better able to reach the minimum initial resource constraint necessary to attain a profitable level of influence production. The heavy fixed-cost nature of the inputs to political influence means that the average cost of influencing policy by large firms will be lower than for small firms. Since small firms can rarely reach the minimum size to participate efficiently in the political process, they must rely on group participation – with all of the intra-organizational differences, lack of control, and consequent weakening of influence that go with it.

However, just as in the case of firms in more concentrated industries, the greater visibility of large firms increases the likelihood of attracting opposition to their political efforts and raises the cost of successfully influencing policy. If large firm size discourages efforts to influence political outcomes, the effect of firm size on political outcomes would be negative.

Legal constraints might also disadvantage larger firms. For example, firms may establish as many political-action committees as they wish, but they are limited by law (the Federal Election Campaign Act Amendments of 1976) to a single $5000 contribution per candidate for each election. By merging, two firms will effectively reduce their combined contribution limit from $10 000 to $5000.

Geographic dispersion

The effect of the greater geographic diversity of conglomerates upon their ability to influence public policy is not clear. If each member of Congress has many constituent groups competing for his attention, and if he allocates his time to their requests in proportion to their likely impact on his reelection, then it follows that an industry must be sufficiently large in any congressional district to pass the minimum threshold to gain recognition. Consequently, for a given industry size, industries with firms located in fewer different geographic areas will be more likely to capture the attention of their representatives and to achieve their political-influence goals. In other words, there are economies of scale in obtaining a hearing for one's views so that a larger single presence in congressional districts produces advantages.

In addition, conflicts of interest between political group members are less likely to occur within specific regions than if the firms have diverse locations. For example, sun-belt versus snow-belt issues may hinder the formation of an interest group. Therefore, geographic concentration may increase the prospect for successful collective action and subsequent political influence.

While geographic concentration may improve the chances for obtaining the attention and support of a sponsor for certain legislation, industries that are highly concentrated geographically may lack the broad-based political support necessary to pass legislation and to have it implemented. The optimal geographic dispersion may be a few areas in which the industry is highly concentrated and clearly significant to the political representatives, with the rest of the industry spread over at least one-half of the districts, so that a majority voting for special legislation favoring the industry can claim a victory for some constituency.

Dispersion might also be inversely related to political efforts and successful outcomes because it may increase the communications and organizational costs of forming an effective political-action group. Thus, the net effect of the greater geographic dispersion of conglomerates upon their ability to influence public policy is ambiguous.

Product diversification

Product diversification is another attribute of conglomerates that may create greater incentives for or efficiency in influencing public policies through the political apparatus. First, diversified firms might find that the cultivation of political gardens for one purpose is also profitable for their other interests. When special problems arise, a diversified firm is more likely to have dealt with them at one time or another in some part of its total operation. Furthermore, diversified firms can mobilize support for their efforts to influence policy from a wider range of sources and are more likely to find support from some important constituencies.

More diversified firms tend to have varied interests that may be affected in contrary ways by a specific policy. For example, if a firm is both an exporter and an importer, which position should it take on tariffs? The importance of this fact for political influence is ambiguous. A conglomerate merger between two firms that previously had produced political influence in opposition to each other might lead to a resolution of the conflict within the firm and a single focused effort at influencing policy. Consequently, conglomerate mergers may increase political power. However, the internal organizational characteristics of firms might inhibit a strict profit-maximizing approach in favor of some negotiated settlement among disputants within a firm. Such settlements might take the form of agnosticism toward controversial issues, thereby eliminating any net effect the competing efforts might have made and, consequently, reducing political influence.

Finally, it has also been argued that diversified firms cannot press as hard on any one issue as a single-purpose organization because they are more likely to jeopardize their success in another area. Therefore, diversified firms might be less successful in influencing policy on any one issue.

Empirical evidence

The systematic empirical studies of the political influence of business fall into two categories: (1) investigations of the effect of economic variables on political instruments such as campaign contributions or lobbying efforts; and (2) studies that relate economic variables directly to political outcomes. Studies of political instruments should be most useful in assessing the validity of the free-rider theory, which predicts greater political involvement by firms in more-concentrated industries. The political-outcome studies are more difficult to interpret since a correlation between economic variables and political results could be the consequence either of greater efforts by firms to influence policy or greater effectiveness in using a given amount of resources to achieve their goals.

Four empirical studies look at political instruments. Pittman's two studies and the study by Marx examine the determinants of campaign contributions.[9,10] Mann and McCormick investigate the relationship between firm attributes and lobbying efforts in California.[11] Eight empirical studies devoted to political outcomes relate the economic environment directly to policy results from three substantive areas: regulation, tariff protection, and tax burdens.[12]

The empirical studies report varied and conflicting results. On the one hand, the studies of political instruments (campaign contributions and lobbying expenditures) agree on the positive effect of market concentration on efforts to influence policy. These results are consistent with the theory of private versus group incentives from which we derive the proposition that effort to influence policy should be determined by the divergence of individual and group interests.

On the other hand, the studies of political outcomes reveal quite diverse results. The three studies of tariff protection report a negative, neutral, and positive effect, respectively, of market concentration on effective rates of protection. Siegfried's study of corporation income-tax rates finds a negative effect of concentration on political influence, but Stigler finds that occupations with local markets, in which market concentration is higher, obtained entry regulation sooner than other occupations. Overall, the tests seem to favor the free-rider hypothesis.

The evidence on firm size is also mixed. Mann and McCormick find that larger firms spend more on lobbying, but not as much more as one would expect on the basis of their size. Salamon and Siegfried find that larger firms have greater success in obtaining special tax favors, but neither Coolidge and Tullock nor Marx find any evidence to support such a conclusion. If larger firms actually devote proportionately less to political lobbying, as Mann and McCormick find, and yet are more successful in achieving their goals, as Salamon and Siegfried find, their relative efficiency advantage in producing political influence (the economies-of-scale argument) can be inferred to be quite large.

Geographic concentration does not appear to matter. Pincus finds that geographically concentrated industries were more effective in obtaining protective tariffs in 1824. This is consistent with the dependence of communications costs on physical proximity at that time. However, the studies that have examined the effect of geographic concentration on contemporary policy have failed to find any systematic relationship between it and political influence. The three studies that looked explicitly at product diversification, the most apparent characteristic of conglomerates, found no net impact on political influence, with the exception of Marx's positive relationship between conglomeration and campaign contributions.

EFFECTS ON WORKER SATISFACTION

A conglomerate merger may affect a worker's satisfaction by altering his employment, wages, or the quality of his work environment. A worker's satisfaction will be reduced if his job is lost, real wage falls, or his work environment deteriorates, *ceteris paribus*. In addition, the satisfaction of an employed worker may decline if his real wage falls more than the increase in the implicit value of his job amenities or if his real wage rises less than the decrease in the implicit value of amenities attributable to the merger. Thus, in order to gauge the impact of a conglomerate merger upon a worker's satisfaction, we must consider its impact upon the probability of employment and upon the wages and amenities enjoyed by workers who remain employed after the merger.

Employment

The level and composition of a firm's employment may be affected by a conglomerate merger for several reasons. In a world of imperfect capital markets, internal financing is normally cheaper than external borrowing. By increasing the size of the internal capital market and/or by increasing stockholders' estimates of the firm's profitability and cyclical stability, the firm's access to capital may be improved and interest costs reduced by a merger. As interest rates decline, the cost of capital goods falls, and producers may be encouraged to substitute capital for labor in the production process. At the same time, the reduced cost of financing will encourage the producer to expand output and to employ more of both capital and labor. The net effect upon employment will depend upon the relative size of these two effects. Workers who are less easily replaced by (or are complementary to) capital will experience a smaller decrease or greater increase in employment. Thus, if skilled workers are complementary to capital, as the capital-skill-complementarity hypothesis suggests, conglomerate mergers may increase the employment of skilled labor relative to unskilled labor.[13] However, if a conglomerate merger improves allocative efficiency sufficiently, employment of both skilled and unskilled labor may increase.

Second, through its effect on total firm size, a conglomerate merger may allow a firm to exploit certain economies of scale in the provision of nonproduction services like marketing, distribution, personnel services, management, and advertising. The actual effect of these economies on the firm's employment will, however, be ambiguous. If employees were underemployed prior to the merger, consolidation of services may result in some reduction in employment; but if the merger improves efficiency and increases output, employment in these services may increase. In addition, the reduction in the cost of providing nonproduction services may encourage firms to perform internally those services that had previously been provided by external consultants. Thus, a firm that had previously employed an outside legal firm may now find it less costly to hire its own legal staff. Of course, even though the firm's employment may increase, the net effect on total employment of such a transfer of services may be zero or even negative.

Third, a conglomerate merger may increase a firm's product and input market power. Increased industrial concentration may encourage employers to reduce output and, consequently, employment. In addition, a merger may increase a firm's input market power. If industrial concentration is increased, the number of purchasers of certain specialized types of labor may be reduced. Further, a conglomerate merger may reduce union bargaining power. Because of the greater diversity of its product line, a conglomerate may be more able to withstand an industrywide strike, and, therefore, may be less willing to accede to union demands. Offsetting this, however, is the possibility that greater firm size and visibility may encourage unions to organize and/or support a strike by employees of a newly consolidated firm, but if the firm's monopsony power is increased by the merger, employment and/or wages may decline.

Thus, the net effect of a conglomerate merger on firm employment is unclear. If the merger improves efficiency, output and employment may increase. If capital costs decline, the firm may be encouraged to substitute capital for labor, and employment, particularly employment of unskilled labor, may decline. If the firm's product and/or input market power increases, employment may decline as well.

Wages and the work environment of employed workers

Empirical studies of firm and industrial wage differentials suggest that average wages are higher in larger firms and in more concentrated industries.[14] These studies suggest that a conglomerate merger may increase (or at least not reduce) an employee's wages. In order to understand the effects of higher wages on a worker's satisfaction, it is important to consider why conglomerates might offer higher average wages than other firms. If the wage is increased to compensate for a decrease in the quality of the employee's work environment, the effect on a worker's satisfaction will be very different than if the wage is increased with no change in the work environment.

Opponents of conglomerate mergers have expressed concern that the higher wages are at the expense of various job- and firm-specific amenities. Their concern is based upon the theory of equalizing differences. In a world of perfect information and complete factor mobility, competitive factor market equilibrium requires that the satisfaction of the marginal worker be equal across firms. Any firm that offers a higher wage must be offering less of some amenities or the market would not be in equilibrium.

A number of features of conglomerate firms suggest that a worker may, on the one hand, indeed enjoy a less satisfactory working environment after a merger. In particular, the high fixed, low variable costs of capital may encourage a conglomerate with higher capital-labor ratios and higher capital-labor complementary to increase work effort, decrease the flexibility in hours worked, and increase job specialization with a resulting increase in job pressure and tedium. In addition the larger work-group size may require that an individual worker compromise more to conform to common group work rules. Finally, greater geographic distance between top management and labor may lead to a feeling of worker alienation.

On the other hand, a conglomerate merger may increase a worker's satisfaction by decreasing the riskiness of a particular job and by increasing the worker's sphere of promotion. Any time an employee accepts a particular job, there is the possibility that the job will be terminated. Because of its greater product and/or geographic diversity, a conglomerate offers greater cyclical stability in employment. In addition, an employee may be more protected from structural unemployment by the possibility of transferring to a new job or new plant within the same firm should his current job become obsolete. Similarly, larger firm size increases the number of job openings potentially available to a worker interested in promotion within the firm.[15]

Empirical efforts to assess the impact of conglomerate mergers upon job satisfaction are practically nonexistent. Dunn found that satisfaction with work environment increased with firm size, holding plant size constant. She also found that satisfaction decreased with plant size – a result that indicates the potential difficulty in extrapolating the results of the more numerous plant studies to conglomerates.[16] Unfortunately, the limited nature of her sample makes any conclusions tenuous. All that can be said is that her results do not appear to support the view that a conglomerate merger will reduce a worker's satisfaction with his work environment.

Is it possible that a conglomerate merger could lead to an increase in a firm's average wage without reducing the job- and firm-specific amenities enjoyed by its workers by an equivalent amount, as Dunn's empirical results suggest? There are several reasons why this might occur.

First, the higher firm wage may simply be a statistical aberration. If a conglomerate merger increases the ratio of skilled to unskilled workers and if skilled workers are paid more than unskilled workers, then the average wage paid by the firm would tend to be higher after the merger even if the merger had no effect upon the wages of skilled and unskilled workers. In this case, average firm wages could increase without affecting an employed worker's satisfaction in any way.[17]

Second, large conglomerates may be more easily organized than smaller firms. If unions push for higher wages, the higher wages may reflect a reduction in the employer's monopsony power. Offsetting this, however, is the fact that a merger may increase an employer's bargaining power with industrial unions as discussed previously.[18]

Third, a conglomerate may find that labor costs may actually be reduced by paying employees a wage greater than the current market-clearing wage. When information in imperfect and factor mobility is limited, wages are not the only cost of employment. Higher wages may reduce recruiting costs by improving a firm's relative market attractiveness. If there are significant diseconomies of scale in hiring at the going wage, a large firm, with a higher absolute number of new hires per period, may choose to raise wages in order to economize on hiring costs.[19]

Higher wages may also reduce turnover costs. An employee will be less likely to leave when alternative market opportunities are not as good as his current job. If labor is more complementary to capital in a conglomerate, firm-specific investment in labor may be higher, and turnover costs may be very large. The conglomerate may choose to pay higher wages in order to protect past investment in labor.[20]

Higher wages may also enable a firm to increase the quality of its employees.[21] For the same amount of recruiting effort, the employer should receive more applications for employment after the wage increase. If the employer's screening system does not decrease in accuracy, labor quality will improve as the number of applicants increases. A conglomerate may be more concerned about labor quality than a single-plant or -product firm since increased work-group size, greater specialization of labor, and geographic diversity may increase labor force complementarity, the importance of the internal labor market as a source of promotion, and the distance between management and labor. Improved labor force quality will reduce the possibility that a single worker will slow the entire production process, improve the quality of workers subject to promotion, and decrease the need for close supervision of workers by management.

In addition, higher wages may allow an employer to forestall the introduction of unions. Since its larger size and greater product and/or geographic visibility may make a conglomerate a more likely target for unionization by unions with a broad industrial base, a conglomerate may choose to offer higher current wages in order to reduce a union's bargaining power and to restrain future labor costs.

If, by offering higher current wages, a firm can reduce total labor costs, such behavior can increase the satisfaction of both stockholders and workers. A compensatory decrease in job amenities would simply reduce the firm's labor market advantage and increase labor costs.

Finally, after a merger, a firm may simply be in a better position to offer higher wages to its employees. If firms are utility- rather than profit-maximizing entities, managers may choose to please employees by offering higher wages than ordinary profit maximization would allow.[22] If a merger improves a firm's profits, the manager's ability to raise wages without incurring the stockholders' wrath is increased. Some evidence suggests that firms in more concentrated industries do share monopoly profits with employees.[23]

Thus, conglomerates may lead to an increase in average firm wages with little or no reduction in job satisfaction. Higher average wages may reflect a difference in labor quality, in the degree of unionization, in hiring or turnover costs, or in ability to offer higher wages as well as a difference in firm- or job-specific amenities. It is not proper to conclude that, because conglomerates offer higher wages, the quality of the work environment must be lower. Further studies of employee's actual perceptions of the work environment are necessary before any statement of the impact of conglomerate mergers on total worker satisfaction may be made.

EFFECTS ON THE DISTRIBUTION OF INCOME

Even if the distribution of rewards does not influence allocative efficiency, the effect of conglomerate mergers upon the distribution of income may be important from a policy standpoint.[24] If an equitable distribution of income is viewed as a good by the majority of the community, if the transactions costs of redistributing income are large, and if conglomerate mergers increase the inequity of the income distribution, then controls on conglomerate mergers might be warranted even if these mergers increase allocative efficiency.

Through its effects on factor payments and charitable contributions, a conglomerate merger can be expected to affect the nominal-income distribution. Through its effects on product prices, the real-income distribution will be affected as well. The character of these effects, however, is far from clear.

In most cases, a merger is undertaken to increase firm profitability.[25] On the one hand, improved capital markets, reduced transactions costs, increased ability to exploit available scale economies in nonproduction services, and added protection from cyclical fluctuations should decrease costs, raise output and factor payments, and reduce final product prices – that is, by increasing allocative efficiency, the merger may increase everyone's nominal and real income. Some parties may, however, gain more than others. The exact effect upon any one individual will depend upon the character of the firm's production function, the nature of the input supply and product demand curves, and the composition of the individual's consumption and input market baskets.

On the other hand, a conglomerate merger may increase firm profits by increasing the firm's product or input market power. If this increased power reduces allocative efficiency, the profit increase will occur at the expense of consumers who are forced to pay higher prices for final products and owners of factors of production who experience a decrease in factor demand. In this case, someone must lose both absolutely and relatively. Thus, the effect of a conglomerate merger upon the level and distribution of income will depend critically upon the source of the improved profitability.

Factor payments

Payments to stockholders

As noted in the previous section, conglomerate mergers are expected to increase firm profitability. As long as potential extra profits are not dissipated in consummating the merger, passed on to factor owners and consumers in the form of higher factor prices and/or lower final good prices, or given away through charity or taxes, stock prices and firm dividends should increase.[26]

The effect upon the distribution of income of this increased return to stockholders will, however, depend upon the distribution of stock ownership. While it is true that within the United States the median income of stockholders exceeds the median income of all individuals,[27] stock ownership is not confined, exclusively, to upper-income groups. Significant numbers of lower-income retirees and middle-income workers, who exercised employee stock options, receive income from dividends. Since a $1 increase in dividend income will have a greater relative effect upon the income of low-income stockholders than that of high-income stockholders, an increase in dividend payments will possibly decrease income inequality.

A simple example illustrates this point. Suppose that four people live in the community with pre-merger incomes as indicated in Table 1. Each individual owns the indicated number of shares of stock in one of the firms that is merging. After the merger, dividends increase by 10¢ a share, and post-merger incomes of all stockholders are as indicated [for example, $100 + 50(.10) = 105$]. In this case, income

Table 1 Hypothetical effects of merger on income distribution

Person	Premerger income of individual	Stockholding in shares	Postmerger income of individual
1	100	50	105
2	50	30	53
3	10	0	10
4	5	20	7
Mean income	41.25		43.75
Coefficient of variation	.925		.909
Gini coefficient	.492		.481

inequality, as measured by either the coefficient of variation or the Gini coefficient, will decrease after the merger. Obviously, a conglomerate merger will be more likely to reduce income inequality via stock price increases if low-income people hold a large share of the merging firms' stocks.

Payments to factor owners other than stockholders

The effect of a merger on payments to factors other than capital is far from clear. It will depend upon how employment and factor prices are affected.

If the merger reduces interest costs, fixed inputs may be substituted for variable inputs in the production process. Thus, more capital goods and skilled labor may be employed while less unskilled labor may be used. At least in the short run, the price of capital goods and skilled labor will increase, reflecting their relatively inelastic supply. Employment of these inputs will increase slightly. The effect upon the price and employment of unskilled labor will depend upon the elasticity of supply of unskilled labor and upon the relative size of the output and substitution effects of the reduced capital costs. Since we expect that the supply curve for unskilled labor is relatively elastic, much of the change in factor payments will reflect employment rather than price changes.

Thus, if a merger reduces output, we would expect to observe a reduction in the employment of unskilled labor with only a moderate reduction in wages. Employment of skilled labor and capital goods will be less affected. The effect on factor prices will depend upon the relative size of the output and substitution effects. If the demand for skilled labor and/or capital goods increases (decreases), prices may increase (decrease) substantially.

The effect upon the distribution of income will depend upon the availability of alternative employment and upon the distribution of factor ownership across income groups. If there is already an excess supply of unskilled labor, the merger may increase the number of unemployed and thus low-income families. The effect upon the rest of the income distribution is less clear. It may become more or less dispersed depending upon the size of the substitution and output effects and the pattern of factor ownership across income groups.

The results of a simulation study by Lankford and Stewart of the effects of a reduction in monopoly power upon the distribution of income within the United States suggest that the effect of a conglomerate merger upon the distribution of income may be rather small.[28] If conglomerates reduce output, average households with incomes greater than $30 000 would appear to benefit at the expense of lower-income households. However, because of differences in households' factor shares within income classes, the impact upon households in the same income bracket may vary greatly. Their results suggest that any increase in monopoly distortion will have only a moderate impact on the inequality of the income distribution – that is, a relatively small number of households will experience substantial gains, but most households will experience a moderate decrease in factor income.

Charitable contributions

Through their effects upon firm contributions to charity, conglomerate mergers may also affect the income distribution. If conglomerates give more money to organizations that aid lower-income groups than other firms, then the income distribution may be made more equal by allowing a merger to be consummated. However, corporate contributions may represent a transfer of gift giving from stockholders whose dividend may decline, from government whose tax revenue is reduced, or from factor owners whose income may fall. A complete analysis of the effect of the gift-giving behavior of conglomerates upon the character of the income distribution would require knowledge of the gift-giving behavior of stockholders, factor owners, consumers, and the government, as well as that of the firm. We only consider the effect of a merger upon the size and distribution of the firm's charitable gifts.

A conglomerate merger may lead to an increase or a decrease in total corporate giving.[29] Due to the mildly progressive nature of the corporate tax structure, the marginal cost of charitable giving will be smaller for firms with higher absolute profits. This suggests that the marginal cost of gift giving may decline after a merger, which should induce a firm to increase charitable giving. Since the last increase in marginal tax rates occurs at an income of $50 000, however, this price effect will only influence the gift-giving behavior of very small firms. Further, if firms undertake charitable giving for the goodwill it creates and if there are significant economies of scale in generating such goodwill, a conglomerate, with its higher absolute earnings, may be in a better position to exploit these economies and, thus, may be more interested in charitable giving. Therefore, while several small firms might not be willing to donate individually in order to have their name appear on the symphony program, they might together be willing to donate a large amount to have their corporate name appear on symphony hall. In addition, if consumers' images of all firms in an industry are affected by their image of one firm so that all firms share the benefits of one firm's attempt to increase its goodwill, firms will have an incentive to underinvest in charitable giving. If conglomerate mergers increase industrial concentration, the importance of this free-rider problem will be reduced. Finally, firms may undertake charitable giving out of purely philanthropic motives. If conglomerate mergers increase total firm earnings, funds available for satisfying these motives will increase.

Conversely, a conglomerate merger may lead to a reduction in total firm giving for several reasons. For example, charitable giving may represent the utility-maximizing behavior of managers or stockholders. If the managers or stockholders of the merging firms have similar philanthropic interests, total giving may decline. One gift by the conglomerate may provide as much satisfaction as two equal-sized gifts by the separate firms had provided prior to the merger. If the managers or stockholders have different philanthropic interests, the lack of agreement may also lead to a reduction in total giving. Rather than promote discord within the firm, giving to groups in dispute may be curtailed. In addition, charitable giving may be regarded as a job amenity by employees. By giving to charities of interest to their employees, employers may be able to reduce wages. If larger work-group size makes agreement on desirable places to give more difficult, the amenity value of and thus the total amount of gift giving may decline. Finally, corporate goodwill need not be confined to a particular product or area. By merging, a firm may be able to capitalize upon the acquiring firm's good name and reduce its investment in charitable giving with no reduction in product demand. A reduction in giving would be particularly likely if there is a limit to how much goodwill can be generated through charitable giving so that the marginal benefit of contributions declines rapidly.

Empirical results indicate that larger firms may give more than smaller firms, but a positive elasticity of giving with respect to income is not sufficient to ensure that a merger will increase total corporate giving. If the income of the conglomerate is not significantly larger than the total income that the merged firms would have earned independently, then the income elasticity must be close to or greater than one to ensure an increase in total corporate contributions. Various estimates of the income elasticity have been made, with the results ranging from .5 to 1, but limitations of each study make definitive conclusions suspect.[30]

In order to measure the effect of increased industrial concentration upon charitable giving, Nelson and Whitehead both considered the effect of the number of firms in an industry upon charitable giving.[31] Whitehead's results supported the view that industrial concentration would increase charitable giving; Nelson's did not. Given the difficulty with using numbers of firms as a measure of concentration, the difference in results may not be surprising. Using four firm seller concentration ratios as a measure of market power, Maddox and Siegfried found that market power had a positive impact on charitable giving.[32]

Finally, a study by the Business Committee of the Arts of corporate arts supporters suggests that firms with local rather than national product markets may tend to contribute more to artistic groups.[33] Thus, if the product markets of a conglomerate have a broader geographic scope than the product markets of the merging firms, total contributions to the arts and, perhaps, to charities, as a whole, might decline after a merger. However, the committee's results need not imply that total contributions will decline. For reasons discussed later, conglomerates may choose to contribute less to the arts and more to other groups.

The interim results of a direct-interview study by Maddox and Siegfried of corporate-giving behavior suggests that total corporate giving may increase after a merger.[34] Of the eighty firms interviewed, five had recently moved their headquarters and fifty-one had either made an acquisition or had been acquired within the last few years. Twenty-four firms felt that contributions to local charities had increased after corporate headquarters were moved out of a community, ten felt they declined, and eighteen reported no change (four could not answer). Thus, over twice as many firms reported an increase in giving in the community that lost headquarters as reported a decrease. Since most firms give more to charities in headquarters cities than in cities with branch plants, this suggests that total gift giving may have increased. Of course, it may be possible that firms are temporarily giving to charities in cities that contain recently acquired firms in order to compensate for disruptions caused by the merger or to increase firm recognition. Further study is required to determine if total firm contributions will increase over the long term.

Conglomerate mergers may affect the choice of organizations that will receive charitable gifts as well as the size of total corporate gifts. As discussed previously, larger work-group size makes gift giving to groups of interest to particular employees less appealing to producers. Similarly, an increase in the number of stockholders and/or managers increases the likelihood that some individual will be opposed to supporting a particular charity. Thus, contributions to religious organizations and political campaigns are likely to be reduced. In addition, the greater a product and geographic market diversity of conglomerates might lead to greater interest in gift giving to organizations with a broader national appeal than to local or special-interest groups. Thus, the results of the Business Committee of the Arts study of corporate arts supporters may reflect the fact that contributions to local art galleries and symphonies are less appealing to firms with national markets.[35]

The effect of such shifts in the targets of charitable giving upon the character of the income distribution will depend upon the chosen charities. If a firm gave to the local art gallery prior to the merger but gives to the United Way after the merger, income inequality might be reduced. However, if prior to the merger the firm gave to the local day-care center, income inequality might be increased if contributions now are given to public television. Further study of the targets of charitable giving is necessary before any statement may be made about the effect of conglomerate mergers on this aspect of the income distribution.

Product prices

If a conglomerate merger leads to an increase in industrial concentration, product price may increase. If a product's price increases, the real income of any individual who would have bought this product prior to the price increase will be reduced. In addition, if producers pass along to consumers at least some part of an increase in input prices, the real income of any individual consuming a good derived from this product will decline as well. The effect on individuals who do not buy this product or any product derived from it is less clear. At least in the short run, prices of goods and inputs complementary to it will fall, while prices of substitutes will increase. The effect on consumers will depend upon the composition of their premerger market basket and the size of these secondary price changes. Some individuals may, conceivably, experience an increase in real income.

Even if everyone's real income falls, the effect on the distribution of real income will depend critically upon the character of the product-demand function. As long as the good is a normal good, higher-income purchasers will experience a larger absolute loss in real income. Since their real income is larger, though, the effect on their real income relative to that of lower-income families is ambiguous. An increase in the price of a normal good may increase or decrease the dispersion in real income. The results of a study by Maddox, Siegfried, and Sweeney of the incidence of product price changes suggest that the real-income distribution effects of product price increases vary greatly across products.[36] Their results suggest that mergers that result in an increase in the price of wine and liquor, furniture, or musical instruments would reduce income inequality, while mergers that result in an increase in the price of cigarettes, drugs, or utilities would increase income inequality. Thus, in order to gauge the impact of a conglomerate merger upon the real-income distribution, particular care must be given to measuring the probable impact of that merger on product prices and to determining the income levels of consumers ultimately affected by the price changes.

A conglomerate merger may increase or decrease the inequality in the nominal- and/or real-income distributions. The effects on payments to factors, charitable gifts, and product price changes are ambiguous. Only careful study of firm's production process, input and product markets, and decision-making behavior can determine the likely impact of a firm's merger upon the distribution of income.

EFFECT ON COMMUNITY WELFARE

Critics of conglomerate mergers have expressed concern that a merger may reduce the quality of life in the community in which the acquired firm is located. Some people feel that this area will become vulnerable to the somewhat arbitrary behavior of a group of managers that has little interest in the community's welfare because of its geographic distance from it. Fear is expressed that plants will be closed, employment growth will be curtailed, and/or that the community that once depended upon the corporate managers for community guidance will now be subjected to the whims of a politically more powerful force that threatens job loss and shows no interest in the external costs of its behavior.[37]

Are these concerns justified? Are conglomerates likely to close plants previously operated by a recently acquired firm? Would these plants have closed anyway, or does their closure represent the arbitrary whim of disinterested managers? Do conglomerates prey upon a community's fear of plant closure, justified or not, in order to exploit their own interests to the possible detriment of the community?

The effects of a conglomerate merger upon plant closures are not clear.[38] Several factors suggest that a conglomerate may be willing to relocate plants in areas outside of the acquired firm's home community, but other factors suggest that conglomerates may be unlikely to terminate a division entirely.

As noted previously, conglomerate mergers may allow firms to exploit certain economies of scale in research and development, advertising, inventory control, and so forth. If these scale economies are more easily exploited when plants are in close proximity, a conglomerate may tend to consolidate plants in one central location. In many cases, however, a firm might simply move corporate activities to the head- quarters city while still maintaining the previous plant for actual production. Never- theless, if significant complementarities exist between production processes, and if one of the acquiring firm's plants has substantial excess capacity, fixed costs might be significantly reduced by consolidating production within that plant. Thus, if joint production is possible, the risk of plant relocation may increase after a merger.

Because of their greater geographic and product diversity, conglomerates may also have greater incentives to close a particular plant. The greater geographic diversity of a conglomerate may reduce the cost of acquiring information concerning resource costs and the location of product markets outside of the acquired firm's immediate area. Thus, a conglomerate may be better able to determine the optimal location for the acquired firm's plant. If the cost of relocation is less than the expected profit gain, relocation might be justified. Further, the greater physical distance between top management and employees may reduce the importance placed upon the disruption of the employees' lives in the plant's location or termination decision; but even if management does have concern for the acquired firm's employees, the greater possibility of internal placement of employees displaced may make it easier for top management to discontinue a division's operation. In addition, the greater the firm's product diversity, the more unlikely it is that the closure of a division will pose a threat to the firm's continuity. Therefore, owners and managers of conglomerate firms may be more willing to close a division currently earning less-than-normal profits. Excess funds that had previously been invested in submarginal enterprises may be invested in activities with higher returns. The closure of the Youngstown Sheet and Tube steel plants may be an example of such behavior.[39]

Merger may also be an important way to ensure a firm's continued operation. Improvements in efficiency due to better access to capital or other scarce resources (for example, research-and-development personnel or superior management) or greater ability to exploit available scale economies may reduce costs enough to turn profitable unit firms into profitable divisions of the conglomerate. Further, where bankruptcy is an imminent possibility, cross-subsidization may allow the more diversified conglomerate to maintain employment temporarily. Greater reserves make it easier to withstand cyclical instability and give the firm added time to turn the business around.

In addition, complementarities between products may encourage conglomerates to maintain unprofitable divisions. The cost of terminating a plant or business will depend upon its relationship to the rest of the firm. Abandoning a business whose product is complementary to others sold by the firm or that shares some distribution channels may involve a potential loss in profits greater than the loss in earnings from the exited business. Similarly, despite a persistent loss, a firm might choose to remain in an industry rather than incur the wrath of a union that also covers members of other more profitable divisions. Thus, once a business has been assimilated into the firm, jointness of costs may make it less easy for a conglomerate to close unprofitable divisions.

Finally, management of conglomerate firms is more highly visible than management of smaller concerns. If there is a stigma attached to closing a plant and admitting a lapse in good business vision, managers of conglomerates may be less inclined to close a plant. This will obviously require that stockholders be sufficiently disinterested in total firm profits so that management can exercise some discretion in plant closings.

In a study of plant closings in rural Iowa, Barkley and Paulsen found that multiplant firms, including conglomerates, were less likely to close plants due to bankruptcy than were single-plant firms.[40] The reasons for this are not clear. On the one hand, conglomerates may have avoided bankruptcy because of greater efficiency or improved cyclical stability. On the other hand, conglomerates may have judiciously avoided acquiring firms headed for bankruptcy. Some evidence suggests that acquired firms may be at least as well managed and profitable as acquiring firms.[41]

In the same study, Barkley and Paulsen found that branch plants of multiplant firms, including conglomerates, were considerably more geographically mobile than single-plant firms. Further, plant closings by multiplant firms were more closely tied to variations in the business cycle than were closings of single-unit plants.[42] This is consistent with the hypothesis that managers of conglomerates are more aware of and responsive to changes in product demand or resource cost.

Thus, a conglomerate may be more willing than a single-product or -plant firm to close a viable local plant; but if this closing improves allocative efficiency, the net social benefit may be positive. While employees and property owners in the original city will suffer, employees and property owners in the new location will benefit. It is quite conceivable that the increase in benefits to the new city and to consumers of the firm's products will exceed the loss to the old community. Thus, legislation to control plant closings or limit conglomerate mergers could reduce total welfare while protecting obsolete plants from closure.[43]

In addition, it should be pointed out that any effort to limit merger possibilities reduces the potential profits and/or increases the risk of starting a new business. By reducing the potential salvage value of a firm, limitations on mergers may reduce the growth of single-unit firms as well. Thus, if conglomerate mergers had been banned at the time these plants were opened, some plants acquired by conglomerates might never have existed.

Even if conglomerates are not more likely to close plants than single-product firms, the ability of conglomerate firms to make communities feel hostage may have important welfare effects. Communities may be more willing to make concessions to conglomerates in the form of reduced taxes, looser pollution-control requirements, greater subsidization of plant or road-construction costs, and so forth. To the extent that these concessions reduce funds for investment in local public goods or lead to an increase in negative externalities, community welfare may be reduced. Some evidence suggests that such concessions are made to large firms with greater geographic scope and are not made to smaller local plants.[44] However, this may depend critically upon the extent of the local firm's buying market power. Small firms in one-employer towns may be just as likely to exploit their market power and cause a less-than-optimal investment in social overhead capital.

In addition, it is felt that because of their greater geographic distance from the community, top management will be less interested in the social affairs of the community in which the acquired firm is based. It is feared that the greater geographic diversity of conglomerates will increase the geographic mobility of middle managers. Increased mobility may reduce the managers' long-term interest in community development and reduce their willingness to assume a leadership role in the community.[45] Whether this fear is justified or not is hard to say. Since input and product markets may be broadened by a merger, charitable and other social contributions on the local level may be less important to continued firm viability. However, the greater size and diversity of conglomerates may increase firm visibility in any market. Failure to continue contributions begun by an acquired firm may have strong negative effects on product demand for all of the firm's products. Further, the level and composition of contributions depends somewhat upon the tastes and preferences of management and stock-holders. Quite possibly, owners and managers of the conglomerate may be more rather than less charitably and socially inclined than the original owners and managers of the acquired firm. The interim results of the study by Maddox and Siegfried of corporate giving behavior suggests that charities in the acquired firm's community do not suffer after a merger.[46]

While no doubt exists that a corporate merger may have significant effects on community welfare, it is not clear whether the net effect will be positive or negative. A merger may breed new life into a less-than-viable local plant or lead to a transfer of the local firm's resources to other divisions of the conglomerates, but even if the merger reduces employment in and/or social commitment to the acquired firm's community, the net social benefit may be positive. In assessing the welfare effects of conglomerate mergers, concerns of parochial interest groups must be distinguished from true net social costs.

CONCLUSIONS

This chapter has reviewed the (mostly ad hoc) theories relating the characteristics of conglomerate firms (large size, market concentration, product diversity, and geographic dispersion) to four social goals: political democracy, worker satisfaction, income distribution, and local community welfare. In each case, we found reasons why conglomeration might increase or decrease the social goal. Consequently, the net impact of conglomeration on these important issues becomes an empirical question. Unfortunately, the empirical evidence on these issues is limited and suffers from severe measurement problems. In view of the myriad of hypotheses concerning conglomerates and the high emotional content of the issues raised in this chapter, more systematic theoretical and empirical research should be of paramount interest to the Washington policymakers.

NOTES

1 Federal Trade Commission, *Economic Report on Corporate Mergers* (Washington, DC, 1969).
2 For an exhaustive review of the literature, see Dennis C. Mueller, "The Effects of Conglomerate Mergers: A Survey of The Empirical Evidence," *Journal of Banking and Finance* (1977): 315–347.
3 John J. Siegfried, ed., *The Economics of Firm Size, Market Structure and Social Performance*, Federal Trade Commission, Bureau of Economics, 1980.
4 US, Congress, Senate, Hearings before the Subcommittee on Antitrust, Monopoly, and Business Rights of the Committee on the Judiciary, 96th Cong., 1st Sess. on S.600, The Small and Independent Business Protection Act of 1979, Part 2, (Washington, DC: US Government Printing Office, 1979).
5 The arguments that conglomerate firms are larger, more geographically dispersed, and have greater product diversification are straightforward. The link between conglomerates and market concentration is less obvious. The case for such a link is made in *Economic Report on Corporate Mergers*, pp. 230–235.
6 Large firm size should also affect the incentives to influence policy since larger firms stand to gain a greater share of whatever benefits are produced. This role of firm size – namely, its impact on the size distribution of firms – is included in the market-concentration argument. Firm size is considered with other things, in particular the size distribution of firms, held constant.
7 See, for example, James M. Buchanan, *The Demand and Supply of Public Goods* (Chicago: Rand McNally, 1968), chapter 5; Anthony Downs, *The Economics of Democracy* (New York: Harper and Row, 1957); and Mancur Olson, *The Logic of Collective Action* (Cambridge, Mass.: Harvard University Press, 1965).
8 Olson, *Logic of Collective Action*.
9 Russell Pittman, "The Effects of Industry Concentration and Regulation on Contributions in Three 1972 US Senate Campaigns," *Public Choice* 27 (Fall 1976): 71–80; and Pittman, "Market Structure and Campaign Contributions," *Public Choice* 31 (Fall 1977): 37–52.
10 Thomas G. Marx, "Political Consequences of Conglomerate Mergers," *Atlantic Economic Journal* 8 (March 1980): 62–63. For more details, see Marx, "Political Consequences of Conglomerate Mergers" (unpublished paper, General Motors Corporation, January 1980).
11 Michael Mann and Karen McCormick, "Firm Attributes and the Propensity to Influence the Political System," in Siegfried, *Economics of Firm Size*.
12 George J. Stigler, "The Theory of Economic Regulation," *Bell Journal of Economics and Management Science* 2 (Spring 1981): 3–21; John J. Siegfried, "The Relationship between Economic Structure and the Effect of Political Influence: Empirical Evidence from the Federal Corporation Income Tax Program" (Ph.D. dissertation, University of Wisconsin, 1972); Charles P. McPherson, "Tariff Structures and Political Exchange" (Ph.D. dissertation, University of Chicago, 1972); Lester M. Salamon and John J. Siegfried, "Economic Power and Political Influence: The Impact of Industry Structure on Public Policy," *American Political Science Review* 71 (September 1977): 1026–1043; Cathleen Coolidge and Gorden Tullock, "Firm Size and Political Power," in Siegfried, *Economics of Firm Size*; Jonathan J. Pincus, *Pressure Groups and Politics in Antebellum*

Tariffs (New York: Columbia University Press, 1977); Richard E. Caves, "Economic Models of Political Choice: Canada's Tariff Structure," *Canadian Journal of Economics* 9 (May 1976): 278–300; and Marx, "Political Consequences."

13 The capital-skill complementarity hypothesis states that the elasticity of substitution of capital for unskilled labor is greater than the elasticity of substitution of capital for skilled labor. See Z. Griliches, "Capital-Skill Complementarity," *Review of Economics and Statistics* (1969), pp. 465–468; and Robert D. Brogan and Edward W. Erickson, "Capital-Skill Complementarity and Labor Earnings," *Southern Economic Journal* 42 (July 1975): 83–88.

14 See, for example, Lucia F. Dunn, "The Effects of Firm and Plant Size on Employee Well-Being," in Siegfried, *Economics and Firm Size*; Leonard W. Weiss, "Concentration and Labor Earnings," *American Economic Review* 56 (March 1966): 96–117.

15 See Frank P. Stafford, "Firm Size, Workplace Public Goods, and Worker Welfare," in Siegfried, *Economics of Firm Size*, for a discussion of the workplace costs and benefits of large firm size.

16 Dunn, "Effects of Firm and Plant Size." The results of plant studies are mixed, but most suggest a negative association between plant size and satisfaction. See L. Porter and E. Lawler, "Properties of Organizational Structure in Relation to Job Attitudes and Job Behavior," *Psychological Bulletin* (1965), pp. 23–51; F. M. Scherer, "Industrial Structure, Scale Economies, and Worker Alienation," in *Essays on Industrial Organization in Honor of Joe S. Bain*, edited by R. Masson and D. Qualls (Cambridge, Mass.: Ballinger, 1976); and John E. Kwoka, Jr., "Established Size, Wages, and Job Satisfaction: The Trade-offs," in Siegfried, *Economics of Firm Size*.

17 See Brogan and Erickson, "Capital-Skill Complementarity," for use of this argument to explain the relationship between industrial concentration and wages.

18 Harold M. Levinson, "Unionism, Concentration, and Wage Changes: Toward a Unified Theory," *Industrial and Labor Relations Review*, January 1967, pp. 198–205; and Martin Segal, "The Relation between Union Wage Impact and Market Structure," *Quarterly Journal of Economics*, February 1964, pp. 96–114.

19 J. C. Ullman, "Interfirm Differences in the Cost of Search for Clerical Workers," *Journal of Business* 41 (1968): 153–165.

20 G. S. Becker, *Human Capital*, 2nd ed. (New York: Columbia University Press, 1975); Stephen A. Ross and Michael Wachter, "Wage Determination, Inflation, and the Industrial Structure," *American Economic Review* 63 (September 1973): 675–692; and Wachter, "Cyclical Variation in the Interindustry Wage Structure," *American Economic Review* 60 (March 1970): 75–84.

21. Albert Rees and George P. Schultz, *Workers and Wages in an Urban Labor Market* (Chicago: University of Chicago Press, 1970), p. 219.

22. Armen A. Alchain and Reuben A. Kessel, "Competition, Monopoly, and Pursuit of Pecuniary Gain," in *Aspects of Labor Economics* (Princeton: National Bureau of Economic Research, 1962).

23 See the empirical results of James A. Dalton and E. J. Ford, Jr., "Concentration and Labor Earnings in Manufacturing and Utilities," *Industrial and Labor Relations Review* 31 (October 1977): 45–60; and Dalton and Ford, "Concentration and Professional Earnings in Manufacturing," *Industrial and Labor Relations Review* 31 (April 1978): 379–384 for possible support for this view. See also Weiss, "Concentration and Labor Earnings," for a contrary view.

24 See Robert Smiley, "Firm Size, Market Power, and the Distribution of Income and Wealth: A Survey"; and F. M. Scherer, "Commentary," in Siegfried, *Economics of Firm Size*, for a discussion of the literature linking the distribution of rewards to allocative efficiency.

25 This may not always be the case. See F. M. Scherer, *Industrial Market Structure and Economic Performance*, 2d ed. (Chicago: Rand McNally, 1980), pp. 127–138, for a discussion of firm motives for merging. However, even if mergers are not undertaken to increase profits, profits may be increased by the merger.

26 See ibid., pp. 138–141; and George Benston, "Conglomerate Mergers: Causes, Consequences and Remedies," in US, Congress, Senate, Hearings before the Subcommittee on Antitrust, Monopoly, and Business Rights of the Committee on the Judiciary, 96th Cong., 1st Sess. on S.600, The Small and Independent Business Protection Act of 1979, Part 2 (Washington, DC: US Government Printing Office, 1979), pp. 215–228, for a discussion of the financial consequences of mergers.

27 The New York Stock Exchange, *Fact Sheet: 1975 Shareowner Census at a Glance*, News Release, 9 December 1975.

28 Ralph Lankford and John F. Stewart, "A General Equilibrium Analysis of Monopoly Power and the Distribution of Income," in Siegfried, *Economics of Firm Size*.

29 The following discussion relies heavily on Katherine E. Maddox and John J. Siegfried, "The Effect of Economic Structure on Corporate Philanthropy," in Siegfried, *Economics of Firm Size*.

30 For a review of the literature on the income elasticity of charitable giving, see Katherine E. Maddox, "Review of the Literature on Corporate Philanthropy" (unpublished manuscript, Vanderbilt University, August 1980). See also Ralph L. Nelson, *Economic Factors in the Growth of Corporation Giving*, Occasional Paper 111, (New York: National Bureau of Economic Research, 1970); Ralph A. Schwartz, "Private Philanthropic Contributions: An Economic Analysis," (Ph.D. dissertation, Columbia University, 1966); and Paul J. Whitehead, "Some Economic Aspects of Corporate Giving" (Ph.D. dissertation, Virginia Polytechnic Institute and State University, 1976).

31 Nelson, *Economic Factors*, p. 61; and Whitehead, "Some Economic Experts."

32 Maddox and Siegfried, "Effect of Economic Structure."

33 Marion R. Fremont-Smith, *Philanthropy and the Business Corporation* (New York: Russell Sage Foundation, 1972), pp. 42–44.

34 Katherine E. Maddox and John J. Siegfried, "The Effect of Market Structure on Corporate Philanthropy: Interim Report on Interview Results" (unpublished manuscript, Vanderbilt University, October 1980).

35 Fremont-Smith, *Philanthropy and the Business Corporation*, pp. 42–44.

36 Katherine E. Maddox; John J. Siegfried; and George H. Sweeney, "The Incidence of Price Changes in the US Economy" (unpublished manuscript, Vanderbilt University, October 1980).

37 See, for example, the testimonies of Douglas Johnson and Martin Yenawine in US Small Business Administration, Office of Advocacy, "Public Hearings on Proposed Take-Over of Carrier Corporation by United Technologies Corporation," Syracuse, NY, 2 November 1979, pp. 31–36 and 165–168.

38 Much of the following discussion is based upon Richard E. Caves and Michael E. Porter, "Barriers to Exit," in Masson and Qualls, *Essays on Industrial Organization*, pp. 39–70.

39 Opinions on the reason for the closure differ. See Benston, "Conglomerate Mergers," pp. 241–242. For a different view, see F. M. Scherer, "Prepared Statement of F. M. Scherer," p. 138 in the same volume.

40 David L. Barkley and Arnold Paulsen, *Patterns in the Openings and Closings of Manufacturing Plants in Rural Areas of Iowa* (Ames: Iowa State University, North Central Regional Center for Rural Development, May 1979).

41 For a review of the literature on the financial aspects of mergers, see Scherer, *Industrial Market Structure*, pp. 138–141; and Benston, "Conglomerate Mergers."

42 Barkley and Paulsen, *Patterns in Openings and Closings*.

43 See Richard A. Posner, "Prepared Statement of Richard A. Posner," in US Congress, Senate, Hearings before the Subcommittee on Monopoly and Business Rights of the Committee on the Judiciary, 96th Cong., 1st Sess. on S.600, The Small and Independent Business Protection Act of 1979, Part 2, (Washington, DC: US Government Printing Office, 1979), p. 11; and Richard B. McKenzie, *Restrictions on Business Mobility* (Washington, DC: American Enterprise Institute, 1979).

44 Roger W. Schmenner, "How Corporations Select Communities for New Manufacturing Plants," in Siegfried, *Economics of Firm Size*.

45 See testimony of Martin Yenawine, in "Public Hearings"; and Bureau of National Affairs, "Conglomerate Mergers: A Study of Competition, Power, and Philosophy" (Washington, DC: Bureau of National Affairs, 1980).

46 Maddox and Siegfried, "Effect of Market Structure."

Siegfried, J. J. and Sweeney, M. J. B. (1981) "The social and political consequences of conglomerate mergers". In Blair, R.D. and Lanzillotti (eds), *The Conglomerate Corporation*, pp. 70–96. Cambridge, MA: Oelgeschlager, Gunn and Hain Publishers, Inc.; and Siegfried, J. J., *The Effects of Conglomerate Mergers on Political Democracy*, pp. 25–52. Reprinted with permission.

Organizational fit and acquisition performance: effects of post-acquisition integration

19

Deepak K. Datta

Mergers and acquisitions have been a fact of organizational life in the US, with corporations investing billions of dollars each year in such ventures. In 1989 alone more than 3400 such transactions were completed, involving a total value in excess of $230 billion (*Mergers and Acquisitions*, 1990). Many senior executives also believe that the pace of merger and acquisition activity is unlikely to slow down considerably in the 1990s despite proposed anti-merger bills in Congress (*Mergers and Acquisitions*, 1987). The continuing popularity of mergers and acquisitions is probably a reflection of the widespread belief among managers that acquisitions provide a quicker and seemingly easier route to achieving growth and diversification objectives. Paradoxically, studies by Porter (1987) and Young (1981) suggest that acquisitions have a high failure rate – nearly half of all acquisitions are rated as being unsatisfactory by managers of acquiring firms. Additional support is available in a study by Ravenscraft and Scherer (1989). They found that the profitability of target firms, on an average, actually declines after an acquisition, suggesting that implementation difficulties probably play a critical role in determining the eventual performance of an acquisition.

Given the strategic and financial implications of acquisitions, it is not surprising that the performance of acquisitions and the variation therein has figured prominently in business research. Prior research in strategic management (e.g. Chatterjee, 1986; Lubatkin, 1987; Salter and Weinhold, 1979; Seth, 1990; Shelton, 1988; Singh and Montgomery, 1987) has generally focused on the role of "strategic fit" and synergistic benefits as determinants of acquisition performance. On the other hand, issues of "organizational fit" have received considerably less attention – the existing literature is limited, fragmented and anecdotal (Buono and Bowditch, 1989; Davis, 1968; Leighton and Tod, 1969; Marks, 1982; Sales and Mirvis, 1984).

"Organizational fit", which influences the ease with which two organizations can be assimilated after an acquisition, can be assessed along a number of dimensions. However, the two areas often mentioned as being particularly important from the perspective of post-acquisition integration are differences in "management styles" (Callahan, 1986; Davis, 1968; Diven, 1984; Seed, 1974), and, in "organizational systems", particularly the "reward and evaluation system" (Diven, 1984; Ferracone,

1987; Hayes, 1979; Magnet, 1984). This paper seeks to examine the relationship between such differences and post-acquisition performance, and also to identify whether the relationship in each case depends on the extent of post-acquisition integration.

The paper is structured as follows: first, the literature on acquisition performance and the importance of organizational fit in terms of management styles and reward and evaluation systems is discussed. Also presented in the following section are the hypotheses tested in this study. Next, the research method used is described, including the selection of the sample, the operationalization of the variables, and the data collection procedure. Third, the results of the statistical analysis are presented and, following that, in the concluding section, the findings and their implications have been discussed.

REVIEW OF RELATED LITERATURE AND RESEARCH HYPOTHESES

The following paragraphs provide a brief overview of the literature on acquisition performance, the importance and influence of organizational differences (in terms of management styles and reward and evaluation systems), and the role of post-acquisition integration in influencing the relationship between organizational fit and performance.

Acquisition performance

The topic of acquisition performance has been at the forefront of academic research in the areas of financial economics, industrial organization, and strategic management. A recent meta-analytic review (Datta, Narayanan, and Pinches, 1990) identified over 40 studies on acquisition performance using the event-study methodology, with most studies originating in the area of financial economics. Most finance studies have examined performance from the perspective of gains accruing to bidding and target firm shareholders as a result of acquisition announcements (see Jarrell, Brickley, and Netter, 1988; Jensen and Ruback, 1983 for excellent narrative reviews of the literature). The contribution of this body of research has undoubtedly been significant; however, the studies have provided only limited insights into factors that influence acquisition performance, or have explained why nearly half of all acquisitions fail to fulfill prior expectations. Generally speaking, studies here have focused on the relationship between issues related to the market for corporate control, especially its competitiveness (e.g. mode of payment, type of transaction, and number of bidders) and shareholder gains. Issues of strategic organizational fit do not feature in these studies.

Recent studies in strategic management have, however, examined the performance implications of "strategic fit" or relatedness. Basing their arguments on the diversification literature and also on the literature in industrial organization, researchers such as Salter and Weinhold (1979) and Lubatkin (1983) have argued that related acquisitions should exhibit superior performance. Compared to unrelated acquisitions, related acquisitions provide greater synergistic benefits arising out of economies of scale and scope. In addition, possibilities of transferring core skills across involved firms are also associated with such acquisitions. Accordingly, empirical studies by Chatterjee (1986), Lubatkin (1987), Seth (1990), Shelton (1988), and Singh and Montgomery (1987) have sought to test the hypothesis that "strategic fit" is positively related to value creation in acquisitions. Their findings, however, have not always been consistent with expectations. Lubatkin (1987), for example, observed that, contrary to what he had hypothesized, horizontal acquisitions did not outperform vertical or conglomerate acquisitions. Similarly, Chatterjee's (1986) study indicates that gains to target firm shareholders in unrelated acquisitions were significantly higher than those in related, non-horizontal acquisitions. Also, in a more recent study, Seth (1990) found that there were no significant differences in the overall value creation (combined for the bidding and target firm) between related and unrelated acquisitions. On the other hand, Singh and Montgomery's (1987) research provides some support for the relatedness hypothesis. They found that while gains to the acquiring firm shareholders in both related and unrelated acquisitions were not significantly different from zero, those to the target firm shareholders were higher in related acquisitions. Additional support has been provided by Shelton (1988), whose study findings suggest that acquisitions which permit bidders access to new but related markets create the most value for shareholders.

The considerable diversity in the findings of the above studies provides strong support to Jemison and Sitkin's (1986) contention that strategic fit, while important, is not a sufficient condition for superior acquisition performance. In other words, while relatedness indicates that potential synergistic benefits may be present, it will result in superior acquisition performance only if synergies can eventually be realized through effective post-acquisition integration. As discussed later, that might not be the case if organizational impediments thwart effective implementation.

Post-acquisition integration

The need for post-acquisition integration of operations in an acquisition is primarily bounded by its objectives. An acquisition might form a part of a strategy of related diversification and, therefore, be expected to provide synergistic benefits. Such benefits could be in the form of operating efficiencies and economies of scale requiring high levels of integration as might be feasible in related acquisitions (Porter, 1985; Salter and Weinhold, 1979). Alternatively, an acquisition could be of an unrelated business, motivated by a desire to improve one's price-earnings ratio or sales growth, and involve little or no integration or sharing of resources (Shrivastava, 1986).

The primary objective in post-acquisition integration of operations is to make more effective use of existing capabilities. Merging firms can reduce unit costs in production, inventory holding, marketing, advertising, and distribution integrating similar departments and functions (Howell, 1970; Rappaport, 1987). However, while, in theory, integration should result in benefits, in reality the picture can be very different. Impediments associated with the integration of operations can result in the acquiring firm being unable to manage the integration of the target firm effectively (Haspeslagh and Jemison, 1987). This is especially true when organizational incompatibilities exist in areas such as management styles, reward and evaluation systems, organizational structures, or organizational cultures: incompatibilities which may negate the potential benefits associated with an acquisition (Lubatkin, 1983; Marks, 1982). In the following paragraphs we discuss the importance of organizational fit as a determinant of post-acquisition performance, and also present the hypotheses examined in this study.

Organizational fit

Differences in management styles

An important element of "organizational fit" in acquisitions is the extent of compatibility in the styles of the acquiring and acquired firm management. Management style has been described as an element of the managerial or the subjective culture of an organization (Bhagat and McQuaid, 1982; Sathe, 1985). It has been conceptualized in the organizations literature (e.g. Covin and Slevin, 1988; Khandwalla, 1977; Miller, 1987) as comprising a number of factors, including the management group's attitude towards risk, their decision-making approach, and preferred control and communication patterns.

Management styles are unique to organizations and may differ considerably across firms – for example, management groups may have very different risk-taking propensities. It is, therefore, not unusual to find that policies and procedures which seem to be reckless and extremely "risky" to one management group appear to another group to be justifiable approaches (Davis, 1968; Freedman, 1985). Similarly, one management group's tolerance for change may be much greater than another. Top management groups might also differ in their approach to decision-making. As pointed out by Mintzberg (1973), while some management teams rely almost exclusively on common sense, gut feelings, and "rules of thumb", others emphasize formalized strategic planning systems, market research, and various management science techniques. In addition, differences can also exist in management groups' beliefs on the desired level of "flexibility" (Burns and Stalker, 1961). For example, one group may believe in loose, informal controls and open channels of communication, while another might stress greater operating control, highly structured channels of communication, and adherence to well-defined job descriptions. Similarly, there might be significant differences in terms of another critical aspect of management style, i.e. "participation", or the extent to which they encourage subordinate "participation" in decision-making (Vroom and Yetton, 1973).

The influence of management styles on organizational performance has been examined in recent strategic management literature (Covin and Slevin, 1988; Kerr, 1982; Leontiades, 1982; Miller, 1987). An acquisition has the effect of bringing together the management groups of two organizations, with styles which might be similar, or alternatively, very different. Significant differences can contribute to, what Buono, Bowditch, and Lewis (1985) call, "cultural ambiguity", a situation characterized by uncertainties concerning whose style or culture will dominate. Generally, the acquiring firm management end up imposing their own style on the management at the acquired firm and, as Hirsch and Andrews (1983) note, this can result in a loss of identity among acquired firm management. This outcome is one of increased anxiety, distrust, and conflict, culminating in a "merger standstill," with declining productivity and poor post-acquisition performance (Ivancevich, Schweiger, and Power, 1987).

In summary, one can argue that while compatibility in management styles facilitates post-acquisition assimilation, major differences in management styles and philosophies can prove to be serious impediments to the achievement of acquisition success (Davis, 1968). As hypothesized by Buono and Bowditch (1989: 134), differences in management styles may be a major reason why mergers and acquisitions often fail to achieve the level of performance predicted by precombination feasibility studies. Additional support is available in the form of case studies

(Callahan, 1986; Lipton, 1982; Rappaport, 1982), which suggest that differences in management thinking and values are important contributors to post-acquisition problems. Thus:

> **Hypothesis 1:** There will be a negative relationship between differences in the management styles of the acquiring and acquired firms and post-acquisition performance.

The extent to which differences in management styles impact acquisition performance is likely to vary depending on the level of interaction required among the two management groups in the post-acquisition management of the combined entity. Consequently, the potential for conflict due to differences in styles is likely to be the highest in acquisitions followed by considerable operational integration (Marks, 1982), given that such acquisitions invariably involve much higher levels of managerial interaction. Also, the cooperation required to manage the integration process might be very difficult to obtain if major differences in management styles exist. Not only are conflicts likely to be more and, therefore, to be less likely to be resolved, it also becomes more difficult to coordinate and control the integration of post-acquisition operations. As argued by Davis (1968: 93), "the likelihood of conflict because of differences in managerial business styles becomes greater in proportion to the extent that the operations of the two companies are expected to reinforce one another."

Since integration of operations makes the coexistence of two different styles virtually infeasible, it inevitably raises the issue of whose style will dominate (generally it is the style of the acquiring firm that prevails). Ensuing conflicts, in turn, tend to reduce the probability that the two management groups will effectively work together towards achieving the goals of the acquisition. On the other hand, as argued by Hayes (1979), organizations with very different management styles can work effectively together after an acquisition if the interaction is limited, as in situations of low post-acquisition integration. The above arguments lead to the following hypotheses:

> **Hypothesis 2:** In acquisitions characterized by high post-acquisition integration, there will be a negative relationship between differences in management styles and post-acquisition performance.

> **Hypothesis 3:** In acquisitions characterized by low post-acquisition integration, differences in management styles will not be related to post-acquisition performance.

Differences in reward and evaluation systems

The reward and evaluation system is widely regarded as one of the most important components of the organizational form (Galbraith, 1977; Kerr, 1982; Murthy and Salter, 1973; Napier and Smith, 1987). Such systems (which define the terms of exchange between individuals and the organization) do vary significantly across organizations, based on factors such as market or industry characteristics and the strategy that the firm chooses to adopt (Balkin and Gomez-Mejia, 1990; Govindarajan and Fisher, 1990; Kerr, 1985; Lorsch and Allen, 1973; Pitts, 1974; Salter, 1973). For example, Lorsch and Allen (1973) found significant differences in the criteria used to evaluate managerial performance across samples of vertically integrated and conglomerate organizations. Diversified conglomerates in their study placed more emphasis on the "end-result" criteria in rewarding managers while integrated firms typically used a combination of end and intermediate results. Pitts (1974) had found variations in the reward and evaluation systems between firms which were acquisitive diversifiers and those which diversified through internal expansion. Similarly, Kerr's (1985) data suggest that the process by which a firm's diversification strategy had been achieved has a major influence on the design of the reward system.

In addition, the literature on strategy implementation suggests that implementation effectiveness and, hence, performance is significantly influenced by the choice of control systems. For example, recent research by Govindarajan and Gupta (1985) highlights the importance of a fit between strategy and control systems in achieving superior performance. Given that a critical component of control systems is the reward and evaluation system, one can reasonably expect that the choice of the reward system during the assimilation process is an important determinant of post-acquisition performance. Certainly, similarities in reward and evaluation systems allow for easier integration of systems; significant differences between the acquiring and acquired firms, on the other hand, can be an important impediment to acquisition implementation (Diven, 1984).

Differences in reward and evaluations systems exist along a number of factors. These include factors related to the evaluation criteria, such as the time period over which the process is focused, indices used to measure performance, and the type of performance indicator used in the evaluation process. In addition to the evaluation criteria, the form and administration of compensation can be important. The system of bonuses and incentives may differ significantly across firms. Thus, managers accustomed to highly leveraged performance bonus (common in many entrepreneurial companies) might find it difficult to adjust to a more bureauratic mode, if required, after an acquisition and vice-versa (Hayes, 1979). As Ferracone (1987) observes, even in acquisitions where marked differences in reward and evaluation systems are not always there, there are often enough dissimilarities to generate considerable conflicts.

With reward and evaluation systems representing an important vehicle in reinforcing organizational culture (Kerr and Slocum, 1987), changes made to the existing system (or the imposition of a new system) after an acquisition are likely to elicit strong reactions. Even speculations on how the system may be altered are sufficient to cause significant anxieties and conflicts, and to lead to unsatisfactory post-acquisition performance. The issue of dysfunctional imposition of the acquiring firm's systems on the acquired firm and its implication for acquisition performance has also been addressed by Jemison and Sitkin (1986). According to them, such imposition can be viewed as the outcome of two forces, namely, defensiveness and arrogance. The former stems from unfamiliarity with the acquired firm's procedures while the latter is generally the outcome of an erroneous belief among acquiring firm management that their systems (including reward and evaluation systems) are superior to those in the acquired entity and should, therefore, be adopted uniformly after the acquisition. The outcome can be detrimental–while a system might have been appropriate and successful in the acquiring firm, it may not be so for the acquired entity. These arguments lead to the next hypothesis:

> **Hypothesis 4:** There will be a negative relationship between differences in the reward and evaluation systems of the acquiring and acquired firms and post-acquisition performance.

Again, the impact of differences in reward and evaluation systems on performance is likely to be more pronounced if post-acquisition plans require substantial integration of operations. In such cases, retention of major differences in reward systems in the post-acquisition phase can create a major morale problem among managers with a perceived inferior system. It then becomes necessary to address and resolve existing differences and bring about uniformity in the reward and evaluation structure, even if it means significant additional expenditure. Therefore, one can hypothesize that, in acquisitions involving high levels of integration, differences in the reward and evaluation systems of the acquiring and acquired firms will have a significant negative impact on post-acquisition performance. On the other hand, if the acquired firm is kept as an autonomous entity and its operations are not integrated with the acquiring firm after the acquisition, it might even be feasible to let the two organizations retain their own systems. Ferracone (1987) provides an example of such an acquisition – one involving a large industrial firm that acquired a leading financial services organization. The acquiring firm management saw the acquired business remaining distinct and autonomous, and were able to adopt a compensation system for the acquired firm which was very different from their own. Thus, in cases where post-acquisition integration is low, differences will probably not have a major impact on acquisition performance. Given the above arguments, the next set of hypotheses examined in this study was as follows:

Hypothesis 5: Differences in the reward and evaluation systems across the acquiring and acquired firms will be negatively related to post-acquisition performance in acquisitions characterized by *high* levels of post-acquisition integration.

Hypothesis 6: Differences in the reward and evaluation systems across the acquiring and acquired firms will *not* be related to post-acquisition performance in acquisitions characterized by *low* levels of post-acquisition integration.

METHODOLOGY

Sample

The study's sample consists of acquisitions valued at $1 million or more in the US manufacturing and mining sectors during the period January 1980–March 1984. The starting point was a list of all acquisitions featured in the acquisition rosters in the quarterly issues of *Mergers* and *Acquisitions*. All partial acquisitions, and also acquisitions by firms who were themselves acquired by 1986, were subsequently excluded from the sample. Moreover, to allow for a minimum assimilation period of 2 years the sample was restricted only to those acquisitions which were completed by March 1984. This screening procedure resulted in a starting sample of 703 acquisitions.

The initial mailing of the questionnaires in May 1986, a follow-up letter, and a second mailing of questionnaires in July resulted in a total of 191 responses. Of the 191 acquisitions, 42 were completed in 1980, 39 in 1981, 38 in 1982, 50 in 1983, and 22 in 1984. The 191 returns represent a response rate of 27 percent, which can be considered satisfactory taking into consideration the fact that the performance of acquisitions is generally viewed by most companies as an extremely sensitive topic. However, complete data on all the variables in this study were available in 173 of the 191 acquisitions.

Potential respondents in the survey were senior executives in acquiring firms – they were identified by comparing the most recent list of senior executives in the acquiring firm with that in the year of the acquisition (using *Moody's Industrial Manuals*). This procedure enabled us to ensure that the executive to whom the questionnaire was mailed was with the acquiring firm at the time of the acquisition and would, therefore, be knowledgeable about the acquisition. In a few cases the executive to whom the questionnaire was sent forwarded it to another person in the organization who, he felt, was more knowledgeable about the particular acquisition. Also, to minimize "survivor bias", respondents were specifically requested to complete the questionnaire even if the acquired firm had been subsequently divested (as long as it had been with the acquiring firm for a period of at least 2 years). In all, of the 191 responses received, 52 were to questionnaires which had been sent to the CEO of the acquiring firm, in 66 cases it was to the President and in 59 cases to a Senior or Executive Vice-President of the firm. The rest (14) were received from Vice-Presidents. Of those who did not participate, 120 (17.5 percent of the sample) provided their reasons for not doing so, citing reasons such as "time pressures", "company policy against participating in surveys", and, quite frequently, "data confidentiality."

Measures

Differences in management style

Differences in management style were measured using an adapted version of instrument developed by Khandwalla (1977). The scale comprised 17 items for measuring differences in the risk-taking propensity of the management groups, extent of participation encouraged in decision-making, approach to decision-making, and emphasis placed on formality (see Appendix for questionnaire items). Respondents were asked to indicate the extent of perceived differences in management styles between the acquiring and acquired firm management along each of these items using a five-point Likert-type scale (1 = very similar, 5 = very different). The Cronbach-α value for the scale was 0.92, providing strong evidence of the reliability of the scale and high inter-item correlation. Principal-components factor analysis with varimax rotation on the items extracted a single factor. An aggregate measure of "differences in management style" was calculated by averaging the scores on all the items in the questionnaire (Koberg, 1987). In a separate question, respondents had also been asked to provide their perception of the aggregate or "overall" difference in the management styles between their and the acquired firm. This measure was highly correlated with the calculated composite score ($r = 0.82$, $p < 0.001$), indicating response consistency.

Differences in reward and evaluation systems

This was measured using a scale identified by Kerr (1982) (see Appendix). Respondents were asked to indicate the extent of perceived differences on a Likert-type five-point scale (1 = very similar, 5 = very different). The Cronbach-α value for the scale was 0.90. Moreover, principal-components factor analysis indicated that all the eight items measuring differences in reward and evaluation systems loaded on a single factor. Again, a composite measure of the difference was calculated for each acquisition in the sample by taking the mean of the item scores, and these too correlated highly ($r = 0.78$, $p < 0.001$) with the overall measures provided by the respondents.

Post-acquisition integration

The extent to which the operations of the acquiring and acquired firms were integrated was measured along various manufacturing/R&D and marketing activities (see Appendix). Principal-component analysis identified two factors – with items on manufacturing integration loading on one and those used to measure marketing integration loading on the other. The Cronbach-α values were 0.91 and 0.90 for the scales measuring post-acquisition integration along manufacturing and marketing activities respectively. Here again, respondents were asked to indicate the extent of post-acquisition integration or consolidation of operations along each item of the scale (1 = very low integration to 5 = very high integration) and the individual scores were then used to calculate a composite index of the extent of post-acquisition integration of manufacturing and marketing functions. These two composite scores were then used to categorize the acquisition in the sample into two subgroups: a "high integration" subgroup which consisted of acquisitions where the composite integration scores along *both* the manufacturing and marketing dimensions were greater than 3.0 (midpoint value in the scale) and a "low integration" subgroup composed of acquisitions where *both* scores were less than 3.0. Seventy-one acquisitions were in the high integration category while 63 were characterized by low levels of post-acquisition integration. However, because of incomplete data the sample sizes in our analysis were 69 and 61 respectively.

Relative size

Various authors (e.g. Kitching, 1967; Kusewitt, 1985) have hypothesized that size differences between the acquiring and acquired firm influence acquisition performance. Kusewitt (1985), for example, found a negative relationship between relative size (ratio of the acquired firm to the acquired firm) and acquisition performance. Kitching (1967), on the other hand, found that acquisitions where the acquired firms'sales were less than 2 percent of the acquiring firm had high failure rates. Given its potential impact, relative size was used as a control variable in this study. It was operationalized as the ratio of the sales of the acquired firm to that of the acquiring firm (in the year before the acquisition).

Acquisition performance

Acquisition performance was measured by asking the respondents for their assessments of the extent to which the acquisition was able to achieve prior expectations in terms of its impact on the performance of the acquiring firm. It was measured along five performance criteria, namely: ROI, EPS, stock price, cash flow, and sales growth, all of which have been widely used in prior research (e.g. Burgman, 1983; Souder and Chakrabarti, 1984). Respondents were asked to (1) rate the performance of the acquisition along each criterion using a five-point Likert-type scale, and (2) assign weights to each criterion according to its perceived importance. The importance scores were used to weight the "performance scores" so that a weighted average "acquisition performance" index could be established for each acquisition. Also, in a separate question, each respondent was asked to provide his opinion of the "overall" performance of the acquisition in question. When compared, the two scores were highly correlated ($r = 0.89$, $p < 0.001$), suggesting consistency of response.

Perceptual measures were used in this study because of the difficulties and problems associated with the use of "objective" measures in measuring post-acquisition performance (Burgman, 1983; Kitching, 1967; Porter, 1987). Accounting measures are typically available in aggregate form (i.e. for the entire corporation) and isolating the performance of the acquisition after controlling for the performance of other units and the impact of other events is difficult, if not impossible. Second, shareholder abnormal gains as a result of an announcement or consummation (used in event studies) do not measure acquisition performance as an outcome but merely reflect the security markets' "*a priori*" expectations (Montgomery and Wilson, 1986). Therefore, they are unlikely to be appropriate measures of post-acquisition performance. In summary, neither accounting nor market measures (abnormal gains) can be used as valid measures of post-acquisition performance. A reasonable alternative is the use of considered management judgement, an approach which is likely to provide a picture of performance which is much closer to reality. This follows the guidelines of Dess and Robinson (1984) who advocate the use of subjective measures when appropriate objective measures are not available (as is the case in this study).

To validate the perceptual performance measure used in this study, an *ex-post* analysis of archival data was done using a randomly selected subsample of 75 acquisitions. Using Predicasts F&S Index, the *Wall Street Journal* index and the ABI Inform database, accounts pertaining to these acquisitions were identified in the business press. However, in 57 of the 75 acquisitions the extent of available information on post-acquisition performance from secondary sources was very limited and, hence, did not provide an opportunity for any meaningful evaluation. In the remaining 18 acquisitions, data from articles, news items, information in annual reports etc., on each acquisition were then carefully examined by an independent and informed evaluator to assess the level of post-acquisition success using multiple criteria, i.e. post-acquisition sales growth, post-acquisition profitability of the acquired division (where the information was available), cash flow changes, importance given to the acquired entity by the acquiring firm after the acquisition, and the opinions expressed by executives and industry analysts. His evaluations of the post-acquisition performance of the 18 acquisitions on a 1–5 scale (with "1" being "very unsuccessful" and "5" being "very successful") were then correlated with the composite measures of "acquisition performance" calculated based on questionnaire data. The zero-order correlation coefficient of 0.77 ($p < 0.001$) between the two sets of scores indicates that the questionnaire responses were reasonably valid measures of post-acquisition performance.

Non-response bias

Given that the response rate was only 27 percent, we checked for possible non-response bias using two tests. First, the respondents and non-respondents were compared along the dimension of average size (measured in terms of sales revenue) for both the acquiring and acquired firms. The calculated t-statistic values of 0.403 and 0.103 for the acquiring and the acquired firm respectively (see Table 1) were statistically insignificant, which suggests that there were no significant differences between the responding and the non-responding groups. Second, given obvious difficulties in comparing the respondent and non-respondent samples across the

Table 1 Comparison of respondents and non-respondents (in terms of $million sales revenue)

| | Respondents | | Non-respondents | | |
	Mean	SD	Mean	SD	t
Acquiring firms	1551.4	3665.4	1644.7	2252.0	0.403
Acquired firms	158.2	809.9	150.6	736.6	0.103

SD = Standard deviation.

Table 2 Comparison of early and late respondents

| | High integration | | | Low integration | | |
Variable[a]	Early (n = 43)	Late (n = 28)	t value	Early (n = 37)	Late (n = 26)	t value
1. Differences in management styles	3.113	3.203	0.655	3.381	3.373	0.046
2. Differences in reward and evaluation systems	3.197	2.900	1.536	3.340	3.119	0.917
3. Acquisition performance	3.093	3.264	0.781	2.925	3.075	0.042

* Variables measured using five-point Likert-type scales.

research variables (differences in management styles, differences in reward and evaluation systems and acquisition performance), we compared the "late" and "early" respondents along these variables. The assumption behind this test for non-response bias (suggested by Oppenheim, 1966) is that the "late" respondents (those responses received after the second mailing) are very similar to non-respondents, given that they would have fallen into that category had a second set of questionnaires not been mailed. Again, as Table 2 illustrates, there were no significant differences between the two groups, providing further evidence of the representativeness of the sample.

ANALYSIS AND RESULTS

Table 3 provides the means and standard deviations of the study variables and also the correlation coefficients between them in the high and low integration subgroups.

Table 3 Correlations, means, and standard deviation of study variables

| | High integration (n = 69) | | | | | | Low integration (n = 61) | | | | | |
Variable[a]	Mean	SD	1	2	3	4	Mean	SD	1	2	3	4
1. Differences in management styles[a]	3.152	0.706	–	–	–	–	3.377	0.681	–	–	–	–
2. Differences in reward and evaluation systems[a]	3.086	0.876	0.27	–	–	–	3.274	0.956	0.50	–	–	–
3. Acquisition performance[a]	3.184	0.883	–0.40	–0.22	–	–	3.010	1.150	–0.32	–0.21	–	–
4. Relative size	0.129	0.242	–0.11	–0.10	–0.08	–	0.168	0.233	–0.08	–0.20	0.05	–

* Measured using five-point Likert-type scales.

Hypotheses 1 and 4 were first tested on the entire sample using the following regression model:

$$PERFORM = \alpha_0 + \alpha_1(RSIZE) + \alpha_2(DIFSTY) + \alpha_3(DIFREW) + \epsilon_1 \tag{1}$$

where

$$
\begin{aligned}
PERFORM &= \text{acquisition performance} \\
RSIZE &= \text{relative size} \\
DIFSTY &= \text{differences in management styles} \\
DIFREW &= \text{differences in reward and evaluation systems}
\end{aligned}
$$

In order to test Hypotheses 2, 3, 5 and 6 we estimated the above equation separately for the high and low integration subgroups.

$$PERFORM = \beta_0 + \beta_1(RSIZE) + \beta_2(DIFSTY) + \beta_4(DIFREW) + \epsilon_2 - \text{high integration} \tag{2}$$

$$PERFORM = \gamma_0 + \gamma_1(RSIZE) + \gamma_2(DIFSTY) + \gamma_3(DIFREW) + \epsilon_3 - \text{low integration} \tag{3}$$

Results of the regression analyses are presented in Table 4. The regression coefficient associated with the DIFSTY variable in the full model was negative and significant ($\alpha_2 = -0.527, p < 0.001$), providing statistical support for Hypothesis 1. In other words, differences in top management style and post-acquisition performance are negatively related after controlling for relative size and differences in reward and evaluation system across all acquisitions. However, no significant relationship was observed between differences in reward and evaluation systems and performance ($\alpha_3 = -0.123, p < 0.17$).[1] Also, as hypothesized, a strong negative relationship was found between differences in management style and acquisition performance in the subgroup with high post-acquisition integration ($\beta_2 = -0.477, p < 0.01$) after controlling for relative size. However, contrary to expectations, a significant negative relationship was also observed in the low integration subgroup ($\gamma_2 = -0.499, p < 0.05$),

Table 4 Relationships between organizational differences and acquisition performance

| Subgroup | No. of cases | Regression coefficients | | | R^2 | Adj R^2 | F |
		RSIZE	DIFSTY	DIFREW			
All acquisitions	173	−0.532 (−1.780)	−0.527*** (−4.467)	−0.123 (−1.378)	0.177	0.162	12.154***
High post-acquisition integration	69	−0.471 (−1.147)	−0.477** (−3.281)	−0.130 (−1.110)	0.191	0.154	5.129**
Low post-acquisition integration	61	0.049 (0.077)	−0.499* (−2.028)	−0.074 (−0.413)	0.109	0.062	2.321

*** $p < 0.001$; ** $p < 0.01$; * $p < 0.05$.
Figures in parentheses represent t-statistics.

suggesting that differences in management style can be an important factor in influencing acquisition performance even in acquisitions characterized by low levels of post-acquisition integration.

Contrary to what had been hypothesized (H5), no significant negative relationship was observed between differences in the reward and evaluation systems and acquisition performance in the high integration sample ($\beta_3 = -0.130$, $p = 0.27$). The direction of the regression coefficient was negative and suggestive of a possible negative impact of such differences on acquisition performance, but in the absence of significant results definite conclusions cannot obviously be drawn. Hypothesis 6 was supported in that no significant relationship was observed between differences in the reward and evaluation systems and acquisition performance in the low integration subgroup ($\gamma_3 = -0.074$, $p = 0.68$).

In addition to the above, the study tested for the equality of coefficients in the regression models for high integration and low integration subgroups using the Chow test (Chow, 1960). The low F-statistic value of 0.59 indicates that the two models (high and low integration) are not statistically different, and suggests that the extent of post-acquisition integration does not significantly influence the relationships between organizational fit and acquisition performance (as had been hypothesized). Additional tests of the potential moderating effects of post-acquisition integration were undertaken using the procedures suggested by Arnold (1982). First, differences in the "strength" of the relationship (measured by correlation coefficients) between differences in management style and acquisition performance across high and low integration subgroups, were examined. A similar test was done for the relationship between differences in reward and evaluation systems and performance. In either case no statistically significant differences in the value of the correlation coefficients across the two subgroups were identified. Second, t-tests used to examine whether post-acquisition integration moderates the "form" of the relationship also did not produce significant results, providing further evidence that post-acquisition integration does not moderate the relationship between organizational fit and performance. Moreover, given that a single measure of post-acquisition integration cannot be obtained (the scale consists of two dimensions), moderated regression analysis (MRA), the alternative procedure suggested by Arnold (1982) and Stone and Hollenbeck (1984) to test for moderating effects, could not be used in this study.

DISCUSSION

This study examined the impact of two key factors pertaining to "organizational fit", namely differences in management styles and reward and evaluation systems on acquisition performance. A negative relationship was hypothesized for both in acquisitions with high levels of post-acquisition integration. In acquisitions with low integration no such relationship was expected. The findings of this study suggest that compatibility of management styles is important to superior performance in acquisitions characterized by both high and low levels of post-acquisition integration of operations. The findings therefore support the observations in case studies which indicate that acquisitions of firms with a different management style can result in conflicts, difficulties in achieving operational synergies, market share shrinkages and poor performance. These findings were not surprising given that most acquisitions are accompanied by significant changes in a relatively compressed period of time – changes which almost inevitably result in enhanced complexity and uncertainty.

These problems are further aggravated by differences in managerial styles and ongoing tensions concerning which style will dominate. One can reasonably expect the level of apprehension to be much higher among acquired firm management, who often react defensively by clinging to their own beliefs and approaches in an effort to reduce uncertainty and preserve their identity. The outcome is likely to be one of conflicts and confrontations contributing to poor acquisition performance.

An interesting finding of this study is that differences in management styles have a negative impact on acquisition performance even in acquisitions characterized by low post-acquisition integration. It was, however, not totally unexpected, suggesting that, while in theory one can visualize keeping the management groups separate – thereby allowing each to maintain its style – in practice it is often not the case. Necessary post-acquisition administrative interactions in such acquisitions mean that the acquiring firm management often end up imposing their own style on the acquired firm. The likelihood is higher when the acquiring firm management believe that they can enhance target firm effectiveness by imposing their style, systems, and culture on the acquired firm. In other words, low post-acquisition integration does not necessarily mean true autonomy. Even in acquisitions followed by low integration of operations the acquired firm is often subjected to very close control and scrutiny. It can take the form of increased reporting, frequent visits by acquiring firm management, and fundamental changes being required of the acquired firm in their management priorities. Also, the studies of Lorsch and Allen (1973) and Hoskisson and Hitt (1988) on diversified firms suggest that financial control is important in the successful management of an acquired firm in unrelated acquisitions characterized by low integration. To the extent that differences in management styles prevent agreements on attendant financial targets, goals, and investment criteria, the task of management control becomes more difficult in such acquisitions. In addition, "arrogance" on the part of the acquiring firm, and a belief that its own style and practices are superior, can lead to the imposition of its style and systems on the acquired entity even if the actual integration of operations undertaken is low (Jemison and Sitkin, 1986). The result may be high post-acquisition turnover among key acquired firm executives. While not explored in this study, the loss of valuable expertise through the departure of key executives can be an important factor affecting performance in such acquisitions (Walsh, 1988).

The study findings suggest that differences in reward and evaluation systems do not have the same kind of negative impact on acquisition performance as differences in management styles in acquisitions characterized by either high or low post-acquisition integration. A possible reason may be that differences in reward and evaluation systems are more easily and quickly reconciled following an acquisition than differences in management styles. Consequently, such differences may not have a major long-term impact on acquisition performance as do problems arising from incompatible management styles (which are deep-rooted, and therefore much more difficult to overcome). Also indicated by the data is the relationship between differences in management style and in reward and evaluation systems, especially in acquisitions characterized by high post-acquisition integration. While management style and reward systems are two different components of the organizational form, it must be remembered that reward systems are often employed to reinforce values, beliefs, and practices in an organization (Kerr and Slocum, 1987). The relationship between the two, therefore, does not come as a major surprise. As observed by Cummings (1984), reward systems in an organization with a high risk-taking management style are likely to be different from one with a risk-averse culture, and a merger of two such organizations can pose significant challenges in the integration phase.

In interpreting the results of this study however, one needs to take into account its limitations. First, this study was limited to the examination of just two of the factors representing "organizational fit", with "relative size" as a control variable. Obviously there are other factors (not included in this study) which potentially influence post-acquisition performance. To the extent that future studies use a more comprehensive and fully specified model, they will not only explain a greater percentage of the variability but also be able to identify possible confounding effects. Second, the data pertaining to a particular acquisition in this study were collected from a single respondent in the acquiring firm. The decision to use a single respondent was partly based on the opinions of executives who participated in the pretest. They strongly felt that use of multiple respondents would significantly increase their reluctance to participate in the study and consequently would have a very negative effect on the response rate. Taking into consideration their views, the fact that response rate on a sensitive topic such as mergers and acquisitions is likely to be low, and the very low response rate in a previous questionnaire-based study by Burgman (1983), we chose to use a single respondent. Certainly, a future study which uses multiple respondents can generate greater confidence in the results. Third, the study relies upon self-report measures. While reliability and validity tests undertaken provide grounds for confidence in the measures, future studies which use multiple data sources and more objective measures will yield stronger results. Finally, the research does not address the level within the acquiring firm at which the acquired firm is managed. A more in-depth future study of a limited number of acquisitions, preferably one where the researcher is provided "inside access," can better address this issue and its implications from the viewpoint of the relationships examined in the paper.

Implications for managers

The findings of this study have important implications from the perspective of executives associated with mergers and acquisitions. In addressing the issue of high failure rate among mergers and acquisitions, a number of authors (e.g. Achtmeyer and Daniell, 1988; Rappaport, 1979) have suggested that the probabilities of success can be significantly improved through systematic planning. Our results imply that such planning, in order to be meaningful, should necessarily include a careful assessment of existing organizational differences, particularly differences in management styles. Unfortunately, in practice, such analysis is either overlooked or given secondary importance. The escalating momentum and the underlying desire to complete transactions quickly often leads to incomplete analysis and premature "solutions" (Jemison and Sitkin, 1986), with organizational considerations often playing a very limited role in merger and acquisition decisions (Hirsch, 1987; Robino and DeMeuse, 1985; Schweiger and Ivancevich, 1985). This is especially surprising when one considers that in a recent survey of 101 CEOs and senior managers of large companies, by the management consulting firm of Egon Zehnder International, the most commonly cited causes for acquisition failure were people and organizational problems (*Mergers and Acquisitions*, 1987).

Another factor contributing to inadequate analysis might be the over-reliance on the services of investment bankers, who typically choose to de-emphasize questions and issues related to organizational fit. As Haspeslagh and Jemison (1987) suggest, it is not because investment bankers believe that qualitative organizational issues are any less important, but often because recommendations based on quantitative data are easier to defend, if legally challenged. Moreover, issues related to management styles and values are highly sensitive and controversial. The tendency, therefore, is to avoid them as much as possible during the pre-acquisition and negotiation phases. However, the findings of this study highlight the importance of including an analysis of key organizational dimensions as an integral part of any acquisition analysis. First, it will help managers gain a more realistic picture of synergistic benefits and, thereby, the true value of the acquisition. Second, considering the likely impact of organizational factors will prompt early thinking on how the acquisition can be best managed, once it is completed. For example, in acquisitions with differences in management styles, significant mental readjustments required for effective integration suggest the need for an atmosphere of open communications and mutual respect among management groups, and facilitating conditions in which each group can better understand the others' perspective.

RESEARCH IMPLICATIONS AND DIRECTIONS FOR FUTURE RESEARCH

From the viewpoint of academic researchers, the findings highlight the importance of taking a broader perspective in their study of acquisition performance. There is a definite need to go beyond issues of relatedness and synergistic benefits, recognizing that the expansion of "two plus two equals five" does not happen automatically. With the findings of the body of research linking "strategic fit" and performance being largely inconclusive, future research should also focus on issues related to post-acquisition implementation. Shrivastava (1986) identifies three types of post-acquisition integration – procedural, physical and managerial/sociocultural. While procedural integration involves the combination of systems procedures, and rules, physical integration entails the consolidation of assets and equipment. Managerial and sociocultural integration, on the other hand, relates to cultural integration, integration of management styles, and changes in organization structure. The findings of this study indicate that one aspect of managerial integration, namely differences in management styles, has an important impact on post-acquisition performance while impediments to procedural integration in the form of differences in reward systems do not play an important role. Future research needs to identify impediments associated with other aspects of the three types of integration towards assessing their impact on acquisition performance.

A very important area for future research relates to the management of acquisitions. As emphasized by Haspeslagh and Jemison (1987), the probability of value creation in mergers and acquisitions stems not from relatedness but primarily on how the interdependencies that contribute to the benefits are managed. While the results indicate that high differences in management style are generally associated with poor performance, not all acquisitions with high differences in management styles in this study exhibited poor performance. Why did some acquisitions with high differences in management styles perform better than others? An interesting area for future research, therefore, relates to the process of implementation, and on how the process can be best managed, particularly in cases where organizational incompatibility poses additional challenges. Another important area for future research is the role and importance of organizational mechanisms in successfully managing the interdependencies that promote resource/skill-sharing. For example, research that explores the importance of task forces in mediating problems and conflicts that emerge out of differences in terms of management styles, cultures, and systems should provide interesting insights. Such questions which involve contingent relationships can probably be appropriately examined using medium-grained methodologies (e.g. cluster analysis or *Q*-type factor analysis) suggested by Harrigan (1983). By combining the generalizability of coarse-grained methodologies (cross-sectional analysis using large data bases) with the detail of fine-grained methodologies (individual case studies) they provide a useful middle ground for examining contingent relationships.

In summary, although researchers such as Buono and Bowditch (1989), Jemison and Sitkin (1986), Hunt (1990), and Marks (1982) emphasize the importance of the implementation, such issues have played a very limited role in the empirical research on mergers and acquisitions. While research attention has primarily been on the potential benefits in such transactions, the high failure rate among acquisitions is a testimony to the fact that anticipated benefits (or synergies) are not easily realized. There is, therefore, a compelling case to extend research on the performance of acquisitions to an examination of the impact of key organizational and behavioral issues. Hirsch, Friedman, and Koza (1990) have emphasized the importance of looking at both the formulation and implementation sides of strategic decisions – and that certainly applies to research on mergers and acquisitions. The paucity of existing research on acquisition implementation provides excellent opportunities for meaningful future research in the area of strategic management. It is hoped that this study represents an important step in that direction, prompting further research which will provide a better understanding of the myriad factors that influence post-acquisition performance.

APPENDIX: QUESTIONNAIRE ITEMS

Differences in management style

1. Approach to management problems (proactive vs reactive and cautious).
2. Degree of emphasis on R&D and innovation.
3. Degree of reliance on external borrowings or stock issues vs funds generated from operations to finance growth.
4. Riskiness of the investments pursued.
5. Usage of sophisticated analytical techniques in decision-making.
6. Importance accorded to the long-term planning of investments and their financing.
7. Reliance on personal experience and judgement rather than on experts.
8. Orientation in decision-making (long-term vs immediate future).
9. Extent to which the communication channels are structured and access to important financial information restricted.
10. Emphasis on adapting freely to changing circumstances without too much concern for past practice.
11. Usage of sophisticated control and information system for tight formal control.
12. Getting personnel to follow formally established procedures.
13. Getting line and staff personnel to adhere closely to formal job descriptions.
14. Participation sought by top management in decision-making relating to product- or service-related decisions.
15. Extent of participation in decision making among top management relating to capital budgeting decisions.

16. Extent of participation in decision-making in decisions related to long-term strategic growth and diversification.
17. Strongly individualistic decision-making by formally responsible executive vs group-oriented consensus decision-making.

Differences in reward and evaluation system

Differences in the evaluation criteria

1. Time period over which the reward and evaluation process focused (short-run vs long-run performance).
2. Type of performance indicator used in the evaluation process (end result vs intermediate performance).
3. Nature of indices used to measure performance (objective indices vs judgmental input of superiors).
4. Performance measures based on divisional vs corporate performance.

Difference in the administration of rewards

5. Form of reward (cash, stock, etc.).
6. Frequency with which rewards are distributed.
7. Extent to which bonuses are linked to the strategic risk incurred.
8. Uniformity of rewards across divisions.

Extent of post-acquisition integration

Production and R&D

1. Manufacturing process.
2. Purchasing.
3. Warehousing (raw materials and finished goods).
4. Maintenance.
5. Research and development.

Marketing

6. Product market served.
7. Distribution channels.
8. Promotion and advertising.
9. Customer service.

ACKNOWLEDGEMENTS

Portions of this paper were presented at the International Conference of the Strategic Management Society, Boston, 1987. Partial funding for this project was provided by the Strategic Management Institute, University of Pittsburgh and University of Kansas General Research Allocation no. 3822-XO-0038. The author wishes to thank John H. Grant, V. K. Narayanan, and N. Rajagopalan for their helpful comments on earlier drafts of this paper, and Shraboni Datta for research assistance. This paper has also benefited significantly from the comments and suggestions provided by two anonymous reviewers.

NOTE

1 Berry and Feldman (1985) suggest computing R_i^2 (the proportion of variance in an independent variable explained by other independent variables) as a measure of the effects of multicollinearity. Multicollinearity is a serious problem if the value is close to 1.0 – for none of the variables in the three regression models estimated in this study was the value more than 0.28.

REFERENCES

Achtmeyer, W. F. and M. H. Daniell. "How advanced planning widens acquisition rewards", *Mergers and Acquisitions*, **23**(1), 1988, pp. 37–42.

Arnold, H. "Moderator variables: a clarification on conceptual, analytic and psychometric issues", *Organizational Behavior and Human Performance*, **29**, 1982, pp. 143–174.

Balkin, D. B. and L. R. Gomez-Mejia. "Matching compensation and organizational strategies". *Strategic Management Journal*, **11**, 1990, pp. 153–169.

Berry, W. D. and S. Feldman. *Multiple Regression in Practice*, Sage, Beverly Hills, CA, 1985.

Bhagat, R. S. and S. J. McQuaid. "Role of subjective culture in organizations: a review and directions for future research", *Journal of Applied Psychology*, **67**(5), 1982, pp. 653–685.

Buono, A. F., J. L. Bowditch and J. W. Lewis. "When cultures collide: the anatomy of a merger", *Human Relations*, **38**(5), 1985, pp. 477–500.

Buono, A. F. and J. L. Bowditch. *The Human Side of Mergers and Acquisitions*, Josey-Bass, San Francisco, CA, 1989.

Burgman, R. J. "A strategic explanation of corporate acquisition success", unpublished dissertation, Purdue University, 1983.

Burns, T. and G. M. Stalker. *The Management of Innovation.* Tavistock, London, 1961.

Callahan, J. P. "Chemistry: how mismatched managements can kill a deal", *Mergers and Acquisitions*, **20**(4), 1986, pp. 47–53.

Chatterjee, S. "Type of synergy and economic value: the impact of acquisitions on merging and rival firms", *Strategic Management Journal*, **7**, 1986, pp. 119–139.

Chow, G. C. "Tests of equality between sets of coefficients in two linear regressions", *Econometrica*, **28**, 1960, pp. 591–605.

Covin, J. G. and D. P. Slevin. "The influence of organizational structure on the utility of an entrepreneurial top management style", *Journal of Management Studies*, **25**(3), 1988, pp. 217–234.

Cummings, L. L. "Compensation, culture, and motivation: a systems perspective". *Organizational Dynamics*, Winter 1984, pp. 33–44.

Datta, D. K., V. K. Narayanan and G. E. Pinches. "Factors influencing wealth creation in mergers and acquisitions: a meta-analytic synthesis". Paper presented at the National Academy of Management Meetings, San Francisco, CA, 1990.

Davis, R. L. "Compatibility in organizational marriages", *Harvard Business Review*, **46**(4), 1968, pp. 86–93.

Dess, G. C. and R. B. Robinson. "Measuring organizational performance in the absence of objective measures: the case of the privately held firm and conglomerate business unit", *Strategic Management Journal*, **5**, 1984, pp. 265–273.

Diven, D. L. "Organizational planning: neglected factor in mergers and acquisition strategy", *Managerial Planning*, July–August 1984, pp. 4–12.

Freedman, A. M. "DuPont trims cost . . .", *Wall Street Journal*, 25 September 1985, pp. 1, 20.

Ferracone, R. "Blending compensation plans of combining firms", *Mergers and Acquisitions*, **21**(5), 1987, pp. 57–62.

Galbraith, J. R. *Organizational Design*, Addison-Wesley, Reading, MA, 1977.

Govindarajan, V. and J. Fisher. "Strategy, control systems, and resource sharing: effects on business-unit performance", *Academy of Management Journal*, **33**(2), 1990, pp. 259–285.

Govindarajan, V. and A. K. Gupta. "Linking control systems to business unit strategy: impact on performance", Accounting, *Organizations and Society*, **10**, 1985, pp. 51–66.

Harrigan, K. R. "Research methodologies for contingency approaches to business strategies". *Academy of Management Review*, **8**(3), 1983, pp. 398–405.

Haspeslagh, P. C. and D. B. Jemison. "Acquisitions – myths and reality", *Sloan Management Review*, **28**(2), 1987, pp. 53–58.

Hayes, R. H. "The human side of acquisitions", *Management Review*, **68**(11), 1979, pp. 41–46.

Hirsch, P. *Pack Your Own Parachute: How to Survive Mergers, Acquisitions, and Other Corporate Disasters*, Addison-Wesley, Reading, MA, 1987.

Hirsch, P. and J. A. Andrews. "Ambushes, shootouts, and knights of the roundtable: the language of corporate takeovers". In L. Pondy, P. Frost, G. Morgan, and T. Dandridge (eds), *Monograph in Organizational Behavior and Industrial Relations*. Vol. 1: *Organizational Symbolism*, JAI Press, Greenwich, CT, 1983, pp. 145–155.

Hirsch, P., R. Friedman and M. P. Koza. "Collaboration or paradigm shift? Caveat emptor and the risk of romance with economic models for strategy and policy research". *Organization Science*, **1**(1), 1990, pp. 87–97.

Hoskisson, R. E. and M. A. Hitt. "Strategic control systems and relative investment in large multi-product firms", *Strategic Management Journal*, **9**, 1988, 605–621.

Howell, R. A. "Plan to integrate your acquisitions", *Harvard Business Review*, **48**(6), 1970, pp. 66–76.

Hunt, J. W. "Changing pattern of acquisition behavior in takeovers and consequences for acquisition processes", *Strategic Management Journal*, **11**, 1990, pp. 69–77.

Ivancevich, J. M., D. M. Schweiger and F. R. Power. "Strategies for managing human resources during mergers and acquisitions", *Human Resources Planning*, **10**(1), 1987, pp. 19–35.

Jarrell, G. A., J. A. Brickley and J. M. Netter. "The market for corporate control: the evidence since 1980", *Journal of Economic Perspectives*, **2**(1), 1988, pp. 49–68.

Jemison, D. B. and S. B. Sitkin. "Corporate acquisitions: A process perspective", *Academy of Management Review*, **11**(1), 1986, pp. 145–163.

Jensen, M. and R. Ruback. "The market for corporate returns", *Journal of Financial Economics*, **11**(1), 1983, pp. 5–50.

Kerr, J. "Assigning managers on the basis of life cycle", *Journal of Business Strategy*, Spring 1982, pp. 58–65.

Kerr, J. "Diversification strategies and managerial rewards: an empirical study", *Academy of Management Journal*, **28**, 1985, pp. 155–179.

Kerr, J. and J. W. Slocum. "Managing corporate culture through reward systems", *Academy of Management Executive*, **1**(2), 1987, pp. 99–108.

Khandwalla, P. N. *The Design of Organizations* Harcourt, Brace, Jovanovich, New York; 1977.

Kitching, J. "Why do mergers miscarry?" *Harvard Business Review*, **45**(6), 1967, pp. 84–101.

Koberg, C. S. "Resource scarcity, environmental uncertainty and adaptive organizational systems", *Academy of Management Journal*, **30**(4), 1987, pp. 798–807.

Kusewitt, J. B. "An exploratory study of strategic acquisition factors relating to performance", *Strategic Management Journal*, **6**, 1985, pp. 151–169.

Leighton, C. M. and G. R. Tod. "After the acquisition", *Harvard Business Review*, **47**(2), 1969, pp. 90–102.

Leontiades, M. "Choosing the right manager to fit the strategy", *Journal of Business Strategy*, **3**(2), 1982, pp. 58–69.

Lipton, S. L. "High technology acquisitions", *Mergers and Acquisitions*, **17**(3), 1982, pp. 30–40.

Lorsch J. and S. A. Allen. *Managing Diversity and Interdependence*. Division of Research, Harvard University, 1973.

Lubatkin, M. "Merger and the performance of the acquiring firm", *Academy of Management Review*, **8**(2), 1983, pp. 218–225.

Lubatkin, M. "Merger strategies and stockholder value", *Strategic Management Journal*, **8**,(1), 1987, pp. 39–53.

Magnet, M. "Acquiring without smothering", *Fortune*, 12 November 1984, pp. 22–30.

Marks, M. L. "Merging human resources", *Mergers and Acquisitions*, **17**(2), 1982, pp. 38–42.

Mergers and Acquisitions. "Trends and findings", **21**(2), 1987, pp. 19–20.

Mergers and Acquisitions. "1989 profile", **24**(6), 1990, p. 57.

Miller, D. "Strategy making and structure: analysis and implications for performance", *Academy of Management Journal*, **30**(1), 1987, pp. 7–32.

Mintzberg, H. "Strategy making in three modes", *California Management Review*, **16**(3), 1973, pp. 44–58.

Montgomery, C. A. and V. A. Wilson. "Mergers that last: a predictable pattern", *Strategic Management Journal*, **7**, 1986, pp. 91–96.

Murthy, K. R. S. and M. S. Salter. "Should CEO pay be linked to results?" *Harvard Business Review*, **51**(3), 1973, pp. 66–73.

Napier, N. K. and M. Smith. "Product diversification, performance criteria and compensation at the corporate manager level", *Strategic Management Journal*, **8**, 1987, pp. 195–201.

Oppenheim, A. N. *Questionnaire Design and Attitude Measurement*, Basic Books, New York, 1966.

Pitts, R. A. "Incentive compensation and organizational design", *Personnel Journal*, **53**(5), 1974, pp. 338–344, 348.

Porter, M. E. *Competitive Advantage: Creating and Sustaining Superior Performance*, Free Press, New York, 1985.

Porter, M. E. "From competitive advantage to competitive strategy", *Harvard Business Review*, **65**(3), 1987, pp. 43–59.

Rappaport, A. "Strategic analysis for more profitable acquisitions", *Harvard Business Review*, **57**, 1979, pp. 99–110.

Rappaport, A. "United Technologies and Mostek: after the acquisition", *Mergers and Acquisitions*, **17**(1), 1982, pp. 49–54.

Rappaport, A. "Converting merger benefits to shareholder value", *Mergers and Acquisitions*, **21**(3), 1987, pp. 49–55.

Ravenscraft, D. J. and F. M. Scherer. "The profitability of mergers", *International Journal of Industrial Organization*, **7**, 1989, pp. 101–116.

Robino, D. and K. DeMeuse. "Corporate mergers and acquisitions: their impact on HRM", *Personnel Administrator*, **30**(11), 1985, pp. 33–44.

Sales, A. L. and P. A. Mirvis. "When cultures collide: issues of acquisitions". In J. R. Kimberly and R. Quinn (eds), *Managing Organizational Transitions*, Irwin, Homewood; IL, 1984, pp. 107–133.

Salter, M. S. "Tailor incentive compensation to strategy", *Harvard Business Review*, **51**(2), 1973, pp. 94–102.

Salter, M. S. and W. A. Weinhold. *Diversification through Acquisitions: Strategies for Creating Economic Value*, Free Press, New York, 1979.

Sathe, V. *Culture and Related Corporate Realities*. Irwin, Homewood, IL, 1985.

Schweiger, D. M. and J. M. Ivancevich. "Human resources: the forgotten factor in mergers and acquisitions", *Personnel Administrator*, **30**(11), 1985, pp. 47–54.

Seed, A. H. "Why corporate marriages fail", *Financial Executive*. December 1974, pp. 56–62.

Seth, A. "Value creation in acquisitions: a reexamination of performance issues", *Strategic Management Journal*, **11**, 1990, pp. 90–115.

Shelton, L. M. "Strategic business fits and corporate acquisition: empirical evidence", *Strategic Management Journal*, **9**(2), 1988, pp. 279–287.

Shrivastava, P. "Post-merger integration", *Journal of Business Strategy*, **7**(1), 1986, pp. 65–76.

Singh, H. and C. Montgomery. "Corporate acquisition strategies and economic performance", *Strategic Management Journal*, **8**, 1987, pp. 377–386.

Souder, W. E. and A. K. Chakrabarti. "Acquisitions: do they really work out?" *Interfaces*. **14**(4), 1984, pp. 41–47.

Stone, E. F. and J. R. Hollenbeck. "Some issues with the use of moderated regression", *Organizational Behavior and Human Performance*, **34**, 1984, pp. 195–213.

Vroom, V. H. and P. W. Yetton. *Leadership and Decision Making*, University of Pittsburgh Press, Pittsburgh, **PA**, 1973.

Walsh, J. P. "Top management turnover following mergers and acquisitions", *Strategic Management Journal*, **9**, 1988, pp. 173–183.

Young, J. B. "A conclusive investigation into the causative elements of failure in acquisitions and mergers", In S. J. Lee and R. D. Colman (eds), *Handbook of Mergers, Acquisitions and Buyouts*, Prentice Hall, Englewood Cliffs, **NJ**, 1981, pp. 605–628.

20 Post-acquisition managerial learning in central east Europe[1]

Roland Villinger

WESTERN ACQUISITIONS IN CENTRAL EAST EUROPE

For decades, a "wall" separated eastern Europe from the rest of the continent. On one side there was controlled ideology and central planning, hierarchical structures, restrictions and rigidity and on the other pluralism, decentralization and markets, open systems and individual responsibility (at least to a certain extent . . .). In the course of 1989 this wall was dismantled by a chain of revolutions in eastern Europe. Since then, all countries in the region have begun to move in the direction of a market-oriented environment. Hungary, (the former) Czechoslovakia and Poland represent the "fast movers" in this transition process. These central east European, "fast-track" reforming countries can be described by their relative success with respect to progress both in structural reforms and in macro stabilization.

A major role in this tremendous transformation process has been (and still is and will be) performed by foreign companies investing financial and human capital in the region. East European governments, on the one hand, hope that the managerial and technological capabilities as well as the financial resources of western investors will contribute to a fast growth of their economies, eventually leading to the standards of living characteristic of developed, western, market-based societies. Thus, the privatization of their previously state-controlled economies has become a high priority on their political agendas. Western companies investing in the region, on the other hand, see attractive opportunities to enter and expand into "new" markets promising high growth rates.

Hence, foreign direct investment especially into Hungary, Poland, the Czech Republic and Slovakia has grown rapidly, exceeding US$ 10 billion for these four countries in the period from 1990 to 1993.

With privatization schemes generating promising investment opportunities, western acquisitions of substantial equity stakes in east European companies have been accelerating, especially from 1991 onwards. According to Ackermann and Lindquist (1992), a total of 207 western equity participations in existing east European enterprises were completed between January 1989 and March 1992, of which 194 took place in the fast moving countries of central eastern Europe mentioned above. East–west joint ventures, and other looser contract-based networks representing various types of co-operation between two or more companies, have admittedly outnumbered western acquisitions in eastern Europe, i.e. takeovers of local companies. However, the picture can change dramatically when the disclosed investment values in conjunction with joint ventures, on the one hand, and acquisitions, on the other hand, are taken into consideration (*East European Investment Magazine 1992*). The values, in terms of equity participation plus committed investments of the largest western acquisitions, involve amounts of several hundred million US$, and the top transactions exceed one billion US$. Thus, western acquisitions are a means of foreign direct investment with substantial economic significance in the transformation of east European countries into market-oriented economies and, consequently societies.

Acquisitions also represent highly interesting phenomena with respect to the organizational and managerial issues involved. Acquisitions tend to lead to "tighter" forms of co-operation between originally separate companies than joint ventures and other forms of alliances. Hence, the acquisition of a controlling equity stake potentially involves a very significant transfer of managerial paradigms and practices as well as an extreme type of clash between two organizations representing different structures and cultures.

In an east–west context, as discussed here, these differences are bound to be particularly pronounced, thus involving substantial organizational challenges. This is obviously due to a crossing of national boundaries and, at the same time, boundaries between (at least formerly) highly different political and economic systems: the socialist, centrally planned countries of eastern Europe versus the market-based societies in the west.

Acquisitions, as analyzed in the study underlying this paper, include all transactions in which a western company takes over an equity stake in an existing, central east European (Hungarian, Czech, Slovakian, Polish) enterprise, thus gaining essential control of the acquired organization's management. These transactions generally take place through privatization, i.e. a sell-off by the respective country's government to private and – in capital-intensive industries – predominantly foreign investors. Only companies engaged in manufacturing industries are included in the study. In many cases the acquired equity stake is a majority stake or, in a number of cases, a 100 percent share of the acquiree. However, even with an equity participation of (slightly) less than 50 percent, the western acquirer – representing a relative wealth of managerial, technological, and financial capabilities and resources – is generally expected to lead the process of adjusting and restructuring the east European business to meet the requirements of market-based competition.

Managing such a challenging "turn-around" situation requires substantial learning on both sides, the western acquirer and the central east European acquiree. While the research work underlying this paper deals with a variety of issues concerning post-acquisition management and learning in central east European organizations, the present paper focuses on aspects of *individual, managerial learning* following acquisitions in Hungary, the Czech Republic, Slovakia and Poland.

POST-ACQUISITION LEARNING

The literature dealing with post-acquisition management shows a clear concentration on one particular aspect: the issue of *integrating* the acquired company into the acquiring organization (Mace and Montgomery, 1962; Brockhaus, 1971; Lindgren and Spangberg, 1981; Lindgren, 1982; Yunker, 1983; Buono and Bowditch, 1989; Larsson, 1989; Scheiter, 1989; Haspeslagh and Jemison, 1991; Walenciak, 1991; Pablo, 1991; Clark, 1991; Shanley and Correa, 1992; Clever, 1993; Gerpott, 1993). The term "*learning*", on the other hand, is only used every now and then in the more recent literature on post-acquisition management. A learning concept or framework has not been systematically developed in a post-acquisition context, so far. This is quite surprising considering the increasing prominence of the notion of learning in academic thought on management and organization since the late '70s and early '80s.

Combining two organizations by means of an acquisition is most frequently justified by the anticipated managerial, operational and/or financial synergies. These synergies are expected to improve development and performance of the combined operations ("2 + 2 = 5" effect), thus reflecting the effective working of the market for corporate control: the new ownership structure puts the acquired company's assets and resources to an economically better use.

Such an impact can be reached through pure size effects due to the integration of acquirer and acquiree, e.g. increased negotiating power with suppliers or better utilization of machinery by producing larger batches. However, progress can also be made by initiating more or less mutual learning processes following an acquisition. Thus, the acquirer and the acquiree can benefit from each others' strengths and specific competencies. Interestingly, Senge uses the term synergy "in the sense of shared learning and vision" (Meen and Keough, 1992: 67).

In fact, two of the five sub-constructs or sub-processes of knowledge acquisition suggested by Huber (1991) in his review essay on organizational learning can be directly related to the impact of acquisitions, as discussed here. Thus, Huber points out the importance of vicarious learning, a form of cross-organizational learning through observing other organizations, or in other words the acquisition of "second-hand experience" (see also Levitt and March, 1988). Another explicitly acquisition-related type of learning is utilized when organizations graft on to themselves components possessing new knowledge (Huber, 1991).

So far, post-acquisition learning has been treated as an opportunity arising from the combination of two companies. However, an acquisition also leads to substantial managerial and organizational challenges. Hence, post-acquisition learning does not only represent an opportunity for improvement, but also a necessity in terms of overcoming the problems following the transaction and dealing successfully with the new organizational situation.

These post-acquisition management problems and, consequently, the amount and quality of learning required are particularly significant when it comes to western investments in eastern Europe. Such an assessment seems to be justified considering that a western acquisition in an east European country not only involves the challenges of combining or integrating two companies, or even two distinct national identities, but also implies a potential clash between highly different societies, both ideologically and culturally, representing (formerly) antipodal political and economic systems. However, the desire to learn in general, and the perceived learning requirements in particular, may very well differ when judged from the western perspective, on the one hand, and the eastern point of view, on the other.

Moreover, many east European companies are more or less uncompetitive when facing a western-style, market-oriented environment. In fact, this is the very reason why east European governments are promoting western investment in their countries: they hope that the transfer of western managerial and operational know-how, as well as capital, will increase their economic power, thus eventually lifting their living standards to the levels enjoyed in developed western countries; in addition, this would obviously increase social and political stability.

To sum up, the aspect of integration can be at the centre of post-acquisition management. However, post-acquisition integration is neither always the right answer, nor is it necessarily the key issue. In the "turn-around" cases typical of acquisitions in eastern Europe, it can well be argued that learning is the central aspect rather than integration: at least in the initial phases of east–west post-acquisition management it may well be more important to transform the east European acquiree than to integrate it into its new western parent organization.

LEARNING AND UNLEARNING IN A DIFFICULT ENVIRONMENT

So far, learning has been introduced as a highly relevant issue in post-acquisition management with a particular focus on the difficult situation in eastern European countries. What has not been provided yet is a clarifying definition of learning in an organizational context.

Learning in organizations: a working definition

Obviously, there is an indefinite number of different, sensible ways of defining learning in organizations. The growing body of literature dealing with this topic reflects this diversity through varying emphases on the range of potentially relevant aspects or perspectives. A decision has to be taken in view of the specific objectives and context of research.

The following working definition is suggested and may serve as an appropriate starting point (compare Fiol and Lyles, 1985: 803; Senge, in Meen and Keough, 1992: 59; Huber, 1991): *Learning in organizations represents the process of developing a potential to improve actions (behaviour) through better knowledge and understanding (cognition).*

Three particularly relevant, basic features of this definition may be briefly explained here. "Organization(al) learning", the term generally used in the relevant literature, has been avoided in the suggested definition. The justification for this decision lies in the prevailing dissension or confusion with respect to the differentiation between individual learning in organizations, on the one hand, and organizational learning (*per se*?), on the other hand (Huber, 1991; Pawlowsky, 1992). The more neutral use of the term *"learning in organizations"* can accommodate both, a condition which appears beneficial for our purposes.

Learning in organizations does *not* equal change in organizations. Learning has a positive connotation. Consequently, it is closely linked to *improvement*. Change, instead, represents a neutral term. The improvement process involved in learning can be *defensive* in the sense of adaptive adjustments in reaction to changes in the inner or outer organizational environment. It can also be *offensive* in the sense of innovative improvements proactively manipulating the organization's environment.

The suggested definition also reflects the fundamentally cognitive nature of learning in business organizations. First of all, learning represents the process of improving knowledge and understanding. The impact of this cognitive process, then, *potentially*, though not necessarily, shows in improved actions. This possible and, of course, desirable impact on the behavioural level (DeGeus, 1988: 72) is fundamentally based on the underlying cognitive improvement. While the behavioural level is directly accessible to observations, cognitive developments are more difficult to determine.

Based on these defining considerations, the phenomenon of learning in organizations can now be approached in a more systematic way. Three key aspects can be pointed out:

> *Who* is (or should be . . .) learning – *subject*
> *what* – *object*
> *where* – *environment?*

These three aspects of learning in organizations will now be touched on as far as they seem relevant in the context of the empirical research introduced in this paper.

The players: learners and learning entities

The issue of differentiating between individual learning in organizations, on the one hand, and organizational learning, on the other hand, has already been raised briefly (Hedberg, 1981; Huber, 1991; Pawlowsky, 1992). Undoubtedly, there are innumerable and complex individual learning processes continuously taking place in all kinds of organizations. Although *individual learning in organizations* refers to improvements in the knowledge and understanding of single employees, it is embedded in the organizational context and thus very much represents a social phenomenon.

Who, however, are the learners or learning entities referred to, when the term *organizational learning*, as opposed to individual learning, in organizations is used? Organizations obviously do not have their own cognitions and, thus, can only learn through individuals (Hedberg, 1981). In other words, individuals are the agents through whom all learning in organizations takes place. Hence, organizational learning is dependent on individual learning processes. The social nature of individual learning in organizations, on the one hand, and the reliance of organizational learning processes on individuals, on the other hand, show the complex interrelatedness of individual and organizational learning. Therefore the mentioned dissension or confusion in the literature with respect to this issue of differentiation is not too surprising.

The fact that organizational learning can only take place through individuals does not necessarily imply that organizational learning is simply the sum of all individual learning within an organization (as related to fulfilling the organization's mission). Depending on the perspective and, consequently, on the definition chosen, it can be more, or less, or both at the same time, indicating a different quality of organizational as compared with individual learning. This issue, however, will not be elaborated here, as the present paper concentrates on individual learning.

Following the acquisition of a central east European enterprise by a western acquirer, the population of learning individuals includes the acquired company's employees and at least those employees within the acquirer who are in some way or other in charge of the management of the acquisition and/or the links with the parent company. While these individuals from both sides can represent all types of organizational roles and hierarchical levels, the focus of this paper is on learning by senior managers in key positions: western expatriate managers or so-called "fly-ins" (supervising or managing the acquiree from their home office) as well as top central east European managers in the acquired company.

The various learning subjects all face their own distinct problems, obstacles and hurdles. As much as their learning history or experience forms a necessary basis for further learning, it can also make it very difficult.

The contents: levels and areas of learning

Moving from the issue of the players, the "who?", in post-acquisition learning, to the question of the "what?" or the contents of learning in an organizational setting takes us to a topic which has been dealt with far more extensively or at least more explicitly in the relevant literature (see the review tables in Fiol and Lyles, 1985: 809, and Pawlowsky, 1992: 205). In fact, it is quite striking how little systematic effort has been put into a clarification of the *subjects* (entities) of learning in organizations, while a comparatively large body of conceptual work has been developed with respect to the *objects* of learning in an organizational context.

Concerning the content of learning in organizations, the basic issue of the cognitive versus the behavioural nature of learning has already been raised briefly in the context of our working definition. A position has been taken focusing on the fundamentally cognitive character of learning in business organizations. Potentially, there is a wide variety of approaches to a differentiation of learning in organizations by its cognitive content. Quite surprisingly, however, in his review of theoretical approaches to organizational learning Pawlowsky (1992) is able to identify a three-level framework which integrates several concepts of learning types suggested by a number of key authors in the field (see also Fiol and Lyles, 1985; Hedberg, 1981; Bateson, 1973; for a post-modern approach Cooper et al., 1992; for an empirical study Burgoyne and Hodgson, 1983). The three distinct levels of learning in organizations can be differentiated based on two aspects: (1) the relationship between the changes in knowledge and the already existing knowledge base, and (2) the learner's initiative.

The first and "lowest" of these learning levels refers to improvements or rather adjustments *within* the boundaries of the existing organizational systems of knowledge. Learning in this sense represents the reactive adaptation to changes in the outer or inner organizational environment. It is targeted towards an optimization of the organization's situation and performance within the existing frameworks. The second of the three learning levels is still reactive in its orientation. However, this intermediate type of learning implies changes of the organizational frameworks: a process of "*reframing*". It leads to modifications of the boundaries or structures of the existing knowledge bases. Learning on this level is oriented towards survival. Learning on the "highest" of the three levels can be referred to as "meta-learning": it is about *learning how to learn* or how to improve the quality of learning processes. Learning in this sense represents reflexive cognitive processes. It is proactive and generative (Senge, 1990b). Learning on this third level aims at creating progress through gaining or developing insights into the organizational purpose. Using the well-known terminology coined by Argyris and Schön (1978) these three learning types can be referred to as "single-loop-learning", "double-loop-learning" and "deutero-learning", respectively.

Undoubtedly, this three-level framework is conceptually elegant. However, it also represents a relatively abstract differentiation of learning types. In a paper by the Centre for International Business and Management (1993) within the Judge Institute of Management Studies at the University of Cambridge a more practical classification of three levels of learning and development is suggested (see also Child et al., 1992). This "categorization has emerged from preliminary field studies of ISA (international strategic alliance) development" (p. 12). The authors distinguish between "three levels concerning respectively the use of techniques, the design of systems and procedures, and strategic understanding" (p. 11). It is not hard to see some parallelism to the above, more abstract three-level framework.

The first, *technical* level refers to learning as the acquisition of new, specific techniques. As possible examples the authors quote specific techniques for quality measurement, specific scientific or engineering techniques, or with respect to managerial knowledge specific techniques for the construction of samples for market research.

The second, *systemic* level relates to learning with regard to new systems and procedures. The focus is on an integrative type of learning, emphasizing coordination, relationships and links. Examples suggested by the authors are: production technologies representing integrated systems of techniques and procedures, production control and budgeting systems, systems defining responsibilities and reporting relationships, and other managerial systems such as the operation of a marketing function.

The third, *strategic* level "involves changes in the mind-sets of senior managers, especially their criteria of business success and their mental maps of factors which are significant for achieving that success" (pp. 11–12). The authors of the paper by the Centre for International Management refer to the relevance of "vision" in this context.

According to Child (1993: 220–221) this last, strategic level of learning represents the key issue in the transition of east European companies:

> (T)he chief area of adaptation and new learning for enterprise managers experiencing the societal transformation towards a market economy is that of developing a strategic understanding. They have to learn to function without the protective paternalism of the centralized hierarchical system and instead to understand the nature of doing business competitively in a relevant domain. (. . .) In terms of the Argyris and Schön (1978) model of learning, the single-loop learning of acquiring new techniques from foreign sources is therefore likely to present far less of a challenge to former socialist managers than will the double-loop learning of understanding and accepting a new cognitive framework for doing business and conducting the task of managing.

Different levels of learning will pose different problems for the learners and learning entities with respect to both the quality or kind of such problems as well as their intensity. Whether, however, it is appropriate to claim that one level of learning is more important than the others seems highly questionable. Improvements on all three levels will be asked for to ensure a successful transition of east European enterprises in order to survive and progress in an internationally competitive, market-oriented environment.

A disadvantage in using either of the two three-level frameworks for practically relevant and accessible, empirical research on learning in organizations lies in the fact that the three respective levels do not possess distinct characteristics: they are not independent of each other – in fact, they build upon each other. The second, *systemic* level of learning, for example, relates to integrated systems of techniques. However, the acquisition of a new, specific technique, representing learning on the first, *technical* level, may lead in many cases to an immediate and direct change of the whole system concerned. Hence, the differentiation between a technical and a systemic level might be theoretically interesting, but hardly feasible in practical terms. Also, what does it really tell about successful learning in a post-acquisition setting? It is not too surprising that learning about an integrated system of techniques is preferable to the acquisition of just a single, specific technique, or that *learning how to learn* represents the most superior level of learning one can achieve.

Consequently, another differentiation of levels or rather areas of learning is used in the present paper to analyze individual, managerial learning in an east–west post-acquisition setting. It is based on a distinction between business skills in general and cross-border management skills in particular. In addition, it separates learning on the level of "tools" or "hard" specific knowledge from learning as the development of a deeper understanding and relevant insights. On this basis, four major types of managerial learning can be identified in our context. The first two relate to business skills in general and are independent of the specific cross-border, post-acquisition situation:

1. Learning in the sense of developing into a generally more effective and efficient manager, i.e. the acquisition of general management insights ranging from organizational leadership to strategic and visionary thinking.
2. The acquisition of specific, applicable, functional know-how and technical competencies, e.g. in the areas of production, marketing, finance or computer systems.

The other two types of managerial learning specifically relate to cross-border management skills:

3. The development of a deeper understanding of and an improved sensitivity for the partner company's and country's culture.
4. The acquisition of the partner's language, thus being able to communicate directly without the use of interpreters.

These latter two forms of learning appear to be of particular significance in cases of acquisitions crossing not only national boundaries, but, at the same time, boundaries between (at least formerly) different sociopolitical and economic systems.

The environment: too much turbulence?

Unfortunately, there are reasons to believe that the highly turbulent conditions characteristic of the east European economies in transition may not be conducive to successful learning processes (Hedberg, 1981; Pawlowsky, 1992). In other words, is there too much change going on in eastern Europe to allow efficient and effective learning in organizations to take place after an acquisition?

Companies operating in eastern Europe, and particularly those in the central east European "fast-track" reforming countries, have been facing and are continuing to face a rapid stream of fundamental changes with respect to their external as well as internal environments. Whole societies are developing from relatively rigid and restrictive socialist or communist systems, towards "open" market-oriented democracies. There is a shift from controlled ideology, central planning and hierarchical structures towards pluralism, decentralization and, consequently, an increased emphasis on individuality. This is leading to a rise in individual responsibility and accountability as well as to fundamentally changed motivational settings with respect to individuals, as well as groups, all kinds of institutions and whole societies. These developments affect, or rather threaten, each and every business organization, targeting it from the outside (customers, suppliers, banks, governmental institutions, etc.) as well as from the inside (employees).

Do these admittedly "hostile" environments lead to organizational inertia or paralysis, i.e. do they block learning, or, rather, do they provide for an increased motivation and inspiration to learn from and improve the situation? According to Hedberg (1981: 14) "Organizations in hostile environments face new problems and are often forced to develop new niches, but their possibilities to learn are often restricted by scarce resources and limited strategic opportunities". Although this might be a generally appropriate conclusion, in the case of a western company making an acquisition in eastern Europe these restrictions should be eased for the acquiree, thus facilitating the occurrence of learning processes. On the other hand, the existence of a western parent company with seemingly "unlimited" resources might also undermine the incentives for improvement, leading back to the phenomenon of soft budget constraints well known from state owned enterprises (not only in eastern Europe!).

Taking on an information processing point of view, the sheer amount and variety of information, ambiguities, inconsistencies and conflicts typical of a high-change situation as currently experienced in eastern Europe might simply result in a stimuli overload for the actors involved. Thus, the extreme environmental complexity and turbulence would prevent successful learning (Duncan, 1972), and the consequent uncertainty might encourage managers to stick to their "old" practices. However, the guidance provided by the western acquirer can help to avoid the potential organizational inertia by controlling the east European employees' exposure to the new.

The learning process necessary in east European enterprises also implies a great amount of forgetting. Differentiating between *unlearning*, on the one hand, and relearning or rather new learning, on the other hand, promises further interesting considerations with respect to the learning process as a whole.

Although crises and confusion as such might not directly provide new learning, they potentially contribute to rapid and radical unlearning. In Hedberg's (1981: 21) words: "Crises, conflicts, dialectics, self-doubt, and hesitancy can facilitate unlearning". However, he also finds that "unlearning is often difficult, and it takes time", and especially "total restructurings are often strongly resisted" (p. 9). Thus, the double problem of facing both new questions and new responses, the need for an extreme shift of paradigm (Kuhn, 1970) or, following Watzlawick et al. (1974), the complete "reframing" in the course of the east European transition process can make unlearning a highly challenging endeavour.

In this context it can also be rewarding to consider the learning history of those involved in the transition. Schein (1993) points out that the unlearning process is not symmetrical. He argues that avoidance behaviour learned through punishment is more stable than behaviour learned through reward – a conclusion taken from the general behaviour theories in individual (human and animal) learning psychology. It may be realistic to assume that socialist or communist societies were controlling their citizens through negative rather than through positive feedback – in other words, relying on punishment rather than rewards. Unfortunately, "People who are punished across a wide range of behavior are likely to limit themselves to very narrow safe ranges or become paralyzed for fear of making mistakes" (Schein, 1993: 87). Consequently, east European employees might often show strong resistance to new learning, because their anxiety will make them "fall back on behavior patterns that were reliable in avoiding punishment in the past" (Schein, 1993: 87).

Following the previous discussion it becomes clear that an appropriate balance between the inspiring and motivating effects of change and, *at the same time*, the reliance on a stable basis, is a necessary condition for successful learning: *learning requires both change and stability*.

In this context it is important to reemphasize that the western acquirers and their representatives do not only represent the "teachers". They have to learn themselves, too, thus continuously trying to improve their understanding of local conditions as well as their coaching skills, but also drawing valuable conclusions for their operations "at home".

RESEARCH METHOD AND SAMPLE: KEY CHARACTERISTICS

In order to study various issues of post-acquisition management in cases of western acquisitions of majority or controlling equity stakes in central east European manufacturing companies, a survey-type approach incorporating some qualitative inquiry was chosen. Particular emphasis was put on aspects of individual learning experienced by the local and western managers involved as well as on other, more aggregate forms of learning and development within the acquired organizations. The intention was to obtain information on as many relevant cases as possible, but to go significantly beyond just scratching the surface in each of these cases. To this end, a set of two questionnaires was developed (both of them in English).

The "*profile*" questionnaire: a general five-page (plus cover) questionnaire asking for factual information on the acquisition and the companies involved. It includes 25 open and closed questions structured in four blocks: (1) entities involved; (2) operational profile of acquired company; (3) top management structure; (4) staffing, personnel and organizational development. The intention was that this "profile" questionnaire should be completed once for each of the participating companies.

The "*experience*" questionnaire: a three-page (plus cover) questionnaire with 11, mainly open, questions relating to the objectives and expectations of acquirer and acquiree, the (subjective) performance of the acquiree, a number of qualitative issues concerning its post-acquisition development, the acquirer-acquiree relationship, and individual as well as collective learning experiences. This "experience" questionnaire was designed to be filled in twice for each of the participating companies. One copy was to be completed possibly by the most senior western manager who has been playing a major role in the acquisition process from the beginning on (expatriate or "fly-in"). A second copy was to be completed preferably by the most senior local (central east European) manager who has been playing a key role in the post-acquisition management efforts and who was already employed by the acquiree before the transaction.

In the period between November 1993 and October 1994 information on 35 cases was collected through mailed questionnaires and a large number of personal interviews (also based on the above set of questionnaires) with western expatriate managers (and also some "fly-ins") as well as local, central east European managers. The western managers involved were generally the most senior western managers holding an active management position in the acquired company, either in its board or on the first management level. The central east European managers involved were in most cases the most senior local managers in the acquiree organization, and often the former Presidents or CEOs of the acquired company before the transaction and subsequent reorganization. In most of the cases included in the sample, it was possible to obtain a complete set of information by using the two questionnaires.

To ensure sufficient post-acquisition management experience, the sample included acquisitions that had taken place before 1993, in all but one of the cases. More than 80 percent of the transactions were completed during 1991 and 1992.

Of the 35 cases analyzed, 14 acquisitions had taken place in Hungary, 12 in the Czech Republic, one in Slovakia, and eight in Poland. This composition of the target countries in the sample reflects the overall distribution of foreign direct investment across these four central east European countries. Of the 35 central east European enterprises included in the sample, 22 were acquired by German or US companies. Other investor nations involved in more than one acquisition are the United Kingdom, Belgium, Austria, Switzerland and the Netherlands. This composition of investor countries in the sample also corresponds with the overall distribution of foreign direct investment in the region.

A variety of different industries is covered in the sample:

- construction materials: seven cases;
- various chemicals and gases: six cases;
- food and beverages: six cases;
- tobacco products: three cases;
- electric and electronic products: three cases;
- other industries: ten cases.

Overall, 19 cases fall into the industrial goods sector, while 16 cases represent consumer goods industries.

In all cases, the acquirer was familiar with the acquiree's industry/ies, in other words, only related acquisitions were found. This is to be expected as a reasonable company will generally not attempt to acquire an organization operating in an unrelated industry within a foreign high-risk environment. In 19 cases, the acquirer's industry portfolio was larger than that of the acquiree. In 14 cases a "perfect match" was found i.e. the acquirer's and the acquiree's industry portfolios were very similar. In two cases, both among the Polish sample, there was a substantial industry overlap, but both the acquirer and the acquiree were also involved in one or more industries not included in the portfolio of the other party.

The average export share of the acquired companies at the time of data collection had reached a level of about 23 percent of their total turnover, following first an initial break-away from eastern export markets and then an increasing penetration of western markets. While the numbers were, on average, at about 30 percent in both the Hungarian and the Czech cases, the Polish average was far lower at less than eight percent. An explanation may lie in the fact that, due to its comparatively larger population, the Polish domestic market has a substantially greater potential than its Hungarian and Czech counterparts. Taking into consideration the relatedness between the organizations involved in the acquisitions (as mentioned above), it is not too surprising that almost 18 percent of the acquirees' outputs (in terms of turnover) were channelled through their acquirers' sales and distribution systems into export markets.

The western acquirers' equity shares in their central east European target companies were on average at 63 percent immediately following the initial transaction. At the time of data collection they had risen to an average of 79 percent. While the Czech, Slovakian and Polish cases lie below this level, on average, the Hungarian part of the sample clearly exceeds the overall averages, with Hungary being perceived as the most "fast-track" of the central east European reforming countries (at least initially). The upgrading has been achieved either through a direct purchase of additional equity or via an incremental dilution of the stake held by other equity owners through operational investments financed entirely or mainly by the western investor. The only other significant owners across the 35 cases included were the acquirees' countries, i.e. state property or privatization agencies, ministries, etc.

The price paid for the initial equity share in the acquired central east European company amounted to US$ 29 million on average. Further capital investments by the western acquirers were US$ 27 million on average at the time of data collection. Additional capital investments planned during the first five post-acquisition years were another US$ 11 million on average. In total, this amounts to an average capital commitment by the western investor companies of US$ 67 million.

Across the whole sample, the central east European acquirees were far smaller – in terms of numbers of employees – than their western acquirers. While the average western investor company included in the sample had more than 40 thousand employees, the average central east European target enterprise only had about 1,400 employees at the time of the transaction.

EMPIRICAL FINDINGS ON POST-ACQUISITION MANAGERIAL LEARNING

Following this brief description of a number of basic characteristics of the cases included in our sample, some key empirical findings on *individual* learning by the senior managers involved will now be presented.

First, western and central east European perceptions of the main skill requirements for expatriate as well as local managers will be shown. These skill requirements will be compared with the most important areas of learning as actually experienced by western as well as central east European managers involved in the post-acquisition management efforts. Finally, the perceived main barriers to successful learning will be analyzed in the light of the skill requirements and actual learning experiences (see Figure 1).

Key skill requirements

Based on our differentiation of four major types of managerial learning in a post-acquisition context, western as well as central east European managers were asked to

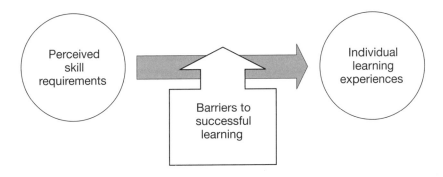

Figure 1   Individual learning at the senior management level – framework for analysis.

rank the following four categories of key skill requirements for expatriate and for local managers in order of perceived importance:

- *Effective and efficient management*, i.e. general ("soft") management competencies ranging from organizational leadership skills to strategic and visionary thinking.
- *Specific* (applicable) *know-how and technical competences.*
- *Sensitivity to the partner's culture.*
- *Command of the partner's language* (thus facilitating direct communication without the need for interpreters).

The answers collected on perceived key skill requirements *for expatriate managers* (see Figure 2) show that, overall, general business skills, independent of the specific cross-border, post-acquisition situation, were rated higher than the two cross-border skill categories. They also show that "hard", specific competencies are generally considered less important that "soft" skills.

Overall, there is a surprisingly clear consensus between western and local managers that the general ability to manage effectively and efficiently represents the most important skill category for expatriate managers, while the command of the partner's language is rated the lowest, on average. Although there are certain differences between the three sub-samples (Hungary, Czech Republic and Slovakia, Poland), the overall picture remains relatively stable across the sample as a whole. Only in the Polish cases was the sensitivity to the local culture considered even less important than language skills, which might be explained by the overall impression that the Polish interviewees appeared, in general, to be more business-focused than their Hungarian or Czech and Slovak counterparts.

There are various reasons which may explain the emphasis on effective and efficient management. First, this category is certainly the broadest of our four types of key managerial skills. Second, as all interviewees were in senior management

	Total Sample		Hungary	Czech Rep. and Slovakia	Poland
Effective and efficient management		3.2	3.0	3.1	3.6
		3.5	3.1	3.5	3.9
Specific know-how and technical competencies		2.9	2.9	2.9	3.0
		2.8	2.9	2.9	2.6
Sensitivity to the partner's culture		2.8	3.0	3.3	1.9
		2.5	2.8	2.6	2.1
Command of the partner's language		2.1	2.0	2.3	2.1
		2.1	2.0	1.9	2.5

Key: ☐ Western/expatriate perspective

▨ ECE/local perspective

Figure 2 Perceptions of key skill requirements for expatriate managers (grading on a scale of averages from 1/least important to 4/most important).

positions, a focus on more general competencies as opposed to very specific skills may have been expected. Third, however, there may be a real perception that, above all, western managers need general management skills in order to successfully face an environment which is new to them and, at the same time, highly turbulent. Finally, the perception may be that central east European managers have to learn most regarding effective and efficient management; therefore, western managers should be particularly competent in this area in order to be able to transfer these skills.

Turning to the perceived key skill requirements *for local, central east European managers*, the importance of the general competency to manage effectively and efficiently is confirmed (see Figure 3). The argumentation supporting this emphasis can follow the lines of the above reasoning in the case of the expatriate managers' key skill requirements.

Again, the cross-border skill categories are ranked lower, on average, than the general business skills. However, the command of the partner's language now ranks second, overall, while the sensitivity to the partner's culture is rated as by far the least important skill category. This latter finding should not be surprising, since the exposure of the local management to the foreign acquirer's culture tends to be rather limited, while expatriate managers are continuously confronted with the acquiree's culture (national as well as company-specific). As for the expatriate managers, specific know-how and technical competences are rated as a skill category of medium relevance.

As above, there is a surprisingly clear, overall consensus between western and local managers' perceptions of key skill requirements.

To sum up, western as well as local perceptions of key skill requirements for the managers involved in post-acquisition situations show a clear emphasis on general management skills, while cross-border skill categories are on average considered less important.

	Total Sample		Hungary	Czech Rep. and Slovakia	Poland
Effective and efficient management		3.4	3.1	3.4	3.8
		3.5	3.4	3.6	3.6
Command of the partner's language		3.0	3.0	2.9	3.3
		2.9	2.6	2.3	3.0
Specific know-how and technical competencies		3.0	3.2	3.1	2.4
		2.8	3.1	3.0	2.4
Sensitivity to the partner's culture		1.9	2.1	1.9	1.5
		1.9	2.3	2.1	1.1

Key: ☐ Western/expatriate perspective

▨ ECE/local perspective

Figure 3 Perceptions of key skill requirements for local/central east European managers (graded on a scale of averages from 1/least important to 4/most important).

Main areas of learning

Did western and local managers actually learn what they should learn according to their own, individual perceptions? An overall encouraging picture emerges when the perceived key skill requirements as described above are brought in contact with the main areas of learning as experienced by western as well as central east European managers.

In the case of *western (expatriate or "fly-in") managers*, learning has taken place especially in the category of general management skills (see Figure 4). Aspects such as leadership, employee motivation as well as patience, team building, management by objectives, flexibility, or the development of long-term visions were frequently mentioned by the interviewees. This can be interpreted as a positive development, since this area of competency has also been rated as the most important skill requirement for western managers involved in post-acquisition settings in central eastern Europe. Thus, this development may be the result of a focus on these skills, based on their perceived importance. It can also be just the outcome of a situation in which western expatriates are continuously facing a new and turbulent environment, leading to a "maturing" of general management skills rather than to the development of specific competencies. However, as above, it may simply reflect the comparatively broad definition of the general management skill category, or be a consequence of the seniority of the managers interviewed.

Learning experiences on this general management level are followed, in terms of perceived frequency, by learning within the category of cultural issues and, less frequently, specific know-how. This also roughly corresponds to the above rating of key skill requirements, where these two categories were assessed as being of average importance. The relatively lower frequency of learning on the level of specific know-how makes sense considering that the western managers should be equipped with these skills as a basic prerequisite for coming to central eastern Europe, since they are generally expected to transfer these specific competencies to their eastern partner companies.

With respect to foreign language skills, there seems to be no learning on the part of the western managers involved. The reasons generally given for this obvious deficit are the lack of time due to the multitude of business problems and the extreme

	Total Sample		Hungary	Czech Rep. and Slovakia	Poland
General management		23	8	8	7
Cultural (systemic/ national) issues		14	8	2	4
Specific know-how		7	2	4	1
Foreign language		0	0	0	0
'Not much'/'none'/ 'nothing'		10	6	3	1

Figure 4 Main areas of learning for western/expatriate managers (frequency of citations, i.e. main areas of learning quoted across the sample, based on the responses to open questions).

difficulty of learning any of the central east European languages concerned. This might lead to an explanation of the low rating of the command of the local language as a key skill requirement for expatriate managers, while the command of the partner's language is rated far higher as a requirement for local managers. The total lack of the actual development of language skills on their part may drive western managers to the defensive claim that the knowledge of the local language is not that relevant anyway. The local managers, on the other hand, may have generally accepted this situation, thus putting more emphasis on learning the respective western language themselves.

Almost 30 percent of the western managers questioned claimed that they had learned "not much", "none" or "nothing". This outcome might be interpreted as the result of the relative "superiority" of western skills and competencies in general or the highly developed experience base of the western expatriate managers in particular. However, it may also be a reflection of either an extremely narrow interpretation of the term "learning", or a certain narrow-mindedness of western managers, who perceive the post-acquisition management setting they are in as a oneway flow of information and experience. It would be surprising, though, if even the most highly experienced western expatriates were not able to find some valid opportunities for learning.

Moving on to the local managers' perspective, learning has been experienced especially in the areas of general management (e.g. strategic and financial thinking, delegation and team orientation, management by objectives, openness, cost consciousness and perfection) and specific know-how, followed, far less frequently, by the acquisition of foreign language skills and the improved understanding of cultural issues (see Figure 5). This also corresponds quite well to the above rating of key skill requirements, except that the actual acquisition of foreign language skills appears to be less frequent than desirable.

The frequency of learning on the level of general management skills experienced by local managers can be explained along the lines of the above interpretation for western/expatriate managers. The acquisition of specific know-how as the second main area of learning experiences for local managers may be due to the immediate,

	Total Sample	Hungary	Czech Rep. and Slovakia	Poland
General management	19	7	5	7
Specific know-how	18	7	6	5
Foreign language	7	1	3	3
Cultural (systemic/ national) issues	7	1	6	0
'Not much'/'none'/ 'nothing'	2	1	0	1

Figure 5 Main areas of learning for local/central east European managers (frequency of citations, i.e. main areas of learning quoted across the sample, based on the responses to open questions).

perceived need for such technical, functional skills, etc. and their direct applicability; in other words, specific know-how can be more readily and easily understood than more "soft" and less "tangible" knowledge and insights.

In two cases, central east European managers claimed that they did not experience any substantial learning in working together with their western partners. In both cases the general level of satisfaction on the central east European side with their western acquirers appeared to be extremely low. Consequently, these negative responses to the question about learning experiences may be understood as a sign of disappointment and an expression of protest by the local managers.

Overall, it may be concluded that the extent to which the different types of learning have been experienced corresponds relatively well to the perceived skill requirements. From both perspectives, a dominance of general business competencies over cross-border skill categories can be observed.

Barriers to successful learning

While the actual learning experiences seem to be relatively well in line with the perceived key skill requirements, an analysis of the managers' perceptions of the main barriers to successful learning reveals a major problem: Difficulties with or the lack of cross-border skills, i.e. the command of the partner's language and a sensitivity towards cultural issues, represent by far the most important barriers to successful learning, although these competencies appeared to be of relatively lesser importance, judging from the analyses presented above.

Starting with the western perspective, language problems are clearly perceived to be the dominant barrier to successful learning following a western acquisition in central eastern Europe (see Figure 6). Although interpreters can be used to ease this problem, a real understanding of the true, underlying meanings is frequently

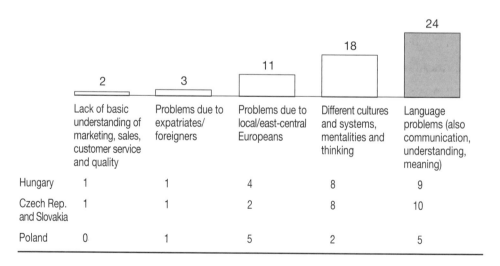

	Lack of basic understanding of marketing, sales, customer service and quality	Problems due to expatriates/ foreigners	Problems due to local/east-central Europeans	Different cultures and systems, mentalities and thinking	Language problems (also communication, understanding, meaning)
	2	3	11	18	24
Hungary	1	1	4	8	9
Czech Rep. and Slovakia	1	1	2	8	10
Poland	0	1	5	2	5

Figure 6 Main barriers to successful learning – the western perspective (frequency of citations, i.e. learning barriers quoted across the sample, based on the responses to open questions).

impossible, if no means of direct communication, i.e. a common language, are available.

Language difficulties are followed by problems due to pronounced differences in cultures and (socio-political and economic) systems as well as mentalities and ways of thinking, leading to an additional potential for misunderstandings. The third main barrier to learning lies, according to the western point of view, in specific problems caused by their central east European colleagues: defensiveness as well as a lack of openness are identified as significant barriers to successful processes of unlearning as well as new learning. Following the above discussion of the east European learning environment, this is hardly surprising: communist societies controlled their citizens through negative rather than positive feedback, thus encouraging avoidance behaviour and generally defensive and secretive attitudes.

Turning to the central east European perspective on learning barriers, language difficulties again represent the dominant problem (see Figure 7). A lack of real communication and understanding is generally blamed for insufficient learning on both sides. As from the western perspective, language problems are followed in terms of importance by difficulties due to the differences in cultures, mentalities and attitudes to business.

A third significant source of learning barriers judged from the local perspective lies in problems due to expatriate or other western employees involved in the post-acquisition management efforts: they are sometimes perceived as "know-betters" who are not willing or able to accept local specifics, thus revealing a lack of both openness and readiness for un-learning on the western side. In addition, the central east European managers also recognize problems on their own part as yet another barrier to successful learning: they tend to misjudge their skills, to fear open communications with their western partners, and, occasionally, they are still highly influenced by the traditions of "the old system".

	Problems due to local/east-central Europeans	Problems due to expatriates/ foreigners	Different cultures, mentalities and attitudes to business	Language problems (also communication, understanding)
	3	5	10	22
Hungary	0	3	1	–
Czech Rep. and Slovakia	2	0	5	7
Poland	1	2	4	8

Figure 7 Main barriers to successful learning – the local/central east European perspective (frequency of citations, i.e. learning barriers quoted across the sample, based on the responses to open questions).

The theoretical discussion in the third section raises the issue that too much environmental turbulence might lead to learning blockages. In spite of the tremendous changes currently under way in central eastern Europe, the "multitude of social, political and economic changes" was only mentioned once in the context of learning barriers. This may well be due to the seniority of the managers involved, allowing them to deal better with change, and even radical change, than other employees. However, it may be that it is easier to acknowledge language problems or to blame "the unavoidable clash of cultures" following a west–east acquisition than to accept one's own difficulties in coping with change.

CONCLUSION

The above analyses provide some indication that managers involved in post-acquisition efforts in central eastern Europe underestimate the relevance of appropriate cross-border skills as compared to general business skills. The knowledge of the partner's language and a sensitivity towards cultural issues seem to be crucial factors for successful learning processes on both sides. However, while deficits in these areas are perceived as the main barriers to successful learning, they are not sufficiently understood as key competences which have to be developed as a basis for the acquisition of general and specific business skills.

Quite surprisingly, the perceptions of the western managers on these issues are remarkably similar, overall, to those of the east central European managers. However, this may well be explained through shared experiences and the ongoing, mutual socialization processes, especially in the higher ranks of the organizations. Also, there are relatively strong similarities between the findings for the different central east European countries included in the sample. This may indicate that the overwhelming systemic and ideological as well as social and economic changes taking place in each of these countries, and the tremendous challenges of a post-acquisition setting are dominating national or rather cultural differences to a certain extent with respect to the issues under consideration. Still, there are noticeable differences between the east European target countries included, which can well be identified and partially explained by differing national characteristics and orientations. However, these differences were not at the core of the present paper, being mentioned only in one instance above, when the overall impression was articulated that, in general, the Polish interviewees may have appeared to be more "business-focused" than their counterparts from other central east European countries.

Interestingly, although language and communication problems are clearly pointed out as the key barrier to successful learning from both sides, there seems to be a consensus that the command of the partner's language is mainly a requirement for eastern managers, and significantly less so for their western partners. The managers' learning experiences confirm this picture: no acquisition of language skills on the western side, some learning of the foreign language on the eastern side. This may be surprising, as it can lead to a situation in which a hundred east European managers have to learn German, instead of a small number of German expatriates learning the local language. However, it may be argued that the language chosen for (future) communications will depend on the expected direction of the "flow of learning" between the two partners. Hence, if it is expected that mainly the eastern managers will learn from their western partners, and not vice versa, western managers (and some of their eastern counterparts as well) may conclude that their eastern colleagues should acquire western language skills in order to be able to absorb as much western know-how as possible. The western managers, though, may not be inclined to learn the local language, as they perceive themselves as the "teachers", and not as the "students". Such an argument in favour of the acquisition of western language skills may gain further support through the redirection of business flows to western countries in many cases. Nevertheless, if western managers were to speak the local language, they could function better as coaches, they would be socially more integrated in their host country, and, consequently, they could become more sensitive to the local culture. This may not only help their communications within the acquired company, but it may also represent a great advantage in dealing with customers or public authorities.

Finally, as a consequence for practical management, western acquirers in central eastern Europe should put more emphasis on language and cultural skills in selecting and training those of their employees who are expected to get involved in post-acquisition management efforts. As such training can be fairly demanding and time-consuming, the use of "re-patriates" (e.g. a Polish-born immigrant to the US) might be intensified, if suitable candidates can be made available inside or outside the acquiring organization. Following an acquisition, language training and cultural awareness workshops etc. should become a main focus of employee development. Thus, the transfer of more directly business-related skills will be substantially facilitated.

NOTE

1 I would like to thank Professor John Child, Niti Dubey-Villinger (both at the University of Cambridge), as well as the anonymous referees for their helpful comments.

REFERENCES

Ackermann, Charbel, and John Lindquist (1992) "Acquiring in eastern Europe: the record to date". *M and A Europe* (May/June): 40–45.

Argyris, Chris, and Don Schön (1978) *Organizational learning: a theory of action perspective.* Reading, MA: Addison-Wesley.

Bateson, G. (1973) *Step to an ecology of mind.* New York: Ballantine.

Brockhaus, W. L. (1971) *The post-merger and post-acquisition integration process in business mergers and acquisitions.* Bloomington, IN: Indiana University Press.

Buono, Anthony F., and James L. Bowditch (1989) *The human side of mergers and acquisitions: managing collisions between people, cultures, and organizations.* San Francisco: Jossey-Bass.

Burgoyne, J. G., and V. E. Hodgson (1983) "Natural learning and managerial action: a phenomenological study in the field setting". *Journal of Management Studies* 20/3: 387–399.

Centre for International Business and Management (1993) "The role of international strategic alliances as agents for the improvement of management practice and corporate performance – an outline proposal for research". Judge Institute of Management Studies, University of Cambridge, April 1993 (internal draft).

Child, John (1993) "Society and enterprise between hierarchy and market" in *Societal change between market and organization.* John Child et al., 203–226. Aldershot: Avebury.

Child, John, and Alfred Kieser (1981) "Development of organizations over time" in *Handbook of organizational design*, Vol. 1. Paul C. Nystrom and William H. Starbuck (eds.), 28–74. Oxford: Oxford University Press.

Child, John, Livia Markoczy, and Tony Cheung (1992) "Managerial adaptation in Chinese and Hungarian strategic alliances with culturally distinct foreign partners". Working Paper, August 1992, The Judge Institute of Management Studies and St John's College, University of Cambridge (Paper presented to the British Academy of Management annual conference, September 1992, University of Bradford).

Clark, P. (1991) *Beyond the deal: optimizing merger and acquisition value.* New York: Harper Business.

Clever, Holger (1993) *Post-merger-management*. Stuttgart: W. Kohlhammer.

Cooper, Robert, Stephen Fox, and Lluis Tarin Martinez (1992) "Preface – postmodern management and organization: the implications for learning 2". *International Studies of Management and Organization* 22/3: 3–10.

DeGeus, Arie (1988) "Planning as learning". *Harvard Business Review* (March-April): 70–74.

Duncan, R. (1972) "Characteristics of organizational environments and perceived environmental uncertainty". *Administrative Science Quarterly* 17: 313–327.

East European Investment Magazine (1992) "Investment activity review: up, up and away". *East European Investment Magazine* (June): 14–25.

Fiol, C. Marlene, and Marjorie A. Lyles (1985) "Organizational learning". *Academy of Management Review* 10/4: 803–813.

Gerpott, Torsten J. (1993) *Integrationsgestaltung und Erfolg von Unternehmensakquisitionen*. Stuttgart: Schäffer-Poeschel.

Haspeslagh. Philippe C., and David B. Jemison (1991) *Managing acquisitions: creating value through corporate renewal*. New York: The Free Press.

Hedberg, Bo (1981) "How organizations learn and unlearn" in *Handbook of Organizational Design*, Vol. 1. Paul C. Nystrom and William H. Starbuck (eds.), 3–27. Oxford: Oxford University Press.

Huber, George P. (1991) "Organizational learning: the contributing processes and the literatures". *Organization Science* 2/1: 88–115.

Kuhn, Thomas S. (1970) *The structure of scientific revolutions*. Chicago, IL: Chicago University Press.

Larsson, Rikard (1989) *Organizational integration of mergers and acquisitions: a case survey of realization of synergy potentials*. Lund: Lund University Press.

Levitt, Barbara, and James G. March (1988) "Organizational learning". *Annual Review of Sociology* 14: 319–340.

Lindgren, Ulf (1982) *Foreign acquisitions: management of the integration process*. Stockholm: Business School Press.

Lindgren, Ulf, and Kjell Spangberg (1981) "Management of the post-acquisition process in diversified MNCs" in *The management of headquarters-subsidiary relationships in multinational companies*. Lars Otterbeck (ed.), 233–253. Aldershot: Gower.

Mace, Myles La Grange, and George G. Montgomery (1962) *Management problems of corporate acquisitions*. Boston: Division of Research, Graduate School of Business Administration, Harvard University.

Meen, David E., and Mark Keough (1992) "Creating the learning organization – an interview with Peter M. Senge, author of 'The fifth discipline: the art and practice of the learning organization'". *The McKinsey Quarterly* 1: 58–78.

Pablo, Amy Lou (1991) "Determinants of acquisition integration level: an evaluation of current theory from a decision making pespective". Unpublished doctoral dissertation. The University of Texas at Austin.

Pawlowsky, Peter (1992) "Betriebliche Qualifikationsstrategien und organisationales Lernen" in *Managementforschung* 2. Wolfgang H. Staehle and P. Conrad (eds.), 177–237. Berlin, New York: Walter de Gruyter.

Schein, Edgard H. (1993) "How can organizations learn faster? The challenge of entering the green room". *Sloan Management Review* (Winter): 85–92.

Scheiter, Dietmar (1989) *Die Integration akquirierter Unternehmungen*. Dissertation, Hochschule St. Gallen. Bamberg: difo-druck schmacht.

Senge, Peter M. (1990a) *The fifth discipline: the art and practice of the learning organization*. London: Century Business (New York: Doubleday).

Senge, Peter M. (1990b) "The leader's new work: building learning organizations". *Sloan Management Review*: 7–23.

Shanley, Mark T., and Mary E. Correa (1992) "Agreement between top management teams and expectations for post acquisition performance". *Strategic Management Journal* 13: 245–266.

Walenciak, Joe Franklin (1991) "Organizational integration following mergers and acquisitions: an archival study of integration strategies". Unpublished doctoral dissertation. University of Arkansas.

Watzlawick. P., J. Weakland, and R. Fisch (1974) *Change*. New York: Norton.

Yunker. J. (1983) *Integrating acquisitions: making corporate marriages work*. New York: Praeger.

Villinger, R. (1996) "Post acquisition managerial learning in Central East Europe". *Organisation Studies*, 17(2), 181–206. Reprinted with permission.

Section 6
Summary and Conclusion

A CEO roundtable on making mergers succeed   21

The M&A Group[*]

The announcement in January 2000 of the merger between America Online and Time Warner marked the convergence of the two most important business trends of the last five years: the rise of the Internet and the resurgence of mergers and acquisitions. M&A activity has been at a fever pitch recently, and all signs point to an even further acceleration of deal making, spurred in large part by the breathtaking influx of capital into the Internet space. Many executives will be placing bets on M&A that will put their companies' futures at stake.

We at the *Harvard Business Review* are very pleased, therefore, to share with our readers a lively discussion of M&A and its role in the new economy by a group of chief executives who all have deep experience in making deals work. In a roundtable held last December at a meeting of the M&A Group in Scottsdale, Arizona, these executives addressed a number of important and timely topics, including the trade-offs between acquiring a company and growing organically, the changing shape of M&A strategy, and the keys to successful integration.

The Editors

Dennis Carey: *I'm sure some of you are familiar with studies suggesting that most mergers and acquisitions do not pan out as well as expected. Has that been your experience? Are mergers and acquisitions worth it?*

Alex Mandl: I would take issue with the idea that most mergers end up being failures. I know there are studies from the 1970s and '80s that will tell you that. But when I look at many companies today – particularly new-economy companies like Cisco and WorldCom – I have a hard time dismissing the strategic power of M&A.

In the last three years, growth through acquisition has been a critical part of the success of many companies operating in the new economy. In fact, I would say that M&A has been the single most important factor in building up their market capitalization. I remember that when I bought McCaw Cellular for AT&T back in 1993, everybody said we'd paid too much. But with hindsight, it's clear that cellular telephony was a critical asset for the telecommunications business, and it would have been a tough proposition to build that business from scratch. Buying McCaw was very much the right thing to do. The plain fact is that acquiring is much faster than building. And speed – speed to market, speed to positioning, speed to becoming a viable company – is absolutely essential in the new economy.

David Bohnett: I agree with Alex. For some Internet companies in particular, M&A is certainly the fastest way to expand and solidify their businesses. That was one of the driving reasons behind our decision to sell GeoCities to Yahoo! in 1999. The two companies had compatible cultures and a similar vision of how the Internet was evolving. But the real reason we came together was that it was a fast way for both of us to continue to build competitive mass and expand our user base.

Ed Liddy: I'm not sure that it's so black and white. Acquisitions are certainly a very good way to add a product line or distribution channel that would be too costly to build from scratch. But they don't replace internal growth or alliances. In my business, as in many of today's knowledge industries, assets go up the elevator in the morning and down again at night. They can walk out the door if they feel disfranchised. The build or buy decision therefore becomes a bit more delicate. I usually like to build internally when I feel confident that we have the product and process knowledge to capitalize on an opportunity quickly. Only if we don't have that knowledge, and if we see a company that provides a good strategic fit, will we go the buy route.

David Komansky: You don't want to fall into the trap of making acquisitions just for the sake of it. Although we've made over 20 acquisitions at Merrill Lynch in the last decade as we've expanded – including a $6 billion purchase of Mercury Asset Management – we didn't set out to make them. We started out with what we considered to be a well-forged, highly tuned strategy and decided between acquisitions and green-field investments depending on which approach we felt would more quickly fulfill our ambitions. And we've had our ups and downs in both situations.

Ed Liddy: I'd just like to say one more thing about the bad rap on M&A. I think one of the reasons for it is that acquisitions are so visible. When they fail, they draw intense notice. But a lot of things in business fail; we've all started projects that didn't work out. The internal failures simply don't get as much attention.

Dennis Carey: *The obvious follow-up questions are, How do you raise the odds of success? How do you choose the right companies to buy or merge with?*

Dennis Kozlowski: Tyco has been very aggressive in making acquisitions. The key thing I've learned is that acquisitions work best when the main rationale is cost reduction. You can nearly always achieve them because you can see up front what they are. You can define, measure, and capture them. But there's more risk with revenue enhancements; they're much more difficult to implement.

Unfortunately, people are often too optimistic about revenues. One of the businesses we're in, for example, is medical products. I've seen a lot of health care businesses think that, just by virtue of having more products, they'll be able to sell more to hospitals or other medical service providers a lot quicker. But it takes a long time to train salespeople to bundle the new products with their existing ones effectively and have them accepted in the market. For one thing, the salespeople have to deal with new competitors – the people already selling the same kinds of products they've just added to their bundle.

Jan Leschly. I'm not sure I'd go along with that entirely. Of course, I'm more famous for the deals I didn't make than for the ones I did! But when we at SmithKline Beecham look at acquisitions, we do focus on revenues because our production costs, once we've developed a drug, are minimal. So if we can increase revenues, we're in great shape. And what really drives revenues in the drug business is R&D; there are enormous opportunities in the new technologies now being developed. When we looked at merging with Glaxo, for example, we were talking about synergies in R&D. By merging the two organizations, we probably could save in the neighborhood of $500 million. That's $500 million more a year we could reinvest in the R&D itself, and that's where the merger's real benefit would be.

In terms of improving growth, though, I'd have to say that we have been much more successful at acquiring products and technologies than at acquiring companies. We have a venture capital fund that invests in start-up biotechnology companies whose products and services we then buy. We invest small amounts – half a million dollars here and a million there – and we put our people on the boards. Once the companies get going, we can decide whether to buy them out completely or not. With large acquisitions, you're buying an awful lot of problems along with the products and technology they bring. Our venture capital investments, though, grow with us, and we can see exactly how they might fit in.

Raj Gupta: Obviously, acquisitions can add value in many ways, and you need to gear your M&A strategy to the needs of your company and the realities of your industry. In the chemical industry, where Rohm and Haas operates, much of the M&A activity is driven by the industry's need to consolidate. Currently, there are more than 200 chemical companies with more than a half-billion dollars in sales. As one analyst put it, a large specialty-chemical company is an oxymoron. With this degree of fragmentation, there's certainly plenty of scope for cutting costs through acquisitions. But cost reduction shouldn't be the sole goal; the most successful companies will be those that can grow, as well.

When we make acquisitions, therefore, our real aim is to create larger platforms for growth. When we bought Morton, the chemical and salt company, we knew we could make significant gains on two fronts. First, we were able to strengthen our technology base by tapping into Morton's expertise in polyurethane adhesives and powder coatings. Second, we were able to bring Rohm and Haas's considerable access to new geographic markets to the Morton portfolio.

Jan Leschly: But acquisitions aren't always a workable way to get into a new geographic market. We've been struggling for the last ten years with how best to build a business in Japan, for example. From a cultural perspective, it would be very difficult for us to acquire a company there. And the Japanese distribution system is so fragmented that we can't feasibly establish a direct presence. So we're trying to find other ways to do business – alliances, joint ventures, and so on.

Dennis Carey: *Looking at the deals we're seeing these days, it seems there's been a shift from buying companies outside your business space to buying ones within your business space. Is that the key to success?*

Mackey McDonald: We certainly view it like that. At VF Corporation, we focus on the core businesses that we know – like jeans and intimate apparel – and we try to bring our core competencies to acquisitions in those areas. An acquisition becomes attractive if it offers us a new consumer segment or geographic market to sell our products to or if it adds new products to one of our core categories. In our business, we find that if we venture too far from our core competencies, the risk isn't worth it. Many of the companies we buy are run by entrepreneurs who generally know a lot more about why they're selling than we know about why they're selling. We like to stick to our core businesses so if we run into problems, we have the resources and know-how to resolve them.

Jan Leschly: That's true for us as well. Not so long ago, the pharmaceutical companies were on an expansion kick. They spread into cosmetics, then got into consumer products, and finally into service businesses. In our case, we've been successful as a pharmaceutical company and as a major consumer health care company. But when we expanded into service businesses, we soon found that service provision is just not one of our core capabilities. We are a company based on innovation. We're good at manufacturing and systems.

Dennis Kozlowski: I've worked at companies that did diversify outside their core businesses, and I can tell you that they were never very successful. They'd take profits from good, established businesses and put the money into the next high technology. But they usually didn't have the management talent to support the new products or the services that they were investing in. Diversification was the main reason for company failures in the 1960s, '70s, and even the '80s. You can come up with quite a list of companies – think of Hanson PLC, ITT, and SCM – that had good ideas and then spoiled them by going out to invest in the next hot business. In contrast, companies that are doing well today are very focused. At Tyco, we have the same core businesses as a $27 billion company that we had when we were just a $200 million company.

Dennis Carey: *Alex, you said earlier that M&A was a critical strategic tool for growth in the new economy. Can you expand on that for us?*

Alex Mandl: As I said before, the need for speed forces companies to acquire rather than build. The smart Internet and communications companies, for example, are using their high market caps as currency to buy companies and quickly solidify their positions as the new economy takes shape. Take WorldCom. Five years ago, I don't think anybody around this table had heard of it. Thanks to a series of rapid and clever acquisitions, it's now one of the top two telecom companies in the world.

No one knows for sure where we're all going to end up. But we know that we need to get there quickly. You need to carve out your space. And the only way to do that is through acquisitions. The pace, in the telecom world at least, is furious, and it's not going to let up until we know who the major players in the broadband world are going to be.

Jan Leschly: Using acquisitions to expand into the Internet space is a much less obvious strategy for those of us who aren't already Internet businesses. A company like SmithKline Beecham faces huge challenges in figuring out what to do with the Internet. Before we can even think about acquisitions, we need to understand the implications of the Net for our business. I really think that when it comes to the Internet, SmithKline Beecham has a leadership crisis. At least, that's the sense I'm trying to create in our organization. I have to make people at the top understand that we have very little knowledge of how to work in the new market space. The people who really understand it are very low in our hierarchy. They have no responsibility, no authority, no money. We're getting into a situation where it's the young people who have to mentor us – not the other way around. That's a huge problem for middle and upper management to realize, and they're understandably reluctant to delegate too much authority to younger people.

David Bohnett: I agree that it's usually very difficult for traditional companies to integrate Internet start-ups. Traditional companies' processes, cultures, and business models don't work in the new economy. In fact, most successful Internet businesses have evolved on their own, relying purely on the commercial possibilities of the Internet. The huge amount of money out there for Internet start-ups, of course, has made it easy for them to do that.

Mackey McDonald: Jan's point reflects our experience in the apparel business as well. In building up our Internet capabilities at VF, we quickly found out that you can't just go buy technology companies. They have a whole different mind-set than apparel companies do, a different pace. It's easier to figure out how to do business in

Japan than in the new technology culture. We've found that the best solution is to form partnerships with independent companies. That's what we are doing with 12 technologies in the business-to-business arena. Also, we can't lose sight of the fact that our business is still heavily dependent on traditional retail channels, and we think a lot more apparel will continue to be sold in stores, not on-line. So when you announce that you're going to compete with your customers – the retailers – and sell direct to consumers, you're bound to run into problems. You don't want to undermine 98% of the business for the sake of a 2% opportunity.

Dennis Carey: *David, you've been working hard to bring Merrill Lynch into the Internet space. Why did you decide to build rather than acquire?*

David Komansky: There was great debate within the firm about that. We could certainly have acquired almost any of the on-line brokerage firms if we had chosen to, and there were those within our organization who wanted to. But we didn't feel that it was the right course. After all, one of the great challenges facing e-companies is building an image and a brand. If you watch TV now, you'll be swamped with e-commerce companies advertising their wares. For us, though, the Merrill Lynch brand is probably our greatest asset. So our strategy is to leverage our name and move the battleground away from price and technology by offering much the same *price* structures as the leading on-line brokers. In our business, technology is going to be a sine qua non, so everyone in the game will have it. But if we can force the game to content, it will be very difficult for other on-line competitors to match what we can provide.

It's certainly been a very, very difficult trip for our organization. Adjusting to the new economy is like trying to change the tires on a 747 in the middle of landing. Something is going to get squeezed somewhere. It took us a long time to get over our denial and accept the fact that the Internet is not a temporary phenomenon but a true change in the marketplace. It had reached the point where we had earned the reputation of being Luddites. Now that's all changed. We recognize that a certain segment of our clientele wants to deal in the virtual environment. Either we provide that opportunity for them or they go over to companies like Schwab.

We still have a lot of work to do in teaching our sales force how to deal with the pricing pressures that the Internet is putting on our business, and the challenges of managing our core businesses along with the Internet are very trying. But I do think that the emotional transition is well behind us.

Dennis Carey: *Let's pick up on that thought and turn to some of the softer issues surrounding M&A. We often hear about deals collapsing because of cultural incompatibilities. What's been your experience with cultural integration issues?*

Jan Leschly: It's a necessary condition for any deal that there be a good rationale for integrating the businesses. But, in my experience, even if the rationale for a deal is terrific, the deal can still fall apart because of cultural differences. Merging a US and a European company, as we have done, is a particularly complicated process. The management styles are totally different. People have different views on how to manage a global organization. Where should management be centralized, and where should it be decentralized? How should you pay people? The British and American philosophies are so far apart on those subjects they're almost impossible to reconcile.

Dennis Kozlowski: I'm not so sure that culture is as important as it's made out to be. I've never seen a deal really fall apart on a culture issue – or any soft issue. Most collapse on price, one way or another, and managers just use soft issues as an excuse.

I accept that companies do have different cultures and that reconciling them can be a lot of work for both sides. But I've been able to live with different cultures and adjust to them.

Bill Avery: Well, having just acquired a European company, I can tell you that there is one cultural difference still very fresh in my mind. Let's say you're not making your budgets because the selling prices of your products are falling. In the US, we'd think, "Well, if prices are going down, we've got to cut costs." But in Europe, some managers may be inclined to say, "Well, prices are falling now, but in a couple of years, they'll go back up." My experience at Crown has been that European management tends to be generally less aggressive in cutting costs than we are here in the US, perhaps because margins traditionally have been higher in Europe. That's a really big culture clash.

At Crown Cork, we think we are very, very good at cost control, so we are working hard to get a more consistent style across the company. In fact, in the packaging industry, our profits are the highest in our categories. When you buy a company outside the US as we did, you really need to know what you're getting into, and that's hard to get at in due diligence.

David Komansky: It's totally futile to impose a US-centric culture on a global organization. We think of our business as a broad road. All we expect people to do is stay on the road within the bounds of our strategy and our principles of doing business. We don't expect them to march down the white line, and, frankly, we don't care too much if they are on the left-hand side of the road or the right-hand side of the road. You need to adapt to local ways of doing things. The only firms in our industry that have been really successful on a global basis are Goldman Sachs, Morgan Stanley, and ourselves. That's because we've been more flexible than investment banks from other countries.

Nicholas Moore: Cultural differences are not just a matter of geography. Different companies can have very different attitudes and ways of working. In merging Price Waterhouse with Coopers, for example; we've had to put together people who've been competing against each other for 40 years. So culture has been a really big part of the equation. You have to build trust, and that takes a lot of managerial attention and time.

Ed Liddy: It's important to remember that you don't always have to have a high degree of cultural integration. You can't try to slam every acquisition into one mold. In the last 12 to 15 months, we've probably made four or five acquisitions. In some cases, we've completely integrated them into Allstate. But in other cases, much to the chagrin of our very good Allstate executives, I've said, "I don't want you to 'Allstate-ize' them. I want them to be separate." In the end, what you do with an acquisition depends on the channels and the products that you and the acquired company are in.

Dennis Carey: *Let's shift to some of the mechanics of integration. How do you approach it, and what are your priorities?*

Raj Gupta: At the beginning of negotiations, you tend to concentrate more on the business portfolio, but as the deal advances, your focus switches to people and processes. And once the deal closes, you often have to move very quickly on those fronts. The first thing you have to do is settle the uncertainty of who's going to report to whom and who's responsible for what. When we bought Morton, we put the new management team in place just 24 hours after announcing the deal. Doing that helped people to focus externally rather than internally. Losing external focus is one of the biggest risks when you integrate two businesses – and that's when you lose people and customers.

Once you've answered the key people questions, then you have to start integrating the basic work processes, computer systems, financial systems, and so on. You shouldn't underestimate the difficulty here. You'll find that you won't always get the information you need to make a timely decision – especially in the early days. That's why it's essential to have the right people in the right places within your organization – people you can trust to use a solid combination of data evaluation and intuition to make the best and fastest decisions for your organization.

Ed Liddy: When we announce an acquisition, we try to have the management structure completely laid out. I think the work of integration really needs to start when you're planning the acquisition because it's tied up with the whole reason you're buying the company. You have to start asking the right questions early. At Allstate, we have an integration team that works hand-in-hand with our strategic-planning area. They'll press the planners: "What's the logic of this acquisition? Is it cost takeout? If it is, what processes do we have that we can transfer to the acquired company to bring it up to a level of performance that we're comfortable with? What can we borrow from them that would help us?" And we communicate, communicate, communicate. We say the same thing over and over again to the acquired company, to ourselves, to Wall Street. That way, a common understanding of what we're trying to do can emerge.

Mackey McDonald: After an acquisition, you have to face a room full of people who want to know, "What happens to me?" If you don't answer that question, they don't hear much else of the presentation. Obviously, you can't say, "Everyone here is fine, and no changes are going to take place." What we try to do is explain the process that will determine the new management structure. If you can show how that's going to work, it does relieve some of the concerns. You've then got to pull in the smartest people you have to implement the changes. It's particularly important to do this for international acquisitions. When we acquired our Wrangler-licensed business from Mitsubishi in Japan, we came across all the culture issues we've been talking about here. We couldn't put in people who would immediately try to Americanize the company. We had to understand the local culture, or at least be willing to learn about it before making any changes.

Jan Leschly: It's extremely important to reach out to the second tier of management quickly. When we acquired Sterling Drug in 1994, we used a consulting company to evaluate all our managers – not just Sterling's – in every single country in which Sterling operated. They did it in just three weeks. It was a tremendous morale boost for Sterling's managers, who didn't feel that they were just being slaughtered. In fact, we had to fill 87 jobs around the world in the integrated operation, and 57 of them were filled by Sterling's managers.

Dennis Kozlowski: A very interesting statistic I once read says that people are normally productive for about 5.7 hours in an eight-hour business day. But any time a change of control takes place, their productivity falls to less than an hour. That holds true in merger situations. Inevitably, people immediately start thinking about themselves. So moving fast and getting the right people in place are extremely important. At Tyco, we look to the companies we acquire to provide those people. We present our objectives and our philosophy, and we look for the people who respond. Often, it's not the top executives but rather the people under them who are the quickest to understand and embrace the new philosophy.

At one company we acquired, we took a group of about 25 people off to a small town in Germany for a long weekend to consider ways of changing the business. They came up with a drastically different organizational structure for the company, which we implemented pretty well 100%. But more important, the company owned those changes. They weren't forced on it by us – they came from within. The more you can create a culture that encourages actions like that, the greater your chances of success. I might add that it's almost impossible to build such a culture when you do hostile acquisitions, which is why we don't do them.

Dennis Carey: *When there are integration problems, where do they tend to arise?*

Tig Krekel: I've been in companies that have been acquired, and I can tell you that people become extremely sensitive to every announcement, to every detail. Where is headquarters going to be located? How many people are going to lose their jobs? The in-house rumor is 400, but the acquiring company says 200. You need constant communication to avoid paralysis and maintain morale.

Another flash point is the customer. In the drive to complete a deal, it's easy to lose sight of the concerns of customers. There's almost never any detailed analysis in due diligence of how the customers will react or of the pros and cons of the deal from their point of view. But if you're in a noncommodity business with a small number of large customers, as we are at Hughes, you really do need to have a handle on who will control those relationships after the deal. You can't have ambiguity when it comes to customers.

Jan Leschly: It's true that merger talk makes a lot of people unhappy. But it can also make a lot of people very happy, and that brings its own problems. Think of all the people who can say, "My goodness, this gives me the chance to retire a little earlier. I get this wonderful package. My stock options are vested. This is a wonderful opportunity for me to get out of here." The potential for an exodus of talent is very real. And it becomes even more real in hostile takeovers. As we speak, think of what's going on inside Pfizer, Warner-Lambert, and American Home Products – three companies in the midst of a whirlwind of takeover talks and rumors. What do you think is happening in those organizations today? Think of the opportunities to recruit from them. Whichever deal gets made, a lot of people will just cash in and leave. At SmithKline Beecham, we spend a lot of time figuring out how to retain people who have just become multimillionaires. What incentives can we give them to stay? In any deal, the impact on talent has to be at the top of the agenda.

Dennis Carey: *One of the most delicate questions in any merger or acquisition is the composition of the board. Although good directors are tough to find, not many are being brought in from acquired companies. Why is that?*

Alex Mandl: It depends on whether people have an interest in joining. Most of the time, board members move on to something else. Craig McCaw, for example, declined a seat on the AT&T board because he realized that he was going to start up new businesses, as of course he has.

I think your comment about it being tougher to find board members really begs the question of why, in today's world, you would want to be on a board. Yes, it's an interesting group of people, and it can be an interesting experience. But I'm amazed, frankly, at how much talk there is in mergers about the importance of combining the two boards. Why is it important that both groups end up on the same board? Taking a board role, it seems to me, might make more sense with an exciting new company, where you might have a significant personal stake and where you can truly help get the company going.

Ed Liddy: We've certainly found very good directors through acquisitions. The challenge is finding people who are prepared to represent the interests of all shareholders, not just the management or the shareholders of the company whose board they were originally on. Clearly, you'll always have an affinity for that part of the organization, but you have to move beyond it. I think most people who sit on multiple boards understand that.

Jan Leschly: I have to say that we've never taken on any board members from our acquisitions. It's not a policy; it's just never happened. It's a different story for mergers, though, where board membership can be a very sensitive issue. It's tough to face your board and tell half of them that they're not going to join the new board. It doesn't exactly create an easy atmosphere. Normally, you just combine the two boards as one big one and then over a year or two it comes down to a normal size again. Of course, most mergers are really acquisitions. People called it a merger when Squibb teamed up with Bristol-Myers. I was president of Squibb at the time, and I can assure you that it was certainly not a merger of equals. It was an acquisition, and the majority, by far, of Squibb's management team was dismissed. If it really had been a merger of equals, that couldn't have happened.

Dennis Carey: *And with that, I'd like to bring to a close what I think has been a very productive discussion. Thank you very much.*

NOTE

* Founded in 1999 by Dennis Carey, along with Jan Leschly and Dennis Kozlowski, the M&A Group calls itself "the club for acquisitive CEOs." The purpose of the group, which currently has 40 members, is to bring together CEOs who are interested in M&A as a business strategy and provide them with a confidential forum to discuss ideas and share experiences. In addition to attending semiannual conferences, members can assess information and interact with professional advisory firms at the group's Web site (www.themagroup.com). The principal participants at the M&A roundtable were Dennis Carey (Moderator), Alex Mandl, David Bohnett, Ed Liddy, David Komansky, Dennis Kozlowski, Jan Leschly, Raj Gupta, Mackey McDonald, Bill Avery, Nicholas Moore and Tig Krekel.

22 Conclusions

Peter J. Buckley and Pervez N. Ghauri

MERGERS AND ACQUISITIONS

Mergers and acquisitions can be approached from a number of perspectives, all of which are represented in this volume:

1. The market for corporate control
2. Transaction cost theory
3. The resource based view of the firm
4. The impact of national and organizational cultures
5. Processes: pre- and post-acquisition strategies.

There are a number of key constituencies on whom M&As directly impact:

1. The acquiring firm including managers, workers, and its shareholders
2. The acquired firm including managers, workers, and its shareholders
3. Potential rival acquirers and non-acquired firms
4. In international M&As, the host country and source country (competitive environment) and welfare impacts.

M&As have external implications for taxpayers, employees, managers and workers in other firms, for consumers and for the pace of technological change. As well as the strategies of actual and potential acquiring firms, the defensive strategies of potential victims also impact on the above groups. M&As have a profound impact on social and political processes as well as the purely business and economic.

The merger wave, which in the early 1990s was considered to be largely an American phenomenon, became a worldwide trend and the latter part of the 1990s and the year 2000 has shown increased M&A activity in other parts. In 1999–2000, Europe led in M&A activities, in 2000 the total value of M&A reached $3.5 trillion (from $0.4 billion in 1990). Out of this, the USA accounted for about $1 trillion and Asia for $144.6 billion, the rest came from Europe (*The Economist*, Jan. 27, 2001, p. 59). In spite of this, more than 50 percent of the M&As are reporting post-merger problems. While in the past, firms have justified these deals arguing for synergistic benefits, more and more M&As are reporting synergistic losses. BMW and Rover, Daimler Chrysler, Union Pacific and South Pacific, Upjohn and Pharmacia, and Boeing and McDonald Douglas are but a few good examples.

INTERNATIONAL M&As

More than 50 percent of the total M&A activities in the last few years have been between cross-border firms. Here ABB (Asea and Brown Boveri), Exxon-Mobil and BP-Amoco and Upjohn-Pharmacia are good examples. A lot of time and energy was spent on "American" vs "European" practices than on achieving synergistic benefits. Daimler Chrysler was taken to court by its biggest shareholder for issuing misleading information. The fact that cross-border M&As place host country assets under the governance of multinational firms and contribute to the growth of an international production system does not necessarily mean that it creates synergistic benefits. As a result of these cross-border mergers, concentration has increased in many industries including: banking, pharmaceuticals, automobiles, telecommunication, insurance, and energy. After the Asian crisis, cross-border M&As in the five main crisis-hit countries accounted for more than 60 percent of the total Asian M&As in 1998–1999. Since cross-border M&As have become an important element in the expansion of the international production system, there is a need for a better understanding of what impact they have on countries, especially the host country (UNCTAD, 2000).

A great omission in the literature on M&As and their performance is that too little attention is given to cultural clashes, while many mergers faced enormous problems due to cultural differences; Bankers Trust and Deutsche Bank, Upjohn and Pharmacia, and Daimler Chrysler are good examples. As put by Mr Hubert of Daimler Chrysler, "We are absolutely happy with the development of the merger, we have a clear understanding: one company, one vision, one chairman, two cultures" (see also the Daimler Chrysler case in Chapter 2). This is also due to the fact that in most M&As more attention is given to the deal rather than to the integration of the companies involved. In many cases, companies ended up with two bosses, two accounting systems and neither side really knew what the other was doing (*The Economist*, Jan. 9, 1999).

ROUNDTABLE ON MAKING MERGERS SUCCEED

The discussion reproduced as Chapter 21 above contains many fascinating insights from experienced M&A executives. The discussion highlights several important advantages of M&As: speed of entry and speed to market, the ability to acquire critical assets, platforms for future growth and entry into new geographical markets. Speed of entry is felt to be particularly critical in the Internet age (see Exhibit 1).

EXHIBIT 1

The Impact of the Internet on formal corporate links

In the past year, a number of deals have been concluded between companies, often competing in the same industry, to create Internet-based business-to-business exchanges. In such arrangements, companies come together on a functional basis to build Internet-based market places without having to establish formal corporate links. Such exchanges enable companies to achieve various objectives, beginning with cost savings, without having those activities housed in the same corporate shell. This applies particularly to Internet-based procurement systems, through which, by streamlining the procurement process, companies aim at reducing procurement expenditures.

Examples of Internet business-to-business exchanges include the tie-up between Hitachi, IBM, LG Electronics, Matsushita Electronics, Nortel Networks, Seagate Technology Selection and Toshiba, known as e2open.com, and the tie-up still under discussion between DaimlerChrysler, Ford and General

Motors, known as Covisint. Covisint, for instance, would offer to its members a comprehensive online market place for the procurement of automotive parts and supplies and other services (e.g. catalogue purchasing and Internet bid events). The respective purchasing departments of the member firms would remain separate, using the exchange as a tool to conduct their independent procurement.

The development of such exchanges raises a number of questions, especially as regards their impact on competition. The combined purchasing power of their members also can significantly affect the bargaining position of suppliers.

Source: UNCTAD World Investment Report 2000, p. 102

Several disadvantages of merger are discussed: the fact that asset values go down as well as up, cultural barriers in international acquisitions and the strategic point that M & As do not replace internal growth and alliances. It is also pointed out that the failure of M&As is often very visible whereas start-ups and new venture failures often go unnoticed.

The discussion of strategy covers related versus unrelated M&As and the need for focus is emphasized. Industry differences are obviously important – it may be that where the purpose of the M&A is to cut costs, that these benefits are more obvious, and more quantifiable than revenue enhancing strategies, where there may be more risk. R&D synergies are suggested to be the major reason for M&As in pharmaceuticals. Keeping the focus on the acquisition of products and technologies rather than companies may be important. Venture capital operations in biotechnology (for instance) are alternatives to M&As. This discussion and the views on the need to integrate Internet startups strongly suggest that M&A strategy should be part of an overall strategy, and not separate from it.

RESTRUCTURING AND FIRE-SALES

The Asian financial crisis of the late 1990s was followed by an upsurge of M&A activity in the formerly successful developing countries of East Asia (Thailand, Malaysia, Indonesia, Philippines and Republic of Korea). The dirigiste development (largely directed by the state) led to over-diversification, over capacity and inflated (property) values and of capital-intensive and scale-driven industries (Zhan and Ozawa, 2001). After the financial collapse, values collapsed and, at lower exchange rates, companies became available at much lower prices when expressed in the acquirer's currency. State encouragement to inward investors in order to attract funds also fuelled the spate of M&As. Reform programmes encouraged more open forms of corporate governance and a move away from bank-finance to stock market financing, thus opening the way for further M&A activity. However, these processes opened up the acquirers to the charge of indulging in "fire-sales" at bargain prices, taking advantage of the distressed state of local businesses. The brakes put on full reform in the host countries slowed down this process, but may have provided fuel for future problems.

REGULATION OF M&As

In case of regulations and antitrust, many firms jump into bed with each other without properly considering regulatory concerns. MCI and WorldCom, two American telecommunication firms were totally surprised by objections to their $37 billion marriage from European regulators (*The Economist*, Jan. 9, 1999). The liberalizations in FDI regimes has encouraged companies to expand through M&As. The international regulatory framework, bilateral investment, and double taxation agreements and the WTO have also supported these trends. In Europe, the EU has stimulated restructuring for national, regional, and cross-border M&As which has resulted in major changes in corporate ownership. One impact of all these changes is that there is an increased acceptance of M&As all over the world, even though there are mixed opinions on their impact on industrial concentration. According to one opinion, cross-border M&As can have a positive effect on competition if the foreign firm takes over ailing domestic firms that would otherwise have been forced out of the market. They can also challenge established domestic firms to create effective rivals. The opposing view is that "monopolizing M&As" can occur in the following situations (UNCTAD, 2000, p. 193):

(1) The acquiring firm was exporting substantially to a market before it buys a competing firm in it.
(2) A foreign firm with an affiliate already in the market acquires another, thereby acquiring a dominant or monopolistic market share.
(3) The foreign firm acquires a market leader with which it has previously competed.
(4) The acquisition is intended to suppress rather than develop the competitive potential of the acquired firm.
(5) A foreign firm with an affiliate in a host country acquires an enterprise in a third country that has been a source of import competition in the host country market.
(6) Two foreign affiliates in a host country merge, although their parent firms remain separate, eliminating competition between the two and leading to a dominant market position.

Although we can accept that higher concentration by itself does not indicate anti-competitive conduct, the crucial issue is that it differs from market to market and from industry to industry. In the United States and the European Union, only a small number of M&As are scrutinized to assess negative impacts on competition. An even smaller number are asked to sell off parts of the business or are prohibited. In the United States, for example, only 1.6 percent of 4679 M&As notified to antitrust authorities resulted in enforcement actions, with only about 1 percent being challenged in the end (US Department of Justice, 2000). In the EU, the situation is not much different. In 1999, only 14 out of 292 M&As (less than 5 percent) were challenged or subject to a second phase investigation, while an additional 19 cases were reported but cleared in the first phase of investigation. In Japan, all 3813 M&As notified in 1998 were cleared, only 2 transactions were revised during pre-notification consultation (ibid, p. 7). This means that the authorities do not believe M&A to be against the public interest even if concentration does increase.

REFERENCES

Harrison, Joan, 2000, "M&A Time Line," *Mergers & Acquisitions*, vol. 35 (8), September, pp. 24–31.
The Economist, 1999, "How to Merge", January 9, pp. 19–21.
The Economist, 2001, "The Great Merger Wave Breaks," January 27, pp. 59–60.

United States Department of Justice, 2000, *International Competition Policy Advisory Committee to the Attorney General and the Assistant Attorney General for Antitrust: Final Report*, http://www.usdoj.gov/

UNCTAD, 2000, "Cross-border Mergers and Acquisitions," *World Investment Report*, New York: United Nations.

Zhan, James and Terutomo Ozawa. 2001. *Business Restructuring in Asia*. Copenhagen: Copenhagen Business Press.

Index

Page numbers in *italics* refer to illustrations and tables; page numbers in **bold** refer to main discussion.